Plato: The Man and His Work

PLATO

THE MAN AND HIS WORK

by A. E. Taylor

MERIDIAN BOOKS *New York* 1957

A. E. Taylor

Born in 1869, Alfred Edward Taylor was Professor of Philosophy at McGill University from 1903 to 1908, at St. Andrew's from 1908 to 1924, and then at Edinburgh until his death in 1945. Among his many books are *The Problem of Conduct, Elements of Metaphysics, The Faith of a Moralist,* and *The Christian Hope of Immortality.*

Meridian Books edition first published October 1956
First printing September 1956

Second printing January 1957

Reprinted by arrangement with The Humanities Press, Inc. from the sixth edition, reprinted 1952

Library of Congress catalog card number: 56:10023

Manufactured in the United States of America

PREFACE

I HOPE two classes of readers may find their account in this book—" Honours students " in our Universities, and readers with philosophical interests, but no great store of Greek scholarship. What both classes most need in a work about Plato is to be told just what Plato has to say about the problems of thought and life, and how he says it. What neither needs is to be told what some contemporary thinks Plato should have said. The sense of the greatest thinker of the ancient world ought not to be trimmed to suit the tastes of a modern neo-Kantian, neo-Hegelian, or neo-realist. Again, to understand Plato's thought we must see it in the right historical perspective. The standing background of the picture must be the social, political, and economic life of the age of Socrates, or, for the *Laws*, of the age of Plato. These considerations have determined the form of the present volume. It offers an analysis of the dialogues, not a systematization of their contents under a set of subject-headings. Plato himself hated nothing more than system-making. If he had a system, he has refused to tell us what it was, and if we attempt to force a system on a mind which was always growing, we are sure to end by misrepresentation. This is why I have tried to tell the reader just what Plato says, and made no attempt to force a " system " on the Platonic text. My own comments are intended to supply exegesis, based as closely as may be on Plato's own words, not to applaud nor to denounce. The result, I hope, is a picture which may claim the merit of historical fidelity. For the same reason I have been unusually careful to determine the date and historical setting assumed for each dialogue. We cannot really understand the *Republic* or the *Gorgias* if we forget that the Athens of these conversations is meant to be the Athens of Nicias or Cleon, not the very different Athens of Plato's own manhood, or if we find polemic against Isocrates, in talk supposed to have passed at a time when Isocrates was a mere boy. If it were not that the remark might sound immodest, I would say that the model I have had before me is Grote's great work on the *Companions of Socrates*. Enjoying neither Grote's superb scholarship nor his freedom from limitations of space, I have perhaps the compensation of freedom from the prejudices of a party.   Whatever bias I may have in metaphysics or in politics, I have tried to keep it out of my treatment of Plato.

I must apologize for some unavoidable omissions.   I have been unable to include a chapter on the Academy in the generation after Plato and Aristotle's criticisms of it ;   I have had to exclude from consideration the minor *dubia* and the *spuria* of the Platonic *corpus* ;   I have passed very lightly over much of the biology of the *Timaeus*.   These omissions have been forced on me by the necessity of saying what I have to say in one volume of moderate compass. For the same reason I have had to make my concluding chapter little more than a series of hints.   This omission will, I trust, be remedied by the publication of a study, "Forms and Numbers," which will, in part, appear in *Mind* simultaneously with the issue of this volume.   The details of the *Timaeus* are fully dealt with in a Commentary now in course of printing at the Clarendon Press.   A brief account—better than none—of the transmission of the Platonic tradition will be found in my little book, *Platonism and its Influence* (1924 ;   Marshall Jones Co., Boston, U.S.A. ;   British Agents, Harrap & Son).

Want of space has sometimes forced me to state a conclusion without a review of the evidence, but I hope I have usually indicated the quarters where the evidence may be sought.   May I say, once for all, that this book is no " compilation " ?   I have tried to form a judgment on all questions, great and small, for myself, and mention of any work, ancient or modern, means, with the rarest of exceptions, that I have studied it from one end to the other.

There remains the grateful duty of acknowledging obligations. I am a debtor to many besides those whom I actually quote, and I hope I have not learned least from many whose views I feel bound to reject.   In some cases I have echoed a well-known phrase or accepted a well-established result without express and formal acknowledgment.   It must be understood that such things are mere consequences of the impossibility oi excessive multiplication of footnotes, and that I here, once for all, request any one from whom I may have made such a loan to accept my thanks.   The recommendations at the ends of chapters are not meant to be exhaustive nor necessarily to imply agreement with all that is said in the work or chapter recommended.   The last thing I should wish is that my readers should see Plato through my spectacles.   I wish here to make general mention of obligation to a host of scholars of our own time, such as Professors Apelt, Parmentier, Robin, Dr.

Adolfo Levi, the late Dr. James Adam, and others, besides those whose names recur more frequently in my pages. The immense debt of my own generation to scholars of an earlier date, such as Grote, Zeller, Diels, Baeumker, Bonitz, is too obvious to need more than this simple reference.

To two living scholars I must make very special acknowledgment. How much I owe to the published writings of my friend and colleague in Scotland, Professor Burnet, will be apparent on almost every page of my book ; I owe even more to suggestions of every kind received during a personal intercourse of many years. I owe no less to Professor C. Ritter of Tübingen, who has given us, as part of the work of a life devoted to Platonic researches, the best existing commentary on the *Laws* and the finest existing full-length study of Plato and his philosophy as a whole. One cannot despair of one's kind when one remembers that such a work was brought to completion in the darkest years Europe has known since 1648. It is a great honour to me that Dr. Ritter has allowed me to associate his name with this poor volume. Finally, I thank the publishers for their kindness in allowing the book to run to such a length.

A. E. TAYLOR

EDINBURGH, *July* 1926

NOTE TO SECOND EDITION

THIS Second Edition only differs from the first by the correction of misprints, the addition of one or two references and the modification of a few words in two or three of the footnotes.

A. E. TAYLOR

EDINBURGH, *March* 1927

NOTE TO THIRD EDITION

APART from minor corrections and some additions to the references appended to various chapters, this edition only differs from its precursors by the presence of a Chronological Table of Dates and an *Appendix*, dealing briefly with the *dubia* and *spuria* of the Platonic tradition. (I have, for convenience' sake, included in this a short account of a number of Platonic epistles which I myself believe to be neither dubious nor spurious, but have not had occasion to cite in the body of the book.) I should explain that this essay was substantially written in 1926, though it has been revised since.

I take this opportunity of mentioning the following recent works, to which I should have been glad to give more specific references in the text, had they come into my hands a little sooner. All will be found valuable by the serious student of Plato.

STENZEL, J.—*Platon der Erzieher*. (Leipzig, 1928.)
SOLMSEN, F.—*Der Entwicklung der Aristotelischen Logik und Rhetorik*. (Berlin, 1929.)
WALZER, R.—*Magna Moralia und Aristotelische Ethik*. (Berlin, 1929.)
TOEPLITZ, O.—*Das Verhältnis von Mathematik und Ideenlehre bei Plato*, in *Quellen und Studien zur Geschichte der Mathematik I. 1.* (Berlin, 1929.)
ROBIN, L.—*Greek Thought and the Origins of the Scientific Spirit*. (E. Tr. from the revised edition of the author's *La Pensée Grecque*, London, 1928.)

A. E. TAYLOR.

EDINBURGH, *July*, 1929

NOTE TO FOURTH EDITION

I HAVE made few changes in this new edition of the text, though I have been led to rewrite one or two paragraphs in the chapter on the *Timaeus* by study of Professor Cornford's valuable commentary on his translation of the dialogue. I have tried to remove misprints and detected errors throughout. Among works important for the student of Plato published since the earlier editions of this book I could mention in particular the following :

FRUTIGER, P.—*Les Mythes de Platon*. (Paris, 1930.)
SHOREY, P.—*What Plato Said*. (Chicago, 1933.)
NOVOTNÝ, F.—*Platonis Epistulae*. (Brno, 1930.)
HARWARD, J.—*The Platonic Epistles*. (E. Tr. Cambridge, 1932.)
FIELD, G. C.—*Plato and His Contemporaries*. (London, 1930.)
CORNFORD, F. M.—*Plato's Cosmology, the Timaeus of Plato translated with a running commentary*. (London, 1937.)
SCHULL, P. M.—*Essai sur la Formation de la Pensée Grecque*. (Paris, 1934.)

A. E. TAYLOR.

CONTENTS

THE following abbreviations have occasionally been used:

E.G.Ph.[3] = BURNET, *Early Greek Philosophy* (3rd edition), 1920.

E.R.E. = HASTINGS, *Encyclopaedia of Religion and Ethics*, 1908–1921.

R.P. = RITTER AND PRELLER, *Historia Philosophiae Graecae* (9th edition), 1913.

PLATO
THE MAN AND HIS WORK

CHAPTER I

THE LIFE OF PLATO[1]

PLATO, son of Ariston and Perictione, was born in the month Thargelion (May–June) of the first year of the eighty-eighth Olympiad by the reckoning of the scholars of Alexandria, 428–7 B.C. of our own era, and died at the age of eighty or eighty-one in Ol. 108.1 (348–7 B.C.). These dates rest apparently on the authority of the great Alexandrian chronologist Eratosthenes and may be accepted as certain. Plato's birth thus falls in the fourth year of the Archidamian war, in the year following the death of Pericles, and his death only ten years before the battle of Chaeronea, which finally secured to Philip of Macedon the hegemony of the Hellenic world. His family was, on both sides, one of the most distinguished in the Athens of the Periclean age. On the father's side the pedigree was traditionally believed to go back to the old kings of Athens, and through them to the god Posidon. On the mother's side the descent is equally illustrious and more his-

---

[1] The chief extant lives are : (a) Apuleius, de Platone, i. 1–4 ; (b) Diogenes Laertius, iii. 1 (critical edition, Basle, 1907) ; (c) Olympiodorus (Platonis Opera, ed. Hermann, vi. 190–195). The least bad of these is (b), which appears to have been originally composed for a lady amateur of Platonic philosophy (φιλοπλάτωνι δέ σοι δικαίως ὑπαρχούσῃ, § 47), not before the latter part of the first century of our era. The one or two references to the scholar Favorinus of Arles may possibly be later marginal annotations by an owner or copier of the text. If they are original, they would bring down the date of the Life to the latter part of the second century A.D. In the main Diogenes Laertius appears to give the version of Plato's life accepted by the literati of Alexandria. But we can see from what we know of the work of Alexandrians like Sotion, Satyrus, and Hermippus, that biographies were already being ruined by the craze for romantic or piquant anecdote before the end of the third century B.C. In Plato's case there is a peculiar reason for suspicion of Alexandrian narratives. The writers were largely dependent on the assertions of Aristoxenus of Tarentum, a scholar of Aristotle who had known the latest generation of the fourth century Pythagoreans. Aristoxenus has long been recognized as a singularly mendacious person, and he had motives for misrepresenting both Socrates and Plato. See Burnet, Greek Philosophy, Part I., p. 153.

torically certain, and is incidentally recorded for us by Plato himself in the *Timaeus*. Perictione was sister of Charmides and cousin of Critias, both prominent figures in the brief " oligarchic " anarchy which followed on the collapse of Athens at the end of the Peloponnesian war (404–3 B.C.). The grandfather of this Critias, Plato's maternal great-grandfather, was another Critias, introduced in the *Timaeus*, whose own great-grandfather Dropides was a " friend and kinsman " of Solon, the great Attic legislator. The father of this Dropides, also called Dropides, the first member of the house who figures in authentic history, was the archon of the year 644 B.C. Besides Plato himself, Ariston and Perictione had at least three other children. These were two older sons, Adimantus and Glaucon, who appear as young men in Plato's *Republic*, and a daughter Potone. Ariston appears to have died in Plato's childhood ; his widow then married her uncle Pyrilampes, whom we know from the allusions of the comic poets to have been a personal intimate of Pericles as well as a prominent supporter of his policy. Pyrilampes was already by a former marriage the father of the handsome Demus, the great " beauty " of the time of the Archidamian war ; by Perictione he had a younger son Antiphon who appears in Plato's *Parmenides*, where we learn that he had given up philosophy for horses.[1]

These facts are of considerable importance for the student of Plato's subsequent career. Nothing is more characteristic of him than his lifelong conviction that it is the imperative duty of the philosopher, whose highest personal happiness would be found in the life of serene contemplation of truth, to make the supreme sacrifice of devoting the best of his manhood to the service of his fellows as a statesman and legislator, if the opportunity offers. Plato was not content to preach this doctrine in the *Republic* ; he practised it, as we shall see, in his own life. The emphasis he lays on it is largely explained when we remember that from the first he grew up in a family with traditions of Solon and accustomed through several generations to play a prominent part in the public life of the State. Something of Plato's remarkable insight into the realities of political life must, no doubt, be set down to early upbringing in a household of " public men." So, too, it is important to remember, though it is too often forgotten, that the most receptive years of Plato's early life must have been spent in the household of his stepfather, a prominent figure of the Periclean *régime*. Plato has often been accused of a bias against " democracy." If he had such a bias, it is not to be accounted for by the influence of early surroundings. He must have been originally indoctrinated with " Periclean " politics ; his dislike of them in later life, so far as it

[1] See the family tree in Burnet, *Greek Philosophy, Part I.*, Appendix I., p. 357. For Pyrilampes, cf. *Charmides*, 158a, and for Demus, *Gorgias*, 481d 5, Aristophanes, *Wasps*, 98. According to *Ep*. xiii. 361e, Perictione was still alive at the date of writing (*i.e.* about 366), but her death was expected, as Plato speaks of the expense of the funeral as one which he will shortly have to meet. Nothing is known of Pyrilampes after the battle of Delium (424 B.C.).

is real at all, is best intelligible as a consequence of having been " behind the scenes." If he really disliked democracy, it was not with the dislike of ignorance but with that of the man who has known too much.

The actual history of Plato's life up to his sixtieth year is almost a blank. In his own dialogues he makes a practice of silence about himself, only broken once in the *Apology*, where he names himself as one of the friends who urged Socrates to increase the amount of the fine he proposed on himself from one mina to thirty and offered to give security for the payment, and again in the *Phaedo*, where he mentions an illness as the explanation of his absence from the death-scene.[1] Aristotle adds the one further detail that Plato had been " in his youth familiar with " the Heraclitean Cratylus, though we cannot be absolutely sure that this is more than a conjecture of Aristotle's own. The later writers of the extant *Lives* of Plato add some details, but these are mainly of a purely anecdotal kind and not to be implicitly trusted. In any case their scraps of anecdote throw no light on Plato's life or character and we may safely neglect them here. All we can be sure of, down to Plato's twenty-sixth year, is that the influence of friendship with Socrates must have been the most potent force in the moulding of his mind. (We may add that if Aristotle's statement about Cratylus[2] really is more than an inference, the Heraclitean doctrine, learned from Cratylus, that the world disclosed to us by our senses is a scene of incessant and incalculable mutability and variation, was one which Plato never forgot. He drew, says Aristotle, the conclusion that since there is genuine science, that of which science treats must be something other than this unresting " flux " of sense-appearances.)

The gossiping Alexandrian biographers represented Plato as " hearing " Socrates at the age of eighteen or twenty. This cannot mean that his first introduction to Socrates took place at that age. We know from Plato himself that Socrates had made the close acquaintance of Plato's uncle Charmides in the year 431, and was even then familiar with Critias.[3] Presumably Plato's acquaintance with Socrates, then, went back as far as he could remember. The Alexandrian tales will only mean that Plato became a " disciple " of Socrates as soon as he was an ἔφηβος or " adolescent," a period of life currently reckoned as beginning at eighteen and ending at twenty. Even with this explanation the story is probably not accurate. Both Plato and Isocrates, his older contemporary, emphatically deny that Socrates ever had any actual " disciples " whom he " instructed," and Plato himself, in a letter written nearly at the end of his life, puts the matter in a truer light. He tells us there that at the time of the " oligarchical " usurpation of 404–3, being still a very young man, he was looking forward to a political career and was urged by relatives who were among the revolutionaries (no doubt, Critias and Charmides) to enter public life

---

[1] *Apology*, 38b 6, *Phaedo*, 59b 10. [2] Aristotle, *Met.* 987a 32.
[3] See the opening pages of the *Charmides*.

under their auspices, but waited to see first what their policy would
be. He was horrified to find that they soon showed signs of lawless
violence, and finally disgusted when they attempted to make his
" elderly friend Socrates," the best man of his time, an accomplice
in the illegal arrest and execution of a fellow-citizen whose property
they intended to confiscate. The leaders of restored democracy
did worse, for they actually put Socrates to death on an absurd
charge of impiety. This, Plato says, put an end to his own political
aspirations. For in politics nothing can be achieved without a
party, and the treatment of Socrates by both the Athenian factions
proved that there was no party at Athens with whom an honourable
man could work. The suggestion clearly made here is that Plato
did not regard Socrates as, properly speaking, a master. He loved
him personally as a young man loves a revered elder friend, and he
thought of him as a martyr. But it was not until the actual execution of Socrates opened his eyes once for all that he gave up his
original intention of taking up active political life as his career.
His original aspirations had been those of the social and legislative
reformer, not those of the thinker or man of science.[1]

Hermodorus,[2] an original member of Plato's Academy, stated
that for the moment the friends of Socrates felt themselves in
danger just after his death, and that Plato in particular, with
others, withdrew for a while to the neighbouring city of Megara
under the protection of Euclides of that city, a philosopher who was
among the foreign friends present at the death of Socrates and
combined certain Socratic tenets with the Eleaticism of Parmenides.
This temporary concentration at Megara presumably would only
last until the feelings aroused in connexion with the *cause célèbre*
had had time to blow over. The biographers narrate that it was
followed by some years of travel to Cyrene, Italy, and Egypt, and
that the Academy was then founded on Plato's return to Athens.
How much of this story—none of it rests, like the mention of the
sojourn in Megara, on the evidence of Hermodorus—may be true, is
very doubtful. Plato himself, in the letter already alluded to,
merely says that he visited Italy and Sicily at the age of forty and
was repelled by the sensual luxury of the life led there by the well-
to-do. His language on the whole implies that most of the time
between this journey and the death of Socrates had been spent at
Athens, watching the public conduct of the city and drawing the
conclusion that good government can only be expected when
" either true and genuine philosophers find their way to political
authority or powerful politicians by the favour of Providence take
to true philosophy." He says nothing of travels in Africa or
Egypt, though some of the observations made in the *Laws* about
the art and music, the arithmetic and the games of the Egyptian
children have the appearance of being first-hand. The one
fateful result of Plato's " travels," in any case, is that he won
the whole-hearted devotion of a young man of ability and

[1] See the full explanation of all this at *Ep.* vii. 324*b* 8–326*b* 4.   [2] D.L., iii. 6.

promise, Dion, son-in-law of the reigning " tyrant " of Syracuse, Dionysius I.[1]

The founding of the Academy is the turning-point in Plato's life, and in some ways the most memorable event in the history of Western European science. For Plato it meant that, after long waiting, he had found his true work in life. He was henceforth to be the first president of a permanent institution for the prosecution of science by original research. In one way the career was not a wholly unprecedented one. Plato's rather older contemporary Isocrates presided in the same way over an establishment for higher education, and it is likely that his school was rather the older of the two. The novel thing about the Platonic Academy was that it was an institution for the prosecution of *scientific* study. Isocrates, like Plato, believed in training young men for public life. But unlike Plato he held the opinion of the " man in the street " about the uselessness of science. It was his boast that the education he had to offer was not founded on hard and abstract science with no visible humanistic interest about it ; he professed to teach " opinions," as we should say, to provide the ambitious aspirant to public life with " points of view," and to train him to express his " point of view " with the maximum of polish and persuasiveness. This is just the aim of " journalism " in its best forms, and Isocrates is the spiritual father of all the " essayists," from his own day to ours, who practise the agreeable and sometimes beneficial art of saying nothing, or saying the commonplace, in a perfect style. He would be the " Greek Addison " but for the fact that personally he was a man of real discernment in political matters and, unlike Addison, really had something to say. But it is needless to remark that an education in humanistic commonplace has never really proved the right kind of training to turn out great men of action. Plato's rival scheme meant the practical application to education of the conviction which had become permanent with him that the hope of the world depends on the union of political power and genuine science. This is why the pure mathematics—the one department of sheer hard thinking which had attained any serious development in the fourth century B.C.—formed the backbone of the curriculum, and why in the latter part of the century the two types of men who were successfully turned out in the Academy were original mathematicians and skilled legislators and admini-

---

[1] I have said nothing of the story related, *e.g.*, in D.L., iii., 18–21, that Dionysius I had Plato kidnapped and handed over to a Spartan admiral who exposed him for sale at Aegina, where he was ransomed by an acquaintance from Cyrene. The story, though quite possible, seems not too probable, and looks to be no more than an anecdote intended to blacken the character of Dionysius, who in fact, though masterful enough, was neither brute nor fool. In spite of the counter-assertion of Diels, it is pretty certainly *not* referred to in Aristotle, *Physics*, B 199b 13. Simplicius seems clearly right in supposing that Aristotle's allusion is to some situation in a comedy. The statement that Dionysius *attempted* to kidnap Plato is made earlier by Cornelius Nepos, *Dion*, c. 2, and perhaps comes from the Sicilian historian Timaeus.

strators, a point on which we shall have a word or two to say in the sequel. It is this, too, which makes the Academy the direct progenitor of the mediaeval and modern university : a university which aims at supplying the State with legislators and administrators whose intellects have been developed in the first instance by the disinterested pursuit of truth for its own sake is still undertaking, under changed conditions, the very task Plato describes as the education of the " philosopher king." The immediate and perceptible outward sign of the new order of things in the Greek world is that whereas in the age of Plato's birth aspiring young Athenians had to depend for their " higher education " on the lectures of a peripatetic foreign " sophist," in the Athens of fifty years later aspiring young men from all quarters flocked to Athens to learn from Isocrates or Plato or both. The travelling lecturer was replaced by the university or college with a fixed domicile and a constitution.

Unfortunately the exact date of the foundation of the Academy is unknown. From the obvious connexion between its programme and the conviction Plato speaks of having definitely reached at the time when he visited Italy and Sicily at the age of forty, we should naturally suppose that the foundation took place about this time (388–7 B.C.) ; and it is easier to suppose that the visit to Sicily preceded it, as the later biographical statements assume, than that it followed directly on its inception. If there is any truth in the statement that the real object of Plato's journey was to visit the Pythagoreans, who were beginning to be formed into a school again under Archytas of Tarentum, we may suppose that it was precisely the purpose of founding the Academy which led Plato just at this juncture to the very quarter where he might expect to pick up useful hints and suggestions for his guidance ; but this can be no more than a conjecture.

We have to think of Plato for the next twenty years as mainly occupied with the onerous work of organizing and maintaining his school. " Lecturing " would be part of this work, and we know from Aristotle that Plato did actually " lecture " without a manuscript at a much later date. But the delivery of these lectures would be only a small part of the work to be done. It was one of Plato's firmest convictions that nothing really worth knowing can be learned by merely listening to " instruction " ; the only true method of " learning " science is that of being actually engaged, in company with a more advanced mind, in the discovery of scientific truth.[1] Very little in the way of actual " new theorems " is ascribed to Plato by the later writers on the history of mathematical science, but the men trained in his school or closely associated with it made all the great advances achieved in the interval between the downfall of the original Pythagorean order about the middle of the fifth century and the rise of the specialist schools of Alexandria in the

[1] *Ep.* vii. 341*d–e*. See the comments on this passage in Burnet, *Greek Philosophy, Part I.*, 220–222.

third. In estimating Plato's work for science it is necessary to take account first and foremost of the part he must have played as the organizer and director of the studies of this whole brilliant group. It was, no doubt, this which induced the first mathematician of the time, Eudoxus of Cnidus, to transport himself and his scholars bodily from Cyzicus to Athens to make common cause with the Academy. Probably we are not to think of Plato as writing much during these twenty years. He would be too busy otherwise, and, as we shall see, there is the strongest reason for thinking that most of his dialogues, including all those which are most generally known to-day, were all composed by his fortieth year, or soon after, while the important half-dozen or so which must be assigned to a later date most probably belong definitely to his old age.

In the year 367 something happened which provided Plato, now a man of sixty, with the great adventure of his life. Dionysius I of Syracuse, who had long governed his native city nominally as annually elected *generalissimo*, really as autocrat or " tyrant," died. He was succeeded by his son Dionysius II, a man of thirty whose education had been neglected and had left him totally unfitted to take up his father's great task of checking the expansion of the Carthaginians, which was threatening the very existence of Greek civilization in Western Sicily. The strong man of Syracuse at the moment was Dion, brother-in-law of the new " tyrant," the same who had been so powerfully attached to Plato twenty years before. Dion, a thorough believer in Plato's views about the union of political power with science, conceived the idea of fetching Plato personally to Syracuse to attempt the education of his brother-in-law. Plato felt that the prospect of success was not promising, but the Carthaginian danger was very real, if the new ruler of Syracuse should prove unequal to his work, and it would be an everlasting dishonour to the Academy if no attempt were made to put its theory into practice when the opportunity offered at such a critical juncture. Accordingly Plato, though with a great deal of misgiving, made up his mind to accept Dion's invitation.

If the *Epistles* ascribed in our Plato MSS. to Plato are genuine (as I have no doubt that the great bulk of them are), they throw a sudden flood of light on Plato's life for the next few years. To understand the situation we must bear two things in mind. Plato's object was not, as has been fancied, the ridiculous one of setting up in the most luxurious of Greek cities a pinchbeck imitation of the imaginary city of the *Republic*. It was the practical and statesman-like object of trying to fit the young Dionysius for the immediate practical duty of checking the Carthaginians [1] and, if possible, expelling them from Sicily, by making Syracuse the centre of a strong constitutional monarchy to embrace the whole body of Greek communities in the west of the island. Also, Plato's belief in the value of a hard scientific education for a ruler of men, wise or not, was absolutely genuine. Accordingly he at once set about the task

[1] *Ep.* vii. 333*a* 1, viii. 353*a*.

from the beginning and made Dionysius enter on a serious course of
geometry. For a little while things looked promising. Dionysius
became attached to Plato and geometry the " fashion " at his court.
But the scheme wrecked on a double obstacle. Dionysius was too
feeble of character and his education had been left neglected too
long, and his personal jealousies of his stronger and older relative
were easily awakened. In a few months the situation became
strained. Dion had to go into what was virtually banishment and
Plato returned to Athens. Relations, however, were not broken off.
Dionysius kept up a personal correspondence with Plato about his
studies and projects, and Plato endeavoured to reconcile Dionysius
and Dion. This proved not feasible when Dionysius not only
confiscated Dion's revenues but forced his wife, for dynastic
reasons, to marry another man. Yet Plato made another voyage
to Syracuse and spent nearly a year there (361–360) in the hope of
remedying the situation. On this occasion something was really
done on the task of drafting the preliminaries to a constitution for
the proposed federation of the Greek cities, but the influence of the
partisans of the old *régime* proved too strong. Plato seems at one
time to have been in real personal danger from the hostility of
Dionysius' barbarian body-guards, and it was with difficulty and only
by the mediation of Archytas of Tarentum that he finally obtained
leave to return to Athens (360 B.C.).

At this point Plato's personal intervention in Sicilian politics
ceases. The quarrel between Dion and Dionysius naturally went
on, and Dion, whose one great fault, as Plato tells him, was want of
" adaptability " and *savoir-faire*, made up his mind to recover his
rights with the strong hand. Enlistment went on in the Peloponnese
and elsewhere, with the active concurrence of many of the younger
members of the Academy, and in the summer of 357 Dion made a
sudden and successful dash across the water, captured Syracuse, and
proclaimed its " freedom." Plato wrote him a letter of congratulation on the success, but warned him of his propensity to carry things
with too high a hand and reminded him that the world would expect
the " You-know-who's " (the Academy) [1] to set a model of good
behaviour. Unfortunately Dion was too good and too bad at once
for the situation. Like Plato himself, he believed in strong though
law-abiding personal rule and disgusted the Syracusan mob by
not restoring " democratic " licence ; he had not the tact to manage
disappointed associates, quarrelled with his admiral Heraclides
and at last made away with him, or connived at his being made
away with. Dion was in turn murdered with great treachery by
another of his subordinates, Callippus, who is said by later writers
to have been a member of the Academy, though this seems hard to
reconcile with Plato's own statement that the link of association
between the two was not " philosophy " but the mere accident of
having been initiated together into certain " mysteries." Plato
still believed strongly in the fundamental honesty and sanity of

---

[1] *Ep*. iv. 320 *c–e*, and for Dion's want of " tact," *ibid*. 321*b*, vii. 328*b*.

Dion's political aims and wrote two letters to the remnants of his party, justifying the common policy of Dion and himself and calling on them to be faithful to it, and making suggestions for conciliation of parties which were, of course, not accepted. As he said in one of these letters, the fatal disunion of parties seemed likely to leave Sicily a prey either to the Carthaginians or to the Oscans of South Italy.[1]

It is not necessary to follow the miserable story of events in Syracuse beyond the point where Plato's concern with them ends. But it is worth while to remark that Plato's forecast of events was fully justified. The " unification of Sicily," when it came at last, came as a fruit of the success of the Romans in the first two Punic wars ; and, as Professor Burnet has said, this was the beginning of the long series of events which has made the cleavage between Eastern Europe, deriving what civilization it has direct from Constantinople, and Western Europe with its latinized Hellenism. If Plato had succeeded at Syracuse, there might have been no " schism of the churches " and no " Eastern problem " to-day.

Nothing is known, beyond an anecdote or two not worth re-cording, of Plato's latest years. All that we can say is that he must still have gone on from time to time lecturing to his associates in the Academy, since Aristotle, who only entered the Academy in 367, was one of his hearers, and that the years between 360 and his death must have been busily occupied with the composition of his longest and ripest contribution to the literature of moral and political philosophy, the *Laws*. Probably also, all the rest of the dialogues which manifestly belong to the later part of Plato's life must be supposed to have been written after his final return from Sicily. A complete suspension of composition for several years will best explain the remarkable difference in style between all of them and even the maturest of those which preceded. It may be useful to remember that of the years mentioned as marking important events in Plato's life, the year 388 is that of the capture of Rome by the Gauls, 367 the traditional date of the " Licinian rogations " and the defeat of the Gauls at Alba by Camillus, 361 that of the penetration of the Gauls into Campania.

See further :

BURNET, J.—*Greek Philosophy, Part I.*, Chapters xii., xv.
BURNET, J.—*Platonism* (1928).
FRIEDLANDER, P.—*Platon : Eidos, Paideia, Dialogos* (1928).
GROTE, G.—*Plato and the other Companions of Socrates*, Chapter v.
RITTER, C.—*Platon*, i., Chapters i.-v. (Munich, 1914.)
WILAMOWITZ-MOELLENDORFF, U. v.—*Platon*. (Ed. 2. Berlin. 1920.)
STENZEL, J.—*Platon der Erzieher*. (Leipzig, 1928.)
  The general historical background of Plato's life may be studied in any good history of Greece. Specially excellent is
MEYER, E.—*Geschichte des Altertums*, vol. v. (Stuttgart and Berlin, 1902.)
ROBIN, L.—*Platon*, pp. 1-8.

CHAPTER II

THE PLATONIC WRITINGS

I

PLATO is the one voluminous author of classical antiquity whose works seem to have come down to us whole and entire. Nowhere in later antiquity do we come on any reference to a Platonic work which we do not still possess. It is true that we know nothing of the contents of Plato's lectures except from a few scanty notices in Aristotle or quotations preserved from contemporaries of Aristotle by the Aristotelian commentators. But the explanation of this seems to be that Plato habitually lectured without any kind of manuscript. This explains why Aristotle speaks of certain doctrines as taught in the " unwritten teaching " (ἄγραφα δόγματα) of his master, and why at least five of the auditors of a particularly famous lecture (that on " The Good "), including both Aristotle and Xenocrates, published their own recollections of it. We must suppose that Plato's written dialogues were meant to appeal to the " educated " at large and interest them in philosophy ; the teaching given to Plato's personal associates depended for its due appreciation on the actual contact of mind with mind within the school and was therefore not committed to writing at all. As we shall see later on, this has had the (for us) unfortunate result that we are left to learn Plato's inmost ultimate convictions on the most important questions, the very thing we most want to know, from references in Aristotle, polemical in object, always brief, and often puzzling in the highest degree.

When we turn to the contents of our manuscripts, the first problem which awaits us is that of weeding out from the whole collection what is dubious or certainly spurious. We may start with the fact that certain insignificant items of the collection were already recognized as spurious when the arrangement of the dialogues which we find in our oldest Plato MSS. was made. By counting each dialogue great or small as a unit, and reckoning the collection of *Epistles* also as one dialogue, a list of thirty-six works was drawn up, arranged in " tetralogies " or groups of four. It is not absolutely certain by whom or when this arrangement was made, though it certainly goes back almost to the beginning of the Christian era and perhaps earlier. It is commonly ascribed by later writers to a certain Thrasylus or to Thrasylus and Dercylides. The date of neither of these scholars is known with certainty. Thrasylus has been usually identified with a rhetorician of that name living under Augustus and Tiberius. But it is notable that Cicero's contemporary, the antiquary M. Terentius Varro, refers [1] to a passage of the *Phaedo* as occurring in the "fourth roll" of Plato, and the *Phaedo* actually happens to be the fourth dialogue of the first "tetralogy." Hence it has been suggested that the arrangement is older than Varro. If this is correct, it will follow that either Thrasylus has been wrongly identified or the arrangement was merely adopted, not originated, by him. On the other hand, this grouping cannot be *earlier* than the first or second century B.C. For Diogenes Laertius [2] informs us that an earlier arrangement of the dialogues in "trilogies" had been attempted, though not carried completely through, by the famous third-century scholar Aristophanes of Byzantium. There is no hint anywhere that the "tetralogies" of Thrasylus admitted any work not regarded as Platonic by Aristophanes or excluded any which he had admitted. We may fairly conclude that the thirty-six "dialogues" were currently regarded as genuine by the librarians and scholars of the third century B.C. As far as the extant dialogues omitted from the "tetralogies" go, there is no question that they are one and all spurious, and no one proposes to reverse the judgment of antiquity on any of them. The same thing is true of the collection of "definitions" also preserved in Plato MSS. There is no doubt that in the main the definitions of the collection are genuinely ancient and Academic. Some of them are actually extracted from the Platonic dialogues ; others are shown to be Academic by their coincidence with Academic definitions used or commented on by Aristotle in his *Topics*. But since some of them can be pretty clearly identified with definitions we can prove to be characteristic of Plato's immediate successors, Speusippus and Xenocrates, we cannot regard the collection as the work of Plato. Our only real problem is whether the list of the thirty-six dialogues must not be further reduced by the elimination of spurious items. Even in antiquity there were doubts about one or two dialogues. The *Alcibiades II* [3] was thought to be unauthentic by some, and the Neoplatonist Proclus wished to reject the *Epinomis*. In modern times doubt has been carried much farther. In the middle of the nineteenth century, especially in Germany, the "athetizing" of Platonic dialogues became a fashionable amusement for scholars ; the *Laws* was pronounced spurious by Ast and, at one time, by Zeller, the *Parmenides*, *Sophistes*, and *Politicus* by Ueberweg and others; extremists wished to limit the number of genuine dialogues to nine. Fortunately the tide has turned, since the elaborate proof of the genuineness of the *Sophistes* and *Politicus* by Lewis Campbell. There is now a general agreement that every dialogue of any length and interest in the list of the thirty-

[1] Varro, *de lingua Latina*, vii. 88. [2] D. L., iii. 61–62.
[3] Athenaeus (506e) records an opinion which ascribed the dialogue to Xenophon.

six is Platonic, and an equally general agreement about the spuriousness of a number of the smaller and less interesting, though there
still remain one or two works about which opinion is divided.   Thus
there is little doubt of the un-Platonic character of the following
works : *Alcibiades II, Hipparchus, Amatores* (or *Rivales*), *Theages,
Clitophon, Minos.* Opinion may be said to be divided about *Alcibiades I, Ion, Menexenus, Hippias Major, Epinomis, Epistles.*
The scope of the present work allows me only to make one or two
very brief remarks on the subject.

As to the now generally rejected dialogues it may be observed
that they are all brief and of no great moment.   Our conception
of Plato as a thinker and a writer is not seriously affected by the
rejection of any of them.   If it were possible to put in a word on
behalf of any of these items, I should like personally to plead for
the short sketch called the *Clitophon*, which seems to be in any case
a mere unfinished fragment, the main purport of which can only be
conjectured.   The style and verve are not unworthy of Plato, and
I believe I could make out a case for the view that the point to which
the writer is working up is also Platonic, as well as important.   Yet
there is the difficulty that the little work appears on the face of it
to be in form a criticism of the parts played by Socrates and Thrasymachus in *Republic I*, and it is hard to think of Plato as thus playing
the critic to one of his own writings.

About all these dialogues we may say at least two things.
There is only one of them (the *Alcibiades II*) which does not seem
to be proved by considerations of style and language to be real
fourth-century work.   And again, there is no reason to regard any
of them as " spurious " in the sense of being intended to pass falsely
for the work of Plato.   They are anonymous and inferior work of
the same kind as the lighter Platonic dialogues, and probably, in
most cases, contemporary with them or nearly so, not deliberate
" forgeries."   Hence this material may rightly be used with caution
as contributing to our knowledge of the conception of Socrates
current in the fourth century.   *Alcibiades II* is probably an exception.   It is the one dialogue in the list which exhibits anything
very suspicious on linguistic grounds, and it appears also to allude
to a characteristic Stoic paradox.[1]   But, even in this case, there is
no ground to suppose that the unknown writer intended his work
to pass current as Plato's.   A little more must be said of the
dialogues which are still rejected by some scholars, but defended
by others.   The *Alcibiades I* has nothing in its language which
requires a date later than the death of Plato, and nothing in its

---

[1] There seems to be a definite polemic running through the dialogue
against the Stoic thesis that every one but the Stoic " sage " is insane.   Cf.
in particular *Alc. II,* 139*c*–140*d*.   (Personally I regard the attack on this
paradox as the main object of the work.)   Hence it cannot date from any
period of the Academy before the presidency of Arcesilaus (276–241 B.C.), with
whom anti-Stoic polemic became the main public interest of the school
For a discussion of the question see *Appendix*, pp. 528–9.

contents which is not thoroughly Platonic. In fact, it forms, as the Neoplatonic commentators saw, an excellent introduction to the whole Platonic ethical and political philosophy. It is just this character which is really the most suspicious thing about the dialogue. It is far too methodical not to suggest that it is meant as a kind of " textbook," the sort of thing Plato declared he would never write. And the character-drawing is far too vague and shadowy for Plato even in his latest and least dramatic phase. In the interlocutors, though they bear the names Socrates and Alcibiades, there is no trace of any genuine individuality—far less than there is even in the anonymous speakers in the *Laws*. It is a further difficulty that on grounds of style and manner the dialogue, if genuine, would have to be assigned to a late period in Plato's life when he is hardly likely to have been composing such work. On the whole, it seems probable that *Alcibiades I* is the work of an immediate disciple, probably written within a generation or so of Plato's death and possibly even before that event.

The *Ion*, so far as can be seen, has in its few pages nothing either to establish its authenticity or to arouse suspicion. It may reasonably be allowed to pass as genuine until some good reason for rejecting it is produced.

The *Menexenus* offers a difficult problem. It is referred to expressly by Aristotle in a way in which he never seems to quote any dialogues but those of Plato, and it seems clear that he regarded it as Platonic.[1] On the other hand, the contents of the work are singular. It is mainly given up to the recital by Socrates of a " funeral discourse " on the Athenians who fell in the Corinthian war. Socrates pretends to have heard the discourse from Aspasia and to admire it greatly. Apparently the intention is to produce a gravely ironical satire on the curious jumble of real and spurious patriotism characteristic of the λόγοι ἐπιτάφιοι, which are being quietly burlesqued. The standing mystery for commentators is, of course, the audacious anachronism by which Socrates (and, what is even worse, Aspasia) is made to give a narrative of events belonging to the years after Socrates' own death. To me it seems clear that this violation of chronological possibility, since it must have been committed at a time when the facts could not be unknown, must be intentional, however hard it is to divine its precise point, and that Plato is more likely than any disciple in the Academy to have ventured on it. (As the second part of the *Parmenides* proves, Plato had a certain " freakish " humour in him which could find strange outlets.) And I find it very hard to suppose that Aristotle was deceived on a question of Platonic authorship. Hence it seems best to accept the traditional ascription of the *Menexenus*, however hard we may think it to account for its character.

The *Hippias Major*, though not cited by name anywhere in Aristotle, is tacitly quoted or alluded to several times in the *Topics* in a way which convinces me that Aristotle regarded it as a Platonic

[1] Aristot. *Rhetoric*, 1415b 30.

work.[1] As the "athetizers" have really nothing to urge on the other side except that the dialogue is not Plato at his best, and that there are an unusual word or two to be found in it (as there are in many Platonic dialogues), I think Aristotle's allusions should decide the question of genuineness favourably.

The *Epinomis* and *Epistles* are much more important. If the *Epinomis* is spurious, we must deny the authenticity of the most important pronouncement on the philosophy of arithmetic to be found in the whole Platonic *corpus*. If the *Epistles* are spurious, we lose our one direct source of information for any part of Plato's biography, and also the source of most of our knowledge of Sicilian affairs from 367 to 354. (As E. Meyer says, the historians who reject the *Epistles* disguise the state of the case by alleging Plutarch's *Life of Dion* as their authority, while the statements in this *Life* are openly drawn for the most part from the *Epistles*.) Documents like these ought not to be surrendered to the "athetizer" except for very weighty reasons.

As to the *Epinomis* the case stands thus. It was certainly known in antiquity generally and regarded as genuine. Cicero, for example, quotes it as "Plato." On the other hand, the Neoplatonic philosopher Proclus (410–485 A.D.) wished to reject it as spurious because of an astronomical discrepancy with the *Timaeus*. Diogenes Laertius also tells us that Plato's *Laws* were "copied out from the wax" by the Academic astronomer Philippus of Opus, adding "and his too, as they say, is the *Epinomis*." It has become common in recent times to assert, on the strength of this remark, that the *Epinomis* is an appendix to the *Laws* composed by Philippus. It ought, however, to be noted that Proclus was apparently unaware that any doubt had been felt about the *Epinomis* before his own time, since he based his rejection wholly on argument, not on testimony. His argument is, moreover, a bad one, since the "discrepancy with the *Timaeus*" of which he complained is found as much in the *Laws* as in the *Epinomis*. The internal evidence of style seems to reveal no difference whatever between the two works. And it may be urged that since the state of the text of the *Laws* shows that the work must have been left at Plato's death without the author's final revision and then circulated without even the small verbal corrections which the editor of a posthumous work commonly has to make in the interests of grammar, it is most unlikely that disciples who treated the *ipsissima verba* of a dead master with such scrupulous veneration would have ventured on adding a "part the last" to the work on their own account. Hence it seems to me that Hans Raeder is right in insisting on the genuineness of the *Epinomis*, and that the remark of Diogenes about Philippus of Opus only means

---

[1] Twice for the unsatisfactory definition of τὸ καλόν as τὸ πρέπον (*Topics*, A5. 102a 6, E5. 135a 13) ; once for the still worse definition of καλόν as τὸ δι' ὄψεως ἢ ἀκοῆς ἡδύ (*Topics*, Z6. 146a 22). That both these bad attempts at definition occur in the dialogue seems to make it clear that Aristotle is alluding to it and not to any other source.

that he did for this work was also transcribed by, or perhaps dictated to, him. (The now customary disparagement of the *Epinomis* seems to me due to mere inability to follow the mathematics of the dialogue.[1])

Professor Werner Jaeger[2] has incidentally done a service to the student of the *Epinomis* in his recent work on the development of Aristotle's thought by showing that there is an intimate connexion between the *Laws* and *Epinomis* and Aristotle's work περὶ φιλοσοφίας, of which only fragments are now extant. In particular, as he shows, there is an immediate connexion between the " fifth " or " etherial " bodily region of the *Epinomis* and Aristotle's famous " celestial matter " of which the " heavens " are assumed to be made (the *essentia quinta* or *materia coelestis*). Professor Jaeger interprets the connexion thus. We have first the *Laws* circulated promptly after Plato's death, then Aristotle's proposals for modifications of Platonic doctrine in the περὶ φιλοσοφίας, finally (all in the course of a year or two), the *Epinomis*, rejoining to Aristotle, and composed by Philippus. While I regard Professor Jaeger's proof of the intimate relation between *Epinomis* and περὶ φιλοσοφίας as important, I think it more natural to interpret the facts rather differently by supposing the *Laws* and *Epinomis* together to have been transcribed and circulated shortly after the death of Plato, and then followed by Aristotle's criticism of Platonic doctrine in the περὶ φιλοσοφίας. This at least leaves Aristotle more leisure than Professor Jaeger's hypothesis for the composition of a work which, as we know it ran to three " books," must have been of considerable compass. Whatever the truth about the *Epinomis* may be, I am at least sure that it is premature to assume that it is known not to be Plato's.

As for the *Epistles*, it is not necessary now to argue the case for their genuineness as elaborately as one would have had to do some years ago. Since Wilamowitz in his *Platon* declared for the genuineness of the very important trio VI, VII, VIII, those who depend on " authority " for their opinions have been in a hurry to protest that these three at least must be accepted. But the acceptance of the three logically carries with it recognition of the correspondence between Plato and Dionysius (II, III, XIII) and the letter of congratulation and good advice to Dion (IV) ; and when these are accepted as Platonic, there remains no good ground for rejecting any of the thirteen letters of our MSS. except the first, which is written in a style wholly unlike the others, and by some one whose circumstances, as stated by himself, show that he can be neither Plato nor Dion, nor have any intention of passing for either. Presumably this letter got into the correspondence by some mistake at a very early date. The twelfth letter (a mere note of half a dozen lines) was apparently suspected in later antiquity, since our

---

[1] For a good recent defence of the dialogue see the discussion in H. Raeder, *Platons philosophische Entwickelung*, 413 ff. and cf. *infra*, pp. 497–8.

[2] Jaeger, *Aristoteles*, c. 2.

best MSS. have a note to that effect.   No grounds have ever been
produced for questioning the authenticity of any of the rest which
will bear examination.   Most of the difficulties raised in modern
times, especially those alleged in connexion with II and XIII,
rest on mere misunderstandings.   It is safe to say that the present
tendency to accept only VI, VII, VIII is a consequence of mere
servile deference to the name of Wilamowitz.   None of these
documents should have needed the imprimatur of a professor as a
recommendation ; their acceptance is bound to lead logically to
that of the rest with the exception of I and *possibly* XII.   As far
as external testimony goes, it is enough to say that Aristophanes
of Byzantium included in his " trilogies " *Epistles* (pretty obviously
our thirteen, or we should have heard more about the matter), and
that Cicero quotes IV, IX, and especially VII (*nobilissima illa
epistula*, as he calls it) as familiar Platonic material.   This, taken
together with the thoroughly Platonic style of the letters, disposes
of the notion that they can be " forgeries."   The art of writing
such prose was already dead in half a century after Plato's death,
and the revival of " Atticism," which might make such a production
barely conceivable, belongs to a time some generations later than
Cicero.[1]

II

To understand a great thinker is, of course, impossible unless
we know something of the relative order of his works, and of the
actual period of his life to which they belong.   What, for example,
could we make of Kant if we did not know whether the *Critique of
Pure Reason* was the work of ambitious youth or of ripe middle age,
whether it was written before or after the discourse on the *Only Possible Demonstration of the Being of a God* or the *Dreams of a Ghost-seer* ?
We cannot, then, even make a beginning with the study of Plato
until we have found some trustworthy indication of the order in
which his works, or at least the most significant of them, were
written.   Even when we have fixed this order, if it can be fixed, we
need, for a completer understanding, to be able also to say at what
precise period of life the most important dialogues were written,

[1] The reader will find an elaborate collection of linguistic and other
arguments against the *Epistles* in the section devoted to them in H. Richards'
Platonica, 254–298, and, as regards most of the series, in C. Ritter, *Neue Untersuchungen ueber Platon*, 327–424.   Most of the alleged objections appear
frivolous, or at best based on misreading of the Syracusan situation.   Why
the German critics in general think that it is in some way " unworthy " of Plato
to have had a " business settlement " with Dionysius such as that to which
Ep. xiii. relates is to me as unintelligible as Wilamowitz's assertion that the
statements of the same letter about the great age of Plato's mother and the
existence of four nieces for whom he may have to provide must be fiction.
Old ladies do sometimes live to over ninety, and any man of sixty may quite
well have four nieces.   The names of Bentley, Cobet, Grote, Blass, E. Meyer,
are enough to show that there is plenty of good " authority " for belief in the
Epistles.   See *Appendix*, pp. 541–544, for further discussion.

whether in early manhood, in mid life, or in old age, and again whether they are an unbroken series of compositions or whether there is evidence of a considerable gap or gaps in Plato's literary activity. These are the questions which we have now to face.

The external evidence supplied by trustworthy testimony only assures us on one point. Aristotle tells us (*Pol.* 1264*b* 26), what could in any case never have been doubted, that the *Laws* is later than the *Republic*. There was also an ancient tradition, mentioned by Proclus and implied in the statement of Diogenes Laertius about Philippus of Opus, that the *Laws* was left by Plato " in the wax," and the " fair copy " for circulation made after his death. The statement is borne out by the frequency in the dialogue of small grammatical difficulties which cannot reasonably be ascribed to later " corruption," but are natural in a faithfully copied first text which has never received the author's finishing touches. Trustworthy testimony takes us no farther than this. Comparison of certain Platonic dialogues with one another yields one or two other results. Thus the *Republic* must be earlier than the *Timaeus*, where it is referred to and the argument of its first five books briefly recapitulated. The *Politicus* must be not earlier than the *Sophistes*, to which it is the professed sequel; and the *Sophistes*, for the same reason, later than the *Theaetetus*. These are all the certain indications furnished by the matter of the dialogues themselves. There *may* be an allusion in the *Phaedo* to a point more fully explained in the *Meno*, and the *Republic* has been supposed to allude to both. Both the *Theaetetus* and the *Sophistes* refer to a meeting between Socrates, then extremely young, and the great Parmenides; and there must be some connexion between these references and the fact that the *Parmenides* professes ostensibly to describe this encounter. But we cannot say that the allusions enable us to determine with certainty whether the *Parmenides* is earlier than both the others, later than both, or intermediate between the two. Raeder has tried to show at length that the *Phaedrus* contains allusions which would only be intelligible to readers who already knew the *Republic*; but there are gaps in his argument, and it has not completely convinced some prominent Platonic scholars. Clearly, if we are to arrive at results of any value, we need a clue to the order of composition of the dialogues which will take us much farther than the few certain indications we have so far found.

In the earlier part of the nineteenth century more than one unsatisfactory attempt was made to provide such a clue. Thus it was at one time held that we can detect signs of comparative youth in the gorgeous rhetoric of certain dialogues, and the *Phaedrus* in particular was often assumed to be the earliest of the dialogues on this ground. But it is obvious that reasoning of this kind is inherently untrustworthy, especially in dealing with the work of a great dramatic artist. Inferences from the manner of the *Phaedrus* are, for example, to be discounted partly on the ground that its rhetoric is largely parody of the rhetoricians, partly because so much of its content is imaginative myth which lends itself naturally to a high-flown diction.   The assumption that works in which there is a large element of semi-poetical myth must be " juvenile " obviously rests on another assumption, for which we have no evidence at all, that we know independently what the personal temperament of the youthful Plato was.   We have only to think of the known chronological order of the works of Goethe to see how unsound a method must be which would require us to regard the second part of *Faust* or *Wilhelm Meisters Wanderjahre* as juvenile productions.   A still more arbitrary assumption underlies the attempt of E. Munk to arrange the dialogues in order on the assumption that the age ascribed to Socrates in a dialogue is an indication of its date.   On the theory that dialogues which represent Socrates as a young man must be early, those which represent him as old, late, we should have to put the *Parmenides*, where Socrates is " very young," at the opening of the series, the *Theaetetus*, which narrates a conversation held just before his trial, at the other end, though the allusion in the one dialogue to the meeting which provides the setting for the other shows that they are probably not to be separated by too long an interval.

The serious scientific investigation of the internal evidence for the order of composition of the dialogues really begins in 1867 with Lewis Campbell's philological proof of the genuineness of the *Sophistes* and *Politicus*.   It has been further developed, sometimes with too much confidence in its results, by a whole host of writers, notably Dittenberger and C. Ritter in Germany, and W. Lutoslawski in this country.   The underlying and sound principle of the method may be simply stated thus.   If we start with two works which are known to be separated by a considerable interval and exhibit a marked difference in style, it may be possible to trace the transition from the writer's earlier to his later manner in detail, to see the later manner steadily more and more replacing the earlier, and this should enable us to arrive at some definite conclusions about the order of the works which occupy the interval.   The conclusion will be strengthened if we take for study a number of distinct and independent peculiarities and find a general coincidence in the order in which the various peculiarities seem to become more and more settled mannerisms.   The opportunity for applying this method to the work of Plato is afforded by the well-authenticated fact that the *Laws* is a composition of old age, while the *Republic* is one of an earlier period, and forms with certain other great dialogues, such as the *Protagoras, Phaedo, Symposium*, a group distinguished by a marked common style and a common vigour of dramatic representation which experience shows we cannot expect from a writer who is not in the prime of his powers.   Growing resemblance to the manner of the *Laws*, if made out on several independent but consilient lines of inquiry, may thus enable us to discover which of the Platonic dialogues must be intermediate between the *Laws* and the *Republic*. There are several different peculiarities we may obviously select for study. Thus one obvious contrast between *Republic* and *Laws* is to be found in the marked decline of dramatic power. A second is that the *Laws* conforms carefully to a whole number of the graces of style introduced into Attic prose by Isocrates, the *Republic* and the other great dramatic dialogues neglect these elegancies. A third line of study which has been very minutely pursued, especially by Lutoslawski, is the examination of special uses of connecting particles throughout the dialogues. Without going into detail, it is enough to say here that the result of these converging lines of study has been to convince students of Platonic language and idiom, almost without an exception, that we can definitely specify a certain group of very important dialogues as belonging to the post-*Republic* period of Plato's life. The group comprises *Theaetetus, Parmenides, Sophistes, Politicus, Timaeus, Philebus, Laws*. The identification of this group of " later " dialogues may be taken as a pretty assured and definite result, not likely ever to be seriously modified.

It is another question whether the employment of the same method would enable us to distinguish more precisely between the earlier and later dialogues belonging to either of the two great groups, so as to say, *e.g.*, whether the *Philebus* is earlier or later in composition than the *Timaeus*, the *Symposium* than the *Phaedo*. When two works belong to much the same period of an author's activity, a slight difference of style between them may easily be due to accidental causes. (Thus in dealing with the *Symposium* we should have to remember that a very large part of it is professed imitation or parody of the styles of others.) Lutoslawski in particular seems to me to have pushed a sound principle to the pitch of absurdity in the attempt, by the help of the integral calculus, to extract from considerations of " stylometry " a detailed and definite order of composition for the whole of the dialogues. It may fairly be doubted whether " stylometric " evidence can carry us much beyond the broad discrimination between an earlier series of dialogues of which the *Republic* is the capital work and a later series composed in the interval between the completion of the *Republic* and Plato's death.

It is possible, however, that some supplementary considerations may take us a little further. Plato himself explains, in the introductory conversation prefixed to the *Theaetetus*, that he has avoided the method of indirect narration of a dialogue for that of direct dialogue in order to avoid the wearisomeness of keeping up the formula of a reported narrative. Now the greatest dialogues of the earlier period, the *Protagoras, Symposium, Phaedo, Republic*, are all reported dialogues, and one of them, the *Symposium*, is actually reported at second-hand. So again is the *Parmenides*, where the standing formula, as Professor Burnet calls it, is the cumbrous "Antiphon told us that Pythodorus said that Parmenides said." The original adoption of this method of narration of a conversation is manifestly due to the desire for dramatic life and colour.

It permits of the sort of record of the by-play between the personages of the story which contributes so much to the charm of the *Phaedo*. But the labour required to keep up the " formula " is so great that it is not surprising that Plato finally dropped it, and that the *Theaetetus* and all the works we find reason to place later are in the form of direct dialogue. To me it seems highly probable, though not certain, that it was the special complication of the formula required for the *Parmenides* which led to the final abandonment of the method, and that we may plausibly infer that the *Parmenides* was written either simultaneously with the *Theaetetus* or immediately before it. Another inference which I should draw with some confidence is that, since no young writer is likely to have made his first prentice experiments in dialogue with so difficult a form, the popular view that the *Protagoras* is one of the earliest of the Platonic dialogues must be erroneous. The certainty and vigour of the dramatic handling of the characters there should prove that the *Protagoras* belongs as a fourth with the *Phaedo, Symposium,* and *Republic* to the period of Plato's supreme excellence as a dramatist and stylist. In particular, it must be a considerably later work than the comparatively undramatic and rather unduly diffuse *Gorgias*, a point which has some bearing on the interpretation of the purpose and ethical teaching of the *Protagoras*.

We may turn next to the question whether it is possible to fix any definite date in Plato's life as a *terminus ad quem* for the earlier series of dialogues, or a *terminus a quo* for the later. Something, I believe, may be done to settle both these questions. I have already referred in the last chapter to the statement made by Plato in *Ep.* vii., written after the murder of Dion in the year 354, that he came to Sicily in his forty-first year already convinced that the salvation of mankind depends on the union of the philosopher and the " ruler " in one person. The actual words of the letter are that Plato had been driven to *say* this " in a eulogy on true philosophy," and this seems an unmistakable allusion to the occurrence of the same statement in *Rep.* 499 ff. It should follow that this most philosophically advanced section of the *Republic* was already written in the year 388–7, with the consequence that the *Republic*, and by consequence the earlier dialogues in general, were completed at least soon after Plato was forty and perhaps before foundation of the Academy. If we turn next to the dialogue which seems to prelude to the later group, the *Theaetetus*, we get another indication of date. The dialogue mentions the severe and dangerous wound received by the mathematician Theaetetus in a battle fought under the walls of Corinth which cannot well be any but that of the year 369. It is assumed tacitly all through that Theaetetus will not recover from his injuries and is clear that the discourse was composed after his death and mainly as a graceful tribute to his memory. Thus, allowing for the time necessary for the completion of so considerable a work, we may suppose the dialogue to have been written just before Plato's first departure on his important practical enterprise at Syracuse. This, as Professor Burnet has said, seems to be the explanation of the magnificent eulogy of the retired and contemplative life, a passage confessed by Plato himself to be an irrelevance so far as the argument of the dialogue is concerned. Plato is giving expression to the reluctance with which he leaves the Academy, at the bidding of duty and honour, for the turmoil and sordidness of the political arena.

Once more, the *Sophistes* seems to give us an approximate date. It is the first of the series of dialogues in which the deliberate adoption of the Isocratean avoidance of hiatus occurs. This would naturally suggest a probable break of some length in Plato's activity as a writer just before the composition of the *Sophistes*. Now it is antecedently probable that there must have been such an interruption between 367 and 360, the year of Plato's last return from Syracuse. His entanglements with Dionysius and Sicilian affairs, combined with his duties as head of the Academy, are likely to have left him little leisure for literary occupation in these years.

Thus we may say with every appearance of probability that there are two distinct periods of literary activity to be distinguished in Plato's life. The first cannot have begun before the death of Socrates ; apart from the absurdity of the conception of Plato as " dramatizing " the sayings and doings of the living man whom he revered above all others, it is fairly plain that the original motive for the composition of " discourses of Socrates " by the *viri Socratici* was to preserve the memory of a living presence which they had lost. It apparently continued down to Plato's fortieth or forty-first year and the opening of the Academy, and it includes all the work in which Plato's dramatic art is most fresh and vigorous. The main object of this incessant activity seems to be to immortalize the personality of Socrates. For twenty years after the foundation of the Academy Plato seems to have written nothing, unless the *Phaedrus*, a difficult dialogue to account for on any theory, falls early in this period. This is as it should be : the President of the Academy would for long enough after its foundation be far too busy to write. Then, probably on the eve of the Sicilian adventure, after twenty years of work the Academy is sufficiently organized to leave its head, now a man of some sixty years, leisure to write the *Theaetetus* and *Parmenides*; but an opportunity for continuous writing does not present itself until Plato's final withdrawal from active personal participation in " world politics." The composition of five such works as *Sophistes, Politicus, Timaeus, Philebus, Laws,* is a notable achievement for any man between the ages of sixty-seven and eighty-one. But we must think of this work as being executed simultaneously with regular oral exposition of the doctrine described by Aristotle as the " philosophy of Plato." It is an entire misconception to relegate this last stage in the development of Plato's thought, as the textbooks often seem to do, to a " senile " year or two subsequent to the close of Plato's activity as a writer. It must have been contemporary with the writing of the whole

" later " group of dialogues, and the man who was still at his death labouring on the *Laws* can never have sunk into " senility."

See further :

BURNET, J.—*Platonism*, Ch. **1**, 4.

CAMPBELL, L.—" *Sophistes* " and " *Politicus* " of Plato (1867), General Introduction.

HACKFORTH, R.—*The Authorship of the Platonic Epistles.* (Manchester, 1913.)

RAEDER, H.—*Platons philosophische Entwickelung.* (Leipzig, 1905.)

LUTOSLAWSKI, W.—*Origin and Growth of Plato's Logic.* (1897.)

PARMENTIER, L.—*La Chronologie des dialogues de Platon.* (Brussels, 1913.)

RITTER, C.—*Untersuchungen ueber Platon.* (Stuttgart, 1882.) ; *Neue Untersuchungen ueber Platon.* (Munich, 1910.)

LEVI, A.—*Sulle interpretazioni immanentistiche della filosofia di Platone.* (Turin, N.D.)

SHOREY, P.—*The Unity of Plato's Thought.* (Chicago, 1903.)

SHOREY, P.—*What Plato Said*, pp. 58–73.

ROBIN, L.—*Platon*, pp. 19–48.

NOVOTNÝ, F.—*Platonis Epistulae.*

HARWARD, J.—*The Platonic Epistles* (Introduction).

NOTE.—I do not deny that Plato's " first period " may have extended into the opening years of his career in the Academy. On my own reasoning this must be so if the *Phaedo* should, after all, be later than the *Republic*. It has been argued (*e.g.* by M. Parmentier) that the *Symposium* must be later than 385, the year of the death of Aristophanes. I doubt, however, whether too much has not been made of the supposed Platonic rule not to introduce living persons as speakers. Callias was alive and active years after any date to which we can reasonably assign the *Protagoras*. Euclides, who was alive and apparently well when Theaetetus received his wound, is more likely than not to have survived the writing of the *Theaetetus*. Socrates " the younger " can hardly be taken to have been dead when the *Politicus* was written. Gorgias *may* have lived long enough to read the *Gorgias*. Simmias, if we may believe Plutarch *de genio Socratis*, was alive and active in 379. That the majority of Plato's personages are characters already dead when his dialogues were written, seems to me a mere consequence of the fact that the dialogues deal with Socrates and his contemporaries.

[It might be urged against the reasoning of the first paragraph of p. 20 *supra* that several, if not all, of the dialogues of Aeschines (certainly the *Aspasia, Alcibiades, Callias, Axiochus*) were of the " narrated " type. But they were narrations of the simplest kind of which the *Charmides* and *Laches* are examples, and such evidence as we have suggests that they are all later in date of composition than the earliest work of Plato.]

CHAPTER III

MINOR SOCRATIC DIALOGUES : *HIPPIAS MAJOR,*
HIPPIAS MINOR, ION, MENEXENUS

LOVERS of great literature have every reason to be whole-heartedly thankful that once in the world's history a supreme philosophical thinker should also have been a superb dramatic artist. But what is to them pure gain is, in some ways, gain at the expense of the average student of " metaphysics." For several reasons it is quite impossible to construct a neatly arranged systematic handbook to the " Platonic philosophy." In the first place, it is doubtful whether there ever was a " Platonic philosophy " at all, in the sense of a definite set of formulated doctrines about the *omne scibile*. Plato has done his best to make it quite clear that he took no great interest in " system-making." To him philosophy meant no compact body of " results " to be learned, but a life spent in the active personal pursuit of truth and goodness by the light of one or two great passionate convictions. It is not likely that, even at the end of his life of eighty years, he fancied himself to have worked out anything like a coherent, clearly articulated " theory of everything." Systematization of this kind commonly has to be paid for by intellectual stagnation ; the vitality and progressiveness of Platonism is probably largely owing to the fact that, even in the mind of its originator, it always remained largely tentative and provisional. If there ever was a Platonic " system," at least Plato himself resolutely refused to write an exposition of it,[1] and we of later times, who do not possess any record of the oral teaching which was clearly intended to be the vehicle of Plato's most personal and intimate thinking, are not in a position to make the lack good. The dialogues will tell us something of Plato's fundamental life-

---

[1] *Ep.* vii. 341*c*: " There does not exist, and there never shall, any treatise by myself on these matters. The subject does not admit, as the sciences in general do, of exposition. It is only after long association in the great business itself and a shared life that a light breaks out in the soul, kindled, so to say, by a leaping flame, and thereafter feeds itself." *Ep.* ii. 314*c*: " I have never myself written a word on these topics, and there neither is nor ever shall be any treatise by Plato ; what now bears the name belongs to Socrates beautified and rejuvenated." That is, all that a teacher can do in philosophy is to awaken in a younger mind the spirit of independent personal thinking ; the dialogues are meant not to expound a " Platonic system," but to preserve the memory of Socrates. One of Plato's grounds for dissatisfaction with Dionysius II was that he had circulated a work professing to expound " Platonism " (*Ep.* vii. 341*b*).

long convictions ; of his " system," if he had one, they hardly tell us anything at all. With Aristotle we are in a very different position. We have lost the " works " in which he recommended his " views " to the world at large, and possess the manuscripts of courses of lectures in which we see him, for the most part, feeling his way to his results through the criticism of others.

Further special difficulties are created for us by certain peculiarities of Plato's literary temperament. Unlike Aristotle, he does not introduce himself and his opinions into his dialogues. He is, in fact, at great pains, with the instinct of the great dramatist, to keep his own personality completely in the background. Socrates is present as one of the speakers in all the dialogues except the *Laws*, and in all except those which we have seen reason to regard as written in late life, Socrates is not only the chief speaker but dominates the whole dialogue by his vivid and strongly marked personality. It can hardly be doubted that in the long list of works written before Plato had found his real vocation as head of the Academy, the main conscious object of the writer is to preserve a faithful and living portrait of the older philosopher.

Even if we accept the view originated about the beginning of the nineteenth century, that Plato has transfigured the personality and teaching of Socrates out of recognition, we are bound, I think, to hold that the transfiguration has been unconscious. We cannot seriously ascribe to Plato deliberate and pointless mystification. This means, of itself, that Plato carefully devotes himself to reproducing the life and thought of a generation to which he did not himself belong, and that whatever indications he may have given us of his personal doctrines have to be given under restrictions imposed by this selection of a vanished age as the background of the dialogues. (Thus we cannot read the *Republic* intelligently unless we bear carefully in mind both that the whole work presupposes as its setting the Athens of the Archidamian war and that this setting had vanished into the past by 413, when Plato was still no more than a boy. So to understand the *Protagoras* we have to remember that we are dealing with a still earlier time, Athens under Pericles shortly before the outbreak of the great war, and that Plato was not even born at the date of the gathering of the " wits " in the house of Callias.) There are only two characters among the host of personages in Plato's dialogues of whom one can be certain that they are not actual historical figures of the fifth century, the unnamed Eleatic of the *Sophistes* and *Politicus* and the unnamed Athenian of the *Laws*. They have been left anonymous apparently on purpose that their creator may be at liberty to express thoughts of his own through them with a freedom impossible in the case of figures who are " kennt men," with characters and views of their own which have to be taken into account.

This is generally admitted on all hands except for the one most important figure of all, that of Socrates. Him, it is still maintained in many quarters, though not so confidently as it used to be maintained thirty or forty years ago, Plato treated without scruple, to the point of putting into his mouth all sorts of theories invented by Plato himself after the death of their ostensible exponent. I cannot myself believe in this extraordinary exception to the general rule, but even if one does believe in it, the general situation is not very seriously affected. Even those who most freely credit Plato with fathering his own views on Socrates commonly admit that some of the views ascribed to Socrates in the dialogues (if only those expressed in the *Apology*) are those of the actual Socrates, and to admit this means admitting at least that we have somehow to distinguish between those utterances of " Socrates " which are really deliverances of " Plato " and those which are not, and it becomes a difficult problem to know on what principle the distinction is to be made. Finally, there is a further difficulty arising from the very life-likeness of the dialogues of the earlier groups. In nearly all of them except the shortest, the conversation wanders, as actual talk does, over a wide field of topics. Metaphysics, ethics, the principles of government, of economics, of art-criticism, of education, may all come under consideration in one and the same conversation. If we try to isolate the topics, putting together under one head all Plato has to say anywhere about economics, under another all his utterances about religion, under a third his views on beauty and the arts, we run the very serious risk of confusing what may be views learned early in life, and very largely taken over receptively from a predecessor, with the very ripest fruits of a life of intense personal thought. (Thus it would be rash to confound in one amalgam utterances about early education taken from the *Republic*, written probably before Plato was forty and at any rate *possibly* more Socratic than Platonic, with others taken from the *Laws*, the *magnum opus* of Plato's old age, where there is no Socrates in question to cause any difficulty.) A work on Platonic philosophy composed on these principles may be an admirably digested " cram-book " ; it is certain to obliterate every trace of the development of Plato's thought. For all these reasons, it seems the better choice between evils, to deal with the different dialogues *seriatim*, even at the cost of some repetition.

Accordingly I propose first to consider what we may call the " Socratic " group among the dialogues, the series of works culminating, so far as ripeness of thought and compass of subjects are concerned, in the *Republic*, grouping the slighter dialogues together but dwelling more fully on the detail of the greater and richer. Next I propose to treat separately each of the great dialogues of Plato's later age in the same way. In both cases I must remind my reader that I do not believe that many results of anything like certainty can be reached in the determination of the precise order of composition of particular dialogues. In the case of the earlier group, which I call Socratic in the sense that they are dominated by the personality of Plato's Socrates, I make no assumption about this order beyond the general one that the four great dialogues which have the widest range of subject-matter and are also reported at second-hand are maturer work than the slighter dialogues which have the form of direct conversation, and presumably also than shorter " indirect " conversations like the *Charmides* and *Euthydemus*. Beyond this, the order in which I shall examine the dialogues has no merit except that of convenience. Similarly the arrangement I shall adopt for the dialogues of later life is not meant to carry any silent chronological implications.

With one or two trifling exceptions most of the dialogues we shall have first to review have an ethical purport. (Perhaps the only complete exception of any importance is afforded by the *Cratylus*.) The interest of many of them is by no means exclusively ethical, sometimes (as in the case of the *Euthydemus*) not ostensibly primarily ethical, but we commonly find that the discussion either begins with, or is found as it proceeds to involve, the great practical issue of the right direction of conduct. It is therefore advisable to begin at the outset by formulating very briefly and in a way which brings out their interconnexion, a few simple principles which we shall find running through the whole of Plato's treatment of the moral being of man. Since we find these principles taken for granted in what has every mark of being Plato's earliest work as well as in his ripest and latest, we may fairly regard them as a legacy from Socrates ; and the most characteristic of them are, in fact, specifically attributed to Socrates by Aristotle, though we have no reason to suppose that Aristotle had any reason for the attribution beyond the fact that the principles in question are put into the mouth of Socrates in the Platonic dialogues, notably in the *Protagoras*. The most bald and straightforward statement of these principles as a whole in the Platonic *corpus* is perhaps that of the *Alcibiades I*, which has every appearance of being intended as a compendium of ethics composed by an immediate disciple and possibly during Plato's lifetime. We may reproduce the main line of argument adopted there and elsewhere much as follows.

The one great standing aim of men in all they do is to attain happiness (*eudaimonia*), in other words to make a success, in the best sense of the word, of life. Every one wants to make a success of his private life ; if a man is conscious of abilities and opportunities which open the way to prominence as a public man, he is anxious to make a success of the affairs of his " city," to be a successful states-man. This is what we mean by being a *good* man ; the *good* man is the man who " conducts his own affairs, those of his household, those of the city, *well*." And the words *good* and *well* are not used here in a narrowly moralistic sense. To conduct your business well means to make a thorough success of it ; the good man is the thoroughly effective man. But to make a thorough success of life means to achieve and possess *good*. We may say then that all men alike desire *good* and nothing but good. A man may conceivably prefer the appearance or reputation of some things to their reality ; *e.g.* a man may prefer a reputation for a virtue he does not possess to the possession of the virtue, or he might prefer being thought handsome or witty to being really so. But no one ever prefers being thought to enjoy good to the actual enjoyment of good. Where good is concerned, every one wishes really to have it, and not to put up with a counterfeit. If a man chooses, as many men do, what is not really good, the reason must be that he wrongly supposes it to be good. No one would ever knowingly choose evil when he might choose good, or leave a good he might have had unchosen. This is the meaning of the famous " Socratic " paradox that " all wrongdoing is involuntary." It is involuntary in the sense that the man who chooses what is bad only chooses it because he wrongly thinks it good. And so with the other " paradox " that no one ever knows the good without acting on his knowledge. It cannot be true that men "know the good but do the bad "; that would imply choice of an evil known to be evil, and such a choice is impossible.

Now when we come to consider the different things which men commonly call " good " and wish to have, we see at once that they are of various kinds. Some of them are material possessions. Many men think that good means just plenty of things of this sort. But we can easily see that material things are not good except for a man who knows how to use them. It would be no good to a man, for example, to have flutes, or musical instruments of any kind, unless he knew how to use them. Flutes are good—for the man who knows how to play on them. Similarly it would be no real good to you to possess all the gold in the world, unless you know how to *use* it. Again, men think that bodily beauty, strength and agility, robust health, are very good things. But health and strength again may be misused ; they are good only for the man who knows how to make the proper use of them. If a man has not this knowledge, but " abuses " his physical advantages, it might be much better for him if he had been less robust and active. The same thing is true of intellectual " parts." A man is not really the better for parts and accomplishments which he does not know how to use rightly. In fact we may say that if health, wealth, and the recognized " good " things are to be really good, it is first of all necessary that the user of these things should be good. Now that which uses all other things, even a man's body, is his *soul*. The soul *is* the man, and everything else that is his is merely something he has or owns. A man, in fact, is a " soul *using* a body " (this is the standing Academic definition of " man ").[1] Hence the first condition of enjoying real good and making a real success of life is that a man's soul should be in a good or healthy state. And the good or healthy state of the soul is just the wisdom or knowledge (*sophia, phronesis*) which ensures that a man shall make the right use of his body and of everything else which is his. Hence the first duty of every man who means to enjoy good or happiness is to " tend his soul," " to

---

[1] For this reasoning see *Alc. I* 119a–133d, *Euthydemus*, 278e–282d, 288d–292e. For the soul as the real " man " which " uses " the body see *Alc. I* 130c.

see to it that his soul is as good as it possibly can be," that is, to get the knowledge or insight which ensures his using everything rightly. And before a man can develop this quality of soul, he must be brought to " know himself," that is, to recognize the imperative need of moral wisdom and the dreadfulness of his present state of ignorance.[1] This is why Socrates taught that " all the virtues are one thing," wisdom or moral insight, and why he insisted that the necessary preparation for the private man or the statesman who means to make life a success is the " tendance of his own soul," and the first step towards this " tendance " is true self-knowledge. The same considerations explain the peculiar character of the mission Socrates believes himself to have received from heaven. He does not claim, like the professional teacher of an " art " such as medicine or music, to have ready-made knowledge to impart to anyone, and hence he denies that he has ever had " disciples." For he does not profess to have attained the wisdom or insight of which he speaks, but only to have attained to the perception that it is the one thing needful for the conduct of life. He claims only that he makes it the business of his life to " tend his own soul " and exhorts all his fellow-citizens, high and low, old and young, to do the same, and that he has a certain power of bringing home to others by his questions the grossness and danger of their ignorance of themselves. His function is simply to impress on all and sundry the misery of the state of ignorance in which they find themselves " by nature " and the importance of " coming out of it." How a man is to come out of this state of nature is not explained anywhere,[2] but in proportion as he does come out of it and advance to true insight, true knowledge of moral good and evil, all the different " virtues " or excellences of character and conduct will automatically ensue from this knowledge.

These fundamental elementary notions will suffice to explain the general character of most of the earliest " Socratic " dialogues. The procedure adopted is commonly this. Some term of moral import for the conduct of life, one of those words which everybody is using as familiar expressions daily without much consideration of their precise meaning, such as " courage," " self-mastery," or even " virtue " itself, is taken and we ask the question whether we can say exactly what it means. A number of answers are suggested and examined, but all are found wanting. None of them will stand careful scrutiny. Usually the result arrived at is a negative one. We discover to our shame that we do not really know the meaning of the most familiar epithets which we use every day of our lives to convey moral approval or censure. This revelation of our own ignorance is painful, but it has the advantage that we have taken a

---

[1] This is the message with which Socrates regarded himself as charged by God to his fellow-citizens and mankind in general (*Apol.* 29*d–e*, 36*c*, 41*c*).

[2] Naturally not. An answer to this question would raise the issues covered in Christian theology by the doctrine of " grace." We must not look for an anticipation of Augustine in Hellenic moral philosophy.

step forward. At any rate, our knowledge of our own ignorance will henceforth prevent our fancying that we really knew when we were repeating some of the formulae which our inquiry has condemned. Now that we know that we do not know what it is so necessary for the conduct of life to know, we are at least left with a heightened sense of the importance of " tendance of the soul " ; we shall not, like the rest of mankind, suppose ourselves to be in spiritual health when we are really inwardly diseased ; our very knowledge of the gravity of our spiritual malady will make us all the more unremitting in our determination to make the attempt to escape from our ignorance the great business of life. This, rather than anything more specific in the way of " positive results," is the conclusion Plato means us to draw from these " dialogues of search." It has been objected to Plato by unsympathetic critics, as he makes some of his characters object it to Socrates, that such a conclusion is not satisfactory. Socrates, Grote thinks, should have exchanged the easier part of critic for that of defender of theses of his own. He would have found that they could be subjected to a dialectic like his own with effects as damaging as those produced on his rivals' theories by himself. The objection misses the mark. Plato's object is not to propound theorems in moral science for our instruction, but to rouse us to give our own personal care to the conduct of our moral life by convincing us of the ignorance we usually disguise from ourselves by acquiescence in uncriticized half-truths and the practical gravity of that ignorance. He wishes to make us think to the purpose about the great concern of life, not to do our thinking for us. From his point of view, complacent satisfaction with false conceptions of good is the deadliest of all maladies of the soul ; if he can make us honestly dissatisfied with our customary loose thinking, he has produced exactly the effect he designed.

We may now, bearing these few simple ideas in mind, consider the arguments of some of the early dialogues.

The Greater Hippias.—The form of the dialogue is the simplest possible ; it is a direct colloquy between Socrates and a single speaker, the well-known polymath Hippias of Elis, who figures also in the *Lesser Hippias*, the *Protagoras*, and a conversation, perhaps suggested by the opening remarks of our dialogue, in the fourth book of Xenophon's *Memorabilia*.[1] The presence of Hippias at Athens implies that the time is one of peace, and, as the first visit of Gorgias to the city is referred to as a past event (282b), the supposed date must be after 427 B.C., and therefore during the years of the peace of Nicias. Hippias is depicted as childishly conceited on the strength of the great variety of topics he is able to expound, and the brilliant financial success which attends him wherever he goes. Even at Sparta—a city where he is often called on matters of state—though no interest is taken in his astronomy and mathematics, he has made a resounding success with a more immediately practical

[1] Xenophon, *Memor.* iv. 4.

subject, a set homily put into the mouth of Nestor on " the kind of fine achievements by which a young man may win high reputation " (286b).   This remark leads on to the main subject of the dialogue, the question what is really meant by the word καλόν, beautiful, which was commonly employed, like its Latin equivalent *honestum*, and our colloquial " fine," to express both physical and moral beauty. Socrates professes to have much trouble in satisfying the question of a certain combative and ill-mannered acquaintance who has reproached him for constantly using the epithets καλόν and αἰσχρόν, " fine " and " ugly," in judgments of value without being able to explain their exact meaning.   Can Hippias help him out of his perplexity ?   (It does not call for much perspicacity to see that the imaginary " rude fellow " who insists on asking awkward questions is no other than Socrates himself.[1])   The precise problem is this. We call an act of remarkable courage a " fine " act, and we say the same thing about an act of outstanding and remarkable justice. The use of the same word " fine " in both cases implies that there is a something (a certain εἶδος, form, or character — the word is little more than a synonym for a " something ") common to both cases, or why do we give them the same name, " fine " ?   What is " the fine itself," " the just fine " (αὐτὸ τὸ καλόν), *i.e.* what is it which is exactly and precisely named when we use the word " fine " ?[2] Hippias, like many interlocutors in Plato, underrates the difficulty of the problem because he confuses the *meaning* of a term with an *example* of it.   He answers that a " fine girl " is, of course, something " fine " (287e).   But this clearly tells us nothing about the *meaning* of " fine."   There are also " fine " horses, " fine " musical instruments, even " fine " pots and pans, like those made by the masters of Attic pottery (288d), and, after all, the beauty of the " fine girl " is relative.   She would not be " fine " by comparison with a goddess (289b).   What then is " the just fine," the character which all " fine " things exhibit ?   (289d).   Here again Hippias makes an elementary blunder.   Anything, he says, is made " fine," if it is gilded, and so " that which by its presence makes a thing fine " may be said to be just *gold* (289e).

But then the objection occurs that Phidias notoriously did not gild the features of his famous chryselephantine Athena, and surely Phidias may be presumed to have known his own business as an artist (290b).   This leads, at last, to a real attempt to *define* " the fine."   The " fine " is " the becoming " or " fitting " or " appropriate " (τὸ πρέπον, 290c).   It would follow from this at once that a soup-spoon of wood, because more " fitting," is more beautiful or " fine " than a golden spoon (291c).   Note that Socrates does not

---

[1] See 288d, where Socrates humorously describes his pertinacious questioner as " no wit, one of the *canaille* who cares nothing for anything but the truth," and where he as good as identifies him with " the son of Sophroniscus."

[2] The characteristic phrases αὐτὸ τὸ καλόν and εἶδος are introduced at 289d without explanation, as something quite familiar.   They bear the same

positively assert this conclusion, as he is represented as doing by interpreters who are determined to see nothing in him but a commonplace utilitarian. He obviously intends to raise a difficulty. It seemed a satisfactory explanation of the procedure of Phidias to say that a statue with a gilded face would not be " beautiful " because the gilding would not be " befitting." Yet, though a common wooden spoon would be more " in place " where one is eating soup than a golden one, it is a *paradox* to say that because the wooden spoon is " in place," it is a thing of beauty. Whatever may be the true answer to the question what " beauty " is, the identification of the aesthetically " fine " with the " befitting " is far too crude a solution.

Hippias evidently feels the difficulty, and is made to fall back again on an illustration, this time from the moral sphere. It is eminently " fine " to live in health, wealth, and honours, to bury your parents splendidly, and to receive in the fullness of days a splendid funeral from your descendants (291d). But this, again, is manifestly no true definition. A definition must be rigidly universal. But every one will admit that Heracles and Achilles and others who preferred a short and glorious to a long and inglorious life, and so died young and left their parents to survive them, made a " fine " choice (292e–293c). The illustration has thus led nowhere, and we have still to discuss the definition of the " fine " as the " fitting " or " becoming " on its own merits. When a thing has the character of being " becoming," does this make it " fine," or does it only make the thing *seem* " fine " ? Hippias prefers the second alternative, since even a scarecrow of a man can be made to look " finer " if he is " becomingly " dressed. But, obviously, if " propriety " makes things seem finer than they really are, " the appropriate " and the " fine " cannot be the same thing (294b). And we cannot get out of the difficulty, as Hippias would like to do, by saying the " appropriateness " *both* makes things " fine " and makes them seem " fine." If that were so, what really *is* " fine " would always *seem* fine too. Yet it is notorious that communities and individuals differ about nothing more than about the question what sort of conduct is " fine " (294c–d). Thus if " appropriateness " actually makes things " fine," the proposed definition may possibly be the right one ; but if it only makes them " seem " fine— (we have seen that the alternatives are exclusive of one another)— the definition must clearly be rejected. And Hippias is satisfied that this second alternative is the true one (294e). (Hume's well-known ethical theory affords a good illustration of the point of this reasoning. Hume sets himself to show that every society thinks the kind of conduct it " disinterestedly " likes virtuous and the

meaning which they have in dialogues where the so-called " ideal theory " is expounded. They mean that which is denoted without excess or defect by a significant name, a determinate character. This is a good illustration of the way in which the " ideal theory " is directly suggested by the everyday use of language. It is assumed that if several things can each be significantly called *x*, then *x* has a determinate significance which is the same in all the cases.

conduct it " disinterestedly " dislikes vicious. He then assumes
that he has proved that these two kinds of conduct really *are*
virtuous and vicious respectively, and that because a society knows
certainly what it likes and what it dislikes, it is infallible in its
judgments about virtue and vice. There is manifestly no connexion between the premises of this reasoning and its conclusion.)
Socrates now (295c) throws out a suggestion of his own for examination. Perhaps it may be that the " fine " is the same as the
" useful." At any rate, by " fine eyes " we seem to mean eyes
which do their work of seeing well, by a " fine " or " handsome "
body one which discharges its various functions well, and the same
considerations seem to hold good of " fine " horses, ships, implements of all kinds, and " fine " social institutions. In all these cases
we seem to call " fine " that which serves the use to which it is to
be put well, and " ugly " that which serves that use badly. The
examples, drawn from a wide range of facts, thus suggest an obvious
generalization, and the use of them to suggest it is an illustration
of what Aristotle had in mind when he specified " inductive arguments " as one of the contributions of Socrates to philosophical
method.[1]

If the definition once given were magisterially proposed for our
acceptance, Socrates would thus stand revealed as a pure utilitarian
in moral and aesthetic theory. But it is, in fact, put forward
tentatively as a suggestion for examination. The examination
is conducted in strict accord with the requirements of the dialectical
method as described in the *Phaedo*.[2] The first step is to see what
consequences follow from the suggested " postulate " ($\dot{v}\pi\acute{o}\theta\epsilon\sigma\iota s$).
If the consequences are found to be in accord with known facts,
and thus so far " verified," the postulate will be regarded as *so far*
justified ; if some of them prove to be at variance with fact, it must
be modified or dismissed, it cannot hold the field as it stands.

What consequences follow, then, from the identification of the
" fine " with the " useful " ? There is one at least which must
give us pause. A thing is useful for what it *can* do, not for what it
cannot ; thus our formula apparently leads to the identification of
$\tau\grave{o}$ $\kappa\alpha\lambda\acute{o}\nu$ with *power* to produce some result. But results may be
good or they may be bad, and it seems monstrous to hold that
power to produce evil is " fine." We must, at the least, modify
our statement by saying that the " fine " is that which can produce
good, i.e., whether the " useful " is " fine " or not will depend on
the goodness or badness of the end to which it is instrumental.
Now we call that which is instrumental to good " profitable "
($\dot{\omega}\phi\epsilon\lambda\iota\mu\acute{o}\nu$) ; thus our proposed definition must be made more
specific by a further determination. We must say " the fine "

---

[1] Aristot. *Met*. M1078b 27. Note that neither Socrates nor Aristotle regards
the " induction " as a proof. The generalization $\tau\grave{o}$ $\kappa\alpha\lambda\acute{o}\nu = \tau\grave{o}$ $\chi\rho\eta\sigma\iota\mu\acute{o}\nu$ has
yet to be tested and may have to be rejected. The testing is the work of
intellectual analysis, or, as Socrates and Plato call it " dialectic."
[2] *Phaedo*, 100a–b, 101d.

is that which is profitable (instrumental to the production of good) (296e).

Even so, we have a worse difficulty to face. We are saying in effect that the " fine "=that which causes good as its result. But a cause and its effect are always different (or, in modern language, causality is always transitive). Hence, if the "fine " is the *cause* of good, it must follow that what is " fine " is never itself good, and what is good is never itself " fine," and this is a monstrous paradox (297a). It seems then that the attempt to give a utilitarian definition of τὸ καλόν must be abandoned.

Possibly we may succeed better with a hedonist theory of beauty. The pictures, statues, and the like which we call " fine " all give us pleasure, and so do music and literature. In the one case the pleasure is got from sight, in the other from hearing. This suggests the new theory that the " fine " is " that which it is pleasant to see or hear " (298a). And we may even get in " moral beauty " under the formula, for " fine conduct " and " fine laws " are things which it gives us pleasure to see or to hear. But there is a logical difficulty to face. We are trying to define the " fine " as " that which it is pleasant to see *and* hear." But, of course, you do not hear the things which it is pleasant to see, nor see the things which it is pleasant to hear. Thus our proposed definition will not be true of either of the classes of things which are " fine," and, being true of neither, it cannot be true of both. We assumed that τὸ καλόν, whatever it may be, must be a character common to all ' fine " things, but " to be seen and heard " is not a character either of the " pleasures of sight " or of the " pleasures of hearing " (300a, b).

Aristotle comments on the fallacy, formally committed in this argument, of confusing " and " with " or," but the real trouble lies deeper. When the reasoning has been made formally sound by substituting " or " everywhere for " and," it still remains the fact that it is hard to say that the " pleasures of sight " and those of hearing have anything in common but their common character of being pleasant, and it has been the standing assumption of the dialogue that all " fine " things *have* some one common character. But the conclusion, which might seem indicated, that the " fineness " which all " fine " things have in common is just " pleasantness " is excluded by the firm conviction of both Plato and Aristotle that there are " disgraceful," morally " ugly " pleasures, *e.g.* those of the sexual " pervert." At the same time, the proposed formula is at any rate suggestive. There must be some reason why the two unmistakably " aesthetic " senses should be just sight and hearing, though the utilization of the fact demands a much more developed aesthetic psychology than that of our dialogue. The equivocation between " and " and " or " is, on Socrates' part, a conscious trap laid for his antagonist, as he shows when he goes on to remark that, after all, it is possible for " both " to have a character which belongs to neither singly, since, *e.g.*, Socrates and Hippias are a couple, though Socrates is not a couple, nor is Hippias. Thus it would be logically possible that " the pleasures of sight and hearing " might collectively have some character which belongs to neither class separately ; but the possibility is nothing to *our* purpose. For we agreed that the " fine " is a character which makes all " fine " things " fine," and obviously a character which " fine sights " do not possess, (though the collection " fine sights *and* sounds " may possess it,) cannot be what makes " fine " sights fine (303*d*). If we look for some common character which distinguishes both pleasures of sight and pleasures of hearing from other pleasures, and so justifies our calling them in particular the " fine " pleasures, the only obvious character is that both are " harmless " and therefore better than other pleasures, (indulgence in which may easily harm our health or character or repute). But this brings us back to our old formula that the " fine " is the " profitable " with the added specification that it is " profitable pleasure " (303*e*). And thus we are faced once more with the difficulty that the " fine " is made productive of good, or a cause of good, with the consequence that the " fine " is not itself good nor the good itself " fine " (304*a*). Thus the result of the whole discussion is negative. We have only learned that though we are always talking about " fine conduct," as though we knew our own meaning, we are really in a state of mental fog of which we ought to be ashamed. We have discovered our own ignorance of what it is most imperative we should know and what we fancy ourselves to know exceptionally well.

It is in this salutary lesson and not in any of the proposed definitions of the " fine " that we must look for the real significance of the dialogue. But it is also suggestive in other ways. The lesson it gives in the right method of framing and testing a definition is more important than any of the tentative definitions examined. Yet it is a valuable hint towards a more developed aesthetic theory that sensible " beauty " is found to be confined to the perceptions of the two senses of sight and hearing, and the illustration of the golden and wooden spoons might well serve as a warning against the dangers of an unduly " rationalistic " aesthetic theory. A wooden porridge-spoon is not necessarily a thing of beauty because it may be admirably " adapted " for the purposes of the porridge-eater. It is a still more important contribution to sound ethics to have insisted on the impossibility of reducing moral excellence (the " fine " in action) to mere " efficiency," irrespective of the moral quality of the results of the " efficient " agent.[1] And the emphatic insistence on the " transitive " character of all causality—a view which pervades all the best Greek metaphysics from first to last— may be regarded as the opening of a discussion which has continued to our own time and has issues of the most momentous kind for the whole interpretation of existence.[2]

[1] Mr. Chesterton remarks somewhere that Fagin was probably an exceptionally " efficient " educator of boys ; the trouble was that he was efficient in teaching them the wrong things.

[2] *E.g.* the cause of Theism is bound up with the position that all genuine causality is " transitive," and that purely " immanent " causality is not caus-

The Lesser Hippias.—This short dialogue, though less ambitious in its scope, is much more brilliantly executed than the *Hippias Major*. Its authenticity is sufficiently established by the fact that Aristotle, though not mentioning the author, quotes the dialogue by name as " the Hippias " ; such explicit references never occur in his work to writings of any " Socratic men " other than Plato.[1] The conversation discusses a single ethical paradox, and its real purport only emerges in the closing words of Socrates.

Socrates opens the talk by quoting an opinion that the *Iliad* is a finer poem than the *Odyssey*, as the hero of the former, Achilles, is a morally nobler character than Odysseus, the hero of the latter. The moralistic tone of this criticism is characteristically Athenian, as we can see for ourselves from a reading of the *Frogs* of Aristophanes, but does not concern us further. The remark is a mere peg on which to hang a discussion of the purely ethical problem in which Socrates is really interested. The transition is effected by the declaration of Hippias that Achilles was certainly a nobler character than Odysseus, since Achilles is single-minded, sincere, and truthful, but Odysseus notoriously *rusé* and a past master of deceit. We see this from the famous lines in the ninth book of the *Iliad*, where Achilles pointedly tells the " artful " Odysseus that he hates the man who says one thing and means another "worse than the gates of Hades " (365*a*). Socrates replies that, after all, Achilles was no more " truthful " than Odysseus, as the context of this very passage proves. He *said* he would at once desert the expedition, but, in fact, he did nothing of the kind, and, what is more, he actually told his friend Aias a different story. To him he said not that he would sail home, but that he would keep out of the fighting until the Trojans should drive the Achaeans back to their ships (371*b*). (This is meant to negative the suggestion of Hippias that Achilles honestly meant what he said when he threatened to desert, but changed his mind afterwards because of the unexpected straits to which his comrades-in-arms were reduced.) It looks then as though Homer, unlike Hippias, thought that the " truthful man " and the " liar " are not two, but one and the same. This is the paradox which Socrates proceeds to defend, and Hippias, in the name of common sense, to deny. Or rather it is the application of a still more general paradox that the man who " misses the mark " (ἁμαρτάνει) on purpose (ἑκών) is " better " than the man who does so " unintentionally " (ἄκων). Popular morality rejects

ality at all. This becomes specially obvious from a study of the famous Aristotelian argument for the " unmoved Mover."

[1] It is barely credible that Aristotle should not have read the admired " Socratic discourses " of Aeschines of Sphettus or the *Alcibiades* of Antisthenes, and it is therefore significant that he never mentions any of these works. We may take it that a named dialogue introducing Socrates *always* means to him a dialogue of Plato, or one regarded by the contemporary Academy as Plato's. And I cannot believe that the Academy itself can have been liable to error about the Platonic authorship of dialogues within a quarter of a century of Plato's death.

a view of this kind as monstrous. It holds that we ought, as Hippias says, to show συγγνώμη (to "make allowances") for involuntary wrong-doing, but that for deliberate wrong-doing there is no excuse. The main interest of the dialogue lies in the line of argument by which Socrates impugns this generally accepted thesis. He proceeds, as usual, by an "inductive" argument, *i.e.* an appeal to analogy. In general, the man who knows most about a subject is of all men the one who can mislead you in his own subject if he chooses to do so. An able mathematician, like Hippias, would be much better able to impose a false demonstration on others than a non-mathematician, who would only commit fallacies unintentionally and incidentally, and thus be led into visible self-contradictions. And the same thing holds good for astronomy (366*d*–368*a*). The same thing is true about arts involving manual dexterity (368*b*– 369*b*). The man who only fails when he means to fail is a much better craftsman than the man who fails unintentionally from incompetence. It is true also of all forms of bodily dexterity. The runner who falls behind only when he means to do so, the wrestler who is thrown when he means to let himself be thrown, is a better runner or wrestler than the man who falls behind his competitor or is thrown against his will, because he "can't help it" (373*c*– 374*b*). So with physical "talents." The man who only makes a false note when he means to do so is a better singer than the man who can't help singing out of tune. And in the world of industry, a tool with which you can make a bad stroke when you mean to do so, is a better tool than one with which you can't help making false strokes. And to come to living "implements," a horse or a dog which does its work badly only when the owner means that it shall, has a "better soul" than one which does the wrong thing when the owner means it to do the right one (374*c*–375*c*). The same thing would be true of a servant. (Bob Sawyer's boy, who took the medicines to the wrong houses because he was ordered to do so, was much more efficient than the sort of boy who blunders about errands because he is too stupid to do what he is told.) We may argue by analogy that our own souls are better if they "go wrong" on purpose than if they do so unintentionally (375*d*). In fact, we may condense the principle of the argument thus. Righteousness or morality (δικαιοσύνη) is either "power" (δύναμις), or "knowledge" (ἐπιστήμη), or both. But the man who *can* do right is better in respect of "power," a more "able" man than the man who cannot ; and the man who knows how to do it has more knowledge than the man who does not. And we have seen that it takes more ability and more knowledge to "go wrong" when you mean to do so, than to blunder unintentionally. And the better man is the man who has the better soul. Hence it seems to follow that "the man who does wrong on purpose, if there is such a person, is a better man than the man who does wrong unintentionally" (375*d*–376*b*). Yet this is such a paradox that Socrates hesitates to assert it, though he does not see how to escape it.

What is the real point of this curious argument ? It is clear, of course, that the main assumption on which it is based is the famous Socratic thesis that " virtue is knowledge," and again, that the method by which the conclusion is reached is the appeal to the analogy of the arts and crafts so constantly employed by Socrates. It is clear also that Plato does not mean us to accept the alleged inference ; he does not seriously think that the deliberate " villain " is morally better than the man who does wrong, in an hour of temptation, against his settled purpose in life ; it is the impossibility of such a doctrine which leads Socrates to say that he cannot commit himself consistently to the conclusion. Yet we cannot take the dialogue as intended to expose and refute either the doctrine that virtue is knowledge, or the use of the analogy from the " arts " as valuable in ethical reasoning. That a man who knows " the good " will, of course, aim at it is a standing doctrine of all Greek ethics ; to suppose that Plato means either to deny this or to reject reasoning from the " arts," would be to treat nearly the whole of the *Republic*, to name no other Platonic dialogues, as a prolonged bad joke. We must therefore find some other method of interpretation.

On reflection we see that the key to Plato's meaning,is really supplied by one clause in the proposition which emerges as the conclusion of the matter : " the man who does wrong on purpose, *if there is such a person*, is the good man." The insinuation plainly is that there really is no such person as " the man who does wrong on purpose," and that the paradox does not arise simply because there is no such person. In other words, we have to understand the Socratic doctrine that virtue is knowledge, and the Socratic use of the analogy of the " arts," in the light of the other well-known Socratic dictum, repeated by Plato on his own account in the *Laws*, that " all wrong-doing is involuntary." It is this, and not the formulated inference that the man who does wrong on purpose is the good man, which is the real conclusion to which Plato is conducting us. And we need have no difficulty about admitting this conclusion, if we bear in mind the true and sensible remark of Proclus about the Platonic sense of the word " voluntary " (ἑκούσιον). In Plato, the voluntary, as Proclus says,[1] means regularly what we really wish to have. Now no man wishes to have what he knows or believes to be bad for him. Many men wish for what, in fact, would be bad for them, but they can only do so because they falsely think the thing in question good. To wish to have a thing *because* you know it would be bad for you would be impossible. As Aristotle puts it, " every one wishes for what *he* thinks good." Many men choose evil in spite of the fact that it is evil, no one chooses it *because* it is evil and he knows it to be so. (Of course he may know or believe that he will be sent to prison or to hell for choosing as he does, but at heart he thinks that it will be " worth his while " to take these consequences, he will be " better off " even after paying this price

[1] Proclus, *in Remp.* ii. 355 (Kroll).

for what he desires.[1]) Thus the proposition " all wrong-doing is involuntary," has nothing to do with the question of human freedom ; it is merely the negative way of stating that a man who really knows what his highest good is, will always act on this knowledge. The man who really knows the good but chooses something else is as much of a nonentity as a round square, and it is just because " there is no such person " that the wildest paradoxes can be asserted about him.

It follows that knowledge of the good is, in one respect, different from every other kind of knowledge, and this difference affects the employment of the analogy from professional and technical knowledge, the sort of thing the " sophists " meant by " knowledge." It is the only knowledge which *cannot* be put to a wrong use ; every other kind of knowledge can be abused, and is abused when it is put to a bad use, as, *e.g.*, when the medical man employs his special professional knowledge to produce disease or death, instead of curing the one or preventing the other. There is a real analogy between " goodness " and the " arts " ; false beliefs about what is good or bad will ruin the conduct of life, as surely as false beliefs about what is wholesome will ruin a man's practical success as a medical man ; but if you press the analogy to the point of arguing that a man can use his knowledge of good for the deliberate doing of evil, as he might use his knowledge of medicine to commit a clever murder, you will be led astray, a truth with which Socrates is made to show himself familiar in Book I. of the *Republic,* when he urges this very point against Polemarchus ; that the analogy has its limits does not prevent it from being a sound analogy within those limits ; that it becomes unsound when you forget them is no reason for denying that virtue really is knowledge, though it is not, like the " goodness " taught by the sophists, mere technical knowledge how to produce certain results, if you happen to wish for them.

Ion.—Little need be said about this slight dialogue on the nature of " poetic inspiration." The main ideas suggested are expounded much more fully in those important Platonic works with which we shall have to deal later. We may, however, make a few remarks about the current conceptions of poetry against which Socrates is made to protest. It is important to remember that the whole conception of " inspiration," so familiar to ourselves, is foreign to the way of thinking of poetry characteristic of the age of Pericles and Socrates. Poets were habitually reckoned, along with physicians, engineers, engravers, and others, as σοφοί, " wits " or " clever men." This means that what was thought distinctive of the poet was not what we call " native genius," but " craftsmanship," " workmanship," " technique." He was conceived as consciously producing a beautiful result by the deft fitting together of words and musical sounds, exactly as the architect does the same thing by the deft putting together of stones. Of all the great Greek poets Pindar is

[1] Cf.   " To reign is worth ambition though in Hell :
Better to reign in Hell, then serve in Heav'n."

the only one who pointedly insists on the superiority of φυά, " native genius," to the craftsmanship (τέχνη) which can be taught and learned; but to our taste conscious workmanship, rather than untaught " inspiration," is the characteristic quality of Pindar himself. *We* should never dream of talking of *his* " native woodnotes wild," or of comparing him with a skylark pouring out its soul in " *unpremeditated* art." Also it was held commonly that the service the poet does us is definitely to " teach " us something—how to fight a battle, how to choose a wife, to retain a friend, or something of that kind. This explains why, in the *Apology*, when Socrates is speaking of his attempts to discover a " wiser man " than himself, he mentions poets along with statesmen as the two classes of recognized σοφοί to whom he first turned his attention (*Apol.* 22c). Since he found that the most admired poets were quite helpless at explaining the meaning of their own finest passages, he came to the conclusion, which he repeatedly maintains in Plato, that poets are not deliberate " craftsmen " at all, (do not compose in virtue of σοφία, *ibid.* 22b,) but that poetry is a matter of " natural endowment " (φύσις) and non-rational " inspiration," and thus became the originator of the conception of the " poet " conventional among ourselves.

Ion, who is represented as an eminent professional rhapsode, shares the current views of the " wisdom " of the poets; it is a matter of " skill " or " art " (τέχνη), and he assents at once to the inference that the professional reciter of poetry absorbs from his study of the poet's works a special measure of their author's " skill." The interpreter of the poet to the audience is, like the poet himself, the possessor of a " craft " or " profession." Yet he has to admit that his own skill as an interpreter is confined to the poetry of Homer; he cannot succeed in declaiming any other poet or explaining the " beauties " of his work; in fact, his interest flags as soon as any poet but Homer is made the topic of conversation. This, as Socrates says, serves to show that the rhapsode's accomplishment is not the result of specialist skill. All the poets, as Ion admits, treat of much the same topics—the conduct of men and women in the various occupations of life, the " things in the heavens and the underworld," and the births and doings of " gods," though Homer treats all these topics better than any one else. Hence if the exposition of a poet were a matter of professional expert knowledge, the same knowledge which makes a man able to appreciate and expound Homer, would equally make him a good critic and expositor of poetry in general. Consequently, Socrates suggests that the conception of the interpreter of the poet as a conscious " craftsman " is mistaken. The poets themselves are not self-conscious " artists "; they compose their works in a mood of " inspiration " in which they are " taken out of themselves," and are temporarily, like " seers " or Bacchanals, vehicles " possessed " by a higher power of which they are the unconscious mouthpieces. In the same way, the " rhapsode " with a special gift for reciting Homer is " inspired " by the poet at second-hand. He becomes temporarily himself the " mouthpiece " of the poet, as the poet is the mouthpiece of the god.   And he in turn " inspires " his hearers by communicating to them, in a non-logical way, something of the " inspiration " he has received from the poet.   Thus poet, reciter, audience, are like so many links of iron, the first of which is " attracted " by a magnet, and in its turn attracts another.   It is evidence for the non-rational character of this influence that the rhapsode for the time actually enters into the feelings of the characters whose speeches he is declaiming, shudders with their fears and weeps over their distresses, and makes his audience do the like, though neither they nor he may really be faced with any danger or distress. So far Ion is not unwilling to go with Socrates, but he is less ready to follow him when Socrates turns to the other chief feature in the popular conception of the poet, and denies that the poet as such is a " teacher " with knowledge to impart to us.   If Homer were really a great teacher of wisdom human and divine, it should follow that a rhapsode, whose profession compels him to be intimately acquainted with Homer's poetry, is also a high authority in all fields of knowledge.   But it is undeniable that a physician would be a sounder judge of Homer's statements about medicine than a rhapsode, and again that a racing man would be better able to appreciate and criticize the advice Nestor gives in the *Iliad* about horse-racing than a professional rhapsode, unless the rhapsode happens incidentally to be a specialist in horse-racing.   If then there really is any department of specialist knowledge which can be acquired by a study of Homer, what is it ?

Ion falls back on the traditional view that at any rate Homer is a specialist in the art of warfare, and that a close student of Homer, such as he himself has been, learns from Homer the " art of the general."   The *Iliad*, in fact, is a first-rate manual of military science, and Ion professes, on the strength of his familiarity with it, to be a great general *in posse*.   But how comes it, then, that he has never attempted to distinguish himself in so eminently honourable a profession ?   If there is no opening in his native city of Ephesus, which is now a subject-ally of Athens, why has he never, like some other aliens, entered the military service of Athens herself ?

Nominally the little dialogue is concerned with the question whether rhapsodes and actors owe their success to professional or expert knowledge, or to some kind of " genius " or non-rational " inspiration."   But it is clear that the real points intended to be made are that the poet himself is not an " expert " in any kind of knowledge and, as poet, has not necessarily anything to teach us. These points are enforced more impressively in other Platonic works, notably in the *Phaedrus*, but the *Ion* has its value, both as a contribution to the psychology of the " rhapsode " (or, as we should say to-day, the actor), and as a particularly clear and simple refutation of the never-dying popular delusion that the function of the poet himself, and consequently of his exponent, is primarily didactic. The type of critic who conceives it to be his business to find

" morals " and " lessons " in the plays of Shakespeare, and regards it as the object of *Hamlet* or *Macbeth* to warn us against procrastination or ambition, has something to learn even from the *Ion*.

Menexenus.—The *Menexenus* offers, in a way, a worse puzzle to the reader than any other work of the Platonic *corpus*, and it is not surprising that its authenticity should be doubted by students of Plato who are in general on the conservative side in questions of genuineness. Externally the evidence for it is good. It is twice cited by Aristotle,[1] and once with a formal title, " the Funeral Discourse," and this seems to show that Aristotle at least believed it to be Platonic. Now the systematic production of works falsely ascribed to eminent authors seems not to occur in the history of Greek literature until long after the time of Aristotle. And again it is not likely that Aristotle, of all men, should have been misinformed about the real authorship of an Academic dialogue. Thus it is hard to believe either that the dialogue is a deliberate forgery or that it is a production of some lesser member of the Academy which has been ascribed by a simple mistake to Plato, as seems to be the case with a few of the minor items of the " canon of Thrasylus." Nor have modern stylometrical investigations given any reason to suspect the little work. Aristotle's allusion thus seems to compel us to accept it as genuine. On the other hand, there are two notorious difficulties which we have to face when we admit Plato's authorship. One is that it is at least hard to see what Plato's object in such a composition can be. The other is that the dialogue commits an anachronism to which there is no parallel anywhere in Plato, and which cannot be unconscious. The body of it is made up of a recital by Socrates of a " funeral oration " on the Athenians who fell in the Corinthian war, and Socrates professes to have heard the speech from the lips of the famous Aspasia, the wife of Pericles. It is certain that Socrates was put to death in the summer of the year 399 B.C., long before the opening of the Corinthian war (395 B.C.). Yet he is made to carry his review of Athenian history down to the pacification dictated by the Persian king, which ended the war in the year 387. Aspasia, the nominal speaker, must have died *before* Socrates. This is implied in the structure of the *Aspasia* of Aeschines, on which see H. Dittmar, *Aeschines von Sphettus*, 45–56. Plato must have violated chronology quite deliberately and with a view to producing a definite effect. But what can we suppose the intention to have been ?

It is idle to suggest that the whole affair is a mere Aristophanic jest, and that Plato only wants to show that he can rival the comedians on their own ground by putting ludicrous " topical allusions " into the mouth of his hero. We cannot reconcile such a use of Socrates, for purposes of pure burlesque, with the tone of reverence and devotion in which Plato continues to speak of Socrates in the letters written at the very end of his own life ; even

---

[1] *Rhetoric*, 1367b 8, 1415b 30.

if one could, we have to remember that Socrates is not being made, as he might be made in a burlesque, to offer a remarkably intelligent " anticipation of the course of events " ; he is represented as commenting on the events of the twelve or thirteen years after his own death *ex post facto*. And we still have to explain why Socrates should pretend that Aspasia too is still a well-known figure at Athens, and that he has learned his discourse from her. Again, we cannot account for this use of Aspasia by appealing to the passage (*Menexenus*, 236b) where Socrates is made to credit her with the authorship of the famous " funeral speech," delivered by Pericles in the first year of the Archidamian war, and reported by Thucydides. Plato's object is not to ridicule oratory of this kind by the insinuation that its tone is what might be expected from a woman and an *hetaera*. The remains of the *Aspasia* of Aeschines of Sphettus, make it clear that the view, which underlies the proposals of *Republic* v., that " the goodness of a woman and that of a man are the same," was a genuine doctrine of Socrates, and that he quite seriously believed in the " political capacity " of Aspasia. His profession of owing his own " Funeral Discourse " to her is, no doubt, only half-serious, but it is quite in keeping with what we know to have been his real conviction. We have therefore to discover the object of the whole singular mystification, if we can, from an analysis of the oration itself.

It will not be necessary to insert here a full analysis, but there are certain points, well brought out in such a commentary as Stallbaum's, which we have to bear in mind. The discourse is framed on the lines we can see from comparison with the extant examples to have been conventional on such occasions. It treats first of the glorious inheritance and traditions of the community into which the future warriors were born and in which they were brought up, then of their own achievements, by which they have approved themselves worthy of such an origin, and finally of the considerations which should moderate the grief of their surviving friends and relatives. In this respect it exhibits a close parallel with the discourse of Pericles in Thucydides, the " funeral speech " included in the works ascribed to Lysias, the *Panegyricus* of Isocrates, the discourse of Hyperides on Leosthenes and his companions in the Lamian war. There are direct verbal echoes of the speech of Lysias, perhaps of that of Pericles, and, I suspect, also of the Isocratean *Panegyricus*, a work of the year 380. The diction again has clearly been modelled on that actually adopted in real encomia of the fallen, and it is this which makes it impossible to use evidence from style to date the dialogue. " Funeral orations " belong to the type of oratory called by the Greeks " epideictic," and demand an artificial elevation of diction and use of verbal ornament avoided in " forensic " pleading and political speaking. Hence all the extant specimens exhibit, to a greater or a less degree, the high-flown and semi-poetical character distinctive of the Sicilian " show declamation " introduced to Athens by Gorgias, and Plato has been careful to preserve this peculiarity. When we examine the contents of the discourse, we see that he has been equally careful to conform to the accepted model. His oration, like those of Lysias and Isocrates, but unlike the really statesmanlike discourse of Pericles, dwells on the topics afforded by mythology for the glorification of Athens, the origination of the cultivation of corn and of the olive in Attica, the contest of Athena with Hephaestus for the patronage of the city, the public spirit and chivalry displayed in such legendary exploits as the protection of the family of Heracles and the rescuing for burial of the corpses of the champions who fell before the gates of Thebes. Lysias and Isocrates both expatiate on these prehistorical events at great length—a length apparently satirized by Socrates in the remark (239b) that they have already received their due meed of celebration from the poets. The speech then proceeds, like those which are apparently its immediate models, to a sketch of the history of Athens down to date, the object of which is to glorify the city on two grounds—its rooted and inveterate antipathy to "barbarians," (242c–e, 245d,) and its unselfish Panhellenism, shown by its readiness always to make sacrifices to preserve the "balance of power" between the different Greek cities by supporting the weaker side in these internal quarrels (244c). The demonstration of the second point in particular leads to a bold falsification of history, by which the fifth century attempts of Athens to dominate Boeotia and the Archidamian war itself are made to appear as heroic struggles against the "imperialism" of other communities. We know enough from Plato of the real sentiments both of himself and of Socrates to understand that this version of history cannot represent the serious convictions of either ; it has all the appearance of satire on the "patriotic" version of history given by Isocrates in an inconsistent combination with Panhellenism. Similarly, after reading the *Gorgias* and *Republic* and the sketch of Athenian history given in *Laws* iii., we shall find it impossible to take the *Menexenus* seriously when it glorifies the existing constitution of Athens as a true aristocracy in which the men who are reputed to be "best" govern with the free consent of the multitude (238d–e). When we are told that at Athens, as nowhere else, "he who has the repute of wisdom and goodness is sovereign," the emphasis must be meant to fall on the words "who has the repute," and the encomium is disguised satire. Probably, then, the real purpose of the discourse is to imitate and at the same time, by adroit touches of concealed malice, to satirize popular "patriotic oratory." It is no objection to such an interpretation to say, what is true enough, that the speech contains noble passages on the duty of devotion to one's State and the obligation of per-petuating its finest traditions. Even the "flag-flapper" who distorts all history into a romantic legend of national self-glorifica-tion, usually has some good arguments, as well as many bad ones, for his "patriotism," and we may credit Plato with sufficient penetration to have seen that satire misses its designed effect unless it is accompanied by intelligent recognition of the good which is mingled with the evil in its objects. (This is why so much of the writing of Juvenal, Swift, Victor Hugo, merely wearies a reader by the monotony of the invective.[1])

If Isocrates is the person against whom the satire of the *Menexenus* is largely directed, we can see an excellent reason why that satire should be so liberally mixed with sympathy. Isocrates was honourably distinguished by his real superiority to mere particularism and his real concern for the interests of Greek civilization as a whole, and in this he and Plato were wholly at one. But, unlike Plato, who regarded the hard and fast distinction between Greek and " barbarian " as unscientific superstition, Isocrates takes the antithesis seriously and tends to regard hate of the barbarian as equivalent to love for civilization. The combination of the two points of view in the *Menexenus* is a fair representation of his lifelong attitude towards affairs. So again the distortion of history by which the most aggressive exploits of Attic imperialism, such as the attempt of Pericles and his friends to dominate Boeotia, and the Archidamian War as a whole, are represented as " wars of liberation," is no very violent parody of the methods of Isocrates when he is anxious, as in the *Panegyricus*, to gratify Athenian partiality for Athens or Athenian dislike of Sparta. One may suspect the same purpose of parody in the false emphasis which is laid in the *Menexenus* on the naval exploits of Athens in the Sicilian expedition as efforts for the " liberation " of the oppressed. Isocrates notoriously held the view that the naval ascendancy of Athens had been a national misfortune, since it had led to the lust for empire, and there are passages in the *Laws* which show that Plato sympathized with this conviction. But it would be a telling criticism of the Isocratean way of manipulating history to show that it could easily be employed for glorifying precisely the side of Athenian history which gave Isocrates himself least satisfaction. You have only to sit as loosely to facts as Isocrates habitually allows himself to do when he wishes to praise or to abuse some one, and you can make Alcibiades into a hero of chivalry who was only doing his duty by the oppressed when he lured Athens on to its ruin by the prospect of the conquest of Sicily ![2] If we read the *Menexenus* in this light, we can perhaps understand the point of the curious anachronism in its setting. The satire of the actual " Funeral Discourse " is so subtly mixed with sympathetic appreciation that it would be easy to mistake the whole speech for a serious encomium—a mistake which has actually been made by a good many interpreters of Plato. The ordinary reader needs some very visible warning sign if he is to approach the discourse with the required anticipation that

---

[1] Cf. the excellent remarks of Sir A. Quiller-Couch, *Studies in Literature*, p. 290 ff.

[2] Lysias takes care to " skip " the Peloponnesian War entirely ; Isocrates does worse. He actually justifies the two great crimes of the enslavement and massacre of the Melians and the destruction of Scione !

its purpose is satirical. The warning is given, for any intelligent reader, by the amazing introduction of Socrates at a date years after his death. It is as though Plato were telling us in so many words that we are dealing with the utterances of a mere puppet who has nothing to do with the great man to whose memory the dialogues in general are a splendid tribute. Even so, the fiction is singular, and hardly to be accounted for unless we realize the presence in Plato himself of a peculiar vein of freakish humour which comes out notably in the singular " antinomies " of the *Parmenides* as well as in the whimsicalities of the *Sophistes* and *Politicus*. It was an " impish " trick to put the discourse of the *Menexenus* into the mouth of a puppet Socrates, and we may be glad that the trick was never repeated, as we are glad that Shakespeare never perpetrated a second *Troilus and Cressida*. The very audacity of the trick is some additional evidence of the genuineness of the dialogue. We can understand that Plato might take such a liberty—once, and in an unhappy moment ; it is surely incredible that a younger member of Plato's *entourage* should have ventured on it at all.

See further :

RITTER, C.—*Platon*, i. 297–308 (*Hippias II*), 359–361 (*Hippias I*), 485–496 (*Menexenus*).

RAEDER, H.—*Platons philosophische Entwickelung*, 92–94 (*Ion*), 94–95 (*Hippias II*), 101–106 (*Hippias I*), 125–127 (*Menexenus*).

APELT, O.—*Beiträge zur Geschichte der griechischen Philosophie* (1891), 369–390 (*der Sophist Hippias von Elis*) ; *Platonische Aufsätze* (1912), 203–237 (on *Hippias I and II*).

KRAUS, O.—*Platons Hippias Minor*. (Prague, 1913.)

DITTMAR, H.—*Aeschines von Sphettus* 1–59 (on the connection of the *Menexenus* with the *Aspasia* of Aeschines. The connection is clearly made out, but I think it an exaggeration to find the purpose of Plato's dialogue mainly in a " polemic " against Aeschines).

CHAPTER IV

MINOR SOCRATIC DIALOGUES : *CHARMIDES*, *LACHES, LYSIS*

WE may group the three dialogues which form the subject of this chapter together for several reasons. From the dramatic point of view all show an advance upon what is likely to have been the earliest form of the Platonic dialogue, the direct presentation of Socrates in conversation with a single interlocutor. The *Lysis* and *Charmides* both profess to be reports of recently held conversations given by Socrates to an unnamed friend or friends, and thus conform to the type of such masterpieces of literary art as the *Protagoras* and *Republic*. The fiction that the dialogue is reported enables Socrates to draw a highly dramatic picture of the persons engaged in the conversation and the circumstances in which it is held. This device is not adopted in the *Laches*, where the method of direct reproduction of the conversation is maintained, but the same advantage is obtained by adding to the number of the interlocutors, so that we have a vivid characterization of three persons, two of them notabilities, besides Socrates himself. All three dialogues, again, are connected by the fact that they deal with Socrates in the special character of older friend and adviser of the very young, and two of them, the *Charmides* and *Lysis* give us an attractive picture of his personal manner as mentor to his young friends. In the cases of *Charmides* and *Laches* Plato has been careful to indicate approximately the period of life to which Socrates has attained, and we see that both are meant as pictures of the master as he was between the ages of forty and fifty, and thus take us back to a time when Plato himself was either an infant or not yet born. It is closely connected with this that both dialogues, and especially the *Laches*, are pervaded by the atmosphere of the Archidamian war and remind us of the fact that Socrates was, among other things, a fighting man. A further point of connexion between these two dialogues is, that they are both concerned at bottom with a difficulty arising directly out of the Socratic conception of virtue as identical with knowledge. Each deals with one of the great recognized virtues demanded from a Greek " good man "—the *Charmides* with "temperance," the *Laches* with " valour " or " fortitude "—and in both cases the discussion follows the same general lines. We are gradually led up to the point of identifying the virtue under consideration with knowledge of the good, and then left to face the difficulty that the identification seems to involve the further identification of this particular virtue with all virtue. If valour, for example, is knowledge of the good, how can we continue to distinguish the soldier's virtue of valour from any other virtue, and what becomes of the popular belief that a man may have one virtue in an eminent degree, and yet be deficient in another—may be, for example, a very brave soldier but very " licentious " ? This problem of the " unity of the virtues " forms the starting-point for the discussion of the *Protagoras*, and cannot be said to receive its full solution until we come to the *Republic*. Thus, by raising it, the *Laches* and *Charmides* prelude directly to what must have been the great achievements of Plato's literary prime of manhood ; this is an additional reason for holding that they must not be placed among his earliest compositions. It is, for example, quite possible, if not even probable, that both may be later works than the *Gorgias*, which still retains the method of simple direct reproduction of a conversation and, for all its impressive eloquence, shows less insight into the more difficult philosophical problems raised by the Socratic conception of morality.

The *Charmides*.—Formally, like several of the dialogues, the *Charmides* has as its object the finding of a *definition*. To us it seems at first pedantic to attach importance, in morals at any rate, to mere definitions of the different virtues. A definition, we are inclined to think, is at best a matter of names, whereas ethical thinking should concern itself directly with " concrete realities." If a man recognizes and practises a noble rule of life, it matters very little by what name he calls the right act, whether he looks at it as an exhibition of courage, or of justice, or of " temperance." The " fine " deed can, in fact, easily be made to wear the semblance of any one of these " virtues." This is true enough, but it would be out of place as a criticism on the Socratic demand for " definitions " in matters of conduct. From the Greek point of view, the problem of definition itself is not one of names, but of things. If our moral judgment is to be sound, and our moral practice good, we must approve and disapprove rightly. We must admire and imitate what is really noble, and must not be led into false theory and bad practice by confused thinking about good and evil. The problem of finding a definition of a " virtue " is at bottom the problem of formulating a moral ideal, and it is from this point of view that we ought to consider it. The important thing is that we should know quite definitely what we admire in conduct and that our admiration should be rightly given to the things which are really admirable. Failure in finding the definition means that we really do not know what we admire, and so long as we do not know this, our moral life is at the mercy of sentimental half-thinking.

The particular virtue selected for discussion is one which bulks very large in all Greek thought about the conduct of life—the beautiful characteristic called by the Greeks *sophrosyne*, and by the Romans *temperantia*. It is easier to indicate from the usage of the language what this moral excellence is, than to find any one name for it in our modern English.   In literature we find *sophrosyne* spoken of chiefly in the following connexions.   As its derivation implies, the word means literally the possession of a " sane " or "wholesome " mind ; *sophrosyne* is thus contrasted with the " folly " of the man who " forgets himself " in the hour of success and prosperity, and " presumes on " his advantages of wealth or power, pushes them to the full extreme in his dealings with the less fortunate.   Or it may equally be contrasted with the " unbalanced " conduct of the fanatic who has only one idea in his head, can only see one side of a situation and is blind to all the others.   In this sense, as the virtue opposed to the pride of the man who forgets that the gods can cast him down as low as they have raised him high, the recklessness of the successful man who forgets that he may himself come to be as much at the mercy of another as others are now at his, the pitilessness of the fanatic who can only see one side to every question, *sophrosyne* covers very much of what we call humility, humanity, mercy. Again, the word is a name for the kind of conduct thought becoming specially in the young towards elders, soldiers towards their superior officer, citizens towards their magistrates.   In this sense it means proper modesty and even covers such minor matters as a becoming outward deportment in speech and gesture.   In still a third sense, it is the characteristic of the man who knows how to hold his imperious bodily appetites, " the desire for meat and drink and the passion of sex," in easy and graceful control, as contrasted with the man who offends us by unseemly and untimely greed of these appetitive enjoyments.   In this aspect, *sophrosyne* is what in good English is still called " temperance," if we take care to remember that it is part of the virtue itself that it is not the imperfect self-restraint of the man who holds himself in check ungracefully and with difficulty, but the easy and natural self-restraint of the man who enjoys being " temperate." [1]   If it does not seem an affectation to use such a phrase, we may say that *sophrosyne* is the spirit of the " disciplined " life.   It is not, as Hume insinuates,[2] a " monkish " virtue, except in the sense that you certainly cannot be a good monk without it.   Neither, as Hume forgot, can you be a good soldier, and that is why in the *Laws* [3] Plato throws *sophrosyne* and valour together, and insists that the former is the major and the harder part of the lesson every good " fighting man " has to master.   The very wide range of the use of the word in literature goes a long way to explain the importance Socrates attaches to a clear and coherent statement of its meaning, and the difficulty the company have in producing such a statement.   The introductory narrative provides an opportunity for a clear indication of the date

[1] Hence Aristotle's sharp distinction throughout the *Ethics* between the σώφρων and the ἐγκρατής or morally " strong " man in whom judgment and " will "—in the Elizabethan sense—are at variance though he habitually compels himself to follow judgment.

[2] *Inquiry into the Principles of Morals*, Section IX. Part I.

[3] *Laws*, 634a–b.

at which the conversation is supposed to take place. Socrates has been serving before the walls of Potidaea, in the campaign of the year 431 with which hostilities between Athens and the members of the Peloponnesian confederacy opened, and has just returned safe and sound, after having displayed his courage and coolness in danger, as we learn from the *Symposium*,[1] by saving the life of Alcibiades. He is then a man of some forty years (Plato, we must remember, is not yet born). He goes direct, on his arrival, to his " wonted haunts," the *palaestrae*, and begins at once to ask questions about the way in which " philosophy and the young people " have been faring in his absence on service (*Charm.* 153*d*). (This, we observe, implies that the interest of young men of promise in Socrates as a wise counsellor was already a reality, eight years before Aristophanes burlesqued these relations in the *Clouds*.) Critias, cousin of Plato's mother, afterwards to be unhappily known as a leader of the violently reactionary party in the "provisional government " set up after the capitulation of Athens to Lysander, but at present simply a young man of parts but with a touch of forwardness and self-confidence, thereupon promises to introduce Socrates to his own cousin Charmides (Plato's uncle, subsequently associated with Critias and his party as the head of the commission set up to dominate the Piraeeus), as a lad of exceptional promise.[2] Socrates had already seen him as a mere child, but he has now grown to be a youth of wonderful beauty and equally wonderful *sophrosyne*. It is agreed that Socrates shall have some conversation with the lad and judge of him for himself.

Socrates leads up playfully to his real purpose, the examination of the boy's spiritual state. Charmides has been complaining of headaches. Socrates professes to have brought back from his northern campaign a wonderful remedy which he has learned from a Thracian.[3] The Thracian, however, had explained that not only can you not treat a local disorder properly without treating the patient's whole body, you cannot treat the body successfully without treating the soul, which is the real seat of health and disease. Hence Socrates is under a promise not to practise the recipe against headache on anyone who is not spiritually sound in constitution. It would be useless if employed on a subject with a deep-seated spiritual disorder. *Sophrosyne* is presupposed in spiritual health ; before Charmides can be treated for his headaches, then, we must find out whether he has *sophrosyne* (*Charm.* 155*e*–158*e*). Now if a man has this or any other character of soul, it must, of course, make

---

[1] *Symposium*, 219–220.

[2] According to Xenophon (*Mem.* iii. 7, 1), it was Socrates himself who first persuaded Charmides to enter public life. But this looks like a mere inference from what is said in our dialogue of the modest and retiring disposition of Charmides in boyhood. If the fact were so, it is singular that no one ever seems to have accused Socrates of " corrupting " Charmides, though he was made responsible for Critias and Alcibiades.

[3] For the reputation of Thrace as a home of this kind of lore—it was the land of Orpheus, we must remember—cf. Eurip. *Alc.* 986 ff.

its presence *felt*, and its possessor will therefore have an opinion of some kind about its nature. (It is not meant, of course, that the possessor of the character need have a " clear and distinct idea " of it, but only that he must have some acquaintance with it ; language about it will have some meaning for him, exactly as language about sight or hearing will mean something to anyone who can see or hear, though it would be meaningless to beings born blind or deaf.) Thus we are led to the question what kind of thing Charmides takes *sophrosyne* to be. As is natural in a mere lad, Charmides fixes first of all on an exterior characteristic, and equally naturally it is a characteristic of *sophrosyne* in the form which would be most familiar to a boy—the form of decent and modest bearing towards one's elders and " good behaviour " generally. One shows *sophrosyne* by walking, talking, doing things generally, in an " orderly and quiet " fashion ; so perhaps we may say that it is " a sort of quietness " ($\dot{\eta}\sigma\upsilon\chi\iota\acute{o}\tau\eta\varsigma$), a " slowness " which may be contrasted with undignified and ungraceful " hurry " (159*b*). This, of course, is true, so far as it goes, only it does not go very far. There is a " hurry " which means that one's limbs or one's tongue are not really under control as they should be. But we want to get behind such mere outward indications to the interior condition of soul from which they spring ; and besides, clearly " slowness," " deliberateness," does not always arise from being " master of one's soul." As Socrates says, in the various physical and mental accomplishments it is what is readily and quickly done, not what is done slowly and with difficulty, that is " well " or " fairly " ($\kappa\alpha\lambda\hat{\omega}\varsigma$) done. He who reads or writes, or wrestles or boxes well, does these things quickly ; he who can only make the proper movements slowly does not do them well. So with accomplishments of the mind. A fine memory or judgment or invention is a quick, not a slow, memory or judgment or invention. Now it is admitted that *sophrosyne*, whatever it is, is something " fine " ($\kappa\alpha\lambda\acute{o}\nu$). Clearly then it cannot be right to fix on " slowness " as what is specially distinctive of *sophrosyne* (159*c*-160*d*). The point is that, in small things as well as in great, the man who is master of his soul is free from " hurry." There is, in a sense, a spacious leisureliness about his behaviour. But this freedom from " haste " and " hurry " is not the same thing as slowness : slowness *may* be, and often is, a mere consequence of awkwardness, of *not* being master of yourself.

Charmides next makes a suggestion which shows a real attempt to get behind the externals of behaviour to the spirit and temper they reveal. *Sophrosyne* makes a man quick to feel shame, and perhaps it is the same thing as modesty ($\alpha\dot{\iota}\delta\acute{\omega}\varsigma$, 160*e*). The boy is still clearly thinking of the form in which *sophrosyne* would be most familiar to a well-bred boy—the sense of being " on one's best behaviour " in the presence of one's parents, one's elders, and in general of those to whom respect is due. (We may compare Kant's well-known comparison of the reverence for the moral law which is, according to him, the specific *ethical* feeling, with the sense of restraint

we feel in the presence of an exalted or impressive personage—the
sort of feeling an ordinary man would have if he were suddenly summoned to an interview with the King or the Pope. There is a real
analogy between the two things ; as Kant says, our feeling in both
cases is primarily one of inhibition or restraint. You don't " loll '
in the King's presence, and a good man is not " free and easy " in
the presence of a moral obligation.) But again, the analogy is only
an analogy, not an identity. *Sophrosyne* cannot be simply identified
with *shamefacedness* (αἰσχύνη) or *modesty* (αἰδώς).[1] For, by
general consent, it is something which is always not merely " fine "
(καλόν) but good (ἀγαθόν), and there is a false modesty which is not
good. As Homer says, " Modesty is not good in a beggar." (Cf.
the Scots saying, " Dinna let yer modesty wrang ye.") The shame or
modesty which makes a man too bashful to tell his full need on the
proper occasion is not good, but *sophrosyne* is always good (160e–
161a).
    This leads to a third suggestion which is more important than
any we have yet met. Charmides has heard some one—it is hinted
that this some one is Critias—say that *sophrosyne* means " attending
to one's own matters " (τὸ τὰ ἑαυτοῦ πράττειν, 161b),[2] and this,
perhaps, may be the true account. It does obviously present one
advantage. The formula is a strictly universal one, applicable to
the whole conduct of life in all its different " ages," not merely to
the kind of conduct appropriate to the young in particular. In a
boy the shyness, or backwardness, of which we have just been speaking is a laudable thing, and " forwardness " a fault, but " shyness "
is far from being a laudable characteristic in a grown man. But
at any age of life it is laudable to " mind your own affairs " and
censurable to be a " meddler " or busybody. Unfortunately, as
Socrates goes on to point out, the phrase " to attend to one's own
matters " is so ambiguous that the new suggestion is something of
a " conundrum " ; we have to guess, if we can, what its author may
have meant (161d). Clearly he cannot have meant that a man
should only read and write his own name and no one else's, or that
the builder or the physician should build his own house or cure his
own body and no other, on pain of being noted for a " meddler."
Life would be intolerable to a community where the rule was that
every one should " attend to his own matters " in the sense that he
must " do everything for himself " (161e). The alleged saying,
then, is what we called it, a pure conundrum. In the *Republic*, as

----

[1] Strictly, αἰδώς is the name for laudable modesty, αἰσχύνη for the backwardness which is not laudable, *mauvaise honte*. But the words are freely
treated as interchangeable.
[2] τὸ τὰ ἑαυτοῦ πράττειν is the conduct which is the opposite of τὸ πολυπραγμονεῖν,
" having a finger in everyone's pie." In Attic life πολυπραγμοσύνη would show
itself, *e.g.*, in that tendency to quarrel with one's neighbours and drag them
into law-suits about trifles which Aristophanes regularly ascribes to his *petits
bourgeois*. Hence ἀπράγμων is in Attic sometimes an epithet of censure—
" inert," " lazy "—but often one of approval—" a quiet decent man," a man
who " keeps himself to himself."

we all know, this very phrase "to mind one's own matters" is adopted as an adequate definition not merely of one type of "virtue," but of δικαιοσύνη, "right-doing," the fundamental principle of the whole moral life. There is no inconsistency between the two dialogues. The point made in the *Charmides* is simply that the phrase as it stands, without further explanation leaves us in the dark. In the *Republic* the necessary explanation has been supplied by the educational theory and moral psychology which precede its introduction, so that when we come to it, it has a very definite significance, and is seen at once to embody the whole content of the Socratic ideal that a man's business in life is the "tendance of his soul." If it had been sprung upon us, without this preparation, in the course of *Republic* i. as an answer to the ethical nihilism of Thrasymachus, it would then have been exactly what Socrates calls it in the *Charmides*—a conundrum.

The defence of the proposed definition is now taken up by Critias. He replies to the objection of Socrates by making a distinction between "doing" (τὸ πράττειν, τὸ ἐργάζεσθαι) and "making" (τὸ ποιεῖν). The shoemaker "makes" shoes for his customers, but in "making" their shoes he is "doing" his own work. The shoes he makes are not his own shoes, but the making of them *is* his "own" trade or work. Here again we are dealing with a real and important distinction ; in the *Republic* we shall learn the true significance of the conception of a "work" or "vocation" which is a man's "own," not because the products of it are to be his "own" property for his own exclusive use, but because it is the contribution he and no one else can make to the "good life." Critias has not, however, thought out the implications of his own distinction, and goes wrong from the start by an elementary confusion of ideas. He appeals in support of the distinction to the saying of Hesiod that "no work is disgraceful," [1] on which he puts a glaringly false interpretation. Hesiod, he says, cannot have meant that no occupation is a base one, for there are base trades like those of the shoemaker and fishmonger, not to mention worse ones. By "work" Hesiod must have meant "making what is honourable and useful," and similarly, when we say that *sophrosyne* is "minding your own matters" or "doing your own work" we mean that it is doing what is "honourable and useful" (163*b–c*).

We might expect that Socrates would fasten at once on the obvious weakness of this definition ; it presupposes that we already know what we mean by "good and useful." We should then be led direct to the conclusion which it is part of Plato's purpose to drive home, that we cannot really know the character of *sophrosyne*

---

[1] ἔργον δ' οὐδὲν ὄνειδος (Hesiod, *O.D.* 311). Xenophon (*Mem.* i. 2, 56–57) states that Socrates was fond of the saying, apparently taking it in the sense that "honest work is no disgrace." His "accuser" twisted it to mean that no one need feel ashamed of anything he does. Comparison with the similar charges of getting an immoral sense out of the poets considered in the *Apologia Socratis* of Libanius, seems to show that what Xenophon has in view is the pamphlet of Polycrates against Socrates.

or any other virtue until we know what good and evil are, and when we know that we have answered the question what virtue is. In point of fact, Socrates prefers to make an unexpected deviation from the direct line of the argument, which raises a still more general issue, and apparently takes us out of the sphere of ethics into that of epistemology. The length of this section shows that it is meant to be the most important division of the dialogue, and we shall need therefore to consider it with some care.

According to the explanation of Critias, a physician who cures his patient is doing something good and useful for both himself and the patient and is therefore acting with *sophrosyne*. But he need not know that he is doing what is " good and useful." (The physician cannot be sure that he will really be the better, or that his patient will be the better, for his services. It *might* be better for the patient that he should die, or for the physician that he should not make the income he does make.) Thus it would seem that a man may have *sophrosyne* without being aware that he has it (164*a–c*). This would not only seem inconsistent with the assumption Socrates had made at the beginning of his conversation with Charmides, but also flatly contradicts the generally accepted view, with which Critias agrees, that *sophrosyne* actually is the same thing as " self-knowledge." (The thought, of course, is that " sanity of mind " is precisely a true understanding of yourself, your strength and your weaknesses, your real situation in relation to gods and men, the kind of self-knowledge which was inculcated by the *Nosce teipsum* [1] inscription in the Delphic temple.) We thus find ourselves embarked on a double question : (1) Is self-knowledge possible at all ? (2) If it is, is it profitable ; has it any bearing on the practical conduct of life ? Or again : (1) What is the object apprehended by self-knowledge ? (2) What is the result it produces ?

The second question is met by Critias with the reply that self-knowledge, like such " sciences " or " arts " as arithmetic and geometry, and unlike such "sciences " or " arts " as building or weaving, has no " product." This is, in untechnical language, the distinction which is more clearly drawn in the *Politicus* and finally takes technical form in Aristotle as the distinction between " speculative " knowledge, which has no further end than the perfecting of itself, and " practical " knowledge, which has always an ulterior end, the making of some thing or the doing of some act. Critias is unconsciously assuming first that self-knowledge is ἐπιστήμη or τέχνη, knowledge of universal rules or principles of some kind, and next that it is " speculative," not " practical " science. The result is that he is virtually confusing the direct acquaintance with one's own individual strength and weaknesses really meant in the Delphian inscription with the " science " of the psychologist. He is taking it for granted, as too many among ourselves still do, that to know psychology and to have a profound acquaintance with your own " heart " are the same thing (*Charm.* 165*d–e.*) Socrates lets this

[1] γνῶθι σαυτόν.

confusion of " direct acquaintance " with " knowledge about " go uncriticized, because his immediate purpose is to raise a more general issue, one which concerns not the *effect* of knowledge, but the *object* apprehended. In all other cases, he urges, that which is apprehended by a " knowledge " or " science " is something different from the knowing or apprehending itself. Arithmetic for example is knowledge of " the even and odd," as we should say, of the characters of the integers. But " the even and odd " are not the same thing as the knowing which has them for its object. (In fact, of course, arithmetic is a mental activity, the integers and their properties are not.) We shall find the same distinction between the " knowing " and the object known in the case of any other " knowledge " we like to take (166*a–b*). Critias admits the truth of this in general, but asserts that there is one solitary exception. The self-knowledge of which he had spoken is this exception; it is quite literally a knowing which " knows itself and all other knowledges," and the virtue *sophrosyne* is no other than this " knowing which knows itself " (166*c*). In effect this amounts to identifying *sophrosyne* with what is called in modern times " theory of knowledge."

We proceed to test this thesis in the true Socratic way by asking what consequences would follow from it. It would follow that the man who has *sophrosyne* would know what he knows and what he does not know but merely " fancies " (οἴεται), and also what other men know and what they only " fancy." Let us once more put our double question, Is such knowledge as this possible, and if it is, is it of any benefit to us ?

There is a grave difficulty even about its possibility. For, in all other cases, we find that a mental activity is always directed on some object other than itself. Sight and hearing do not see or hear sight or hearing; they see colours and hear sounds. Desire is never " desire of desire " but always desire of a pleasant object ; we do not wish for " wishing " but for *good*. What we love is not " loving " but a beloved person, what we fear, not fear but some formidable thing, and so forth. That is, it is characteristic of mental activities of all kinds that they are directed upon an object *other than themselves* (167*c*–168*a*). It would be at least " singular " (ἄτοπον) if there should be a solitary exception to this principle, a " knowing " which is not the knowing of a science (μάθημα) of some kind, but the " knowing of itself and the other knowings " (168*a*). Knowing, in fact, is always a knowing of something, and so *relative* to an object known ; its " faculty " is to be *of* something (168*b*), and so where there is knowing there must be a known object, just as where there is a " greater than " there must always be a " less " *than* which the greater is greater. Hence, if there is anything which is greater than itself, it must also be less than itself ; if anything which is double of itself, it must also be half itself, and so on. If " seeing " can see itself, " seeing " itself must be coloured. Some of these consequences are patently absurd, *e.g.* that there should be a number which is greater than, and by consequence also less than itself : if it is not so obvious that seeing cannot see itself, and that sight, by consequence, is not a colour, the position is at any rate difficult to accept. It would require a great philosopher to decide the question whether any activity can be its own object, and if so, whether this is the case with the activity of knowing, and we have not the genius needed to determine the point (168*b*–169*b*). But in any case, we may say that such a supposed " knowing of knowing " cannot be what men mean by *sophrosyne* unless it can be shown that it would be " beneficial " to us, as *sophrosyne* admittedly is (169*b*–*c*).

(So far then, the point of the argument has been the perfectly sound one that no mental activity is its own object. Manifestly this is true of the knowing of the epistemologist, as much as of any other activity. If there is such a science as the " theory of know-ledge," its object will be " the conditions under which knowledge is possible." But these conditions are not the same thing as anyone's knowing about them. The doctrines of the *Critique of Pure Reason*, for example, are one thing and Kant's knowing or believing these doctrines is another.)

We can now take a further step. Let us concede, for the pur-poses of argument, that there is such a thing as a " knowing of knowing." Even if there is, it is not the same thing as " knowing *what* you know and *what* you do not know," and therefore is not the self-knowledge with which Critias has been trying to identify *sophrosyne*. Critias does not readily take in the distinction, which has therefore to be made gradually clearer by illustrations. Sup-pose a man to " know about knowing," what will this knowledge really tell him ? It will tell him that " this is knowledge " and " that is not knowledge," *i.e.* that this proposition is true, that proposition is not certainly true. But to know so much and no more would certainly not be enough for the purposes of the practitioner in medicine and statesmanship. The physician needs not merely to know that " I know such and such a proposition," he needs to know that the true proposition in question is relevant to the treatment of his patients. In other words, it is not enough for him to know what *knowledge* is, he needs to know what *health* is, and the states-man similarly must know not merely what knowledge is, but what *right* is. *Ex hypothesi* they will not learn this from a science which has knowledge as its object, but from medicine, of which the object is health in the body, or from politics, which knows about " right." Thus we must not say that the man who has only " knowledge of knowledge " will know *what* he knows and *what* he does not ; we may only say that that he will know the bare fact *that* he knows or does not know. (The meaning is, for example, that a man who was a mere epistemologist and nothing more might be aware that when he says, " So many grains of arsenic are fatal, " he is saying something which satisfies all the conditions required for genuine scientific knowledge ; but, if he only knew epistemology and nothing else, he would not even know that he must not administer fatal doses of arsenic to his fellow-men.) Thus if *sophrosyne* is the same thing as

a " knowledge of knowledge," the man who has it will not be helped
by it to distinguish a genuine practitioner from a pretender in
medicine or in anything else. To distinguish the true physician
from the quack, you need to know not epistemology, the " knowledge of knowledge," but medicine, the " knowledge of things
wholesome and unwholesome." The true judge of medical theory
and practice is not the epistemologist but the medical specialist, and
no one else (169d–171c). And this conclusion seems to dispose of
the worth of *sophrosyne*, if we were right in identifying it with a
" knowledge of knowledge." A self-knowledge which taught us to
know, in the first instance, our own strength and weakness, and, in
the second place, the strength and weakness of others, and so
enabled us to be on our guard against self-delusion and imposture,
would be of the highest value for the conduct of life. But we have
just seen that all that the epistemologist as such could possibly
tell about himself or anyone else would be merely whether he really
knew epistemology (171c–e).

The point to which all this leads us up is manifestly that though
sophrosyne is a knowledge of something, it cannot be a " knowledge
about knowledge," nor can this be what was really meant by those
who have insisted on self-knowledge as the one thing needful for a
happy life. It is clearly indicated that the sort of knowledge of
ourselves really needed as a guide to practice is knowledge of good and
evil and of the state of our souls in respect of them, a view which
would immediately lead to the further result that all the genuine
virtues are at bottom one and the same thing, knowledge of the good,
and the distinctions commonly made between the different types
of virtue at best conventional. (It is incidentally a further valuable
result of the argument that it has vindicated the autonomy of the
various sciences by exposing the pretensions of the " theory of
knowledge " to judge of scientific truths on *a priori* grounds, and
making it clear that in every case there is no appeal from the verdict
of the expert in a specific science, so long as he claims to be the final
authority *in his own speciality*.)

The main purpose of the discussion becomes apparent when we
reach its final section. Even if we waive all the difficulties we have
raised, and admit that *sophrosyne* really is a " knowledge of knowledge," and that such a knowledge is, (as we just said that it is
not,) " knowing *what* we do know and what we do not," would this
supposed knowledge be of any value for the direction of life ?
It is clear, of course, that if we had such a knowledge, and directed
our actions by it, everything would be done " scientifically " (κατὰ
τὰς ἐπιστήμας, ἐπιστημόνως). Our medical men, our soldiers, our
sailors, all our craftsmen in fact, would be real experts ; lives would
not be lost by the blunders of the incompetent physician or strategist
or navigator, clothes would not be spoiled by the bungling of their
makers ; we may even imagine that " prophecy " might be made
" scientific," and that we could thus have confident anticipations of
the future, and, if you like, we may suppose ourselves equally

correctly informed about the past (a suggestion which curiously recalls Du Bois-Reymond's fanciful picture of his omniscient "demon"[1]). But we should be none the happier for all this knowledge unless we had something more which we have not yet mentioned—knowledge of good. Without this we might know all about healing the sick, sailing the sea, winning battles, but we should not know when it is *good* that a sick man should recover, or that a vessel should come safe to port, or a battle be won. If our life is to be truly happy, it is this knowledge of our good which must take the direction of it; apart from that knowledge, we may be able to secure the successful accomplishment of various results, but we cannot make sure that anything will be "well and beneficially" done. But *sophrosyne* by our assumed definition is not this knowledge of good; even when we waived all other difficulties about it, we still retained the thesis that it is a "knowledge about knowledges," a "science of sciences." Thus *sophrosyne* seems to fall between two stools; it is not the knowledge of good which would really ensure happiness. It is not even a knowledge which will ensure that the practitioners of the various "arts" shall be experts and practise their callings with success; for we have just seen that it is the specialist in each department and not the man who knows the "theory of knowledge" who is the final judge in his own department. *Sophrosyne*, if we accept the proposed definition of it, even with the most favourable interpretation, thus seems to be of no practical value whatever (171*d*–175*a*). Yet this conclusion is so extravagantly paradoxical that it clearly cannot be sound. We can only suppose that the fault is with ourselves; our notions on the subject must be hopelessly confused. This is unfortunate, as it makes it impossible to employ the Thracian's recipe for the cure of Charmides, but there is no help for it. (Of course, the real, as distinct from the dramatic, conclusion has already been reached in the suggestion that what is really needed for the direction of life is the knowledge of good, and that this knowledge is something quite different from any of the recognized special "sciences" or "arts." The purpose of the dialogue is to show that serious examination of the implications of the current conceptions of *sophrosyne* conducts us straight to the two famous Socratic "paradoxes" of the unity of virtue and its identity with *knowledge* of good.)

The Laches.—The *Laches*, which we may now treat more briefly, aims at reaching these same results by starting with the current conceptions of the great fighting-man's virtue—courage or valour or fortitude. As in the *Charmides*, the discussion is accompanied by an interesting introduction which enables us to refer it to a definite period in the life of Socrates. Lysimachus and Melesias, the undistinguished sons of two of the greatest Athenians of the early fifth century, Aristides "the just" and Thucydides, the rival of Pericles, are both anxious that their own sons should rise to distinction, and therefore that they should receive the careful education which

[1] Du Bois-Reymond, *Ueber die Grenzen des Naturerkennens*, 17 ff.; Ward, *Naturalism and Agnosticism*, i. 40 ff. (ed. 1).

their own parents were prevented by their preoccupation with public affairs from bestowing on themselves. They have just witnessed a public exhibition given by one Stesilaus, who professes to be able to teach the art and mystery of fighting in full armour, and have brought with them two of the most famous military men of the day, Laches and Nicias, in order to get their opinion on the advisability of putting the lads under such an instructor.

Socrates also has been present at the display, and at the recommendation of Laches, who witnessed and highly admired his presence of mind and courage in the disastrous retreat of the Athenian forces from Delium (424 B.C.), he is taken into consultation (*Laches*, 180a–b). It now comes out that Sophroniscus, the father of Socrates, had been a lifelong friend of Lysimachus, and that Socrates himself is a person of whom Lysimachus has heard the boys speak as an object of great interest to themselves and their young companions (180d–e). Laches, as it comes out later, knows nothing of him except his admirable behaviour on the field of Delium (188e), but Nicias is perfectly familiar with him and his habit of turning every conversation into a searching examination of the state of his interlocutor's soul (187e–188b). These allusions enable us to date the supposed conversation pretty accurately. It falls after Delium in 424, but not long after, since it is assumed that Laches, who fell at Mantinea in 418, is still burdened by the cares of public office (187a–b). The references to the comparative poverty of Socrates—it is not said to be more than comparative (186c)—may remind us that Aristophanes and Amipsias both made this a prominent feature in their burlesques of him (the *Clouds* of Aristophanes and the *Connus* of Amipsias), produced in 423. It points to the same general date that the two old men should be thinking of the speciality of Stesilaus as the thing most desirable to be acquired by their sons. After the peace of Nicias, which was expected to put an end to the struggle between Athens and the Peloponnesian Confederation, it would not be likely that fathers anxious to educate their sons well should think at once of ὁπλομαχία as the most promising branch of education. We thus have to think of the conversation as occurring just about the time when Aristophanes produced his delightful caricature of Socrates as a guide of youth ; Socrates is a man of rather under fifty ; Nicias and Laches, as Plato is careful to remind us (181d), are older men, and Lysimachus and Melesias quite old and " out of the world." [1]

The two military experts, as it happens, are of different minds

---

[1] The same approximate date is suggested by the allusion to the famous Damonides, or Damon, of Oea. Nicias expresses gratitude to Socrates for having procured an introduction to Damon for his son Niceratus. Laches professes to think Damon a mere spinner of words and phrases, but Nicias retorts that it is not for him to judge, since he has never even met the man (200b). The assumption is that Damon is living in retirement from society generally. Since he was one of the two " sophists " who " educated " Pericles (Isocr. xv. 235), he must have been born, like his colleague Anaxagoras. about 500 B.C., so that his advanced age will account for his seclusion

about the practical value of the proposed instruction in the conduct of spear and shield. Nicias, who is represented all through as the more intellectual of the two, is inclined to recommend it on the grounds that a soldier needs to know how to handle his weapons, that he is likely to find skill of fence serviceable in actual fighting, that it may awaken in him an interest in other branches of the military art, such as strategy, finally that the training produces grace and agility and banishes awkwardness (181e–182d). Laches, a brave fighting-man with no intellectual capacity, takes a different view. He holds that the " proof of the pudding is the eating of it." There cannot be much in this technical skill, for we see that the Spartans, who ought to be the best judges of things military, set no store by its professors, and the professors themselves avoid Sparta like the plague. They reap their harvest from communities who, by their own admission, are backward in warfare. (This is an excellent little bit of dramatic characterization ; Laches is mentally too dull to see the obvious explanation that the professionals take their wares to the market where the need for them is likely to be most felt.) Besides, in actual warfare, the professional masters of fence never distinguish themselves.[1] Laches remembers having seen this very professor make himself a laughing-stock by his clumsy handling of a complicated weapon of his own forging (182d–184c).

In this disagreement of the experts, Socrates is now called upon to give the decisive opinion. But, as he says, a question of this kind is not to be settled by a majority of votes. The deciding voice should be left to the expert, the man who really knows, even if he were found to be in a minority of one. But who is the expert to whom we ought to appeal in the present case ? Not the mere expert or connoisseur in ὁπλομαχία. The problem is really concerned with the " tendance " of the young people's souls, and the expert to whom we must appeal is therefore the expert in " tending " his own soul, the man who can achieve " goodness " in himself and, by his influence, produce it in others (185a–e). Now, if a man really is an expert, he may take either of two ways of convincing us of his claims. If he has learned his skill from others, he can tell us who his teachers were, and convince us that they were competent.[2] If he has picked it up for himself, as expert knowledge is often picked up, he can point to its results, he can give us examples of persons who have been made better by his influence on them (186a–b). Socrates confesses himself to be no expert, but maliciously suggests that the case may be different with the two generals. They are richer than he, and may have been able to pay " sophists " for instruction in the art of " tending the soul " ; they are older and more experienced, and so may have discovered the secret for themselves

[1] In the *Republic* Socrates himself is made to propose a training for his young men from which all specialism of this kind is expressly excluded (*Rep.* iii. 404a ff.).
[2] We shall see the full significance of this when we come to examine the *Protagoras.*

(186c). At any rate, they must be experts, or they could not pronounce on a question in which only the expert is competent with such confidence and readiness. (The insinuation, of course, is that, as we might expect from their disagreement, neither is a real "expert"; both are talking about what they do not understand.)

We may, however, contrive to avoid the demand for direct evidence that there is an expert among us. For if a man really knows what, e.g., good sight is, and how to produce it in a patient, he can tell us what sight is; if he cannot, he is manifestly not a specialist in the treatment of the eye. So, in the present case, the man whose judgment we need is the expert in "goodness," which makes our souls better souls. If a man cannot even say what goodness is, it would be waste of time to take his advice on the kind of education which will produce it. Thus the original question whose judgment is authoritative in the problem of education may be replaced by the question who knows what goodness is. And this question may be, for convenience, further narrowed down. For our present purpose, judging of the worth of the art of the professional teacher of skill with shield and spear, it will be sufficient to consider only one "part" of goodness—courage or valour. A competent judge on the question whether the accomplishment makes its possessor a better soldier must at least be able to say what courage is (189d–190e). We have now got our ethical question fairly posed : What is it that we really mean to be talking about when we speak of ἀνδρεία—manliness, valour, courage—as one of the indispensable points of manhood? Laches, the less thoughtful of the two professional soldiers, thinks that any man can answer so simple a question off-hand. "A man who keeps his place in the ranks in the presence of the enemy, does his best to repel them, and never turns his back—there is a brave man for you" (190e). Thus, just as in the *Charmides*, we start with a proposed definition of an interior state of soul which confuses the state itself with one of its common and customary outward expressions. The further course of the discussion will reveal the double defectiveness of this formula. It is not even adequate as a description of the conduct of the fighting-man himself, and fighting is far from being the only business in life which demands the same qualities as those we expect from the good soldier. As usual, Plato is anxious to insist upon the real identity of the spiritual state under the great apparent variety of its outward manifestations. To discover that other occupations than those of warfare also call for the "soldierly" virtues is a long step towards discovering the essential unity of the "virtues" themselves.

Even Laches is ready to admit at once that a feigned withdrawal is a proper manoeuvre in warfare, as is shown by the practice of the Scythians, the pretended retreat by which the Lacedaemonians drew the Persians from their defences at Plataea, and other examples (191a–c). He is even ready to allow that fighting is not the only situation in which courage may be shown. A man may show himself a brave man or a coward by the way he faces danger at sea, poverty, disease, the risks of political life ; again, bravery and cowardice may be shown as much in resistance to the seductions of pleasure and the importunities of desire as in facing or shirking pain or danger, a consideration which, incidentally, shows the artificial nature of the popular distinction between valour, the virtue of war, and *sophrosyne*, the virtue of peace and non-combatants (191*d–e*). (It is this passage of the *Laches* which Aristotle has in view in the *Ethics* where he distinguishes valour in the "primary" sense of the word from the very kind of conduct here called by the name.[1] The disagreement, however, is a purely verbal one. Aristotle does not mean to deny that the qualities in question are indispensable to the good life, nor that there is a close analogy between them and the quality of the soldier, which justifies a "transference" of the name *valour* to them. He is concerned simply, in the interests of precise terminology, to insist that when we speak of "putting up a good fight" against disease, financial distress, temptation, and the like, we are using language which originally was appropriated to the actual "fighting" of actual soldiers, and Aristotle's purpose in giving the series of character-sketches which make up this section of the *Ethics* requires that he shall describe the various "virtues" in the guise in which they are most immediately recognizable by popular thought.)

Now that he sees the point, Laches replies very readily that there is a certain spirit or temper which is to be found universally in all the examples of courageous behaviour Socrates has produced. They are all cases in which a man "persists" in the face of opposition or risk of some kind. Hence he proposes as the definition of courage that it is in all cases a certain καρτερία, "persistence," "endurance," "sticking to one's purpose" (192*c*). This definition clearly has some of the qualities of a good definition. When you speak of courage as a "persistence of soul," just as when we commonly use the word "resolution" as a synonym for it, you are really trying to indicate the spirit which underlies all the manifold expressions of the quality. And it is, of course, true that persistence or resolution is a characteristic of courage ; the brave man is one who "sticks it out." But, as a definition, the formula is still too wide. All courage may be persistence, but all persistence is not courage. In the technical logical language which makes its appearance in Plato's later dialogues, we need to know the "difference"[2] which discriminates persistence which is courage from persistence which is not. Since unwise persistence, mere obstinacy, is a bad and harmful thing, whereas we certainly mean by courage something we regard as eminently good, it looks as though we might remedy the defect of our formula by saying that "wise persistence" (φρόνιμος καρτερία) is courage (192*d*). But the question now arises *what* wisdom we mean. A man may wisely calculate that by persisting in expenditure he will make a commercial profit, but we should hardly regard this as an example of courage. When a

---

[1] *E.N.* iii. 6, 1115*a* 7 ff.   [2] διαφορά, διαφορότης (*Theaetet.* 208*d* ff.).

physician persists in refusing the entreaties of his patient for food which he knows would be bad for the patient, we do not think the physician has shown any particular courage. In warfare, we do not commend the courage of a force which " holds out " because it knows that it is superior in numbers and still has the stronger position and is certain of reinforcement. It is just the " persistence " of an inferior force, with a worse position and no hope of relief, that impresses us as singularly courageous. So we think more of the courage of the man who acquits himself well in the cavalry though is he an unskilled rider, or the man who makes a plucky dive into deep water though he is a poor swimmer, than we do of the persistence of the man who acquits himself well because he has mastered these accomplishments. (E.g., we think Monmouth's raw countrymen showed great courage at Sedgemoor in putting up a fight against the Household troops; we do not commend the courage of the Household troops because they " held out " against a crowd of peasants.) This looks as if, after all, it is " unwise " persistence (ἄφρων καρτέρησις) rather than " wise " which is the true courage. We have plainly not found the right formula yet, and shall have to call on ourselves for the very quality of which we have been speaking, " persistence " in the inquiry, if we are to approve ourselves " courageous " thinkers (192c–194a). We must not miss the point of this difficulty. Socrates does not seriously mean to suggest that " unwise " resolution or persistence is courage. His real object is to distinguish the " wisdom " meant by the true statement that courage is " wise resolution " from specialist knowledge which makes the taking of a risk less hazardous. The effect of specialist knowledge of this kind is, in fact, to make the supposed risk unreal. The man whom we admire because we suppose him to be rightly taking a great risk is, in reality, as he himself knows, taking little or no risk. Our belief in his courage is based on an illusion which he does not share. But it is true that we do not regard the " unwise " persistency of the man who takes " foolish " risks as true courage. What we really mean is that the brave man faces a great risk, being alive to its magnitude, but faces it because he rightly judges that it is good to do so. The " wisdom " he shows is right judgment of good and evil, and this is what Socrates means to suggest.

At this point Nicias comes into the discussion. He has " often " heard Socrates say that a man is " good " at the things he " knows " (ἄπερ σοφός, 194d) and "bad" at the things he does not know (ἃ ἀμαθής). If this is true, as Nicias believes it to be, courage, since it is always a good quality or activity, will be a σοφία or ἐπιστήμη, a knowledge of some kind. It is clearly not the same thing as any form of specialist technical knowledge, for the reasons we have already considered. But it may well be that it is " the knowledge of what is formidable and what is not " (ἡ τῶν δεινῶν καὶ θαρραλέων ἐπιστήμη, 194e); i.e. the truly brave man may be the man who knows, in all the situations of life, what is and what is not a proper object of fear. This suggestion is plainly a step in the right direction, as it incorporates the important distinction between specialist knowledge and the kind of knowledge which might conceivably be the same thing as virtue, the distinction which would be made, in the fashionable terminology of our own day, between knowledge of facts and knowledge of values. Laches, however, who is in a bad temper from his own recent rebuff, treats the theory as a mere piece of mystification, and can hardly be brought to express his objections to it in decently civil language. A physician or a farmer knows the dangers to which his patients or his cattle are exposed, but such knowledge does not constitute courage (195b). The objection shows that Laches has missed the whole point of the definition, as Nicias goes on to observe. The physician may know that a patient will die or will recover ; he does not know whether death or recovery is the really " formidable " thing for the patient. It may be that it is recovery which would in some cases be the " dreadful " thing, but medical science cannot tell us which these cases are; (e.g. a man might use his restored health in a way which would bring him to public disgrace worse than death, and, of course, his medical man cannot learn from the study of medicine whether this will happen or not [1]). Even the " seer " can only predict that a man will or will not die, or lose his money, that a battle will be won or lost ; his art cannot tell him which event will be better for the man or the State (195e–196a). This is, of course, exactly the reply which might be made to Laches' criticism from the Socratic standpoint. But it still leaves something to be said which Socrates is anxious to say. In the first place, if courage is knowledge of some kind, we must deny that any mere animal can be brave. In fact, the truly brave will be a small minority even among men. Must we say, then, that there is no difference in courage between a lion and a deer, a bull and a monkey ? Laches thinks the suggestion a sufficient refutation of what he regards as the sophisticated nonsense of Nicias, but, as Nicias observes, its edge is turned if we distinguish between natural high temper and fearlessness (τὸ ἄφοβον) and genuine courage (τὸ ἀνδρεῖον, 196d–197c). So far Nicias is simply insisting on what we shall see from the *Phaedo* and *Republic* to be the Socratic view.[2] Native fearlessness is a valuable endowment, but it is only in a human being that it can serve as a basis for the development of the loyalty to principle we call courage, and it is only in " philosophers " that this transformation of mere " pluck " into true valiancy is complete. But there is a further difficulty which Nicias has left out of account. By a " formidable thing " or " thing to be feared " we mean a *future* or impending *evil*. Now there is no science of *future* good and evil distinct from the science of good and evil

[1] So in Dickens's *Great Expectations* it is " better for " the returned convict that he dies in the prison hospital, since, if he had recovered, he would have been sent to the gallows for returning from transportation. The hero is *glad* to hear on each inquiry that the patient is " worse."

[2] The distinction is more obvious to a Greek than to ourselves, since the *vox propria* for " brave " is ἀνδρεῖος, " manly," and to call a brute " manly " is felt to be at least a straining of language.

simpliciter, just as there is no special science of "*future* health and disease " or of "*future* victory and defeat." There is simply the science of medicine or of strategy, and these sciences apply indifferently to past, present, and future. So our definition, if we are to retain it, must be amended ; we must say that courage is " knowledge of good and evil," without any further qualification (198*d*–199*e*). But as now amended our formula covers not merely a part but the whole of goodness. If it is a definition at all, it is the definition of " goodness," not of one of several different varieties or departments of " goodness " (199*e*). Yet it is commonly held that courage is not the whole of " goodness " ; a good man needs to display other virtues, such as " justice " and *sophrosyne.* It appears then that, after all, we have not answered the question what *courage* is. So far from being competent to choose masters for the education of the boys, we all need to go to school ourselves, if only we could find a teacher (201*a*).

Thus the dialogue has led us to the same result as the *Charmides.* If we try to explain what any one great typical moral virtue is, we find ourselves driven on to define it as " the knowledge of what is good." Every virtue thus seems on examination to cover the whole field of the conduct of life, and none can be in principle distinguished from any other. Yet it is commonly thought, and we shall see in dealing with the *Republic* that there are facts of experience which strongly support the view, that the different virtues are so really distinct that a man may be eminent for one and yet no less eminent for the lack of another, (as the typical soldier is commonly thought to be at once braver and more licentious than the ordinary peaceable civilian). We are forced by our intellect to accept the Socratic " paradox " of the unity of virtue, but we have to explain how the " paradox " is to be reconciled with the facts upon which popular moral psychology is based. How the reconciliation is effected we shall be able to say when we have studied the *Protagoras, Phaedo,* and *Republic.* The all-important point, on which too many interpreters went wrong in the nineteenth century, is to understand that, to the end of his life, Plato never wavered in his adherence to the " paradox " itself.

Lysis.—The dialogue is linked with the *Charmides* by its setting, which presents another charming picture of the manner of Socrates with promising boys ; some of the problems of moral psychology it suggests point forward to one of the supreme achievements of Plato's literary prime, the *Symposium.* It is specially interesting as the unnamed source from which Aristotle derives most of the questions discussed in a more systematic way in the lectures which make up the eighth and ninth books of the *Nicomachean Ethics.* (The extensive use of the *Lysis* in these books of itself disposes of the misguided attack made on its authenticity by some nineteenth-century scholars.)

The subject of the discussion is Friendship, a topic which plays a much more prominent part in ancient than in modern ethical literature, for easily assignable reasons. It is quite untrue to say that the Greeks " had no family life," but it is true that owing to the neglect of the education of their women, the family tended to be more a close " business partnership " than a centre of intellectual interests and spiritual emotions. Again, though conjugal affection could be a real thing in the Hellenic world, for the same reasons, romantic love between the sexes had little scope for the moralizing and spiritualizing effects we are accustomed to ascribe to it. " Passion " was relatively more prominent, " affection " much more secondary, in the sexual life of Periclean Athens than in that of any community which has been stamped by Christian traditions. In the Greek literature of the great period, Eros is a god to be dreaded for the havoc he makes of human life, not to be courted for the blessings he bestows ; a tiger, not a kitten to sport with.[1] Love, as known to the classical writers, is a passion for taking, not for giving. Hence in life, as seen from the Hellenic point of view, there are just two outlets for the spirit of eager unselfish devotion. It can show itself in a high impersonal form, as absolute devotion to the "· city " which is the common mother of all the citizens. For the man who, like most of us, needs a personal object of flesh and blood for passionate affection and self-sacrifice, there is the lifelong friend of his own sex, whose good is to him as his *own*. This is why, in Aristotle's *Ethics*, an elaborate study of friendship immediately precedes the culminating picture of the " speculative life," in which man puts off the last vestiges of his human individuality to lose himself in the contemplation of God. We may suspect that those who condemn the tone of Greek ethics as " self-centred "have usually " skipped " these books in their reading of the *Ethics*, and forgotten that they are only the remains of what was once a vast literature.[2]

Plato's interest in the *Lysis* is partly a psychological one. He is fascinated by the mystery of the attraction which can draw two human beings so close, that each is to the other as dear or dearer than himself, as modern philosophers have been by the mystery of the attraction of a particular woman for a particular man. What does A see in B rather than in C, to account for this attraction ? But he has also a more specifically ethical purpose, as will appear from an analysis of his argument. As usual, we shall find the fundamental conceptions of the Socratic morality, the doctrine

[1] Cf. Bevan, *Hellenism and Christianity*, 93–94.

[2] There are linguistic difficulties about any precise reproduction of the argument of the *Lysis* in English. φιλεῖν can only be rendered " to love," *i.e.* with the love of affection (not that of sexual desire). But for φίλος, used as a substantive, we have to say " friend," while the adjective has to be rendered in various ways. If we said regularly either " friendly " or " dear," we should obscure the reasoning, since " friendly " means definitely " a person feeling affection," and " dear " a " person towards whom affection is felt." Either rendering would make nonsense of the question, whether our φίλοι are those whom we " love " or those who " love us." Further, when the adjective is used about things, like wine and the like, we cannot render it by either. We have to say that a man " likes " wine or horses. This must be my apology for the shifts to which I have been driven.

of the " tendance " of the soul and the dependence of happiness upon *knowledge* of good, emerging from the paradoxes in which the discussion appears to entangle itself.

The introduction of the dialogue closely resembles that of the *Charmides.* Socrates is taking a walk outside the city wall from the suburb of the Academy on the N.W. to the Lyceum on the E., when he is accosted by some of his young friends and drawn into a *palaestra* to make the acquaintance of Lysis, a beautiful and modest boy passionately admired by Hippothales, one of the elder lads. Hippothales, in fact, as the others complain, makes a nuisance of himself by inflicting on them endless bad poems, in which he belauds the antiquity, wealth, and splendid renown of the family of Lysis. Socrates good-naturedly banters Hippothales on the mal-adroitness of attempting to make a " conquest " by flatteries which would be more likely to spoil the recipient, by making him arrogant, conceited, and domineering, and is then invited to enter the *palaestra* and give a practical example of the kind of conversation really appropriate to a " lover " (*Lysis*, 203*a*–207*c*).

(The tone which Socrates adopts in his conversation with Lysis discloses quietly but unmistakably the difference between his own conception of a romantic attachment and that of his fashionable young companions. The tacit presupposition is that the " true lover's " desire is for the real felicity of the beloved ; his passion is thus an entirely pure and disinterested thing, a form of φιλία, " affec-tion," not of selfish lust ; and this, no doubt, is why Socrates can open the argument by examples drawn from wise parental affection.[1])

Lysis has parents who love him dearly. Since they love him so well they are, of course, anxious for his " happiness." Now a man cannot be happy if he is not his own master and cannot " do what he desires," " have his own way." Yet the very parents who are so devoted to the boy's happiness will hardly let him have his own way about anything. He is not allowed to drive his father's horses or mules, though a hired coachman or a groom who is a slave is allowed to do as he thinks good with them. He is even made to go to school under the conduct of a *paedagogus* and, though the man is a slave, has to do what he tells him. When he comes back from school, he may not do as he pleases with his mother's wools and implements for spinning and weaving ; he would even be whipped if he meddled with them. This does not look like being happy or being one's own master (207*e*–209*a*).

Lysis gives the boyish explanation that he is not yet old enough to meddle with such matters. But the real reason cannot be one of age. There are things in which he is allowed to have his own way. When his parents want him to read aloud, to write or to sing, he is allowed to have his own way about the order in which he reads or

[1] The brutal selfishness of the fashionable ἐραστής is the theme of Socrates homily in the *Phaedrus*, on the text " that one's favours should not be granted to a ' lover.' " Cf. the proverb quoted at the end of the homily, that this sort of " love " is the ' love of the wolf for the lamb " (*Phaedrus*, 238*c*–241*d*).

writes words and about tuning the strings of his instrument, because these are things which he *knows* how to do. Any man, or any body of men, will be ready to let us manage any kind of business at our own discretion, if only it is believed that we know *how* to do it better than anyone else. When you *know* how to handle an affair, every one will trust you to handle it ; no one will interfere with your action if he can help it ; the affair will really be *your* affair and you will be *free* in dealing with it. But our best friends will be the first persons to check us from having our own way in matters we do not understand ; they will not be *our* affair, and we shall be " under the control of others," " not our own masters " in handling them (209*a*–210*b*). The reason is that we are " unprofitable," " useless " (ἀνωφελεῖς), in matters we do not understand. But we cannot expect anyone to " love " us for our " uselessness." If we are " wise," everybody will be our friend, because we shall be " good and useful " ; if we are not, even our parents and relatives will not be our friends. Thus the sample conversation is made to lead up to the point that to be happy and to be free is the same thing as to have true knowledge. Socrates adds, with a sportive play on words, that it is absurd, μέγα φρονεῖν, " to have a high mind," to be conceited, about matters we do not know, and where, therefore, we haven't a " mind " of our own at all (ἐν οἷς τις μήπω φρονεῖ). This is, of course, directed against the vanity of the pride of family which we were told Hippothales encouraged in Lysis (210*b*–*d*).

Some by-play follows here, and when the argument is resumed it is with a different interlocutor. This is a device for calling our attention to the fact that the main issues of the dialogue have not yet been raised ; they are to be looked for, not in the example of the right way of conversing with an ἐρώμενος, but in the apparently more desultory talk which is to follow. Socrates remarks that though he has always thought a good friend the most precious possession a man can have, he himself does not so much as understand how a friend is acquired. Young people who have had the good fortune to form a passionate friendship in their earliest days could, no doubt, enlighten him out of their experience. In this way we make the transition to the main problem of the dialogue, the question : What is the foundation of the personal attraction of one man for another ?

" If one man loves another, which is the friend of the other—the lover of the loved, or the loved of the lover, or does this make no difference ? " *I.e.*, where there is a one-sided affection of *A* for *B*, does this entitle us to say that *A* and *B* are " friends " ? If not, does it entitle us to call *one* of them a " friend," and, if so, which is the friend ? Are my friends the persons who love me or the persons whom I love ? The difficulty lies in the existence of unrequited affection. *A* may be strongly attracted to *B*, while *B* is indifferent to *A*, or even repelled by him. Can we talk of friendship in cases of this kind ? Or should we say that there is not friendship unless the attraction is reciprocal ? It seems most reasonable to hold that the relation of friendship only exists when there is this reciprocal affection. In that case nothing is φίλον to you unless it " loves you back." To a Greek this creates a linguistic difficulty. When he wishes to say that a man is " fond of " anything—wine, for example, or wisdom—he has to form a compound adjective with φιλο for its first component, φίλοινος, φιλόσοφος, or the like, much as when a German wishes to say that he is fond of animals he has to call himself a *Tierfreund*. Language thus seems to be against the view just suggested, but there are undeniable facts on its side ; very young children may feel no love for their parents, and may feel actual " hate " when they get a whipping, but the parent, even when he punishes the child, is its " best friend." This suggests that it is being loved that makes a friend. If you love me, I am your friend, whether I love you or not (212*b*–213*a*).

But a difficulty arises when we remember that, by parity of reasoning, it should follow that it is *being* hated which makes a man an enemy : (if you hate me, I am your enemy, though my heart may be full of nothing but goodwill to you, or though I may not know of your existence). This leads to the paradox that when *A* feels love to *B*, but *B* hates *A*, *A* is being hated by a friend and *B* loved by an enemy, and thus the same couple may be said to be at once friends and enemies, a contradiction in terms (213*b*).

If we revise our view and say that it is not being loved but loving that makes a friend, so that he who loves me is my friend, whatever my attitude to him may be, the same paradox equally follows, since I may love a person who cannot abide me. Since we began by setting aside the view that reciprocal affection is necessary for friendship, we seem thus to have exhausted all the possibilities, and to have shown that there is no such relation as friendship (213*c*).

The absurdity of this shows that we must have made a false start. We must go over the ground again, and we may take a hint from the poets, who talk of friendships as " made in heaven.' God, they say, " draws like to its like." The scientific men who write cosmologies also make use of this principle of " like to like ' to account for the distribution of bodies in the universe. Perhaps this may be the secret of friendship ; the drawing of *A* to *B* may be one case of a great universal principle which underlies the structure of the universe. Yet, on closer examination, we see that unfortunately, so far as the relations of men are concerned, the principle of " like to like " cannot be, at best, more than half the truth. Bad men are not made friends by being " drawn together." The more closely they are drawn together, the more each tries to exploit the other, and the more hostile they become. Perhaps the poets knew this, and really meant to say that a bad man, being without principle, is an unstable and chameleon-like being. He is a " shifty " fellow, who is perpetually " unlike " and at variance with himself, and *a fortiori* unlike and at variance with every one else. Hence the poets perhaps meant to hint that only men of principle, the good, are really " like " one another, and that friendship can only exist between the good (213d–214e).

Yet, when we come to think of it, there is a worse difficulty to be faced. If one thing can act on another and influence it in any way, can the two be exactly alike ? Must there not be some unlikeness, if there is to be any interaction ? And if one party is wholly unaffected by the other, how can the one "care for " (ἀγαπᾶν) the other ? What " comfort " (ἐπικουρία) can the one bring to the other ? And how can you feel friendship for that which you do not care for ? If good men are friends, the reason must be in their goodness, not in their "likeness " (*i.e.* they must be good in *different* ways, so that their respective goodnesses supplement each other, 214e–215a). And this, again, seems impossible. For the good man is ' sufficient for himself " in proportion as he is good. He therefore feels no need of anything but himself. But he who feels no need does not " care for " anything, and he who does not care for a thing can have no affection for it. By this account there can be no friendships between the good ; being " self-sufficient," they will not miss one another in absence or have any occasion for one another's offices when they are together. On what ground, then, should they " set a value " on one another (215a–b).[1]

Again we have gone off on a false track. Socrates once heard some one say that likeness is the source of the keenest rivalry and opposition, but extreme unlikeness the source of friendship. There is poetic authority for this in the Hesiodic saying about " two of a trade," and, in fact, we see that it is so. The rich and the poor, the feeble and the strong, the ailing man and the physician, are brought into friendly association precisely because they are unlike ; each needs the services of the other (*e.g.* the rich man needs industrious and honest servants, the poor need an employer who has wherewithal to pay for their industry ; the sick man needs the physician's skill, the physician needs the fee for it). In fact, said this speaker, the attraction of *unlikes* is the key to cosmology.[2] Everything in nature needs to be tempered by its opposite : the

[1] Obviously we are here raising a question of vast significance. In its extreme form it is the question whether there can be, as Christianity assumes, a love of God for the sinner, or indeed whether God can love anything but Himself. Socrates is raising a difficulty, but not solving it. It is true that the better a man is, the less does the removal of friends, by accident or estrangement or death, wreck his life. In that sense the good man is " sufficient to himself."

[2] Note the way in which it is assumed throughout the dialogue that Socrates is quite familiar with the theories of the cosmologists, and that his young friends will recognize allusions to them. This is strictly in keeping with the standing assumption of the *Clouds* as well as with the autobiographical section of the *Phaedo*. The conception of φιλία in particular as " attraction of unlike for unlike " comes from Empedocles and the Sicilian medicine which goes back to him ; the thought that one opposite is the τροφή, " food " or " fuel," of the other is that of Heraclitus. Heracliteanism was actually represented at Athens in the time of the Archidamian war by Cratylus ; from the speech of Eryximachus in the *Symposium* we see that the Sicilian medical ideas were at home there also.

hot by the cold, the dry by the moist, and so on, for everything is " fed by " its opposite—the familiar doctrine of Heraclitus. Thus it would be tempting to say that friendship is a case of attraction between opposites. Yet if we say that, we shall at once fall an easy prey to those clever men, the ἀντιλογικοί, who love to make a man contradict himself. For they will say that hatred and love are a pair of extreme opposites, and so are " temperance " and profligacy, or good and evil. Our principle would thus require us to believe that a man will generally be most attracted to the very persons who detest him, that a remarkably temperate man will make his bosom friend of a notorious profligate, and the like. But manifestly these statements are not true. So once more we have come to no result. Neither simple " likeness " nor simple " unlikeness " can be the secret of the attraction between friends (215c–216c).[1] We may attempt a more subtle explanation. Perhaps the truth is that in friendship one party is good, the other " neither good nor bad," the only alternative of which we have yet taken no account. (The suggestion is that the relation is regularly one between the possessor of some excellence and some one who aspires to the excellence but has not yet attained it. The friend to whom we are drawn is what we should like to become.) We may illustrate by a simple example from medicine. Health is a good thing, disease a bad thing ; the human body may be said to be neutral, because it is capable of both. Now no one cares about the doctor, so long as he is well. But when he is afraid of being ill, he welcomes the doctor. He does this not when he is at his last gasp, but before, when he apprehends illness, *i.e.* when he is neither in full health nor beyond help. We may say that this is a case in which " that which is neither good nor bad becomes friendly to that which is good because of the presence of what is evil " (217b). And here we must make a careful distinction. " Some things are such as to be themselves such as that which is present to them, others are not " (217c). Thus if the golden locks of a boy are daubed with white paint, " whiteness " is present to them, but they are not themselves white (since, of course, the paint can be washed off). But when the boy has become an old man, " whiteness " will be " present " to his hair in a different sense ; his hair will *itself* be white. (The only object of these remarks is to warn us against supposing that when Socrates speaks of the " presence " of what is evil to what is " neither good nor bad," he is using the term in the sense in which it is employed when we explain the possession of a predicate by a thing by saying that the corresponding form is " present " to the thing. In this sense παρουσία, " presence " of the form, is an equivalent for μέθεξις, the " participation " of a thing in the form, as we see from the free use of both expressions in the *Phaedo*.[2] It is assumed that

---

[1] *I.e.* it is not true either that any and every " likeness," nor yet that every and any " unlikeness," can be the foundation of friendship.

[2] Cf. *Phaedo*, 100d, where Socrates says that we may call the relation of form to sensible thing παρουσία or κοινωνία or " whatever you please " (εἴτε ὅπῃ

the technical language of the theory of forms is so familiar a thing that Socrates needs to warn the lads not to be misled by it ; an odd representation if the whole theory had been invented by Plato after Socrates' death.)

The theory, then, works out thus. So long as a thing is not yet itself evil, the " presence " of evil makes it desire the corresponding good ; when the thing itself has become evil, it has lost both desire and affection for good. This explains why neither those who are already wise, like the gods, nor those who are simply ignorant are " lovers of wisdom " ($\phi\iota\lambda\acute{o}\sigma o\phi o\iota$). " Philosophers," as we are also told by Diotima in the *Symposium*, are between the two extremes— on the way to wisdom, but only on the way. They are aware of their ignorance and anxious to get rid of it. The theory naturally appeals to the lads, since a boy's enthusiastic devotions are regularly attachments of this kind to some one older than himself whom he admires and wants to grow like (216c–218b).

Still, on reflection Socrates finds a fatal flaw in this attractive solution of his problem. If we revert to our illustration, we observe that the patient is attached to his physician " because of something " and " for the sake of something." He values the doctor *because* he is afraid of illness and *for the sake* of health, and of these disease is bad and " hateful " to him, health is dear or welcome ($\phi\acute{\iota}\lambda o\nu$) and good. Thus, if we generalize the principle, we must state it more exactly than we did at first. We must say, " That which is neither good nor bad is friendly to that which is good *because* of that which is bad and hateful, and *for the sake* of that which is good and welcome." Now, passing by all merely verbal points to which exception might be taken, this statement implies that whatever is dear, or welcome, or friendly ($\phi\acute{\iota}\lambda o\nu$) to us, is welcome as a *means* to something else, just as the physician's skill is welcome as a means to keeping or recovering health. But health itself is surely also welcome ($\phi\acute{\iota}\lambda o\nu$). Are we to say that it too is only welcome as a means to something ? Even if we say this, sooner or later we are bound to come upon something which is dear to us simply on its own account, and is that for the sake of which all other " dear " things are dear. A father whose son has swallowed hemlock will be eager to put his hand on a jar of wine. But he only cares for the jar because it holds the wine, and he only cares about the wine because it will counteract the poison. It is his son, not a sample of Attic pottery or of a particular vintage, about whom he is really concerned. So long as a thing or person is only " dear " to us for the sake of something else, it is only a *façon de parler* to call it " dear." What is really " dear " to us is " just that upon which all our so-called affections terminate " ($\grave{\epsilon}\kappa\epsilon\hat{\iota}\nu o$ $a\mathring{\upsilon}\tau\grave{o}$ $\epsilon\mathring{\iota}$ $\mathring{o}$ $\pi\hat{a}\sigma a\iota$ $a\mathring{\upsilon}\tau a\iota$ $a\mathring{\iota}$ $\lambda\epsilon\gamma\acute{o}\mu\epsilon\nu a\iota$ $\phi\iota\lambda\acute{\iota}a\iota$ $\tau\epsilon\lambda\epsilon\upsilon\tau\hat{\omega}\sigma\iota\nu$, 220b). (Thus the question about the secret sources

---

$\delta\grave{\eta}$ $\kappa a\grave{\iota}$ $\mathring{o}\pi\omega\varsigma$† $\pi\rho o\sigma\gamma\epsilon\nu o\mu\acute{\epsilon}\nu\eta$). Elsewhere in the dialogue the form is said to " occupy " ($\kappa a\tau\acute{\epsilon}\chi\epsilon\iota\nu$, a military metaphor) the thing, the thing to " receive " ($\delta\acute{\epsilon}\chi\epsilon\sigma\theta a\iota$, again a military metaphor) or to " partake in " ($\mu\epsilon\tau\acute{\epsilon}\chi\epsilon\iota\nu$) the form.

of affection has brought us face to face with the conception of the *summum bonum*, which is the source of all secondary and derivative goodness, 218*b*–220*b*.)

We have thus eliminated from our last statement the clause " for the sake of that which is good and welcome." Will the rest of the formula stand criticism ? Is it true that what we " care for " is "good" and that we care for it " because of " (to escape from) evil ? If the second of these statements is sound, it should follow that in a world where there were no evils, we should no longer care about anything good, any more than we should value medicine in a world where there was no disease. If this is so, then our attitude to the supreme object of all our affections is unique. We care about the secondary objects of affection " for the sake of something welcome to us " (φίλον), *i.e.* because they are means to this primary object ; but we must say of the primary object of all affection itself that we care for it " for the sake of the unwelcome " (ἐχθρόν), if we should really value it no longer in a world where there were no evils. Perhaps the question, as we put it, is a foolish one, for who can tell what might or might not happen in such a world ? But our experience of the world we live in teaches us as much as this. To feel hungry is sometimes good for us, sometimes harmful. Suppose we could eliminate all the circumstances in which being hungry is harmful, hunger would still exist, and so long as hunger existed we should " care for " the food which satisfies it. (Even in a socialist Utopia where every one was sure of sufficient food, and every one too healthy and virtuous to be greedy, men would still have " wholesome appetite " and care about their dinners.) This is enough to dispose of the theory that we only care about good as an escape from evil (220*b*–221*c*).

Thus our formula seems to have gone completely by the board, and the course of the argument has suggested a new one. It seems now that the cause of all attachment (φιλία) is desire (ἐπιθυμία), and that we must say " what a man *desires* is dear to *him* and *when* he is desiring it." (Thus we arrive at a purely relative definition of τὸ φίλον, probably intentionally modelled on the famous relativist doctrine of Protagoras that " what a man thinks true *is* true—for *him*, and so long as he thinks it so.") We may proceed to develop this thought a little farther. A creature which desires regularly desires that of which it is " deficient " (ἐνδεές). So we may say that " the deficient " (τὸ ἐνδεές) is " attached " (φίλον) to that of which it is " deficient." And deficiency means being " deprived " of something. (The " deficient " creature is " defective " ; it is without something it must have in order to be fully itself.) " Passion " (ἔρως), friendship, desire, then, are all felt for something which " belongs to one's self " (τὸ οἰκεῖον). Friends or lovers, thus, if they really are what they profess to be, are οἰκεῖοι to one another ; they " belong to " one another ; each is, as we might say, a " part of the other " in " soul, or temper or body " (κατὰ τὸ τῆς ψυχῆς ἦθος ἢ τρόπους ἢ εἶδος). A thing for which we feel affection is then something φύσει οἰκεῖον to ourselves, "our very own." It follows that since each party to the affection is thus "the very own " of the other party, affection must be reciprocal, and Socrates is careful to apply this lesson by adding that "a genuine lover " must be one who has his love reciprocated. (This is plainly intended as a comment on the current perversions of "romantic " passion. Reciprocated affection was the last thing the pervert could expect from his παιδικά, a point of which we shall hear more in the *Phaedrus*. The fashionable ἐραστής, it is meant, is not worthy of the name of a lover at all (221*d*–222*b*).)

Formally the dialogue has ended in a circle, or seems to have done so. If τὸ οἰκεῖον, "what belongs to one's self," is also τὸ ὅμοιον, "what is like " one's self, we have contradicted our earlier conclusion that friendship is not based on "likeness." If we try to escape from the contradiction by distinguishing between τὸ οἰκεῖον and τὸ ὅμοιον, it is attractive to say that all good things are οἰκεῖα to one another (in virtue of their common goodness), all bad things οἰκεῖα in virtue of their badness, and all "neutral" things again οἰκεῖα. But this would contradict our decision that friendship is impossible between the bad. Or if we identify τὸ οἰκεῖον, what is one's own, with τὸ ἀγαθόν, one's good, we should have to say that friendship is only possible between two men who are both good, and this again would contradict another of our results (222*b–e*).

In ending in this apparently hopeless result, the *Lysis* resembles a much more famous dialogue, the *Parmenides*. In neither case need we suppose that Plato's real intention is to leave us merely befogged. The way in which the thought that what is most near and intimate to each of us (τὸ οἰκεῖον) is the *good* is kept back to the very end of the conversation suggests that this—that man as such has such a "natural good," and that it is the one thing worth caring for in life—is the thought he means the discussion to leave in our minds. If we go back to the various proposed explanations of the secret of friendship with this thought in our minds, it may occur to us that they do not, after all, formally contradict one another. The common bond between the parties to associations which are all correctly called "friendships " may be different in different cases. Or rather, the bond between the "friends " may in every case be association in the pursuit of some "good," but goods are of very different levels of value, and "friendships " may exhibit the same variety of levels. Thus it may be that the full and perfect type of friendship can only be based on common pursuit of the true supreme good, and in that case friendship in the fullest sense will only be possible between "the good." Yet there may be associations between men founded on the common pursuit of some good inferior to the highest (*e.g.* the common pursuit of the "business advantage " of both parties, or the common pursuit of amusement or recreation). These would be "friendships " but of a lower type, and it may quite well be the case, *e.g.*, that a good man and a bad one. or even two bad men may be associated in this inferior sort of " friendship." Such, at least, are the lines on which Aristotle in the *Ethics* develops a theory of friendship in which all the conflicting points of view of our dialogue are taken up, and each is found to have its relative justification.

See further :

RITTER, C.—*Platon*, i. 284–297 (*Laches*), 343–359 (*Charmides*), 497–504 (*Lysis*).

RAEDER, H.—*Platons philosophische Entwickelung*, 95–99 (*Laches Charmides*), 153–158 (*Lysis*).

STOCK, ST. GEORGE.—*Friendship* (*Greek and Roman*) in *E.R.E.* vol. vi.

CHAPTER V

MINOR SOCRATIC DIALOGUES: *CRATYLUS,*
EUTHYDEMUS

BOTH the dialogues to be considered in this chapter have
something of the character of "occasional works." Both
are strongly marked by a broad farcical humour, which is
apparently rather Socratic than Platonic ; we meet it again, *e.g.,*
in the comic fury of the satire in some parts of the *Republic,* but it
is quite unlike the grave and gentle malice of such works as the
Parmenides and *Sophistes.* The mirth, especially in the *Euthydemus,*
has something of the rollicking extravagance of Aristophanes, and,
according to the *Symposium,* there really was a side to Socrates
which made him congenial company for the great comic poet.
(Both men could relish wild fun, and both could enjoy a laugh at
themselves.) In neither of our two dialogues is the professed main
purpose directly ethical, though the Socratic convictions about the
conduct of life incidentally receive an impressive exposition in
the *Euthydemus.* It seems impossible to say anything more precise
about the date of composition of either than that stylistic considerations show that both must be earlier than the great dramatic
dialogues, *Protagoras, Symposium, Phaedo, Republic.* Since the
Cratylus is a directly enacted drama with only three personages,
while the *Euthydemus* is a reported dialogue with numerous personages and a vigorously delineated " background," this second is
presumably the more mature work of the two.

Cratylus.—The personages of the dialogue other than Socrates
are two, Hermogenes and Cratylus. Hermogenes is well known
to us as a member of Socrates' *entourage.* Both he and Cratylus
figured in the *Telauges* of Aeschines,[1] where Socrates was apparently
made to criticize the squalor affected by the extreme Orphic and
Pythagorist *spirituali.* We learn from Plato (*Phaedo* 59b) that
Hermogenes was present at the death of Socrates. Xenophon
mentions him several times and professes to owe some of his information to him. He was a base-born brother of the famous,
or notorious, " millionaire " Callias, son of Hipponicus, the muni-
ficent patron of " sophists " (*Crat.* 391c), but himself poor, and
apparently on no very good terms with his brother. As Callias
was connected by marriage with Pericles, the appearance of him
and his brother among the associates of Socrates is one of the many

---

[1] See *E.R.E.*, art. SOCRATES, and H. Dittmar's *Aeschines von Sphettus,*
213–244. He and Callias are prominent figures in Xenophon's *Symposium.*

indications that the philosopher stood in early life in close relations with the Periclean circle.   Of Cratylus we apparently know only what Aristotle has told us in his *Metaphysics*,[1] that—as we could have inferred from our dialogue itself—he believed in the Heraclitean doctrine of universal " flux," and that he carried his conviction of the impermanence of everything to the length of refusing to name things, preferring to point at them with his fingers.   (The use of a significant name would suggest that the thing named really had some sort of relatively permanent character.)   But one may reasonably suspect the story of being no more than an invention of some wag which Aristotle has perhaps taken too seriously.[2]   According to Aristotle, Plato had been "familiar " with him, and derived from him his rooted conviction that sensible things, because of their complete impermanence, cannot be the objects of scientific knowledge.

It is not clear whether Aristotle means to place this connexion of Plato with Cratylus before or after the death of Socrates, but presumably he means that it was before that event, since he says that it belonged to Plato's youth.   The fact is likely enough, since Cratylus seems to have been one of Socrates' associates.   (We must not suppose Aristotle to mean that when Plato associated with him he had not yet met Socrates ; the close relations of Socrates with Critias, Charmides, Adimantus, Glaucon, show that Plato must have been acquainted with him from early childhood.)   We need not believe, and we can hardly believe, that the influence of Cratylus really counted for much in determining Plato's own thought ; he would not need any special master to inform him that sensible things are mutable.   Most probably Aristotle, who only knew Plato in Plato's old age, has exaggerated the importance of an acquaintance which had really no great significance.   In any case, the tone of the whole dialogue requires us to suppose that both Cratylus and Hermogenes are youngish men, decidedly younger than Socrates.[3]   The " dramatic date " of the conversation is hardly indicated with certainty.   If we may suppose, what seems to me most likely, that the " curfew regulations " in Aegina, alluded to at 433*a*, were connected with the Athenian military occupation of the island in 431, this would suggest a date not too long after the beginning of the Archidamian war, when Socrates would be in the early forties, and the other two perhaps twenty years younger.

[1] Aristotle, *Met.* 987*a* 32, 1010*a* 12.

[2] Since Cratylus appears in our dialogue as holding that many of the names by which we actually call things are not their " real names," the point of the jest may have been less recondite.   It may lie in his uncertainty what the " real name " of a given thing is.   A good deal of fun might obviously be got out of this, *e.g.*, in a comedy.

[3] This was certainly true of Hermogenes, since his elder brother Callias was still alive and active in public affairs at a date when Socrates, if he had still been living, would have been a centenarian.   The active career of Callias hardly begins until the end of the f h century.   The youth of Cratylus is expressly remarked on by Socrates at the end of the dialogue (440*d*, ἔτι γὰρ νέος εἶ).

This is further borne out by the reference (386d) to Euthydemus as a person whose views are of interest. We shall see below that the *Euthydemus* requires to be dated at latest not after 421 or 420.[1] The ostensible subject of discussion is the origin of language. Are names significant by "nature" (φύσει), in virtue of some intrinsic appropriateness of the verbal sign to the thing signified, or only significant "by convention" (νόμῳ), *i.e.* arbitrary imposition ? Cratylus takes the first view ; there is a natural " rightness " of names which is one and the same for every one, Greek or barbarian (383b). If you call a thing by any other name than its own intrinsically " right " name, you are not naming it at all, even though you are using for it the word which every one else uses. Hermogenes is on the side of " convention " or arbitrary imposition ; he holds that whatever we are accustomed to call anything is, for that reason, the name of the thing. The dispute is referred to Socrates, who is careful to explain that he cannot decide the question with expert knowledge, as he has never attended the expensive fifty-drachma lecture of Prodicus on the right use of language ; he can only contribute the suggestions of his native mother-wit (384b).[2]

The issue under consideration is thus only one aspect of the famous " sophistic " antithesis between " nature " and " social usage " which we know to have been the great controversial issue of the Periclean age. The fancy that if we can only discover the original names of things, our discovery will throw a flood of light on the realities named, seems to recur periodically in the history of human thought. There are traces of it in Heraclitus and Herodotus ; in the age of Pericles it was reinforced by the vogue of allegorical interpretations of Homer, which depended largely on fanciful etymologies. Much of the dialogue is taken up by a long series of such etymologies poured forth by Socrates under what he himself declares to be " possession " by some strange personality. It is

[1] Reference is made several times in the *Cratylus* to a certain Euthyphro who exhibited the phenomena of " possession " (ἐνθουσιασμός). This may be the same person who gives his name to the dialogue *Euthyphro*, and was attempting to prosecute his own father for murder in the spring of the year 399. There is no difficulty about the chronology if we suppose that at that date Euthyphro, whose manner is that of an elderly rather than a very young man, was a year or two over fifty, and his father seventy-five or more. But the identification, though accepted by eminent scholars, seems precarious. There is nothing about the religious fanatic Euthyphro to suggest that he was subject to " possession." It is true that Socrates playfully calls him a μάντις (*Euthyph.* 3e), but μαντική had many forms.

[2] It is not suggested that it was poverty which prevented Socrates from attending the lecture. It seems clear that Socrates was not really poor until his middle age. As Burnet has said, the way in which the comic poets dwelt on his poverty when they attacked him in 423, suggests that his losses were then fairly recent. In the *Protagoras*, which takes us back before the Archidamian war, he appears to have a house of his own with a courtyard, and at least one servant (310b, 311a), and speaks of himself in a way which implies that he could at need have helped to pay Protagoras on behalf of his young friend (311d, ἐγώ τε καὶ σὺ ἀργύριον ἐκείνῳ μισθὸν ἕτοιμοι ἐσόμεθα τελεῖν ὑπὲρ σοῦ). Hence the absence of any reference to poverty is perhaps an indication of " dramatic date."

plain that we are not to find the serious meaning of the dialogue here, especially as, after delighting Cratylus by a pretended demonstration that language supports the Heraclitean philosophy, since the names of all things good contain references to movement, and the names of all bad things to arrest of movement, he turns round and produces equally ingenious and far-fetched etymological grounds for supposing that the original " giver of names " must have held the Eleatic doctrine that motion is an illusion, since all the names of good things appear to denote rest or stoppage of motion. Obviously, we are to take all this as good-humoured satire on attempts to reach a metaphysic by way of " philology " ; as far as etymologies go, a little ingenuity will enable us to get diametrically opposite results out of the same data.

The real purpose of the dialogue, so far as it has any purpose beyond the preservation of a picture of Socrates in one of his more whimsical moods, is to consider not the *origin* of language, but its use and functions. If we consider the purposes which spoken language subserves, we shall see that if it is to be adequate for those purposes, it must conform to certain structural principles. Hence the formula of the partisans of " convention " that the " right name " of anything is just whatever we agree to call it, makes language a much more arbitrary thing than it really is. A " right name " will be a name which adequately fulfils all the uses for which a name is required, and thus one man's or one city's vocabulary may name things more rightly, because more adequately, than that of another. But so long as the purpose for which names are required is adequately discharged by any vocabulary, things will be rightly " named " in the vocabulary. The names for things will not have the same syllables and letters in Greek and in a " barbarian " language, but if the purposes for which speech is required are equally well achieved in both languages, both names will be equally " true " names for things. So the partisans of φύσις, who hold, like Cratylus, that there is one particular combination of sounds which is the one and only " right name " of a given thing, are also only partly right. They are right in thinking that the right assignment of names is not arbitrary, but depends on principles of some kind, and that a nomenclature which " every one agrees in using " may, for all that, be a bad one ; they are wrong in thinking that if a given succession of sounds is a " right name " for a certain thing, no other such combination can be its " right name." The *Cratylus* is thus not so much concerned with the " origin " of language, as with the principles of philosophical and scientific nomenclature, though it contains many incidental sound observations about those analogies between the different movements of articulation and natural processes which seem to underlie the " onomatopoeic " element in language, as well as about the various influences which lead to linguistic change.

Hermogenes, at the outset, adopts an extreme form of the view that language is wholly arbitrary. If I like to call a thing by a certain name that *is* its name for me, even in the case of my inverting the usage of every one else. Thus, if I call "horse" what every one else calls "man," "horse" really is my private name, the name in my private language (ἰδίᾳ, 385*a*) for that being, as truly as "man" is its name "in the language of the public" (δημοσίᾳ). Now this assertion raises a very large question. A name is a part, an ultimate part, of a λόγος or statement. Statements may be true or they may be false ; they are true if they speak of realities (ὄντα) as they really are, false if they speak of them otherwise. But if a whole "discourse" or "statement" may be either true or false, we must say the same about its parts. Every part of a true statement must be true, and thus, since there are true and false λόγοι, there must be true and false names (385*c*). This looks like a fallacy, but we shall see that it is not really one if we note carefully the use Socrates makes of the distinction. His point is the sound one, that language is a *social* activity; it is primarily an instrument of communication. A "name" given by me privately to something which everybody else calls differently does not discharge this function ; it misleads, is a bad instrument for its purpose. This is what Socrates means by calling it a "false" name. It is a spurious substitute for the genuine article which would do the work required.

This disposes of the suggestion of a purely "private" language peculiar to the individual, but still it may be reasonably maintained that at any rate though the names "barbarians" give to things are not the same as those used by Greeks, they are just as much the "true names" of things as the Greek words (385*e*). *I.e.* we may urge that the plurality of languages shows that language is an arbitrary thing, though it depends on the *arbitrium* of a group, not of a single man. But if names are arbitrary, is the reality (οὐσία) of the things named equally arbitrary? If a thing's name is just whatever some one likes to call it, is the thing itself just whatever some one thinks it to be? Protagoras actually held that everything really is for any one just what he thinks it to be, so long as he thinks it to be so, and Hermogenes reluctantly admits that he sometimes feels driven to accept the view, strange as it is. However, we may perhaps dismiss it with the remark that it leaves no room for distinguishing wiser and less wise men, since it says that every one's beliefs are true—for him and no one else, and just as long as he holds them. But it seems the most patent of facts that some men are good, and therefore wise, and some wicked and therefore unwise. Yet we can hardly go to the opposite extreme with Euthydemus, who says that all statements whatever are true, always and "for every one." This would equally lead to the view that there is no distinction between the virtuous and the vicious, and consequently none between wisdom and the lack of it [1] (386*d*)

---

[1] Since, if Euthydemus is right, you can always truly predicate both virtue and vice of any subject whatever. Formally, Protagoras says that a proposition is true only when it is being believed by some one ; Euthydemus, that what we

Now if neither of these doctrines can be true, " objects " (τὰ πράγματα) clearly have some determinate real character of their own (οὐσίαν τίνα βέβαιον) which is independent of our " fancy " ; and if this is so " activities " (πράξεις) will also have a " nature " or " reality " (φύσιν) of their own, since " activities " are one form of " object " (ἔν τι εἶδος τῶν ὄντων, 386e). Hence, if we want to perform an act, we cannot do it in any way and with any instrument we please. We must do it in the way prescribed by the nature of the object we are acting on, and with the " naturally proper " instrument (ᾧ πέφυκε). For example, in cleaving wood, if we are to succeed, we must split the wood " with the grain " and we must use a naturally suitable implement. Speaking of things and naming them is an activity (πρᾶξις), and what we have just said applies therefore to naming. If we want to name things we must name them not just as the fancy takes us, but " as the nature of the objects permits and with the instrument it permits." The instrument or tool for naming things is, of course, the name itself. We may define a name as " an instrument by which we inform one another about realities and discriminate between them " (388b–c, ὄνομα ἄρα διδασκαλικόν τί ἐστιν ὄργανον καὶ διακριτικὸν τῆς οὐσίας). In all the crafts (weaving, for example) one craftsman (e.g. the weaver) has to make a proper use of some implement which has been properly made by some other craftsman (e.g. the carpenter, who makes the wooden implements which the weaver uses). Now from our definition of a name we see at once who is the expert craftsman who " uses " names as his tools ; he is the " teacher " or " instructor " (ὁ διδασκαλικός). But who is the other expert who makes the tools which the teacher uses ? According to the very theory from which we started, they are made by νόμος, " social usage." Hence we may say that they are the manufacture of the " legislator," the institutor of social usage. And legislation is not work that anyone can do, " unskilled labour " ; it is " skilled labour," work for an expert, or professor of a τέχνη. Clearly then, it is not correct to say that anyone whatever can arbitrarily give names to things (386d–389a). (Thus the result so far is that, since the function of language is the accurate communication of knowledge about things, the vocabulary of " social usage " will only be satisfactory when it supplies a nomenclature which corresponds to the real agreements and differences between the things named.)

Well, what would the expert in establishing usages have before his mind's eye in assigning names ? We may see the answer by considering the way in which the carpenter works when he makes a κερκίς for the weaver. He " keeps his eyes on " the work the κερκίς is meant to do in weaving—its function. If one of his articles breaks while he is making it, of course he makes a fresh one, and in making it he does not " fix his eye " on the spoilt and broken κερκίς but on the form (εἶδος) with an eye to which he had been

all disbelieve is as true as what we all believe.   Both positions make science impossible.

making the one which broke (389b). It is this " model " κερκίς, kept by the carpenter before his mind's eye in making all the different wooden κερκίδες, which best deserves the name of αὐτὸ ὃ ἔστιν κερκίς, " just the κερκίς, " the κερκίς and nothing else " (ib.). There are three points to be got hold of here. (1) The carpenter cannot give the tools he makes for the weaver just any shape he pleases ; the shape or form of the κερκίς is determined, independently of anyone's fancy, by the work it is meant to do. (2) Strictly speaking, when the carpenter is said in common parlance to *make* a κερκίς, what he does is to put the form, which is the " natural " or " real " κερκίς, into the wood on which he is working.[1] (3) And though the shape of a κερκίς is something fixed, it will be reproduced by the carpenter in different material, according as the implement is wanted for weaving different sorts of cloth (*e.g.*, you would need the wood to be harder for work on some kinds of material than on others). We may transfer these results to the case of the " legislator " who makes names. The letters and syllables, like. the wood of the carpenter, are the material into which he has to put " the real name " (ἐκεῖνο ὃ ἔστιν ὄνομα). Differences in the material will not matter, in this case any more than in the other, so long as the resulting instrument answers its purpose. This is why, though the sounds of a Greek word and those of the " barbarian " equivalent may be very different, each is a true name if it discharges the function of a name adequately (389b–390a). (It should be noted that all through this passage the technical language of the doctrine of forms is used without explanation. Plato assumes that Hermogenes and Cratylus may be counted on to know all about it. To my own mind, it is just the frequency with which this assumption is made, apparently without any consciousness that it calls for any justification, which is the strongest reason for refusing to believe that the whole doctrine was " developed " by Plato or anyone else after the death of Socrates.)

Who, then, decides whether a given piece of wood has really received the " form of κερκίς," as it should have done ? Not the expert who makes the implement (the carpenter), but the expert who will have to use it (the weaver). And this is a general rule. The man who makes an implement must " take his specifications " from the man who is to use it. Thus we arrive at a distinction

---

[1] According to the well-known statements of Aristotle (*Met.* 991b 6, 1080a 3, 1070a 18, *al.*), the Academy of his own day held that there are no " forms " of artificial things. No doubt the statement is true, but it has no bearing on the form of κερκίς in the *Cratylus* or that of κλίνη in *Republic* x. Aristotle is speaking of the theory as he knew it, *i.e.* after 367, and it is notorious that this version of the doctrine has to be learned from his writings, not from Plato's. The only character in the dialogues of Plato's later life who ever says anything about the doctrine is Timaeus, and he speaks pretty much as Socrates is made to do in the earlier dialogues. In the *Cratylus* there is no suggestion that the εἶδος is a sort of supra-sensible " thing." It is just a " type " to which the manufacturer's articles must conform, and its independence means simply that the structure of the κερκίς is determined by its function, independently of anyone's caprice.

afterwards explicitly formulated in the *Politicus* and reproduced as fundamental in the opening paragraphs of the *Nicomachean Ethics*, the distinction between superior and subordinate " arts," the rule being that it is the " art " which uses a product that is superior, the " art " which makes it that is subordinate.   This will apply to the case of the " legislator " who makes names.   There must be a superior expert, whose business it is to judge of the goodness of the names, namely, the expert who is to use them, and he can be no other than the expert in asking and answering questions, that is the " dialectician " or metaphysician.   The " legislator " who is to bestow names rightly must therefore work under the superintendence and to the specifications of the " dialectician," the supreme man of science.   (In other words, the test of the adequacy of language is not mere " custom," but its capacity to express the highest truth fully and accurately.)

Cratylus, then, is right in thinking that language depends on " nature," and that names can only rightly be given by a man who " fixes his eye on the real ($\phi\acute{\nu}\sigma\epsilon\iota$) name and can put its form into letters and syllables " (389*a*–390*e*).[1]   At any rate, this is how the matter looks to Socrates, though, as he had said, he cannot go on to convince Hermogenes by explaining which names are the " right " ones.   For that one must go to the professional sophists, such as Protagoras, or, since Hermogenes has no money to pay them, he might ask his brother Callias to teach him what he has learned from Protagoras on this very subject (391*a*–*c*).   Perhaps we can hardly do this, since Hermogenes has already decided against the main principle of Protagoras' book on *Truth*.   But something can be done, to make a beginning, with Homer.   He sometimes gives two names for a thing, that used by " gods " and that used by " men," and in such cases we sometimes find that the name used by the " gods " is significant (*e.g.*, we call a certain river Scamander, but the gods call it " the Yellow River," $\Xi\acute{a}\nu\theta\sigma\varsigma$).   Or again he tells us that Hector's son was called Scamandrius by the women, but Astyanax by his father and the men.   Now, on the average, the men of a society are more intelligent than their women-folk,[2] and their name for the boy is presumably his " right " name.   And,

---

[1] It is, of course, with intentional humour that Socrates forgets that Cratylus had meant something quite different when he said that names are " by nature."   Note the repeated insistence on the point that Greek has no necessary superiority over a " barbarian " language (like, *e.g.*, Persian).   The notion that " barbarians " are intrinsically inferior to Hellenes, so prominent in Isocrates and Aristotle, is foreign to the Platonic dialogues, though it is recognized as a fact that Hellenes show more aptitude than Egyptians and other peoples for science.   The all-round inferiority of the non-Hellene is not a Socratic or Platonic doctrine.   That the point should be insisted on in a discussion about language is all the more interesting since $\beta\acute{a}\rho\beta\alpha\rho\sigma\varsigma$ seems originally to have meant one who " jabbers "—like a swallow, as Clytaemnestra says in Aeschylus.

[2] This is given as a mere statement of fact, and in a place like the Athens of the fifth century it was true.   It is not implied that it ought to be so, or need be so.   Indeed, as we shall see, Socrates held that it need not be so.

in fact, we see that it has a significance which makes it appropriate. The name means " Burgh-ward," and is therefore very suitable to the son of Hector who " warded " Troy so effectually (391a–392e).

Once started on this trail, Socrates proceeds to propound a host of derivations of names—proper names of heroes and gods, and common nouns—with the general purpose of showing that in their original form, often widely different from that to which we are accustomed, they have a " connotation " which makes them specially appropriate. There is no need to follow this part of the conversation in any detail, all the more since Socrates professes to be surprised by his own readiness and suggests that he must have been infected by an abnormal " possession " from having just left the company of the " inspired " Euthyphro (396d). We could hardly be told more plainly that the extravagances which are to follow are meant as a caricature of the guesses of " etymologists " working in the dark without any scientific foundation.[1] But, like a wise man, Socrates mixes some sense with his nonsense. Thus it is a sound principle, whatever we may think of some of the applications made of it, that proper names of men and gods are likely to have been originally significant, though their meaning has been lost through linguistic changes. It is sound sense again to say (398d) that we may often be put on the true track by considering archaic forms which are obsolete in current speech, or peculiar dialectical variants (401c). So again Socrates is quite right in calling attention to the presence of " barbarian " words in the current vocabulary (409e), though the use he makes of the fact as a convenient way out of a difficulty whenever he is at a loss is manifestly jocular (421c–d). The jocularity is even more patent when he pretends (402a) to make the sudden discovery, which he then rides to death, that the ancient names of the gods and a host of other words show that the creators of the Greek language were Heracliteans, or (409b) that the name Selene conveys the discovery, connected at Athens with the name of Anaxagoras, that the moon shines by reflected light. It is no surprise to us when, after a long interval of more serious discussion, we find him (437a ff.) expressing his doubts whether after all etymology might not be made to bear equal witness to Parmenides and his doctrine of the absolute motionlessness of the real.

We come back to seriousness at 422a with the reflection that, after all, the process of derivation cannot go on for ever. We must, in the end, arrive at a stock of primitive names, the ABC (στοιχεῖα) of all the rest. How are we to account for the appropriation of each of these to its *signification*? We may do so if we reflect that language is a form of gesture. If we were all deaf and dumb we

---

[1] Probably, if only we had adequate literary records of the Periclean age we might find that a good many of the etymologies are specimens of the serious speculations of the persons satirized. Few of them are much more extravagant than, *e.g.*, the derivation of κῆρυξ from κήρ hinted at in Euripides, *Troad.* 425.

should try to communicate information by imitating with our own
bodies the shapes and movements of the things to which we wanted
to call attention. Now we can imitate in the same way by vocal
gestures. If a man could reproduce the " reality " of different
things by the vocal gestures we call " letters " and " syllables," he
would be naming the various things (423a–424b). The primitive
names may be supposed to have been produced by this method of
imitation. We may test this suggestion and judge of the " rightness " of these primitive words by making a careful classification
of the elementary components of our speech—the vowels, consonants,
and so forth—and considering the movements by which they are
produced. We shall ask whether there are not analogies between
these various processes and processes in nature at large, and whether
primitive names do not seem to be composed of sounds produced
by movements analogous with those of the things they signify,
allowance being made for a considerable amount of variation for
the sake of euphony and greater ease of articulation. We might,
to be sure, save ourselves trouble by simply saying that the primitive words were invented by gods or " barbarians " of long ago,
but this would be shirking the chief problem which the scientific
expert in the theory of language has to face (425d–426b). Socrates
therefore ventures, with misgivings, to state some of his observations on the subject. The pages in which he does so (426b–427d)
have often been commended for their penetration, but the subject
has more interest for the student of phonetics than for the philosopher, and we need not delay over the details. What is of real
interest to others than specialists in phonetics is the discernment
shown by the insistence on the general principle that speech is to be
regarded as a species of mimetic gesture, and the clear way in
which such vocal gesture is distinguished from direct reproduction
of natural noises and the cries of animals (423c–d).

Hitherto the conversation has been a dialogue between Socrates
and Hermogenes ; Cratylus now replaces the latter as interlocutor.
He is delighted with all that Socrates has said—no doubt because
Socrates has professed to find Heracliteanism embodied in the very
structure of language—and thinks it could hardly be bettered. But
Socrates himself has misgivings, and would like to consult his second
thoughts. (What the by-play here really hints is that we are
now to come to a discussion to which Plato attaches greater importance than he does to the entertaining etymological speculations
on which so much time has been spent.)

We said that name-giving is a trade, and that the workman
(δημιουργός) who makes names is the " legislator." Now in general
there are better and worse workmen in any trade ; we should expect,
then, that there are degrees of goodness and badness in the names
made by different legislators (i.e. linguistic tradition, of which the
νομοθέτης is a personification, approximates more or less nearly,
in the case of different idioms, to the ideal of a " philosophical "
language). Cratylus denies this, on the ground that a word either

is the right name of a certain thing, or is not that thing's name at all, but the name of something else. There cannot be any intermediate degree of " rightness " in this case. If you call a thing by the name of something else, you are not speaking of the thing in question at all ; (*e.g.* to say " Hermogenes " when you meant Cratylus, is trying to say " what is not," and that is impossible). You cannot say *nothing*. Whenever you speak you must be saying *something*. Not only must you mean (λέγειν) something, but you must enunciate (φάναι) something. Hence when a man uses any but the " right name " Cratylus holds that he merely makes a senseless noise, like a " sounding brass " (ψοφεῖν ἔγωγ' ἂν φαίην τὸν τοιοῦτον, μάτην αὐτὸν ἑαυτὸν κινοῦντα, ὥσπερ ἄν εἴ τις χαλκίον κινήσειε κρούσας, 430*a*). In other words, you cannot make a statement which is significant and yet false. Every statement is either true or meaningless. The difficulty here suggested only seems fanciful to us, because the explanation of it given for the first time in Plato's own *Sophistes* has become part of our current thought. To say " what is not " does not mean to say what is simply meaningless, but only to say what means something *different* from the real facts of the case. Until this had been explained, there was a double difficulty for the Greek mind in understanding how it is possible to speak falsely. Partly the difficulty is due to the accident of language that the word εἶναι is ambiguous : it means " to be " or " to exist " ; in Greek, especially in the Ionic Greek, which was the original tongue of science, it also means " to be true," as when Herodotus calls his own version of the early life of Cyrus τὸ ἐόν, " the true narrative," or Euripides in Aristophanes speaks of the story of Phaedra as an ὤν λόγος, " an over-true tale." Behind the merely verbal ambiguity there is further a metaphysical one, the confusion between " what is not " in the absolute sense of " blank nothing," and " what is not " in the merely relative sense of " what is other than " some given reality. So long as you confuse " what is not " in this relative sense with what is just nothing at all, you must hold it impossible to say significantly " what is not " (*i.e.* to make a false statement which has any meaning). This explains why, in the age of Pericles and Socrates, it should have been a fashionable trick of ἀντιλογικοί or ἐριστικοί, pretenders who made a show of intellectual brilliance by undertaking to confute and silence every one else, to argue that no statement, however absurd, if it means anything, can be false. The most violent paradoxes must be true, because they *mean* something, and therefore he who utters them is saying " what is." Plato regularly connects this theory of the impossibility of speaking falsely with the philosophy of Parmenides, and its unqualified antithesis between " what is " and mere non-entity. He means that the doctrine arises as soon as you convert what Parmenides had meant for a piece of physics into a principle of logic. Cratylus, to be sure, is a follower not of Parmenides, who regarded change of every kind as an illusion, but of Heraclitus, who thought change the fundamental reality. But he is led by a different route to the same result. Whether you start with the premise that "what is not," being just nothing at all, cannot be spoken of, or with the premise that to call a thing " out of its name " must be to speak of something else and not of the thing in question, in either case the conclusion has to be drawn that you cannot significantly say what is false, since that would be to speak of a given thing and yet not to speak of it " as it is." [1]

Though this issue of the possibility of significant false statement has been raised, we need not go to the bottom of it for our present purposes. (In fact, Plato's own logical studies had presumably not yet led him to the complete solution.) It is enough to remember that we have already agreed that a name is a " representation " ($\mu i\mu\eta\mu a$) of that which it names. It is like a portrait, except that the portrait is a visible, the name an audible, representation. Now we might take the portrait of a woman for a portrait of a man ; we should then be connecting the portrait with the wrong original, but still it would be a portrait of *some* original. We do the same thing when we misapply a name ; it does not cease to be a name because we apply it to the wrong thing. Again, a portrait is not an exact replica. One artist seizes points which another misses, and thus there may be a better and a worse portrait, and yet both are portraits of the same original. Why may not the same thing be true of the primitive names in language ? Why may not a name be an imperfect but real " representation " of that for which it stands ? (This would explain why the primitive names in different languages may all be genuine " vocal gestures," denoting the same thing, in spite of the differences between them.) Cratylus suggests that the analogy with portraiture does not hold. A bad portrait may leave out some characteristic of its original, or put in something not present in the original, and yet be a recognizable portrait of the man. But in the case of a name, if, for example, we put in or leave out a single letter, we have not written *that* name at all.

---

[1] It has been the fashion, especially in Germany, for a generation and more, to connect the paradox about false-speaking specially with the name of Antisthenes, and to regard all the references to it in Plato as direct attacks on that rather insignificant person. This seems to me quite unhistorical. The standing assumption of Plato is that the ἀντιλογικοί are quite a numerous and fashionable body. Socrates even refers to them in the *Phaedo* (90*b*), where Antisthenes is supposed to be present (59*b*) and all possibility of an attack on his own old friend is out of the question. The one dialogue of Plato's early life in which they are singled out for special satire is the *Euthydemus*, and we see from the *Cratylus* itself that Euthydemus really was a well-known personage who held views of this kind. Isocrates too (x. 1) implies that the " eristics " who maintain the paradox are a fairly numerous body of the generation before his own. For this reason it seems to me out of the question to find attacks on Antisthenes in any of the Platonic dialogues in which Socrates is the principal figure. Whether in the later dialogues, when Socrates has fallen into the background, Plato ever criticizes Antisthenes on his own account, is another question with which we shall not be concerned until we come to deal with the *Parmenides* and *Sophistes*, though I believe we shall find reason to think that there also he has very different antagonists in view.

We may reply that it is not with quality as it is with number. Any addition or subtraction will make, *e.g.*, the number 10 another number (such as 9 or 11), but a " representation " may be like the original without reproducing it in its details. Thus the portrait-painter reproduces the outward features and complexion of his sitter, but leaves out everything else. The sitter has entrails, movement, life, thought ; the picture has none, and yet it is a picture of him. In fact, if it did reproduce the whole reality of the sitter, it would not be a portrait at all but a reduplication of the man himself. Full and complete reproduction is thus not the kind of " rightness " we require in a portrait, and we have already recognized that a name is a kind of portrait of which vocal gesture is the medium (430*a*–433*b*).

If we are agreed so far, we may now say that a well-made name must contain the " letters " which are " appropriate " to its signification ; *i.e.* those which are " like " what is signified (*i.e.* the vocal gestures which compose the name must have a natural resemblance to some feature in that which it names ; a name which contains inappropriate sounds may be still a recognizable name if some of its components are appropriate, but it will not be a well-made one). The only way of escaping our conclusions would be to fall back on the view that names are purely conventional and arbitrary. This is impossible, since in any case there must be some sort of natural appropriateness about the elementary components of vocal gesture to lead the imposers of names in the making of their first conventions, just as there must be in nature colouring materials appropriate for the reproduction of the tints of a face if there is to be such an art as portraiture. But we can see that " convention " and the arbitrary play their part in language too. Thus there is a " roughness " about the sound of the letter *r* which makes it appropriate in the name of anything hard and rough, while there is a smoothness of articulation about *l* which makes it inappropriate for the same purpose. Yet this letter actually occurs in the very word σκληρός itself, and even Cratylus must admit that " thanks to custom " he knows what the word means. It discharges its function as a name none the worse for containing an inappropriate sound (433*b*–435*b*). In particular we should find it quite impossible to show that the names of the numerals are made up of gestures naturally appropriate to signify those particular numbers. The principle of natural significance, however sound, is a most uncertain guide in etymological studies (435*b*–*c*).

We revert to a position we had laid down at the outset. The " faculty " (δύναμις) or function of a name is to convey instruction (διδάσκειν). Does this imply that a man who has knowledge of names will also have a corresponding knowledge of the realities (πράγματα) for which the names stand ? Cratylus is inclined to think so, and even to hold that the knowledge of names is the *only* way to the knowledge of things. Not only is the understanding (τὸ μανθάνειν) of words the one way to the understanding of things; *inquiry* into language is the only road of inquiry and discovery. The one way to *discover* the truth about things is to discover the meanings of names (436a). But obviously this would put all science in a very unfavourable position. The study of names will only at best show what the givers of the names *supposed* to be the truth about things, and how if these name-givers were wrong in their suppositions? Cratylus holds that we need not feel any anxiety on the point. The best proof that the " giver of names " was one who knew all about things is the consistent way in which all names support one and the same theory about things. Has not Socrates himself shown that they all point to the Heraclitean doctrine of the flux (436c)? Unfortunately this is not conclusive; if you start with false initial postulates you may be led to gravely erroneous conclusions, and yet these conclusions may be quite compatible with one another, as we see in the case of certain geometrical false demonstrations.[1] The supreme difficulty in any science is to be sure that your initial postulates themselves are true (436c–d). And, on second thoughts, we may doubt whether the testimony of language is quite so self-consistent as we had fancied. There are many words which seem to indicate that the " giver of names " was an Eleatic rather than an Heraclitean (437a–c), and it would be absurd to decide on the truth of such incompatible views by appeal to a " numerical majority " of derivations.

In any case, the view Cratylus is maintaining is self-contradictory. He holds that the inventors of the first names must have known the truth about things in order to give each its " true " name, and also that the truth about things can only be discovered by the study of names. How then did the *original* makers of names discover it? Perhaps, says Cratylus, the first names were of a superhuman origin; language began as a divine revelation, and its divine origin guarantees the " rightness " of the primitive names. If that is so, then both our sets of derivations cannot be sound, or, as Cratylus says, one set of words cannot be real " names " at all (438c). But the question is, which set—those which suggest the " flux " or those which suggest that movement is an illusion—are real names? We cannot decide the issue by appeal to other words, for there are no other words than those employed in language. The appeal will have to be to the realities words signify, and we shall have to learn what these realities are, not from words, but "from one another and from themselves " (438e). Besides, even if we admit that the truth about things can be learned by studying their names, since well-made names, as we have said, are " likenesses "

---

[1] 436d. διαγράμματα here seems, as in some other passages in Plato and Aristotle, to mean " proofs " rather than " figures." One might illustrate the point by reference to the entertaining section of De Morgan's *Budget of Paradoxes* which deals with James Smith the circle-squarer. Mr. Smith's method of proving his thesis (that π = 3⅛) was to assume it as a postulate, and then show that it led to consequences compatible with itself and with one another. He forgot to ask whether it did not lead also to consequences incompatible with independently known truth.

of the things they name, it must be a nobler and more assured method to study the reality (ἀλήθεια) directly in itself, and judge of the merits of the " likeness " from our knowledge of the original than to try to discover from a mere study of the " likeness " whether it is a good one, and what it represents (439a). How a knowledge of realities is to be acquired it may take greater thinkers than ourselves to say, but it is satisfactory to have learned that at least we cannot acquire it by the study of names (439b).

Socrates keeps the point on which he wishes to insist most until the end. Whatever the opinion of the framers of language may have been, the Heraclitean doctrine of universal impermanence cannot be true. There are such things as " Beauty " and " Goodness " (αὐτὸ καλὸν καὶ αγαθόν) and other realities of that kind. Even Cratylus admits this at once. He does not extend his doctrine of impermanence to the realm of "values." Now *they* cannot be everlastingly mutable ; they are what they are once for all and always. You could not call anything " *the* so-and-so " (αὐτό, 439d), if it had no determinate character but were merely mutable. And the merely mutable could not be known. What is known is known as having this or that determinate character, but if the doctrine of " flux " is true, nothing ever has such determinate character. Not to mention that knowing as a subjective activity also has a determinate character, so that in a world where everything is incessantly becoming something else, there could be neither objects to be known nor the activity of knowing. But if knower (τὸ γιγνῶσκον), object known (τὸ γιγνωσκόμενον), Beauty, Good, are real, the Heraclitean doctrine cannot be true. We will not now ask which of these alternatives is the right one, but we may say that it does not *look* a sensible procedure for a man to have such confidence in names and their givers that he hands over his soul to "names" for "tendance," and asserts dogmatically that all men and all things are sick of a universal "defluxion" and as leaky as a cracked pitcher (440a–d). This is the issue which young men like Cratylus and Hermogenes should face seriously and courageously and not decide in a hurry (440d). Thus the dialogue leaves with us as the great problem, or rather the two aspects of the same great problem of all philosophy, the metaphysical problem of the reality of the forms and the moral problem of the right " tendance of the soul." [1]

Euthydemus.—The dialogue, as we have said, has more of the spirit of broad farce than any other work of Plato ; it would be possible to see in it nothing more than an entertaining satire on " eristics " who think it a fine thing to reduce every one who opens his mouth in their company to silence by taking advantage of the

[1] I can see no reason to fancy that the dialogue is intended as a polemic against the nominalism of Antisthenes in particular. A.'s preoccupation with names, like the choice of the themes for his extant declamations. only shows that he was influenced by the general tendencies of the " sophistic " age. I am wholly sceptical about theories which represent the Platonic Socrates as engaged in attacks on one of his own companions.

ambiguities of language. Even if this were Plato's main object, it would still be a reasonable one. An attempt to detect and expose the principal fallacies *in dictione* would be a useful contribution to the as yet only nascent study of logic. It is thus not surprising that Aristotle should have made frequent use of the dialogue in his own systematic essay on Fallacies, the *de Sophisticis Elenchis*. But the real purpose of the dialogue is more serious and proves to be a moral one, arising out of the claim of the sophists of the Periclean age to be able to " teach goodness." A man who undertakes this task must be prepared to win the adherence of a pupil by satisfying him first that " goodness," the secret of a satisfactory life, can be taught ; and next, that the speaker is one of the experts who can teach it. No one will go to school to you unless you can persuade him that you have something important to teach, and that you are competent to teach it. This accounts for the rise of a distinct branch of literature, the " protreptic " discourse, which aims at winning the hearer's assent to the idea that he must live the " philosophic " life, and encouraging his confidence that a particular teacher will show him how to do it. To this type of literature belonged, among other works, Aristotle's famous *Protrepticus* and Cicero's almost equally famous Latin imitation of it, the *Hortensius*, both now unhappily lost. The true object of the *Euthydemus* is to exhibit the directness, simplicity, and power of Socratic " protreptic," addressed to a young and impressionable mind ; the fooleries of the two sophists afford an entertaining background, without which the picture would not produce its full effect. We might suppose Plato to have felt that to a careless observer the close cross-questioning characteristic of Socrates must seem very much the same sort of thing as the futile sporting with words on which the ordinary " eristic " plumes himself. By pitting the one thing directly against the other he drives home his point that, for all their apparent minute hair-splitting, the questions of Socrates are no idle displays of ingenuity, but have the most momentous and most truly practical of all objects ; their purpose is to win a soul from evil for good.

In form the *Euthydemus* is a narrated drama. Socrates describes to his old friend Crito, with a great deal of humour, a mirthful scene in his favourite haunt, the *palaestra* near the Lyceum, at which he had been present the day before. The supposed date can only be fixed by consideration of a number of bits of internal evidence. It is, as we see from *Euthydemus*, 271c, " many years " after the foundation of Thurii (444 B.C.), and must be before the year of the great scandal about the " profanation of the mysteries," just before the sailing of the Athenian Armada for Sicily (416–5), since Axiochus of Scambonidae, father of the lad Clinias who figures as respondent, was one of the principal persons ruined by the affair.[1] A date not later than about 420, and possibly a little earlier, seems to fit all the

[1] For the ruin of Axiochus, the uncle of Alcibiades the person whose destruction was the main object of the raisers of the scandal, see Andocides, i. 16.

MINOR SOCRATIC DIALOGUES 91

indications. The centre of attraction in the dialogue is the beautiful and modest Clinias ; it is on his person that Euthydemus, whom we have already met in the *Cratylus*, and his brother Dionysodorus, natives of Chios who had been among the original settlers of Thurii, but found themselves banished in the years of faction which followed on the foundation of the city and have since then haunted Athens and her dependencies, make the experiment of displaying a new educational discovery, a method of instantaneously " teaching goodness." Hitherto they had taught, like other professionals, the art of fence on the field and in the law-courts ; their crowning achievement is a recent invention which they are anxious to parade and Socrates to witness. It proves, in fact, to be simply " eristic," the trick of stopping a man's mouth by catching at the natural ambiguities of language. Perhaps it is an indication of date that Socrates is made to lay the stress he does on the contrast between this latest marvel and the now familiar art of effective forensic pleading which had been the thing taught by Protagoras and the earliest " sophists." The two men, however, are described as elderly, so that they will be at least as old as Socrates himself, and we must remember that though Socrates was the first Athenian to interest himself in logic, it had been founded by Zeno, who cannot at most have been more than ten years younger than Protagoras. Hence too much must not be made of this point.[1] The serious business of the dialogue is opened by Socrates in a short speech, laying down the main lines it is to follow. Clinias is a lad of great promise and illustrious connexions ; it is of the first moment that he should grow up to be a thoroughly good man. The sophists are therefore invited to prove the value of their latest discovery by convincing him " that one must give one's attention to goodness and philosophy " (275*a*). They fall to work at once by asking a series of questions so con-structed that they can only be answered by " Yes " or " No." and that the respondent can be equally silenced whichever answer he gives. The first question—from its recurrence elsewhere we may infer that it was a " stock " puzzle—turns on the double sense of the word μανθάνειν, which means primarily to " learn " ; but derivatively, in colloquial language, to " understand," " take the

[1] The pair of " eristics," Euthydemus and his brother Dionysodorus, are natives of Chios who had been among the first settlers at Thurii (this is implied by the tense of ἀπῴκησαν at 271*c*), but had been exiled thence and have spent " many years " περὶ τούσδε τοὺς τόπους, *i.e.* Athens and the islands of the Aegean (271*c*). The date of the foundation of Thurii is 444. Socrates is ἤδη πρεσβύτερος (272*b*), " not exactly a young man," but no more ; this suggests an age not far off fifty, but probably something short of it. Perhaps the allusion of 272*c* to the figure he cuts among the boys in the music-class of Connus is best taken as a humorous reference to some shaft aimed at him in the *Connus* of Amipsias (exhibited in 423), and in that case, we must suppose that play to be still a recent work. Alcibiades is spoken of at 275*a* in a way which implies that he is already in the prime of manhood. 286*c* refers to Protagoras in a way which seems to mean that he is already dead. But since Plato insists that Protagoras was a generation older than Socrates (*Protag.* 317*c*) and also says that he died at about seventy (*Meno*, 91*e*), this does not take us with certainty much below the year 430.

meaning of " a statement. The eristic method of the two brothers may be reproduced in English by taking advantage of the double sense which " learning " happens to bear in our own language. Who are learners, the wise or the ignorant, *i.e.* those who already know something or those who do not ? There is here a triple *équivoque*, since the " wise " (σοφοί) may mean " clever, intelligent " pupils, as well as persons who already know the thing to be taught, and the " ignorant " (ἀμαθεῖς) may mean " the dull, stupid," as well as those who are ignorant of a given subject. The lad takes the question to mean, " Which class of boys learn what they are taught, the clever boys or the dull ones ? " and answers, " The clever." But, it is retorted, when you lads were learners in reading or music, you did not yet know these subjects and therefore were not " wise " (σοφοί) about them, and so must have been " ignorant " (ἀμαθεῖς). And yet again, in your schooldays, it was not the " dull " (ἀμαθεῖς) among you, but the quick or clever (σοφοί) who " took in " (ἐμάνθανον) what the schoolmaster dictated. *Ergo*, it is the σοφοί, not the ἀμαθεῖς who " learn." (As we might say, the dull don't get learning from their schoolmasters, but the quick (275*d*–276*c*)).

A new puzzle is now started. When a man learns something, does he learn what he knows or what he does not know ? (This again is a standing catch, intended to prove the paradox that it is impossible to learn anything, to get new knowledge.) The natural answer is that a man learns what he does not already know, since learning means getting fresh knowledge. But when a schoolmaster dictates something to you, you " learn " the sense of the passage (you take in its meaning). What he dictated is a series of " letters," but you must have " known " your letters before you could do dictation. Thus when you " learn," you must already " know " the thing you are learning. Yet, *per contra*, to learn means to get knowledge, and no one can get what he already has. *Ergo*, after all, it is what you do not know that you learn (276*e*–277*c*).

It is clear, of course, what the origin of " eristic " of this kind is. Euthydemus and his brother are borrowing and degrading the logical method of Zeno.[1] In Zeno's hands, the deduction of apparently contradictory conclusions from the same premisses had a legitimate object. The intention was to discredit the premisses themselves. And in fact, Zeno's antinomies do establish the important result that the postulates of Pythagorean mathematics are incompatible with one another and require revision (*e.g.* it is indispensable to Pythagorean geometry that every straight

[1] This is made especially clear twice over (275*e*, 276*e*), by the whispered remark of Dionysodorus that his brother will " catch the boy out " equally whichever way he answers the question. This construction of " antinomies," to show that the affirmation and the denial of the same proposition are equally impossible, was the special contribution of Zeno to the development of logical method. There is also probably intentional point in the way in which we are reminded of the connexion of the brothers with Thurii—the place, of all others, where they would be most certain to meet Eleatics.

line should be capable of bisection, and yet, on the Pythagorean principles, a line may contain an odd number of "points" and therefore be incapable of bisection, because you cannot "split the unit "). With eristics like Euthydemus this hunting after "antinomies," perfectly legitimate when intended as a criticism of presuppositions which lead to an "antinomy," becomes a mere delight in entrapping the respondent into contradicting himself by mere neglect to guard against ambiguity in words, and its object is not to detect error but to produce admiration for the ingenious deviser of the ambiguous formula. This is the point on which Socrates now fastens. The two "sophists" care nothing about convincing Clinias of the need for "goodness and philosophy "; their concern is merely to make a display of their own cleverness. Accordingly, Socrates interrupts the performance. He professes to think that what has gone before is not meant as any sample of the "wisdom " of the brothers. It is a mere piece of "fun," like the sportive preliminaries which precede initiation into the Corybantic rites, or, as we might say, like those popularly supposed to precede an initiation into freemasonry. So far the two great men have merely been playing a "game " with the lad, enjoying a "practical joke " at his expense ; no doubt the serious part of their "protreptic " is yet to come. Before it comes, Socrates would like to show, by a conversation of his own with the boy, what, in his "foolish and amateur fashion " (ἰδιωτικῶς τε καὶ γελοίως), he supposes the drift of such exhortations must be, though, of course, he fully expects to be left in the shade by two such eminent professionals (277d–278e).

There follows at once a simple statement, in clear language such as a mere boy can follow, of the root ideas of Socratic ethics. Of course every one of us wants εὖ πράττειν, to "fare well," to "make a success of life." And equally, of course, making a success of life means having "abundance of good " (πολλὰ ἀγαθά). Now what things is it good to have ? "The first man you meet "will mention some of them : wealth, health, beauty, bodily advantages in general, good birth, a position of influence and respect. But there are other good things than these, or at least other things which Socrates and Clinias regard as good : sophrosyne, justice, courage, wisdom. Is the list of goods now complete ? Perhaps we have left out the most important of all, "good luck " (εὐτυχία), without which any other advantages may turn out to be disguised curses. And yet, on second thoughts, we have not forgotten it. For wisdom is itself εὐτυχία. Who have the best "luck " or "good fortune " in playing musical instruments, in reading and writing, in navigation, warfare, medicine ? The men who know how to do these things— expert musicians, sailors, soldiers, physicians. One would, e.g., think it a great piece of luck in war to be serving under a competent and not under an incompetent commander. In general, wisdom or knowledge (σοφία) leads to efficient achievement (εὐπραγία) and so to "good fortune." If we have wisdom, then we may expect "success," "good fortune" (τὸ εὐτυχεῖν) in the department of practice which our "wisdom" covers (278e–280a).

On reviewing these results, we see ground to criticize one of them, the statement that we shall be happy and "make life a success" (εὐδαιμονεῖν καὶ εὖ πράττειν) if we "have abundance of good things." To *have* them will not benefit us unless we also *use* them, any more than it would benefit an artisan to have the materials and tools of his trade if he never used them. So, e.g., "wealth" is of no benefit unless we *use* it. And it would not be enough to say that we must not only have the various good things but use them. We must add that, to be happy, we must use them *right*. They are, in fact, dangerous tools ; if you use them in the wrong way you do yourself a harm ; it would be better to leave them alone than to use them wrongly. Now in all crafts and businesses it is the expert's *knowledge* (ἐπιστήμη) of his craft which enables him to use his materials and implements in the right way, and the same thing holds good of health and wealth and the goods in popular esteem generally. *Knowledge* enables us to use wealth, health, and all other "advantages" rightly, and to achieve success (εὐπραγία). If a man had all other possessions besides wisdom and were not directed by "sense" (νοῦς) in his undertakings, the less he undertook the fewer blunders he would make, and the happier he would be. It would be happier for him to be poor than rich, timid than courageous, sluggish and dull rather than of active temper and quick perception, since the less he undertook the less mischief he would do. In fact, none of the things we began by calling good can be called unconditionally (αὐτὰ καθ' αὑτά) good. They are better than their opposites when they are conjoined with the wisdom to make a right use of them (φρόνησίς τε καὶ σοφία), but worse when they are disjoined from it. It follows that, properly speaking, there is just one thing good, wisdom, and just one bad thing, ἀμαθία, "dullness," stupidity (280b–281e). (Compare the precisely similar line of reasoning by which Kant reaches the conclusion that the good *will* is the only thing which is unconditionally good, because it is the only good which cannot be misused.)

We may draw a final conclusion. We now see that since happiness depends on wisdom and knowledge, the one end after which every man should strive is to become "as wise as possible." Hence what we should crave to get from our parents, friends, fellow-citizens, alien acquaintances, before everything else, is just wisdom. One should be ready to "serve and slave" and render "any service that is comely" [1] to any man for the sake of wisdom ; that is to say, provided that wisdom can really be taught and does not "come by accident" (ἀπὸ ταὐτομάτου), a difficult question which we have not

---

[1] ὁτιοῦν τῶν καλῶν ὑπηρετημάτων, 282b. The qualification is inserted because ἐρασταί have been mentioned, and Socrates wishes to guard himself against being supposed to include chastity as one of the prices which may be paid for "wisdom." His attitude on that point is as unqualified as Plato's own in the *Laws*.

faced. If we may assume that wisdom can be taught, we have satisfied ourselves of the absolute necessity of pursuing it, "being philosophers" (282a–d).

Socrates has really given us so far only half of a "protreptic discourse" such as would be to his mind. He has led up to the conclusion that happiness depends on the direction of life and conduct by knowledge, but has not so far told us what knowledge in particular it is of which we cannot make an ill use. It is fundamental for his purpose that we should distinguish such knowledge from every recognized form of expert professional knowledge, and the distinction will be made later. For the present we return to the "comic relief" of the fooleries of Euthydemus and his brother, which become increasingly absurd, precisely in order that the heightened contrast of tone shall mark the second part of Socrates' discourse, when we reach it, as the most important thing in the whole dialogue. For the present he proposes that the "professionals" shall now take up the argument at this point, and decide the question whether one needs to learn every kind of "knowledge," or whether there is one special knowledge which conducts to happiness. Or, if they prefer, they may go over the ground he has already covered and do so in a less amateurish fashion. Of course they do neither ; their object is simply *épater les bourgeois*, and Dionysodorus, the older of the two, sets to work at once to administer a thoroughly sensational shock. Can Socrates and the others, who profess to feel so much affection for Clinias, be serious in saying that they are anxious that he should become "wise" ? For their language implies that he is not yet what they wish him to become. They say they want him to "be no longer what he now is"; but to wish a man to "be no longer" is to wish that he may perish—a pretty wish on the part of one's "affectionate friends" (283a–d). (Here again we are on Eleatic ground, and we see that it is not for nothing that Plato reminds us repeatedly that his two sophists had lived at Thurii. The argument that nothing can change, because that which "becomes different" is becoming "what it is not," and therefore becoming nothing at all, derives directly from Parmenides as soon as his physics are converted into logic, and, like the rest of the puzzles connected with it, only gets its solution when we come to the distinction between absolute and relative not-being introduced in the *Sophistes*. In our dialogue Plato is not seriously concerned with the solution of these difficulties ; what he is con cerned with is the futility of regarding them as a preparation for the conduct of life, and the *moral* levity of the professors who make a parade of them.) The immediate effect of the sally of Dionysodorus is to call forth from Ctesippus, an older lad deeply attached to Clinias, an angry complaint of the "falsity" of the accusation, and this gives Euthydemus an opening for airing his principal piece of "wisdom," which we have already met in the *Cratylus*—the doctrine that all statements are true, or, as he puts it now, that "it is impossible to speak falsely," for the reason that whenever you make a statement, you must either be saying " what is " or saying " what is not." In the first case, you are telling the truth, for to " say what is," is truth-speaking. As for the second case, " what is not " is just nothing at all, and no one can speak and yet say " nothing "; whoever speaks at all is saying something (283e–284c). The regular corollary is promptly drawn that οὐκ ἔστιν ἀντιλέγειν, no man can contradict another, since there can be no contradiction unless both parties are speaking of the same " thing " (the logical subject must be the same in the two state-ments). But since you cannot speak of a thing " as it is not," in the case of apparent contradiction, one or both parties would have to be speaking of " what is not," and this is impossible. If the two parties are making significant statements at all, since such statements must be statements of " what is," they must be talking about two different subjects, and so there is no contradiction (285d–286c).[1]

It is characteristic of Socrates that he insists at once on calling attention to the practical bearings of this piece of logical paradox. It implies that two men cannot even think contradictory pro-positions ; if a false statement is impossible, mental error is impossible too, and from this it follows that no one can commit an error in *practice* (ἐξαμαρτάνειν ὅταν τι πράττῃ), and the claim of the brothers to be able to *teach* goodness must therefore be an empty one, for their teaching is superfluous.[2] Dionysodorus eludes the difficulty partly by insisting that his present assertion should be considered on its own merits independently of anything he may have said before, and partly by catching at the phrase which Socrates has used, that he cannot understand what the statement " means " (νοεῖν). How can a statement be said to " mean " anything ?[3] The conversation is rapidly degenerating into mere personalities (λοιδορία) when Socrates saves the situation by repeating his former suggestion that the eminent wits from Thurii are still only engaged on the " fun " which is to introduce their serious wisdom. They need to be pressed a little more, and we shall then get at last to the earnest. This gives him an excuse

---

[1] Note that at 286c Socrates describes this paradox as " stale," and ascribes it to " Protagoras and men of a still earlier date," as, in fact, it does follow from the ἄνθρωπος μέτρον doctrine. This should dispose of the fancy that Antisthenes is specially aimed at in the dialogue. The " still older " person meant is presumably Parmenides, who expressly denies that " what is not " can be spoken of or named.

[2] Exactly the same point is urged against Protagoras at *Theaetet.* 161 c–e. But in that dialogue, where Plato's main purpose is epistemological, Socrates is careful to consider whether Protagoras might not make a rejoinder to this criticism (166a–168c), and to examine the soundness of the rejoinder (171e–172b, 178a–179b).

[3] The quibble turns on the uses of the word νοεῖν, which signifies (a) to think, to intend, to purpose, (b) to *mean* or *signify*. The sophist pretends to take the expression " your words mean so-and-so," in the sense that they " intend " or " think," and asks how anything but a ψυχή can possibly " think " anything. There is the same *équivoque* in the distinction in English between " to mean " and " to mean to " say or do something.

for returning to his own specimen of serious " protreptic " at the point where he had left off.

We saw that the one thing needful for the conduct of life is knowledge. But what kind of " knowledge " ? Of course, the knowledge which will " profit " us, " useful knowledge." Now what kind of knowledge is that ? It cannot be any kind of knowledge which merely teaches us how to *produce* something without also teaching us how to *use* the thing we have produced. This enables us to dismiss at once all the specialized industrial arts, like that of the maker of musical instruments, none of which teach a man how to use the thing they have taught him to make. In particular, this consideration applies to the art of the λογοποιός, which looks so imposing. We might think that this art of composing effective speeches is just the kind of knowledge we need for the conduct of life, since it teaches us how to make the " charm " or " spell " which is potent against those most deadly of enemies, angry and prejudiced dicasteries and *ecclesiae*. Yet, after all, the important thing is to know how to *use* the " spell," but the λογοποιός only teaches you how to *make* it.[1] There might be something to say for the soldier's profession, the art of catching a human prey ; but, after all, the hunter does not know how to use the game he captures, but has to pass it on to the cook or *restaurateur* ; and in the same way the commander who " captures " a city or an army has not learned from his profession what to do with his capture when he has made it. The military art, then, is clearly not the supreme art needed for the right conduct of life (288*b*–290*d*).[2]

Incidentally we note that the claim of any of the purely speculative branches of knowledge, the mathematical sciences, has been disposed of by this criticism. The mathematicians also are, in their way, " hunters " on the trail of " realities " (τὰ ὄντα). But though their διαγράμματα (here again the word means " proofs "

---

[1] The point here, as in the *Gorgias*, which classes " rhetoric " with " swimming " as a device for preserving your life, is that the patron of the λογοποιός is normally one of the well-to-do minority of whom the Periclean democracy were naturally suspicious precisely because democracy really meant the " exploitation " of this class for the benefit of the " proletarian." From the well-to-do victim's point of view, effective public speaking is exactly what it is called here, a " spell " to put the watchful, hostile *belua* of democracy to sleep ; from the democrat's point of view, it is a trick by which the μισόδημος gulls the simple citizens into taking him for the " people's friend."

[2] Socrates is made to assert that this criticism was delivered by Clinias on his own account ; Crito thinks such a mere boy could not have shown such acuteness, and hints that the remark must really have come from Socrates himself (290*e*). This is dramatically in keeping with the picture Plato has drawn of Crito—a dull, honest man. But the real point is that the " protreptic " of Socrates is effective in the right way ; it elicits from a younger mind flashes of insight which would have been impossible but for the way in which the preceding questions have led up to them. This is the true answer to the criticism of Grote that anyone can ask puzzling questions. The peculiarity of the Socratic question is not to be puzzling, but to be enlightening.

rather than " figures ") " find " the quarry, the mathematicians
do not know how to "treat " it ; that task, if they have any sense,
they leave to the διαλεκτικός, the critical philosopher.[1] On
scrutiny, the " art " which seems to have the best claims to supremacy is the βασιλικὴ τέχνη, the " art of the king," *i.e.* statesmanship. If there is any " speciality " which can secure happiness,
it should certainly be that of the man who knows how to govern
and administer the community (since, of course, no one except a
paradox-monger would deny that " human well-being " is what all
true statesmanship takes as its end). But with this result we seem
to have come round in a complete circle to the same point from
which our argument set out. It is clear that statesmanship
(ἡ πολιτικὴ τέχνη) is the supreme master-art ; generals and other
functionaries are only servants of the statesman. He *uses*, as
means to his end—the well-being of the state—victory in war and
all the other results which the generals and the rest *make* ; and we
have seen already in the *Cratylus* that the art which uses a product
is always the master-art in relation to those which made the product.
But the statesman too has something to produce ; he uses the
products of all the other " craftsmen " as means to producing
something himself, and this something must be something beneficial, and therefore good. Now we had already satisfied ourselves
that knowledge is the only thing which is unconditionally good.
Hence, if statesmanship is really the art of the conduct of life, such
results as wealth, civic independence, freedom from party strife,
must be its mere by-products ; its main product must be wisdom
and goodness. Yet what wisdom and goodness does true statesmanship produce in those on whom it is exercised ? It does not
aim at making them all " good " shoemakers or " good " carpenters,
or " good " at any other special calling. Apparently we must
say that the knowledge which the art of the statesman produces in
us is the knowledge of itself. But what use do we make of this
knowledge of statesmanship ? Perhaps its use is that it enables us
to make other men good. But then we come back to the old
question, " Good at *what* ? " We seem to have reached the conclusion that happiness depends on knowing how to make other
men good at knowing how to make yet other men (and so on *ad
indefinitum*) good at knowing . . . no one can say precisely what
(291a–292e).

[1] The point becomes clear if we think of the relation of a Pythagorean
geometer to the typical διαλεκτικός Zeno. The mathematicians " track " or
" hunt down " truths like the Pythagorean theorem, but they are so far from
knowing what to " do with them " that it is left for a διαλεκτικός like Zeno
to show that the discovery itself leads to consequences which are fatal to
some of the postulates of the Pythagorean geometer (such as the incommen-
surability of the " side " and the " diagonal "). The last word on the
question what can be " made of " the results of the sciences rests with the
critical " metaphysician," who has to test the claims of these sciences to give
a finally satisfactory account of " the real." Note the complete acceptance
here of the " primacy of the *practical* reason," which is as characteristic of
Socrates and Plato as of Kant.

The serious positive purpose of the argument, which has incidentally slipped into becoming a direct conversation between Socrates and Crito, is not hard to discover. The knowledge on which the right conduct of life and the right government of men alike depend is not knowledge of the way to meet any one particular type of situation or to discharge any one particular calling or function ; it is knowledge of good, or, to put the point in more modern phraseology, knowledge of absolute moral values. On the Socratic assumption that knowledge of this kind is always followed by corresponding action, and is therefore the only knowledge which is guaranteed against all possible misuse, the question *for what* we are to use it becomes superfluous ; we do not " use " it as a means to some ulterior end at all, we simply act it out. To put the matter in the Greek way, every " art " is an " art of opposites " ; that is, may be used for a bad as well as for a good end. The special knowledge of toxicology which makes a man a medical specialist may also make him a dangerous secret poisoner. The intimate knowledge of the Stock Exchange and share market which makes a man an excellent trustee for the fortune of his ward will also make him a particularly dangerous " fraudulent trustee " if he applies it for dishonest ends. But " knowledge of the good " is in a unique position which distinguishes it from all special professional or technical knowledge, the thing with which the " sophists " and their pupils regularly confuse it. It too, in a sense, is " of opposites, " since to know what is good involves knowing that what is incompatible with good must be evil. But, on Socratic principles, this knowledge is not a knowledge of opposites in the sense that it can be put to either of two opposite uses, a good one and a bad one. The possession of the knowledge carries along with it the possession of the " good will." We thus recover the fundamental positions of the Socratic ethics from the apparently fruitless argument. The reason why the positive result is not stated is simply that the object of Socrates' " protreptic " is not to do another man's thinking for him and present him with ready-made " results," but to stimulate him to think along the right lines for himself, so that when the " result " emerges, it comes as a personal conviction won by a genuine personal exercise of intelligence. Hence Socrates is represented as breaking off at the point we have reached, and appealing to the two distinguished strangers to help him out of the " squall " in which he seems to be threatened with shipwreck. As we should expect, they do nothing of the kind, but fall to their old trick. Socrates does not need any help, for they will prove to him that he already has the knowledge for which he is seeking. He knows some things, *ergo* he has knowledge ; but one cannot both have knowledge and not have it, *ergo* he knows everything. And so, for the matter of that, does every one else (293*a–e*). Euthydemus and his brother have, in fact, a sort of universal infallibility ; they know all trades and the answers to all the most trifling speculative questions. This, says Socrates, must be the great truth to which all that has gone before was the playful prelude.[1]

From this point onwards the dialogue becomes increasingly farcical as the two brothers go on to develop one absurdity after another, until Socrates, the only member of the company who has preserved his gravity, takes his leave of them with many ironical compliments and the advice to take care, in their own interests, not to cheapen the price of their wisdom by too many public exhibitions. There is no need to follow in detail the whole series of ludicrous paralogisms which precedes this *finale*. Aristotle found good material in it for his own study of fallacies, but Plato's object is ethical rather than logical, as has been already said.[2] The extreme absurdity of the performances by which the brothers follow up the second and more important part of the " protreptic " argument are merely meant to throw that section of the dialogue into the strongest relief.   The one comment it may be worth while to make is that the standing rule of " eristic," by which the respondent is expected to reply to each question exactly as it has been put, without raising any objection to its form or qualifying his answer by the introduction of any *distinguo*, however simple, of itself provides exceptional opportunity for the perpetration of every kind of " fallacy in the diction." From this point of view much of the dialogue might be said to be a criticism of the method of question and answer as a vehicle of philosophic thought.   It is clear, and Plato may have meant to hint this, that the method is the most uncertain of weapons unless the questioner combines intelligence with absolutely good faith ; this is why it may be a powerful weapon of criticism in the hands of Socrates, but is nothing but an instrument of sophistry in those of a Euthydemus whose only object is to make men stare.

At the end of Socrates' narrative, Plato adds a sort of appendix, a page or two of direct conversation between Socrates and Crito. Crito observes that the remark had already been made to him by a certain writer of speeches for the law-courts who fancied himself a " great wit " (πάνυ σοφός), that the disgraceful scene in the Lyceum was enough to show that " philosophy " is " mere waste of time " (οὐδὲν πρᾶγμα), for the professionals who had just been making egregious fools of themselves were actually among its most eminent

---

[1] We are still dealing with the misuse of Eleatic doctrine. The proof of the infallibility of every one is made to turn on the principle of contradiction *plus* the neglect of qualifying conditions. We cannot both have knowledge and not have it ; if you know anything, you have knowledge, and therefore have all knowledge. This is just the Eleatic doctrine that there is no half-way house between " what is " and blank nonentity, transferred from physics to logic. Whenever we come on ἀντιλογικοί we are safe in looking for the influence of Zeno.

[2] Note that at 301*a* Socrates, without any explanation, falls into the technical language of the so-called " ideal " theory when he says that καλὰ πράγματα are different from αὐτὸ τὸ καλόν, though a certain κάλλος " is present " to them, and that this peculiar Socratic use of the word παρεῖναι is even made the subject of a jest.

living representatives. The critic who made the remark was not himself a political man, nor had he ever addressed a law-court, but had the reputation of being a skilled professional composer of speeches for litigants (304b–305c). Socrates replies that these men, who, as Prodicus once said, are on the border-line between politics and philosophy, are always jealous of the philosopher ; they think he keeps them out of rightful recognition. The truth is, that the man who tries to combine two callings is regularly inferior in both to the man who confines himself to one. *If* the philosophic life and the life of affairs are both good things, the man who tries to play both parts is certain to be inferior in each to the specialist in his own line (305c–306d).

It has naturally been suspected that there is some personal allusion underlying these remarks, and the view has often been taken that Plato is aiming a shaft on his own account at his rival Isocrates. It is true, of course, that during the lifetime of Socrates, Isocrates was known only as a λογογράφος or composer of speeches for the courts, but that some time early in the fourth century he gave up this profession for that of presiding over a regular institution for the preparation of young men of promise for a political career. It is true also that Isocrates called the kind of education he bestowed on his pupils his " philosophy," and that he affected to look down on the severely scientific studies of Plato's Academy as " useless " and unpractical. From Plato's point of view, it would be highly *à propos* to speak of Isocrates as " on the border line " between a politician and a philosopher, and inferior to each in his own department—except that one might doubt whether Plato did really think Isocrates inferior in statesmanship to the commonplace Athenian men of affairs of his own time.

Yet I think the identification quite impossible. At the date indicated by all the allusions of the *Euthydemus* Isocrates would still be no more than a lad, whereas the person spoken of by Crito is already a λογογράφος of established repute. Still less could Socrates, *at this date*, be supposed to anticipate that Isocrates would some day lay claim to the reputation of a philosopher. (The case is rather different with the express references of the *Phaedrus* to Isocrates, since, as we shall see, the date of that dialogue is supposed to be later.) We must suppose Socrates to be alluding rather to some well-known figure of the time of the Archidamian war. There is no reason why there should not have been more than one personage of the age to which Callicles and Thrasymachus belong who fancied himself as a blend of the philosophical thinker and the practical " statesman." The remains of Antiphon " the sophist," for example, suggest by their character that he might perfectly well be the person intended, and we know from a notice preserved by Xenophon [1] that he was among the acquaintances of

---

[1] Xen. *Mem.* i. 6. It is important to note, as Professor Burnet has done, that the information cannot depend on Xenophon's personal recollections, but must have been taken from some source describing Socrates as he

Socrates. It is true that there is no direct proof that he was a writer of speeches for the law-courts, but there is no reason why he may not have been. In fact, it does not seem to me by any means established that Antiphon the " sophist " and Antiphon of Rhamnus, the famous politician and λογογράφος, are two distinct persons.[1] And I feel sure that we have no right wantonly to attribute to Plato the anachronisms which a reference to Isocrates in our dialogue would imply, nor is there, in point of fact, any real evidence that there ever was any personal ill-feeling between Isocrates and Plato.[2] The real object of the passage is probably simply to recognize the fact that to a good many persons the dialectic of Socrates must have seemed much on a par with the frivolities of Euthydemus and his brother, and to hint that, if we choose, we may discover the real difference between the two things from the dialogue itself, as we certainly can.

See further :

> RITTER, C.—*Platon*, i. 450–462 (*Euthydemus*), 462–496 (*Cratylus*).
> RAEDER, H.—*Platons philosophische Entwickelung*, 137–153.
> STEWART, J. A.—*Plato's Doctrine of Ideas*, 34–39 (*Cratylus*.)
> WARBURG, M.—*Zwei Fragen zum Kratylos*. (Berlin, 1929.)

---

was at the time of the Archidamian war. This gives it all the more historical value.

[1] The question should probably be decided, if decided at all, on linguistic and stylistic grounds. But are the remains of the " sophist " extensive enough to permit of effective comparison with those of the λογογράφος ? And to what extent should we expect to find a λογογράφος exhibiting in his compositions for the courts the peculiarities of his personal literary style ? Professor S. Luria calls my attention in particular to two articles by Bignone in the *Rendiconti del R. Istituto Lombard. di scienze*, 1919, pp. 567 f., 755 ff., as establishing the non-identity of the two men. I regret that I have not myself seen these essays.

[2] On this point see the remarks of Burnet, *Greek Philosophy, Part I.*, 215. Isocrates may have enjoyed aiming his shafts at the Academic mathematics, but the deliberate adoption of Isocratean tricks of style in the *Sophistes* and the other later dialogues seems to show that Plato is not likely to have borne him any malice on account of his inability to appreciate science.

CHAPTER VI

SOCRATIC DIALOGUES : *GORGIAS, MENO*

THE *Gorgias* is a much longer work than any we have yet
considered, and presents us with an exposition of the Socratic
morality so charged with passionate feeling and expressed
with such moving eloquence that it has always been a prime
favourite with all lovers of great ethical literature. The moral
fervour and splendour of the dialogue, however, ought not to blind
us, as it has blinded most writers on Platonic chronology, to certain
obvious indications that it is a youthful work, earlier in composition,
perhaps, than some of those with which we have been concerned.
We might have inferred as much from the mere fact that Plato
has adopted the form of the direct dialogue for so considerable a
work, and thus missed the chance of giving us a description of the
personality of Gorgias to compare with his elaborate portrait of
Protagoras. Personally, I cannot also help feeling that, with all
its moral splendour, the dialogue is too long : it "drags." The
Plato of the *Protagoras* or *Republic*, as I feel, would have known
how to secure the same effect with less expenditure of words ;
there is a diffuseness about our dialogue which betrays the hand
of the prentice, though the prentice in this case is a Plato. For
this reason I think it a mistake in principle to look, as some have
done, for an ethical advance in doctrine as we pass from the
Protagoras to the *Gorgias*. As we shall see when we come to deal
with the *Protagoras*, the ethical doctrine of the dialogues is identical
and it is inconceivable to me that any reader of literary sensibility
can doubt which of the two is the product of a riper mastery of
dramatic art. Beyond this general statement that the *Gorgias* must
be an early work, and probably a work dating not many years after
the death of Socrates, I do not think it safe to hazard any conjecture as to the date of composition.[1]

[1] We shall see when we come to deal with the *Republic* that it, and consequently any dialogues which precede it, must be dated not much later than
387, within twelve years of Socrates' death. If the *Gorgias* falls early in this
period, we must place its composition quite soon after that event, while the
feelings connected with it were still in their first freshness in Plato's mind.
Professor Wilamowitz-Moellendorf, in his *Plato*, i. 221, ii. 94–105, makes an
ingenious attempt at a more exact dating. He starts from the curious misquotation of Pindar's well-known lines about νόμος, as given by all our best MSS.
at *Gorgias* 484b (where the text has been corrected back again in all the printed
editions). He rightly, as it seems to me, holds that the misquotation is what
Plato actually wrote, and then goes on (again, I believe, rightly) to infer from

It is unusually difficult to determine the date at which the conversation is supposed to be held. It has sometimes been supposed that a reference made by Socrates to some occasion when he was a member of the committee of the βουλή who had to preside over the meetings of the ἐκκλησία, and raised a laugh by his ignorance of the formalities to be observed in " putting the question " (*Gorg.* 473*e*), has to do with the events of the trial of the generals at Arginusae, where we know from both Plato and Xenophon that Socrates actually was one of the presiding committee. If this interpretation were certain, we should have to suppose the conversation to fall somewhere in the last year of the Peloponnesian war, when Athens was fighting with her back to the wall for her very existence. There are certainly no signs in the dialogue that this situation is presupposed ; it seems rather to be taken for granted that the political and commercial life of the city is in a normal condition. Moreover, as Burnet has said, the democracy was in no laughing mood at the trial of the generals, and we thus seem forced to suppose that the reference is to some unknown incident which happened on some former occasion when Socrates was a member of the βουλή.[1] On the other side, it would appear from the opening sentences of the dialogue that Socrates is as yet a complete stranger to Gorgias and his profession, and this suggests that Gorgias is in Athens for the first time. There seems no good reason to deny the statement of Diodorus Siculus that Gorgias visited Athens first as a member of the embassy sent thither by his native city, Leontini, in the year 427, and such a date would fit in very well with certain other indications in the work, *e.g.* the reference to the " recent " death of Pericles,[2] and the statements about the almost despotic power of the Athenian demagogue.[3] (These would suit the time when the place of Pericles was being taken by Cleon and men of his stamp to perfection.) Possibly, too, the date

Libanius' *Apology of Socrates* that the accusation of misquoting Pindar had figured in the pamphlet of Polycrates against Socrates published somewhere about 393. His final inference is that the accusation was based on this passage of the *Gorgias*, which must thus be anterior to the pamphlet of Polycrates. I hope to suggest reasons for believing that the misquotation in Plato is conscious and made for a legitimate purpose. At this point I merely wish to observe that it cannot have been the foundation of an accusation against the memory of Socrates for two conclusive reasons : (1) that in any case a misquotation in Plato would be no proof of anything against Socrates, and (2) that the person who is made by Plato to misquote Pindar is not Socrates, but Callicles, who is arguing against him. Polycrates, to judge from the line Isocrates takes with him (Isoc. xi. 1–8), was pretty much of a fool, but it is hard to believe that he could have used a misquotation put by Plato into the mouth of Callicles to damage the reputation of Socrates. At the same time, I feel no doubt that the *Gorgias* was written as early as Professor Wilamowitz holds, and most probably earlier.

[1] This is quite compatible with the statement of *Apology*, 32*b* 1. Socrates says there that he has been a member of the βουλή. He does not say that he had only served once in that capacity. See Burnet's note in *loc. cit.* The best historians hold that Xenophon has made a slip in saying that Socrates was the ἐπιστάτης at the famous trial.

[2] *Gorgias,* 503*c*.   [3] *Ibid.* 466*c*.

would not be too early for the allusion to the handsome Demus, the son of Plato's own stepfather Pyrilampes, as a reigning beauty, though there may be a very small anachronism here since Aristophanes first mentions the craze for Demus in the *Wasps*, which belongs to the year 422.[1] On the other side, again, we find the *Antiope* of Euripides quoted as a well-known and popular work,[2] and the date of that tragedy seems to be *c.* 408. The career of Archelaus of Macedon, again, comes in for a good deal of discussion,[3] and it has commonly been inferred from Thucydides that his reign did not begin until 414–413, though disputed successions and the simultaneous existence of several pretenders to the crown were so common in Macedonia that we cannot build very confidently on such data. It is very unfortunate that we have no independent information about Callicles of Acharnae, who appears in the dialogue as a cultivated and ambitious young man who has lately entered political life, though the mere fact that Plato specifies his deme is enough to show that he is an actual man, and not, as has been suggested, an *alias* for some one. If he really attempted to act up to the Nietzschian theories ascribed to him in the dialogue, it may not be wonderful that no record of his career has survived. In the names which Plato gives as those of his immediate associates we recognize some which were prominent in the second half of the great war, but, of course their early days would belong to its first half. On the whole, the arguments for an early dramatic date seem to preponderate, though the references to the *Antiope* and the usurpation of the Macedonian crown by Archelaus, especially the second, seem to create a little difficulty.[4]

The characters of the dialogue besides Socrates are four—Gorgias, the famous " orator " of Leontini, whose well-known rhetorical devices for adding pomp and glitter to language represent the first stage in the development of a literary prose style rising above colloquialism or bald narration of matter of fact and yet remaining prose; Polus of Agrigentum, his enthusiastic disciple and admirer; Callicles of Acharnae, of whom we only know what Plato has thought fit to tell us; and Chaerephon, the lean, impetuous, and apparently rather superstitious companion of Socrates, whom

[1] *Gorgias*, 481*d*, Aristoph. *Wasps*, 89.

[2] *Gorgias*, 484*e*–486*d*. Since Aristotle appears to have been the first person to attempt to construct a chronology of the Attic drama by making a collection of *didascaliae*, I should have attached no importance to this particular point but for the fact that if the commonly accepted view about the date of the *Antiope* is correct Plato must pretty certainly have seen the performance himself.

[3] *Ibid.* 470*d*–471*d*.

[4] The way in which Nicias is mentioned at 472*a* certainly seems to assume that he is living and at the very height of his prosperity. This would exclude any date much later than the sailing of the Syracusan expedition in 415. The difficulties seem to me to be created by the very wealth of topical allusions for which the dialogue is remarkable. It would be very hard, in the absence of something like the complete files of a newspaper, to make so many of these allusions without falling into a small error here or there, and there were no newspapers or gazettes at Athens.

Aristophanes finds so useful as a butt.[1] The precise scene is not indicated ; apparently it is not in the house of Callicles, who is acting as host to the distinguished visitor, but in some public place where Gorgias has been giving a display of his gifts.[2] The ostensible subject of the conversation must be carefully distinguished from the real subject. Professedly the question propounded for dis- cussion is the new speciality which Gorgias has introduced to Athens, the art of impressive speech ; the points to be decided are whether it is really an " art " at all, and if it is, whether it is, as Gorgias claims, the queen of all other " arts." But to discover the real object of the work we need to look carefully at the general construction of the argument, and particularly at the end of the whole composition. If we do this, we find that the dialogue really consists of three successive conversations of Socrates with a single interlocutor ; it has, so to say, three scenes, each with two " actors." In the first conversation between Socrates and Gorgias the topic of conversation really is the character and worth of the " rhetori- cian's " art ; in the second, between Socrates and Polus, we find that the rival estimates of the worth of rhetoric depend on sharply contrasted ethical convictions about the true happiness of man. In the final conversation with Callicles, where the tone of the dialogue reaches its level of highest elevation, all secondary questions have fallen completely into the background and we are left with the direct and absolute conflict between two competing theories of life, each represented by a striking personality. The true object of the whole work thus emerges : it is to pit a typical life of devotion to the supra-personal good against the typical theory and practice of the " will to power " at its best. We are to see how the theory of the " will to power," expounded by a thoroughly capable, intelligent, and far from merely ignoble champion, like Callicles, and the " practice " of it as embodied in Periclean Imperialism look from the point of view of a Socrates, and also how the convictions and career of a Socrates look to the intelligent worshipper of " strength " ; and when we have looked at each party with the eyes of the other, we are to be the judges between them. Life and the way it should be lived, not the value of rhetoric, is the real theme, exactly as the real theme of the *Republic* is not the merits and demerits of com- peting political and economic systems, but " righteousness, temper- ance, and judgment to come."[3]

[1] For the leanness, cf. Aristoph. *Clouds*, 502-503 ; for the impetuousness, *Apology*, 21a, σφοδρὸς ἐφ' ὅτι ὁρμήσειεν ; for the superstition, Aristoph. *Birds*, 1553 ff., where his taste for things ghostly is burlesqued by making him the fraudulent confederate who plays the " spirits " in Socrates' *séances*.

[2] Or perhaps we are to suppose that Socrates and Callicles meet in the street, and that the scene changes to the house of Callicles after the opening courtesies.

[3] The *Gorgias* stands in sharp contrast with the greatest of the dialogues in respect of the way in which the three sections of which the argument consists are marked off, like scenes on the Greek or French stage, by the putting forward of a new respondent to bear the brunt of the argument. Where his dramatic genius is at its highest, Plato is accustomed to interweave the

Formally the dialogue opens in a familiar way. Socrates is anxious to discover the precise character of the *art* or " speciality " (τέχνη) professed by Gorgias, the art of " rhetoric." It is, as Gorgias says (449*d*), an art of " speech " or " discourse " (περὶ λόγους), and as such it makes those who possess it skilled in " speaking," and therefore, since speech is the expression of thought or intelligence, makes them intelligent (δυνατοὺς φρονεῖν, 450*a*) about something. But this is far from an adequate definition. We may say that " arts " are of two kinds : the operations of the one kind are wholly or chiefly manual, those of the other kind are purely or principally effected by λόγοι, " discourses " (450*d*), a first intimation of the distinction, which becomes fundamental in Plato's later dialogues and in the philosophy of Aristotle, between " theoretical " and " practical " sciences. Now rhetoric is not the only " art " of the second kind ; there are many others, such as theoretical and practical arithmetic (ἀριθμητική and λογιστική), geometry, medicine, and others, in which manual operations play no part or a subordinate one ; but Gorgias certainly does not mean to say that he teaches medicine or mathematics. To complete the definition we need to know what is the subject-matter with which the " discourse " of the rhetorician is concerned, as the " discourse " of the arithmetician is concerned with " the odd and even " (*i.e.* with the properties of the integer-series (451*a–d*)). Gorgias thinks it enough to say that the subject-matter is " the most important of human concerns " (τὰ μέγιστα τῶν ἀνθρωπείων πραγμάτων), " the supreme interests of mankind." But a statement of this kind, which attempts to define by means of a mere formula of laudation, is ambiguous, since there are different opinions on the question what is the " great concern " of man. A physician might say that it is health, an economist or a business man that it is wealth. Hence, though Gorgias may be right in his estimate of his art, the estimate itself presupposes an answer to the ethical question what is the chief good for man (452*d*). Gorgias replies that the chief good for man is ἐλευθερία, freedom, in the sense of having his own way and being able to impose his will on his fellow-citizens, and that it is rhetoric, the art of persuasive or plausible speech which produces this good (452*d*). Thus the thought is that " power " is the chief good and that rhetoric, the art of persuasion, is the supreme art, because, in the life of a city like Athens, persuasive eloquence is the great weapon by which the statesman acquires power ; the persuasive speaker gets his policy adopted by the *ecclesia*, his financial schemes by the βουλή, and successfully impeaches his opponents and defends his partisans before the *dicasteria*. The secret of a Pericles, for example, is simply his command over the resources of persuasive eloquence. Gorgias holds that he can teach this secret to a pupil, and that is why he regards his own τέχνη as the supreme achievement of the human

threads of his plot more subtly. This, again, is a fair ground for an inference about the place of the dialogue in the series of Plato's works.

intelligence.[1] It should be noted that the hint is thus given early
in the dialogue that the real problem to be discussed is the ethical
question, not formally reached until we come to the scene in which
Callicles is the respondent, whether " power," unchecked freedom to
do as one likes and to make others do as one likes, *is* the highest
good. The dispute about the "merits" of the art of rhetoric is
wholly subservient to this ethical purpose and is mainly introduced
because, in a Greek democracy, facility and persuasiveness in speech
were necessarily the chief instruments by which such " power "
was to be attained.[2]

We know now what Gorgias means by " rhetoric " : he means
an " art " of persuasion. It is an " art " because it is, or claims
to be, reducible to intelligible principles ; its end or aim is to
" persuade " men to accept the views of the practitioner, and
so to make them consenting instruments of his will. But the
definition has the fault of being too wide : it does not, in fact,
state the specific differentia of the orator's accomplishment.
There are other " arts," including that of the arithmetician, of
which we might equally say that they are arts by which men are
persuaded to accept the specialist's opinion, since they " teach "
us certain truths, and he who is taught is certainly persuaded of
the things taught him. We must ask then, further, what *kind*
of persuasion does rhetoric employ, and about what *matters* does
it produce persuasion ? (454*a*). Gorgias replies that rhetoric is
the kind of persuasion employed " before dicasts and mobs in
general," and that it persuades about " matters of right and
wrong," *i.e.* it is the art of effective public speaking on questions of morality (454*b*). This at once suggests an important
distinction. Persuasion or conviction (τὸ πιστεύειν) may be produced by instruction or without it. In the first case, a man
is not only persuaded to hold an opinion, he is led to *knowledge* ; in the second, he is convinced but does not really *know*
that his conviction is true. Now obviously a " mob " cannot be
conducted to knowledge on grave and complicated issues in the
short time required for the delivery of an effective speech. The
orator, therefore, must be a practitioner of the mere persuasion
which does not produce real knowledge. We must expect, then,

[1] We are certainly dealing here with a thesis actually maintained by
Gorgias. For in the *Philebus*, Protarchus remarks (*Phileb.* 58*a–b*) that he
had often heard Gorgias maintain that the art of persuasion is far superior
to all others, because the man who possesses it can make every one do his
will and do it voluntarily. Obviously the reference is not to the *Gorgias*
itself (though 458*c* implies that an audience is present at the discussion),
but to some statement actually made in a discourse of Gorgias. *Gorgias*
452*d* ff. clearly refers to the same statement and probably reproduces it
with close fidelity.

[2] We might say, in fact, that the great weakness of ancient democracy was
that it really meant government by irresponsible orators, as modern democracy tends to mean government by equally irresponsible " pressmen."

that such a man will not attempt to persuade his audience about matters which obviously demand special technical knowledge, such as naval and military engineering, but only about " right and wrong " (which are popularly held not to be questions for specialists). Yet, as Gorgias observes, the greatest naval and military con- structions of Athens—the dockyards, the harbours, the "long walls " —were undertaken not at the instigation of engineering specialists, but at that of Themistocles and Pericles, who were eminent " orators," but not engineers.   In fact, you .will find that before any public audience a skilful orator will always succeed in proving more " convincing " than an " expert " who is no orator, even on questions which fall within the expert's province.   The " orator " who knows nothing of medicine, for example, will always be more persuasive, even on a medical question, than the medical specialist who is no orator.   In general, the man who is merely an " orator " who understands his business will be able to pass himself off before the public as a consummate authority in matters where he has no real technical knowledge at all, and this is precisely the secret of his power.   (The trick is that habitually employed in our own age by the able and eloquent advocate "speaking from his brief," and the view of Gorgias amounts to holding that states- manship is just a matter of consummate skill in speaking from a brief.)   To be sure, bad men may employ this formidable weapon for the worst of ends, but that is not the fault of the teacher from whom they have learned to use it, but their own.   It is as absurd to blame the teacher for a pupil's abuse of the art as it would be to hold a boxer or fencing-master responsible for a foul blow struck by one of his pupils (455a–457c).   Thus we see that Gorgias makes no claim to " teach goodness."   It is important that his pupils should make a right, not a wrong, use of the weapons he teaches them to use, but his concern is merely to teach the " manage " of the weapons.

There is an obvious weak point in this commendation of the orator's art, and Socrates fastens on it at once.   The " orator," by Gorgias' own account, is no " expert," and the " mob " or " crowd " before whom he succeeds in silencing the real expert are not experts either.   Thus, on the showing of Gorgias himself, oratory is a device by which an ignorant man persuades an audience equally ignorant with himself that he understands a question better than the expert who really knows about it.   Does this apply to the moral issues with which the " orator " will be largely concerned ? Does he need to know no more about right and wrong, honour and dishonour, than about, e.g., naval engineering or medicine ?   If he does need knowledge of this kind, where is he to get it, since Gorgias has explained that it is not his own business to impart it ?   Gorgias, rather inconsistently, suggests that, in case of need, a pupil might incidentally get the knowledge of right and wrong from himself ; in any case, he needs to have it.   The " orator " must be δίκαιος, " a moral man."   (If he were not, of course, he might make the

worst use of his oratorical skill.)   But if he is "a moral man,"
he will not have the wish to do wrong.   At this rate, a true orator
would never abuse his skill, and this seems inconsistent with the
former contention that when an orator does misuse his art, the
blame lies with himself and not with his teacher (457*c*–461*b*).

So far our results have come to this : it has at least been suggested that a statesman, who owes his power in a democracy to
skill in persuasion, need not be an expert in any of the technical
arts, but does require sound moral principles, though it is not
quite clear how he is to come by them.   Here Gorgias retires from
the argument, and his place is taken by his younger disciple and
admirer Polus, who is prepared to break with conventional views
about morality, as the respectable Gorgias is not.   According to
Polus, Socrates has taken an unfair advantage of the conventional
modesty which had led Gorgias to disclaim the status of a professional teacher of right and wrong.   The disclaimer was a mere
piece of good manners, and Socrates has himself committed a
breach of manners in pretending to take it seriously.   Polus also
insists that Socrates shall play the part of "respondent" and
submit his own definition of rhetoric for examination, as Socrates,
in fact, is quite willing to do.   According to this definition, which
opens the second of the three sections of the dialogue, rhetoric is
not an "art," a matter of expert knowledge, at all.   It is a mere
empirical "knack" (ἐμπειρία, τριβή), and more precisely, a
"knack of giving pleasure" (462*c*).   In this respect it is like
confectionery.   The confectioner pleases the palates of his customers by a clever combination of flavours, and the "orator"
in the same way "tickles the ears of the groundlings" by attractive
combinations of words and phrases.   It is meant that neither
confectionery nor oratory is really an application of rational principles ; you cannot lay down rules for either, since both are mere
tricks of gratifying the tastes of a body of patrons, and in each case
the trick depends on nothing more scientific than a tact which
cannot be taught but only picked up by long personal experience
of successes and failures.   There is thus nothing "fine" about
either ; they are both branches of a "knack" for which the proper
name is κολακεία, "humouring the moods of a patron,"[1] "acting
the parasite."

We may, in fact, distinguish four species of this κολακεία,
each of which is a spurious counterfeit or "ghost" (εἴδωλον) of a
real science or art.   We start from the now familiar Socratic con-

---

[1] The word must not be translated "flattery."   The successful demagogue
often scores his point better by "slanging" his audience than by flattering
them.   In the language of the fifth century, κόλαξ meant what the new
comedy calls παράσιτος, the "trencherman" or sycophant or toady who keeps
his place at a great man's table by compliance with his moods, like the
"hangers-on" of Gaunt House in Thackeray.   The thought of Socrates is
that the "statesman" who supposes himself to be imposing *his* will on the
"many-headed monster" is merely adroitly "pandering" to the creature's
lusts.   This is the verdict of philosophy on all successful "opportunism."

ception of the " tending " of a thing. There is a double art of tending the body, that is, of keeping it in a state of health and fitness, and a corresponding double art of tending the soul. In the case of the body, the two arts of " tending " have no common name ; they are those of " gymnastic," bodily culture (which sets up the ideal of true bodily " fitness "), and medicine (whose function it is to restore the " unfit " to health). The art of " tending " the soul has a single name ; it is called πολιτική, " statesmanship " : but it also has two branches, legislation (νομοθετική), which sets the standard of spiritual health, and " justice " (or righteousness, δικαιοσύνη), which corrects and repairs disease in the soul. Each of these four is a genuine art ; it aims at the good or true best condition of body or soul, and thus rests on a scientific knowledge of good and evil. The regulations of " gymnastic " and medicine are based on knowledge of what is wholesome for the body, those of the legislator and the judge on knowledge of what is wholesome for the soul. But each of the four arts has its counterfeit, and the counterfeit differs from the true art in taking as its standard the pleasant and not the good. Thus the confectioner is a counterfeit of the physician. The physician aims at prescribing the diet which will be wholesome for us, the confectioner at prescribing that which will please our palates. Now it is possible to know what diet is wholesome, but you can only discover what diet will please a man's palate by guesses based on long acquaintance with his moods and whims, and even when you guess right, the dishes you prepare will commonly not be good for your patron.

In the same way, κομμωτική, the " art," if you could call it so, of bodily adornment (the calling of the *friseur*, the professional beautifier, the jeweller, and many others), is a parody of the genuine art of the trainer. " Gymnastic " makes the body inherently attractive and graceful by training it in the exercises which produce genuine grace, agility, and vigour ; κομμωτική mimics this real art by producing a sham grace and charm effected by the artifice of cosmetics, fashionable clothes, and the like. (Here, again, there is no real standard, nothing but the caprice of the passing " fashion.") So with the arts which have to do with the health of the soul. The sophist professes to teach goodness, but what he teaches as goodness is merely the kind of life which is likely to recommend itself to his auditors ; the " orator " claims to be the physician of the disorders of the body politic, but the measures he recommends only persuade his audience because he is careful to recommend what is agreeable to their mood of the moment. Thus we may define rhetoric by saying that it is the counterfeit of one part of " politics," namely, of justice (463a–466a).[1]

Polus urges in reply that rhetoric cannot be a form of κολακεία,

---

[1] The most extravagant " public man " always insists that he is only advocating the " just rights " of his nation, or church, or class. But a " just right " in his mouth means, in fact, whatever his supporters are keenly set on demanding.

since the "hanger-on" is a disreputable character, whereas the "orator" is the most powerful person in the community, and, it is implied, the figure of highest consequence. He can use his influence to secure the banishment of anyone he pleases, to confiscate his goods, even to procure his execution. Thus he is virtually an autocrat with no superior. Socrates admits the fact, but denies the inference that either orator or autocrat is really powerful, if by "power" you mean anything which it is good for a man to have. The autocrat, recognized or unrecognized, no doubt always does "as he thinks good," but for that reason he never does "what he wishes" (466e). And it is not good for a man to do "as he thinks good" if his thinking is false. To explain the point more fully, we may put it thus. There are many things which we do, not for the mere sake of doing them, but as means to something else, as when a man drinks a disagreeable medicine at his doctor's order, for the sake of recovering health, or follows the fatiguing and dangerous calling of the sea with a view to making a fortune. In all such cases, where a thing is done as a means to some ulterior end, it is the ulterior end, not the disagreeable or indifferent means to it, that the man wishes for.[1] And he wishes for the end because he thinks it a good. So when we put a man to death, or banish him, or confiscate his property, we always have an ulterior end. We only do these things because we think they will be "useful" in view of that end. If the autocrat, then, is mistaken in supposing that such steps will "be for his good," if they are really bad for him, he is not doing "what he wished," and should not be called "powerful." (The thought is thus that every one really wishes for good, no one wishes for evil. "The object of every man's desire is some *good* to himself." To be really powerful means to be able to get good ; it is weakness, not power, to "do whatever you please," if the consequence is that you reap evil and not good (466a–469e).)

We now pass to the direct enunciation of the main ethical doctrine of the dialogue. This is elicited by the unmannerly remark of Polus that, whatever Socrates may be pleased to profess, he would certainly envy the man who could forfeit, imprison, or kill anyone he pleased. Socrates replies that he would not. The man who inflicts such things on another, even when they are righteously deserved, is not to be envied ; the man who inflicts them undeservedly is miserable and pitiable. What is more, he is more pitiable and miserable than the unfortunate innocent victim, since to commit injustice is much worse than to have to suffer it. Socrates himself would, of course, like Candide in a similar case,

---

[1] Note that in the course of this argument (at 468a) Socrates talks of things "participating" in good and "participating" in evil, using the very word (μετέχειν) which appears in connexion with the theory of Forms as technical for the relation between the "particular thing" and the "universal" we predicate of it. Since it cannot reasonably be doubted that the *Gorgias* is a considerably earlier work than the *Phaedo*, this creates a grave difficulty for those who suppose that the theory is an invention of Plato's own, expounded for the first time in the *Phaedo*.

" choose neither the one nor the other," but if he had to choose, he would much rather suffer the crime than commit it (469a–c). Polus treats this view as a ridiculous paradox. He admits that any man with a knife under his cloak might claim to be " powerful," in the sense that he can, like the autocrat, kill any one he has a mind to kill, but for one thing, the certainty of punishment. Impunity must be stipulated for as one of the conditions of " power," but a child could refute Socrates' view that it is only " better " to kill, banish, and confiscate at will when these acts are done " justly." One has only to consider the very latest example from contemporary life, that of Archelaus, who has made himself king in Macedonia. His whole career has been one of rebellion and murder, but he has gained a throne by it. By Socrates' theory he ought to be the most wretched of men, but he is, in fact, the happiest, and there is not a man in Athens, not even Socrates, who would not dearly like to change places with Archelaus (469c–471d). An appeal of this kind is, however, an *ignoratio elenchi* in the most literal sense. Even if every one but Socrates would be willing to go into the witness-box on behalf of Polus, it is possible that a solitary witness may be a witness to truth, and the testimony of numbers on the other side erroneous. Socrates will not consider his own case as established unless he can produce one solitary witness to it, the antagonist himself (472b). In other words, the appeal must be to argument and not to authority. The first step we must take is to define the issue at stake as precisely as we can. It is, in fact, the most important of all practical issues, the solution of the question, " Who is the truly happy man ? " Polus maintains that a man may be happy but wicked ; Socrates denies this. As a corollary, there is a secondary disagreement. Polus holds that the wicked man, to be happy, must go unpunished ; Socrates, that such a man is in any case unhappy, but more unhappy if he escapes punishment than if he suffers it, and he must try to convince Polus on both points (472d–474c).

The precise point of disagreement between the opposing views now receives a still more exact definition. Polus is still so far under the influence of current moral conventions that he admits at once that to commit a wrong is more " ugly " or " disgraceful " (αἴσχιον) than to suffer one, but he declines to draw the further inference that the " uglier " thing must also be the greater evil. He distinguishes, as Socrates refuses to do, between the good (ἀγαθόν) and the " fine " or " noble " (καλόν), and consequently also between the " ugly " (αἰσχρόν) and the evil (κακόν). The task of Socrates is to show that these distinctions are unreal The argument runs as follows. When we distinguish between " fine " bodies, colours, sounds, callings (ἐπιτηδεύματα) and others which are " ugly " or " base," our standard is always either " benefit " or " pleasure." By a " fine " shape or colour or sound, we mean one which is either serviceable or immediately agreeable in contemplation or both. The same thing holds good when we speak of " fine " or " noble "

usages (νόμοι) and callings in life, or of the " beauty " of a science.[1]
We mean that the usage or business or science in question either is
highly beneficial or " creates in the disinterested spectator a pleasing
sentiment of approbation," or both, a view which delights Polus
by its apparent Hedonistic implications.   It follows that by calling
anything " ugly " or " base," we must mean that it is either dis-
serviceable, or painful, or both.   Also, that when we say " A is
finer than B," we must mean that A is either more pleasant or
more useful than B, or both more pleasant and more useful.   And
when we call A " more ugly " than B, we mean that it is either
more harmful or more painful, or both.   Now we are agreed that
the commission of wrong (τὸ ἀδικεῖν) is an " uglier " thing than the
suffering of it (τὸ ἀδικεῖσθαι), and it is certainly not the case that it is
more painful to commit the crime than to have it committed on
you.   It must follow that the commission of the wrong is the more
harmful, i.e. the more evil course, the worse course.   Now no one
can rationally prefer an alternative which is at once the worse
and the more " ugly " of those open to him, and Socrates has thus
established his main point out of the mouth of his antagonist
(474c–476a).   We come now to the proof of the corollary.

We begin with a consideration of general logic.   Wherever
there is an agent (ποιῶν) there is a correlative "patient"
(πάσχων), a thing or person which is acted upon.   Also the
modality of the activity gives rise to strictly correlated qualifications (πάθη) in agent and patient.   If the agent, e.g., strikes a
sudden, or a severe, or a painful blow, the patient is suddenly,
severely, or painfully struck.   If the agent " cuts deep," the patient
is " deeply cut," and so forth.   Now to be punished for a crime is
to be the patient in a relation in which the inflictor of the penalty
is the agent.   Hence, if the agent inflicts the penalty deservedly or
justly, the patient undergoes it deservedly or justly.[2]   And, as
Polus does not deny, what is just is " fine," and therefore, as we
have seen, either good or pleasant.   Hence the man who is justly
punished has something good done to him (since no one will suggest
that he finds the punishment pleasant).   He is benefited by what
is done to him.   We may go on to specify the nature of the benefit.
Goods and evils may be classed under three heads : good or bad

[1] Note that the " induction " is exactly parallel with that of the famous
speech of Diotima (Symposium, 210a ff.), when the successive stages in the
ascent to the contemplation of Beauty are delight in one person's bodily beauty,
in bodily beauty universally, in beauty of soul and character, beauty of
occupations and usages (ἐπιτηδεύματα and νόμοι), beauty of sciences (ἐπιστῆμαι).
The more carefully the Platonic dialogues down to the Republic are studied,
the more of a piece we find their teaching to be, and the harder it becomes to
trace any " development " within them.

[2] Observe once more that the logical principle presupposed here of the
interconnexion between the modalities of correlates is that which is used in
the Republic to establish the reality of the distinction between the " parts in
the soul "(Rep. iv. 438b–e).   Both passages presuppose the existence of a
good deal of recognized logical doctrine as early as the time of the Archi-
damain war.

conditions of fortune (χρήματα), of body, of soul. A bad condition of fortune is poverty; of body, weakness, disease, deformity. The corresponding bad state of soul is wickedness (ἀδικία), and admittedly wickedness is the " ugliest " of the three. Yet it is certainly not more *painful* to be wicked than to be destitute or physically ill. By our preceding reasoning, therefore, it must be very much more evil or harmful. Badness of soul is thus the very greatest evil to which a man is exposed, and thus we get back to the fundamental principle of the whole Socratic ethics (476b–477e).[1]

One further step remains to be taken. There is an " art " which covers each of the three kinds of evil. Business (χρηματιστική) releases us from poverty, medicine from physical disease, " justice " administered by a competent judge from wickedness. The judge who passes sentence on the criminal is thus a physician of the soul, and his calling is a " finer " one than that of the healer of the body, because he cures a graver disease. In both cases the process of treatment is disagreeable but salutary for us. And again, in both cases, the happiest condition is to be in bodily or spiritual health, and so not to need the physician. But in both also, the man who is cured of a grave disease by a sharp treatment is much less badly off than the man who has the disease without receiving the cure. Thus a man like Archelaus who lifts himself by successful crime above all possibility of correction is like a man with a deadly disease who refuses to submit to the surgeon. The claim advanced for rhetoric, then, that it enables its possessor to " get off " when he is called to account for his misdeeds, is wholly vain. The best use a man who has fallen into crime could make of eloquence would be to expend it in denouncing himself and ensuring that he shall receive from the judge whatever chastisement may be needed to restore his soul to health. If eloquence is to be used to enable the criminal to " get off " the penalties of his misdeeds, it would be appropriate to reserve this employment of it for the case of our mortal enemies, as the deadliest injury we can inflict (477e–481b).

So far we have been concerned simply with an emphatic statement of the thesis that to do wrong is always worse than to suffer it, with the inevitable corollary that it is worse to do wrong with impunity than to be punished. With the opening of the third scene of Plato's drama we proceed to the application of these moral principles to the theory of statesmanship and government. That this application is the principal theme of the dialogue is indicated both by the fact that this part of the work is longer than both the others together, and by the introduction of a new spokesman whose case is presented with an unmistakable gusto quite absent from all that has gone before. The new speaker is a certain Callicles of Acharnae, of whom we learn little more than that he has recently begun to aspire to a prominent place in Athenian public life. He is

---

[1] Note the assumption of the threefold classification of goods as goods of soul, body, and "estate," as something quite familiar (*Gorg.* 477a ff.). This too, then, is clearly pre-Academic.

one of the very few characters in Plato's dialogues of whose historical reality we have no independent evidence, but it should be clear from the very vigour with which his character is drawn that he is a genuine man of flesh and blood. His intervention at once gives a more realistic touch to the dramatic picture and lifts the argument to a distinctly higher level. Polus was not only half-hearted in his professed rejection of conventional moral convictions, but also wanting in moral seriousness. He had nothing more inspiring to say in support of his eulogy of the " tyrant " than that it is a pleasant thing to be able to gratify all your passions without apprehension of consequences. Clearly, established morality is in no danger from the assaults of worldlings of this type, least of all when they are mere literary gentlemen talking for talking's sake. Callicles is quite another matter. His morality, like Nietzsche's, may be an inverted one, but it is one with which he is in downright earnest. He has a definite ideal which carries him off his feet, and, though it is a false ideal, Plato plainly means to make us feel that there is a certain largeness about it which gives it a dangerous fascination. To be fascinated by it, indeed, you need to have a certain greatness of soul ; it is notable that Callicles himself is wholly above the appeal to the mere enjoyability of being able to gratify ignoble cupidities, of which Polus had made so much. The ideal he is defending is that of the men of action for action's sake, the Napoleons and Cromwells, and it is his conviction that there is a genuine moral right on which the ideal rests. His imagination has been fascinated by the vision of a Nature whose law is that " the weakest goes to the wall," and he sees the life of human societies in the light of this vision. He is as earnest as Carlyle in his conviction that superior ability of any kind gives the moral right to use the ability according to your own judgment and without scruples. Hence he feels that in rejecting " conventionalism " in morals he is not rejecting morality itself ; he is appealing from a petty and confined morality of local human conventions to an august morality of " Nature " or " things-as-they-are." The case for the partisans of φύσις in the fifth-century dispute about φύσις and νόμος could not well be argued more persuasively, and it is Plato's purpose that it shall be argued with the maximum of persuasiveness with a view to its thorough refutation.

If Socrates is in earnest and his theory is true, Callicles says, the whole of our actual social life is organized on wrong lines ; our whole conduct is " topsy-turvy." Socrates does not deny this, but replies that he and Callicles are lovers of two very different mistresses, " philosophy " and the Athenian democracy. Socrates' mistress, " philosophy," has taught him to speak her language, and, unlike the mistress of Callicles, she always holds the same language. It is she, not her lover, whom Callicles will have to refute.[1] Callicles

---

[1] 481d.   Here comes in the humorous reference to the mortal " sweetings " of Socrates and Callicles respectively, Alcibiades and Demus, son of Pyrilampes. We know from Aristophanes (*Wasps*, 98) that Demus was the fashion-

thinks the task will not be difficult if once we make the distinction between mere " convention " and Nature, or " reality." Polus had only been silenced because he had not the courage to say what he really thought. He deferred to the tradition of the average respectable man by saying that it is " uglier " to commit a wrong than to suffer one. But this is a mere convention of weaklings, set up for their own protection. In " reality " to commit a wrong or aggression is noc the " ugly " thing ; the " ugly " thing is to have it committed on you. It is weaklings, slaves, persons who cannot stand up for themselves like men, who have to " put up " wrongs ; the strong are aggressive and commit what the conventions of the weak call " wrongs." If we look at φύσις, " things-as-they-are," we see that the stronger animal regularly pushes the weaker aside. Human life displays the same features, if we look at it on the large scale. By what right, for example, but that of the stronger did Darius attack the Scythians or Xerxes the Greeks ? Their proceedings may have been unlawful by the standard of the self-interested conventions of the weak, but they had Nature's right—the right of the strong to impose his will on the weak—on their side ; indeed, the conqueror is acting in strict accord with " Nature's νόμος " [1] in disregarding our paltry human νόμοι. When a really strong man—in fact, the Übermensch—appears, he will soon tear up our " contracts " and " formulae," and prove himself what he really is " by right of nature," the master of us all, as Pindar hinted in his well-known eulogy of the piratical feat of Heracles who drove the cows of Geryones " without leave asked or price paid." [2]

able beauty at Athens in the year 422. So far the jest makes for giving the *Gorgias* a dramatic date in the Archidamian war. But the supposed relations between Socrates and Alcibiades could also be used playfully in the *Symposium*, the assumed date of which is the year 416, so that the argument is not conclusive. If Socrates is thinking of the profession of the " Paphlagonian," to the personified Attic Demus in Aristophanes (*Knights*, 732, φιλῶ σ', ὦ Δῆμ', ἐραστής τ' εἰμὶ σός), this would also make for the earlier date.

[1] *Gorg.* 483*e*, κατὰ νόμον γε τὸν φύσεως. The first occurrence, so far as I know, in extant literature, of the ominous phrase " law of Nature." Callicles, of course, intends the words to be paradoxical—" a convention, if you like, but Reality's convention, not a human device."

[2] *Gorg.* 484*b*. I agree with Wilamowitz that the misquotation by which the MSS. made Callicles credit Pindar with saying that νόμος ἄγει βιαιῶν τὸ δικαιότατον " does violence to the most righteous claim " (whereas the poet wrote δικαιῶν τὸ βιαιότατον, " makes the most high-handed action just ") comes from Plato and should not be " corrected," as it has been by all the editors. (Callicles expressly says that he does not know the lines accurately.) But I doubt the cogency of the far-reaching inferences, including one as to the date of composition of the dialogue, which Wilamowitz bases on the misquotation. I should conjecture that Plato makes it quite deliberately, and that the verses had been actually quoted in this form by the champions of φύσις against νόμος in the fifth century. We must remember that in the time of Socrates there were no " official " texts at Athens, even of the Attic dramatists ; still less would it be possible to secure the text of a foreign poet against misquotation. In the *Apologia Socratis* of Libanius (fourth century A.D.) Anytus is represented as having made a point of this particular misquotation at the trial of Socrates. This probably means, as Wilamowitz holds, that the complaint occurred in the pamphlet of Polycrates against Socrates, published some

As for what Socrates has said about the lessons of philosophy, philosophy is a graceful accomplishment in a young man, but to take it in earnest in mature life is ruin.   It unfits a man for the life of action, leaves him ignorant of the laws of the community, the principles of public and private business, and the real passions of his fellow-men, like Amphion in the *Antiope* of Euripides.   One should cultivate philosophy up to a certain point, when one is a lad, but a grown man should lay it aside with the toys of his boyhood.   It is unmanly in a man of ability and ripe years to take no part in affairs and sit whispering " with a parcel of lads in a corner."[1]   Callicles pushes the point " in a spirit of friendship " ; Socrates is a man of admirable natural parts, but his way of life has left him at the mercy of anyone who wishes to do him a harm. If he were falsely accused on a capital charge, he would be quite incapable of making an effective defence—more's the pity (481c–486d).   Socrates professes himself delighted to have such an opponent to deal with, a man who is at once " educated," sincere (as is shown by the fact that his professed view of the proper place of philosophy in man's life is one which Socrates knows him to hold in common with several distinguished associates), and perfectly frank in speaking his mind without any deference to the conventions. If we can convince a man with these qualities of the soundness of our view of life, there can be no reasonable doubt of its truth. But first we must be quite clear on the point that, in the doctrine of Callicles, " better " is a mere synonym of " stronger " and " worse " of " weaker."   If this is granted, as it is, then, since " the many " are stronger than one man, *their* conventional usages are the usages of the stronger, that is to say, of the better, and should be regarded as the " naturally fine " (κατὰ φύσιν καλά).   But *their* convention is just what Callicles has been denouncing, the convention that aggression is wrong and that to commit it is " uglier " than to suffer it.   Thus the antithesis between " nature " and " convention " on which Callicles had based his argument is unsound. This, says Callicles, is mere catching at a word.   He never meant by the " stronger " (κρείττους) those who are merely superior in muscle and brawn (ἰσχυρότεροι).   A *canaille* of slaves would, at that rate, be stronger and better than the " strong man."   By the " stronger " he really meant " the wiser " (φρονιμώτεροι), the " men of parts."   " Natural right " is that " the better and wiser should rule and have the advantage over (πλέον ἔχειν) the worse " (486d–490a).

years after 399 B.C.   But the complaint cannot have been based on our passage, where it is Callicles, not Socrates, who misquotes.
    [1] *Gorg.* 485d 7.   Plato has sometimes been thought to have fallen here into attributing his own way of life in the Academy to Socrates.   But (a) it is most unlikely that the Academy existed when the *Gorgias* was written ; (b) from Plato's account it appears that most of the conversations of Socrates with his young friends *were* held " in a corner," in places like the gymnasium of the Lyceum or the *palaestra* of Taureas, so that Callicles' language is perfectly appropriate.

But what exactly may this mean ? If food and drink are to be distributed to a company of men of varying physique, and there is just one physician among them, he is certainly the "wisest" in matters of diet, and it may be reasonable that he should regulate the distribution by his orders; but is he to get the biggest ration, even if he should be the greatest invalid of the party? Should the weaver always have the biggest and finest clothes or the maker of shoes the biggest shoes and most of them ? Naturally not ; Callicles really means that the "strong" are men with the intelligence to know how a city may be "well administered," and the daring to carry out their designs (οἳ ἂν εἰς τὰ τῆς πόλεως πράγματα φρόνιμοι ὦσι, ὄντινα ἂν τρόπον εὖ οἰκοῖτο, καὶ μὴ μόνον φρόνιμοι ἀλλὰ καὶ ἀνδρεῖοι, ἱκανοὶ ὄντες ἃ ἂν νοήσωσιν ἐπιτελεῖν, 491b). It is right that such men should be sovereign in the State and "have the advantage" (πλέον ἔχειν) of their subjects.

Should we add that the best men are also sovereigns over themselves in the popular phrase, i.e. can govern their own passions ? No ; for in the nature of things the great man is one who has great passions and is intelligent and daring enough to secure them full gratification. The popular commendation of temperance is a mere trick by which the weaklings of the "herd," who have not manhood enough to live the best kind of life themselves, enslave their "natural superiors" (492a). If a man is born to a throne, or has the manhood to win his way to a throne, it would be base and bad in him not to rise above the conventional "temperance" and "justice" of the herd, and reap the full benefit of his capacity for himself and his friends. In the capable, lawless self-will (τρυφὴ καὶ ἀκολασία καὶ ἐλευθερία, 492c) are virtue and happiness ; regard for the "unreal catchwords" (τὰ παρὰ φύσιν συνθήματα) of the vulgar is contemptible. Thus the ideal of Callicles, like that of Nietzsche, is the successful cultivation of the *Wille zur Macht*, and his "strong man," like Nietzsche's, is a being of the type of Caesar Borgia as conceived in popular legend.[1]

The thesis of Callicles and the moralists of the "will to power" then is that one "ought" (δεῖ) to have violent desire and gratify it to the full ; to "want nothing" is the condition of a stone. But perhaps, as Euripides said, what we call life is really death. There is a rival view, developed by a certain wise man of Italy, that the tale of those who are condemned in the underworld to draw water in leaky pitchers is an apologue descriptive of the death-in-life

[1] Cf. Blake, *Marriage of Heaven and Hell*:." Those who restrain Desire do so because theirs is weak enough to be restrained ; and the restrainer or Reason usurps its place and governs the unwilling. And being restrained, it by degrees becomes passive, till it is only the shadow of Desire." The recently discovered Oxyrhynchus fragments of Socrates' contemporary, Antiphon "the sophist," have revealed to us one of the quarters in which these conceptions found literary expression in the age of the Archidamian war. It is, I believe, of Antiphon among others that Plato is thinking when he makes Glaucon declare that this same theory is widely current in his own circle (*Rep.* ii. 358b).

of the service of the passions. The leaking pitcher, or sieve, is
" the part of the soul in which our desires are " ; the more gratification you give them, the more they crave, and this impossibility
of ever contenting them shows the intrinsic absurdity of the
attempt.[1] And it is clear that if one had to fill a number of vessels
from a few scanty springs, a man who did not care whether his
vessels were sound or cracked, and who allowed a vessel to run over,
would have a very difficult task. The man who made sure that
his pitchers were sound and that none of them ran over would be
much more successful. Callicles, however, thinks this simile
misleading. When the vessel has been filled, you can get no more
enjoyment out of the process of " filling " it ; the enjoyment
($\dot\eta\delta o\nu\dot\eta$) depends on the continuance of the flow. To get it, you
must always have room for " more " to flow in (494b).[2] (Callicles
thus assumes the psycho-physical theory according to which pleasure
is or accompanies—the theory hardly distinguishes these alternatives—the " filling-up " or making good of a process of " depletion " in the organism, pain the process of " depletion " itself.
The doctrine is familiar to us from Plato's acceptance of it, so far
as the satisfaction of physical appetites are concerned, in the
Republic and Philebus, and Aristotle's vigorous polemic against it
in the Nicomachean Ethics. Plato rejects it, except for these cases,
and the rejection of it is the basis of the important distinction of the
Philebus between " pure " or " neat " and " mixed " pleasures.
It is taught more unreservedly by the Pythagorean Timaeus at
Tim. 64a–65b, and we see from Aristotle's polemic that it was fully
accepted by Speusippus and the extreme anti-Hedonists of the
Academy. Its origin is pretty clearly to be found in the medical
doctrine of Alcmaeon, according to which all disease is disturbance
of the state of $\iota\sigma o\nu o\mu\dot\iota\alpha$ (" constitutional balance ") between the
hot, the cold, the moist, and the dry in the organism. The im-
mediate assumption of Callicles that $\dot\eta\delta o\nu\dot\eta$ and $\pi\lambda\dot\eta\rho\omega\sigma\iota\varsigma$ may

---

[1] Gorg. 498a–c. Note (1) that, as Burnet says, the allusion to the Italian
" sage " seems plainly meant for Philolaus or some contemporary Pythagorean ; (2) that the unexplained mention of " the part of the soul in which
the $\dot\epsilon\pi\iota\theta\upsilon\mu\dot\iota\alpha\iota$ are " presupposes the doctrine of the " tripartite soul " more
fully explained in Rep. iv., which must thus be, as there is much in the
Republic itself to indicate, of Pythagorean origin, as Posidonius is known to
have asserted (Burnet, Early Greek Philosophy[3], 278, n. 2). It is evidence of
the same thing that the doctrine is taught also in Plato by the Italian Pythagorean Timaeus, who cannot be supposed to have learned it from Socrates
just before delivering his own discourse. (3) The tale of the cracked pitchers
is not connected by Plato with the Danaïds. His version represents it as
describing the future destiny of the " uninitiated " ; this suggests Orphic
provenance.

[2] Cf. Hobbes, Leviathan, c. xi. : " There is no such Finis ultimus (utmost
ayme) nor Summum Bonum (greatest Good) as is spoken of in the Books of
the old Morall Philosophers. Nor can a man any more live, whose Desires
are at an end, than he, whose Senses and Imaginations are at a stand. . . .
So that in the first place, I put for a generall inclination of all mankind, a
perpetuall and restlesse desire of Power after power, that ceaseth onely in
Death."

be equated shows us that this doctrine was a commonplace in cultivated circles of the age of Socrates.)

Obviously, if happiness depends on such a process of unending
" filling-up," it demands a similarly unending process of " depletion."
If water is always to be running into the pitcher, it must also be
always running out at the cracks. Would it then be intense happiness to have a continual itch, provided one could go on endlessly
getting the gratification of chafing the itching place ? You must
admit this if you mean to be serious with the theory.[1] What is
more, the life of a catamite must be eminently happy, if he can only
get a perpetual series of satisfactions for his unnatural *prurigo*. For
all his " freedom from convention," Callicles objects to this particular " transvaluation of values," but you cannot avoid it so
long as you persist in identifying good with pleasant. To condemn
any kind of gratification, you must distinguish good from pleasant,
and this Callicles admits he cannot consistently do (495*a*).

We proceed next to consider the identification of good and bad
with pleasure and pain on its merits. Two difficulties occur to us
at the very outset. (*a*) Good and bad are " contraries " ; you
cannot predicate both at once of the same subject, nor can you
deny both at once. A man cannot have both predicates at once, nor
" get rid " of both at once. Pleasure and pain are not opposed in
this way. *E.g.*, when a hungry man is satisfying his hunger by a
square meal, he feels at once the pleasure of appeasing the hunger
and the painfulness of the still unappeased hunger which urges
him to eat more. When his hunger is sated and he leaves off, the
pleasure and the pain are both at an end. But it is just at this
point, where both the pleasure and the pain are over, that the man
reaches the good to which eating ministers, the restoration of normal
equilibrium in his organism.[2] (*b*) Callicles himself makes a dis
tinction between " good " men and " bad " ones, the " good,"
according to him, being the intelligent and bold, the " bad " the
silly or timorous. He must hold, therefore, that good is " present
to "[3] the former and not to the latter. But he cannot deny that
fools and cowards feel pleasure and pain at least as keenly as the

---

[1] Dante, it may be remembered, regards such a life as a torment for the
damned, and the worst of the damned (*Inferno*, xiv. 40, xv. 131, xxix. 76 ff.).

[2] The presupposed doctrine is that explained at length in the *Philebus*,
that the satisfactions of appetite attend on the process (γένεσις) by which
a " depletion " of the organism is made good. Thus they are (*a*) preceded
by a painful consciousness of " want " (ἔνδεια), and (*b*) are not, even while
they last, wholly pleasurable. Their piquancy and intensely exciting character depends on the tension between satisfied want and the persistence of
still unsatisfied want. This is why these pleasures are " mixed," not " neat "
(καθαραί).

[3] *Gorg.* 497*e*, " We call good men good in virtue of the presence of good
things " to them (ἀγαθῶν παρουσίᾳ). παρουσία has here precisely the sense
it bears when used in connexion with the forms in the *Phaedo*. The predicate
" good " is predicable of a certain man because he " has " goodness of some
kind or other, is " possessed of " good. On a Hedonist theory this means that
" X is good " always implies " X is enjoying pleasure," and it is this implication Socrates is calling in question.

intelligent and daring, if not more keenly, since cowards, for example, seem to feel more distress in the face of the enemy and more delight at their disappearance than brave men do. Thus there are empirical objections to the identification of pleasure with good (495c–499b).

Callicles extricates himself for the moment in the only way possible to a Hedonist in a " fix." Like Mill, he declares it obvious that " pleasures differ in quality"; there are better pleasures and worse pleasures, and it is unfair in Socrates, as Mill said it was in his opponents, to neglect the distinction. For example, a pleasure which contributes to bodily health is good, one which is detrimental to health is bad, and the same thing is true of pains. The rule for choice is that we should choose the good pleasures and pains and avoid the bad ones. In fact, Callicles is prepared to admit now that pleasure is a *means* to good (500a). But the right selection of pleasures will demand a " competent expert "; not every one can be trusted to make it.

We are thus brought face to face with the final problem raised by our dialogue. Socrates and Callicles stand respectively for two antithetical ideals in life, the one for the " life of philosophy," the other for the " life of action " as followed by a man of affairs in the Athenian democracy. The choice between these competing ideals is the ultimate practical problem, and it is this issue which is to be decided by the " competent judge." The distinction we have been forced to make between the pleasant and the good shows that the qualifications of the competent judge must not be based (as Mill tries to base them) on an empirical acquaintance with the flavours of pleasure (a thing of which the empiric understands neither the character nor the cause, 501a), but on a true τέχνη, which knows about the *good* of the soul as medicine does about the good of the body ; in fact, Socrates means, moral science is to prescribe the soul's regimen as medicine prescribes the regimen of the body (501b–c).[1]

Now there is certainly one class of " rhetoricians," *i.e.* practitioners of the use of language to work on men's feelings and imaginations, who are empirics of the type of the confectioner, namely, the poets. Their standard is always simply the " taste " of their public. They aim at pleasing this taste, and incidentally gaining their own advantage by doing so, without troubling themselves in the least whether their productions will make any one a better man. And what is poetry, when you divest it of the addition of tune, rhythm, and metre, but rhetoric—the effective use of language ? Has the rhetoric of an Athenian politician any saner basis ? Does the politician aim at the improvement of his public, or merely at gratifying their moods (501d–502e) ? [2]

[1] Thus Socrates disposes in advance of Mill's preposterous appeal to a jury of pleasure-tasters devoid of all ethical preferences. From his point of view, to consult judges with such a " qualification " about pleasures would be like selecting medicines by the agreeableness of their tastes.

[2] The whole indictment of poetry in the *Republic* is contained in principle in what is said here about its character as a " mere mechanic " trick of pleasing

Callicles thinks that, though the suggestion of Socrates may be true about some statesmen, there are others who really are guided by regard for the good of their fellow-citizens. He could not say so much for any living man of affairs, but it is true of the great men of the past, from Themistocles to the recently dead Pericles. They *did* make Athenians " better " by their careers. Socrates will not admit this. Themistocles and the rest made Athens great, if it is greatness to gratify all your cravings and passions, good and bad alike. But the scientific practitioner in any department must have an ideal before him into accord with which he sets himself to bring the material on which he works, as, *e.g.*, the physician has an ideal standard of health which he tries to reproduce in his patients. Has there ever been a statesman in Athens who, in the same way, has had an ideal of character, " goodness of soul," and set himself to promote it in the citizens ? The physician, unlike his counterfeit the confectioner, aims at producing in a human body a definite " order and regulation " (τάξις καὶ κόσμος) ; the statesman, if he is more than a mere unprincipled empiric, should aim at doing the same thing for the human soul. This is to say that his purpose should be to produce " temperance and justice " (σωφροσύνη καὶ δικαιοσύνη) in the souls of his public. The object of a statesman and orator *secundum artem* is the production of national character. If the ἐπιθυμίαι of the citizens, the " national " aspirations and ambitions, are unhealthy and evil, the public man who is not a mere " toady " will aim at repressing them, and so making the national soul " better " by " chastisement " (505*b*–*c*).

Callicles is so disgusted with this return of the argument to the apparent paradox which had led to his intervention in the discussion, that Socrates is left to act as respondent to his own questions as he draws to his formal conclusion. Good is not the same thing as pleasure ; it depends universally on " order and rightness and *art*," and shows itself in a condition of " regulation and orderliness." This means that the temperate or " disciplined " soul is the good soul, the " unchastened " (ἀκόλαστος), " undisciplined " soul is bad. The former acts " appropriately to the situation " in all the situations of life, and consequently acts well, does well, and is " happy " ; the latter, not meeting the situations of life with the appropriate responses, is not merely bad but unhappy, especially if it is not held in check by " chastisement." These are the principles on which public no less than private conduct should be organized ; the life of the " superman " or of the " superstate " is simply that of a bandit, and a bandit has the hand of gods and men against him. He does not know how to " communicate " or " go shares " (κοινωνεῖν), but all social life depends on " communica-

and amusing   That poets aim merely at pleasing the taste of an audience, good or bad, was a current view. Herodotus uses it (ii. 116) to explain why Homer adopted a " false version " of the story of Helen, Euripides (*H.F.* 1341–6) to discredit the whole poetical mythology. In the δισσοὶ λόγοι it occurs more than once as an objection to the appeal to poets on questions of morality that their standard is ἀδονά, not ἀλάθεια.

tion." Indeed the "wise" (the Pythagorean men of science) say that "communication" or "reciprocity" ($\kappa o\iota\nu\omega\nu\acute{\iota}a$) is the basis not only of all human affections and moral virtues, but of the whole physical order of heaven and earth. "Geometrical equality" is the great law of the universe (508a),[1] and this is why the "wise" call the universe $\kappa\acute{o}\sigma\mu o\varsigma$, "the *order* of things." In setting up $\pi\lambda\epsilon o\nu\epsilon\xi\acute{\iota}a$, "going beyond the limit," as a principle for life, Callicles has forgotten his geometry. But if these convictions are sound, we must also admit Socrates' paradox that the best use an offender can make of rhetoric is to ensure his own conviction. Callicles was right in saying that Socrates' rule of life left him at the mercy of an aggressor, but wrong in thinking the position "ugly." The "ugliness" is not in the suffering but in the perpetrating of aggression. To escape this conclusion you must show that the principle that "wickedness is the greatest of evils to its possessor" is false (509e).

To commit wrong, then, is the worst evil which can befall a man ; to have to submit to it, though a lesser evil, is also an evil. In neither case will the mere purpose to avoid the evil avail of itself to secure its end. To avoid being wronged you also need "power" or "strength." And, since we long ago agreed on the principle that wrong-doing is "involuntary," a consequence of error, you need to secure yourself against it by acquiring some "power or $\tau\acute{\epsilon}\chi\nu\eta$, organized knowledge" (510a).[2] If you want to avoid being wronged, you must either be an "autocrat" or a friend of the sovereign body, whatever it may be ($\acute{\epsilon}\tau a\hat{\iota}\rho o\varsigma$ $\tau\hat{\eta}\varsigma$ $\acute{\upsilon}\pi a\rho\chi o\acute{\upsilon}\sigma\eta\varsigma$ $\pi o\lambda\iota\tau\epsilon\acute{\iota}a\varsigma$, 510a). In an autocracy this means that you must be a "creature" of the autocrat; in a democracy, like Athens, you must make yourself a favourite with your "master" the populace, and conform yourself to its moods and prejudices. In neither case have you secured yourself against the greater evil of committing wrong. On the contrary, to be a favourite with either autocrat or populace you must sink to their moral level and sympathize with their injustices. Callicles thinks this only sensible, for the "leviathan" will kill you if you do not humour it. But this plea rests on the assumption that life at any cost and on any terms is supremely desirable, even at the cost of moral corruption. It amounts to basing the high claims made for rhetoric on the view that rhetoric is an art of saving your skin. No doubt it is ; the politician is constantly saving his skin by his plausible speech. But swimming

---

[1] $\iota\sigma\acute{o}\tau\eta\varsigma$ $\acute{\eta}$ $\gamma\epsilon\omega\mu\epsilon\tau\rho\iota\kappa\acute{\eta}$, *i.e. proportion*, "equality of *ratio*." It is called so, in contradistinction to "arithmetical" or absolute "equality," because of the part it plays in the geometry of "similar" figures. The "wise" meant are the Pythagoreans who were the discoverers of the various elementary "progressions," or, as the Greeks called them, $\acute{a}\nu a\lambda o\gamma\acute{\iota}a\iota$, "proportions," and gave the name $\kappa\acute{o}\sigma\mu o\varsigma$ to what had before them been called $o\acute{\upsilon}\rho a\nu\acute{o}\varsigma$. For the thought we might compare Kant's insistence on the principle of *Gemeinschaft* and reciprocal interconnexion in nature.

[2] Cf. *Ep*. vi, 322d, where Plato recommends Erastus and Coriscus to the "protection" of Hermias on much the grounds here spoken of.

and seamanship save your skin too, and are not thought of supreme moment for a gentleman's education. An ordinary skipper will bring you, your family, and all your belongings safe from Egypt or the Pontus, but he asks a very modest fare, and his calling is thought a very humble one. And this is as it should be, for the skipper has really done a man who is hopelessly diseased in body or soul no real service ; it would be better for such a man to go to the bottom (511c–512b). So an ordinary engineer may save the lives of a whole community by the machines he builds, but a man like Callicles regards the engineer as a " base mechanic " and would not dream of intermarriage with his family. If mere life is the highest good, why should not all these " mechanics " advance the same claims which are put forward on behalf of rhetoric (512c–d) ? The truth is that the important thing is not to live long, but to live well ; is a man likely, or is he not, to attain that end by conforming himself to the spirit and temper of the community, e.g. of the Athenian δῆμος, as he must do if he means to be a " public man " (512e–513c) ?

" Impressive, but not convincing," is the verdict of Callicles on all this. Convincing or not, however, it is plain that *if* we aim at a statesmanship which is more than successful " parasitism " [1] (κολακεία), a statesmanship which is a genuine *art* of " tendance of our fellow-citizens," our chief problem will be to promote national *character* ; it is no true service of the State to increase its wealth or power, unless its citizens are fitted by their character to use wealth or wield power [2] (514a). On the hypothesis, then, our fitness for the statesman's calling depends on our possession of a *science* (ἐπιστήμη), in fact, on our *knowledge* of moral values. Now an expert can establish his claim to be an expert in two ways : (*a*) by pointing out the master from whom he has learned his knowledge, (*b*) by pointing to the results in which his knowledge has been embodied. If a man can satisfy neither of these tests, we cannot take his claims to be an expert seriously. No one would give an appoint-

---

[1] We might perhaps use a biological analogy to bring out better the full meaning of the distinction between the κόλαξ and the genuine " craftsman " which runs all through the dialogue. The κόλαξ or " trencherman " of social life lives, and lives, according to the vulgar estimate, well by living on his patron (whom he really depraves by " pandering " to his vices), exactly as the parasitical organism fattens itself on the tissues of its unfortunate " host." So the empiric in statesmanship, the " opportunist," makes a " good thing " for himself of depraving the national character and lowering the national ideals. The best comment on the view Socrates takes of the influence of the " orators " on national life is the humorous caricature of the same thing in the scene of Aristophanes (*Knights*, 725 ff.) where the sausage-seller and the Paphlagonian bid against each other for the lucrative post of pimp-in-chief to Demus. Aristophanes and Socrates agree in their estimate of the νῦν πολιτικοί.

[2] Cf. the lesson, *e.g.*, of the *Euthydemus* that wealth and power are good or bad according as the " soul " which is to *use* them is good or bad. Note that there is once more a tacit allusion to the apologue of the " three lives." " Wealth " and " power " are the ends of the " body-loving " and " distinction-loving " lives respectively, ἐπιστήμη the end of the " philosophic " life.

ment as a public physician to a candidate who could not prove
that he had effected any cures as a private practitioner. So an
aspirant to statesmanship may fairly be expected to satisfy us
that he has " in private practice " made the souls or characters
of his fellow-men better. How do the famous public men of Athens,
from Miltiades to Pericles, stand this test (515*d*) ? It is Socrates'
conviction that one and all fail under it. Pericles, as every one is
saying, made the Athenians worse, not better ; he made them
" idle, cowardly, talkative, and greedy " (515*e*). The best proof
of this is the notorious fact that at the end of his career, they actually
turned on him and found him guilty of embezzlement.[1] The conviction was, to be sure, iniquitous, but whose " tendance " of the
animal *civis Atticus* had taught it these iniquitous ways ? The
" tendance " of Pericles himself (516*a–d*). He made the animal
" wilder," and this disposes of his claim to be a statesman. The
same is true of Cimon and Miltiades : the very wrongs they ended
by suffering from the δῆμος prove that they too had made their
" cattle " worse by their treatment (516*d–e*).[2] None of these
famous men was even skilled in the spurious " parasitic " kind of
rhetoric—for each of them ended by displeasing the common
patron (517*a*).

You may say that, after all, these must have been great men,
for their " public works " (*e.g.* the creation of the Athenian navy,
the building of the walls, docks, and the like) speak for them. And
this really proves that they were, so to say, good " domestics " or
" personal servants " of Demus ; they knew how to provide their
master with the things he desired. But what they did not know—
and true statesmanship consists in knowing just this—was how to
get him to desire what is really good (517*b*).[3] To call them statesmen is like calling a confectioner or a fancy baker a specialist in
hygiene and medicine ; it is to compare a subordinate " art,"
which makes things, with the master-art which " uses " them
aright (517*e*–518*c*). If a man made that confusion, his cooks and
confectioners would soon ruin his constitution, and he would lay
the blame for his want of wholesome appetite on the inferiority of
his present cook as compared with his old one. Callicles is making

---

[1] 515*e*, ταυτὶ γὰρ ἔγωγε ἀκούω κτλ. Socrates means that this is the verdict
to be heard on all sides now that Pericles is dead and his dominance is at an
end. He would " hear " this, of course, from many quarters. It is, *e.g.*, the
view of Aristophanes and apparently of the contemporary comic dramatists
generally. The statement that Pericles had made Athenians " lazy and
greedy " διὰ τὴν μισθοφορίαν refers, of course, to his establishment of the
dicasts' μισθός. The picture of Philocleon and his friends in the *Wasps* is
an admirable illustration of the point.

[2] Socrates would have the Old Comedy on his side in what he says about
Pericles ; the point about Miltiades and Cimon is made to show that the heroes
of Aristophanes and the anti-Pericleans are in the same condemnation.

[3] 515*e*, οὐδ' ἐγὼ ψέγω τούτους ὥς γε διακόνους εἶναι πόλεως. Pericles and the rest
have no claim to be " physicians of the commonwealth," but they were competent purveyors, major-domos, and butlers. So much Socrates will concede,
but no more.

precisely the same blunder. The real authors of the disorders of the " body politic " were the " statesmen " of the past who ruined the constitution of the public by filling it with " harbours and docks and such stuff, without justice and temperance." When the " cold fit " of the disorder arrives, the sufferer will lay the blame for his disorder on Alcibiades, or perhaps Callicles himself, who are at worst only minor contributors to the mischief.[1] When the public turns and rends one of its leaders in this fashion, he usually complains of its injustice. But the complaint is as ludicrous as that of the sophists who profess to teach their pupils " goodness," and then accuse them of cheating them of their fees. The very complaint shows that neither sophist nor politician can do what he professes to do ; the one cannot make his pupils " good," the other cannot promote the real good of the " people " (517b–520a). Of the two pretenders, there is a certain advantage on the side of the sophist. The art he caricatures, that of the legislator, is a nobler thing than the art of the judge, as that of the physical trainer who keeps the body fit is nobler than that of the physician who banishes disease. If either pretender really believed in himself, he would exercise his calling *gratis* ; a man who can make an individual or a people " good " has no need to take precautions against ungrateful or unfair treatment (520c–e).[2]

What, then, did Callicles mean when he recommended Socrates to take up " public life " ? Did he mean that Socrates should be a physician to the public or merely a " toady " and " body-servant " ? The truth is that Socrates himself is the only real statesman of his time, for he is the only Athenian who aims in his use of speech not at giving pleasure but at doing real good to those with whom he speaks. He may very possibly be dragged into court as a " corrupter of youth," and if that should happen, his condemnation is certain, for he would be the physician pleading against the confectioner before a jury of children of whom he had already spoken.[3] But he would die innocent of offence, and the dreadful thing is not to die, but to enter the unseen world with a soul laden with guilt (521a–522e).

[1] This allusion to a possible turning of the δῆμος against Alcibiades seems to make it clear that the supposed date of the conversation must at any rate be well before the event which fulfilled the prophecy—the scandal about the " profanation of the mysteries " in 415. Observe the contempt expressed by Callicles at 520a for the professional " teachers of goodness." This is strictly in keeping with his theories about the superman, since no one can teach you to be a superman ; you have to be born one.

[2] Is this an allusion to the anecdote told by later writers about Protagoras and his defaulting pupil ? Or, more probably, is not the story to which Plato alludes a contemporary jest into which the name of Protagoras was worked before the time of Aristotle ?

[3] We might at first be surprised to find Socrates at what seems to be an early stage in his career contemplating the possibility of prosecution for " corrupting the young." But we should compare *Apology,* 18b ff., where Socrates insists that the prejudice against him and his influence goes back to the old caricatures of the comic poets, who charged him with useless speculations and " making the worse argument appear the better."

The argument of the dialogue is now complete. We reach the climax of the Socratic ethics of the " tendance of the soul " with the declarations that statesmanship is nothing but the practice of this same " art " on the large scale, that its indispensable basis is knowledge of moral values, and that the apparent " mugwump " Socrates is in fact the one man of his age and city who is leading the real " active life," because he has himself, and tries to communicate to every one else, a moral faith and moral ideals. He alone, in a world of " opportunist " careerists, is doing work which will last, because he alone is building on a rock. What makes the *Gorgias* so important in spite of its *longueurs*, is that, more fully than any other dialogue, and with an intenser πάθος, it works out the application of the conception of " tendance of the soul " to the whole complicated business of life. Formally, the conversation is prolonged for a few pages, to give Socrates the opportunity to drive home the exceeding horror of sin by an imaginative myth of judgment after death, the earliest in order of composition of Plato's masterpieces in this kind. The basis of the story, in this case, seems more strictly Orphic and less Pythagorean than in the companion pictures of the *Republic* and *Phaedo*. The scenery, " the meadow where the three ways meet," [1] the judges before whom the dead appear, the original division of the universe into heaven, earth, and the underworld, used as the *motif* for the tale, are all familiar to us as features of the Orphic mythology. On the other hand, nothing is said of the Pythagorean reincarnation which plays so prominent a part in the eschatology of the *Republic*, *Phaedo*, and *Phaedrus*. This presumably means that that doctrine is no part of the serious convictions of Socrates or Plato, and this may be why Socrates expressly says at 524b that he accepts the present account of the judgment as true, without any warning, such as he gives in the *Phaedo*, against pressing its details.

The main thought of the myth is the impossibility of escaping the scrutiny of the eye of the divine judge. In the old days, men were judged while still in the body, and the stains and sores of the soul often escaped notice, especially when the party to be judged was a great man, who appeared with all the splendours of external pomp and circumstance. To prevent such mistakes, the judgment has now been placed after death, that the soul may appear at the tribunal naked, without the " tunic " of the body. This ensures that its destiny shall be decided by its worth, not by the station it has held on earth. We shall find Plato preaching the same doctrine of a divine judgment which neglects nothing and can make no

---

[1] The three ways are the roads which lead (*a*) from earth to " the meadow," (*b*) from the meadow to heaven, (*c*) from the meadow to hell. As usual, hell is depicted in the main as a purgatory for the not wholly depraved. A few incurables are detained there permanently as a warning to others, but these are chiefly " supermen " of the Napoleonic type. Ordinary human weakness is regarded as " curable." Not all " statesmen " take the road to destruction. Aristides " the just " is instanced as an example of a man who filled high office nobly and went " straight to heaven " (526b).

error, in the tenth book of the *Laws*, without any mythology at all. In the *Gorgias*, the point to notice is the tone of earnestness with which Socrates is made to profess the doctrine as his own personal faith. This representation is quite incompatible with the singular view that " the historic Socrates " was an agnostic on the problem of immortality. If Plato misrepresented his master in the matter, the misrepresentation did not begin with the *Phaedo*. He must have ended the *Gorgias* with a deliberate mystification.[1]

The Meno.—There are points of contact between the *Meno* and the *Gorgias* which make it convenient to consider them together, though the main purpose of the *Meno* connects it rather with two more mature dialogues, the *Phaedo* and the *Protagoras*, as well as with the *Apology*. The dramatic setting of the dialogue is of the simplest. It is a conversation between Socrates and the young Thessalian Meno, who is attended by at least one slave, broken by an interlude which brings on the scene the prominent politician Anytus, afterwards the instigator of the proceedings against Socrates. Where the conversation takes place we are not told, except that it is, of course, somewhere in Athens. The dramatic date can be readily fixed by reference to the facts about Meno recorded in Xenophon's *Anabasis*. Meno joined the expedition of Cyrus the younger against his brother Artaxerxes II at Colossae in the middle of March 401 B.C. (*Anab.* i. 2, 6), rendered the important service of being the first of the Greek adventurers to declare for Cyrus openly when the army had reached the Euphrates and its real objective became clear (*ibid*. i. 4, 13), and was present with

[1] I may here append a very brief statement about the conclusion which seems to me safest on the question of the dramatic date of the dialogue. As I have said, I think the tone of the reference to a possible revulsion of feeling against Alcibiades excludes any date later than about 416. The main difficulty to set against this conclusion is the free use made by both Callicles and Socrates of the *Antiope* of Euripides, which is assumed to be a familiar and popular work. The scholiast on Aristophanes' *Frogs* 53 refers to the play as " recently produced " at the time of production of the *Frogs* (405 B.C.), and implies that it was a later work than the *Andromeda* (produced in 412 along with the *Helena*, both of which are burlesqued by Aristophanes in the *Thesmophoriazusae*, a play of the year 411). Unless Plato has forgotten the real date of a play of which he probably saw the first performance, there must be some error in the scholiast's reckoning. The references to the actual state of affairs throughout the dialogue suggest that Pericles has not yet found a successor recognized as such by admirers like Callicles. The picture of the power actually wielded by the " orators " seems to me so completely in keeping with the tone of Aristophanes' *Knights* and *Wasps*, that I would suggest that the most suitable date is during the career of Cleon, somewhere about 424–422, or at most a little later. As the demagogues had been able to disgrace Pericles at the end of his life, 427 would be a possible date, but I think rather less likely. We need not suppose that Gorgias is in Athens for the first time, or that he had only came there once. Andron, the best known of the associates of Callicles, is specially connected for us with the events of 411–410 ; he had been a member of the " four hundred," but, like Critias, took a prominent part in the overthrow of that body, being the proposer of the psephism which " attainted " its leading spirit, the orator Antiphon. But in the *Gorgias*, no doubt, we are to think of him as, like Callicles, only just beginning his career.

the others at the battle of Cunaxa. The rivalry between Clearchus and Meno, after the battle, led directly to the capture of the principal Greek leaders by Tissaphernes and the death of Clearchus (*ibid.* ii. 5, 27 ff.). Meno, with the rest, was sent a prisoner to the Persian court, where he was executed after a year's confinement (*ibid.* ii. 6, 29). Xenophon, who was a fervid admirer of the stupid and brutal Clearchus, gives Meno the worst of characters. One may discount a great deal of this, but the general impression that the man was a spoilt and petulant boy, only half civilized, is borne out by Plato's dialogue. Xenophon does not mention Meno's age at death, but implies that he was still a mere lad (ἔτι ὡραῖος, he says) when he was put in charge of the 1500 men he brought to the expedition. Hence we shall hardly be far wrong if we suppose his presence in Athens to be connected with the forthcoming enterprise. This means that we must date it not long before his arrival in Colossae. We must thus think of Socrates as an old man, within two or three years of seventy, and of the conversation as taking place after the restoration of the democracy in 403, when Anytus was one of the two or three most powerful and respected public men. The *Meno* then, unlike any of the dialogues we have so far considered, is dated at a time which would be compatible with supposing Plato to have been actually present at the conversation and to be describing it from his own recollections.[1] The dialogue opens with an abruptness hardly to be paralleled elsewhere in the genuine work of Plato by the direct propounding of a theme for discussion ; there are not even the ordinary formalities of salutation. May we argue that this indicates that its composition belongs to the very earliest years of Plato's literary activity ? This would be an important consideration, since, as no one denies, the whole characteristic metaphysics of the *Phaedo*, the theory of forms and the doctrine of " reminiscence," are explicitly taught in the *Meno*. In any case there ought to be no doubt that the *Meno* is a cruder and earlier work than either of the two great dramatic dialogues with which it is most intimately connected, the *Phaedo* and the *Protagoras*, and this of itself would be enough to prove that the *Phaedo* is not, as has been supposed, a first publication of an important philosophical discovery.

The question raised by Meno (70a) is one directly suggested by the activity of Protagoras and the other " teachers of goodness " (ἀρετή). Can " goodness " be taught, or, if not, can it be acquired

[1] The *only* other " Socratic " discourses for which this would be *possible*, so far as I can see, are the *Apology* (where Plato mentions his own presence). *Theaetetus* and *Euthyphro*, (?) *Philebus*. It would consequently be possible for the *Sophistes* and *Politicus* also, though the fiction by which the *Theaetetus*, with which these dialogues are especially connected, is represented as read from notes made by Euclides is probably intended to suggest that Plato is not a κωφὸν πρόσωπον in these discourses. These facts suggest that, except in the case of the *Apology*, Plato means us to think of himself as absent even in the one or two instances when he might, so far as date goes, have been present : his intention is to suppress his own personality altogether.

by "*practice*"—is it ἀσκητόν? If it can be acquired neither by instruction nor by practice, is it " naturally " inborn, or how do we come by it ? This is just the point at issue between the champions of νόμος and the partisans of φύσις in the time of Socrates. (For the Socratic answer to the problem we need to go partly to the *Protagoras*, still more to the elaborate account of the training proposed for the " auxiliaries " and the " philosopher kings " of the *Republic*. Plato's own final position has to be learned from the educational sections of the *Laws*. At present it will be enough simply to state summarily the results reached in the *Republic*. There is no formal discussion of the problem in the dialogue, but the solution of it is given implicitly in the educational programme laid down in the course of books iii.–vii. Socrates' solution there depends on a *distinguo*. There are two distinct levels of " goodness," one which will be sufficient for the ordinary good citizen and even for the " auxiliaries," the executive force of society, and a higher, indispensable to the statesmen who have to direct the whole of the national life and determine its standard. For those whose business in life is to obey rules based on the ideals of the true statesman, all that is necessary is a discipline in absolute loyalty to the traditions in which the ideals are embodied, and this discipline is secured by the moulding of temper, taste, and imaginations described in *Republic* iii.–iv. Such an education, however, does not result in personal insight, but at best in loyalty to a noble rule of life taken on trust. The " goodness " of the classes who are " under authority " is thus not μαθητόν but ἀσκητόν, a result not of enlightenment but of discipline. But in the statesman who has to create the national tradition, something more is needed. He must know, as a matter of personal insight, what the true moral " values " are. The statesman is therefore required to possess a " philosophic " goodness, based on direct personal insight into the structure of the universe and man's place in that structure. Such insight can only be won by the mind which has been trained in arduous scientific thinking for itself, and is therefore " knowledge," and, like all knowledge, comes by " teaching "; but this teaching is no mere communication of " results." A man is not made a thinker of the first order by any imparting of " information," but by stimulating in him the power and the ambition to think for himself. This is why the one effective method of teaching in philosophy and science is the association of an older and a younger mind in the prosecution of an " original research.")

To return to the *Meno*. Meno's question, flung out in an airy way as though it could be disposed of in a sentence, cannot really be answered without facing one still more fundamental. We cannot expect to know how " goodness " is produced until we know what it is. And this is more than anyone at Athens, and most of all Socrates, professes to know. We are thus brought back to the problem of definition which has met us already in other dialogues (71c–d). According to Meno, this problem is no real problem at

all. Gorgias could have told Socrates what goodness is, or, if
Socrates has forgotten what Gorgias has to say, Meno, whose
admirer Aristippus had been a patron of Gorgias, can remind him.
There are a variety of " goodnesses " (ἀρεταί). The goodness of a
man is to have capacity for public affairs, to be a valuable ally and
a dangerous enemy, and to know how to hold his own ; that of a
woman is to look after " the home " and to obey her husband ; and
there are yet other goodnesses appropriate to a child, an elderly
man, a slave, and so forth. In fact, every age of life and every
social station has its own peculiar goodness (72a). (Thus we have
once more the confusion of definition with enumeration.) These
commonplaces, however, do not answer our question. We want
to know what the οὐσία, or essentia of " goodness " is, and this
must be something in respect of which the " goodnesses " of male and
female, old and young, bond and free, do not differ, a " single
identical pattern " (ἐν εἶδος, 72c), in virtue of which the common
name ἀρετή is bestowed.[1] Consider the analogy of health or
strength. One might say, as Meno has done, that there is " health
in a man " and " health in a woman," " manly strength " and
" womanly strength," and that they have their differences. And
Meno himself must admit that " in respect of being health " or
" in respect of being strength " masculine health and strength
do not differ from feminine.[2] There is a single " pattern " of
health (ἐν πανταχοῦ εἶδος) in all healthy beings, and similarly
with strength. So, since we can speak of a good man and of a good
woman, there must be some one " pattern " of goodness in man
and woman, young and old. (In the language of to-day, " goodness " must be a determinable, of which the " goodness of a man,"
the " goodness of a woman," and the rest are the determinants.)
We may note that this position, which arises at once from the
application of the theory of forms to human conduct, is of first-

[1] The " something which is the same in all cases " and justifies the use of a
common name is successively spoken of as οὐσία (what the thing is, its
quid) (72b), as a single εἶδος, pattern (72c, d, e), as something which " pervades "
all the cases, διὰ πάντων ἐστίν (74a), is the same " over them all," ἐπὶ πᾶσι ταὐτόν
(75a). All these are names for the objective reality indicated by the employment of a common predicate of many subjects, and the abundance of them
presupposes the existence of an already rather elaborate logical doctrine
founded on the metaphysics of forms. Linguistically, οὐσία is the most
interesting of them, since in this sense it is a loan-word from Ionic science ;
the only familiar meaning in the Attic of the fifth century was the legal one,
" estate," " property, personal or real." On the probability that the philosophical meaning of the word comes from the Pythagoreans, see Burnet's note
on Euthyphro, 10a 7. As to εἶδος, criticism has not shaken my conviction
that its philosophical use is a development from its source in Pythagorean
mathematics—" regular figure."

[2] That in a sense there is male health and female health is clear from the
simple fact that there are professors of and treatises on gynaecology. But
the εἶδος of health, namely, that it is " equilibrium in the constituents of the
organism," holds good for both sexes. The thesis that the " goodness " of a
woman is the same as that of a man was ascribed to Socrates also by Aeschines
in his Aspasia, and is thus a genuine tenet of the Socratic ethics (cf. Burnet,
art. SOCRATES, in Encyclopaedia of Religion and Ethics, xi. 667).

rate importance for both logic and ethics. In logic it means that there is no third alternative between realism and nominalism. A universal, unambiguously employed, signifies something or it does not. If it signifies anything, that something is not an arbitrary fiction of my mind ; if it signifies nothing, there is an end of all science. Science stands or falls with " objective reference." [1] In ethics the doctrine means that there really is one moral standard for all of us, male or female, Greek or barbarian, bond or free. There really is one " eternal and immutable " morality, not a variety of independent moral standards, one perhaps for the " private man " and another for the " nation " or its politicians, or one for " the herd " and another for the " superman." The particular application of this conviction to the case of man and woman is shown to be genuinely Socratic by the fact that it not only appears in *Republic* v. as the principle on which Socrates justifies the participation of women in public life, but is also implied in the fragments of the *Aspasia* of Aeschines as his reason for asserting the capacity of women for the tasks of war and statesmanship. [2]

Meno is inclined at first to deny the position. But he has to admit that both what he regards as man's work and what he calls woman's work are only well done if they are performed with *sophrosyne* and justice, and similarly that wilfulness (ἀκολασία) and unfairness are faults alike in children and in elderly men. Thus *sophrosyne* and justice emerge as characteristic of human goodness, irrespective of age, sex, or status. There is then such a thing as a " goodness in virtue of which all human beings are good " ; can Meno remember what Gorgias supposed this goodness to be ? He suggests that it may be " capacity to command " (ἄρχειν οἷόν τ' εἶναι τῶν ἀνθρώπων, 73*d*). But what then about a child or a slave (who, of course, show their " goodness " not by giving orders, but by obeying them) ? And again, one may give unjust commands, and this can hardly be goodness, since it is not disputed by Meno that justice is a virtue and injustice a vice. We must at least qualify the statement by saying that goodness in man is the capacity

[1] We could not meet the argument by falling back on Aristotle's well-known doctrine of the " analogous " employment of universals. True as that doctrine is, it remains also true that in its strict and primary (κύριον) sense the universal can still be asserted of a plurality of subjects, and to be significant must be asserted of each and all of them in the same sense. Thus, even if it be granted, that there is no one common " goodness " of all things, *e.g.* that there is no more than an analogy between the goodness of a good razor and that of a good man, the Aristotelian ethics is based on the view that there is a " human goodness " which is one and the same for all men ; there is not one goodness of Peter and a different and merely analogous goodness of Paul. Peter and Paul have to be pronounced good or bad by the *same* standard. Aristotle's attempt in the *Politics* to justify the conventional prejudice which sets up a different moral standard for the two sexes amounts to a denial of the moral unity of humanity, and contradicts the very principles on which his own ethics are constructed.

[2] See the collection of these fragments in H. Dittmar's *Aeschines von Spheltos.*

to command justly (73*d*). This at once raises the question whether commanding justly is goodness or only ἀρετή τις, *one* form of goodness ; in fact, in the language of a more developed logic, whether we are not confusing a genus with one of its own species. We may illustrate the confusion by a simple example. It would be false to say that " circularity is figure " (σχῆμα), though true to say that it is *one* figure among others (73*e*). There are other figures besides circles, and Meno admits that there are " many " forms of goodness besides justice. Our attempt at definition has failed ; like the original enumeration, it has left us with *many* goodnesses instead of one (74*b*).

Perhaps we may get a hint of the kind of statement we really want if we go back to our illustration of the circle. There are many figures (σχήματα) of which the circle is only one, just as there are many colours, of which, *e.g.*, white is one among others. But we might try to define figure in a way which would express what is common to all figures, by saying, for example, that " figure is the one thing which always accompanies colour," " the sole inseparable concomitant of colour " (ὃ μόνον τῶν ὄντων τυγχάνει χρώματι ἀεὶ ἑπόμενον, 75*c*). It is true, as Meno remarks, that such a " definition " would involve the undefined term " colour." A pugnacious eristic would ignore this criticism ; he would retort that he had done his part in giving his own definition and that any amendment of it was the business of his antagonist. But we are not disputing for victory, and Socrates is ready to meet the criticism by attempting a better definition. Meno will admit that he knows what mathematicians mean by a " boundary " ; if we say then that " figure is the boundary of a solid " (στερεοῦ πέρας), the statement will hold good universally and exclusively, and not be open to the criticism that it introduces a second " unknown " (76*a*).

Meno should now attempt a similar definition of goodness, but irrelevantly insists that Socrates shall go on to define colour. This, as Socrates says, is the mere whim of a capricious " beauty," but he will comply with it. Meno at any rate will be satisfied by a definition based on the doctrine of Gorgias, which is derived from the " efflux " theory of Empedocles.[1] Assuming this theory, we may say that colour is " an efflux from surfaces which fits into the passages of the visual apparatus and is sensible " (ἀπορροὴ σχημάτων ὄψει σύμμετρος καὶ αἰσθητός, 76*d*), a definition which Meno thinks

[1] For the Empedoclean theory of the part played by these " effluxes " and the " passages " in the sense-organs into which they fit, see Theophrastus *de Sensu*, 7–9, and the criticism of Aristotle *de Generat.* A 324*b* 25ff., *de Sensu*, 437*b* 23ff., with the striking fragment 84 of Empedocles, quoted by Aristotle, *de Sensu*, 437*b* 26 [*R.P.* 177*b*, *c*] ; Burnet, *Early Greek Philosophy*³, 246–249. The definition is based on the Empedoclean theory because Gorgias, as a Sicilian, is assumed to be in accord with the biological views of the founder of Sicilian medicine. Quintilian iii. 1, 8 [*R.P.* 232] gives it as the " tradition " that Gorgias had originally been a " disciple " of E. Cf. D.L. viii. 58–59. In the *Timaeus* Plato makes his spokesman, who is represented as holding the principles of the Sicilian medicine, give the same account of colours. (*Tim.* 67*c*–68*d*.)

admirable, though Socrates calls it "stagy" and says it is inferior to that just given of figure.[1]

Meno at last makes an attempt at the definition of goodness. It is "to desire the fine things and to be able to secure them" (ἐπιθυμοῦντα τῶν καλῶν δυνατὸν εἶναι πορίζεσθαι, 77b). But the statement is doubly open to criticism. (a) It implies that it is *possible* to desire what is not "fine," that is, to "desire evil." But, in fact, no one can or does desire what he knows to be evil, for that would be equivalent to the impossibility of desiring to be unhappy (77c–78b). The first clause of Meno's definition is thus superfluous, and it reduces to the statement that goodness is "ability to secure goods." (b) By "goods" he means, as he explains, such things as wealth, health, and high civic and social distinction (the ends, be it noted, of the "body-loving" and "distinction-loving" lives). But we cannot call ability to get these things by any means, fair or foul, *goodness*; it would be truer to say that the virtuous man is *in*capable of gaining fortune or position by foul means. So we have to introduce the qualification that goodness is capacity to secure good things "by righteous" or "honest" means, or something to that effect. Now righteousness, honesty, or whatever other qualifications we introduce, have already been admitted to be "parts" of goodness, so that we are in effect saying that goodness or virtue is attaining certain ends by the practice of some specific virtue (*i.e.* we introduce one or more of the determinants of a given determinable into a proposed definition of that determinable itself, and thus commit a vicious "circle," 77b–79e). We are thus no nearer to a satisfactory definition than we were before.

Meno is half inclined to lay the blame for the collapse of the argument on Socrates, who, he says, has the reputation of always being bepuzzled himself and communicating his bewilderment to others. He benumbs men's wits as the fish called νάρκη benumbs their muscles if they touch it. In any other company Meno would have plenty to say about "goodness," but in the presence of Socrates he is "paralysed." In any foreign city Socrates would run a real risk of being arrested for sorcery. Socrates has to admit the accusation, with the reservation that the comparison with the νάρκη is only apt on the assumption that the creature itself is as "numb" as its victims. The difficulties his conversation creates in others are only the reflection of those he finds in his own thinking. But if Meno will adventure on the definition of "goodness" over again, he will do his best to examine the new result (80 a–d). At this point Meno again tries to run off on an irrelevant issue. He brings up the "sophistic" puzzle which we have already met in

[1] Why does Socrates prefer the definition of figure to that of colour? Presumably because the second implies a detailed physical and physiological speculation which is highly problematic; the other presupposes only the principles of geometry, and geometry is an indubitable "science." The definition of colour is τραγική, "stagy," because it makes a show with grand words which are only a cover for imprecision and uncertainty.

the *Euthydemus,* that " inquiry " is impossible because you cannot inquire after something you already know, nor yet after what you do not know (since, in the second case, you would not even recognize the object you were looking for, if you should succeed in finding it). This dilemma, however, would cease to be a difficulty if there should be truth in a doctrine which Socrates has learned from " priests and priestesses who have been at the pains to understand their professional duties " and also from Pindar and other poets. The doctrine is that our soul is immortal and our present life only one episode in its history. If this is so, the soul must long ago have " learned " everything, and only needs to be " put in mind " of something it has temporarily forgotten in order to regain its knowledge by diligent following of the clue provided by " reminiscence." Learning, in fact, is just a process of " re-call " (ἀνάμνησις), and for this reason the sophistic argument to show that it is impossible to learn a new truth is a mere appeal to mental indolence (80e–82a). (As we are encountering the doctrine of " recollection " for the first time, it is worth while to note what the exact point of it is. It must be observed that it is not a theory of " innate ideas," or " innate knowledge," in the popular sense of the words. We are not supposed to bring any actual knowledge into the world ready-made with us. On the contrary, we are said to " have learned " truth but to have lost it again, and we have to recover what we have lost. The recovery requires a real and prolonged effort of steady thinking ; what " recollection," or more accurately " being reminded," does for us is to provide the starting-point for this effort. In the *Phaedo,* this is illustrated by the way in which chance " associations " will start a train of thinking, as when the sight of an absent friend's belongings or his portrait sets us thinking of the friend himself. The main emphasis thus falls not on the Orphic doctrine of pre-existence and re-incarnation, which Socrates professes to have learned from poets and priests, but on the function of sense-experience as suggestive of and pregnant with truths of an intelligible order which it does not itself adequately embody or establish. And the philosophical importance of the doctrine is not that it proves the immortality of the soul,[1] but that it shows that the acquisition of knowledge is not a matter of passively receiving " instruction," but one of following up a personal effort of thinking once started by an arresting sense-experience. But for this " suggestiveness " of sense-experience the *ignava ratio* of the eristic, " you cannot learn the truth from any teacher, because unless you know it already, you will not recognize it for the truth when he utters it," would be valid. We see, then, why both Socrates and Plato hold that " knowledge " can only be won by

---

[1] In the *Phaedo* itself the argument is found insufficient to meet the formidable difficulty raised by Cebes that even if pre-existence is true, it gives us no guarantee that we shall continue to be after the dissolution of our present body. For the illustrations from " association," see *Phaedo,* 73c ff.

personal participation in " research " ; it cannot simply be handed on from one man to another.[1]

An illustration of the principle that " learning " is really " being reminded of something," *i.e.* is the following up by personal effort of the suggestions of sense-experience, may now be given. Socrates calls forward the lad who is attending on Meno, after satisfying himself that the boy can understand a question in plain Greek, but has never been taught any mathematics, and undertakes to show how he can be brought to see geometrical truths for himself by merely asking appropriate questions which enable the answerer to correct his own first hasty thoughts. The point to be established is that the areas of squares are proportional to the second powers of the lengths of their sides, and in particular that the area of a square described on the diagonal of one previously described is double the area of the original figure.[2] We are to think of Socrates, of course, as drawing the requisite figure, which will be found in any commentary on the *Meno*, in the sand as he speaks. The boy's first thought is that if we want to make a square with twice the area of a given one, we must make its sides twice as long. (That is, he argues, " since $2^2 = 2 \times 2$, $4^2 = 2 \times 4$.) He is easily made to see for himself that this cannot be true (since $4 \times 4 = 16$), and amends his first answer by suggesting that the side of the second square should be to that of the first as 3 to 2 (*i.e.* he suggests that $3^2 = 8$). Again it is easy to get him to see that this is impossible (since $3 \times 3 = 9$). The length of the line we require must be greater than that of our original line, but less than half as great again ($\sqrt{2} > 1 < \frac{3}{2}$). And with a few more questions, the lad is led to see that the line we require as the base of our second square is no other than the diagonal of our original figure ($82b–85b$).[3] The point insisted on is that the lad starts with a false proposition, is led to replace it by one less erroneous, and finally by one which, so far as it goes, is true. Yet Socrates has " told " him nothing. He has merely drawn diagrams which suggest the right answers to a series of questions. The only " information " he has imparted to the slave is that a certain line is technically called by " the sophists," *i.e.* " professionals," a " diagonal." Everything else has been left to the boy to think out for himself in response to the suggestions provided by Socrates' diagrams and questions. Yet undeniably

[1] See the language on this point of Plato, *Ep.* vii. 341c. Perhaps I may refer to the statement of the theory in my little volume, *Platonism and its Influence* (Boston, U.S.A., 1925) c. 2, as well as to Burnet, *Greek Philosophy, Part I.*, pp. 220–222.

[2] The particular theorem is chosen, no doubt, because of the importance of the " side and diagonal " as the most elementary instance of a pair of " incommensurable " magnitudes.

[3] Thus, to put it arithmetically, what has been proved is that $\sqrt{2}$ lies somewhere between 1 and 1·5. In the famous passage *Rep.* 546b ff. it is made clear that Socrates, in fact, knows quite well how to construct the whole series of fractions which form the " successive convergents " to $\sqrt{2}$. For his purpose here it is enough to consider the " second convergent," $\frac{3}{2}$, and to show that this is too large a value.

the lad began by not knowing something and ended by knowing it. Thus he " brought up the knowledge from within " (ἀναλαβὼν αὐτὸς ἐξ αὐτοῦ τὴν ἐπιστήμην), and such a process is " being re-minded," " recalling " something. We infer then that the slave once " had " the knowledge he had forgotten, and since he has never in this life been " taught " geometry, the " once " must have been " before he was a man," [1] and thus we see that the soul is immortal. (Socrates, however, hastens to remark that he would not care to be too confident about anything in the theory except the main point that it proves that we can arrive at truth and thus saves us from the sloth and self-neglect which are natural conse-quences of the eristic *ignava ratio* (86b).[2])

We have wandered away far from our original question about the teachability of goodness, and Meno is anxious to have that answered without further digression. The humour of the situation is that this is impossible. We cannot really expect to know whether goodness or anything else can be taught unless we first know what the thing in question *is*, as we have admitted that we do not. But we may give a tentative and provisional answer to the question ἐξ ὑποθέσεως, subject to an initial postulate, *sous condition*. Only we must make another digression to explain what we mean by this restriction. If you ask a geometer whether a certain problem is soluble, he may often have to say that he does not know whether the problem has a perfectly general solution or not, but that he can give a solution for it, subject to a specified restriction. This is illustrated for us by the example of a problem about the inscription of a triangle of given area in a circle of given diameter. The geo-meter may be unable to say whether the inscription can be effected unless the data are further specified by some restricting condition. He will then answer that " I cannot solve your problem as it stands, but *if* the area in question satisfies the condition X, the inscription is possible." [3]   So we, in our present state of uncertainty

[1] The same way of speaking about our ante-natal condition as the " time when we were not yet men " is characteristic of the *Phaedo*. It implies that the true self is not, as is commonly thought, the embodied soul, but the soul *simpliciter*, the body being the instrument (ὄργανον) which the soul " uses," and the consequent definition of " man " as a " soul using a body as its instru-ment." Since that which " uses " an implement is always superior to the implement it uses, this definition merely embodies the Socratic conviction that the soul is the thing of supreme value in us.

[2] The caution should not be understood to mean that Socrates doubts the *fact* of immortality. His firm belief in that is the assumption of the *Phaedo* and is really presupposed by *Apolog.* 40c–41c. He means, as he says, that he will not go bail for the λόγος ; it is not really a complete demonstration of pre-existence and immortality, as is frankly admitted in the *Phaedo*, though, no doubt, it suggests their possibility. The real reason why Socrates attaches so much importance to the doctrine of " reminiscence " (ἀνάμνησις) is independent of the use of it as an argument for " survival." One should be careful to bear in mind that ἀνάμνησις does not properly mean in the theory " remember-ing," but " being reminded of " something. Sensible experiences are always " suggesting " to us " ideal " standards which none of them actually exhibit.

[3] The precise character of the restriction imposed by the geometer in Socrates' illustration has been a matter of much dispute, which is due partly

about the true character of goodness, can only answer Meno's question *sous condition* If goodness is knowledge, *then* it is something which can be taught, *i.e.* according to the theory of learning we have just laid down, something which can be " recalled to mind " (ἀναμνηστόν, 87b) ; if goodness is anything other than knowledge, it cannot be taught. (We now see the real purpose of the introduction of the doctrine of ἀνάμνησις. The object is to show that though the " teachability " of goodness is a direct consequence of the Socratic principle that " goodness is knowledge," Socrates does not mean, as some of the " sophists " seem to have done, that a man can become good by any mere passive listening to the " instructions " of a lecturer, since no knowledge whatever is acquired in this way ; *all* " learning " is an active response of personal thought and effort to the " hints " derived from a more mature fellow-learner.)

Goodness, then, can be taught, if goodness is knowledge and not otherwise, and we are thrown back on the antecedent question whether goodness is or is not knowledge. (Thus we conform to the rule of order laid down at *Phaedo* 101c–e. We first consider what are the " consequences," συμβαίνοντα, of a " postulate " ; only when we are clear on this preliminary question do we go on to ask whether the " postulate " itself can be " justified.") To answer our new question, we have again to start with an unproved " postulate," the ὑπόθεσις that ἀρετή is a *good* thing. (No question arises of a " justification " of *this* ὑπόθεσις, because both Socrates and Meno accept it as common ground ; it is an ἱκανόν τι such as is spoken of in the passage of the *Phaedo* about logical method.) It follows at once that if knowledge is the only good, " goodness " or " virtue " (ἀρετή) must be knowledge ; if there are other goods besides knowledge, it is *possible* that ἀρετή may be one of these other goods (87d). Thus we find ourselves driven in the end to face the ultimate question whether knowledge is not the *only* good, or at any rate an indispensable constituent of all good. This question is now treated in the way already familiar to us. Whatever is good is " beneficial " (ὠφελιμόν), *i.e. does* us good. Now the commonly recognized goods are such things as health, physical strength, comeliness, and we may add, wealth. But none of these is " unconditionally " good ; all *may* " harm " their possessor ; they benefit him when they are rightly used but harm him when they are misused. So with the commonly recognized good characters of the " soul," of which Socrates proceeds to give a list. Courage, in the popular sense, covers " daring " or " venturesomeness " (θάρρος) of every kind. But though venturesomeness combined with sound sense (νοῦς) is beneficial, senseless daring is harmful to its possessor, and the same thing is true of σωφροσύνη, " appetitive coldness," retentive memory, and qualities of soul generally. To

to uncertainty about the technical terminology of geometers in the fifth century. For our purpose it is sufficient to grasp the main point that there are such restrictions. It is, *e.g.*, obvious that some restricting condition must connect the area of the given triangle with the radius of the given circle. For a correct solution see A. S. L. Farquharson in *C.Q.*, xvii. 1 (Jan. 1923).

be beneficial, they must be accompanied by intelligence or understanding ($\phi\rho\acute{o}\nu\eta\sigma\iota\varsigma$); they, too, are harmful when misused. We infer, then, that the goodness of all other good things is conditional on the " goodness of soul " of the possessor, and this again conditional on his intelligence ($\phi\rho\acute{o}\nu\eta\sigma\iota\varsigma$). It follows that intelligence, or some specific form of intelligence ($\mathring{\eta}\tau o\iota$ $\sigma\acute{v}\mu\pi a\sigma a$ $\mathring{\eta}$ $\mu\acute{e}\rho o\varsigma$ $\tau\iota$), is identical with " goodness," and therefore that " men are not good by nature," *i.e.* goodness is not a matter of congenital *endowment* (as Callicles maintains in the *Gorgias* for example, 87*d*–89*a*).[1]

This last inference admits at once of empirical verification, for if goodness were congenital endowment, we could detect its presence in early life, and so we could secure a succession of true statesmen by merely selecting the properly endowed natures in early life and bringing them up " under guard," carefully isolated from all risks of contamination.[2] Yet, on second thoughts, we may see reason to distrust our identification of goodness with knowledge. If it were knowledge, surely there would be professional teachers of it and they would have " pupils." But there does not appear to be any such " profession." It is lucky for us that Anytus has just taken a seat by our side at this point of the conversation. He is the son of a worthy citizen who made a fortune by steady intelligence and industry; the popular judgment is clearly that he has had an excellent early training and education, as is shown by his repeated election to high offices. His opinion on the question whether there are " teachers of goodness " ought therefore to be highly valuable (89*b*–90*b*).

(Why does Plato introduce Anytus at this particular point? Note that he is not supposed to have heard the preceding discussion, which he would have been quite incapable of appreciating. He comes up to the bench on which Socrates and Meno are sitting, and joins them just in the nick of time, as they are beginning to consider the problem about the professional teachers of goodness. Nor is there any appearance of " irony " in what is said about him; unlike Xenophon, Plato never suggests that Anytus had any discreditable private motives for supporting the prosecution of Socrates. The irony of the passage only concerns Anytus to the same degree

---

[1] Note again the exact correspondence of the Socratic argument for the identity of virtue and knowledge with Kant's argument for the thesis that the only unconditional good is the " good will." Kant's further proposal to make conformity with the bare form of a universal imperative the direct and sufficient criterion of right action might be said to be simply a reckless development of one side of the Socratic ethics, its " intellectualism," in unreal isolation from its " eudaemonism."

[2] It might be objected, is not this selection, here assumed to be impossible, actually proposed as the very foundation of the " ideal state " in the *Republic*? The answer is No. In the *Republic* it is, of course, recognized that endowment counts for something, and therefore there is an early initial selection of promising future " guardians." But educational tradition counts for much more; hence the length at which the problem of the creation of a right educational tradition is discussed, and the provision for promotions and degradations at all stages according as the subject under education justifies or belies his early " promise."

as the whole of the Athenian public who respect and trust him. It is clearly meant that, to the measure of his intelligence, Anytus is an able and public-spirited man who deserves the trust he receives. This defect, one which he shares with the whole Athenian public, is simply that he is an *esprit borné*. He has the average Athenian democratic prejudice against men who are " too clever," the *intelligentsia*, and the average Athenian's incapacity for ever calling his own prejudices in question, and it is just because he is such a " representative man " that the public trust him. The purpose of bringing him in is clearly to make us realize the violence of the Athenian prejudice against the " intellectuals," and the inability of even a well-to-do and " educated " public man to discriminate between Socrates and the " intellectuals by profession." If Socrates could be so misconceived by the " leaders of public opinion," we understand how he came to be prosecuted without needing to impute his fate to anything worse than honest stupidity.)

If you wish a young man to learn a science such as medicine or an accomplishment such as flute-playing, to whom do you send him ? You always select a teacher who claims to be a professional expert, and for that very reason charges a fee for his instructions ; you would never think of putting him under a mere " amateur " who does not make a profession of imparting his own skill. It should seem, then, that statesmanship, the science of the right conduct of affairs and the right manage of life must, by parity of reasoning, be learned from the specialists who claim to have made a profession of teaching its principles, and consequently, like all professionals, charge a fee—that is, from the " sophists, as men call them." Anytus has the profoundest horror of the whole profession ; they are, he says, as every one can see, mere depravers and corrupters of all who frequent their lectures. Yet it is difficult to accept this view of them. It would be a unique fact that any class should make a paying profession of visibly spoiling the materials entrusted to it.[1] In point of fact, Protagoras made a considerable fortune by the trade of " teaching goodness," and he exercised it for over forty years. Thus there was plenty of time for him to be found out in, but he never was found out, and his high reputation has survived him to this day, and he is not the only example in point.[2] Anytus is quite sure, though he is thankful he has never in his life had to do with a sophist, that the sophist is a designing scoundrel,

[1] *E.g.* the medical profession would not continue to provide anyone with a living wage if medical men really killed off their patients. In real life a " faculty " of Sangrados would be " found out." Anytus supposes that the " sophists " *have* been found out, and yet contrive to grow fat on their quackery.

[2] I think we are bound to take the observations about Protagoras (*Meno*, 91d–e) quite seriously. Socrates seriously means that the lifelong success of Protagoras, and the high esteem in which he was and is held, show that the democratic view that there was nothing at all in him, that he was " a palpable and mischievous impostor," is far too simple to account for the facts. Protagoras may not have been all he supposed himself to be, but there must have been *something* in him to inspire such long-continued trust and veneration.

and the society which does not make penal laws to suppress him a silly dupe. But, however true his views may be—though by his own showing he must be arriving at them by " divination "—they are not to the point. The question is not who are the corrupters of youth, but who are the " teachers of goodness " from whom the young may learn the true principles of the conduct of life. Anytus holds that we need specify no particular professional teachers ; the conduct of life can be learned from any " decent " Athenian, and he has learned it from his father, who learned it again from his. It is simply a matter of imbibing an hereditary tradition—a view illustrated in the *Protagoras* by the way in which children pick up their mother-tongue or their father's trade without any formal teaching or apprenticeship (*Protag.* 327e ff.). To doubt the possibility of this would amount to denying that there have been " good men " in Athens (90c–93a).

Socrates does not deny that there are and have been at Athens men who are " good at citizenship " (ἀγαθοὶ τὰ πολιτικά),[1] but what he does doubt is whether such men have also been competent *teachers* of the goodness they practise. The difficulty is that the sons of these men have all proved either worthless or insignificant. Thus they clearly did not teach their goodness themselves to their sons, and it is notorious that even those of them who, like Themistocles, were careful to have their sons trained in mere elegant accomplishments, never sent them to anyone for special education in " goodness." The obvious inference is that the " good Athenians," whom Anytus regards as competent teachers of goodness, do not think themselves or anyone else competent to teach it ; they must have supposed that goodness is not the kind of thing which can be taught. Anytus is so chafed at having to listen to such unsparing criticism of the eminent figures of the national history that he misses the point and relapses into silence with an angry warning to Socrates that the Athenian democracy is no safe abode for a man who will not learn to bridle his tongue,[2]—a plain hint, on Plato's part, that

---

[1] It has been suggested by Th. Gomperz that these words are meant to soften down the asperity of the declaration of the *Gorgias* that none of the great figures of Athenian democracy was a true statesman, and even that the chief motive of Plato in writing the *Meno* was to placate a public opinion naturally irritated by such utterances. This seems to me hopelessly fanciful. (*a*) There is really no " recantation " in the *Meno*. The democratic leaders had been denied in the *Gorgias* to be statesmen on the ground that they were empirics, whereas statesmanship is a *science*. According to the *Meno*, these same leaders are so convinced that their own " goodness " is not teachable that they make no attempt to get it taught to their sons. This is just the criticism of the *Gorgias* put in other words. (*b*) In one respect the *Meno* goes further than the *Gorgias*. That dialogue had conceded Athens at least one genuine statesman, Aristides " the just " (*Gorgias*, 526b). In the *Meno* Aristides figures among the rest of the famous men who must have supposed that goodness cannot be taught, since he never had it taught to his son (*Meno*, 94a).

[2] Hannibal Chollop's advice to Mark Tapley, " You had better crack us up, you had," is much the same as that Anytus gives to Socrates, and in both cases the warning is probably not meant unkindly.

it was just this sort of unsparing and impartial free speech about the democracy and its leaders which caused the mistaken but intelligible suspicion of *incivisme* to attach to the philosopher (93*b*–95*a*). That Socrates was really in the habit of employing these criticisms is clear from the fact that the very same use of the argument about statesmen and their sons occurs both in the *Protagoras* and in the *Alcibiades*.

The sophists may, in any case, be dismissed from the discussion, since Meno, on the whole, agrees with Anytus that they cannot teach goodness and thinks it a point in favour of Gorgias that he disclaimed the pretension. In fact, most men, like the poet Theognis, find themselves unable to make up their minds whether goodness is teachable or not. They say " Yes " and " No," according to their moods. Goodness is thus in a uniquely unfortunate position. The claims of the professional teachers are generally disbelieved, and the persons whose practice is generally admired cannot make up their own minds whether their specialty can be taught. It looks as though there were neither teachers nor learners of goodness, and consequently that it is not a thing which can be taught. But how, then, is it ever produced, as we must admit that it is ? On second thoughts, we see a way out of the difficulty. Knowledge is not the only thing which is beneficial in practice. A right belief ($\delta\rho\theta\dot\eta$ $\delta\delta\xi a$) will direct practice as satisfactorily as genuine knowledge. A guide who had a right belief about the road to Larissa would take you there as successfully as one who really knew the way. For practical purposes, then, a right belief is as good as knowledge—but for one trifling drawback. There would be no practical difference, if you could make sure that a man will always retain his right belief. But beliefs are like the fabled statues of Daedalus, which can walk away if they are not fastened to their place. The statues are fine pieces of work, but their price is naturally low if they are loose. So a correct belief is a fine thing, if it will only stay with you, but it will not stay long unless you fasten it down $a\dot\iota\tau\dot\iota a s$ $\lambda o\gamma\iota\sigma\mu\hat\wp$ " by thinking out the reason why " of it (98*a*), and this process is what we have already called " being reminded " ($\dot a\nu\dot a\mu\nu\eta\sigma\iota s$). When we have thought out the " reason why," the belief becomes knowledge and is abiding. We may apply this distinction to the solution of our problem.

The " eminently good men " of Athens plainly do not owe their usefulness as political leaders to knowledge, for if they did, they could teach " statesmanship " to others. Themistocles and the rest were therefore not " scientific statesmen," not $\sigma o\phi o\dot\iota$ (99*b*)— the conclusion also reached in the *Gorgias*—and it is absurd to think they owed all their achievements to accident. Their successes must have been due to " correct opinions " ($\epsilon\dot v\delta o\xi\dot\iota a$, 99*b*). They were much on a level with givers of oracles and diviners, who often say very true things without knowing it (since the responses are delivered in a sort of temporary " frenzy "). Thus we may class together " seers," poets, and statesmen, as beings who all say and do brilliant things without really knowing what they are saying or doing, because they are all acting in a state of "possession," though Anytus, perhaps, will not like our conclusion (95b–99e).[1] To sum up, then : goodness is neither inborn nor yet learned from teachers, but arises from a happy irrational "divine possession" (θείᾳ μοίρᾳ ἄνευ νοῦ), unless, indeed, there could arise a statesman who could teach statesmanship to others. His "goodness" would be to that of other men what substance is to shadow. We must, however, remember that our conclusion is tentative ; we cannot say with certainty how goodness arises until we have answered the still outstanding question what it is. In the meanwhile Meno would be doing Athens a service if he could make Anytus more sympathetic with our point of view (99e–100c).

The full meaning of these last remarks only comes out when we read them in the light of the *Republic* and *Phaedo*. The "statesman who can make another a statesman" is just the philosopher-king of the *Republic*, where the crowning achievement of the "ideal state" is to make provision for the permanent teaching of a statesmanship which is *science*, clear intellectual insight into fundamental moral principles, not a succession of "inspired" adventures, and the provision takes the form of a system of thorough education in hard scientific thinking which culminates in the direct apprehension of "the good." In the light of this educational scheme, we can see that the main object of the concluding argument in the *Meno* is to distinguish between a higher and a lower kind of goodness. The higher kind is that which the *Republic* calls the goodness of the philosopher, and it is based upon certain and assured personal knowledge of the true scale of goods, and is therefore "abiding." The lower kind, which is at best a "shadow" of true goodness, is based on "opinions" which are true, but are not knowledge, and therefore not to be counted on as permanent ; in fact, it rests on acceptance of a sound tradition of living which has not been converted into personal insight into the scale of goods. This is all which is demanded in the *Republic* even of the soldiers of the State ; their goodness is loyalty to a tradition of' noble living in which they have been brought up, but of which they have never even asked the reason why, life by an exalted standard of "honour." Since there are sound elements in the moral tradition of any civilized community, it is possible for an Athenian statesman in whom the best traditions of his city are inbred to "profit" the State by goodness of this inferior kind, "popular goodness," as the *Phaedo* calls it. But security for permanent continuance in well-doing is only to be had when a sound traditional code of conduct has been converted into "knowledge" by understanding of the

---

[1] Socrates regards the achievements of a Themistocles or a Pericles as "wizardry," but he does not mean this as a compliment. "Possession" was popularly regarded as a kind of disease, and we have only to go to Aristophanes to see what the current estimate of χρησμῳδοί and θεομάντεις was. The effect of his classification is much that which might be produced to-day by speaking together of "ventriloquists, mediums, and cabinet ministers."

" reason why," that is by personal insight into the character of good and personal understanding of the place of each of the " goods " of life in the hierarchy of good. Thus the true statesman would be the Socratic philosopher who understands the principle that the " tendance of the *soul* " is the supreme business of both individual and State, and judges soundly of the nature of the "spiritual health" at which the " tendance " aims. Of course, we readily see that " philosophic goodness," being thus identical with *knowledge* of true good, must be " teachable," if you go to work the right way, whereas a " goodness " which does not repose on apprehension of principles cannot be taught ; it can only be " imbibed " by habituation in conformity to a tradition. The vacillation of mankind in their attitude to the teachability of virtue is thus to be explained by the ambiguity of the word "goodness " ; men are dimly aware that real goodness depends on grasp of intelligible principles and thus ought to be teachable, but they confuse this real goodness with its shadow, loyalty to an established tradition *qua* established, and common experience shows that this, however it is to be secured, cannot be secured by teaching. The contributions of the dialogue to the theory of knowledge, the exposition of the doctrine of " reminiscence " and of the principles of method, with all their importance, are meant to be secondary to this main result ; the account of pre-existence and immortality, again, is strictly subordinate to the theory of ἀνάμνησις itself. It would be a complete misunderstanding to find the main purport of the dialogue in these things, though there is no reason to doubt that they were connected in the personal *Welt-Anschauung* of Socrates with his main tenet, the supreme worth of the ψυχή and its specific good, knowledge.

See further :

RITTER, C.—*Platon*, i. 391–449 (*Gorgias*), 476–484 (*Meno*).
RAEDER, H.—*Platons philosophische Entwickelung*, 111–125 (*Gorgias*), 130–137 (*Meno*).
THOMPSON, W. H.—The *Gorgias* of Plato.
NETTLESHIP, R. L.—*Plato's Conception of Goodness and the Good* (*Lectures and Remains*, i. 238–394).
DIÈS, A.—*Autour de Platon*, ii. 414–418, 462–469.
STEWART, J. A.—*Myths of Plato*, 1–76 (*Introduction*), 114–132 (*The Gorgias Myth*) ; *Plato's Doctrine of Ideas*, 24–29 (*Meno*), 29–34 (*Gorgias*).
STENZEL, J.—*Platon der Erzieher*, 147–178.

CHAPTER VII

SOCRATIC DIALOGUES: *EUTHYPHRO, APOLOGY, CRITO*

I HAVE reserved these well-known dialogues for consideration at this point for the simple reason that it is difficult to separate them from the *Phaedo*; thus it is natural to make the treatment of them the immediate prelude to a study of the four great works in which Plato's dramatic genius shows itself most perfect. I do not mean to imply that I regard the whole series of dialogues which centre round the trial and death of Socrates as uninterruptedly following one another in order of composition. As I have already explained, I do not feel satisfied that we are safe in saying more on the question than that the slighter works we are considering must, at least in the main, be regarded as earlier than the four great dramatic dialogues. It is possible, perhaps even probable, that at any rate the *Apology* may have been written before several of the works we have already dealt with, but the probability need not affect our treatment if it is true, as the present analysis tries to show, that there is no serious variation in the doctrine of Plato's dialogues until we come to the series unmistakably shown by style to be later than the *Republic*. In treating of the whole series of these " dialogues of the trial and imprisonment " I shall avail myself fully of the commentaries of Professor Burnet (*Euthyphro, Apology, Crito*, 1924; *Phaedo*, 1911); this will make it possible to aim at a brevity which I should have been only too glad to secure for some other parts of this book.

   1. *Euthyphro.*—On all questions connected with the scene and personages of the dialogue, see Burnet's *Introductory Note*, to which I would only append the following remarks. It is not certain that the Euthyphro of our dialogue is the person of the same name whom we have encountered in the *Cratylus*, though this is possible. If the two men are one and the same, we shall clearly have to think of Euthyphro as now in middle age and his father as a man of some seventy-five or more. To my own mind, the tone of the conversation is consistent with these suppositions and inconsistent with regarding Euthyphro as in any sense young. (He is a familiar figure in the *ecclesia* which he often addresses.) I fully agree with Burnet that the supposed proceedings by Euthyphro against his father as a murderer must be historical fact ; the situation is too *bizarre* to be a natural fiction. Also I think it clear that legally

Euthyphro had no case and was probably non-suited by the *Basileus*, but I would add that in all probability Euthyphro himself counted on this issue. His object, as he explains at 4c, is to clear *himself* from the religious pollution incurred by being in any way accessory to a φόνος. If he files an information against his father, even with full knowledge that it will be dismissed on technical grounds, he has done all that a scrupulous conscience can require. Any possible " pollution " will henceforth rest not on him but on the authorities, and he would probably feel himself free for the future to live in ordinary family relations with his father. This is presumably what he wished to do. We need not suppose that he expects or desires any grave consequences to happen to the old gentleman. As to the main purpose of the dialogue, again, I think Burnet is clearly right. As both Plato and Aeschines represent, Socrates had lived in association with religious ascetics and mystics of the Orphic type ; every one also knew that he had been formally convicted of some kind of religious innovation. The natural inference would have been that he was himself a sectary much of the same type as Euthyphro, as Euthyphro seems to suppose. It was a duty of piety to his memory to make it clear that his views on religion were very different from those of a sect who found the " deep things of God " in stories like those of the binding of Cronus and the mutilation of Uranus—tales which had nothing to do with the official worship of Athens and were repulsive to the ordinary Athenian. It is equally clear that Euthyphro is not intended, as has often been said, to represent " Athenian orthodoxy," *i.e.* the attitude of the dicasts who voted for the conviction of Socrates, since, as Burnet points out, he instinctively takes the side of Socrates as soon as he has heard the nature of the charge against him, and classes Socrates and himself together as theologians exposed to the unintelligent derision of the " vulgar." [1]

Ostensibly the problem of the dialogue is to determine the real character of ὁσιότης, "piety," or as we should probably say now, " religion," that part of right conduct which is concerned with man's duty to God. As usual, no final result is expressly arrived at, but the interest lies in the comparison of two different conceptions of what " religion " is. The conclusion to which we seem to be coming, but for an unexpected difficulty, is that religion is the " art of traffic between man and gods," or the art of receiving from the gods and giving to them (*Euthyphro*, 14d, e). On the face of it, this is a view of religion thoroughly in keeping with the more sordid side of the ancient State cultus, which was very much regulated

---

[1] See the full treatment of all this in Burnet, *op. cit.* pp. 2–7. As to the ordinary Athenian estimate of the Hesiodic stories about Uranus and Cronus, see Aristophanes, *Clouds*, 904, Isocrates, xi. 38–40. How far the Athenians were from taking Cronus seriously is sufficiently shown by the simple fact that κρόνος is Attic for " old Methusalem " or " Rip van Winkle." Even the allusion of Aeschylus, *Ag.* 168 ff., has a touch of contempt for the unnamed being who is now " down and out" (τριακτῆρος οἴχεται τυχών) and the " bully " who preceded him (παμμάχῳ θράσει βρύων).

on the *do ut des* principle. It exactly hits off, for example, the spirit of *religio* as understood in the early days of the Roman republic. Hence it is not surprising that more than one editor (Adam, Burnet) should have found the real point of the dialogue in a hint thrown out, but not followed up, a little earlier (*Euthyphro*, 13e), that religion should rather be thought of as the co-operation of man with God towards some noble result ($\pi\acute{a}\gamma\kappa\alpha\lambda\text{ov}$ $\check{\epsilon}\rho\gamma\text{ov}$) which is left unspecified. It is at least certain that the making of this point is one of the main objects of the discussion, and that the view is shown to arise directly out of the application to religion of the notion of " tendance " ($\theta\epsilon\rho\alpha\pi\epsilon\acute{\iota}\alpha$), so fundamental in the Socratic ethics. But I think it would probably be mistaken to suppose that the other formula is intended to be rejected as conveying a selfish and sordid conception of religion. In the sense put upon it by ordinary Athenian practice, and apparently by Euthyphro himself, that religion consists in knowing how to perform a ritual worship which will procure tangible returns for the worshipper, the formula is, no doubt, sordid enough and wholly at variance with the conception of God and the service of God attributed to Socrates throughout the dialogues. But this interpretation is not the only one which could be put on the phrase. If we think rightly of the blessings for which it is proper to pray, it will be a worthy conception of religion that it *is* an intercourse between man and God in which we offer " acceptable sacrifice " and receive in return the true goods of soul and body.[1] And there can be no doubt both that " praying and sacrificing aright " are $\delta\sigma\iota\acute{o}\tau\eta s$ and that $\delta\sigma\iota\acute{o}\tau\eta s$, since it is virtue or a part of virtue, is in the Socratic view an $\epsilon\pi\iota\sigma\tau\acute{\eta}\mu\eta$ or $\tau\acute{\epsilon}\chi\nu\eta$, an application of knowledge to the regulation of practice. Plato himself, who deals with the regulation of institutional religion at length in the *Laws*, would have had nothing in principle against such a formula, rightly interpreted. The early Academy seem to have been right in including among their definitions of " piety " ($\epsilon\mathring{v}\sigma\acute{\epsilon}\beta\epsilon\iota\alpha$) alternative formulæ which are obviously conflations of the different suggestions of our dialogue, " a faculty of the voluntary service of the gods ; right belief about honouring the gods ; the science of honouring the gods." [2] Hence I do not feel at liberty to treat the two suggestions about the nature of religion as meant to be exclusive of one another.

A very brief analysis of the argument will enable us to re-

---

[1] Cf. the model of an acceptable prayer offered by Socrates, *Phaedrus*, 279c, and the conception of $\delta\alpha\acute{\iota}\mu\text{ov}\epsilon s$ as the middlemen in the " traffic between man and God " in the speech of Diotima reproduced by Socrates in *Symposium*, 202e.

[2] [Plat.] *Def.* 412e 14, $\delta\acute{v}\nu\alpha\mu\iota s$ $\theta\epsilon\rho\alpha\pi\epsilon\nu\tau\iota\kappa\grave{\eta}$ $\theta\epsilon\mathring{\omega}\nu$ $\mathring{\epsilon}\kappa\text{o}\acute{v}\sigma\iota\text{os}\cdot$ $\pi\epsilon\rho\grave{\iota}$ $\theta\epsilon\mathring{\omega}\nu$ $\tau\iota\mu\mathring{\eta}s$ $\acute{v}\pi\acute{o}\lambda\eta\psi\iota s$ $\mathring{o}\rho\theta\acute{\eta}\cdot$ $\mathring{\epsilon}\pi\iota\sigma\tau\acute{\eta}\mu\eta$ $\pi\epsilon\rho\grave{\iota}$ $\theta\epsilon\mathring{\omega}\nu$ $\tau\iota\mu\mathring{\eta}s$. Cf. the definition of $\mathring{a}\gamma\nu\epsilon\acute{\iota}\alpha$ (*ibid.* 414a 12), $\tau\mathring{\eta}s$ $\theta\epsilon\text{o}\mathring{v}$ $\tau\iota\mu\mathring{\eta}s$ $\kappa\alpha\tau\grave{\alpha}$ $\phi\acute{v}\sigma\iota\nu$ $\theta\epsilon\rho\alpha\pi\epsilon\acute{\iota}\alpha$, and of $\delta\sigma\iota\text{o}\nu$ (*ibid.* 415a 9), $\theta\epsilon\rho\acute{a}\pi\epsilon\nu\mu\alpha$ $\theta\epsilon\text{o}\mathring{v}$ $\mathring{a}\rho\epsilon\sigma\tau\grave{\text{o}}\nu$ $\theta\epsilon\mathring{\omega}$. That the Academic definitions of our Plato MSS. in the main belong to the earliest days of the Academy is shown by the frequent appeals made to them in Aristotle, especially in the *Topics*. In some cases the testimony of Aristotle enables us to refer a definition specifically to Speusippus or Xenocrates as the author.

discover in the *Euthyphro* the principal points of both ethical and metaphysical doctrine with which we are already familiar.

The act for which Euthyphro is arraigning his father, we must remember, is specifically an offence against religious law, not a civil wrong, and Euthyphro does not profess to be in any way actuated by motives of humanity or regard for civil right. He is afraid of incurring religious " pollution " by living in household relations with a " sacrilegious person," and wishes to safeguard himself. It is implied that the average Athenian, who is shocked at his procedure, is ignorant of or indifferent to the religious law in which Euthyphro considers himself an expert. Obviously, then, as a " doctor in theology " he may be presumed to know what we might call " canon law " in its entirety, not merely the paragraphs of it which deal with homicide. Hence Socrates, as a person shortly to be accused of irreligion, appeals to him as an expert for an answer to the question what " piety " (τὸ εὐσεβές) or " religious duty " (τὸ ὅσιον) is in its genuine character. There must be some one character which belongs to all action which is " *religiously* right " (ὅσιον), and an opposite character which is shown in all action which is religiously wrong. There must be a definition of " religious obligation," and we want to know what it is. It is noticeable that this common character of the " religiously right " is at the outset spoken of as a single ἰδέα (*Euthyphro*, 5*d*) and subsequently as an εἶδος (6*d*) and an οὐσία (11*a*). This is the language familiar to us as technical in the so-called Platonic " theory of Forms," but it is represented as understood at once by Euthyphro without any kind of explanation. It seems quite impossible to escape the conclusion that from the very first Plato represented Socrates as habitually using language of this kind and being readily understood by his contemporaries.[1]

Like so many of the interlocutors in these early dialogues of Plato, Euthyphro at first confuses definition with the enumeration of examples. " Religious duty " is to proceed against the party guilty of an offence against religion, whether it be a homicide or a sacrilegious theft, or any other such crime, without being deterred by any regard for the ties of blood ; to neglect this duty is " irreligious " (5*d–e*). We have the best of examples for this, that of Zeus himself who " chained " his own father. Of course, if this statement is taken to be more than a production of instances, it would be delightfully " circular," since it makes *religious* duty amount to active opposition to *irreligion*. Socrates prefers to regard the statement as a mere illustration and simply repeats his request for an account of the " one form " in virtue of which

[1] There is indeed an important point on which Socrates is represented as needing to explain himself in the *Phaedo* ; he has to explain at some length how the theory of Forms bears on the problem of " coming into being and passing out of being." We may readily believe that *this* would need some explaining to most persons, but the meaning of the words, ἰδέα, εἶδος, and the reality of the existence of " forms," is simply presupposed in the *Phaedo*, as elsewhere, without any explanation or justification.

all religious duties are religious. This leads to a first attempt at definition : " the religious is what is pleasing to the gods, the irreligious what is not pleasing to them " (6e). This is, in form, a good definition ; whether it is sound in substance remains to be seen. The difficulty is that, according to Euthyphro himself, dissensions and enmities exist among the gods.[1] Now it is not every disagreement which leads to quarrels and enmities. A difference of opinion about number, size, or weight is readily settled by an appeal to counting, measuring, or weighing. It is when we come to disagreement about moral questions—"right and wrong, fine and ugly, good and bad "—that it is hard to find a standard by which to settle the disagreement, and this is why it is regularly differences of this kind which lead to quarrels and factions among us [2] (7c–d). We may fairly reason that if the gods quarrel and fight, it is over the same questions ; they quarrel about right and wrong, and each party will be pleased by what it regards as right and offended by what it thinks wrong. Thus what pleases one god may offend another, and the same act will be, in that case, both religious and irreligious (8a). Cronus, for example, can hardly be supposed to approve of Euthyphro's present proceedings.

Euthyphro's way of meeting the difficulty is to commit in an undisguised form the circle already implied in his original statement. There are points, he urges, on which all the gods would agree ; they would all agree, for example, that wrongful homicide ought not to go unpunished. (Thus he suggests that the definition might run that religious acts are those which the gods approve unanimously, with the explanation that the class " acts unanimously approved by the gods " is identical with the class of rightful acts.) But the suggestion makes matters no better. No one, not even the defendant in a prosecution for homicide, ever denies that *wrongful* homicide, or any other wrongful act, ought to be punished. The issue at stake is always which of the two parties is in the wrong and what is the precise character of the wrong committed. If the

---

[1] These " wars in heaven " refer principally to the stories of the dethronement of Cronus and the Titans and the war of the gods with the giants, to which allusion has already been made. They are part of the Orphic and the Hesiodic theogonies. Socrates does not believe such stories (*Euthyphro*, 6a–c) and it is easy to show that they were not taken seriously by Athenians in general, but Euthyphro has expressly avowed his belief in them and still stranger tales (6b), and it is he who is offering the definition. Hence the objection is perfectly valid against him.

[2] The passage is noteworthy. Plato is fond of assimilating the use of a true " scale of values " to the employment of number, measure, and weight. We may fairly conjecture with Burnet that the suggestion comes from Socrates. Knowledge of good, by enabling us to estimate correctly the relative worth of different " goods," would reduce our heated quarrels about our " rights " to a problem in " moral arithmetic." There is much truth in this. In the bitterest of such quarrels both parties often sincerely wish for no more than their " fair due." The trouble is that they cannot agree on the question how much that is. Compare Leibniz's hope that a perfected " symbolic logic " would reduce all philosophical disputes to the working of a " calculation."

gods are at variance, then, their difference cannot be on the question whether a wrongful act should be punished, but on the very different question what acts are wrongful. How do we know, for example, that different gods might not be of different mind about the rightness or wrongfulness of the step Euthyphro is now taking ? This, however, is only a minor difficulty. We may allow Euthyphro to put his definition in the amended form, " The religious is that which the gods approve and the irreligious that which they disapprove unanimously." But we still have to ask the graver question, " Is a religious act religious because the gods approve it, or do they approve it because it is religious ? " (8b–10a).

(The question is one which has played a prominent part in ethical controversy in later days. It amounts to asking whether acts of piety, or more generally virtuous acts, derive their character of being right from the mere fact of being commanded, or are commanded because they are antecedently *intrinsically* right. Are the " commandments of God " arbitrary ? Is moral obligation *created* by the imposition of a command ? This is, in effect, the thesis of both Hobbes and Locke, and is what Cudworth is denying in his treatise on *Eternal and Immutable Morality*, when he sets himself to argue that acts are good or bad " by nature " and not by " mere will." The same issue reappears in a different terminology in the objection taken against Hutcheson's doctrine of an " implanted moral sense " by those who urged that on the theory in question our Creator might have given us an inverted " moral sense," and then the promotion of human misery would have been our highest duty.) [1] The point is too fine to be taken at once by a man of Euthyphro's type, and therefore has to be explained at a length which we find superfluous. The difficulty hardly exists for us, because we are accustomed from childhood to the distinction between the active and passive " voices " of a verb. In the time of Plato there was, as Burnet reminds us, no grammatical terminology ; the very distinction between a verb and a noun is not *known* to have been drawn by anyone before Plato himself, and that in a late dialogue, the *Sophistes*. The point to be made is the simple one that a definition of an οὐσία cannot properly be given by means of a verb in the passive voice (Burnet, *loc. cit.*). That is, it is no answer to the question what something is, to be told what some one or something else does to it. In more scholastic terminology, a formula of this kind would be a definition by means of a mere " extrinsic denomination," and would throw no light on the *quiddity* of the *definiendum*. [2] (It must be remembered that

---

[1] The problem was also a prominent one in the age of Scholasticism. It is against the view that obligation is created by command that St. Thomas (*S.C.G.* iii. 122) says that fornication is not sufficiently proved to be sinful by alleging that it is an " injury to God." " For we only offend God by doing what is against our own good." It therefore still remains to show that the conduct in question is " against our own good."

[2] Of course such definitions are common enough ; *e.g.* you could not define " trustee " except by a verb in the passive voice or its equivalent. But what

in a question of moral science we are not concerned with a purely *nominal* definition, like those of mathematics, the mere interpretation of a new symbol by a combination of symbols already familiar. The definition of a *character* such as ὅσιον is inevitably a *real* definition, and this is why Socrates calls it a discourse about an οὐσία.)

The principle to be laid down is that when something happens to, or is done to, a thing there is always a correlated person or thing who is the doer. Thus if a thing is carried, or is seen, there is some one or something who carries or sees that thing. And when we use a " passive " participle or adjective to characterize anything, we do so *because* something is being done to the thing by something else. (Thus, it is meant, if a thing is being seen by some one it is a " thing seen " or *visible* (ὁρώμενον), but you could not argue that because a thing is visible some one must actually be seeing it.[1]) In other words, a passive participle or adjective of passive sense is always a *denominatio extrinseca*. Now a thing which is liked or approved (φιλούμενον) comes under this rule ; " it is not because it is a-thing-approved that some one approves it ; it is because some one actually approves it that it is a-thing-approved " (10c.) But this consideration is fatal to our proposed formula, if the formula be taken as a definition of τὸ ὅσιον. If " all the gods " approve the " religious act," that, as Euthyphro concedes at once, is because the act *is* " religious " ; its character as ὅσιον is the *cause* of their approbation. The " extrinsic denomination " thing-approved-by-the-gods, on the other hand, only belongs to τὸ ὅσιον as a consequence of the *fact* that the gods approve it. Thus the formula does not tell us what the character on the ground of which the gods approve certain acts *is* (its οὐσία), but only something which happens to these acts, namely, that the gods approve them ; it tells us an " affection " (πάθος) of the " religious," not its *quiddity* (11a).[2]

Thus we have to begin the work of looking for a definition of the " religious " over again. Our definitions keep running away from us, like the mythical statues of Daedalus, the reputed ancestor

you are really defining in this case is a relation, the relation of the trustee to the " truster." In the case of τὸ ὅσιον we are attempting to define a *quality* (πάθος), and it is no definition of this quality to say that " the gods like it."

[1] Berkeley, it is true, *seems* sometimes to be arguing as though we could infer from the fact that a thing is visible, the further fact that some one is always seeing it. But even he would hardly have argued that if a thing is eatable, some one must be eating it.

[2] It is tacitly assumed that if the gods approve *x, y, z* . . . they do so for an intelligible reason. There is some character common to *x, y, z* over and above the " extrinsic denomination " of being in fact approved, and this character is the ground of the approbation. On the use of the words οὐσία, πάθος (the most general name for anything, mode, quality, relation, etc., which can be asserted of a subject), see Burnet's notes, *loc. cit.* The way in which the terms are used without explanation implies that they are part of an already familiar logical terminology.

of Socrates.[1] Socrates must have inherited, much against his will, a double portion of his ancestor's gift, for it seems that he can bestow mobility on other men's " products " as well as on his own. But he will try to do what he can to remedy the trouble. At this point (12a) the discussion makes a fresh start—a start, we may note, due to the direct suggestion of Socrates, whose part in the dialogues is by no means so exclusively that of a mere critic of others as is sometimes fancied. What is the relation of τὸ ὅσιον (religion) to δικαιοσύνη (duty, obligation, morality in general) ? We both admit that whatever is religious (ὅσιον) is " dutiful " or " right " (δίκαιον) ; can we convert the proposition *simpliciter* and say that whatever is right is religious ? *I.e.* is all duty duty to God ? Euthyphro has the difficulty which seems to beset all beginners in logic in seeing that the universal affirmative proposition does not admit of simple conversion, and the point has to be made clear to him by examples. All reverence (αἰδώς) is fear, but it is not true that all fear (*e.g.* fear of illness) is reverence. All odd integers are numbers, but all numbers are not odd. Reverence is a " part " of fear as " odd number " is of number. In the more developed logical terminology of Aristotle, the thing would, of course, be expressed by saying that reverence and odd number are *species* (εἴδη) of the *genera* fear and number, but Plato, who sits loose to terminology, except when it is needed for the purpose immediately in hand, habitually uses the word " part " (μόριον, μέρος) for what we still call the *membra dividentia* of a logical " division." When the point has been explained to him, Euthyphro at once answers that τὸ ὅσιον is only one part of τὸ δίκαιον—that is, in modern language, that duty to God is not the whole of the duty of man, but one specific branch of it. Thus, like the mass of mankind, he believes in a plurality of distinct " virtues." Man has, *e.g.*, a certain set of " duties to God," and another distinct set of duties to his fellow-men, and it would follow that you might specialize in one of these branches of duty but neglect the others. You might be strong in " religion " but weak, *e.g.*, in honesty, like the legendary Welshman who " had a wonderful gift in prayer but was an awful liar." From the Socratic point of view, this would be impossible. *All* virtue is knowledge of good, and consequently any one real virtue, if you live up to it, will prove to cover the whole of human conduct. The " content " of morality and that of religion would thus alike be the whole sphere of human conduct, and it would be quite impossible in principle to distinguish a man's " religious " from his " moral " duties. At bottom, the reason why the *Euthyphro* ends negatively is the same as that which accounts for the formally negative result of the *Laches* or *Charmides*, the fact that genuine " goodness " is a unity.

---

[1] For the point of the jest, see Burnet, *loc. cit.* It would be *spoilt* if there were any truth in the later story that Socrates was actually the son of a sculptor and had practised the calling himself, as any intelligent reader ought to see.

This is suggested at once for us in 12*d*. If " religion " is a " part " of morality, we must go on to ask " which " part it is ; *i.e.*, to use the technical phrase which meets us as such for the first time in the *Theaetetus*, we must ask for the " difference " which marks off " religious " duties from the rest of our duties. We may suggest that τὸ δίκαιον can be divided into two species, the " cult " or " service " (θεραπεία) of the gods and the cult or service of man ; the former will be religion (12*e*). The thought is that all morality is service, and that service falls under two mutually exclusive heads, the " service of God," and " the service of man," a view still widely popular. (From Socrates' point of view, of course, the view would be false ; you cannot serve man without in the very act serving God, nor serve God without serving man.)

To follow the argument to which this third attempt at a definition gives rise, we have to remember that the word θεραπεία was in use in two special connexions. It was used of the *cult* of a deity by his worshipper (cp. our objectionable use of the phrases " divine service," " Sunday services "), or of a great man by his courtiers, and of the " tending " of men or animals by professionals such as physicians and grooms (the sense of the word from which Socrates developed his conception of the " tending of one's soul " as the supreme business of life). The problem is to determine in which, if either of these senses, religion is to be called the " service " of God. If we start with the second sense, that in which the professional trainer of hounds or oxherd may be said to " tend " or " serve " the hounds or oxen, we see that the aim of such tendance is always to make the " tended " better, to get the dogs or oxen into the pink of condition and keep them so. But we cannot suppose that religion is the service of God in this sense. No one would say that by performing his " religious duties " he "makes his gods better " (13*a–c*). We, must mean " service " in the very different sense in which slaves are said to " serve " or " tend " their owner. Now the " service " of a slave consists in acting as an instrument or " understrapper " in carrying out his owner's business ; it is a form of ὑπηρετική, " co-operating as a subordinate with a superior for the achievement of some result " (13*d*).

Now we can say at once what the result to which the slave of a medical man contributes under his master's direction is ; it is the curing of the master's patients. So the slave of a builder contributes as a subordinate to the construction of a ship or a house. If, then, " serving God " means contributing as an underworker contributes to the business of his superior, if it is " co-operation as an instrument," what is the great work to which *we* contribute " under the gods "? (13*e*). (No answer is given to the question in our dialogue. None could be given by a man like Euthyphro who keeps his morality and his religion in separate " water-tight compartments," and Socrates naturally does not answer his own question. But it is not hard to discover from other dialogues what the Socratic answer would be. The great business of man, we know, is to " tend " his own soul, and so far as he can the souls of all who come into contact with him, to "make them as good as possible." We shall find him, in the *Phaedo* and elsewhere, describing this course of life as "assimilation to God" (ὁμοίωσις θεῷ). Thus we shall not go far wrong if we say that the "great and glorious work of God" is to be the source of order and good to the universe, and that we "contribute under God" to that work in the degree to which we bring order and good into the little "world" of our own personal life and that of the society to which we belong. Such an answer would, of course, presuppose the "unity of the virtues," and break down all barriers between the service of man and the service of God, morality and religion ; it would make irreligion a breach of morality and laxity of morals an offence against religion.)

Euthyphro's inability to follow the thought of Socrates throws him back on what had all along been his implied position, the position of the fanatic who divorces religion from morality. "If a man knows how to please the gods by his words of prayer and his acts of sacrifice—that is religion, and that is what makes private families and public commonwealths prosperous" (14*b*). In briefer phrase, religion is "a science of sacrificing and praying" (14*c*). (Euthyphro, of course, takes the word "science" employed by Socrates to mean simply correct knowlege of the ritual to be observed.) Now in sacrificing we give something to the gods and in prayer we ask something from them. So we may finally put Euthyphro's thought into this definition (the fourth and last of the dialogue), "Religion is the science of asking the gods for things and giving things to them" (14*d*). Now the right way of asking will be to ask for what we really need, and the right way of giving will be to give the gods what *they* want of us, and thus religion turns out to be "an art of traffic between men and gods" (ἐμπορικὴ τέχνη θεοῖς καὶ ἀνθρώποις παρ' ἀλλήλων, 14*e*). But traffic is, of course, a transaction between two parties for mutual advantages ; one "cannot be buyer and seller too." What one party to the traffic between gods and men gets out of the transaction is obvious ; the gods send us all the good things we enjoy. But what "advantage" (ὠφελία) do they get from us ? No "profit," says Euthyphro, but "honour and thanks and gratitude" (τιμή τε καὶ γέρα καὶ χάρις, 15*a*). "The religious act "thus turns out to be "that which is grateful (κεχαρισμένον) to the gods," and this brings us back to the very definition we have already had to reject, that "the religious" is τὸ τοῖς θεοῖς φίλον, "what the gods approve" (15*e*) ; so that we are no nearer knowing what religion is than when we began our discussion.

As I have said, the gentle satire on the unworthy conception of religion as a trade-enterprise carried on by God and man for their mutual benefit ought not to blind us to the fact that the definition of it as *knowing* how to ask from God and how to make a return to Him is capable of being understood in a genuinely Socratic sense. The very introduction into this formula of ἐπιστήμη as the *genus* of religion should indicate that it contains a suggestion we are meant to follow out. "Imitation," says the proverb, "is the sincerest form of flattery." And we may add that the "imitation of God " shown in a life devoted to the "tendance of the soul" is the one acceptable τιμή and the true thanksgiving for the goods we receive from God. So understood, the formula that religion is asking the right things from God and making the right return does not contradict but coincides with the other formula that it is co-operation as agents "under God " in a great and glorious "work."

2. *Apology*.—The *Apology* is too well known to require any elaborate analysis, though it must not be passed over without some remarks on points of general interest. Apart from its strictly historical interest as a professed faithful reproduction of the actual language of Socrates at the memorable trial, it has a philosophical interest as a picture of the life of " tendance of the soul " adopted with full consciousness and led at all costs to its appropriate and glorious end. What is depicted is the life of a " martyr " of the best type as seen from within by the martyr himself ; the object of the picture is to make us understand why the martyr chooses such a life and why the completion of his career by the martyr's death is a *corona* and not a " disaster." In our more commonplace moods we are accustomed to think of martyrdom as a highly dis-agreeable duty ; perhaps it must not be shirked, but we feel that, to be made tolerable to our imagination, it must be " made up " to the martyr by an " exaltation " to follow it. Plato means us rather to feel that the martyrdom is itself the " exaltation " : *in cruce gaudium spiritus ; ambula ubi vis . . . non invenies altiorem viam supra, nec securiorem viam infra, nisi viam sanctae crucis.* The *Apology* is the Hellenic counterpart of the second book of the *Imitatio*.

For the considerations which make it certain that in substance Plato has preserved the actual speech of Socrates (which, as he lets us know, he himself heard), see Burnet's *Introductory Note* and the works referred to there. We must, of course, understand that, like all the circulated versions of celebrated speeches (those of Aeschines and Demosthenes in the matter of the " Crown," for example), the published speech is supposed to have been "revised " in accord with the canons of prose-writing. Plato has, no doubt, done for the defence of Socrates what men like Demosthenes did for their own speeches before they gave them to the world. At the same time we clearly have no right to assume that the process of revision and polishing involves any falsification of fundamental facts. That what we possess is in substance a record of what Socrates actually said is sufficiently proved by the single consideration that, though we cannot date the circulation of the *Apology* exactly, we can at least be sure that it must have been given to the world within a few years of the actual trial, and would thus be read by numbers of persons, including both devoted admirers of the philosopher and hostile critics (and presumably even some of the judges who had sat upon the case), who would at once detect any falsification of such recent facts.[1] It should also be added that even the subtle art by which Socrates, while professing to be a mere "layman" in forensic oratory, actually makes his speech conform to precedent in its general structure, an art most readily appreciated by following Burnet's careful analysis, is certainly not a mere stylistic "improvement" by Plato. The *Gorgias* and *Phaedrus* would be mere mystifications if it were not the fact that, for all his contempt for the ideals of contemporary "rhetoric," Socrates was quite familiar with its recognized methods and principles. Indeed, the *Apology* might be said to afford an ironical illustration of the paradox of the *Gorgias* about the uses which may legitimately be made of rhetorical devices. Socrates is in the position of an accused party, and he makes a "defence" which has been felt from the time of Xenophon onward to be something very much like an avowal of guilt. This is exactly in accord with the principles of the *Gorgias*. Socrates is accused of an offence, and in the eyes of an average Athenian, though not in his own, he has done what amounts to the commission of that offence. Consequently he uses impressive eloquence, not to veil the facts but to put their reality in the clearest light. He is, and for many years has been, a "suspected character," and the whole "defence" consists in insisting on the point and explaining that the suspicion has been inevitable. Even the act of which an ordinary advocate would have made the most as evidence of "sound democratic sentiments," Socrates' defiance of the order of the "Thirty" in the affair of Leon (*Apol.* 32c–d), is deliberately introduced by a previous narrative of an event of which such an advocate would have been careful to say nothing, or as little as possible, Socrates' opposition to the δῆμος at the trial of the Arginusae generals. Thus what might have been used by a man like Lysias to make an acquittal morally certain is actually employed by Socrates as an opportunity to warn the court that they must expect from him no sacrifice of conviction to "democratic sentiments." From the point of view of a Lysias, Socrates must have been "throwing away the ace of trumps" by using the story of his defiance of the Thirty as he does.

The very singular historical circumstances of the trial of Socrates have been better explained in Professor Burnet's notes to his edition of the *Apology* and the chapter on the "Trial" in *Greek Philosophy, Part I.*, than anywhere else. I shall therefore refer the reader to those works for full discussion, contenting myself with an indication of the points which seem most important.

Though the actual prosecutor was Meletus, every one knew that the real instigator of the whole business was Anytus, one of the two

---

[1] In particular, it is quite unthinkable that Plato should have invented the few words, addressed to friends and supporters after the court had voted the penalty of death, with which the *Apology* closes. Modern writers, who think it "impossible" that Socrates should have spoken after sentence had been pronounced, are simply transferring the procedure of a modern European court of justice to the Athens of the fifth century. For the opportunity the case would give for the making of the remarks, see Burnet, *Apology*, p. 161.

most admired and trusted leaders of the restored democracy. Since Anytus was in one and the same year assisting the prosecution of Socrates but helping the defence of Andocides on the very same charge of " irreligion," we cannot suppose motives of fanaticism to have had anything to do with his action. We may fairly suppose that what he attributed to Socrates was the " corruption of the young men," and that this meant exercising an influence hostile to the temper of unquestioning loyalty to the democracy. That this crime, if it is a crime, was one of which Socrates was guilty can be proved from the *Apology* itself, where his capital point is that he is ready to encounter the hostility of the πλῆθος or of any one else at the bidding of conscience. Such criticisms of the heroes of the old democracy as we read in the *Gorgias* and *Meno* are additional evidence, though, in fact, a " practical politician " like Anytus would need no evidence beyond the notorious intimacies between the philosopher and men like Alcibiades, Critias, and Charmides. But there was a reason why Anytus could neither put his real case forward without disguise of some kind nor appear as the actual prosecutor, and this reason has rightly been insisted on by Burnet. The worst " offences " of Socrates had been committed under the old democracy and all open reference to them was banned by the Act of Oblivion forbidding all questioning of citizens for anything done before the archonship of Euclides. Anytus had himself been one of the foremost promoters of this Act and could therefore neither himself prosecute, nor instigate anyone else to prosecute, acts covered by this amnesty. It was necessary to put forward some further pretext for proceeding and to find a nominal prosecutor who would make the pretext the main charge in his indictment. This explains why, to judge from the *Apology*, the precise nature of the " corruption of the young " by Socrates was left so much in the dark that we only discover what is meant by reading rather carefully between the lines of the defence. It also explains the selection of " irreligion " as the accusation to be pressed home and of Meletus as the nominal prosecutor. Burnet is plainly right in holding that it is most improbable, since the name Meletus is a rare one, that there should have been two men of that name, one of whom prosecuted Socrates and another Andocides for the same offence in the same year. If, as is probable, the prosecutor in both cases was the same man, and the speech " against Andocides " preserved to us under the name of Lysias that delivered by Meletus in the prosecution of Andocides—whether it is a composition of his own, or one written by Lysias to be spoken " in character," we see at once why Meletus was selected. The speech against Andocides is that of a sincere but hopelessly crazy fanatic—the very man to make the right sort of tool for a political intrigue just because he combines absolute honesty with the simplicity of a half-wit. Such a man would throw himself heart and soul into the prosecution of an *impie*, none the less effectively because, as is clear from the line taken by Socrates in his defence, neither he nor

anyone else knew precisely what the "impiety" consisted in.
(It is also worth notice that according to Andocides Meletus was
one of the party who executed the illegal arrest of Leon, in which
Socrates refused to be concerned, and thus, as a man who had
contracted the pollution of φόνος, ought to have been in the dock
himself on the very charge he was bringing against less guilty folk.
That Socrates disdains to make a point of this is strictly in keeping
with his character.) As to the meaning of the "impiety" charged
against Socrates, all that we learn from the *Apology* is that Socrates
regards it as having something to do with the caricatures of his
earlier scientific pursuits in the *Clouds* and other comedies, where
men of science in general are represented as having no respect for
the gods of the current official worships. No doubt this statement
is correct, as far as it goes, but there must have been something
more behind the indictment of Socrates. The fact that Andocides
was tried on the same charge about the same time for a ritual offence
and found it necessary in his defence to go into the whole old
scandal of the "mutilation of the Hermae" and the "profanation
of the mysteries" seems, as Burnet has urged, to give us the key
to the secret. Alcibiades and other prominent men among the
associates of Socrates had been deeply implicated in the affair
of the "mysteries," and this would, no doubt, be in the minds of all
the judges. Socrates makes no allusion to the matter in his defence, but this only proves what we should expect from the whole
tenour of his life, that, even in defending himself on a capital charge,
he was scrupulous to observe the spirit of the law by which
offences before the archonship of Euclides had been "amnestied."
Meletus is likely to have been less cautious.

We cannot well acquit Anytus of having stooped to instigate
a proceeding in which he was ashamed to take the principal part,
and of having used a tool whom he must have despised. But this
is no more than has often been done by politicians who, as the
world goes, are counted high-minded. His object was simply to
frighten away from Athens a person whose influence he believed to
be undesirable, much as Dutch William resorted to trickery to
frighten King James out of England—an act for which he is eulogized
by Macaulay. Socrates might have preserved his life by going
away before trial, as it was customary to do when there was any
doubt about acquittal. Indeed Plato is careful to let us see that
even when the case came into court, escape would have been easy.
The verdict of guilty, even after the uncompromising speech of the
accused had been delivered, was only obtained by a small majority.
We may safely infer that an opposite verdict could pretty certainly
have been secured by a little deference to popular opinion, a little
adroit silence about one or two incidents and stress on others—
such as the excellent military record of the accused—with a few
words of regret for the past and promise of cautious behaviour in
future. Even without any of this, it is clear that if Socrates had
chosen to propose a moderate fine as a sufficient penalty, the offer

would have been accepted. (Not to mention that he could readily have escaped during his unexpected month of detention in custody, and that public opinion would not have blamed him.) The accusers had no wish to have the guilt of any man's blood at their doors ; Socrates himself forced their hand. Without any desire for a martyrdom, they had created a situation in which there must inevitably be one, unless the other party would compromise with his conscience, and a martyrdom Socrates determined they should have. This is what he means (*Apology*, 39*b*) by saying that both sides must abide by their τίμημα. Socrates holds in conscience that his conduct has been that of a public benefactor, his opponents that it amounts to crime worthy of death. They would like a confession from himself that their estimate is correct ; if by act or word he would admit this, they are willing not to inflict the penalty. They do not wish to inflict death, but they do wish for the admission that it is deserved. *If* it is deserved, says Socrates, let it be inflicted ; you shall be compelled to " have the courage of your opinions."

In dealing with the analysis of the *Apology* we have to start by understanding that the real and serious defence of Socrates, which is made to rest on his conviction of a special divine mission to his fellow-countrymen, does not begin until we reach page 28*a*. What goes before (*Apol.* 17*a–27e*) is introductory matter, and is concerned with two preliminary points, the explanation of the prejudices which have grown up about Socrates (18*a–24b*), and a proof that the accuser himself cannot say, or at any rate dares not say, what he really means by his charges (24*b–27e*). Throughout the whole of the preliminary pages we must expect to find abundant traces of the whimsical humour which the enemies of Socrates in Plato call his " irony " ; at every turn we have to allow for the patent fact that he is " not wholly serious " ; the actual defence of his conduct through life, when we reach it, is pure earnest. (It is important to call attention to this, since the well-known narrative of the part played by the Delphic oracle in the life of the philosopher belongs to the preliminary account of the causes of the popular misconceptions about him, and has to be taken with the same allowance for his native humour as the account of the burlesques on him by the comic poets. The claim to be conscious of a special mission, imposed not by " the gods," nor by " Apollo," but " by God," comes from the actual defence. The two things have very little to do with one another, and are treated in very different tones ; nothing but misconception can come of the attempt to confuse them. Similarly the point of the " cross-examination " of Meletus has repeatedly been missed by commentators who have not seen that the whole passage is humorous, though with a humour which is deadly for its victim.)

(*a*) *Plea for an Impartial Hearing and Explanation of the Existing Prejudices unfavourable to the Speaker.*—The speech opens in a very usual way with an apology, mainly playful, for the speaker's unacquaintance with the diction of the courts, and a request to be allowed to tell his story in his own way (17a–18a). The one piece of downright earnest in this exordium is the insistence that the supreme business of " oratory " is to tell the truth—a business in which the speaker may claim to be more than a match for his accusers. Like every one who wishes for an impartial hearing, he is first bound to remove any prejudices the audience may have conceived against him. It will not be enough to deal with the attempts the prosecution has just made to create such prejudices ; there is a more inveterate prejudice dating from old days ; the judges who are to decide the case have heard long ago that Socrates is a " clever man " who " busies himself about things aloft and under the earth, and makes the weaker cause appear the stronger "—the double accusation of being a physicist and being an " eristic," which is, in fact, made in the *Clouds* of Aristophanes. " Intellectuals " of this type are popularly suspected of disregard of the gods ; the charges were made in comedies which many of the judges must have seen a quarter of a century ago, in boyhood, when impressions are easily made ; they have never received any rejoinder ; what is more, they have been repeated since of *malice prepense* [1] by a host of anonymous slanderers, and it is these vague prejudices rather than the accusations of the present prosecutors that are likely to stand in the way of a fair trial (18a–e).

The sufficient answer to all this is that Socrates is not responsible for the nonsense he is made to talk in the *Clouds*. His judges themselves must know whether they ever heard him discourse on such topics. But he is careful to add that he means no disparagement to knowledge of this kind ; if it exists.[2] Neither is it true that he has ever made a " profession " of " educating men " ; *i.e.* he is not one of the professional teachers of " goodness," though, again, he is far from disparaging so splendid a calling. If he really could " teach goodness," he says humorously, he would not, like Evenus, do it for a paltry five minae. He would know how *se faire valoir* (20b).

How then has he got the name for being " clever " or " wise " ? Here comes in the well-known tale of the Delphic oracle and its response to Chaerephon, that no man living was wiser than Socrates. Socrates says that he was at first staggered by this pronouncement, and set to work to prove Apollo of Delphi—never a *persona grata* at Athens, for excellent reasons—a liar. With this view he went round looking for a wiser man than himself in the various sections of society. He began with the " statesmen," but soon found that though they fancied themselves very wise, they certainly had no

---

[1] φθόνῳ καὶ διαβολῇ, 18d. It is implied that there was no real ill-feeling on the part of the comic poets who started these stories. They meant no more than fun. We can see for ourselves that this is true of Aristophanes.

[2] *Apol.* 19c. As Burnet points out, *loc. cit.*, what is said here is quite in keeping with the representation of the *Phaedo* that Socrates was deeply interested in all these matters in early life, until he discovered that he " had no head for them " (an expression itself to be taken playfully).

wisdom. Next he tried the poets with much the same result. He found that they were hopelessly incapable of explaining what they meant in their finest work ; this showed that the poet, like a possessed person, speaks under the influence of a genius and inspiration of which he is not master.[1] Finally, he turned to the artisans ; they were less disappointing than " statesmen " and poets, since it turned out that they did know something. They knew their own trades. Unfortunately they fancied that because they knew their trades, they must equally be competent to judge of the greatest questions (*e.g.*, no doubt, as Burnet has said, how to govern an empire).[2] It seemed then as though the Delphic god was not lying after all ; he was merely speaking in riddles, the notorious trick of his trade. He meant to say that human wisdom is such a sorry affair that the wisest man is one who, like Socrates, knows that he does *not* know anything to boast of (*Apol.* 20a–23b).

Naturally enough, the victims of this experiment did not take it any too kindly, and the matter was made worse by the young folk, sons of wealthy and leisured citizens, who accompanied Socrates, " without any pressing on his part " (αὐτόματοι, 23c ; *i.e.*, they were not in any sense " pupils "), for the sport to be got out of the thing, and even tried to practise the trick themselves. Their victims, of course, complain that Socrates is the ruin of the young people. When they are asked how he ruins them, shame prevents the reply, " By exposing the ignorance of us older men," and so they fall back on the old charges against scientific men in general, the accusation of irreligion and " making the weaker case the stronger." The present prosecutors are the mere mouthpieces of this idle talk (23c–24b).

(b) *Direct Reply to Meletus*.—Socrates now turns to the charges actually brought against him by the prosecution, with which he deals very curtly. The humour of the situation is that the prosecutor cannot venture to say what he means by either of his charges without betraying the fact that, owing to the " amnesty," the matters complained of are outside the competency of the court. What he really means by the " corruption of the young " is the supposed influence of Socrates on Alcibiades, Critias, Charmides, and others who have been false to the democracy ; the charge of irreligion is connected with the scandals of the year 415. But to admit this would be to invite the court to dismiss the case. Hence, when Meletus is pressed to explain what he means, he has to take refuge in puerile nonsense. The judges could understand the situation and, no doubt, enjoy it amazingly ; many modern commentators have been badly perplexed by the " sophistical " character of Socrates' reasoning simply because they have not set them-

---

[1] As Burnet says, *loc. cit.*, Euripides would be about the first of the " tragedians " to whom Socrates would apply his test. We have seen already that Socrates held the " modern " view of poetry as dependent on " inspiration."
[2] Compare Mr. Chesterton's *mot* about " the authority which obviously attaches to the views of an electrical engineer " on the existence of God or the immortality of the soul.

selves to realize the difficulty of Meletus' position. They have missed the irony of Socrates' pretence that a prosecutor who is fanatically in earnest is merely playing a stupid practical joke. Meletus professes to have detected Socrates depraving the young. If he has, clearly he must be able to say who improve them. Under pressure, Meletus has to fall back on the view that any good Athenian improves the young by his association with them (because his influence is exerted in favour of the moral tradition of society, exactly as we have found Anytus maintaining in the *Meno*, and shall find Protagoras explaining more at length in the dialogue called after him). Socrates stands alone in making young people worse by his influence on them (25e). Now this is contrary to all analogy ; if you consider the case of horses or other domestic animals, you find that they are improved by only a few, the professionals who understand the art of training them ; they are spoiled when entrusted to anyone else. Moreover, a man must be very dull not to see that he would be acting very much against his own good by depraving the very persons among whom he has to live. No one would do such a thing on purpose (the Socratic doctrine that " no one does evil voluntarily "). If a man makes so grave an error involuntarily, the proper course is not to prosecute him but to open his eyes to his mistake. But Meletus, by prosecuting Socrates, makes it clear that he thinks him capable of the absurdity of purposely trying to deprave the very persons whose depravity would expose him to risk of harm at their hands (25c–26b).

Again, in what particular way does Socrates " deprave " his young friends ? No open allusion to the facts really meant being permissible, Meletus has to fall back on the reply that the depravation consists in incitement to the religious offence alleged in the indictment. Socrates sets the example of irreligion (26b). This brings us to the consideration of this accusation on its own account. Socrates professes to be quite unable to understand what can be meant by the statement that he " does not worship the gods of the city but practises a strange religion.[1] If Meletus means any-

---

[1] As to this accusation, see Burnet, *loc. cit.* It is quite certain on linguistic grounds that the meaning of the phrase that Socrates οὐ νομίζει τοὺς θεοὺς οὓς ἡ πόλις νομίζει is that he does not conform to the *cultus*, does not "worship" the official gods, not that " he does not *believe* in their existence." Aristophanes is punning on this sense of the word νομίζειν when he makes Socrates explain to Strepsiades that ἡμῖν θεοὶ νομισμ' οὐκ ἔστι (" the gods are not legal tender *here* "). It is certain also that in the additional clause ἕτερα δὲ δαιμόνια καινά, δαιμόνια is adjective, not substantive, and that the sense is therefore, " but practises certain other unfamiliar religious observances." The meaning of this is made clearer by comparison with the *Clouds*, where Socrates is represented as combining the functions of a scientific man with those of president of a conventicle of ascetics. It was true that the Ionian men of science used the word θεός in a wholly non-religious way for whatever they took to be the primary body (this is why in the *Clouds* Socrates swears by Respiration and Air, and prays to " the Clouds "), and also that Socrates was an associate of Orphic and Pythagorean ascetics, like Telauges in the dialogue of Aeschines called by that aame, who had a religion of their own not officially recognized by the State. So far there is an intelligible basis for the

thing, he must presumably mean that Socrates is an atheist. (Meletus does not really mean this, and Socrates knows that he does not mean it. But he cannot explain what he really means without risking the collapse of his case, and Socrates is fully entitled to embarrass him for his own and the court's amusement. He despises the charge too much to take it seriously.) If this is what he means, and he dares not explain that it is not, his charge refutes itself. A man cannot be both an atheist and the votary of a " strange religion " ; to make an accusation of this kind is simply wasting the time of the court [1] (26e–27e).

(c) *The Vindication of Socrates' Life and Conduct* (28a–35d).— We come at last to Socrates' serious defence of his character, not against the frivolous charges on which he is being ostensibly tried but against grave misconceptions of old standing. He is well aware that his life is at stake, a thing which has happened to many a good man in the past and will happen again. But there is nothing dishonourable in such a situation. A man's part is to stand loyally, in the face of all risks, to the part which he has judged to be the best for himself, or to which his commander has ordered him. Socrates himself has acted on this principle in his military career, when his superior officers have commanded him to face dangers. Still more is it his duty to be loyal to the command of God which, as he is persuaded, has enjoined him to " spend his life in devotion to wisdom and in examining himself and his fellows " (28e). The real atheism would be to disobey the divine command. Disobedience would be a known evil, but the death with which he is threatened if he does not disobey may, for all he knows, be the greatest of good. Hence if he were offered acquittal on the condition of abandoning " philosophy," with certain death as the alternative, he would refuse acquittal. For God is more to be obeyed than any human law-court. For that reason, so long as life is in him, Socrates will never cease urging on every man the duty of " care for wisdom and truth and the good of his soul " and the relative unimportance of care for health or fortune. That is God's commission to him, and if Athens only knew it, his " service " ($ὑπηρεσία$) [2] of God is the greatest blessing that could befall the

---

reference to the $δαιμόνια\ καινά$. But it is still unexplained what ground there is for saying that Socrates does not worship the gods of the city, and it is this part of the charge on which Socrates fastens. It seems to me that Burnet is right in supposing that what is really meant is the old affair of the " profanation of the mysteries." The " psephism of Diopithes " has nothing to do with the matter. All " psephisms " before the year of Euclides were invalidated (*Andocides* i. 86).

[1] Formally, the argument is rather more elaborate. A man who concerns himself with $τὰ\ δαιμόνια$ (the " supernatural," as we might say) must believe that there are $δαίμονες$ (" supernatural beings ") ; these $δαίμονες$ are either themselves " gods " or are the " offspring of gods," and in either case, a man who believes in them cannot be an atheist. This is pure *persiflage*, but it is as good as Meletus and his backer Anytus deserve.

[2] Compare what has been already said in connexion with the *Euthyphro* about the conception of religion as serving God in the production of a $πάγκαλον$ $ἔργον$. Socrates pleads that his whole life has been dedicated to this work.

whole community (30a). If he "corrupts the young" at all, it must be by preaching to them his unchanging conviction that "it is not wealth which makes worth (ἀρετή), but worth makes wealth and all else good." His present speech is not made to save his own life—Anytus and Meletus may procure his death, but the really dreadful thing is not to lose your life but to *take* a life wrongfully (the thesis of the *Gorgias*)—he would save his fellow-citizens from misusing the gift God has bestowed on them, and is not likely to give them a second time, a gadfly whose buzzing prevents that high-bred but somnolent animal "the People" from drowsy sloth (30c–31c).

It may be asked why a man with such a mission has never attempted to act as a *public* monitor and adviser.[1] Well, the fact is that the "mysterious something" which has warned Socrates all his life against "unlucky" proceedings has always checked any attempt to take part in public life. *Et pour cause :* a democracy (πλῆθος) soon puts an end to anyone who defies its humours in the cause of right. Hence it was a condition of the exercise of the mission that it should be exercised on individuals, not on the multi-tude (31c–32a). In fact, Socrates has only twice been called upon by his mission to come into conflict with authority, once when he withstood the popular sentiment by refusing to be accessory to the unconstitutional steps taken against the generals after Arginusae, and once, more recently, when he disregarded the illegal command of the "Thirty" to arrest Leon. In both cases he ran a great personal risk, and in the second, might well have lost his life but for the downfall of the "Thirty" (32a–e). As for the charge of de-moralizing his "pupils," he has never had any "pupils," though he has never refused to communicate his convictions freely to every one (33a–b) as his mission required of him.[2] He is ready to summon the parents and elder brothers of the young men who have associated with him as witnesses that none of them have been made worse by his companionship (33d–34b).

The defence is now, in substance, concluded, and we have reached the point at which it was customary to make an appeal

---

[1] The implication is that a man of the remarkable gifts of Socrates, who carefully abstains from putting them openly at the service of the community, though he is believed to have employed them freely for the service of men like Alcibiades, must be a formidable anti-democratic conspirator.

[2] Note that in denying that he ever had μαθηταί, Socrates is still referring to the suspicion connected with his relations with prominent persons who are now dead. From Isocrates xi. 5, we learn that the pamphleteer Polycrates made it a principal charge that Alcibiades had been Socrates' pupil, just as Aeschines the orator (i. 173) says the same thing about Critias. Isocrates relates that Alcibiades had never been " educated " by Socrates, thus agreeing with Plato and Xenophon (*Mem.* I. 2, 12 ff.). Socrates is too scrupulously observant of the "amnesty" to explain himself, but it is Alcibiades and Critias, not younger unknown men like Plato and Aeschines of Sphettus, whom he means by his supposed "disciples." The reference to the " divine sign " at 31c is playful, like other allusions of the kind in Plato. The real reason why Socrates took no part in active politics is the one he goes on to give, that he knew the hopelessness of such an attempt.

to the clemency of the court for the sake of one's family and connexions. Socrates declines to follow the usual course, not because he has not dependents, friends, and relatives to whom he is bound by natural ties, but because the procedure would be unworthy of his character and an attempt to seduce the court from its duty. That would be a real "impiety." The issue must now be left in the hands of God and the judges (34*b*–35*e*).

The object of the pages which follow (36*a*–38*b*) is to explain why Socrates did not, after conviction, secure his life by proposing a moderate fine as an alternative penalty, as he clearly could have done. This must have been felt as a real difficulty by common-place persons even among the philosopher's friends, as we see from the absurd explanation given by Xenophon (*Apol.* 1–8) that Socrates deliberately provoked his own execution in order to escape the infirmities of old age. It has to be explained that his real motive was a worthy one. To propose any penalty whatever would amount to admitting guilt, and Socrates has already told the court that he regards himself as a minister of God for good to his countrymen. Hence he cannot in consistency propose any treatment for himself but that of a distinguished public benefactor, a place at the public table (σίτησις ἐν πρυτανείῳ). It should be noted that, strictly speaking, this is the τίμησις which Socrates offers as an alternative to the death-penalty demanded by the accusers. The whimsical mood has returned on him after the intense earnestness of the defence of his life and character. He urges that as he regards himself as a benefactor he can only propose the treatment of a benefactor for himself. The subsequent offer to pay the trifling sum of a mina (only raised to one of thirty minae at the urgent instance of friends) is made with the full certainty that the court, which has just heard Socrates' real opinion of his deserts, will reject it. The real issue is not whether a prophet of righteousness is a major or a minor offender, but whether he is a capital traitor or the one true "patriot," and Socrates is determined that the court shall not shirk that issue, as it would like to do. (As to the sum of thirty minae which Socrates' friends offer to pay for him, one should note (*a*) that in *Epistle* xiii. Plato, writing a generation later, mentions it to Dionysius II as a good dowry for anyone but a very rich man to give his daughter and that this estimate is borne out by a careful examination of all the references to dowries in the fourth-century orators, (*b*) that, though Plato and Apollodorus are joined with Crito as "security," the main burden of payment would, no doubt, fall on the wealthy Crito. The family of Plato are not likely to have been particularly well off just after the failure of the revolution in which its most prominent members had taken the losing side.[1] As we see from the speeches of Lysias belonging to this

---

[1] Cf. what Xenophon makes Charmides say about his own finances at *Symp.* 29 ff., where there seems to be an (anachronistic) allusion to the effects of the "Decelean" war.

period, the downfall of Athens in 404 had been followed by a widespread commercial crisis. Socrates' friends are making what, in the circumstances, must have been a very strenuous effort to save him. This is why they " ask for time " instead of offering to pay money down.[1])

In the concluding remarks of the speech made after the voting on the penalty, note in the first place how clearly it is recognized that Socrates has forced the issue, and that he could have secured his acquittal by simply " asking for quarter " (38d–39b). This is, of course, true of every typical martyr. Martyrdom is dying when you could escape if you would compromise a little with your conscience ; in this sense every martyr forces the issue. Anytus would rather not have killed Socrates, just as the average Roman proconsul would rather not have condemned Christians, or as Bonner (as appears even from the partial accounts of his enemies) would much rather not have sent Protestants to the stake. But it is not the business of the martyr to make things easy for the forcer of consciences.

In the impressive words of encouragement directed to his supporters (39e–41c), the important thing to note is that, contrary to the absurd opinion of many nineteenth-century writers, Socrates makes his own belief in a blessed life to come for the good perfectly plain. The best proof of this is that to which Burnet has appealed, comparison of his language with the brief and hesitating phrases in which the Attic orators are accustomed to allude to the state of the departed. In this respect the *Apology* agrees completely with the *Phaedo*, when we allow for the fact that in the former Socrates is speaking to a large audience, most of whom would not share his personal faith. No one but a convinced believer would have said half what he is made to say about his " hope " (not to mention that the " divinity " of the soul is at bottom the reason why the " tendance " of it is so much more important than that of the body, and, as Rohde long ago observed, to the Greek mind "immortality " and "divinity " are equivalents). The specific allusions of 41a to Hesiod, Musaeus, Orpheus and the Orphic judges of the dead, also make it clear that Socrates' convictions are not meant as simply inferences from "natural theology "; we have to see in them the influence of the Orphic religion, though the *Euthyphro* and the second book of the *Republic* show that Socrates thought very poorly of the ordinary run of " professing " Orphics in his own time.

3. *Crito.*—The *Euthyphro* and *Apology* between them have made us understand what Socrates meant by religion, and why his sense of duty to God forbade him either to evade prosecution or to purchase his life by any concessions. There is still one question connected with his death to which the answer remains to be given. Owing to unexpected circumstances, a month elapsed between

---

[1] This is implied in the mention of " security " (αὐτοὶ δ' ἐγγυᾶσθαι, 38b). Socrates could clearly have paid down the " one mina " of which he had spoken.

condemnation and execution. His friends took advantage of this delay to provide means of escape ; Socrates might still have avoided drinking the hemlock if he would have walked out of his prison, but he refused. Why was this ? No one would have thought the worse of him, and there would have been no question of a compromise with the leaders of the democracy. Persons who held with Socrates himself that the whole proceedings against him had been frivolous, and that he had been condemned for an offence which he had not committed, by a court which had no competence, might fairly be puzzled to know why he thought it a duty to refuse the means of escape. This is the point to be cleared up in the *Crito*. The explanation depends on an important distinction which the ordinary man to this day finds it hard to draw. The condemnation was in point of fact, as Socrates himself insisted, iniquitous. He was quite innocent of any real impiety. But it was strictly legal, as it had been pronounced by a legitimate court after a trial conducted in accord with all the forms of law. And it is the duty of a good citizen to submit to a legal verdict, even when it is materially false. By standing a trial at all, a man " puts himself on his country," and he is not entitled to disregard the decision to which he submits himself, even if his country makes a mistake. The " country " is entitled to expect that the legally pronounced sentence of a legitimate court shall be carried into effect ; there would be an end of all " law and order " if a private man were at liberty to disregard the judgment of the courts whenever he personally believed it to be contrary to fact.

Even so, there is a further point to be considered. We have seen that, strictly speaking, the court was not competent to take account of the offences which the prosecutors really had in mind, and that Socrates shows himself aware of this in the *Apology* when he cross-examines Meletus. It might, then, be urged that if Socrates had escaped he would not have been disregarding the decision of a competent court ; is it wrong to disrespect the sentence of an *in*competent one ? Two things need to be remembered : (*a*) the court thought itself competent, and Athenian law made no provision for the quashing of its findings as *ultra vires* ; (*b*) this being so, for an individual man who had all his life set the example of strict and complete compliance with the νόμοι of the city to follow his private judgment on the question of the competency of the court would have been to stultify the professions of a lifetime. Plato himself, in the same situation, Adam says, would probably have chosen to escape. This may be, but the second consideration just mentioned would not have applied to Plato in 399. A young man of under thirty, whose most important relatives had just four years before lost their lives in the cause of " oligarchy," could not be considered as having thrown in his lot definitely with the democracy and its νόμοι ; his position would have been really different from that of an old man of the Periclean age. The argument, used by Socrates, that to have neglected the opportunity to settle elsewhere is equivalent to a compact to live by the νόμος of the city, would have been inapplicable to a younger man who, in fact, had never had the option in question. Thus, in the last resort, there is a "subjective" and personal element in the considerations which lead Socrates to feel that he would be belying his whole past by escaping. Plato's object is not to lay down a categorical imperative for the guidance of all the wrongfully condemned, but to throw light on the motives of an individual great man. (Whether Plato would himself have chosen to escape, if he had been placed in the same situation *in his own seventieth year*, is another question. Much would depend on his view as to the work which might remain to him to do elsewhere.)

The dramatic *mise-en-scène* is necessarily exceedingly simple. The conversation is *tête-à-tête* between Socrates in his apartment in the prison of the Eleven and Crito, unless we count the "Laws" into whose mouths the last word of the argument is put as an unseen third party to the talk. The time is in the "small hours" before dawn, while it is still dark. Crito, who brings the news that the "sacred vessel" on whose return Socrates will have to die has just been sighted off Sunium, has been some time watching Socrates as he sleeps, when Socrates wakes from a strange dream and the conversation ensues. Crito fears that Socrates, whose sentence will be executed the day after the vessel reaches port, has only one more night to live ; Socrates, on the strength of his dream, expects, as turned out to be the fact, that the boat will not make so quick a voyage and that his death will be deferred another day. (In his interpretation he evidently takes the "fair and comely woman" of 44a for the "fetch" of the approaching vessel, and her "white garments" for its gay white sails.) This brief introduction leads straight to the conversation in which Crito puts the case for escape, to which Socrates replies point for point. (a) The friends of Socrates will suffer in reputation if he persists in dying. It will be supposed that they were too mean to find the money necessary for corrupting his jailers. The answer is that "decent folk" will know better than to think anything of the sort, and what the "many" think does not matter (44c). (b) Unfortunately it does matter what the "many" think. The power of popular prejudice is shown only too plainly by the present position of Socrates himself. *Answer :* the "many" are powerless to do much in the way of either good or ill, for they can neither make a man wise nor make him a fool ; hence it matters very little what they do to him (44d). (c) Perhaps Socrates is really thinking of the interests of his friends, who will be exposed to "blackmailers" (συκοφάνται) [1] if he breaks prison, and be forced to pay these persons to hold their tongues. He need not consider that point ; his friends are in duty bound to take the risk and, besides, these worthies

---

[1] As Burnet points out *loc. cit.*, the source of the annoyance caused by "sycophants" was the procedure of Attic law, which left it to the "common informer" (Ἀθηναίων τῷ βουλομένῳ) to institute prosecutions for offences against the "public."

are not very expensive to satisfy. If Socrates has a delicacy about exposing Crito to the risk, his "foreign" friends, Simmias, Cebes, and others, are ready to open their purses (45a–b).[1] He need have no difficulty in finding an abode where he will be made welcome. Crito himself has relations with powerful men in Thessaly who would honour his friend and act as his protectors (45c) (d) Besides, it is not even morally right that Socrates should throw away his life. That would be gratifying the very men who have prosecuted him. Also it would be deserting his family, and an honourable man has no right to disregard his obligations to his children. Thus refusal to escape will look like a display of unmanly cowardice in both Socrates and his friends (45c–46a).

Socrates begins his formal reply by saying that all through life it has been his principle to act on his deliberate judgment of good. He cannot feel that the judgments he expressed in his defence before the court are in any way affected by the result of the trial. If he is to take Crito's advice, he must first be convinced that there is something unsound in these principles ; it is useless to work on his imagination by setting up bugbears. The strength of Crito's case all through has lain in the appeal to "what will be thought of us." Now formerly we both held that it is not every opinion nor the opinions of every man which matter. Socrates is still of the same mind about this, and so, as he has to confess, is Crito. We should attach weight to the opinion of those who know (the φρόνιμοι), and disregard the opinion of those who do not. For example, in the matter of bodily regimen the physician and the trainer are the experts who know, and their approval or disapproval ought to count, whereas a man who followed by preference the approvals and disapprovals of the "many," who are laymen in such matters, would certainly suffer for it in bodily health. The same principle applies to matters of right and wrong, good and bad, such as the question we are now considering, whether it will be right or good for Socrates to break prison. We have not to take into account the opinions of the "many," but those of the one expert, if there is such a man, by neglecting whose advice we shall injure "that which is made better by right but depraved by wrong." (That is, the soul ; the argument is from the standing analogy between health in the body and moral goodness in the soul.)

Further, we agree that if a man has ruined his physical constitution by following the opinions of the "many" and disregarding those of the medical expert, life with a ruined physique

---

[1] The point is that "aliens" would run no risks from the συκοφάνται because they could get out of Attic territory in a few hours. The purpose for which Simmias is said to have brought money at 45b 4 is not to appease the συκοφάνται, from whom a Theban could suffer no trouble. From the *Phaedo*, Simmias appears to have spent the month between the trial and death of Socrates at Athens, but this need not exclude a journey to Thebes to procure money to pay the warders who were to connive at Socrates' escape. Hence, as I now see, I was wrong in my *Varia Socratica* in supposing that Meletus is one of the persons meant by the reference to blackmailers.

is not worth preserving. But " that in us, whatever it is, in which wickedness and righteousness have their seat " is not less but more precious than the body. (Much less, then, is life worth preserving if this—that is, the soul—is vitiated.) Crito has therefore raised a wrong question. We ought to ask not what " the many " will think of Socrates' behaviour or that of his friends, but what will be thought by the man who " understands " right and wrong. True, the " many " can put you to death if you disagree with them ; but then another principle which both Socrates and Crito hold as strongly since the recent trial as before it is that the all-important thing is not to live but to live a *good* life, and that living a good life means the same thing as living *aright* (δικαίως). The real question to be answered then is, " Would it be *right* for me to take my leave of this place without a public discharge ? " All the other considerations which Crito has raised are irrelevant (46b–48e).

Again, we both still retain our old conviction that to commit a wrong is, in all conditions, a bad thing for the man who commits it (the thesis of the *Gorgias*). It follows that we must hold, contrary to the opinion of the " many," that a man must never repay wrong by retaliatory wrong (ἀνταδικεῖν), and therefore that we must never repay ill-treatment by ill-treatment (ἀντικακουργεῖν κακῶς πάσχοντα). In a word, no treatment received from another ever justifies wronging him or treating him ill, though this is a conviction so opposed to the code of the " many," that those who accept and those who reject it cannot even discuss a problem of practice with one another (οὐκ ἔστι κοινὴ βουλή, 49d). Socrates and Crito can only discuss the course Socrates is to adopt because they agree about this initial principle (49a–e).

Next, ought a man, on these principles, to keep his word when he has given it (assuming that what he has promised to do is *in se* morally right),[1] or may he break it ? Of course, he must keep it. Our immediate problem, then, reduces to this. If Socrates leaves the prison without a public discharge, will he, or will he not, be wronging the very party whom he ought to be most careful not to wrong ? Will he be keeping a right and lawful pledge, or will he be violating it ? Let us consider what the Laws, or the State, might have to say if they could take us in the act of " making our lucky " (μέλλουσιν ἀποδιδράσκειν). This appeal to the personified figure of the State or the Laws is, as Burnet says, in principle a Platonic " myth." Its function is the same as that played in other dialogues by the vision of the Judgment to come. That is, it does not carry the argument further, but brings it home powerfully to the imagination. Artistically the function of the picture is to evoke a mood of ideal feeling adequate to the elevation of the ethical demands of

---

[1] δίκαια ὄντα, 49e. This is inserted to exclude a promise to do what is *impermissum in se*. Socrates' view is that a promise to do what is in itself illicit is null and void. But we see in the sequel that the tacit " compact " by which Socrates is pledged to the νόμοι or κοινόν of Athens involves nothing but what is strictly *licitum*.

Socraticism on the conscience, to arouse unconditional " reverence " for the dignity of the moral law as that which demands and justifies the philosopher's martyrdom.   So far, and no further, it acts as the sight of the Crucifix does on a Christian.   The conception of society implied, as something too obvious to need explanation, is the same which underlies all the versions of the doctrine of " social contract," a doctrine naturally familiar to the members of a society which knew from its own experience how legislation is made.   But it gives us the fundamental truth of the theory of " contract " un-contaminated with any element of historical error about the first origins of " society."   The thought is that a man who has cast in his lot with the community by accepting its " social system " all through life has tacitly bound himself to support the organization on which the social order depends, and cannot in honour go back from his pledge for the sake of his p rsonal convenience.   This is what is really meant by the much-misrepresented doctrine of " passive obedience," and it is interesting to remark that Socrates thus combines in himself the " nonconformist's " reverence for " conscience " and the " non-juror's " reverence for the " powers that be."   He is the one absolutely consistent " conscientious objector " of history, because, unlike most such " objectors," he respects the conscience of τo κoινόν as well as his own.

The Laws might complain that Socrates would by an *évasion* be breaking his own " compact," and that without the excuse that the compact had been made under duress, or obtained by false representation or without sufficient time for consideration.[1]   He has had a life of seventy years for reflection and in all this time has never attempted to adopt a new domicile, but has absented himself less than almost any other citizen from Athens.   Thus he cannot plead any of the recognized excuses for regarding his assent to live under the laws of the city as anything but free and deliberate. (Of course the meaning is not that Socrates could have been " naturalized " in some other community ; but he might have chosen to live as a resident alien under the protection of another society, or as a colonist at *e.g.* Amphipolis or Thurii.)   The whole course of his life bears silent witness that he has accepted the system of institutions into which he had been born, and it is an integral part of the system that an Athenian citizen shall respect the decisions of the duly constituted courts.   He is not at liberty to reject the jurisdiction because in his own opinion the decision of a court does him a material wrong (50c).   To run away to escape the execution of the court's sentence would be following up the exalted speeches he made before the judges by the conduct of the paltriest of eloping slaves.   If he does break his " compact," what good can he expect to accrue to his connexions or himself ?   His family and friends will certainly run the risk of

[1] *Force majeure*, fraudulent misrepresentation, insufficient time for con-sideration, are thus recognized as the three conditions which might, severally or conjointly, make a promise void.

banishment or loss of property. As for himself, suppose he makes his escape to a neighbouring city such as Thebes or Megara, which have good institutions, and where, as we know, he would find warm friends, he must be looked on by all honest citizens as an enemy, who has defied one society and may be expected to do the same by another, and thus will fairly be under the suspicion of being a " corrupter " of the young who may associate with him. If, to avoid such reproach, he takes refuge in a disorderly and lawless community, what kind of life does he propose to lead ? For very shame, he cannot continue his professions of devotion to " goodness and law " with his own conduct staring him in the face. Even in so lawless a society as that of Thessaly, he might for a while live under the protection of Crito's connexions there, and they might find the story of his successful escape from prison an excellent joke, but he must expect to hear the painful truth about his behaviour as soon as he offends anyone. Even if he escapes that disgrace by making himself a general toady, his life will be that of a "trencherman " and parasite, and what will become of all his fine professions about right and goodness ? As for the final appeal which Crito had made to his parental affections, what good will such an existence do to his children ? Does he propose to bring them up as hangers-on in Thessaly ? If they are to grow up as free men and citizens at Athens, will his friends neglect them more because he has removed to the other world than they would if he had removed to Thessaly ? Besides, the plea will be useless when life is over at last and a man has to stand before the judges of the dead. If Socrates abides execution now, he will have a good defence before that tribunal. He will appear as an innocent victim of the injustice not of law, but of individuals who have abused law for his destruction.[1] If he does not, he will have to answer for having done what lay in him to shake the authority of law itself, and must expect to have the law itself against him in the next world as well as in this. It is this appeal which rings in the ears of Socrates and makes him deaf to the voice of Crito, nor can Crito find anything to set against it. We must, therefore, be content to follow the path along which God is leading us (50a–54e).

See further :

BURNETT.—*Euthyphro, Apology, Crito.* (Oxford, 1924.)
RIDDELL.—*Apology* of Plato. (Oxford, 1867.)
BURNET.—*Early Greek Philosophy, Part I.*, Chapter IX. 180–192.
RITTER, C.—*Platon*, i. 363–390.
RITTER, C.—*Sokrates.* (Tübingen, 1931.)
TAYLOR, A. E.—*Socrates.* (London, 1932.)

---

[1] 54b. This is, in fact, the fundamental distinction on which Socrates founds his whole argument. When a man is legally but wrongly convicted of an offence he has not committed, the wrong is inflicted not by the law, but by the persons who have misused the law. Anytus, not the law, has done Socrates a wrong. But the prison-breaker is doing what he can to make the whole social system ineffective. *His* conduct is a direct challenge to the authority of law itself.

CHAPTER VIII

THE *PHAEDO*

WE are now to consider the group of four great dialogues which exhibit Plato's dramatic art at its ripest perfection. It may fairly be presumed that they all belong to one and the same period of his development as a writer, a view borne out by a cautious and sane use of the available "stylometric" evidence. Outwardly they have all the same form, that of a conversation supposed to have taken place before a numerous audience and subsequently described either by Socrates himself (*Protagoras, Republic*), or by one of the original auditors (*Phaedo, Symposium*). We have already found Plato using this difficult literary form for comparatively short dialogues (e.g. *Charmides, Euthydemus*), but it is a more arduous task to keep it up successfully throughout a work of considerable compass ; as we have seen, in the dialogues which there is other reason for thinking later than the *Republic*, it is only adopted once (in the *Parmenides*), and there is a formal explanation of its abandonment in the *Theaetetus*. This is good reason for thinking that Plato's great achievements in this kind belong neither to his more youthful nor to his later period of literary activity, but to his prime of maturity as a writer (which need not, of course, coincide with his ripest maturity as a thinker). I do not think there is any satisfactory method of dating the four dialogues themselves in the order of their composition. We may reasonably presume that the *Republic*, as the work of greatest range and compass among them, must have taken longest to write, and was the last to be completed. It also contains what looks like a concealed reference to the *Phaedo* (*Rep.* 611*b* 10), though the fact is by no means certain.[1] Now there is one consideration which perhaps allows us to fix an approximate date in Plato's life for the writing of the *Republic*. In *Ep.* vii. 326*b*, where Plato is describing the state of mind in which he paid his first visit to Italy and Sicily, he says that he had been driven to state, in a eulogy of genuine philosophy (ἐπαινῶν τὴν ὀρθὴν φιλοσοφίαν), that humanity will never escape its sufferings until either true philosophers occupy political office

---

[1] The " other arguments " (ἄλλοι λόγοι) for immortality referred to in passing *may* mean those which Plato's readers would know from the *Phaedo*, but they may equally well mean those which readers of Socratic literature would know to be current among Orphics or Pythagoreans generally. Thus the words cannot be pressed as an argument for the priority of the *Phaedo*.

or political " rulers," by some happy providence, turn to philosophy. It seems impossible not to take this as a direct allusion to
Republic vi. 499*b*, where the same thing is said, almost in the same
words, as part of a " eulogy " of true philosophy. Since Plato
also says (*Ep.* vii. 324*a*) that he was about forty years old at the
time of his voyage, this seems to give us 387 B.C. as an approximate
date for the writing of the *Republic*, or, at least, of its central and
most difficult section, and we are led to think of his dramatic
activity, culminating in the four great " reported dialogues," as
marking the late thirties of his life. Beyond this, so far as I can
see, we have no means of going. We cannot tell, for example,
whether the *Phaedo* is earlier or later than the *Symposium*, or either
earlier or later than the *Protagoras*. My own reason for taking the
Phaedo before the other two is simply that it connects outwardly
with the events of Socrates' last day, and consequently illustrates
the same side of his thought and character as the three dialogues
we have just examined.

As in the case of these three dialogues, I must be content to a
considerable extent to refer my reader to Professor Burnet's commentary for treatment of details. The scene of the conversation
is laid at Phlius, where Phaedo of Elis, apparently on his way home
from Athens, relates the story of the last hours of Socrates to a
party of Phliasian admirers of the philosopher who have not yet
had any account of the details. The one member of this party who
is named is Echecrates, independently known to us as a Pythagorean.
Hence Burnet is probably not far wrong in supposing the story to
be told in the " meeting-house " of the local Pythagoreans. The
surroundings will thus harmonize with the general tone of the conversation, in which the two principal interlocutors are also pupils
of an eminent Pythagorean, Philolaus. It should be noted that
these two speakers, Simmias and Cebes, are both represented as
young, and that they evidently belong to the group of Pythagoreans
in whom the religious side of the original movement has been completely overshadowed by the scientific. It is Socrates who has to
recall them to the very conceptions which are at the root of Pythagorean religion, and persuade them that their scientific " developments " are inconsistent with the foundations of that religion. We
need also to be alive in reading the *Phaedo* to two important facts
which are sometimes forgotten. One is that Socrates himself is
very careful to qualify his assent to the main tenet of the Orphic
and Pythagorean faith, the deathlessness of the soul, by cautious
reserve as to the details of the eschatology in which that faith has
found expression. He is sure that he will leave this world to be
with God ; he is very far from sure about the rest of the Orphic
scheme of rewards and punishments. The other is that we must
not take the *Phaedo* by itself for a complete expression of the whole
spirit of Socraticism. It sets Socrates before us in the last hours
of his life, and dwells on just the side of his thought and character
which would be sure to be most prominent in the given situation,

but we should misconceive his doctrine if we did not integrate the picture of the *Phaedo* with such a representation of the philosopher in the midst of life as we get, for example, in the *Protagoras*, where the underlying body of doctrine is identical but the situation wholly different and the emphasis correspondingly different. Probably the directest way to an understanding of the influence and personality of Socrates would be to read and meditate these two great dialogues together, interpreting each in the light of the other. (It is worth observing that Aristotle seems to have done something of the kind. His views about the philosophy of Socrates as a whole seem to be derived chiefly from the *Phaedo* ; when he has occasion, in his own *Ethics*, to discuss the Socratic theses about the conduct of life, it is demonstrable that the unnamed source of his information is primarily the *Protagoras*.)

There can be no doubt that Plato intends the reader to take the dialogue as an accurate record of the way in which Socrates spent his last hours on earth, and the topics on which he spoke with his intimate friends in the face of imminent death. This is indicated, for example, by the care shown to give a full list of the names of the persons present. Most of these were probably still living when the *Phaedo* was circulated ; it is quite certain that this was the case with some of them, *e.g.* Euclides and Terpsion, who, as we see from the *Theaetetus*, were still alive and active thirty years later ; Phaedo, the actual narrator, who is represented in the dialogue as still a mere lad ; Aeschines of Sphettus, and others. Though Plato is careful to mention and account for his own absence, it is quite certain that he must have been fully informed of the facts, since the statement that he spent some time after the death of Socrates with Euclides and Terpsion at Megara comes to us on the excellent authority of his own pupil Hermodorus. We are therefore bound to accept his account of Socrates' conduct and conversation on the last day of his life as in all essentials historical, unless we are willing to suppose him capable of a conscious and deliberate misrepresentation recognizable as such by the very persons whom he indicates as the sources of his narrative. This supposition is to my own mind quite incredible, and I shall therefore simply dismiss it, referring the reader who wishes for discussion of it to the full Introduction to Burnet's edition of the dialogue.

The purpose of the dialogue is not quite accurately described by calling it a discourse on the " immortality of the soul." To us this suggests that the main object of the reasoning is to prove the soul's endless survival, and *nothing* more. But to the Greek mind ἀθανασία or ἀφθαρσία regularly signified much the same thing as " divinity," and included the conception of ingenerability as well as of indestructibility. Accordingly, the arguments of the dialogue, whatever their worth may be, aim at showing that our souls never began to be quite as much as at proving that they will never cease to be. But neither of these positions is the main point of the reasoning. The subject of the dialogue is better indicated by the name used by Plato himself in *Ep.* xiii. 363*a*, where it is said to be " the discourse of Socrates about the ψυχή." The immediate and principal object of the whole conversation is the justification of the life of "tendance of the soul " by insisting on the *divinity* of the human soul, and on " imitation of God " as the right and reasonable rule of conduct ; the immunity of the soul from death is a mere consequence, though an important consequence, of this inherent divinity. The argument is, in the proper sense of the phrase, a *moral* one ; the worth and dignity of the soul afford reasonable grounds for hoping that death is, to a good man, entrance on a better life, an " adventure " which he may face with good comfort—the summary of the whole matter given by Socrates himself at 114*d*–115*a*.

A possible misconception which would be fatal to a real understanding of the dialogue is to look upon the members of the series of arguments for immortality as so many independent substantive " proofs," given by the author or the speaker as all having the same inherent value. Any careful study will show that they are meant to form a series of " aggressions " to the solution of a problem, each requiring and leading up to the completer answer which follows it. In particular, Plato is careful, by skilful use of dramatic by-play and pauses in the conversation, to let us see what he regards as the critical points in the argument. These pauses are principally two, that which occurs at 88*c*–89*a*, where the narrative is interrupted by a short dialogue between Phaedo and Echecrates, and 95*e*–100*a*, where Socrates relates the story of his early difficulties with the physical " philosophy " of Empedocles, Diogenes, and others. It is evidently meant that the two outstanding difficulties which must be faced by the philosophical defender of the doctrine of immortality are the " epiphenomenalist " theory of consciousness and the " mechanical theory of nature," the one represented for us in the *Phaedo* by the " objection " of Simmias, and the other by that of Cebes.

As I shall point out later on, Plato himself in the *Laws* specifies just these theories as being at the root of all irreligious philosophizing, and it would still be true to say that to-day they constitute the speculative basis for most of the current denials of human immortality. We are thus directed to find in the *Phaedo* a statement of the position of Socrates on these two perennial issues ; for Plato's own personal attitude towards them we need to look primarily to the express refutation of the " unbeliever " in the tenth book of the *Laws*. The background presupposed in one refutation is the science of the fifth century, that of the other is the Academic science of the fourth, but both agree in the assertions (*a*) that mental life is not the effect of bodily causes, and that physical reality itself— " coming into being and passing out of being "—is not explicable in purely mechanical terms. This—apart from the impressive picture of the fortitude of the true philosopher in the moment of death—is the main lesson of the *Phaedo*.

The immortal narrative must be passed over in the present

connexion with just one word. It may not be superfluous to associate ourselves with Burnet's protest against the absurd charge of " hardness " as a husband which has been brought against the dying Socrates. It is clear that his wife and infant son are supposed to have spent the last night of his life with him in the prison. They are conducted home at the opening of the discourse (60a) for the reason at which Socrates himself hints later on (117d), because Xanthippe is, naturally enough, on the verge of a " nervous breakdown," and Socrates desires to spare both her and himself. The children and the "ladies of the family " reappear again at the end (116b) for a final interview in the presence of no witness but Crito, the oldest friend of the family, and we are expressly told that the interview was a lengthy one. Phaedo cannot describe this eminently private scene, because he had not witnessed it, but it is the mere fact that he was not present which has given rise to mis-understanding (assisted, perhaps, by the incapacity of modern sentimentalists to understand the reticence of all great art).

THE ARGUMENT OF THE DIALOGUE

I. STATEMENT OF THE MAIN THESIS (60b–70b)

The main issue of the dialogue is made to emerge in a simple and natural way from the remark of Socrates that the genuine " philosopher " is one who is ready and willing to die, though he would regard it as " criminal " to put an end to his own life (61c). (That is, he trusts that death is the entrance on a better state, but holds that we may not force the door ; we must wait for it to be opened to us in God's good time. The Pythagorean origin of the absolute veto on suicide is indicated by the allusion to Philolaus at 61d.) This may seem a paradox, but it is intelligible if we con-ceive of man as a " chattel " (κτῆμα) of God, just as a slave is a " chattel " of his owner, and therefore has no right to dispose of his own life, as it does not belong to him. Socrates would not like to commit himself entirely to the Orphic dogma that while we are in the body we are "in ward," i.e. undergoing penal servitude for ante-natal sin, but he thinks it at least adumbrates this truth that " we men are chattels of the gods " (62b),[1] and therefore may not dispose of ourselves as we please. (The kind of κτῆμα (" chattel ") meant is clearly a δοῦλος, who is, as Roman lawyers put it, in the

---

[1] For the doctrine in question see in particular the important fragment of Clearchus the Peripatetic quoted by Burnet *loc. cit.* I think it clear that the φρουρά means " house of detention," not " post of military duty." To the passages making for the former interpretation quoted by Burnet add Plutarch, *de sera numinis vindicta*, 554d. The ἀποδιδράσκειν of 62b 5 exactly suits a prisoner " breaking prison," but not a sentry leaving his post, for which we should need αὐτομολεῖν. Socrates' refusal to commit himself to the " mystical " dogma is important. It makes it clear at the start that, in spite of all ap-pearances to the contrary, it is no part of the object of the dialogue to prove " pre-existence " and " transmigration."

dominium of his owner and therefore has no " proprietary right " in his own body.) Yet in saying this we seem to be merely replacing one paradox by another. If we are the " chattels " of the gods, that means that we are under the "tendance" of good and wise owners who know what is best for us much better than we do ourselves. Death would seem to mean being released from this tendance and left to look after ourselves. Surely a wise man would think such an *emancipatio* a thing to be dreaded (exactly, that is, as a shrewd slave would be very unwilling to be "freed" from a first-rate owner and left to fend for himself (62*d*)). The paradox would be a very real one if Socrates were not convinced that after death one will equally be under the care of good and wise gods, and perhaps—though of this he is not equally sure (63*c*)—in the company of the best men of the past. This is the faith (ἐλπίς) which gives him courage to face death, and he will try to impart it to his friends. Thus the thing to be proved is primarily not the " natural immortality" of the soul. A proof of immortality, taken by itself, would not be adequate ground for facing death in a hopeful spirit. It would be quite consistent with holding that we only leave this world to find ourselves in a much worse one. What is really to be proved, if possible, is that "the souls of the just are in the hand of God " after death as much as before. Socrates, like all great religious teachers, rests his hopes for the unseen future in the last resort on the goodness of God, not on the natural imperishability of the human ψυχή. (So in the *Timaeus* (41*a*–*b*), it is the goodness of the Creator's will which guarantees the immortality even of the " created gods," *i.e.* the stars.) What is to be shown, in fact, is that the faith and hope with which the " philosopher " faces death is the logical consequence and supreme affirmation of the principles by which he has regulated his whole life. To lose faith when you come to die would be to contradict the whole tenour of your past life ; for, though the world may not know it, the life of " philosophy " itself is nothing but one long " rehearsal " (μελέτη) [1] of dying (64*a*). Possibly, indeed, the " world " would say that it does know this well enough ; it knows very well that " philosophers " are " morbid " creatures who are only half alive, and that it serves them right to eliminate them (a plain allusion to the Aristophanic caricature of the φροντισταί as

---

[1] *Not* " meditation " of death. μελέτη means the repeated practice by which we prepare ourselves for a performance. It is used of the " practising " of a man training for an athletic contest, and again of the " learning by heart " of such a thing as a speech which you have procured from a λογογράφος and want to have " perfect " when the time for deliverance comes. No doubt, then, it was also the word for an actor's " study " of his " part." (Cf. *répétition* as used of the rehearsals of a play or a symphony in French.) The thought is thus that " death " is like a play for which the philosopher's life has been a daily rehearsal. His business is to be perfect in his part when the curtain goes up. Note that, as Burnet says (*Phaedo*, 64*b* 3 n., *E.G.Ph.*[3], 278 n. 1), it is implied throughout the argument that " philosophy " has the special sense, which is clearly Pythagorean, of devotion to science *as a way to the salvation of the soul.*

living " ghosts "). Only the world is mistaken on one small point ; it does not understand the sense in which the philosopher uses the word " death," and that is what we must explain (64b). It is all the more necessary to attend to the explanation that it is really the key to the whole of the *Phaedo*, and that its significance has been often misapprehended by both admirers and critics down to our own time as completely as by the δῆμος of Thebes or Athens.[1]

To put the matter quite simply, death, as every one understands, is the " release " of the soul from the body ; in other words, it is the achievement of the soul's independence. Now we can see that what the philosopher has been aiming at all his life long is just to make the soul, as completely as he can, independent of the fortunes of the body. We can see this from the following considerations : (a) The philosopher sets no great store on the gratifications of physical appetite, and disregards the " tendance of the body " in general (fine clothes and foppery) " beyond what is needful."[2] What he " tends " is the soul, and that is why the " mass of men " think him as good as a ghost or corpse (64c–65a). (b) In his pursuit of knowledge he finds the limitations of the body a hindrance to him in more ways than one, and is always doing his best to escape them. He soon discovers the grossness and untrustworthiness of our senses, even of the two most acute of them, sight and hearing, and tries to arrive at truth more accurate and certain than any which the evidence of sense could furnish. This is why he trusts to thinking rather than to sense ; but in thinking the soul is independent of the body in a way in which she is not independent in sensation. (This is, of course, strictly true. Socrates would probably be thinking primarily of the danger of trusting to a " figure " in mathematics, a danger which will be mentioned a little further on. It is equally true that, even in our own times, when the scientific man is so abundantly supplied with " instruments of precision," we have always to allow for a margin of unknown error in all conclusions depending on data derived from sense-perception ; absolute accuracy and certainty can only be obtained, if at all, in " pure " science which makes no appeal to sense, even for its data.) So pleasurable or painful excitement derived from the body also gravely interferes with the prosecution of truth. (One is hampered in one's scientific work when one's head aches or one's liver is out of order.) (c) The supreme objects of our studies, " *the* right," " *the* good," " *the* beautiful," " figure," " health," in short, *the* " reality " (οὐσία) investigated by any science is always something which none of the

---

[1] Socrates' point is that—to use the language of Christian mystics—the " world " confuses a dying life with a living death. The " philosopher " is out for " dying into life " ; the world thinks he is making his existence a death in life, but it is really the worldling who is " dead while he lives."

[2] 64e, καθ᾽ ὅσον μὴ πολλὴ ἀνάγκη αὐτῶν. This is inserted to show that Socrates has no sympathy with the gratuitous slovenliness of persons like the Telauges of Aeschines' dialogue or his own companion Antisthenes. He does not regard " dirt " as a mark of godliness.

senses perceives, and the less we depend on any of them—the less, that is, we substitute " sensing " for "thinking" in our science—the nearer we come to apprehending the object we are really studying (65*d*–66*a*).[1] Having all these considerations in mind, we may fairly take a " short cut " (ἀτραπός) to the conclusion that so long as we have the body with us it will always be a hindrance to the apprehension of " reality " (τὸ ἀληθές) as it is. At the best we lose much valuable time by being obliged to take care of the body. If it gets out of condition, our quest of "the real " (τὸ ὄν) is even more hindered. Bodily wants and the passions connected with them—which, incidentally, are the causes of business and war, the two great occupations of the " active life "—leave us hardly any opportunity or leisure for the pursuit of knowledge. And even in the scanty time we are able to devote to the things of the mind, the body and its needs are constantly " turning up " and diverting our attention. Thus the man who is really " in love with knowledge " must confess that his heart's desire is either only to be won after death, when the soul has achieved her independence of her troublesome partner, or not at all. While we are in the body, we make the nearest approach to our supreme good just in proportion as we accomplish the concentration of the soul on herself and the detachment of her attention from the body, waiting patiently until God sees fit to complete the deliverance for us. When that happens, we may hope, having become unmixed and undiluted intelligence, to apprehend undiluted reality. Meanwhile the life of thinking itself is a progressive purifying of intelligence from the alien element and a concentration of it on itself. The philosopher is the only type of man who makes it the business of his life to accomplish this purgation and concentration and so to win spiritual independence. This is why we may call his life a " rehearsal of death," and why unwillingness to complete the process would be ridiculous in him (66*c*–68*b*). The conception set before us in these pages is manifestly the Hellenic counterpart of the " mystical way " of Christianity. The underlying ideas of both conceptions are

---

[1] That is, the object studied by any science is always what Socrates calls an εἶδος or ἰδέα, though the technical term is not yet introduced. It is important to note the immediate and emphatic assent of Simmias to this statement (65*d*). He is clearly supposed to have learned all about the matter from his Pythagorean teachers. The examples are taken from ethics (δίκαιον, ἀγαθόν, καλόν), mathematics (μέγεθος), medicine (ὑγίεια, ἰσχύς). Of course you can see μεγέθη, but it is quite true that you cannot see μέγεθος. So you can see or draw approximately elliptical lines, but you cannot even approximately draw "the general conic " or "the curve of the third order." If you did try to draw them and relied on some characteristic of your figure as a property of the curve on no better evidence than that of your eyes, you would soon be led into error about the " reality " you are investigating. A thorough empiricist would have to go to much wilder extremes. He would, for example, have to hold that it is quite uncertain whether, if you only went on counting long enough, you might not come on two odd integers without an even one between them, or on a highest prime number, or even on an integer which is neither odd nor even. These things are actually maintained by some empiricist mathematicians, but they would be the death of ἐπιστήμη.

that there is a supreme good for man which, from its very nature, cannot be enjoyed " in this life." The best life is therefore one which is directed to fitting ourselves for the full fruition of this " eternal " good beyond the limits of our temporal existence. In both cases this means that the highest life for man while on earth is a " dying life," a process of putting off the old man with the affections and the lusts and becoming a " new creature." The constant presence of this aim makes the life of devotion to science, as conceived by Socrates and his friends, a genuine *via crucis*. And they, like the Christian mystics, conceive of the best life as one of contemplation, not of action. The ultimate aim of the " philosopher " is not to *do* things, but to enjoy the vision of a reality to which he grows like as he looks upon it, the ideal already expressed in the apologue of the " three lives " popularly ascribed to Pythagoras. We must be careful, however, to guard ourselves against two insidious misconceptions. For all the stress laid on " purification " of the mind from contact with the body, we must not suppose that Socrates is thinking of a life of mere negative abstentions.

The whole point of the insistence on unremitting preoccupation with thinking as the philosophic form of " purgation " is that the object of the renunciation of the philosopher is to make his life richer ; by " purification " from external preoccupations, his intelligence becomes more and more intense and concentrated, just as, *e.g.*, alcohol becomes more potent the more nearly your specimen is " pure " alcohol. Nor must one suppose that the contemplative life, because it is not directed ultimately on action, is one of indolence or laziness. Socrates, who claims in our dialogue to have spent his whole life " in philosophy," was busy from morning to night with his " mission." Probably, when we remember the way in which Plato in the seventh *Epistle* insists on the political character of his own original ambitions and on his lifelong conviction that the business of the philosopher among men is to be a statesman, we may infer that he would not himself at any time have subscribed to the doctrine of the *vita contemplativa* without a great deal of explanation and reservation. Even the Pythagoreans who formulated the doctrine had stood alone among the scientific schools in playing an important part, as a society, in the politics of the early fifth century. They only became a merely scientific society when their political activities had been crushed by revolution. But it may well be that the ablest men of action feel even more strongly than the rest of us that the " conduct of business," the carrying on of commerce, governing, and fighting cannot be its own justification. To be everlastingly " meddling " seems an end not worthy the dignity of human nature ; at bottom we all want not to *do* something but to *be* something. To make " doing things " your ultimate object is merely to take " Fidgety Phil who couldn't keep still " as your model of manly excellence. It has been said with truth that the great " practical reforms " which have proved of lasting value have mostly been the work of men whose hearts were all the time set on something different.

If a man, then, plays the craven when death comes, we may be sure he is no true "lover of wisdom," but a "lover of the body," which is as much as to say a man whose heart is set on wealth (a φιλοχρήματος) or on "honours" (a φιλότιμος), or both at once (68c. This direct allusion to the Pythagorean "three lives" is, of course, intentional.) On the other hand, the philosopher will be marked by eminent courage and eminent "temperance" in the popular sense in which the word means control over one's physical appetites. In fact, when we come to reflect, there is something paradoxical about the courage and temperance of the rest of mankind. They are courageous in the face of danger because courage serves to protect them against death, which they fear as the worst of evils. Thus their very valour is rooted in a sort of cowardice. (As an Indian says of the English in one of Kipling's tales, "they are not afraid to be kicked, but they are afraid to die.") And the decent (κόσμιοι) among them keep their lusts in hand because they think they will get more pleasure by doing so than by giving way, so that "slavery to pleasure" is the source of what they call their "temperance." But the truth is that real virtue is not a business of exchanging pleasures and pains against one another. Wisdom is the true "coin of the realm" for which everything else must be exchanged, and it is only when accompanied by it that our so-called "virtues" are genuine goodness (ἀληθὴς ἀρετή). Without it, the kind of goodness which is based on the "calculus of pleasure and pain" is no more than a painted show (σκιαγραφία).[1] The Orphic saying is that "many carry the narthex but few are real βάκχοι," and we might apply this to our purpose by taking the "real βάκχος," who genuinely feels the "god within," to mean the true philosopher. Of these chosen few Socrates has all his life tried to become one; with what success he may know better in a few hours (68b–69e).[2]

II. THE ARGUMENTS FOR IMMORTALITY

In substance, what has gone before contains Socrates' vindication of his attitude in the face of death. But, as Simmias remarks, the whole vindication has tacitly assumed that there is an hereafter. Now most men find it very hard to believe that the soul

---

[1] 69a 6–c 3. On the text and grammar of this sentence, which have undergone much corruption, see Burnet, *loc. cit.*, where it is also pointed out that σκιαγραφία does not mean an "imperfect outline," but a stage-painting in which, *e.g.*, a flat surface is made to look like the façade of a temple. The point is not that "vulgar" goodness is "imperfect" but that it is illusory.

[2] In this context Socrates' claim can hardly be understood to mean less than that he had been a "follower of the way." We cannot well believe that Plato invented this, still less that he had anything to do with "the way" himself.

is not "dispersed like smoke" when a man dies, and Simmias shares their difficulty. To complete his "case" Socrates must therefore satisfy us that the soul continues to be, and to be intelligent after the death of the "man." Accordingly he now proceeds to produce three considerations which point to that conclusion. It is not said that they are demonstrative. Simmias had asked only for πίστις (conviction), not for demonstration, and Socrates professes no more than to consider whether immortality is "likely" (εἰκός) or not. In point of fact, the first two proofs are found to break down and the third, as Burnet observes, is said by Socrates (107*b* 6) to need fuller examination. Thus it is plain that Plato did not mean to present the arguments as absolutely probative to his own mind. The argument he does find convincing and develops at great length in the *Laws* is put briefly into the mouth of Socrates in the *Phaedrus*, but no mention is made of it here.[1]

(*a*) THE FIRST ARGUMENT (70*c*–77*d*).—This argument itself falls into two parts, a (70*c*–72*e*) and β (72*e*–77*d*) ; the two have to be considered in conjunction to make anything which can be called a proof, and what they go to prove is not "immortality" but merely that the soul continues to be "something" after death. It is not simply annihilated. This, of course, is only the first step to establishing what is really in question, the persistence of intelligence beyond the grave.

(a) *First Reason for holding that the Soul is not simply annihilated at Death* (70*c*–72*e*).—There is an ancient doctrine (it is, in fact, Orphic) of rebirth, according to which a soul which is born into this world is one which has come back from "another world" to which men go at death. This, if true, would establish our point. To look at the matter from a more general point of view, we see that the world is made up of "opposites" (ἐναντία)—such as hot, cold ; great, small ; good, bad. Now if a thing "becomes bigger" it must have first been "smaller," if it becomes hotter it must have been cooler, if it becomes "better" it must have been "worse," and so on. So we may say universally that whatever comes to be, comes to be "out of its opposite," and that to correspond to each pair of opposites, there are two antithetical processes of "becoming." Hot and cold are opposites, and similarly there are the two processes of contrasted sense, "becoming hotter," "becoming

---

[1] It is the argument from the "self-moving" character of the soul (*Phaedrus*, 245*c* 5–246*a* 2, *Laws*, x. 893*b* 6–896*d* 4). Why is nothing said of this argument in the *Phaedo* ? It has been suggested that the reason is that the argument is an invention of Plato's own and that he had not thought of it when he wrote the *Phaedo*. I do not think this likely, since the argument is really in principle that of Alcmaeon of Crotona, and is thus much older than Socrates (Aristotle, *de Anima*, A2. 405*a* 30). I should suggest a different explanation. The argument starts from the reality of motion. But this would have been denied by the Eleatic Euclides and Terpsion, and Socrates wishes to base his reasoning on premisses his company will admit. We must remember also that Euclides and his friend were very probably the persons from whom Plato derived most of his knowledge of the last hours of Socrates

cooler." All this will apply to the case of life and death. Being alive and being dead are opposites, just as being awake and being asleep are. And we have agreed that everything comes to be " out of its opposite." The living must come from the dead, and the dead from the living, and thus here, as elsewhere, there will be two opposed processes, corresponding to the two opposed conditions of being alive and being dead. We see and have a name for one of these processes, that by which a living being becomes dead ; we call it dying. But there must, on our principle, also be an antithetic process of " coming to life " which terminates in actual birth. In fact, if the whole process were not cyclical, life would ultimately perish, and there would be only a dead universe left. Thus the drift of the argument is simply to confirm the " ancient doctrine " of rebirth by showing that it is only one case of the universal natural law of cyclical " recurrence." The illustrations from the alternation of sleep and waking seem to show that Socrates is thinking primarily of the way in which this " law of exchange " had been assumed as the fundamental principle of the philosophy of Heraclitus, with whom death and life, sleeping and waking, are explicitly co-ordinated (Her. Fr. 64, 77, 123, Bywater). But the general conception of the world as made up of " opposites " which are generated " out of one another " was, of course, a commonplace of the earliest Greek physical science (cf. Burnet, *E.G.Ph.*[3], p. 8). Socrates' Pythagorean auditors, in particular, would be at once reminded of their own table of " opposites " by reasoning of this kind.

(It is easy to see that the reasoning is neither cogent nor, if it were, probative of what we want to prove. As Aristotle was afterwards to explain more fully, the whole conception of the generation of opposite " out of " opposite is vitiated by an ambiguity in the phrase " out of." A thing which grows cool has previously been warmer, but it is not true that " heat " is a stuff or *matter* out of which " cold " is made. In Aristotelian language, the thing which grows cool has lost the " form " of " the hot " and acquired the " form " of the cold ; the original " form " has not itself been made into an " opposite " form. Again, it is simply assumed, without warrant, that cyclical alternation is the universal law of all processes. To us there is no absurdity in the view that living organisms should finally vanish, or that differences of temperature should cease to exist. If the " principle of Carnot " could be taken to be true without any restriction, we should have to regard these consequences as inevitable. For the purposes of Socrates, however, it is sufficient that the reasoning should be based on assumptions which would be granted as common ground by his audience ; it is not necessary that they should be admitted by anyone else. Still, even when his assumptions are granted, nothing follows so far beyond the bare admission that the soul which has passed from this world to the other, and will, in turn, come back from the other world to this, has some sort of reality in the interval ; it has not become a mere nothing. To admit so much would, of course, be compatible with the crudest kind of materialism, and would do nothing to justify the conviction Socrates means to defend, the belief that the soul which has won its independence has passed to a " better " life.[1] Hence the necessity for a combination of this line of reasoning with that which is next introduced.)

(β) *The Argument from the Doctrine of Reminiscence* (72e–77d).— Cebes observes that we might have reached our conclusion, independently of the doctrine of recurrence, by arguing from Socrates' habitual position that what we call " learning " a truth is really being " put in mind " of something we had forgotten. If this is true, we must at one time have known all that in this life we have to be " reminded " of. Our souls must have existed " before we were men," and presumably therefore may continue to exist when we have ceased to be men. (This argument, if sound, brings us nearer to the conclusion we want, since it goes to prove that the soul not only was " something " but was fully intelligent before it had been conjoined with the body.) The main argument for this doctrine of reminiscence, we are told, is the one already considered in the *Meno*, that a man can be made to give the true solution of a problem by merely asking him appropriate questions, as we see particularly in the case of problems of geometry.[2] The answer is produced from within, not communicated by the questioner.

[1] Note that Socrates himself in the end throws over the principle of universal cyclical recurrence. His " hope " is that the final destiny of the righteous soul is to be with the gods and to live endlessly " apart from the body " (114c). This would be a swallowing up of death by life just as impossible on the principle of recurrence as the universal reign of death. He is, in fact, borrowing from two pre-philosophical traditions, that of endless " reincarnation " and that of the soul as a fallen divinity destined to regain its forfeited place among the gods. These traditions are not really concordant with one another, and it is the second which really represents his personal faith.

[2] ἐάν τις ἐπὶ τὰ διαγράμματα ἄγῃ (73b) may mean literally " if one shows the man a diagram," but since διαγράμματα sometimes means simply " geometrical *proofs* " (e.g. Xenophon, *Mem.* iv. 7, 3, where the δυσσύνετα διαγράμματα seem to mean simply " intricate demonstrations "), probably we should not press the literal sense of the word here. It is an interesting point that though Cebes knows all about the doctrine and attaches importance to it, Simmias, who appears later on as having gone further than Cebes in dropping the religious side of Pythagoreanism, has forgotten it. I think we may infer two things from the passage. (a) The doctrine of reminiscence was not originated by either Socrates or Plato, since Cebes knows both what it is and what is the recognized " proof " of it. It is presumably a piece of old Pythagoreanism which the " advanced " members of the school had dropped or were dropping by the end of the fifth century. (This explains why we never hear anything about it in Plato's later writings.) (b) I suggest that the connexion with immortality comes about in this way. To judge from the Orphic plates found at Thurii and elsewhere, the original idea was that what the soul has to be reminded of is her divine origin and the dangers she will have to surmount on her way back to the abode of the gods. The Orphic plates are, in fact, buried with the votaries to serve them as a kind of Baedeker's guide. The conversion of this piece of primitive theology into a theory of the *a priori* character of mathematics will be part of the spiritualization of old theological traditions due to the mathematician-saint Pythagoras.

Hence the answerer is plainly in possession of the truth which the questioner elicits. Socrates points out that the conclusion might be reached by a simple consideration of what we call " association." When you see an article belonging to an intimate friend, you not only see the article, but think of the owner, and that is what we mean by saying that the coat or whatever it is, " reminds " us of its owner (" association by Contiguity "). Again, when you see a portrait, you think of or " are reminded " of the original (" association by Resemblance "). Thus you may be " reminded " of something both by what is *unlike* it (" Contiguity ") and by what is *like* it (" Resemblance "). In the second case we also note whether the likeness is complete or not (*e.g.* whether the portrait is a good one or a bad one).

Well, then, let us consider a precisely parallel case. In mathematics we are constantly talking about " equality "—not the equality of one stone to another stone, or of one wooden rod to another wooden rod, but of the " just equal " (αὐτὸ τὸ ἴσον), which is neither wood nor stone—and we know that we *mean* something by this talk. But what has put the thought of the " just equal " into our minds ? The *sight* of equal or unequal sticks, or something of the kind. And we note two things. (*a*) The " just equal " is something different from a stick or a stone which is equal to another stick or stone ; we see the sticks or stones, we do not see " mathematical equality." (*b*) And the so-called equal sticks or stones we do see are not exactly, but only approximately, equal. (Even with instruments of precision we cannot *measure* a length without having to allow for a margin of error.) Thus plainly the objects about which the mathematician reasons are not perceived by the eye or the hand ; the thought of them is *suggested* to him by the imperfect approximations he sees and touches, and this suggestion of *B* by *A* is exactly what we mean by "being reminded of *B* by *A*." But *A* cannot remind us of *B* unless we have already been acquainted with *B*. Now from the dawn of our life here, our senses have always been thus " reminding us " of something which is not directly perceptible by sense (*i.e.* perception has always carried with it estimation by an " ideal " standard). Hence our acquaintance with the standards themselves must go back to a time before our sensations began, *i.e.* to a time before our birth. We have argued the case with special reference to the objects studied by the mathematician, but it applies equally to all other "ideal standards," like those of ethics, the good, the right ; in fact, to everything which Socrates and his friends called a " form." The only alternative to supposing that we had antenatal acquaintance with these " forms " would be to say that we acquired it *at the moment* of birth. But this is absurd, since we are quite agreed that we bring none of this knowledge into the world with us ; we have to recover it slowly enough from the hints and suggestions of the senses. We conclude then that if " the kind of being we are always talking about," that is the " forms," exist, and if they are the standard by which we interpret all our sensations, it must be equally true that our souls also existed and were actively intelligent before our birth (76d–e). (One should note several things about the way in which the doctrine of the " forms " is introduced into this argument. For one thing, we see that there is no room in the theory for " innate ideas " in the strict sense of the word, and that there is no question of a knowledge acquired independently of experience. The whole point of the argument is that we should never be " put in mind " of the " forms," but for the suggestion of the senses. Again, the most important feature of the process of " being reminded " is that sense-perceptions suggest standards to which they do not themselves conform. The same visual sensations which suggest the notion " straight " to me, for example, are the foundation of the judgment that no visible stick is perfectly straight. The " form " is thus never contained in, or presented by, the sensible experience which suggests it. Like the " limit " of an infinite series, it is approximated but never reached. These two considerations, taken together, show that the theory does full justice to both parts of the Kantian *dictum* that " percepts without concepts are *blind*, concepts without percepts are empty." [1] We may also note, as Burnet has done, that the stress laid on the point that the sensible thing always falls short of a complete realization of the " form " means that sensible things are being treated as " imitations " (μιμήματα) of the " form," a view we know from Aristotle to have been Pythagorean. It is quite untrue to say that the " imitation " formula only appears in Plato's latest dialogues as an improvement on his earlier formula of " participation." In the *Phaedo* itself Socrates starts with the conception of things as " imitating " forms ; " participation " will only turn up at a later stage in the argument.)

Simmias is particularly delighted with this argument precisely because, as he says, it proves the ante-natal existence of the soul to be a consequence of the doctrine of Forms, and that he regards as the most clear and evident of all truths (77a). (This delight, by the way, would be quite unintelligible on the theory that the doctrine was an invention of Plato.) But, as he goes on to say after a moment's reflection, to prove that the soul " arose " before our birth is not to prove that it will survive death, and it is against the fear of death that Socrates has to provide an antidote. Formally, as Socrates says, the point would be established if we take arguments (α) and (β) together. (β) has proved the pre-

---

[1] It is very important to remember that on the theory there are no " forms " except those which sense-experience suggests, or, to use the language which will meet us later in the dialogue, there are no " forms " which are not " participated in " by sensible particulars. The " forms " are not Kantian " things in themselves." But equally the " form " is not " the sensible thing rightly understood," for the first fact you discover about any sensible thing, when you begin to understand it, is, in Socrates' phrase, that " this thing is trying (βούλεται) to be so-and-so, but not succeeding" (74d). This implies a " realistic " metaphysic ; from the point of view of " nominalism," " terminalism," or " conceptualism," the whole doctrine is nonsense.

existence of the soul, (a) will prove—on the assumption that the alternate cycle of birth and death is endless—that the souls of the dead must continue to exist in order that men may continue to be born. But the " child in us " which is afraid of the dark is not to be quieted so readily, and we must try the effect of a more potent " charm " on him (77a–78b).

(b) SECOND ARGUMENT FOR IMMORTALITY (78b–84b).—This argument goes much more to the root of the question, since it is based not on any current general philosophical formula, but on consideration of the intrinsic character of a soul. In Aristotelian language, the first proof has been " logical," the second is to be " physical." The reasoning adopted lies at the bottom of all the familiar arguments of later metaphysicians who deduce the immortality of the soul from its alleged character as a " simple substance," the " paralogism " attacked by Kant in the *Critique of Pure Reason*. The " proof," as Kant knew it from the writings of men like Wolff and Moses Mendelssohn, is a mere ghost of that offered in the *Phaedo*. Socrates' point is not that the soul is a " simple substance,"—he had not so much as the language in which to say such a thing—but that it is, as the Orphic religion had taught, something *divine*. Its " deiformity," not its indivisibility, is what he is anxious to establish ; the indivisibility is a mere consequence. Hence he is not affected by Kant's true observation that discerption is not the only way in which a soul might perish. No doubt it might perish, as Kant said, by a steady diminution of the intensity of its vitality, *if it were not divine*,[1] but what is divine in its own nature is in no more danger of evanescence than of discerption.

Simmias had spoken of the possible " dissipation " of the soul at death. Now what sort of thing is liable to dissipation and what not ? Obviously it is the composite which, by its own nature, is liable to be dissipated ; the incomposite, if there is such a thing, should be safe from such a fate. And it is reasonable to hold that whatever maintains one and the same character in all circumstances is incomposite, what is perpetually changing its character is composite. Thus for the crude contrast between the " simple " and the composite, we substitute the more philosophical antithesis between the permanent and the mutable. (This takes us at once to ground where Kant's criticism would not affect us. If the soul is, in any sense, immutable, it is so far secured against the lowering of intensity of which Kant speaks.) In the kind of being of which we speak in our scientific studies, the being we are always trying to define—the " forms," in fact—we have a standard of the absolutely immutable. " Just straight," " just right," " just good," are once and for all exactly what they are, and are invariable.

---

[1] And yet, does not Kant's argument rest on the erroneous assumption that if a series has the lower limit o, o must actually be a *term* of the series ? But he is at least right in saying that survival as a " bare monad " would not be the kind of immortality from the thought of which any man could derive hope or comfort.

But the many things which we call by the same names as the
" forms " are in perpetual mutation. (The " good " man loses his
goodness, the " handsome " garment its beauty, and so on.) Now
these latter mutable things are all things you can touch or see or
apprehend by one or other of the senses ; the immutable " standards "
are one and all apprehensible only by thought ($\delta\iota\alpha\nuo\iota\alpha\varsigma \lambda o\gamma\iota\sigma\mu\tilde{\omega}$).
This suggests that we may recognize two types of objects, each type
having a pair of characters—the invisible and immutable, and the
visible and mutable.[1]   Also we are agreed that we have a body and
have a soul.   To which of our types does each of these belong?
Clearly the body can be seen, the soul is invisible (of course " seen "
and " unseen " are being used here *per synecdochen* for " sensed," "not
sensed," respectively).   In respect of this character there can be no
doubt of the type to which each belongs.   What about the other pair
of contrasted characters ?   As we said before, when the soul relies
on the sense-organs in her investigations she finds the objects she
is studying perpetually shifting, and loses her own way ($\pi\lambda\alpha\nu\tilde{\alpha}\tau\alpha\iota$)
among them.   When she relies on her native power of thinking
and attends to objects which are strictly determinate and unchanging, she finds her way among them without uncertainty and
confusion, and it is just this condition of the soul we call " wisdom "
or intelligence ($\phi\rho\acute{o}\nu\eta\sigma\iota\varsigma$).   This would indicate that the soul
herself belongs more truly to the type with which she is most at
home, the immutable, whereas the body certainly belongs to the
mutable.[2]
    Again, in the partnership of soul and body, it is the soul which
is rightly master and the body servant (the thought which the
Academy crystallized in the definition of man as a soul *using* a
human body as its instrument).   Now it is for the divine to command and rule, for the mortal to serve and obey ; hence it is the
soul in us which plays the divine, the body which plays the mortal
part.   (This brings us at last to the point on which Socrates really
means to insist, the " deformity " or " kinship with God " of the

[1] This is identical at bottom with Dr. Whitehead's recent distinction
between " objects " and " events," *e.g.* between " Cambridge-blue " and
" Cambridge-blue-here-and-now."   Dr. Whitehead, I think, does not expressly
say that it is only events which can be " sensed," but that is really implied in
his language.   I *see* " Cambridge-blue-occurring-here-and-now " ; the *object*
" Cambridge-blue," which does not " happen," is suggested to me by my sensation of what is " happening ".   I *recognize* it, am " put in mind of it " by the
event which happens.   Cf. *Principles of Natural Knowledge*, p. 81 : " Objects
are entities recognized as appertaining to events ; they are the recognita amid
events.   Events are named after the objects involved in them."   This is
precisely the doctrine of " forms " and of " recollection."
    [2] Of course it is not said that the soul is absolutely immutable.   This
would not be true ; we can change even our most deeply cherished scientific
and moral convictions.   But it is true that, by contrast with the body, the
soul emerges as the relatively immutable.   My intellectual and moral convictions do not undergo " adaptive " modifications to a changing environment
with the readiness shown by my organism.   My body, for instance, will adapt
itself to a great climatic change more readily than my mind to a society with
a different morality or religion from my own.

soul. In view of the standing Greek equation of "immortal" with "divine," the formal inference to the immortality of the soul follows as a matter of course.)

The soul, then, is relatively the permanent and divine thing in us, the body the merely human and mutable. We should therefore expect the body to be relatively perishable, the soul to be either wholly imperishable or nearly so. And yet we know that, with favourable circumstances,[1] even a dead body may be preserved from corruption for ages, and there are parts of the body which seem all but indestructible. Much more should we expect that a soul which has made itself as far as possible independent of the mutable body, and has escaped by death to the divine and invisible, will be lifted above mutability and corruption. But if a soul has all through life set its affections on bodily things and the gratifications of appetite, it may be expected to hanker after the body even when death has divorced them, and be dragged down into the cycle of births again by this hankering. We may suppose that the place in the animate system into which it is reborn is determined by the nature of its specific lusts, so that each soul's own lusts provide it with its appropriate "hell," the sensual being reborn as asses, the rapacious and unjust as beasts of prey, and so forth. The mildest fate will be that of the persons who have practised the "popular goodness" misnamed temperance and justice without "philosophy" (*i.e.* of those who have simply shaped their conduct by a respectable moral tradition without true insight into the good, or, in Kantian phrase, have lived "according to duty," though not "from duty"). These, we may suppose, are reborn as "social creatures," like bees and ants, or as men again, and they make "decent bodies" as mankind goes. The attainment of "divinity" or "deiformity" is reserved for the man who has resolutely lived the highest of the three lives, that of the "lover of wisdom," and subdued his lusts, not like the "lover of wealth" from fear of poverty, nor like the "lover of honour" from concern for his reputation, but from love of good. This explains the reason why the lover of wisdom lives hard. It is because he knows that what a man comes to feel pleasure and pain about becomes his engrossing interest. To find your joy and woe in the gratifications of the body means to come to be bound up with its fortunes, and this bars the way to deification and binds you down to the wheel of birth. It is for the sake of this supreme good, "deification," that the lover of wisdom denies "the flesh." To consent to its motions would be to act like Penelope, who unwove by night what she had spent the day in weaving. Now a man whose whole life has been an aspiration to rise above mutability to deiformity will be the last person to fear that the new and abiding

---

[1] The meaning of ἐν τοιαύτῃ ὥρᾳ (80c) has been much disputed. From a comparison with *Tim.* 24c 6, *Phileb.* 26b 1, *Critias,* 111e 5, I take the meaning to be "climate," though I cannot produce another example of the singular of ὥρα in that sense.

deiform self which is being built up in him will be unbuilt by the event of death.[1]

(I make no apology for having drawn freely on the characteristic language of Christian mysticism in expounding this argument. Under all the real differences due to the Christian's belief in the historical reality of the God-man, the ideal of Socrates and the Christian ideal are fundamentally identical. The central thought in both cases is that man is born a creature of temporality and mutability into a temporal and mutable environment. But, in virtue of the fact that there is a something " divine " in him, he cannot but aspire to a good which is above time and mutability, and thus the right life is, from first to last, a process by which the merely secular and temporal self is re-made in the likeness of the eternal. If we understand this, we shall be in no danger of supposing that Socrates is merely anticipating the jejune argument from the indivisibility of a " simple substance," or that the Kantian polemic against Wolffian rationalism seriously affects his reasoning. The thought is that the real nature of the soul has to be learned from a consideration of the nature of the specific " good " to which it aspires. A creature whose well-being consists in living for an " eternal " good cannot be a mere thing of time and change. In this sense, the morality of the Platonic dialogues, like all morality which can command an intelligent man's respect, is from first to last " other-worldly.")

FIRST INTERLUDE (84c–85b).—At this point the thread of the argument is broken ; a general silence ensues, but Simmias and Cebes are observed to be whispering together, as though they were not quite satisfied. Artistically the break serves the purpose of lowering the pitch of the conversation and relieving the emotional strain. It also has a logical function. Impressive as the moral argument for immortality is, there are scientific objections to it of which we have so far heard nothing, and these deserve to be carefully stated and adequately met, since we cannot be called on to accept any view of man's destiny, however attractive, which contradicts known scientific truth, nor is Socrates the man to wish, even in the immediate presence of death, to acquiesce in a faith which is not a reasonable faith. That would be simple cowardice (84e). He has just broken out into his " swan-song," and like the swans, his fellow-servants of the Delphic (? Delian) god, he sings for hope and joy, not in lamentation. He is therefore robust enough in his faith to be only too ready to hear and consider any objections.

OBJECTIONS OF SIMMIAS AND CEBES (85c–88c).—Simmias thinks, like a modern " agnostic," that certainty about our destiny may be unattainable. He would at heart like to be able to appeal to

[1] Like Spinoza, but without, like him, being hampered by a naturalistic metaphysic, Socrates holds that the man who lives best has the soul of which the greatest part is eternal, i.e. the more thoroughly you live the philosophic life, the less is the personality you achieve at the mercy of circumstance, even if the circumstance is the change we call death.

"revelation" (a λόγος θεῖος, 85*d*) on such a question, but agrees that, in the absence of a revelation, one should resolutely examine all human speculations on the problem, and adopt that which will stand close scrutiny best. The difficulty he feels about Socrates' reasoning is that what he has said about the soul and the body might equally be said about the "melody" of a musical instrument and the strings which make the music. The strings are visible and tangible bodies, are composite and perishable, the music is invisible, incorporeal, and "divine." But it would clearly be absurd to argue that, for this reason, the music still exists and sounds "somewhere" when the instrument is broken. Now it is "our belief" that the body is like a musical instrument whose strings are its ultimate components, the hot, cold, moist, and dry, and that the soul is the music this instrument gives out when these 'strings" are properly tuned. If this is so, we may grant that the soul is "divine," like all beauty and proportion, but we must also grant that disease and other disturbances of the constitution of the organism break the strings of the instrument or put them out of tune, and this makes it impossible to argue that because the *débris* of the broken instrument continues to exist after the fracture, *a fortiori* the music must persist still more immutably (85*e*–86*d*).

Cebes has a different objection. He does not attach much importance to the epiphenomenalism of Simmias, but he complains that nothing has really been proved beyond "pre-existence," which has been all along regarded as guaranteed by the doctrine of "reminiscence." Even if we grant that the soul, so far from being a mere resultant of bodily causes, actually makes its own body, this only shows it to be like a weaver who makes his own cloak. In the course of his life he makes and wears out a great many cloaks, but when he dies he leaves the last cloak he has made behind him, and it would be ridiculous to argue that he cannot be dead because the cloak which he made is still here, and a man lasts longer than a cloak. So the soul might make and wear out a whole succession of bodies—indeed, if it is true that the body is always being broken down by waste of tissue and built up again by the soul, something of this sort happens daily. But even if we go so far as to assume that the soul repeatedly makes itself a new body after the death of an old one, it may be that, like the weaver, it exhausts its vigour sooner or later, and so will make a last body, after the death of which the soul will no longer exist. And we can never be sure that the building up of our present body is not the last performance of such a worn-out soul, and consequently that the death we are now awaiting may not be a complete extinction (86*e*–88*b*).

These objections, Phaedo says, struck dismay into the whole company, with the single exception of Socrates. For they appeared to dispose of the whole case for immortality, and, what was worse, they made the hearers, who had been profoundly impressed by Socrates' discourse, feel that they would never be able to put any confidence in their own judgment again, if what had seemed to be completely proved could be so easily disposed of. Plato is careful to interrupt the narrative at this point still more completely, by allowing Échecrates to add that he sympathizes with the general consternation, since he too has hitherto been strongly convinced that the soul is the " attunement " of the body and is therefore anxious to know how Socrates met the difficulty (88c–e).

The purpose of all this by-play is to call attention to the critical importance of the two problems which have just been raised. We are, in fact, at the turning-point of the discussion. The " moral " argument based on the divinity of the soul, as proved by the character of the good to which it aspires, has been stated in all its impressiveness, and we have now to consider whether " science " can invalidate it. To use Kantian language, we have seen what the demand of " practical reason " is, and the question is whether there is an insoluble conflict between this demand and the principles of the " speculative reason," as Echecrates and the auditors of Socrates fear, or, in still more familiar language, the question is whether there is or is not an ultimate discord between " religion " and " science."

As to the source and purport of the two objections it may be enough to say a very few words. That of Simmias, as is indicated by the remarks of Échecrates, is represented by Plato as based on the medical and physiological theories of the younger Pythagoreans. It is a natural development from the well-known theory of Alcmaeon that health depends on the ἰσονομίη or " constitutional balance " between the constituents of the organism. The comparison with the " attunement " of the strings of a musical instrument would be suggested at once by the Pythagorean discovery of the simple ratios corresponding to the intervals of the musical scale. From this to the conclusion that " mind " is the tune given out by the " strings " of the body, the music made by the body, is a very easy step ; and since we now know that Philolaus, the teacher of Cebes and Simmias, had specially interested himself in medicine, we may make a probable conjecture that we are dealing with his doctrine (which is also that of his contemporary Empedocles, Frs. 107, 108). Since the same doctrine appears in Parmenides (Fr. 16), it was clearly making its way among the Pythagoreans by the beginning of the fifth century, though it is, of course, quite inconsistent with their religious beliefs about re-birth in animal bodies : (on all this, see E.G.Ph.³ 295–296).

In principle the theory is exactly that of modern " epiphenomenalism," according to which " consciousness " is a mere by-product of the activities of the bodily organism, the " whistle," as Huxley said, given off by the steam as it escapes from the engine. A satisfactory refutation of it must *ipso facto* be a refutation of the whole epiphenomenalist position.

The source of the difficulty raised by Cebes is different. His allusion to the alternation of waste and repair in the organism at once suggests a Heraclitean origin ; he is thinking of the view of

Heraclitus that the apparent stability of " things " lasts just so long as the antithetical processes of the " way up " and the " way down " balance one another, and no longer. (For the evidence of Heraclitean influences on fifth-century Pythagoreanism, see *E.G.Ph.*[3] Index, *s.v.* Hippasos; *Greek Philosophy, Part I.,* 87–88.) How " modern " Cebes' point is will best be seen by reflecting that the Heraclitean theory of " exchanges " is really a dim anticipation of the modern principle of the conservation of energy. The argument is, in effect, one quite familiar in our own times. If we reject epiphenomenalism and admit interaction between mind and body, it is argued that the mind must part with " energy " in acting on the body, and Cebes, like a modern physicist appealing to the principle of Carnot, holds that this loss of energy cannot be made good indefinitely. A time will come when the effective energy of the ψυχή has been wholly dissipated. Thus his criticism, like that of Simmias, is precisely of the kind which a man of science is tempted to urge against the belief in immortality in our own day. The one difference between the two positions is that the objection of Simmias is primarily that of a biologist, the difficulty of Cebes is that of a physicist. Cebes may also be said in a way to be anticipating Kant's criticism of the argument from the " simplicity " of the soul. His conception of the soul as perishing by wearing out her stock of vitality answers pretty closely to Kant's conception of a gradual sinking of the " intensity " of " consciousness " to the zero-level.

SOLUTION OF THE SCIENTIFIC DIFFICULTIES (88*e*–102*a*).—This section of the dialogue falls into three subdivisions. There is first a preliminary discourse by Socrates intended to warn us against being disgusted with serious thinking by the occurrence of difficulties and so led into mere " irrationalism," next a discussion of the difficulty of Simmias, and then a longer treatment of the much more fundamental problem raised by Cebes, this last subdivision receiving a special narrative introduction of its own.

(a) *The Warning against Misology* (89*a*–91*c*).—Socrates, alone of the company, shows himself calm and even playful in the presence of the bolt—or rather bolts—just shot from the blue. The " argument," at any rate, shall be " raised again," if he can perform the miracle. But whether he succeeds or not, he would at least utter a solemn warning against " misology," irrationalism. Distrust of reason arises much in the same way as misanthropy, distrust of our fellows. The commonest cause of misanthropy is an unwise confidence based on ignorance of character. When a man has repeatedly put this ignorant confidence in the unworthy and been disillusioned, he often ends by conceiving a spite against mankind and denouncing humanity as radically vicious. But the truth is that exalted virtue and gross wickedness are both rare. What the disillusioned man ought to blame for his experience is his own blind ignorance of human nature. So if a man who has not the art of knowing a sound argument from an unsound one has found himself repeatedly misled by his blind trust in unsound " discourses," there is a real danger that he will lay the blame on the weakness of our intellectual faculties and end as a mere irrationalist.[1] To avoid this fate, when we find our most cherished convictions apparently breaking down under criticism we must lay the blame not on the inherent untrustworthiness of " discourse " but on our own rashness in committing ourselves to an uncriticized position. We will therefore reconsider our case and try to meet the objections which have been brought against us, in the spirit of men who are contending honestly for truth, not for an argumentative victory.

(β) *The Objection of Simmias removed* (91c–95a).—In the first place, it may be pointed out that the difficulty raised by Simmias is incompatible with his own professed principles. He avows himself satisfied now by what had been already said that knowledge is " reminiscence," and that, consequently, our souls existed before they wore our present bodily guise. Plainly that cannot be the case if the soul is an " epiphenomenon," the melody given out by the body, the " whistle of the engine," to recur to Huxley's version of the same doctrine. The musical instrument must pre-exist and its strings be screwed up to the right pitch before the melody can be there. We may assert either that all knowledge is " reminiscence " or that the soul is an epiphenomenon ; we must not assert both propositions at once. And Simmias himself has no doubt which of the two positions has the better claim to acceptance. The doctrine of " reminiscence " has been deduced from the " postulate " ($\dot{v}\pi\dot{o}\theta\epsilon\sigma\iota s$) of the reality of the " forms," a principle which Simmias has all through accepted as certain. The epiphenomenalist theory of the soul rests on nothing more than a plausible analogy, and we all know how deceptive such analogies can be—in geometry, for example (92d).

(There is real point in Socrates' *argumentum ad hominem*, independently of the assumption of pre-existence. We may compare the story of W. G. Ward's crushing reply to Huxley, who had just explained mental life to his own satisfaction by epiphenomenalism *plus* the laws of association, " You have forgotten *memory*," *i.e.* the fundamental fact of the *recognition* of the past as past. As Huxley had to admit, his scheme could give no account of recognition, and without presupposing recognition it would not work.)

But the epiphenomenalist theory is not merely incompatible with our unproved postulate about " forms " ; it is also demonstrably false on independent grounds. There are two things which are characteristic of every " attunement " or " melody " ; every " attunement " is completely determined by its constituents, and no " attunement " admits of degrees. If a pair of vibrating strings

---

[1] The description of the misologist would equally cover both the case of the man who ends in pure scepticism and that of the man who takes refuge in a blind faith in what he openly avows to be irrational. Socrates stands for a *fide; quaerens intellectum* against both " universal doubt " and indifferentism and blind fideism or " voluntarism." Hence the partisans of the one call him a " dogmatist," those of the other an " intellectualist."

have one determinate ratio, the interval their notes make will be the fourth, and cannot possibly be anything else ; if they have another determinate ratio, the interval will be the fifth, and so on. Again, a string either is "in tune" or it is not, and there is no third alternative. Between any pair of notes there is one definite interval ; they make that interval exactly and they make no other. C and G♭, for example, make an interval as definite, though not as pleasing, as C and G. "No attunement is more or less of an attunement than any other." What inferences about the soul would follow from these two considerations, if the soul is an "attunement" ? It would follow at once from the second thesis that no one soul can be more or less of a soul than any other. But we have to reckon with the recognized fact that some souls are better or worse than others. Now there seems to be a real analogy between goodness and being "in tune," and between badness and being "out of tune." Either then we should have to express this difference by saying that one "attunement" (the good soul) *is* more "attuned" than another (the bad soul), and our own admissions forbid us to say this ; or we must say that the good soul not only is an "attunement" but *has* a second further "attunement" within itself, and this is manifestly absurd. If a soul is an "attunement," we can only say that every soul is as much an "attunement" as any other, and this amounts to saying that no one soul is morally better or worse than another, or even that all souls, since all are precise "attunements," are perfectly good. But this denial of differences of moral worth is manifestly ridiculous. The argument is, then, that epiphenomenalism is incompatible with the recognition of differences of moral worth, and that these differences are certainly real. A theory which conflicts with the first principles of ethics must be false, since these principles are certain truth.

(The argument, though stated in a way unfamiliar to us, is precisely that which weighs with men who are in earnest with ethics against a philosophy like Spinoza's. Though Spinoza does not make "consciousness" depend causally on the organism, for *practical* purposes his theory of the independent "attributes" works out in the same way as epiphenomenalism. The ψυχή, though not causally dependent on the constituents of the organism, is supposed to be *mathematically* determinable as a function of them. Consequently, just as Simmias has to allow that no "attunement" is more or less an "attunement" than any other, Spinoza holds a rigidly nominalist doctrine about "human nature." There is really no such thing as a "human nature" of which Peter or Paul is a good specimen, but Nero a very bad one. Nero is not, properly speaking, a bad specimen of a man ; he is a perfect specimen of a Nero. To say that he may be a perfect Nero, but is a very bad man, is judging by a purely arbitrary and "subjective" standard. (See *Ethics*, Part I., Appendix, Part IV., Preface.) But, if this is so, Spinoza is undertaking an impossible task in writing a treatise on the good for man and the way to obtain it.)

Again, we have to consider the consequences of the thesis that an " attunement " is a determinate function of its constituents. Given the constituents, the musical " interval " between them is also once and for all completely given. Now the most potent fact about our moral life is that it is a conflict or struggle between an element whose rightful function is to dominate and direct, and a second whose place is to obey and be directed. The soul is constantly repressing the desires for gratification of appetites connected with the body. (It is not meant, of course, that the *whole* of moral discipline consists in subduing such elementary appetites ; they are taken as examples because they are the simplest and most obvious illustration of a principle.) The moral life is a process of *subjugation* of the " flesh " and its desires to the " godly motions of the spirit." The " spirit " which dominates the " flesh " clearly cannot be itself just the " attunement " or " scale " constituted by the ingredients of the " flesh." If this were so, the state of soul at any moment should be simply the resultant and expression of our " organic " condition at that moment, and there should be no such experience as the familiar one of the division of " spirit " or " judgment " against " flesh " or " appetite." (Here, again, the criticism is conclusive for a serious moralist against all forms of epiphenomenalism. The epiphenomenalist is tied by his theory to a " one-world " interpretation of human experience ; morality presupposes a " two-world " interpretation. Its very nature is to be a " struggle " between a higher and a lower. If man were merely a creature of time, or again if he were simply eternal, the struggle could not arise ; its tremendous reality is proof that man's soul is the meeting-place of the two orders, the temporal and the eternal, and this, of itself, disposes of the *simpliste* theory of human personality as a simple function of the passing state of the " organism " or the " nervous system." The epiphenomenalist psychophysics merely ignore the most important of the " appearances " which a true account of moral personality ought to " save." Like all the arguments of the dialogue, this reasoning, of course, presupposes the objective validity of moral distinctions ; to the denier of that ὑπόθεσις it will bring no conviction.)

(γ) *The Difficulty of Cebes discussed* (95a–102a).—As has been said already, the difficulty raised by Cebes is of a much more serious kind than that of Simmias. As the subsequent history of psychology has proved, epiphenomenalism is after all a thoughtless and incoherent theory based on hopelessly misleading analogies and incompetent to take account of the obvious facts of mental life. The theory on which Cebes is relying is a very different matter ; he is appealing to the first principles of a " mechanical " philosophy of nature. Put in modern language, his contention comes to this, that the action of mind on body presupposed in ethics cannot be reconciled with the principles of natural science except by supposing that mind " expends energy " in doing its work of " direction." If this expenditure of energy goes on without compensation, a time must come when the available energy of the mind is exhausted. Thus the issue raised is at bottom that which is still with us, of the universal validity of the postulates of a mechanical interpretation of nature.

Does the guiding influence of intelligence on bodily movement come under the scope of the two great laws of the Conservation and the Degradation of Energy ? If it does, we must look with certainty to the disappearance of our personality after the lapse of some finite duration ; if it does not, the principles of mechanics are not of *universal* application. The development of Energetics in the nineteenth century has enabled us to state the problem with a precision which would have been impossible not merely to Plato, but even to Descartes or Leibniz, but in principle the problem itself has remained the same under all these developments ; Socrates in this part of the *Phaedo* is dealing with the very question which is the theme, for instance, of James Ward's *Naturalism and Agnosticism.*

The importance of the problem demands that we should formulate it with very special care. We may state it thus. Granting the " real distinction of mind from body," it is possible that in every act of intercourse with the body the mind parts with energy which it cannot recover ; if that is so, its progress to destruction begins with its very first entrance into contact with a body, and the completion of the progress is only a matter of time (95d). Now in discussing this problem we are driven to face a still more fundamental one, the question of " the causes of coming into being and passing out of being "(95e), that is, the question of the adequacy of the whole mechanical interpretation of Nature. Socrates' object is to persuade his friends that no single process in Nature is adequately explained by the mechanical interpretation. He can most readily carry them with him by first giving an account of his own personal mental history and the reasons why he gave up the mechanical philosophy in early manhood. This brings us to the

SECOND INTERLUDE (95e-102a).—*The Origin of the Socratic Method.*—(For the, to my mind, overwhelming evidence that the narrative which follows is meant by Plato as a strictly historical account of the early development of Socrates I must refer to Burnet's detailed notes in his edition of the dialogue. The main point is that the general state of scientific opinion described can be shown to be precisely that which must have existed at Athens in the middle of the fifth century, and cannot well have existed anywhere else or at any later time. The " scientific doubts " of which Socrates speaks are all connected with two special problems—the reconciliation of Milesian with Pythagorean cosmology, and the facing of the contradictions Zeno had professed to discover in the foundation of Pythagorean mathematics. It is assumed that the system of Anaxagoras is the last great novelty in physics, and there are clear references to those of Diogenes of Apollonia and of Archelaus. This fixes the date to which Plato means to take us back down to the middle of the fifth century, a consideration which disposes at once of the preposterous suggestions that the narrative is meant as a description either of Plato's own mental development or of the development of a "typical" philosopher. Of course, Plato cannot tell us at first-hand what Socrates was doing and thinking more than twenty years before his own birth, but he has, at least, taken care that his story shall be in accord with historical probabilities, and we may fairly presume that some of the information employed in constructing it came to him directly from Socrates himself. Thus we have as much evidence for its accuracy as we can have for that of any narrative of events related by a narrator born a quarter of a century after the period he is describing.[1])

The general drift of the narrative is as follows. As a young man, Socrates had felt an enthusiasm for "natural science" and made himself acquainted with the biological theories of the Milesians, the Heracliteans, Empedocles, the psychology of Alcmaeon, the flat-earth cosmologies of the Ionians and the spherical-earth cosmologies of the Italian Pythagoreans, as well as with the mathematical subtleties of Zeno about the "unit" and the nature of addition and subtraction. The result of all this eager study was to induce a state of *dubitatio de omnibus*; so far from discovering the cause of all processes, Socrates was led to feel that he did not understand the "reason why" of the simplest and most everyday occurrences. At this point he fell in with the doctrine of Anaxagoras that "mind" is the one cause of order everywhere. The doctrine appealed to him at once, from its teleological appearance. If all the arrangements in the universe are due to intelligence, that must mean that everything is "ordered as it is best it should be," and Socrates therefore hoped to find in Anaxagoras a deliverer from all scientific uncertainties. He expected him to solve all problems in cosmology, astronomy, and biology by showing what grouping of things was best, and consequently most intelligent. But when he read the work of Anaxagoras, he found that its performance did not answer to its promise. Anaxagoras made no use of his principle when he came to the details of his cosmology ; he merely fell back on the same sort of mechanical causes ("airs" and "waters") as the rest of the cosmologists. Like them, he made the fatal mistake of confusing a cause, or *causa principalis*, with "that without which the cause would not act as a cause," *causae concomitantes* or "accessory conditions." This was much as though a man should say that the reason why Socrates is now sitting quietly awaiting death, instead of being in full flight for Thebes or Megara, is the condition of his sinews, muscles, and bones. The real reason is

---

[1] The autobiographical pages of our dialogue are thus the ancient counterpart of Descartes' *Discours de la méthode pour bien conduire sa raison* with the interesting differences, (1) that though both philosophers are concerned to simplify philosophy by getting rid of a false and artificial method, Descartes' object is to revive the very "mechanical" interpretation of nature which Socrates rejected, and (2) that Socrates left it to the piety of another to do for his mental history what Descartes did for himself.

that he judges it good to abide by the decision of a legally constituted court ; if he judged otherwise, if he thought flight the more
reasonable course, his bodily mechanism would be in a very different
condition. Of course, if he had not this apparatus of bones and
sinews and the rest, he could not follow up his judgment, but
it remains true that it is his judgment on the question which
really determines whether he shall sit still or run. This is precisely what we mean by saying that Socrates acts νῷ, rationally
or intelligently.

The disappointment, Socrates says, confirmed his opinion that
he was " no good " (ἀφυὴς ὡς οὐδὲν χρῆμα) [1] at natural science,
and must try to find some way out of his " universal doubt " by
his own mother-wit, without trusting to " men of science," each of
whom only seemed to be able to prove one thing—that all the others
were wrong. His description of the " new method " reveals it to
us at once as that which is characteristic of mathematics. It is a
method of considering " things " by investigating the λόγοι or
" propositions " we make about them. Its fundamental characteristic is that it is deductive. You start with the " postulate,"
or undemonstrated principle, which you think most satisfactory
and proceed to draw out its consequences or " implications "
(συμβαίνοντα), provisionally putting the consequences down as
" true," and any propositions which conflict with the postulate
as false (100*a*). Of course, as is made clear later on, a " postulate "
(ὑπόθεσις) which is found to imply consequences at variance with
fact or destructive of one another is taken as disproved. But the
absence of contradiction from the consequences of a " postulate "
is not supposed to be sufficient proof of its truth. If you are called
on by an opponent who disputes your postulate to defend it, you
must deduce the postulate itself from a more ultimate one, and
this procedure has to be repeated until you reach a postulate which
is " adequate " (101*e* 1), that is, which all parties to the discussion
are willing to admit. (We hear more of this part of the method in
Rep. vi. 510–511, where we discover that the ideal goal of the method
is to deduce the whole of science from truths which are strictly
self-evident, but nothing is said of this in the *Phaedo*.) The most
important special rule of the method, however, is that, also insisted
on by Descartes, that a proper order must be observed. We are
not to raise the question of the truth of a " postulate " itself until
we have first discovered exactly what its consequences are. The

---

[1] Of course this is said humorously. It is the man who can discourse
learnedly about " airs " and " waters "—we might say about " electrons "
and " electric fields "—and yet ignores the distinction between " cause " and
" accessory conditions " who is really, from Socrates' point of view, ἀφυὴς ὡς
οὐδὲν χρῆμα for the work of hard thinking. Later on (99*c*), Socrates calls
the method he fell back on a δεύτερος πλοῦς, or " second-best " course. As
the phrase originally refers to taking to the oars when the wind prevents
using the sails, the suggestion is that Socrates' method is " second-best "
rather in being slower and harder than the slap-dash dogmatism of the physicists than in leading to inferior results.

confusion of these two distinct problems is the great error of the
ἀντιλογικοί (101e). In spite of his humorous depreciation of
his proceeding as that of an amateur, Socrates has evidently, like
Descartes, reflected carefully on the nature of geometrical method,
and, like him, he is proposing to introduce the same method into
scientific inquiry in general. An illustration, he says, may be given
by considering his own familiar practice of " postulating " such
" forms " as " the good," " beauty," and the rest. He intends, in
a few minutes, to show that if this " postulate " is made, the immortality of the soul will follow as an implication (100b). (There
is no question of proving the " postulate " itself, as the whole
company are ready to concede it.) At this point we leave the
autobiographical narrative and pass to an application of the
" postulate " of " forms " to the theory of causation, which
is a necessary preliminary to the final argument for immortality
(100c–102a).

What Socrates intends to explain is what we have learned from
Aristotle to call " formal " causality, but he has no technical
terminology ready to hand and therefore makes his meaning clear
by examples. If we ask *why* something is beautiful, we may be told
in one case, " because it has a bright colour," in another " because
it has such-and-such a shape." The point that Socrates wants to
make is that such answers are insufficient. There must ultimately
be one *single* reason why we can predicate one and the same character, beauty, in all these cases. Having a bright colour cannot be
the cause of beauty, since the thing we call beautiful on the strength
of its shape may not be coloured at all ; having a particular shape
cannot be *the* cause of beauty, since we pronounce things which
have not that shape to be beautiful, on the strength of their colour,
and so on. Hence Socrates says he rejects all these learned explanations and sticks to the simple one that universally the reason
why anything is beautiful is that " beauty " is " present to it,"
or that it " partakes of " beauty. The thought is that whenever
we are justified in asserting the same predicate univocally of a
plurality of logical subjects, the predicate in every case names one
and the same " character." It is these characters which Socrates
calls " forms." We might call them " universals " if we bear two
cautions carefully in mind. They are not to be supposed to be
" ideas in our minds " or anything of that sort ; they are realities
of which we think. Also, as the case of " beauty " is well adapted
to show, a " form " may be " present " to a thing in very varying
degrees. A thing may be very beautiful, or it may be only very
imperfectly beautiful, and it may well be that nothing is super-
latively and completely beautiful. We should also note that the
precise character of the relation which Socrates calls " presence "
or " participation " or " communication " (κοινωνία) is nowhere
explained, and his hesitation about the name for this relation (100d)
may perhaps mean that he feels that there is an unsolved problem
involved by his " postulate." There obviously is such a problem.

We naturally ask ourselves at once what else a particular sensible thing is, besides being a complex of " forms " or " characters." As far as the *Phaedo* goes, we are not told that the thing is any more than a " bundle of universals." The attempt to say what else it is has played a prominent part in later philosophy. Plato's answer has to be collected with difficulty from Aristotle's scattered notices of his informal oral discourses. Aristotle and the mediaeval Aristotelians tried to answer the same question by their doctrine of " matter " and " form," Scotus by the difficult doctrine of *haecceitas*. But there is no evidence that Socrates had any answer to the difficulty. The immediate point is simply that if we admit the existence of " forms," we must say in every case that the " cause " or " reason " why a predicate β can be asserted of a thing a is that a corresponding " form " B " is present " to a, or that a " partakes of " the " form " B. How it has come to do so is a different question, and we must not suffer ourselves to be led away on a false trail. (The question is, *e.g.*, " Why is this thing now beautiful ? What do I mean by calling it so ? not, What had to be done to it before I could call it so ?) [1]

We might seem here to have lost sight of the insistence on teleology which had marked Socrates' comments on Anaxagoras, but there is really a close connexion between " end " and " formal cause," as Aristotle was to show at length. To say that the primary problem is always to explain what a thing is by reference to its " form " carries the implication that we have to explain the origins and rudimentary phases of things by what the things are, when they are at last there, not to explain what they are by discoursing on their origins, and this is precisely what we mean by taking a " teleological " point of view. But it would take us too far away from the *Phaedo* to discuss the full implications of such teleology.[2]

At the point we have reached, the narrative of Phaedo is once more broken in order that Echecrates, as a mathematician, may express his high approval of Socrates' doctrine of method (which, in fact, is pretty plainly inspired by the example of Zeno in his famous polemic, the point of which was to show that there must be something amiss with the " postulates " of the early Pythagorean

---

[1] The importance of Socrates' warning against substituting some other problem for that of the formal cause is well illustrated by the perpetual confusion in our own times between explaining what a thing is and theorizing about its origin. Thus we are incessantly being offered speculations about the way in which morality or religion or art may have originated as if they were answers to the question what art or religion or morality is.

[2] One obvious implication may just be mentioned. As the earlier stages in our own life can only be fully explained in the light of what we were then going to be, so to explain a man's life as a whole we need to know not only what he is now, but what he may yet grow to be. Thus the problem of our ultimate destiny is strictly relevant to the ethical problem proper, on what principles we ought to regulate our present conduct. It is idle to say that it " makes no difference to ethics " whether the soul is immortal. It ought to make all the difference, just as it makes all the difference to the rules of the nursery that babies do not remain babies.

geometers, since they could be shown to lead to pairs of contradictory implications). We then embark formally on the

(c) THIRD (AND FINAL) PROOF OF IMMORTALITY (102a–107b).— The " forms " had entered incidentally into both the proposed proofs which have been already examined. In this final proof we are offered a direct deduction of immortality from the fundamental postulate that the " forms " exist. This marks the argument as intended to be the climax of the whole reasoning, since the proof, if successful, must be recognized as complete by Cebes or any one else who regards the reality of the " forms " as the basis of his whole philosophy.

We have, in the first place, to stipulate for an unusual accuracy of expression which is necessary if we are to avoid fallacy. We commonly speak, for example, of one man as taller or shorter than another. We say Simmias is taller than Socrates but not so tall as Phaedo. On the face of it this looks as though we were calling Simmias at once tall and short, and therefore asserting the simultaneous presence in him of two " opposed " Forms. But all we really mean is that Simmias *happens* to be relatively taller than Socrates and shorter than Phaedo. It is not " in virtue of being Simmias " (*en sa qualité de Simmias*) that these things can be predicated of him. The distinction here taken is that between essential and accidental predication since made familiar to us all by Aristotelian logic. Or, in scholastic terminology, it is the distinction between an intrinsic and an extrinsic denomination. The point has to be made, because the force of the argument now to be produced depends on the fact that it deals entirely with *essential* predication.

This being premised, we may go on to assert (a) that not only will no " form," *e.g.* magnitude, combine with an opposed " form," but further, " the magnitude *in us* will never admit the small " (102d). That is, not only can we dismiss at once as false such assertions as that " virtue is vice," " unity is plurality," but we can also equally dismiss any proposition in which a subject, other than a " form," of which that form is *essentially* predicated, is qualified by a predicate opposed to that which attaches to it *essentially* in virtue of the " form " under consideration. Thus, if " shortness " were an essential predicate of Socrates, we could say that " Socrates is tall " must be false ; it is only because a given stature is an " accident " of Socrates that it is possible to say of him at one date that he is short, but at another (when he has grown) that he is " tall." (Or to take an example which perhaps illustrates the point even better, not only is it absurd to say that virtue itself is vice, it would also be absurd to say " the virtues *of the old pagans* were splendid vices," if we meant such a phrase as anything more than a rhetorical exaggeration.) When a " form " opposite to that which is *essential* to a certain thing " advances " to " occupy " the thing, the original " form " cannot subsist side by side with its rival in joint occupation of the ground. It must either " beat its retreat " (ὑπεκχωρεῖν) or be " annihilated " (ἀπολωλέναι). (The metaphors, including that indicated in the last phrase, ἀπολωλέναι, are all military.) And this statement is quite consistent with that of our first " proof " about the generation of " opposites " from one another. For we were talking then about " opposite *things* " (πράγματα), and meant that a *thing* which becomes cool must have been warm, a thing which becomes big must have been small. Now we are talking about the predicates or characters of the things, and mean that *hot* does not become *cold* nor *cold hot*. The two positions are thus fully compatible with each other (103*b*).

(β) We can make a further assertion which will conduct us straight to the conclusion we want. There are certain things which are not themselves " forms," but of which participation in a given form is an essential character. Thus fire is not " warmth " nor is snow " cold." But fire will not " admit " the form " cold," nor snow the form " warmth." Fire is never cool nor snow hot. As we said already, when " cold " attempts to " occupy " fire, or heat to " occupy " snow, an *essential* character of the thing must either " withdraw " or be " annihilated," and in either case the thing, the fire or the snow, is no longer the thing it was. But we may now add that in cases like that of fire and snow, when each of a pair of subjects has predicated of it *essentially* " participation " in a form " opposite " to one in which the other member of the pair *essentially* participates, the same thing will occur. Thus " cold " is essentially predicated of snow and " hot " of fire. And we may say not only the snow will " retire " or be " annihilated " rather than allow itself to be " occupied " by heat, but further that snow will not abide the " advance " of fire. It *melts* and ceases to be snow when you expose it to fire. (This is a case of the alternative of " annihilation." The snow, so to say, allows itself to be " cut up " in defence of its " position " when the forces of the fire make their onslaught.) So again the number "three" is not the same thing as " the odd," or " odd number," since there are many other odd numbers, but it " participates " *essentially* in the " form " odd. (It is true that " three " and the other numbers, unlike fire and snow, are also themselves spoken of freely in this and other dialogues as " forms," but Socrates makes no difficulty about treating the " participation " of a sensible thing in a " form " and the " participation " of one " form " in another as examples of the same relation. As we might put it in the terminology of modern " logistic," he does not discriminate between the relation of an individual to a class, and the relation of total inclusion between one class and another.) Consequently " whatever is occupied " by the " form " three is also " occupied " by the accompanying " form " odd ; the cardinal number of every " triplet " is an odd integer. Hence no triplet will allow itself to be " occupied " by the " form " even number. You cannot make an even triplet (*e.g.*, when a man's fourth child is born, the class " children of So-and-so " does not become an even triplet ; it ceases to be a triplet as well as to be " odd." This is an example of the alternative of " withdrawal " or " retreat," since " oddness " is not, like low or high temperature, a character which can be " destroyed." The whole " universe " might conceivably be reduced to a uniform low temperature, but not the number-series to a series with all its terms even.)

We now apply these results to the case of the soul. Life is a necessary concomitant of the presence of a soul, as illness is of the presence of fever, or heat of the presence of fire. A soul always brings life with it to any body in which it is present. Now there is an " opposite " to life, namely, death. Hence we may say that a soul will never allow itself to be occupied by the opposite of the character it always carries with itself. That is, life may be essentially predicated of the soul and therefore death can never be predicated of it. Thus the soul is, in the literal sense of the word, " undying " (ἀθάνατος) ; that is, the phrase " a dead soul " would be a *contradictio in adjecto*. So much has now been actually demonstrated (105e).

Of course this does not take us the whole of the way we wish to go. What has been " demonstrated," and would probably not be denied by anyone, is that, properly speaking, "death " is a process which belongs to the bodily organism. It is the body which dies, speaking strictly, not its "mind." But to prove that there is no such thing as a " dead soul," though there are dead bodies, does not prove that the soul continues to live after the body has died, and Socrates is well aware of this. His demonstration, on his own admission, leaves us with an alternative : since " dead " cannot be predicated of a soul, the soul must either be annihilated or must " retire " when the body dies. Socrates' faith is that the second member of the alternative is correct, but the emphatic " so much has been demonstrated " of 105e 8 seems to show that, when all is said, this remains for him an article of faith, not a demonstrated proposition of science. Our decision between the two alternatives will depend on the question whether the soul is not only " undying " but " imperishable " (ἀνώλεθρος). If it is, then we may safely say that what befalls it at death is merely " withdrawal elsewhere." He is not actually called on to argue this fresh point, since his auditors at once assert their conviction that if what is " undying " is not imperishable, nothing can be supposed to be so, whereas there are, in fact, imperishables, such as God, and " the form of life." Thus, in the end, the imperishability of the soul is accepted as a consequence of the standing conviction of all Greek religion that τὸ ἀθάνατον = τὸ θεῖον = τὸ ἄφθαρτον. It is the soul's " divinity " which is, in the last resort, the ground for the hope of immortality, and the divinity of the soul is a postulate of a reasonable faith which the dialogue never attempts to " demonstrate." The last word of Socrates himself on the value of his demonstration is that its " primary postulates " (*i.e.* the " forms " and the divinity of the soul) really demand further examination (107b 5).

THE PRACTICAL BEARING OF THE DISCUSSION (107c–108c).— This brings us to the real moral of the dialogue. As we have just seen, even if we are satisfied with the deduction of immortality from the doctrine of " forms," that doctrine itself is a postulate which is not exempt from reconsideration. But the mere admission that the hope of immortality is not irrational has a profound significance for the conduct of life. It follows that the " tendance of the soul " is incomparably the most serious of human interests, and the danger of neglecting this " tendance " the most awful to which we can expose ourselves. If death ends all, it may not matter so much what sort of soul a man has, since, in a few years, his wickedness will end with his life. But if the soul lives for ever, it takes with it into the unseen world nothing but its own intrinsic character for good or evil, and its unending future depends on that. This is really what the Orphic stories about the judgment of the dead should teach us. On the character we bring with us into the unseen world, our company there will depend, and our happiness and misery will depend on our company. As in the *Gorgias* and *Republic*, the hope of immortality is thus used for a moral purpose. The value of faith in it is that it drives home the question what manner of men we ought to be, if there is an endless future before us, and thus invests the choice for moral good and evil with an awful importance it would otherwise not have (*Phaedo* 107c ; *Rep.* 608b, 621b–d. Plato enlarges on the same theme on his own account at *Laws*, 904a–905b). In the end, for Socrates and Plato, no less than for Kant, immortality is a postulate of the " practical " use of "reason." [1]

I do not propose to make this chapter longer by dwelling either on the impressive myth in which Plato fits an imaginative picture of the future lot of the virtuous and the vicious into a framework supplied partly by a scheme of astronomy which seems to be Pythagorean, and possibly, as the admiring comment of Simmias at 109a suggests, due to Philolaus, and subterranean geography which manifestly comes from Empedocles, or on the famous description of the last earthly moments of Socrates. I must be content to refer the reader to Burnet's commentary, and, for a study of the influence of the picture on later eschatology, to Professor J. A. Stewart's *Myths of Plato*. It is useless to discuss the question how much in these myths of the unseen represents a genuine " extra-belief " of either Socrates or Plato, and how much is conscious " symbolism." Probably neither philosopher could have answered the question himself. But we must bear in mind that Socrates regularly accompanies these stories with the warning (e.g. *Phaedo*, 114d) that no man of sense would put much confidence in the details, and that the one thing of serious moment is that we should

---

[1] If the question is asked whether the faith defended in the *Phaedo* is a belief in "personal" immortality, I can only reply that, though the language of philosophers was not to acquire a word for "personality" for many centuries, the faith of Socrates is a belief in the immortality of his ψυχή, and by his ψυχή he means the seat or *suppositum* of all we call "personal character," and nothing else. "Tendance of the soul" is precisely what we call the development of "moral personality."

live as befits men who are looking for a city that does not yet appear, and that the real object of " tending the soul " is to make us fit for citizenship in the eternal (*Phaedo*, 115*b*). From the historical point of view, the supremely interesting feature of this particular myth is that it is an attempt to get into one picture the flat earth of the old Ionian science and the spherical earth of the Pythagoreans, as Burnet notes. This is done by imagining the sphere of the earth to be of enormous magnitude and to contain a number of shallow depressions like that of the Mediterranean Each of these depressions will look very much like the flat earth of Anaximenes or Anaxagoras or Democritus. As Burnet says, some such reconciliation of the two cosmographies may have suggested itself at Athens in the middle of the fifth century to some one ; it would be absurd to suppose that it could ever have been entertained by contemporaries of Plato.

See further :

BURNET.—*Plato's Phaedo* (Oxford, 1913); *Greek Philosophy, Part I.*, Chapters IX.-X.
RITTER, C.—*Platon*, i. 532–586.
RAEDER, H.—*Platons philosophische Entwickelung*, 168–181.
NATORP, P.—*Platons Ideenlehre*, 126–163.
STEWART, J. A.—*Myths of Plato*, 77–111 (*The Phaedo Myth*) ; *Plato's Doctrine of Ideas*, 39–47.

NOTE.—Plutarch's essay *de Genio Socratis* is rich in interesting traditions about Simmias and the Pythagoreans at Thebes. It describes Pelopidas and his fellow-conspirators, who recaptured the citadel of Thebes from the Spartans in 379, as meeting for their enterprise in the house of Simmias. Plutarch, as a Boeotian, was well informed on Theban matters and his story presumably has historical foundations.

CHAPTER IX

THE *SYMPOSIUM*

THE *Symposium* is perhaps the most brilliant of all Plato's achievements as a dramatic artist ; perhaps for that very reason, it has been worse misunderstood than any other of his writings. Even in its own day it was apparently quite misapprehended by Xenophon, if one may judge by the tone of the very inferior imitation of it in his own piece of the same name. Xenophon was led by the form of the dialogue to suppose that it is meant to deal with the sexual passion and to pit against it a *Symposium* of his own, which has as its climax a eulogy of the pleasures of married life. Our own and the last generation, with the poison of Romanticism in their veins, have gone farther and discovered that the dialogue anticipates William Blake's " prophecies " by finding the key to the universe in the fact of sex. This means that such readers have sought the teaching of the *Symposium* in the first instance in the Rabelaisian parody of a cosmogony put very appropriately into the mouth of Aristophanes. The very fact that this famous speech is given to the great γελωτοποιός should, of course, have proved to an intelligent reader that the whole tale of the bi-sexual creatures is a piece of gracious Pantagruelism, and that Plato's serious purpose must be looked for elsewhere. Similarly, it is more from the *Symposium* than from any other source that soul-sick " romanticists " have drawn their glorification of the very un-Platonic thing they have named " platonic love," a topic on which there is not a word in this or any other writing of Plato. We must resolutely put fancies like these out of our heads from the first if we mean to understand what the real theme of the dialogue is. We must remember that Eros, in whose honour the speeches of the dialogue are delivered, was a cosmogonic figure whose significance is hopelessly obscured by mere identification with the principle of " sex." We must also remember that the scene is a festive one, and that the tone of most of the speeches is consequently more than half playful, and rightly so, as the gaiety of the company is meant to set off by contrast the high seriousness of the discourse of Socrates. It is there that we are to find Plato's deepest meaning, and when we come to that speech we shall find that the " love " of which he speaks the praises is one which has left sexuality far behind, an *amor mysticus* which finds its nearest modern counterpart in the writers who have employed the imagery of *Canticles* to set forth the love of the soul for its Creator.

In form the dialogue is an indirectly reported drama. The actual narrator, Apollodorus of Phalerum, a friend of Socrates (who is mentioned at *Apol.* 38*b* as one of the persons who offered to give security for a fine of thirty minae, and at *Phaedo* 117*d* as breaking into hysterical tears when Socrates drained the hemlock, and again by Xenophon as a constant attendant on the master, at *Mem.* iii. 11, 17), repeats to some friends the story of the banquet held in honour of the first tragic victory of the poet Agathon. Apollodorus is too young to have been present, but had the story direct from an eyewitness, Aristodemus, of the deme Cydathenaeum, apparently the same person as the Aristodemus whom Xenophon makes Socrates take to task (*Mem.* i. 1, 4) for his neglect of public worship. The time of narration is supposed to be " a good number of years " (172*c*) after Agathon's retirement from Athens. When that was we do not know, except that it was after the production of Aristophanes' *Thesmophoriazusae* (411) and before that of the *Frogs* (405), so that the actual narration must be supposed to be given some time in the last few years of the fifth century. The real object of introducing all these particulars seems to be to remind us that Plato himself could not have been present at the banquet, and does not therefore pretend to guarantee the historical accuracy of the narrative in detail.

It is more interesting to remark the careful way in which the spirit of the time is kept up in the account of the banquet itself. Not only is the occasion itself, the first public victory of a new poet, a festive one, but the year is one in which the temper of the Imperial city itself was exceptionally joyous and high. The date is only a few months before the sailing of the great Armada which was confidently expected to make the conquest of Sicily a mere stepping-stone to unlimited expansion, possibly to the conquest of Carthage (Thuc. vi. 15) ; the extraordinary tone of ὕβρις characteristic of Alcibiades in the dialogue becomes much more explicable when we remember that at the moment of speaking he was the commander-designate of such an enterprise and drunk with the ambitions Thucydides ascribes to him quite as much as with wine. We note that Aristophanes also is depicted as he must have been at the height of his powers, when the *Birds* and the *Lysistrata* were yet to be written, not as the broken man, whom Plato might have known personally, who could sink to the tiresome dirtiness of the *Ecclesiazusae*. In a few months' time the whole situation was changed by the scandal about the Hermae and the profanation of the mysteries ; Alcibiades was an exile at Sparta, bent on ruining the city which had disgraced him, and there is good reason to think that at least two other speakers in our dialogue (Eryximachus and Phaedrus) were badly implicated in the same affair.[1] For the δῆμος itself, the year may be said to have been the crisis of its fate. It had staked its all on a great aggressive bid for *Weltmacht* and the bid failed. The city never recovered the loss of men and material ;

[1] For the evidence see Burnet, *Greek Philosophy, Part I.*, 190–191.

the commander of whom she had made a deadly enemy was the man who taught the thick-witted Spartans where to deal her the wound which would, in the end, prove fatal. It is part of Plato's consummate art that he hints at nothing of this. He fixes the mood of the time and of the man of the time, " flown with insolence and wine," with complete objectivity and without after-thought, as a background to set off the figure of " philosophy " incarnated in Socrates.[1]

INTRODUCTION (172a–178a).—Aristodemus, then, related that, the day after Agathon's victory, he met Socrates in very unusual " festal array," on his way to Agathon's dinner-party and accepted his proposal to join him. On the way Socrates fell into one of his ecstasies and left his companion to enter Agathon's house, where he was warmly welcomed, alone. Agathon knew enough of Socrates' habits not to be startled by learning that he was standing " tranced " in the doorway of the next house. He did not make his appearance until dinner was half over, when he took his seat by Agathon in the gayest of humours. When the dinner was finished, the party resolved, on the advice of the physician Eryxi-machus, that there should be no enforced deep " potting " and no flute-playing. They would entertain themselves, as sensible men should, with discourses. Phaedrus, another member of the party, had often remarked on the singular fact that though so many persons and things have been made subjects of eulogy, no one has as yet made an adequate eulogy of Eros.[2] It would be a good way of spending the evening if each member of the party would deliver such a eulogy, beginning with Phaedrus, as the source of the pro-posal. Socrates fell in at once with the suggestion which, he declared, suited him admirably, as the " science of love " was the only science he possessed.

The main object of this little introduction is plainly to call our attention to a marked feature in the character of Socrates. He is at heart a mystic and there is something " other-worldly " about him. We shall hear a great deal more about this later on from Alcibiades when he describes Socrates' long " rapt " in the trenches before Potidaea, an experience which may have had a great significance

---

[1] I do not think it necessary, with Mr. R. G. Bury, to look for any hidden meaning in the references made by Apollodorus to a less accurate narrative of the scene given by a certain Phoenix. These touches are intended merely to suggest that the incidents had aroused a good deal of interest and been much talked about. I do not believe that there is any reason to suppose that Plato is replying to charges made in the κατηγορία Σωκράτους of Polycrates anywhere in our dialogue. If he had done so, we should probably have learned something about the matter from Xenophon or from the *Apologia* of Lib-anius (which shows signs of a knowledge of Polycrates' pamphlet).

[2] Mr. Bury naturally reminds us that there is a chorus about Eros in the *Antigone* and another in the *Hippolytus*. But the ode of the *Antigone* (781–801) deals with the ruin and havoc Eros causes and the crimes to which he prompts even " the just." That of the *Hippolytus* (525–564) is similarly a prayer against his " tyrannical " violence. Neither can be called a eulogy. Cf. E. Bevan, *Hellenism and Christianity*, pp. 93 ff.

for his " mission." A minor experience of the same kind is introduced at the outset to prepare us for this narrative and for the high " other-worldliness " of Socrates' own discourse on Eros. But, as with other great mystics, Socrates' other-worldliness is compatible with being a " man of the world " in the best sense and knowing how to adapt himself readily to the mood of the gayest of companies. (It is worth noting that the biographers of the fervent " ecstatic " St. Francis Xavier dwell on precisely the same combination of qualities as part of the secret of his influence over company of every kind, and that Xavier himself, in his instructions to his remplaçants, lays almost as much stress on the importance of knowing how to win men by being " good company " as on that of intense secret devotion.)

Speech of Phaedrus (178a–180b).—Phaedrus is known to us chiefly from the part he plays in the dialogue called after him, where he appears as an amateur of rhetoric and a fervid admirer of the fashionable stylist of the moment, Lysias, in contradistinction to Socrates, who regards Lysias as intellectually inferior to the, as yet, little known Isocrates. Socrates is made to say of him there (*Phaedrus*, 242b) that he has been the cause of more " discourses," either by delivering them himself or being the occasion of their delivery by other men, than any living person, if we leave Simmias of Thebes out of account. If we may trust the list of names inserted in Andocides i. 15, he was among the persons accused, a few months after Agathon's dinner, of having " profaned the mysteries " (unless, though this is not so likely, the reference is to some other Phaedrus). In Lysias xix. 15 he is said to have fallen into poverty, but " not through vicious courses." There is a well-known epigram in the *Anthology*, ascribed to Plato, which makes him an ἐρώμενος of the author, but, since Phaedrus was a man in 416 when Plato was a small boy, this is chronologically impossible.[1]

The speech of Phaedrus is properly made jejune and commonplace, for a double reason. As a point of art, it is necessary to begin with the relatively tame and commonplace in order to lead up by a proper *crescendo* to the climax to be reached in the discourse of Socrates. And the triviality and vulgar morality of the discourse is in keeping with the character of the speaker as depicted for us in the *Phaedrus*. Phaedrus understands by Eros sexual passion, and particularly passion of this kind between two persons of the same sex. At Athens these relations were regarded as disgraceful both by law[2] and, as the next speaker in our dialogue will remind us, by general opinion, but literature shows that they

[1] Of course the Phaedrus of the epigram might be another person. But when we find Agathon and Phaedrus figuring in an ἐρωτικὸς λόγος by Plato and also appearing as ἐρώμενοι in epigrams ascribed to Plato, it is surely most likely that the epigrams were composed and fathered on Plato by some later author who had read the *Symposium* and forgotten that it is Socrates and not Plato who poses playfully there as an ἐρωτικός.

[2] For the attitude of Attic law to παιδεραστία, the great source of information is the speech of Aeschines against Timarchus.

were in fact cultivated particularly by the "upper classes" as part of the general craze for imitation of Sparta. It is important to remember that all such aberrations were strongly disapproved by the *viri Socratici*. The present dialogue and the *Phaedrus* are complete evidence for the theory and practice of Socrates ; Plato's attitude in the *Laws* is the same. At *Laws* 636*b* it is made a special reproach to Sparta to have set an example of such "corruptions," and their complete suppression in a really moral society is taken as a matter of course at 841*d*.[1] Xenophon's attitude is the same.

The argument of the speech is that Eros is entitled to honour on two grounds—(*a*) his *noblesse*, as proved by his antiquity, and (*b*) the advantages he bestows on us. The first point is established by an appeal to Hesiod and the cosmogonists generally, who presuppose Eros—the impulse to generation—as an original first principle of the universe. It is brought in as a regular commonplace of encomiasts, who are fond of dwelling on the "pedigree" of their hero. (Socrates regarded this pride of birth as pure vanity as he tells us at *Theaetet.* 175*a*–*b*, where he criticizes the common run of panegyrists on this ground.) The second point is supposed to be proved by the argument that "love" is the most powerful of incitements to ambition. A lover will do anything and endure anything to win the admiration of his "beloved" and avoid disgracing himself in his eyes. (Note then that Phaedrus has no conception of any "good" surpassing that of the "lover of honours.") Hence an army of "lovers," if one could be raised, would be invincible. In short, the great service which Eros renders to men is that he inspires them with μένος ("prowess"). (This was, in fact, exactly the view taken in Spartan and other Dorian communities, where "homo-sexual love" in its coarsest form was encouraged because it was believed to contribute to military "chivalry."[2]) The point is illustrated by the cases of Alcestis who died for her "love" Admetus, and Achilles who died for his "lover" Patroclus. Heaven rewarded this devotion by restoring Alcestis to life [3] and translating Achilles to the "isles of the blest." Orpheus, a mere "chicken-hearted" musician, was not allowed to recover his Eurydice, because he had not the "pluck" to die for her but sneaked down to the house of Hades without dying. In substance, then, the speech simply amounts to a defence of an unnatural practice on the plea of its military value. It is an apologia for the theory and practice of Sparta.

[1] These considerations show that we must not put a gross interpretation on the passing remark of Socrates at *Rep.* 468*c*. The reference is merely to innocent marks of affection and admiration which the younger people are to show to the brave soldier, and is half playful in tone.

[2] On this aspect of the subject see in particular the instructive article of Bethe (*Rheinisches Museum*, lxii. 438 ff.).

[3] *Symp.* 179*b*. Apart from the play of Euri·· les, which Phaedrus probably has in his mind, this is the first reference i· extant Greek literature to the famous story

In manner it is a poor and inadroit " encomium " of a common-place type.[1]

Speech of Pausanias (180c–185c).—Pausanias is virtually an unknown figure to us. He appears also in the Protagoras (the supposed date of which must be roughly some twenty years before 416), in company with Agathon, then a mere stripling, and Socrates is there made to say playfully that he should not be surprised if the pair are " lovers " (Prot. 315d). Xenophon has dutifully worked him in in his own imitation of the Symposium (viii. 32), where he is said to be the " lover of the poet Agathon " and to have " defended homo-sexual vice."[2] This, however, is merely a Platonic reminiscence. Xenophon has taken the remark of Socrates in the Protagoras with dull literalness and gone on to attribute to Pausanias the remark about an " army of lovers " actually made in our dialogue by Phaedrus.

The speech of Pausanias, unlike that of Phaedrus, really does attempt to take account of specifically Athenian moral sentiment, and is much more elaborately worked out in point of form. He is dissatisfied with Phaedrus on moral grounds, because he has drawn no distinction between worthy and criminal " love." The distinction is even prefigured in mythology, which recognizes a difference between a " heavenly " Aphrodite, daughter of Uranus without any mother, and a " vulgar " (πάνδημος) Aphrodite, daughter of Zeus and Dione. Since Aphrodite is the mother of Eros, we must consequently distinguish between a " heavenly " and an earthly or " vulgar " Eros. The one is admirable, the other not. In fact—so far Pausanias agrees with Socratic ethics—there is a right and a wrong in all human activities, and consequently there must be a right and a wrong way of " being in love."

The " low " form of love has two characteristics : (1) its object may be of either sex, and (2) what it loves in that object is the body rather than the soul, and this is why the vulgar lover prefers his beloved to be empty-headed (ἀνόητος) and therefore an easy quarry. The " heavenly " love is all masculine in his composition. The object of this love is therefore always male and the passion is free from " grossness " (ὕβρις). It is directed not on the young and pretty but on an object just on the verge of manhood, a person whose character promises assured lifelong friendship.

To this distinction corresponds the apparently self-contra-dictory character of the Attic " use and wont " in respect of Eros. In some communities, such as Elis and Boeotia, the " vulgar " and the more refined Eros are both permitted, in the Ionian cities both are regarded as disgraceful. This is because Eleans and Boeotians

---

[1] Cf. Bury, Symposium, p. xxv. But he is unjust to the " sophists " in suggesting that it is a fair specimen of their performances, and I think he would be nearer the mark if he had said that the moral standpoint of the speech is that of an average Spartan, than he is in speaking of " the average citizen " of Athens.

[2] For another clear echo of our dialogue, cp. Xen. op. cit. ii, 26 with Symp. 198c 3. There are plenty of others.

THE *SYMPOSIUM*   215

are dull and stupid; Ionians have been inured to slavish conformity
to institutions which serve the purposes of their Persian masters.
Eros, philosophy, bodily culture, are all discouraged by the Persians
as influences unfavourable to acquiescence in despotism. At
Athens and Sparta (this last statement can hardly be strictly true)
social custom is not so simple.   Use and wont are divided ; public
opinion " loves a lover " and sympathizes with all his extravagances,
but the young, on the other hand, are expected to resist his advances
and promises, and parents and relatives take all possible care to
protect their charges against them.   (Just as in a " romantic "
society it is thought honourable in a man to practise "gallantry,"
but the point of female honour to be " cruel " to the gallant.)   The
explanation of this apparent contradiction is that the difficulties
put in the way of the " lover " are intended to make it certain that he
loves with the higher and celestial kind of Eros, directed to the soul,
and that the " beloved " is won not by the wealth or social position of the lover but by his genuine " goodness " and " intelligence."
    In some respects the speech is morally on a higher level than
that of Phaedrus.   It is a real contribution to the discussion to
introduce as fundamental the distinction between a noble and an
ignoble " love."   And Pausanias is so far following a right instinct
when he makes the noble " love " independent of obvious physical
prettiness and attractiveness and maintains that its object is a
consortium totius vitae in the fullest sense of the words.   So far he is
in accord with the distinction we should draw ourselves between
the love that is little more than a sensual weakness and the love
which can lead to a " marriage of true minds."   To this extent, I
cannot agree with the disparaging estimate of Mr. Bury (*Symp.*
xxvii).   That Pausanias conceives of a *consortium totius vitae* as only
possible between a younger and an older *male* is to be explained by
the Attic neglect of the intellectual and moral education of the
womenfolk of the citizens.   There is no possibility of the " shared
life " where one of the partners is an intelligent human being and
the other a spoilt child or a domestic animal, and it is fair to remember this when we find Pausanias assuming that all love of
women belongs to the ignoble kind.   On the other hand, Pausanias'
conception of the noble Eros is pitched far too low.   As his inclusion
of Sparta as one of the places where the distinction is recognized
would be enough to show, he quite definitely means to give his
approval to what Socrates and Plato, like ourselves, regard as not
merely " guilty " but " unnatural," provided that it is made the
basis for a permanent life of intimate devotion. ·The persons on
whom he bestows unqualified admiration as having achieved the
perfection of human excellence are just those whom Socrates is
made to treat in the *Phaedrus* much as we should treat the " knight "
who is spurred to chivalrous exploits by a love which, though
" sinful," is not *merely* " carnal."   (Unlike Socrates, Pausanias
would clearly never have understood why Sir Lancelot came short
in the spiritual quest of the Sangraal.)   He does, indeed, expect

passion to be "sanctified" by being pressed into the service of "goodness," but his conception of "goodness," if it is not as crude as that of Phaedrus, who makes it equivalent to mere "prowess," is still unspiritual. Harmodius and Aristogiton who "slew the tyrant" furnish him with his standard of "noble love" and its services to man. On the formal merit of the speech, as judged by the rules of "epidictic" introduced to Athens by Gorgias, see the remarks of Mr. Bury in his edition of the dialogue (Introduction, xxvii–xxviii).

Interlude and Speech of Eryximachus (185c–188e).—We must not forget that we are listening to the speeches delivered at a gay party by guests, many of whom are in a merely festive humour. The grave moral issues which have been raised by the magnification of Eros will receive their proper treatment when we come to the great discourse of Socrates, but before Plato can so much as introduce that, he must raise the imaginative level of the conversation to a pitch at which the first crude glorification of "passion" only survives in an undertone. Otherwise, there will be far too violent a "modulation into a different key." This function of desensualising the imaginative tone of the dialogue is to be achieved by making the speech of Socrates follow directly on one by Agathon, which is a brilliant but passionless and fanciful tissue of jewelled conceits. Even this needs to have the way prepared for it, if we are not to be conscious of too violent a change of mood. Hence the two interposed speeches of Eryximachus and Aristophanes with the little interlude which introduces them. The tone of this part of the dialogue is wholly playful, and I think it would be a mistake to regard it as anything more than a delightful specimen of "Pantagruelism." The numerous persons who are unhappily without anything of the Pantagruelist in their own composition will continue, no doubt, to look for hidden meanings in this section of the *Symposium*, as they look for them in Rabelais, and with much the same kind of success. Fortunately, we need not imitate them, any more than we need take Rabelais' book to be a disguised treatise on the "new monarchy."

It was now, we are told, the turn of Aristophanes to speak, but as he was impeded by a hiccough, the physician Eryximachus undertook to speak out of order as well as to prescribe for the poet's "passing indisposition." Hidden allusions have been suspected in this simple incident, but without reason. Aristophanes, one of the sturdy topers of the party (176b), is held up, when his turn to speak comes, by an accident which is a small joke in itself ; the medical man of the group, who also happens to be a sober soul (176c) not able to carry much liquor, gives him professional aid and fills up what would otherwise be a gap in the evening's programme. There is nothing here which calls for a "serious" explanation.

Eryximachus is presumably the same person as the Eryximachus who was implicated in the business of the "profaning of the mysteries" (Andoc. i. 35) ; at least, there was a certain Acumenus

who was also among the denounced (*ibid.* i. 18), and the name is
a very unusual one, so that it looks as though the denounced persons
were our physician and his father. He is, we might almost say,
the F.R.S. of Agathon's party, and all his behaviour is strictly
in character. He announces himself from the first as a very
" moderate drinker," and, as Mr. Bury observes, takes his departure
later on, as soon as the scene has become one of wild revelry. His
speech is carefully adapted to his character and profession. It is,
in fact, under the guise of a panegyric of Eros, a little discourse
on the principles of " science," especially of medical science. The
scientific, and particularly the medical man, is the real repository
of the secrets of love. The style of the speech is appropriately
sober, free from the artifices of rhetoric and marked by a plentiful
use of professional terminology. We may, with Mr. Bury, call
him a " pedant," if we do him the justice to believe that the pedantry
is, of course, part of the fun of the evening and is presumably
intentional. The learned man is presumably amusing himself,
as an eminent man of science might do to-day in an after-dinner
speech, by making a little decorous " game " of his own professional
occupations. I see no need to suppose that *Plato* intends any serious
satire on the " science " of the speaker, especially as it represents
the views of the Sicilian medical school, the very type of biology
from which both Plato and Aristotle draw the biological analogies
which play so large a part in their ethics.

Eryximachus opens his speech by giving emphatic assent to
the distinction between a good and a bad Eros, but protests against
looking for the effects of these contrasted forces exclusively in the
souls of men. They can be traced everywhere in the structure of
the universe, no less than in the human organism.[1] This may be
illustrated from medicine. The healthy and the diseased constituents of the body have both their " cravings " ; there are wholesome appetitions and morbid appetitions. The business of medical
science is to gratify the one and check the other. We might define
the science as " knowledge of the body's passions for repletion and
evacuation," and the man who can tell which of these " passions "
are healthy and which " morbid," and can replace the morbid
cravings in his patient by healthy ones, is the complete physician.
The body is, in fact, composed of " opposites " which are at strife
with one another, the hot, the cold, the dry, the moist, etc. ; medicine is the art which produces " love and concord " between these
opposites. The task of " gymnastic," agriculture, music, is precisely similar, and this may be what Heraclitus meant by saying,
" It is drawn together in being drawn apart," and talking of the
" concord of opposites," though his language is inadequate, since
in the establishment of " concord," the previous " opposition " is

---

[1] 186*b*, καὶ κατ' ἀνθρώπινα καὶ κατὰ θεῖα πράγματα, *i.e.* not only in biology but
in physics. The θεῖα here gets its meaning from the habit, universal in
Ionian science, of giving the name θεός or θεοί, in a purely secular sense, to
the assumed primitive body or bodies.

cancelled out and disappears. In music, again, we can distinguish the " good " and the " bad " Eros. The " good Eros " is exemplified by those scales in which a really cultivated taste takes pleasure, the " bad " by those which tickle the fancy of the vulgar. So in the wider world of the physicist, a good and healthy climate is a right and equable " temperament " (κρᾶσις) of heat and cold, rain and dry weather, a bad climate is an instance of the " violent " Eros ; it is an unhealthy " blend " of heat and cold, dry and wet weather. Astronomy thus is another science of " love." So, there is a " good " and a " bad " Eros of gods and men ; a religious and an irreligious way of sacrificing and interpreting signs and portents, and the professional knowledge of the priest and seer becomes another example of the science of Erotics.

Thus the point of the speech is to insist on the cosmic significance of Eros. The underlying thought is that nature is everywhere made up of " opposites," which need to be combined or supplemented by one another ; they may be combined either in proportions which make for stability, and then the result is temperate climate, health, prosperity, tranquillity, or in proportions which lead to instability, and the result is then cataclysms of nature, disease, misfortune, violent and unwholesome excitement. The business of science in all cases is to discover the proportions upon which the " good " results depend. The sources of the doctrine are easily indicated. We detect the influence of the Heraclitean conception of the balance of " exchanges " as the explanation of the seeming permanences of the world-order, the Pythagorean doctrine that all things are combinations of " opposites," and of the special biological working out of the thought which is characteristic of the philosophy of Empedocles, the founder of Sicilian medicine. The general point of view, as German scholars have pointed out, is much like that of some of the treatises of the Hippocratean *corpus*, notably the περὶ διαίτης α', in which the attempt is made to find a speculative foundation for medicine in the Heraclitean cosmology. The only inference we are entitled to draw is that the main ideas of Sicilian medicine could be presumed to be generally known to cultivated persons at Athens in the last third of the fifth century, as is, in fact, shown abundantly by the use made of analogies based upon them all through the ethical dialogues of Plato, For the argument of the *Symposium* itself the chief function of the speech is to divert attention from the topic of sex, as must be done if sex itself is to be treated with the necessary philosophic detachment in the discourse of Socrates, and to call attention to the universal cosmic significance of the conception of the reconciliation of " opposites " in a higher " harmony." This preludes to the discourse of Socrates, where we shall find that the principle has actually a *supra-cosmic* significance. Meanwhile, the introduction of this thought of Eros as a " world-building " principle provides the starting-point for the brilliant and characteristic burlesque cosmogony put into the mouth of Aristophanes.

Speech of Aristophanes (189*a*–193*d*).—To the general reader, this is perhaps the best-known section of the whole dialogue, and one of the best-known passages in the whole of Plato. It is the more important to avoid misapprehending its purpose, which is simply humorous and dramatic. We should note that the speech itself is introduced by a thoroughly Aristophanic jest, and that the poet tells us in so many words that he means to live up to his profession by being " funny." The speech itself may be very briefly summarized. In the beginning man was a " round " creature with four arms and four legs and two faces, looking different ways, but joined at the top to make a single head. There were *three* " sexes," if we can call them so, of these creatures, the double-male, double-female, and male-female, the first derived from the sun, the second from the earth, the third from the moon, which is at once a " luminary " and an " earth." But as yet there was no sexual love and no sexual generation. The race procreated itself by a literal fertilization of the soil. These creatures were as masterful as they were strong and threatened to storm heaven or blockade it, as we learn from the old traditions about the " giants." As a measure of safety, Zeus split them longitudinally down the middle and reconstructed them so that their method of propagation should henceforth be sexual. Since then, man is only half a complete creature, and each half goes about with a passionate longing to find its complement and coalesce with it again. This longing for reunion with the lost half of one's original self is what we call " love," and until it is satisfied, none of us can attain happiness. Ordinary wedded love between man and woman is the reunion of two halves of one of the originally double-sexed creatures ; passionate attachment between two persons of the same sex is the reunion of the halves of a double-male or a double-female, as the case may be. If we continue in irreligion, it is to be feared that Zeus may split us again, and leave us to hop on one leg with one arm and half a face.

As I have said, the brilliance of this fanciful speech must not blind us to the fact that it is in the main comedy, and that the real meaning of the dialogue must not be looked for in it. Plato is careful to remind us that the speaker is a professional jester ; he is too good an artist to have made the remark without a purpose, or to have discounted the effect of the disccurse of his hero Socrates by providing his dialogue with two centres of gravity. To be sure, there are touches of earnest under the mirth of his Aristophanes, as there always are under the wildest fun of the actual historical Aristophanes. There is real tenderness in Aristophanes' description of the love-lorn condition of the creature looking for its lost " half," and a real appreciation of unselfish devotion to the comrade who is one's " second self." Aristophanes shows more real feeling than any of the speakers who have been heard so far. It is also true that he is making a distant approximation to the conception, which Socrates will develop, of love as the longing of the soul for union with its true good. But the distance is even more marked

than the approximation. The goal of love, as Socrates conceives ·
it, is not incorporation with a mate of flesh and blood, nor even
lifelong "marriage" with a "kindred mind," but the ἱερὸς γάμος
of the soul with the "eternal wisdom" in a region "all breathing
human passion far above." The passion Aristophanes describes
is that which finds its most lapidary, perhaps its most perfect
expression in Dante's canzone *Così nel mio parlar voglio esser aspro*,
not that which animates the *Paradiso*, the "female love" which
Blake would have us give up before we can see "eternity." It is
in keeping with this that Aristophanes, like Pausanias, relegates
the love of men for women to the lowest plane, on the ground that
the woman is the "weaker vessel," the "earthy" ingredient in our
original composition, thus denying the Socratic and Platonic tenet
that "the goodness of a man and of a woman are the same," and
proves his point by the allegation (192a) that those who are sensible
of female attractions show themselves inferior in "politics." (Like
Pausanias, he has no conception of any worthier life than that of the
"lover of honours.")

We may put the discourse in its true light by a consideration
of its obvious sources. In the first place, I think it is clear that in
composing the speech Plato had in view the brilliant burlesque of
an Orphic cosmogony in Aristophanes' own *Birds* (693–703), where
also Eros is the great primitive cosmic active force. From the *Birds*
comes again the suggestion of the danger that the gods might run
if the turbulent round-bodied creatures cut off the supply of sacrifices, the very method by which the birds of the play reduce
Olympus to unconditional surrender. As for the details of the
story, I think it is clear that they are a humorous parody of
Empedocles. Creatures in whom both sexes are united figure in
his cosmology (Fr. 61), along with the "men with the heads of
oxen" and similar monsters, as appearing in the early stages of the
evolutionary cycle to which we belong, the period of the world's
history in which "strife" is steadily disintegrating the "sphere" by
dissociating the complexes into their constituent "roots." This
is enough to provide a hint for the construction of the whole narrative. We know that the theories of Empedocles became known at
Athens in the fifth century. The *Phaedo* represents Socrates and
his friends as well acquainted with them, and Aristotle tells us that
a certain Critias—we may safely identify him with Plato's great-
grandfather, the Critias of the *Timaeus* and *Critias*—had expressly
adopted one of them, the view that "we think with our blood."[1]
As the *Clouds* and *Birds* are enough to prove, Aristophanes was
fairly well at home in the doctrines of the men of science of whom
he made fun, and it is quite in keeping with Plato's dramatic
realism that he should be made to burlesque Empedocles, exactly
as he has burlesqued Diogenes and the Orphic cosmologists in his
extant comedies. It is from this humorous burlesque (carefully
"bowdlerized" to suit Christianized ethics, *bien entendu*), that the

[1] *de Anima*, 405b 6.

popular misconceptions about so-called " platonic love " seem to have taken their origin.

There are now only two members of the party who have still to speak, Agathon and Socrates. A little by-play passes (193e–194e), which has no purpose beyond that of enhancing our anticipation and making it clear that their speeches are to be the " event " of the evening. It is worth noting that Plato is ready on occasion to turn the humour against the foibles of his own hero. Socrates is allowed, after his fashion, to put an apparently simple question, simply that he may be called to order ; if he were not checked, the programme would be ruined by the substitution of a dialectical discussion for a eulogy. To be sure, when it comes to Socrates' turn to speak, he gets his way after all and we are plunged into dialectic whether we like it or not ; this is part of the fun.

The two speeches marked out as supremely important are wrought with even more art than any of those which have preceded. In form, as in matter, they exhibit the tension between opposites which is the life of a drama at its acutest pitch. Agathon is morally commonplace, cold in feeling, superficial in thought, for the lack of which he compensates by a free employment of all the artificial verbal patterns popularized by Gorgias ; his encomium is a succession of frozen conceits with no real thought behind them— *littérature* in the worst sense of the word. Socrates is, as usual, simple and direct in manner ; he begins what he has to say in the usual conversational tone of his " dialectic," though, before he has done, the elevation of his thought leads to a spontaneous elevation in style, and he ends on a note of genuine eloquence which leaves all the " fine language " of Agathon hopelessly in the shade. He is on fire with his subject, but with the clear. white-hot glow of a man whose very passion is intellectual. He thinks intensely where Agathon, and fine gentlemen like him, are content to talk prettily. And we are not allowed to forget that Agathon's profession is the " stage " ; he is the " actor," impressing an audience with emotions he simulates but does not feel ; Socrates is the genuine man who " speaks from the heart " and to the heart. (Note the adroit way in which this point is worked in at 194b.)

Speech of Agathon (194e–197e).—The whole speech is a masterly parody of the detestable " prose-poetry " of Gorgias, as will readily be seen by comparing it with the specimens of the original article which time has spared to us. It may be summarized, when divested of its verbal extravagances, as follows. Previous speakers have ignored the main point which a eulogy should make ; they have talked about the gifts of Eros to men rather than about his intrinsic qualities. It is these on which the eulogist should dwell. (1) Eros is the most beautiful of all gods ; for (*a*) he is the youngest of all, not the oldest as Phaedrus and his cosmologists pretend. The " wars in heaven " would never have happened if Eros had held sway then. Also he is eternally fair and young and consorts with youth, not with " crabbed age." (*b*) He is " soft " (ἁπαλός) and tender, and that is why he makes his dwelling in the tenderest place he can find, the soul, and only in souls whose temper is yielding (μαλακόν). (c) He is " pliant " (ὑγρὸς τὸ εἶδος), can wind his way imperceptibly in and out of the inmost recesses of the soul. (d) He is comely and lovely and bright of hue, and that is why he will not settle and gather honey from a body or soul which is " past its flower." (2) He has all the virtues : [1] (a) justice, for he neither does nor suffers violence. He cannot suffer from it, for love is unconstrained, and he never inflicts it, for all things are his willing slaves and *nemini volenti fit iniuria*. (b) Temperance, for he " masters all pleasures " (an idle verbal quibble). (c) Valour, for he can master Ares, the "warrior famoused for fights." (d) Wisdom ; he is the author of medicine, as Eryximachus had said ; he inspires poetry in the most unpoetical and must therefore be himself a supreme poet. He shows his wisdom, further, in being the contriver of all generation and the teacher of all crafts. It was love, love of the beautiful, which inspired the various gods who were their discoverers. In the beginning, when necessity held sway, heaven itself was a place of horror ; the birth of Eros has thus been the cause of all that is good in heaven and on earth. In short, Eros is the giver of peace among men, calm in air and sea, tranquil sleep which relieves our cares, mirth, jollity—and here the speech loses itself in a torrent of flowery phrases, which " bring down the house," as they were meant to do.

We see, of course, as Plato means that we shall, the barrenness of thought which all this euphuism cannot conceal. In a way, the praise of Eros, in Agathon's mouth, has " lost all its grossness," by transmutation into unmeaning prettiness, but it has incidentally lost all its reality. The discourse has all the insincerity of the conventional petrarchising sonneteer. Like the sonneteering tribe, Agathon is so intoxicated by his own fine-filed phrases, that he is evidently not at all clear which Eros he is belauding, the " heavenly " or the " vulgar." For the euphuist's purpose, this really does not matter much ; the theme of his discourse is to him no more than a peg on which to hang his garlands of language. There had been real feeling, under all the burlesque and the grossness, in the speech of Aristophanes ; from Agathon we get only " words, words, words." Socrates indicates as much in the humorous observations which introduce his own contribution to the entertainment. He really began to be afraid, as Agathon grew more and more dithyrambic, that he might be petrified and struck dumb by the " Gorgias' head." He bethought himself, now that it was too late, that he had been rash in undertaking to deliver a eulogy at all. In the simplicity of his heart, he had supposed that all he would have to do would be to say the best which could be truthfully said of his subject. But it now appears that the eulogist is expected to glorify his subject at all " costs," regardless of truth. This is more than Socrates engaged

---

[1] Note that the list of the "cardinal virtues " is taken for granted as familiar. Thus it is no discovery of Plato or of Socrates.

to do, or can do. Like Hippolytus in the play, he is "unsworn in soul," and must be allowed to deliver his speech in his own artless fashion, telling the truth and leaving the style to take care of itself, or the result may be a ridiculous collapse. And he must make one more little stipulation. Perhaps Agathon would answer one or two questions, so that Socrates may know where to make a beginning. Thus, we see, the philosopher contrives to get his way after all—we are to have "dialectic," in other words, thinking, as well as fine talking, as part of our programme (198*b*–199*c*).

Dialectical Interrogation of Agathon by Socrates (199*c*–201*c*).— The purpose of this little interlude, as Socrates had said, is to make sure that his own encomium, which was to "tell the truth," shall begin at the right starting-point. In other words, we are to be brought back to reality, of which we have steadily been losing sight. Eros, "love," "craving," is a relative term; all Eros is Eros *of* something which is its correlate, and it is meant that this correlate is a *satisfaction*. This would be clear at once in Greek, but is a little obscured for us in English by the ambiguity of our word "love." In English there are at least three quite distinct senses of the word "love," and much loose sentimental half-thinking is due to confusion between them. If we would be accurate, we must distinguish them precisely. There is (1) "love of complacency," the emotion aroused by the simple contemplation of what we admire and approve, the "love to the agent" of which the moral-sense school speak in their accounts of moral approval. We may feel this towards a person wholly incapable of being in any way affected for good or bad by our acts or affecting us by his, as when we glow with attachment to the great and good of whom we have read in history. There is (2) "love of benevolence," which prompts us to confer kindnesses on its object or to do him services. This love we may feel to the good and the evil alike. It may show itself as active gratitude to a benefactor, as pity for the unfortunate or the sinful, and in many other guises. There is finally (3) "love of concupiscence," *desirous* love, the eager appetition of what is apprehended as our own "good." It is only this *desirous* love which can be called ἔρως in Greek.[1]

Eros, then, is always a desirous love of its object, and that object is always something not yet attained or possessed. Agathon had said that "love of things fair" has created the happiness of the gods themselves. But if Eros "wants" beauty, it must follow that

---

[1] Hence when Euripides says ἐρᾶτε, παῖδες, μητρός, he means a great deal more than we can express by saying "love your mother." He means that the sons of such a mother as his heroine are to be "in love" with her; she is to be to them their true mistress and "dominant lady," as Hector in Homer is "father and mother" to Andromache. One might illustrate by saying that in Christianity God is thought of as loving all men with "love of benevolence," and the righteous with an added "love of complacency," but as loving no creature with "love of concupiscence." The good man, on the other hand, loves God with love of concupiscence, as the good for which his soul longs, and with love of complacency, but could hardly, I suppose, be said to love God with *amor benevolentiae,* since we cannot do "good turns" to our Maker.

he does not yet possess it, and therefore is *not* himself " ever fair,'
and in the same way, if he " wants " good, he cannot himself *be*
good. At this point Socrates closes his conversation with Agathon and
enters on his " discourse," having found the ἀρχή for it. The
questioning of Agathon is no piece of mere verbal dexterity. It is
indispensable that we should understand that the only Eros deserving of our praises is an *amor ascendens*, a desirous going forth
of the soul in quest of a good which is above her. And this going
forth must begin with the knowledge that there is *something* we
want with all our hearts but have not yet got. As the old Evan-
gelicals said, the first step towards salvation is to feel your *need* of
a Saviour. " Blessed are they which *hunger* . . . for they shall be
filled." The soul which is to be love's pilgrim must begin by feeling
this heart-hunger, or it will never adventure the journey. This is
the ἀρχή demanded by Socrates for any *hohes Lied der Liebe* which
is to " tell the truth."

Speech of Socrates (201d–212c).—Though Socrates had affected
to make his " dialectic " a mere preliminary to the " discourse " he
was contemplating, he actually contrives to turn the discourse itself
into " dialectic," genuine thinking, by putting it into the mouth of
one Diotima, a priestess and prophetess of Mantinea, and relating
the process of question and answer by which the prophetess had
opened his own eyes to understand the true mysteries of Eros.
The purpose is that his hearers shall not merely follow his words and
possibly be agreeably affected by them, but shall follow his *thought*.
They are to listen to the " conversation of his soul with itself."
At the same time, I cannot agree with many modern scholars in
regarding Diotima of Mantinea as a fictitious personage ; still less
in looking for fanciful reasons for giving the particular names Plato
does to the prophetess and her place of origin. The introduction of
purely fictitious named personages into a discourse seems to be a
literary device unknown to Plato, as has been said in an earlier
chapter, and I do not believe that if he had invented Diotima he
would have gone on to put into the mouth of Socrates the definite
statement that she had delayed the pestilence of the early years
of the Archidamian war for ten years by " offering sacrifice " at
Athens. As the *Meno* has told us, Socrates did derive hints for
his thought from the traditions of " priests of both sexes who have
been at pains to understand the *rationale* of what they do," and the
purpose of the reference to the presence of Diotima at Athens about
440 is manifestly not merely to account for Socrates' acquaintance
with her, but to make the point that the mystical doctrine of the
contemplative " ascent " of the soul, now to be set forth, was one
on which the philosopher's mind had been brooding ever since his
thirtieth year. This, if true, is very important for our understanding of the man's personality, and I, for one, cannot believe that
Plato was guilty of wanton mystifications about such things. At
the same time, we may be sure that in reproducing a conversation

a quarter of a century old, Socrates is blending his recollections of the past with his subsequent meditations upon it, as normally happens in such cases. He sees an episode which had influenced his life profoundly in the light of all that had come out of it, much as St. Augustine in later life saw the facts of his conversion to Christianity in a changed perspective, as we are able to prove by contrasting the *Confessions* with the works composed just after the conversion.

To all intents and purposes, we shall not go wrong by treating the " speech of Diotima " as a speech of Socrates. We can best describe the purpose of the speech in the language of religion by saying that it is the narrative of the pilgrimage of a soul on the way of salvation, from the initial moment at which it feels the need of salvation to its final " consummation." In spite of all differences of precise outlook, the best comment on the whole narrative is furnished by the great writers who, in verse or prose, have described the stages of the " mystic way " by which the soul " goes out of herself," to find herself again in finding God. In substance, what Socrates is describing is the same spiritual voyage which St. John of the Cross describes, for example, in the well-known song *En una noche oscura* which opens his treatise on the *Dark Night*, and Crashaw hints at more obscurely all through his lines on *The Flaming Heart*, and Bonaventura charts for us with precision in the *Itinerarium Mentis in Deum*. The Christian writers see by a clearer light and they have an intensity which is all their own, but the journey they describe is recognizably the same—the travel of the soul from temporality to eternity. In Greek literature, the speech, I think we may fairly say, stands alone until we come to Plotinus, with whom the same spiritual adventure is the main theme of the *Enneads*. Unless we have so much of the mystic in us as to understand the view that the " noughting " and remaking of the soul is the great business of life, the discourse will have no real meaning to us ; we shall take it for a mythological *bellum somnium*. But if we do that, we shall never really understand the *Apology* and the other dialogues which deal with the doctrine of the " tendance of the soul," a simple-sounding name which conceals exactly the same conception of the attainment of " deiformity " as the real " work of man." In the *Phaedo* we have had the picture of a human soul on the very verge of attainment, at the moment when it is about to " lose itself in light." In the *Symposium* we are shown, more fully than anywhere else in Plato, the stages by which that soul has come to be what it is in the *Phaedo*. We see with Plato's eyes the interior life of the soul of Socrates.

The desirous soul, as was already said, is as yet not " fair " or " good " ; that is what it would be and will be, but is not yet. But this does not mean that it is " foul " and " wicked." There is a state intermediate between these extremes, as there is a state intermediate between sheer ignorance and completed knowledge— the state of having true beliefs without the power to give a justification of them (ἄνευ τοῦ ἔχειν λόγον δοῦναι). This may be expressed mythologically by saying that Eros is not a " god," nor yet a " mere mortal," but a δαίμων or " spirit," and a mighty one (202d–e). According to the received tradition, " spirits " stand half-way between mortality and divinity ; they convey men's prayers to the gods, and the commands, revelations, and gifts of the gods to men ; intercourse between gods and men has them as its intermediaries. Eros is one of these " spirits " (203a). His birth answers to his function. He is the child of Poros son of Metis (Abundance, son of Good Counsel), by the beggar-maid Penia (Need), conceived in heaven on the birthday of Aphrodite, and he inherits characters from both his parents. He is, like his mother, poor, uncomely, squalid, houseless, and homeless. But he has so much of the father about him that he has high desires for all that is " fair and good," courage, persistence, endless resourcefulness, and art in the pursuit of these desires. He is the greatest of " wizards and wits " (δεινὸς γόης . . . καὶ σοφιστής), he " pursues wisdom all his life long " (φιλοσοφῶν διὰ παντὸς τοῦ βίου). He is neither god nor mortal, but lives a " dying life," starving and fed, and starving for more again.[1] He is your one " philosopher " ; gods do not aspire to " wisdom," for they already have it, nor yet " fools," for they do not so much as know their need and lack of it. " Philosophers," aspirants after wisdom, of whom Eros is chief, are just those who live between these two extremes.[2] They feel the hunger for wisdom, the fairest of things, but they feel it precisely because it remains unsatisfied. The conventional representation of Eros as the " ever fair " is due to a simple confusion between the good aspired to and the aspirant after it (201e–204c).

When the thin veil of allegory is removed, we see that what is described here is simply the experience of the division of the self characteristic of man, when once he has become aware of his own rationality. Rationality is not an endowment of which man finds himself in possession ; it is an attainment incumbent on him to achieve. Spiritual manhood and freedom are the good which he must reach if he is to be happy, but they are a far-away good, and his whole life is a struggle, and a struggle with many an alternation of success and failure, to reach them. If he completely attained them, his life would become that of a god ; he would have put off temporality and put on an eternity secured against all mutability. If he does not strive to attain, he falls back into the condition of the mere animal, and becomes a thing of mere change and mutability. Hence while he is what he is, he is never at peace with himself ; that is the state into which he is trying to grow. It is true, in a deeper sense than the author of the saying meant, that *der Mensch ist etwas das überwunden werden muss* (we are only truly men in so far as we are becoming something more). (That the " temporal "

---

[1] The βίος φιλόσοφος, we might say, has as its motto *quasi morientes et ecce vivimus ; tanquam nihil habentes et omnia possidentes.*

[2] Cf. the classification of rational beings ascribed to the Pythagoreans, "gods," "men," "beings like Pythagoras" (φιλόσοφοι). Aristot. Fr. 192, Rose.

in us which has to be put off is always spoken of by Socrates as " ignorance " or " error," not as " sin," has no special significance, when we remember his conviction that the supreme function of " knowledge " is to command and direct, to order the conduct of life towards the attainment of our true *good*.)

It will be seen that Socrates is formally deferring to the dictum of Agathon about the proper disposition of the parts of an encomium. He has dealt with the question what the intrinsic character of Eros is ; he now proceeds to the question of his services to us (τίνα χρείαν ἔχει τοῖς ἀνθρώποις). What is it that, in the end, is the object of the heart's desirous longing ? Good, or—in still plainer words—happiness (εὐδαιμονία). All men wish happiness for its own sake, and all wish their happiness to be " for ever." (*Weh spricht, Vergeh ! Doch alle Lust will Ewigkeit.*) Why, then, do we not call all men lovers, since all have this desirous longing ? For the same reason that we do not call all craftsmen " makers," though they all are makers of something. Linguistic use has restricted the use of the word ποιητής (" maker ") to one species of maker, the man who fashions verse and song. So it is with the name " lover " ; all desirous longing for good or happiness is love, but in use the name " lover " is given to the person who longs earnestly after one particular species of happiness—τόκος ἐν καλῷ (" procreation in the beautiful ")—whether this procreation is physical or spiritual (καὶ κατὰ τὸ σῶμα καὶ κατὰ τὴν ψυχήν, 206*b*).

To explain the point more fully, we must know that maturity of either body or mind displays itself by the desire to procreate ; beauty attracts us and awakens and fosters the procreative impulse, ugliness inhibits it. And love, in the current restricted sense of the word, is not, as might be thought, desire of the beautiful object, but desire to impregnate it and have offspring by it (desire τῆς γεννήσεως καὶ τοῦ τόκου ἐν καλῷ). (It is meant quite strictly that physical desire for the " possession " of a beautiful woman is really at bottom a "masked" desire for offspring by a physically " fine " mother ; sexual appetite itself is not really craving for " the pleasures of intercourse with the other sex " ; it is a passion for *parenthood*.) And we readily understand why this desire for procreation should be so universal and deep-seated. It is an attempt to perpetuate one's own being " under a form of eternity," and we have just seen that the primary desire of all is desire to possess one's " good " and to possess it for ever. The organism cannot realize this desire in its own individuality, because it is in its very nature subject to death. But it can achieve an approximation to eternity, if the succession of generations is kept up. Hence the vehemence of the passion for procreation and the strength of the instincts connected with mating and rearing a brood in all animals. The only way in which a thing of time can approximate to being eternal is to produce a new creature to take its place as it passes away. Even within the limits of our individual existence, the body " never continues in one stay " ; it is a scene of unending waste made good by repair. Our thoughts and emotions too do not remain selfsame through life. Even our knowledge does not "abide " ; we are perpetually forgetting what we knew and having to "recover " it again by μελέτη ("study," "rehearsal "). It is only by giving birth to a new individual to take the place of the old that the mortal can " participate in deathlessness " (208b).[1]

The passion for physical parenthood, however, is the most rudimentary form in which the desirous longing for the fruition of good eternal and immutable shows itself, and the form in which Diotima is least interested. Her main purpose is to elucidate the conception of spiritual parenthood. If we turn to the life of the " love of honours "—note that this reference (208c) implies that in what has been said about the physical instincts we have been considering the " body-loving " life—the passion for " fame undying " which has led Alcestis, Achilles, Codrus, and many another to despise death and danger is just another, and more spiritualized, form of the " desirous longing for the eternal." Thus, just as the man who feels the craving for physical fatherhood is attracted by womankind and becomes " exceeding amorous," so it is with those whose souls are ripe for the procreation of spiritual issue, " wisdom and goodness generally " ; the mentally, like the physically adult looks for a " fair " partner to receive and bear his offspring (209a–b). He feels the attraction of fair face and form, but what he is really seeking is the " fair and noble and highly dowered " soul behind them. If he finds what he is looking for, he freely pours forth " discourse on goodness and what manner of man the good man should be, and what conduct he should practise, and tries to educate " the chosen soul he has found. The two friends are associated in the " nurture " of the spiritual offspring to which their converse has given birth, and the tie is still more enduring than that of literal common parenthood, inasmuch as the offspring which are the pledges of it are " fairer and more deathless." Examples of such spiritual progeny are the poems of Homer and Hesiod, and still more the salutary institutions and rules of life left to succeeding ages by Lycurgus and Solon and many another statesman of Hellas or " Barbary " ; some of these men have even been deified by the gratitude of later generations (209e).[2]

---

[1] This has absurdly been supposed to be inconsistent with the doctrines of the *Phaedo*, and it has even been argued that the *Symposium* must have been written before Plato discovered the doctrine of immortality expounded there. In point of fact, there is no inconsistency. According to both dialogues the " body " belongs to the " mortal " element in us, and perishes beyond recall. Hence *man*, according to the *Phaedo*, is strictly mortal ; what is immortal is not the man, but the " divine " element in him, his ψυχή, as has already been explained. There is not a word in the *Symposium* to suggest that the ψυχή is perishable. Hence no inference about the priority of the one dialogue to the other can be based on comparison of their teaching.

[2] The allusion to " temples " erected to deified statesmen presumably refers to Oriental communities in which the " laws " were traditionally ascribed to remote " divine " rulers. The Greeks did not deify their legislators. At *Laws* 624a the Cretan speaker, indeed, attempts to claim Zeus as the author

The desirous longing for an eternal good, however, has far
higher manifestations than these, and Diotima will not take it on
her to say whether Socrates is equal to making the ascent to them,
though she will describe them, and he must try to follow her.[1]
(The meaning is that, so far, we have been talking only about what
is possible within the limits of the two lower types of life : we have
now to deal with the more arduous path to be trodden by the
aspirant to the highest life of all, that of " philosophy.") He who
means to pursue the business in earnest must begin in early life
by being sensible to bodily beauty. If he is directed aright, he
will first try to " give birth to fair discourses " in company with
one comely person. But this is only the beginning. He must
next learn for himself [2] to recognize the kinship of all physical
beauty and become the lover of " all beautiful bodies." [3] Then
he must duly recognize the superiority of beauty of soul, even
where there is no outward comeliness to be an index to it. He
must be " in love " with young and beautiful souls and try to bring
to the birth with them " fair discourses." Next, he must learn to
see beauty and comeliness as they are displayed in ἐπιτηδεύματα
and νόμοι, avocations and social institutions, and perceive the
community of principle which comely avocations and institutions
imply. Then he must turn to " science " and its intellectual
beauties, which will disclose themselves to him as a whole wide
ocean of delights. Here again, he will give birth to " many a
noble and imposing discourse and thought in the copious wealth of
philosophy "—that is, he will enrich the " sciences " he studies with
high discoveries.

of the νόμοι of Crete, but he knows, of course, that the traditional author
of them was Minos, who was not a god, and so says they may " in fairness "
be credited to Zeus (because, according to Homer, Minos " conversed " with
Zeus).

[1] Much unfortunate nonsense has been written about the meaning of
Diotima's apparent doubt whether Socrates will be able to follow her as she
goes on to speak of the " full and perfect vision " (τὰ τέλεα καὶ ἐποπτικά, 210a 1).
It has even been seriously argued that Plato is here guilty of the arrogance of
professing that he has reached philosophical heights to which the " historical "
Socrates could not ascend. Everything becomes simple if we remember
that the actual person speaking is Socrates, reporting the words of Diotima.
Socrates is as good as speaking of himself, and naturally, Diotima must not
say anything that would imply that he is already, at the age of thirty, assured
of " final perseverance." In the *Phaedo*, speaking on the last day of his life
to a group of fellow-followers of the way, Socrates can without impropriety
say that he has " lived as a philosopher to the best of his power."

[2] αὐτὸν κατανοῆσαι, 210a 8. The αὐτόν seems to be emphatic. The necessity for a " director " (ὁ ἡγούμενος) is admitted for the first step of the progress
only. The rest of the way must be trodden at one's own peril, by the " inner
light." Yet there is a return to the conception of " combined effort " at
210e 6, ἐπὶ τὰς ἐπιστήμας ἀγαγεῖν.

[3] It is not meant that this widening of outlook must act unfavourably on
personal affection. The thought is that *intelligent* delight in the beauty of
one " fair body " will lead to a quickened perception of beauty in others,
just as genuine appreciation of your wife's goodness or your friend's wit
will make you more, and not less alive to the presence of the same qualities in
others.

Even so, we have not reached the goal so far ; we are only now coming in sight of it. When a man has advanced so far on the quest he will *suddenly* descry the supreme beauty of which he has all along been in search—a beauty eternal, selfsame, and perfect, lifted above all mutability. It is no " body," nor yet even a " science " or " discourse " of which beauty could be *predicated*, but that very reality and substance of all beauty of which everything else we call beauty is a passing " participant " ; the unchanging light of which all the beauties hitherto discerned are shifting reflections (211*b*). When this light rises above his horizon, the pilgrim of Eros is at last " coming to port." The true " life for a man " is to live in the contemplation of the " sole and absolute Beauty " ($\theta\epsilon\omega\mu\epsilon\nu\omega$ $a\dot{v}\tau\dot{o}$ $\tau\dot{o}$ $\kappa a\lambda\acute{o}\nu$), by comparison with which all the " beauties " which kindle desire in mankind are so much dross. Only in intercouse with It will the soul give birth to a spiritual offspring which is no " shadow " but veritable " substance," because it is now at last " espoused " to very and substantial reality.[1] This and only this is the true achieving of " immortality." Such was the discourse of Diotima, and Socrates believes it himself and would fain persuade others that Eros (" desirous longing ") is the truest helper we can have in this quest after immortality. This is what he has to offer by way of a eulogy on the " might and manhood " of Eros (212*b–c*).[2]

The meaning of the discourse is clear enough. In the earlier stages of the " ascent " which has just been described, we recognize at once that " tendance of the soul " or care for one's " moral being " which Plato regularly makes Socrates preach to his young friends as the great business of life. That the work of " tendance of the soul " must go further than the development of ordinary good moral habits and rules, that it demands the training of the intellect by familiarity with the highest " science," and that the task of the true philosopher is, by his insight into principles, to unify the " sciences," and to bring the results of ripe philosophical thinking to bear on the whole conduct of life, is the same lesson which is taught us in the *Republic* by the scheme propounded for the education of the philosophic statesman. As in the *Republic*, the study of the separate sciences leads up to the supreme science of " dialectic " or metaphysics, in which we are confronted with the principles on which all other knowing depends, so here also Socrates describes the man who is coming in sight of his goal as descrying " one single science " of Beauty (210*d* 7). And in both cases, in the final moment of attainment, the soul is described as having got beyond " science " itself. Science here passes in the end into direct " contact," or, as the schoolmen say, " vision," an apprehen-

[1] *Symp.* 212*a* 4. The allusion is to the tale of Ixion and the cloud which was imposed on him in the place of Hera, and from which the Centaurs sprang. All loves but the last are, in varying degrees, illusions.

[2] 212*b*, $\dot{\epsilon}\gamma\kappa\omega\mu\iota\acute{a}\zeta\omega\nu$ $\tau\dot{\eta}\nu$ $\delta\acute{v}\nu a\mu\iota\nu$ $\kappa a\grave{\iota}$ $\dot{a}\nu\delta\rho\epsilon\acute{\iota}a\nu$ $\tauo\hat{v}$ $\ddot{\epsilon}\rho\omega\tau o\varsigma$. The $\dot{a}\nu\delta\rho\epsilon\acute{\iota}a$ is specified because the pilgrimage is so long and arduous that it is no easy thing to " play the man " to the end of it. It is a warfare against " flesh and blood."

sion of an object which is no longer " knowing about " it, knowing propositions which can be predicated of it, but an actual possession of and being possessed by it.   In the *Republic*, as in the *Symposium*, the thought is conveyed by language borrowed from the " holy marriage " of ancient popular religion and its survivals in mystery-cults.   Here it is " Beauty " to which the soul is mated ; in the *Republic* it is that good which, though the cause of all being and all goodness, is itself " on the other side of being." [1]

We must not, of course, especially in view of the convertibility of the terms καλόν and ἀγαθόν which is dwelt on more than once in our dialogue, be misled into doubting the absolute identity of the " form of good " of the *Republic* with the αὐτὸ τὸ καλόν of the *Symposium*.   The place assigned to both in the ascent to " being and reality " is identical, and in both cases the stress is laid on the point that when the supreme " form " is descried, its apprehension comes as a sudden " revelation," though it is not to be had without the long preliminary process of travail of thought, and that it is apprehended by " direct acquaintance," not by discursive " knowledge about " it.   It is just in this conviction that all " knowledge about " is only preparatory to a direct *scientia visionis* that Socrates reveals the fundamental agreement of his conception with that of the great mystics of all ages.   The " good " or αὐτὸ τὸ καλόν is, in fact, the *ens realissimum* of Christian philosophers, in which the very distinction between *esse* and *essentia*, *Sein* and *So-sein* falls away.   You cannot properly predicate anything of it, because it does not " participate " in good or any other " form " ; it *is* its own *So-sein*.   Consequently, the apprehension of it is strictly " incommunicable," since all communication takes the form of predication.   Either a man possesses it and is himself possessed by it, or he does not, and there is no more to be said.   This does not mean that the " most real being " is *irrational*, or that by " thinking things out " we are getting further away from it, but it does mean that we cannot " rationalize " it.   We cannot give its constituent " formula," so to say, as we could that of an ellipse or a cycloid.   You might spend eternity in trying to describe it, and all you found to say would be true and reasonable, so far as it goes, but its full secret would still elude you ; it would still be infinitely rich with undisclosed mystery   As the Christian mystics say, God may be apprehended, but cannot be comprehended by any of His creatures.   That is why He is " on the other side of being." The " deiform " do not " think about " God, they live Him.   This does not mean that " myth " is something in its own nature superior to scientific truth, a misconception on which Professor Burnet has said all that is necessary.   *Because* " vision " is direct, the content of a " tale " or " myth " cannot really convey it.   A " tale " is as much a mere form of " knowing about " as a scientific description, and as a form of " knowing about " it is, of course, inferior.   In

[1] *Rep.* 508*b* 9.   For the metaphor of the " holy marriage," cf. e.g. *Rep.* 490*b*, 496*a*.

fact, all the mystics insist on the point that the direct vision of supreme reality is not only incommunicable, it cannot even be recalled in memory when the moment of vision has passed. You are sure that you " saw " ; you cannot tell what you saw even to yourself. This is the real reason why, as Burnet says, Plato never uses " mythical " language about the " forms," but only about things like the soul, which he regards as half real, partly creatures of temporality and change. We should note, however, that the supreme reality which is apprehended in the culminating vision is never said in Plato to be God, but always the supreme " form." It is the *good* which is the Platonic and Socratic *ens realissimum*.

The position of God in the philosophy of both seems to me ambiguous and not fully thought out. Formally, Plato's God is described in the *Laws* as a perfectly good soul ($\dot{a}\rho\dot{\iota}\sigma\tau\eta$ $\psi\upsilon\chi\dot{\eta}$). This ought to mean, as Burnet clearly holds it to mean, that God too is only half-real, and belongs on one side to the realm of the mutable. I confess that I do not see how to reconcile such a position with the religious insistence on the eternal and immutable character of God which meets us everywhere in Plato. We could not meet the difficulty by supposing that God is an imaginative symbol of the " good," since the whole point of Plato's Theism is, as we shall see, that it is by the agency of God that the " participation " of the creatures in the good is made possible. Thus God is not identical with the good, and it seems equally impossible to suppose that God is simply a " creature " participating in good. I can only suppose that there was a really unsolved conflict between the Platonic metaphysics and the Platonic religion. In fact, the adjustment of the two became a cardinal problem for Plotinus and the Neoplatonic succession.[1] We shall not be in a position to deal with the topic properly until we come to speak of Plato's latest written works and the " unwritten doctrines " expounded in the Academy.

Plato clearly means, in spite of Diotima's words of caution, to present Socrates in the *Symposium* as a man who has in his supreme hours attained the " vision " for himself, and for that very reason impresses his fellow-men by his whole bearing as being not of their world though he is in it. We could have inferred at least that he was steadily treading the road to " unification " with the supreme reality from the close correspondence of the description of that road by Diotima with what Plato elsewhere represents as his hero's course of life. But naturally enough, Socrates cannot be made to boast of the supreme achievement with his own lips, and this is why Alcibiades, the most brilliant living specimen of the " ambitious life," is introduced at this point. We are to gather from his famous narrative of the impression Socrates made on him in their years of close intercourse, and the hold the recollections of those years still

---

[1] The Neoplatonic way of dealing with the problem, by making " The One " the source from which $\nu o\hat{\upsilon}s$ and its correlate $\tau\dot{a}$ $\nu o\eta\tau\dot{a}$ directly emanate, definitely subordinates the " forms " to God. Through Augustine this view passed to St. Thomas and still remains part of Thomistic philosophy

have on his conscience and imagination, what could not well be said in any other way, that Socrates has " seen," and that the vision has left its stamp on his whole converse with the world. Perhaps there is a further thought in Plato's mind. Socrates, we might say, is the man who has renounced the world to find his own eternal " life " ; Alcibiades, naturally endowed with all the gifts required for " philosophy," but a prey to the lusts of the flesh and the eye and the pride of life, is the man who might have " seen " if he would, the man who has made the " great refusal " of sacrificing the reality for the shadow. He has chosen for the world and has all the world can give. We are made to look on the two types side by side, and to listen to the confession of the triumphant worldling in the full flush of triumph, that he has chosen the *worser* part. On the panegyric of Socrates by Alcibiades (215a–222b), it is not necessary to dwell here. Its importance is for the understanding of the characters of Socrates and of Alcibiades, not for any contribution it makes to our comprehension of the Socratic or the Platonic philosophy. It shows us Socrates in act following the route of the pilgrimage already described by Diotima. One should, of course, note, in order to avoid some strange misconceptions, that the famous story told by Alcibiades of his own " temptation " of Socrates (216d–219d) is meant to go back to a time when Alcibiades, who fought in the cavalry before Potidaea in 431–30, was still a mere boy, little more than a child (217b). We must date the events somewhere between 440 and 435, when Socrates would be in the earlier thirties. This being so, it is important to observe that even then his fame for wisdom was such that Alcibiades could think no price too high to pay for the benefit of " hearing all that he knew," We must also, of course, understand that Socrates is to be thought of as a man still young enough to feel the charm of beauty in its full force, and to feel it in the way characteristic of the society of his age, but too full of high thoughts to be vanquished by " the most opportune place, the strong'st suggestion his worser genius can." He moves through a brilliant and loose-living society like a Sir Galahad, not because he is not a man of genuine flesh and blood, but because his heart is engaged elsewhere, and he has none to spare for " light loves." This testimony, coming from Plato, is enough to dispose once and for all of the later gossip of Aristoxenus and the Alexandrians who collected such garbage. We must also, I think, with Burnet, recognize that the prominence given to the account of Socrates' "rapt " for four-and-twenty hours at Potidaea (220c–d) is intended to suggest that this was the outstanding " ecstasy " of his life, and left an ineffaceable mark on his whole future. It can hardly be a coincidence that the earliest " missionary " effort of Socrates related by Plato, his attempt to convert Charmides, is dated immediately after his return from the campaign of Potidaea.[1] For the rest, Socrates' remarkable power of adapting

[1] *Greek Philosophy, Part I.*, 130, 138–142 ; E.R.E. xi. 670, col. 1. Professor Burnet has fallen into an oversight in the first of these passages when he makes

himself in appearance to the tone and manner of the world, and yet contriving without any visible effort to bring with him the suggestion of being all the while in constant contact with the other " unseen " world which is at once so near and so far is one of the best-known characteristics of the greatest " contemplatives " ; the stress laid on the point helps to strengthen our conviction that we are presented with a realistic portrait of an actual man. (The same " adaptability " is noted as eminently distinctive of Xavier by his biographers. Xavier recalls Socrates too by the " gaiety " of which the biographers speak as the most striking feature of his conversation.)

On the description of the scene of revelry with which the " banquet " ends, I need only make one remark. We are told (223d) that when the new morning broke, Socrates, Aristophanes, and Agathon were the only persons in the party who were equal to continuing the conversation, and that Socrates was left by Aristodemus trying to convince the two dramatists that the man who can compose a tragedy τέχνῃ, " by his art," can also compose a comedy. Much ingenuity has been wasted on the interpretation of this remark, and it has even been supposed to be a kind of prophecy of Shakespeare's " tragi-comedies," which are neither tragedies, nor yet comedies in the sense in which we give that name to the brilliant personal burlesques of the Attic " old comedians." The real meaning lies on the surface. As we have seen, Socrates dissented from the current view that poets are σοφοί and their productions works of conscious " art." He held that they depend on " genius " or " inspiration," and cannot themselves explain their own happiest inspirations. His point is thus that the inability of Agathon to compose comedies and of Aristophanes to write tragedies, is a proof that neither of them is a σοφός, working with conscious mastery of an " art." Both are the instruments of a " genius " which masters *them*, not wielders of a tool of which they are masters. The passage should really be quoted, not as an excuse for gush about Shakespeare, but as an illustration of what Socrates says in the *Apology* about his attempts to " refute the oracle " by finding a σοφός among the poets and their failure. In fact, he fails here. His two auditors are half asleep after their night of merriment and " do not quite take the point " (οὐ σφόδρα ἑπομένους νυστάζειν, 223d 6).

See further :

RITTER, C.—*Platon*, i. 504–531.
RAEDER, H.—*Platons philosophische Entwickelung*, 158–168.
NATORP, P.—*Platons Ideenlehre*, 163–174.
BURY, R. G.—*Symposium of Plato*. (1909.)
ROBIN, L.—Platon, *Le Banquet*. (Paris, 1929.)
LAGERBORG, R.—*Platonische Liebe*. (Leipzig, 1926.)
STEWART, J. A.—*The Myths of Plato*, 397–450 (*The Two Symposium Myths*) ; *Plato's Theory of Ideas*, Pt. ii.
STENZEL, J.—*Platon der Erzieher*, 209–241.

the " rapt " take place at a time of " hard frost." The time was high summer (*Symp.* 220d 1).

CHAPTER X

THE *PROTAGORAS*

IF there is any Platonic dialogue which can challenge the claim of the *Symposium* to be its author's dramatic *chef d'œuvre* it is the *Protagoras*, with its brilliant full-length portrait of the famous Protagoras and its mirthful sketches of the two minor " sophists," Prodicus and Hippias. The very life-likeness of the narrative has led to grave misunderstanding of the philosophical significance of the dialogue. It has been assumed that so lively a work must be a youthful composition, and this has led to the further supposition that its teaching must be " undeveloped," as compared with that of *e.g.* the *Gorgias*. By way of providing Plato with a crude " early ethical doctrine," for the *Gorgias* to correct, it has then been discovered that the *Protagoras* teaches the Hedonism of Bentham, a misconception which makes the right understanding of its purpose wholly impossible. We shall see, as we proceed, that the dialogue does not teach Hedonism at all ; what it does teach is something quite different, the Socratic thesis that " all the virtues are one thing—knowledge," and that its philosophical purpose is simply to make it clear that this thesis is the foundation of the whole Socratic criticism of life. The absurdity of regarding the dialogue as a juvenile performance is sufficiently shown by the perfect mastery of dramatic technique which distinguishes it. No beginner, however endowed with genius, produces such a masterpiece of elaborate art without earlier experiences of trial and failure. He has first to learn the use of his tools. And it is worth noting that Aristotle must have regarded the dialogue as a particularly ripe and masterly exposition of the Socratic moral theory, since he has taken directly from it his own account in the *Ethics* of the characteristic doctrines of Socrates.[1]

[1] *E.N.* 1116*b* 4, Socrates thought that courage is knowledge, a reference to the lengthy treatment of this point at *Protag.* 349*d* ff. (rather than, as suggested by Burnet in his commentary on the *Ethics*, to the *Laches*); 1144*b* 18, Socrates held that all the " virtues " are φρονήσεις (an allusion probably to the assertion of this in *Protagoras* and *Phaedo*) ; 1145*b* 23 ff., Socrates denied that there is such a state as ἀκρασία in which " passion " commits a " rape " on judgment, δεινὸν γὰρ ἐπιστήμης ἐνούσης, ὡς ᾤετο Σ., ἄλλο τι κρατεῖν καὶ περιέλκειν αὐτὴν ὡς ἀνδράποδον (a verbal allusion to *Protag.* 352*c*); 1147*b* 15, οὐδ' αὕτη (*sc.* ἡ κυρία ἐπιστήμη) περιέλκεται διὰ τὸ πάθος (another echo of the same passage) ; 1164*a* 24, on Protagoras' method of charging for his services, looks like a loose reminiscence of *Protag.* 328*b* 6–*c* 2 ; *E.N.* 1109*b* 6 is a plain reminiscence of *Protag.* 325*d* 6 ; *E.E.* 1229*a* 15 is a direct allusion to *Protag.* 360*d* 4, as is also 1230*a* 7 ff. ; 1246*b* 34 echoes *Protag.* 352*c*. Though Aristotle never names the dialogue, he evidently appreciated its importance.

In form, the dialogue is once more a narrated drama, but, like the *Republic*, with a slightly less complicated formula than the *Symposium*. Socrates himself gives an unnamed friend, with whom he meets in a public place in Athens, an account of a brilliant company from whom he has only just parted. The method of indirect narration is once more necessary, because Plato wishes to impress it on us that the date of the gathering was before his own time. From the jocular opening remarks we learn that Alcibiades is only just becoming old enough to be spoken of as a " man." Since Alcibiades served at Potidaea in 431, this will take us back at least to the beginning of his " ephebate," which cannot be put later than 433, and is more naturally put at least a year or two earlier. (For it would be unreasonable to suppose that he must have been called out for a hard and distant service as soon as he had the minimum age qualification.) Thus we are at a period before the opening of the Archidamian war. This accounts for the presence, on the most friendly terms, of distinguished men belonging to states shortly to be official enemies of Athens, and for the complete absence of any hint that inter-state relations are in any way disturbed. (Hippias of Elis could hardly be made to glorify Athens as he does at 336*c*–338*b*, and to preach a homily on the " internationalism " of *Kultur* if the war-clouds were already gathering.) The time is thus the Periclean age ; Athens is at the very height of her opulence and glory, and Socrates must be thought of as a man of about thirty-five. Of the other figures in the drama, the most important, Protagoras of Abdera, is an older man. He says (317*c*) that he is advanced in years and might easily be the father of any one present, and subsequently (320*c*) alleges his superior age as a graceful excuse for conveying his views in a fable, " as a man may in talking to his juniors." Thus we are directed to think of him as a generation or so older than Socrates, and therefore a man at any rate, approaching sixty-five.[1] Prodicus and Hippias will be roughly men of Socrates' age. The scene is laid in the house of the famous " millionaire " Callias, son of Hipponicus,

---

[1] This would throw back the birth of Protagoras to some time not very far from 500 B.C. and make him a contemporary of Anaxagoras. The Alexandrian chronologists made him some fifteen years younger, and they have mostly been followed by modern writers. It seems to me, as to Professor Burnet, that we must accept Plato's statement. He must have known whether Protagoras really belonged to the generation before Socrates, and could have no motive for misrepresentation on such a point. All through the dialogue the advanced age of Protagoras is kept before the reader's mind, so that Plato is not simply falling into an oversight. The Alexandrians obviously depend on one of their usual arbitrary constructions. The foundation of Thurii (444) was their regular " fixed era " for events of the Periclean age, and as Protagoras was known to have had to do with legislating for Thurii, they fixed his ἀκμή to the year of its foundation. The restoration of Protagoras to his true date enables us finally to dispose of the fable of his prosecution (in 415 or in 411) for " impiety," a story which bears the marks of its futility on its face. From the references of the *Meno* we see that Protagoras must have died during the Archidamian war, and that he ended his life in high general repute.

of whom we read in the *Apology* that he had spent more money on
" sophists " than any living man. He must be supposed to be
quite young, since his activity as a man of affairs begins at a much
later date. Aristophanes makes a topical joke about his presence
at the battle of Arginusae and his renown as a lady-killer in the
Frogs [1] (405 B.C.). In the speech of Andocides on *the Mysteries*
he figures as the villain of the story, the party who, according to
Andocides, is instigating the prosecution in pursuance of a personal
grudge, and we hear endless scandal about his domestic affairs.
From Lysias xix. (delivered between 390 and 387) we learn that the
family capital, which had once been believed to amount to two
hundred talents, had now shrunk to two. (We must take into account
the economic revolution which followed on the collapse of Athens
in 404.) We hear of Callias from time to time in the *Hellenica* of
Xenophon. He was commanding the Athenian force at Corinth
on the famous occasion (390 B.C.) when Iphicrates cut up the Spartan
mora with his peltasts (*op. cit.* iv. 5, 13), and was one of the representatives of Athens at the criticai congress held at Sparta early
in 371, two or three months before the battle of Leuctra. Hence
the agreement then concluded between the Athenian and Peloponnesian confederacies has been generally known as the " Peace
of Callias." His important social position at Athens can be gauged
from the facts that he held by heredity the position of " Torch-
bearer " in the Eleusinian mysteries and *proxenus*, or, as we might
say, " Consul " for Sparta. For a proper historical appreciation
of Socrates it is important to note that Plato represents him, at
this early date, as associating with persons like Callias and Alcibiades, both connected with the Periclean circle, on equal terms,
and being in high consideration with both them and the most
eminent of the foreign " wits." [2]

We cannot rate too high the importance of the *Protagoras*
as the fullest and earliest exposition of the character and aims of the
sophistic " education in goodness." Nowhere else in Greek literature have we an account of the matter comparable for a moment
to that which Plato has put into the mouth of Protagoras himself.
There is really no reason why we should feel any distrust of the
strict " historicity " of the statements. Plato stood near enough
to the Periclean age to be excellently well informed of the facts.
He could form his conclusions not merely from what he might be
told by men of an elder generation who had known Protagoras, or
actually taken his course, but from the work or works of the distinguished sophist himself. (The silly tale of their destruction is
refuted not only by the way in which it is assumed in the *Theaetetus* that all the parties to that conversation are familiar with

---

[1] *Frogs*, 432. For an earlier Aristophanic allusion to Callias as a spendthrift
and *coureur de femmes*, cf. *Birds*, 284–6. He had already been attacked as a
" waster " and patron of sophists by Eupolis in his Κόλακες (421 B.C.).

[2] See the compliment paid him by Protagoras at 361e, and observe that
it is assumed to be based on an acquaintance begun still earlier on a former
visit of Protagoras to Athens.

them, but by the express statement of Isocrates.[1]) He stood far enough away from it to have no personal motive for misrepresentation of any kind, and, in point of fact, the personality and the ideas of Protagoras are treated all through the dialogue with respect and understanding, though we are made to see what his limitations are. His exposition of his programme is done with as much " gusto " as anything in the whole of Plato's works ; so much so that some worthy modern critics have even discovered that Protagoras is the real hero of the dialogue who is meant to be commended at the expense of the *doctrinaire* Socrates. Preposterous as this exegesis is, the fact that it has been given in good faith is the best proof that the dialogue is no satirical caricature, so far as Protagoras is concerned. He is depicted as a man of high aims and sincere belief in the value of the education he gives ; his one manifest foible is that he is not conscious of his own limitations, and in that respect, according to the *Apology*, he is only on a level with all the other " celebrities " of the Periclean age.

If we discount the little exchange of pleasantries between Socrates and his unnamed acquaintance (309*a*–310*c*), which merely serves the purpose of dating the interview of Socrates and Protagoras by reference to the age of Alcibiades at the time, the dialogue falls into the following main sections : (1) an introductory narrative, preparatory to the appearance of Protagoras on the scene (310*a*–316*a*) ; (2) a statement by Protagoras of the nature of the " goodness " he professes to be able to teach, followed by a series of " sceptical doubts " urged by Socrates against the possibility of such an education, which are, in their turn, replied to by Protagoras at great length (316*b*–328*d*) ; (3) an argument between Socrates and Protagoras leading up to the Socratic " paradox " of the unity of the virtues, which threatens to end in an irreconcilable disagreement (328*d*–334*c*) ; (4) a long interlude in which the conversation resolves itself for a time into the discussion of a moralizing poem of Simonides (334*c*–348*c*) ; (5) resumption of the argument begun in (3), with the further developments that the one thing to which all forms of " goodness " reduce is seen to be " knowledge," and the consequence is drawn that " all wrong-doing is error " (348*c*–360*e*) ; (6) a brief page of conclusion in which both parties to the discussion admit the need of further inquiry and take leave of one another with many courtesies (360*e*–362*a*). This general analysis of itself shows that the central purpose of the dialogue is to exhibit clearly the ultimate ethical presuppositions of the Socratic morality and the " sophistic " morality at its best, and to show exactly where they are in irreconcilable opposition. The one serious exegetical problem we shall have to face is that of discovering the connexion of the discussion of the poem of Simonides with what precedes and follows.

---

[1] Isoc. x. 2, νῦν δέ τίς ἐστιν οὕτως ὀψιμαθής, ὅστις οὐκ οἶδε Πρωταγόραν καὶ τοὺς κατ' ἐκεῖνον τὸν χρόνον γενομένους σοφιστάς, ὅτι καὶ τοιαῦτα καὶ πολὺ τούτων πραγματωδέστερα συγγράμματα κατέλιπον ἡμῖν ;

I. Introductory Narrative (310*a*–316*a*).—The narrative is given in a tone of humour marked by touches of satire, which is directed not against Protagoras but against the excessive adulation bestowed on him by his younger admirers, and to a less degree against the self-importance of second-rate " professors " of the type of Prodicus. Its main object, however, is to insist on the great importance of education in " goodness," if such an education is to be had, and thus to raise our interest to the appropriate pitch, before Protagoras and his programme are actually put before us. Socrates has been roused from sleep in the " small hours " by his young friend Hippocrates, who has just heard of the arrival of Protagoras, and is anxious not to lose a moment in getting an introduction to him and putting himself under his tuition. As it is still too early to think of disturbing the great man, Socrates and the lad walk about for a time in the αὐλή of Socrates' house, conversing to pass the time. The drift of the conversation is that by profession Protagoras is a " sophist," but Hippocrates is not proposing to study under him in order to enter the " profession " itself ; he would be degrading himself by such a course. His object is, like that of the pupil of an ordinary schoolmaster or trainer, to get " culture " (παιδεία) as a free gentleman should. That is to say, he is about to put his " soul " into the hands of a professional " sophist " to be " tended." (The point intended is that " culture " is a much more serious thing than is commonly supposed. It really means the moulding of the " soul " for good or ill.) Hence, before we take such a risk, we ought to be quite clear on the point " what a sophist is," *i.e.* to what ends it is his profession to shape us. He is a σοφός or " wit," as his name shows,[1] but we might say as much of a painter. We want to know further on what his " wit " is exercised, of *what* accomplishment he is master. Hippocrates makes the obvious suggestion that the particular accomplishment of the sophist is the skilful use of speech—the " art " which, in fact, the pupils of Protagoras were specially anxious to learn from him. But any skilled professional can speak well and to the point about his own technicality, and in teaching us that technicality, he will make us also able to speak properly about it. Thus the all-important question is, What is it of which a " sophist " as such is by profession a teacher ?—and Hippocrates cannot answer this question (312*e*).[2]

Clearly then, Hippocrates is taking a great risk and taking it

[1] 312*c*. It is assumed that the popular etymology of σοφιστής made it a derivative from σοφός and εἰδέναι, σοφιστής = ὁ τῶν σοφῶν ἰστής.

[2] Hippocrates makes the suggestion that the " sophist's " speciality is to be δεινὸς λέγειν, of course, because the special skill of which Protagoras notoriously boasted was the power to " make the weaker argument the stronger," by stating the case forcibly and plausibly. " Advocacy " is what the young men of Athens pay Protagoras to teach them. Socrates' point is that the worth of his teaching as a " culture for the soul " depends on *what* he " advocates " and teaches others to advocate. Even from the most utilitarian point of view, to be a clever advocate is not the one and only requisite for a statesman.

in the dark. He would be slow to trust the care of his body to a particular adviser, and would do all he could to be sure of such a man's competence before he became his patient. How much more foolish to put that much more precious thing, his soul, into the hands of a recently arrived foreigner, without any consultation with older and more responsible friends and relatives, and actually without knowing the real character of the stranger's profession! We might suggest that the sophist is by profession a sort of importer and retailer (ἔμπορός τις ἢ καπηλός) of foreign articles of spiritual diet (a suggestion taken up again with a good deal of humour in a much later dialogue, the *Sophistes*). The "food of the spirit" is, of course, "studies" or "sciences" (μαθήματα), and we need to guard against the risk that the purveyor of this sustenance may deceive us, as other vendors often do, about the quality of his merchandise. The ordinary vendor praises the wholesomeness of his wares, but without really knowing anything about the matter. You would do well to take the advice of a medical man before you patronize him. So if one could find a "physician of souls," it would be desirable to take his advice before patronizing the spiritual wares vended by Protagoras. This is all the more important that you cannot carry away samples of his wares, as you might of a food for the body, and examine them at your leisure before consuming them. "Sciences" have to be taken direct from the vendor into the soul itself, and if they are unsound articles the mischief is thus done at the very time of purchase. You and I, says Socrates, are still too young [1] to judge for ourselves what is wholesome diet for the mind. But we can, at any rate, go and hear what Protagoras has to say about his merchandise, and take the advice of others accordingly, before we commit ourselves (314b).

We need not delay over the lively description of the scene in the house of Callias, the crowd of visitors, and the figures of those lesser lights Prodicus and Hippias. Some of the party must have been mere boys ; Socrates says this, in so many words, of Agathon, and it must be as true of Charmides, who was still a mere lad in the year of Potidaea. Plato has been reprimanded for making fun of the invalidism of Prodicus, but for all we know, Prodicus may really have been a *malade imaginaire* at whom it is quite fair to laugh. It is interesting to note that all the speakers of the *Symposium* are present except Aristophanes, who would be little more than a child at the supposed date of our dialogue.

---

[1] ἡμεῖς γὰρ ἔτι νέοι. Note the repeated insistence on the comparative youth of Socrates. Plato is determined that we shall not forget the date to which he has assigned the conversation. I should suppose that his reason is that he knew or believed that Socrates, as a fact, did meet Protagoras at this date, and that this was the most important occasion on which the two met, just as he mentions in the *Phaedo* that Socrates first learned Anaxagoras' doctrine about νοῦς from hearing some one "read aloud," as he said, "from a book of Anaxagoras," simply in order to make the historical point that the two men had not actually met.

(I should have mentioned in speaking of the *Symposium* that Aristophanes must be the youngest of the speakers in that dialogue, a man of about twenty-eight.)

II. THE PROGRAMME OF PROTAGORAS (316*b*–328*d*).—As soon as Protagoras makes his appearance, Socrates, who already knows him personally, opens the business on which he has come. His young, well-born, and wealthy friend Hippocrates has political aspirations which he thinks might be furthered by studying under Protagoras. But a preliminary interview is desirable. Protagoras is of the same opinion, and is glad of the chance of explaining his aims as a teacher, since the profession is one in which a man cannot be too careful of his own reputation. Men feel a natural ill-will towards a brilliant stranger when they see the young men of promise preferring his company and instructions to those of their own most eminent countrymen. This is why all the most influential " educators " have preferred to disguise their real practice, from Homer's time on, and have professed to be poets, physicians, musicians, anything but what they really are. Protagoras plumes himself on his own courage in taking the opposite course and frankly avowing that his calling is to " educate men." His boldness has proved the wiser course, for in a long professional career he has escaped all serious consequences of the popular prejudice.[1] So he has nothing to conceal and is ready to expound his aims with complete frankness. The whole company thereupon forms itself into an audience for the promised exposition.

Socrates now repeats the question he had already put to Hippocrates ; what precise benefit may be expected from study under Protagoras ? The answer Protagoras gives is that a pupil who comes to him will go away daily " better than he came," (318*a*. This establishes the formal equivalence of the notions of " educating men " and " teaching goodness.") But this statement needs to be made more precise. *Any* master of a speciality might say as much. If you studied under Zeuxippus, you would improve— in drawing, if under Orthagoras—in flute-playing. But in what will you improve daily if you study under Protagoras ? The question, says Protagoras, is rightly and fairly put, and the answer is that his pupil will daily improve, not in knowledge of astronomy or geometry (like the pupils of the polymath Hippias), but in what is the great concern of life, " prudence in the management of one's private affairs and capacity to speak and act in the affairs of the city." That is, Protagoras undertakes to teach us not how to be

[1] 316*b*–317*c*. Protagoras is, of course, speaking playfully when he suggests that Homer, Simonides, and others were really " sophists " who tried to escape unpopularity by passing themselves off for something different. But we may infer from his remarks (1) that the popular, and very natural, feeling against the professional sophist really existed in Athens in the Periclean age, and is not, as Grote supposed, an invention of Plato and the Socratic men ; (2) that Protagoras was actually the first man avowedly to practise the " educating of men " or " teaching of goodness " as a paid profession. Unless these are facts, there is no point in what Plato makes him say.

good specialists, but how to be good men, and what, to a Periclean Athenian, is the same thing, good active citizens. He is really claiming to be able to teach "statesmanship" (319*a*). (This, of course, *was* precisely what aspiring young Athenians paid him to teach them.)

There can be no doubt that this is the most important thing a man could teach, if it is really true that statesmanship can be taught. But Socrates feels a perplexity on the question whether statesmanship *is* teachable. It is hard to disbelieve in the claims of a famous man like Protagoras who has been pursuing his profession for so many years ; on the other hand, there are considerations which make the other way, and Socrates now proposes to state them. We must observe that he does not undertake to prove that statesmanship cannot be taught, nor does he commit himself to any of the views he goes on to present. He merely urges that, seeing the quarter from which they come, they cannot be simply dismissed, but have to be met. The argument is one from what Aristotle calls εἰκότα, the probabilities of the case.

The Athenians have a great name for being a "clever" people, and it is not likely that an opinion held very strongly by such a people should be a mere delusion. Now *the Athenian public* would appear to hold that "goodness" cannot be taught. For it is singular that though they will only accept public advice on what are admittedly matters for expert knowledge from properly qualified advisers, they listen to an opinion on the statesmanship of a proposed course of action without any such regard for qualifications. They will listen, on a point of naval construction, to no one who is not known either to be an expert himself or to have studied under experts. But when the issue is one of statesmanship—that is, one of the goodness or badness, the rightfulness or wrongfulness, of a proposed public act—they treat any one man's opinion as equally deserving of a hearing with another's ; they make no demand here that a man shall be an approved "expert" or have learned from one.

And this is not merely the attitude of the "general" ; the individuals who are regarded as our wisest and best statesmen show by their conduct that they hold the same view. They neither teach their own "goodness" to their sons nor procure masters of it for them, but leave it to chance whether the young men will pick up this goodness for themselves. The example selected, in this instance, is that of Pericles. Thus Socrates argues the case by appealing, in Aristotelian fashion, first to the opinion of the "many" and then to that of the "wise," the acknowledged experts. It is not likely that a very widespread conviction should be merely baseless ; it is not likely that the convictions of "experts" should be merely baseless ; it is still less likely that both parties should be victims of the same delusion. The point is raised simply as a difficulty ; Socrates is quite ready to listen to a proof from Protagoras that, after all, both parties are wrong. The question is thus not whether goodness can be taught or not, but whether Protagoras can satisfy Socrates that it is teachable, in other words, whether goodness can be taught on the principles and by the methods of Protagoras.

In dealing with the reply of Protagoras, we must be careful to remember that his case is not established by the mere fact that there is a great deal of truth in what he says, so far as it goes. What is required is that he should make out sufficient justification for his claim to be able to teach statesmanship as a speciality, exactly as another man might teach geometry or medicine. If we keep this point carefully in view, it will be found that, though what Protagoras says is true enough, as a vindication of his own claim it is a complete *ignoratio elenchi*.

He begins by indicating his position by means of a fable about the culture-hero Prometheus. At the making of living creatures, Epimetheus was charged with the work of distributing the various means of success in the " struggle for existence " among them ; Prometheus was to act as supervisor and critic. Epimetheus managed the distribution so badly that when he came to deal with mankind, the various serviceable qualities had already been used up on the lower animals ; none were left for man, who would thus have been helpless and defenceless if Prometheus had not stolen from heaven fire and the knowledge of industrial arts. (In plainer words, man is not equipped for self-preservation by a system of elaborate congenital instincts, and he is handicapped also by physical inferiority : he has to depend for survival on intelligence.) In the " state of nature," however, intelligence and the possession of fire were not enough to secure men against their animal competitors ; they had further to associate themselves in " cities," and this gave occasion for all kinds of aggression on one another. (One may compare Rousseau's speculations about the opportunity given by the social impulses of mankind to the exploitation of the many by the able and unscrupulous few.) Hence Zeus intervened to preserve the human race by sending Hermes to bestow on them δίκη and αἰδώς, the sense of right and conscience. But Zeus expressly commanded that these gifts were not to be confined, like *e.g.* skill in medicine, to a few specialists ; they were to be distributed to every one, since " political association " is impossible on any other terms (322*d*). Hence the behaviour of the Athenian *ecclesia,* which has surprised Socrates, is reasonable and right. " Political goodness " is wholly a matter of justice and " temperance," and no member of the community is a layman or outsider where justice and temperance are concerned ; every " citizen," in fact, is an expert in the virtues. This is also why we expect a man who is a layman in other accomplishments to confess the fact, and ridicule him if he pretends to an accomplishment which he does not possess. But when it comes to " justice," or " temperance," or any other " goodness of a citizen," we expect a man to pretend to it, even if he does not possess it ; hypocrisy is a tribute we expect vice to pay to virtue (323c). Similarly we may easily satisfy ourselves that the Athenian people really believe that " goodness " can and must be taught, by reflecting that they never " admonish " or " correct " those who suffer from defects which they cannot help. A man is not reprimanded or corrected for being ugly or undersized or sickly ; he is pitied. But men are properly reprimanded and punished for moral delinquencies, and the whole object is that the reprimand or punishment may be a " lesson " to the offender or to others not to offend in the future. The very existence of criminal justice is thus proof that " goodness " is held to be something which can be taught (323c–324d). (This does not mean that either Protagoras or Plato rejects the " retributive " theory of punishment. The " retributive " theory means simply that before a man can be held liable to punishment, he must by his acts have given you the *right* to punish him. You are not entitled to inflict a penalty simply because you think the suffering of it would " do the man good " ; the penalty must be preceded by the commission of an *offence*. No sane theory of the right to punish can ignore this.)

The little fable about Prometheus has already revealed Protagoras to us as a strong believer in the view that morality is dependent on νόμος, the system of conventions and traditions embodied in the " usages " of a civilized community. As we follow his explanation we shall find him laying still more stress on this point. Like Hobbes, he holds that in a " state of nature," there would be no morality to speak of, and the lack of it would make human life " poor, nasty, brutish, and short." He declares himself strongly opposed to the view of some of his rivals, that " citizen goodness " is a thing that comes by " nature," in other words, that men are born good or bad. He is wholly without any belief in the moral goodness of the unspoiled " savage " and, in fact, looks on morality as a product of civilization, a matter of imbibing a sound social tradition. Such a view would seem to suggest that, since, as we have just been told, every civilized man has to be a " specialist " in justice and temperance, there is no room and no need for the expert teacher of goodness, a conclusion which would make Protagoras' own professional activities superfluous. Hence he goes on, at once, to explain that he does not mean to deny that goodness can be taught or that there are expert teachers of it. You do not imbibe it unconsciously ; it is a thing which comes by teaching and training (323d). His position is that, in a civilized society, life is one long process of being taught goodness, and every citizen is, in his degree, an expert teacher. But there are a few exceptionally able teachers with a special vocation for their function, who do what every good citizen is doing, but do it better, and Protagoras himself is simply one of these.

In support of this view he makes an eloquent and telling speech on the educational process to which the civilized man is all through life subjected, as a consequence of the very fact that he is a member of a society with social traditions. Even in infancy parents, nurses, servants, are all busy teaching a child by precept and example that "this is right" and "that is wrong." The elementary schoolmaster next takes up the same task. The boy's reading lessons are passages from the poets, full of sound moral instruction, and the preceptors from whom he learns to read and write and tune his lyre pay more attention to his conduct than to anything else. So the trainer in bodily exercises makes it his prime business to teach hardihood and manliness of temper, the first requisites of a future soldier. When "school days" are over, and the boy enters on manhood, the city by its laws sets before him a rule for the whole conduct of his life, and penalizes him if he does not learn from this rule how "to govern and be governed." Thus the citizen's life is one unbroken progressive process of learning goodness (325c–326e). It is this very universality of the teaching which explains the puzzle about the sons of statesmen. If any of the "accomplishments" of which Socrates had spoken, for example flute-playing, were held by some community to be so important that every citizen must acquire it, and every one was anxious to communicate his own knowledge of it to others, what would happen? The citizens of such a community would not all be first-rate performers. Any one of them would be a much better performer than an average member of a community which did not insist on the accomplishment ; but the very universality of the instruction would lead to differences between the individual citizens, based on their more or less marked natural aptitude. Where the means of instruction were open to all, and their use compulsory for all, proficiency would be most manifestly in proportion to aptitude. If no one but the son of a musician learned music, or no one but the son of an expert in "goodness" learned goodness, we might reasonably expect that the sons of musicians would always be our most successful musicians and the sons of "good men" our best men. Just because every one "learns," this does not occur in an actual society, and Socrates' paradox is thus seen to be no paradox at all. If he would compare the worst men in a civilized society, like that of Athens, not with imaginary "noble savages," but with real savages, he would soon discover on which side the superiority lies (326e–327e). And as for his argument that there is no provision of a special class of expert teachers of goodness, we may reply that neither are there special experts to whom a child has to be sent to learn to speak its mother-tongue, or to whom the son of an artisan must be apprenticed to learn his father's business. In both cases, the child picks up the knowledge from its "social environment." Besides, there are some men, like Protagoras himself, who have a special and superior gift for teaching goodness, and their pupils do make exceptional progress (327e–328d).

The reply to Socrates' doubts looks plausible, and has apparently traversed all the points of his case. But the plausibility is, after all, only apparent. If we look more closely, we shall see that the whole argument depends on simply identifying " goodness " with the actual traditions of an existing civilized state. What you do imbibe, as Protagoras has said, from parents, servants, school-masters, daily intercourse with your fellow-Athenians, is nothing but the νόμος, the social tradition, of the group in which you live. In a different social group, at Megara for example, the same in-fluences of the social environment would be equally powerful, but the type of character they would tend to produce would be in many ways different. Thus the theory expounded by Protagoras can only be accepted as satisfactory if one assumes, as he has tacitly done, that morality is entirely " relative," that is, that there is no moral standard more ultimate than the standard of respectability current in a given society. If this is conceded, Protagoras has made out his main contention that " goodness " can be, and actually is, learned as a consequence of birth into a society with a definite tradition. But the whole point of the Socratic identification of morality with " knowledge " is that morality is not any more " relative " than geometry. The traditions of Athens are no more an ultimate standard in matters of right and wrong than they are in questions of mathematics. In other words, what Protagoras really means by " goodness," if his argument is to be conclusive, is just the medley of uncriticized traditions which Socrates calls in the *Phaedo* " popular goodness " and opposes to " philosophic goodness," as the imitation to the reality. Goodness, as Socrates understands it, is a matter not of traditions but of insight into principles. Now this, to be sure, *is* " knowledge," and must there-fore be capable of being taught. But the kind of goodness Protag-oras must have in mind when he says that any Athenian citizen, as such, is a teacher of it, is something which, as his own illustration about the boy who picks up his father's trade rather naïvely in-dicates, is not got by teaching of principles at all, but merely picked up, in the main, automatically. Without knowing it, Protagoras has really admitted that such goodness is what the *Gorgias* had called a mere " knack."

Hence it follows that there is a certain inconsistency between Protagoras' main position and the vindication of his profession with which he concludes his speech. To make the whole speech con-sistent, we should have to understand him to be claiming for him-self a certain exceptional ability in catching the tone of the " social tradition " of Athens, or any other community he visits, and communicating that tone to his pupils. Now it would, in the first place, be something of a paradox to maintain that a brilliant foreigner from Abdera can so successfully take the print of the social traditions of every community where he spends a few weeks, that a lecture from him will impress that tone on a young man more effectively than lifelong intercourse with a society in which it is dominant. It would be bad manners, at least, for a brilliant Frenchman or American to profess that a few weeks spent in this country had enabled him to understand the " tone and temper of the British people " better than any of us understand it for ourselves." [1] If " goodness " is knowledge, we can understand that a Chinaman, knowing nothing of " British traditions," may have lessons of first-rate importance to impart to us in it ; the claim becomes absurd if goodness means, in us, simply thorough conformity to the traditions of British respectability. The claim to be an expert teacher of goodness is only justifiable on the Socratic view that goodness is something eternal and immutable. It is in flat contradiction with the relativism professed by Protagoras. The further development of the discussion will make it still clearer that it is bound to end in an irreconcilable divergence because, from the first, the parties to the conversation have meant different things by " goodness."

III. THE UNITY OF THE " VIRTUES " (328*d*–334*c*).—There is just one " little " point Socrates would like to have cleared up, before he can profess himself completely satisfied. Protagoras had specified *two* qualities as bestowed on mankind by Zeus—the sense of *right* ($\delta\iota\kappa\eta$), and conscience ($\alpha\iota\delta\omega\varsigma$) ; he had gone on to mention piety and *sophrosyne* also as constituents of " goodness." Does he mean that " goodness " is an aggregate of which these characters are distinct constituents ($\mu\acute{o}\rho\iota\alpha$), or are we to understand that " conscience," " sense of right," " *sophrosyne*," " piety," are synonymous ? He meant to be understood in the former sense. But did he mean that the constituents are constituents in the way in which eyes, nose, and ears are constituents of a face, or in the sense in which the smaller volumes contained in a homogeneous mass (like a lump of gold) are constituents ? *i.e.* have the different " virtues " each its own constitutive formula, or is there only one such formula ? The question is one on which a practical teacher of goodness is bound to have a definite opinion, because it has a very direct bearing on his educational methods. On the first view, a man might " specialize " in one virtue (for example, courage), while his neighbour might prefer to specialize in some other, just as one man may specialize in diseases of the respiratory organs and another in disorders of the digestive system, or as one man may become a crack oarsman, another a fast bowler. (Or again, a man might set himself to acquire " goodness " by specializing first in one of its " parts " or " branches " and then in another, like Benjamin Franklin.) But on the second view, the principle of goodness will be exactly the same in whatever relation of life it is displayed. A

---

[1] That Protagoras actually took the line here suggested seems to follow from the well-known passage of the *Theaetetus* where the question is raised how Protagoras could reconcile his doctrine of " Man the measure " with his own claim to be able to *teach* " goodness." Socrates suggests that Protagoras might have pleaded that what he does for his pupils is not to give them " truer " views—a thing impossible on the *Homo mensura* theory—but to give them "more useful " views (*Theaetetus*, 166a–168c). This amounts to the suggestion of the text, that Protagoras believes himself to have a special aptitude for appreciating the tone of the current tradition of a community and impressing it on his hearers.

man who *really* acquires one " virtue " will have to acquire all simultaneously (329e).

Protagoras at once adopts the first alternative, that which recommends itself to average common sense. For he thinks it obvious that there are many brave but licentious men, and many " fair-dealing " men (δίκαιοι), who are far from " wise." (Note the way in which the " quadrilateral " of the four great virtues is thus taken for granted by Protagoras, as by other speakers in Plato, as something already traditional.) [1]

A view of this kind implies that each form of " goodness " has a *function* (δύναμις) of its own, distinctive of it, and radically different from the function of any other form. (We have already seen that this view, widely current in ordinary society, is in sharp opposition to the Socratic theory, in which the great difficulty of defining a given " virtue " is that we regularly find ourselves driven to adopt a definition which is equally applicable to every other virtue.) We proceed to treat this position in the recognized Socratic fashion by examining its consequences. It will follow that " justice," to take an example, has a definite function, " piety " or " religion " another and a different function. Justice is not piety, and religion is not justice. But we cannot adopt the monstrous moral paradox that justice is impious, or that religion is " unjust," or wrong, though this would seem to follow from the complete disparity between the " functions " of the different virtues just asserted by Protagoras.[2] Hence Protagoras himself is driven to take back what he had just said about the radical disparity of the different forms of goodness. The matter is, after all, not so simple as all that ; there is some vague and unspecified resemblance between such different " parts " of goodness as piety and justice, though we cannot say exactly what or how close the resemblance is (331e). The reference to the scale of colours or hardnesses as illustrating the point (331d) shows that the meaning is that one virtue somehow " shades off " into a different one, though you cannot say exactly where the boundary-line should be drawn, as white shades off into black through a series of intermediate grays.

To expose the looseness of this way of thinking and speaking, Socrates resorts to another simple argument. Wisdom has been included by Protagoras in his list of forms of goodness, and the contrary opposite of wisdom is ἀφροσύνη (" folly "). But *sophrosyne*

[1] It seems to me that the same allusion must underlie the curious phrase of the poem of Simonides for the Scopadae shortly to be discussed, where the " complete " good man is called " four-cornered " (τετράγωνος ἄνευ ψόγου τετυγμένος). Presumably we are dealing with a Pythagorean τετρακτύς. It should be clear, at any rate, that the " quadrilateral " is no invention of Plato, since he represents it as familiar to so many of his fifth-century characters.

[2] The reasoning (331a ff.) does not really commit the error of confounding otherness with contrary opposition. The point of the passage is actually to make the distinction, though in simple and non-technical language ; the suggestion that not-just (μὴ δίκαιον) = unjust (ἄδικον) is made only that it may be at once rejected.

is also a virtue which we ascribe to men who act "rightly and beneficially." Now *sophrosyne* means by derivation moral "sanity," and *its* contrary opposite, the conduct of those who act "wrongly and harmfully," is consequently *aphrosyne* ("folly"). For it is a principle of logic, which we can illustrate by an abundance of obvious examples, that ἓν ἑνὶ ἐναντίον (every term has one and only one definite contrary). Further, what is done "in contrary senses" (ἐναντίως) must be done "by contraries," *i.e.* in virtue of contrary characters in the agents. Thus if we can oppose what is "foolishly" done to what is "sanely" or "temperately" done, we may also oppose "folly" to *sophrosyne*, temperance, moral sanity. But we have already opposed wisdom and folly as contraries. On the principle then that one term (here "folly") has one and only one contrary opposite, wisdom and *sophrosyne* must be identified. Thus either we must abandon a fundamental logical principle, or we must give up the distinction between wisdom and *sophrosyne*, as our former argument was meant to show that we must give up the distinction between justice and piety (or religion).

(The reasoning here appears at first sight to turn on a mere "accident" of language, the fact that profligacy happens to be spoken of in Greek as "folly." When we reflect on the familiarity of the corresponding expressions in all languages which have an ethical literature, we should rather infer that the fact is no accident, but valuable evidence of the truth of the main tenet of Socratic morality. The thought underlying the linguistic usage is clearly that all morally wrong action is the pursuit of something which is not what rightly informed intelligence would pronounce good, and it is always wise to pursue what is truly good and foolish to prefer anything else.)

The next step in the argument is this. We have seen ground for identifying justice with piety and wisdom with temperance or moral sanity. This leaves us, so far, with two great types of "goodness," justice, regard for right, and moral sanity. But may we not further identify these two ? Can we really say of any act that it is "unjust," a violation of some one's rights, and yet that it is "morally sane" (σῶφρον) or "temperate" ? As a man of high character, Protagoras says that he personally would be ashamed to make such an assertion, but he knows that the "many" would make it. We may therefore examine the assertion simply as a piece of the current ethics of respectability, to see what it is worth (333*b*–*c*).[1] We must be careful, then, to bear in mind that, from

---

[1] Observe that the highly prized virtue, courage (ἀνδρεία), seems to have fallen into the background. This is a piece of Plato's dramatic art. The identification of the other commonly recognized virtues with one another is comparatively easy. But to the popular mind there *is* something " irrational " in high courage ; it " ignores " the risks which " rational calculation " would take into account. The identification of courage with knowledge will therefore be the great *crux* for a rationalist moralist. Hence the discussion of ἀνδρεία is deliberately reserved for the second half of Socrates' argument.

the present onwards, Protagoras is avowedly acting as the dialectical advocate of a current morality which he personally regards as defective. It is not Protagoras of Abdera but the current ethics of respectability, for which he consents to appear as spokesman, that is on its trial. The question is whether a man who is acting "unjustly" can be acting with *sophrosyne*. In our time, as in that of Pericles, the average man would say that this is quite possible. A man may be "temperate" enough, he may be clear of all "licentiousness," but he may be greedy or ambitious and quite unscrupulous about infringing the "rights" of other men in pursuing his greed or ambition. (Macaulay's character of Sunderland would be in point here as an illustration [1]) In fact, it is proverbial that profligacy is a vice of youth and hot blood, avarice and ambition vices of "cold" later age, and the "old young man" (like Joseph Surface) has always been specially unpopular with the ordinary satirist, who is commonly indulgent to the "rake," unless he happens to be an elderly rake. Socrates' conviction, like that of Dante, who punishes the prodigal and the miser in the same circle, is that Charles Surface and Joseph are brothers in the spirit, no less than in the flesh ; the antithesis of the Sheridans and Macaulays between the "generous" and the "mean" vices, is a false one ; there are *no* "generous vices," and no "milksop" virtues.

Formally, the argument is not allowed to reach a conclusion ; Protagoras, finding his case hard to defend, tries to take refuge in irrelevancy by diverting attention to the theory of the "relativity" of good. Socrates has started with the linguistic identification of "temperance" with moral sanity. The man who behaves with moral sanity is the εὖ βουλευόμενος, the man who acts "with good counsel." Hence if a man can in the same act be both temperate and unjust, it must be possible to act with good counsel in violating a "right." But a man only shows himself to be acting with good counsel when he "succeeds" or "does well" by disregarding that right. Socrates is thus taking advantage of the ambiguity of the expression εὖ πράττειν, which may either mean "to act well," or simply to "succeed in doing what you are proposing to do." How he would have continued the argument is indicated by his next question, "Do you recognize the existence of *goods*?" He means, having got the admission that injustice is only "well-advised" when it is successful injustice, to argue that no injustice really does "succeed" in procuring the aggressor on another man's rights what he is really aiming at getting, real good or well-being; it is always unsuccessful because it always involves sacrificing the good of the soul to something inferior (the thesis of the *Gorgias* and of the closing pages of *Rep.* i.). But the moment he shows his hand by

and we are prepared for it by the long half-comic interlude in which the poem of Simonides is canvassed ; this is Plato's way of indicating that it is the hardest and most important section of the dialogue.

[1] " He had no jovial generous vices. He cared little for wine or beauty ; but he desired riches with an ungovernable and insatiable desire," etc. etc. (*History*, c. 6).

asking whether "good things" do not mean "what is beneficial to man," Protagoras tries to escape the development he foresees by delivering a wholly irrelevant homily on the thesis that what is good for one animal may be bad for another, and what is good for man taken externally as a lotion, may be very bad if taken internally, in short that nothing can be pronounced good absolutely and unconditionally. This is, of course, a direct and simple application of Protagoras' own principle of "man the measure" to ethics, and the facts to which Protagoras appeals are all real facts; only they have no bearing on the issue at stake. It is true that I may be poisoned by drinking something which would have done me good if I had used it as an embrocation, that I should damage my health if I tried to live on the diet on which a horse thrives, and so forth. It does not in the least follow that there are not "good activities of the soul," which are absolutely good in the sense that it is good that any man should exhibit them at any and every time, and that scrupulous respect for "rights" is not one of these goods, and possibly the best of them. In common fairness, we may suppose that Protagoras is alive to this, and that he is simply doing his best for his client, the ethics of the average man, by diverting the attention of the audience from the weak point of his case.[1]

IV. INTERLUDE.—*The Poem of Simonides* (334c–348a).—At this point the conversation threatens to end in a general confusion, and the interrupted argument is only resumed after a long and apparently irrelevant episode. The main reason for the introduction of the episode has already been explained. The argument for the Socratic "paradoxes" makes a severe demand on the reader's power of hard thinking, and the most difficult part of it is yet to come. The strain of attention therefore requires to be relaxed, if we are to follow Socrates to his conclusion with full understanding. Plato also wants an opportunity to produce two striking dramatic effects. He wishes to contrast the manner of the "sophist," who is highly plausible so long as he has the argument to himself, but gets into difficulty the moment he is confronted by close criticism with the manner of Socrates, who cares nothing for eloquent plausibility and everything for careful and exact thinking. And he wants to provide a part in the drama for the secondary characters, Prodicus and Hippias; they will get no chance of a "speaking part" while Protagoras and Socrates occupy the centre of the stage. Hence I think we should take the whole of this long interlude as intended mainly to be humorous "relief," a gay picture of the manners of cultivated Athenian society in the later years of the Periclean age, and not much more.

The fun opens with the humorous pretence of Socrates that, in

[1] To judge from the *Theaetetus*, Protagoras had actually made the obvious application of the *Homo mensura* doctrine to ethics for himself (Burnet, *Greek Philosophy, Part I.*, 116–7). It leads directly to that identification of "virtue" with what a respectable society actually approves which is the foundation of his explanation of his own educational theory and practice, and is common ground to "subjectivists" in ethics.

kindness to his " shortness of memory," Protagoras should curb
his eloquence and make his answers to questions as brief as he can.
(The self-depreciation is, of course, fun. Socrates means that he
would like fewer words and more thought ; but the implied criticism
has to be made with due regard for " manners.") Protagoras is a
little huffed by the suggestion that the other party to the discussion
should prescribe the character of his responses ; Socrates politely
expresses his regret for the weakness to which he has referred, and
discovers that he has an engagement elsewhere, and the party
thus seems to be on the point of dissolution, when the auditors
intervene to prevent such a misfortune. The point of chief interest
in the general conversation thus caused is provided by the entertaining burlesque of Prodicus, the great authority on the right
use of words. All he really has to say is that the audience who
listen to a discussion should give a fair hearing, without fear or
favour, to both parties, and assign the victory to the party who
makes out the better case. But his remarks are so disfigured by
the mannerism of stopping to discriminate each of the terms he
uses from some other with which it might conceivably be confused,
that it takes him half one of Stephanus's pages to make his remark.
It is clear that the real Prodicus (who, as we must remember,
actually survived the execution of Socrates, and so must have
been a well-remembered figure to many of the first readers of our
dialogue) must have been very much of a formal pedant in manner,
or the stress laid on the point by Plato would be unintelligible.
No doubt we are also to understand that the defect is being exaggerated for legitimate comic effect. But it is not likely that the
exaggeration is very gross. Prodicus was trying to make a beginning with the foundations of an exact prose style, and it would
be quite natural that, once impressed with the importance of distinguishing between " synonyms," he should ride his hobby to
death. We know from the remains of Varro's *de lingua Latina*, from
Quintilian, Aulus Gellius, and others, to what lengths the men who
attempted to perform the same services for Latin were prepared to
go, and it is likely that if the writings of the " sophists " had been
preserved, we should have found that Prodicus was not outstripped
by his Roman imitators. There is no trace of any personal malice
or dislike in the entertaining sketch Plato has given us. Hippias
is allowed to make a speech of about the same length, *his* main
point being to mark his disagreement with the partisans of " convention," and his conviction that the whole company, in spite of
the differences of " conventional " political allegiance, are all
" naturally " fellow-citizens. His tone is exactly that of a cosmo-
politan eighteenth-century *philosophe*. Since Xenophon (*Mem.*
iv. 4) pits Hippias and Socrates against one another as champions
of φύσις and νόμος respectively, this cosmopolitanism is presumably
a real trait of Hippias, though we cannot be sure that Xenophon
is not simply developing a hint taken from the *Protagoras* itself.
But even so, his representation shows that he thought Plato's

little picture true to life in its main point. None of the interveners in the general conversation shows any sense of the real bearing of the argument which has just broken down. All treat it as a mere contest of verbal skill between two parties, each of whom is " talking for victory." In the end, a heated disagreement is only avoided by the consent of Protagoras to submit to further cross-questioning, if he may first be allowed to deliver another speech. He absolutely declines Socrates' proposal to submit himself to be questioned and to give an example of what he thinks the right way to meet criticism (338*d*–*e*). The scene which ensues can hardly be understood as anything but broad comedy. Protagoras, having carried his point about the delivery of a set speech on a theme of his own choosing, remarks that it is an important part of " culture " to understand the poets and criticize their perform-ances, and that he will accordingly now expound and criticize a poem composed by Simonides for the Scopadae. This is a task suggested naturally by the previous course of the conversation, as the contents of the poem have to do with " goodness."

Unfortunately the poem (Fr. 3 in the *Anthology* of Hiller-Crusius, 12 of Schneidewin) has to be reconstructed from the *Protagoras* itself, and the reconstruction can be neither complete nor certain, so that we are not entitled to speak with too much confidence about the precise drift of the poet. The general sense, appropriate enough in an encomium of a half-barbaric Thessalian chief, seems to be that it is idle to expect complete and all-round " goodness " in any man ; there are difficult situations out of which no human goodness comes with credit. We must be content to call a man " good," if his general conduct shows regard for right (δίκα), if he never misbehaves without highly extenuating circumstances ; absolute superiority to circumstance can only be expected in a god. The impression one gets is that one is reading a paid panegyric on a magnate against whom there is the memory of some shocking deed or deeds which the eulogist wishes to excuse or palliate by the " tyrant's plea, necessity." [1]

The point on which Protagoras fastens is this. Simonides takes occasion to comment unfavourably on the saying commonly ascribed to Pittacus that " it is hard to be good " (χαλεπὸν ἐσθλὸν ἔμμεναι). But he has just said the very same thing himself in almost the same words (ἄνδρ' ἀγαθὸν μὲν ἀλαθέως γενέσθαι χαλεπόν). He has thus committed the absurdity of censuring Pittacus for the very sentiment he has just uttered as his own (339*d*).

Socrates now seizes the opportunity to defend the poet by the aid of Prodicus and his famous art of discriminating between words. The point, he says, is that whereas Pittacus had said that it is hard

---

[1] Simonides writes much as a poet would have to do if he were composing an ode in praise of William III and felt that he could not be silent about the murder of the De Witts and the Glencoe massacre. The apologetic tone shows that his hero had done something which was regarded by most persons as highly criminal.

to be (ἔμμεναι) good, Simonides says that it is hard to become, (γενέσθαι) good; "to be" is one thing, "to become" another, and thus there is no formal contradiction between denying that it is hard to be good and asserting that it is hard to become good. But, objects Protagoras, this distinction only makes matters worse for Simonides; if he denies that it is hard to be good, he must mean that it is easy to possess goodness, and the common sense of all mankind is against him. Socrates is ready with a rejoinder. Possibly Simonides, like his fellow-Cean Prodicus, was a votary of precision of speech, and regarded the employment of χαλεπόν in the sense of "difficult" as a misuse of words, just as Prodicus objects to the common colloquial use of the word "awful" (δεινός) in such phrases as "awful wealth" (δεινὸς πλοῦτος), on the ground that only bad things can properly be called "awful." Let Prodicus, as a fellow-countryman, tell us what Simonides really meant by χαλεπόν. Prodicus at once says he meant κακόν ("bad").[1] If that is so, Pittacus was, from his Lesbian ignorance of the exact meaning of a Greek word, unconsciously uttering the senseless statement that "it is bad to be good," and Simonides was right in objecting this to him. Prodicus at once accepts this explanation, but Protagoras naturally rejects it as ridiculous. "So it is," says Socrates, "and you may be sure Prodicus is only making fun of us" (341d).

(So far, it is clear that the whole tone of the passage about Simonides is playful. Plato is laughing, as he often does, at the fifth-century fashion of trying to extract moral principles from the remarks of poets, especially of poets with a reputation, like Simonides, for worldly wisdom and a shrewd regard for the interests of "number one." The mock-respectful discussion of another dictum of the same poet in Republic i. is couched in exactly the same tone. The solemn pedantry of Prodicus is a second subject of mockery. But the main stroke is aimed at the superficiality of Protagoras. With all his eloquence about the value of a critical study of "literature," his ideal of criticism is to fasten on the first and most obvious weak point, and make an end of the matter. He has shown his cleverness by catching Simonides in a verbal contradiction; he does not see the need of an attempt to understand the drift of his poem as a whole, or to consider whether the apparent contradiction will vanish when taken in the light of the general context. We are all only too familiar with this sort of "criticism," which aims at nothing more than the commendation or censure of individual phrases, while it lets "the whole" go unregarded.)

Socrates now undertakes to propound an interpretation which will pay due regard to the meaning of the whole poem (342a). He introduces it by some general observations, the tone of which ought

---

[1] The suggestion is not quite so absurd as it looks, absurd as it is. χαλεπόν, in the sense "a hard thing to bear," may often be paraphrased by κακόν without injury to sense. Cf. Pindar's τερπνῶν χαλεπῶν τε κρίσις ("issues of weal and woe"), or Homer's χαλεπὸν γῆρας (Il. Θ 103) ("grim old age"), and the like.

to settle the question whether we are to take his exegesis in earnest or not. Crete and Sparta are really the most philosophical communities in the Greek world, and "sophists" abound there more than anywhere else; but they conceal the fact from mankind at large by passing themselves off as rough fighting-men, and by vigilantly discouraging intercourse with other cities, so that they may keep their wisdom for their own exclusive benefit. This is why the ordinary Spartan startles you from time to time by the pungency and pertinence of his "dry" and brief apophthegms. They are all the product of this unique "Spartan culture." The famous "seven sages"—the list of them given in this passage is the earliest extant—were all trained in this school, and Pittacus was one of them. Hence his saying "it is hard to be good" was much admired as a piece of this sententious "philosophy," and Simonides, being an ambitious man, wished to win a great reputation by refuting it. This is the object of his whole poem (342a–343c).

(It ought not to have to be said that this whole representation of Sparta and Crete, the least "intellectual" communities of Hellas, and the two which Socrates himself takes as his models in *Republic* viii. in describing the State which has made the mistake of "neglecting education," is furious fun. Socrates is diverting himself by his whimsical suggestions that the "laconizing" fashionables of other cities, who affect the dress and appearance of prize-fighters, are all the while imitating the wrong thing, the pretence under which the Spartans disguise their real interests, and that the "superiority of Sparta" is really based not on military prowess and success but on intellectual eminence. And if the explanation which introduces the exposition of the poem of Simonides is thus sheer fun, we are bound in common sense to expect that the exposition will turn out to be mainly fun too.)

We are now given the professed exegesis of the poem, which is only arrived at by a series of violences done to its language. Simonides must be understood as correcting the saying "it is hard to be good" by saying "no, the *truly* hard thing is not to be, but to become a thoroughly good man, though this is possible. To *be* permanently good is not hard, but absolutely impossible for a man; it is only possible to a god." A *man*, as Simonides goes on to say, cannot help proving "bad" when he is "struck down" by irretrievable misfortunes. Now no one who is already down can be struck down. Hence Simonides must mean by a "man," an "expert," a wise and good man, and his meaning is shown by the fact that he goes on to say that a man is "good" as long as he "does well" ($\pi\rho\acute{a}\xi\alpha\varsigma$ $\mu\grave{\epsilon}\nu$ $\gamma\grave{a}\rho$ $\epsilon\hat{\upsilon}$ $\pi\hat{a}\varsigma$ $\acute{a}\nu\grave{\eta}\rho$ $\acute{a}\gamma\alpha\theta\acute{o}\varsigma$). For the man who "does well," or "succeeds" in anything is the man who *knows* how the thing ought to be done, the man who "does ill" is always the man whose *knowledge* fails him. Simonides is thus made, by an arbitrary exegesis, to bear witness to the Socratic doctrine that "goodness" and knowledge are the same (345b). His meaning is that it is hard to become good but impossible for

man to be permanently good, because of the limitations and imper-
fections of all human *knowledge*.

The rest of the poem develops the same thought. In particular, when the poet says that he will " praise and love the man
who does no deed of shame willingly," (ἑκών ὅστις ἔρδῃ μηδὲν αἰσχρόν,)
we are not to take his words in what seems their natural grammatical
sense. The " cultured " Simonides must be supposed to know
that it is a vulgar error to suppose that anyone would do evil
voluntarily. Hence the ἑκών must be taken by an extravagant
hyperbaton with the words which precede it, so that the sense is,
" I *readily* praise and love the man who does no deeds of shame "
(though my profession sometimes unfortunately requires me to pay
constrained compliments to " tyrants " who have committed
crimes).

Though there have been commentators who have taken
Socrates' exposition of the poem as perfectly serious, the blunder
ought to be impossible to any man with a sense of humour or of the
necessity of maintaining a dramatic unity of spirit throughout a
scene. We have been prepared for the discussion of the verses by
an introductory homily on the devotion of Sparta to " culture,"
which is manifestly the merest playful humour ; we are fairly
entitled to suspect Socrates whenever we find him pretending to
discover deep philosophic truth in the compositions of any " poet,"
and particularly in those of the poet who had become a byword for
his adroit and profitable flatteries of " the great " ; his purpose
should be made unmistakable by the forced character of the verbal
constructions he is driven to advocate. Clearly we are dealing
with an amusing " skit " on the current methods of extracting
any doctrine one pleases from a poet by devices which can make
anything mean anything. Socrates is amusing himself by showing
that, if he chooses to play at the game, he can beat the recognized
champions, just as in the *Parmenides* Plato amuses himself by
showing that he can, if he likes, outdo the constructors of " antinomies " in the use of their own weapons. The one thing in the
whole of the " lecture " on the verses of Simonides which is not
playful is Socrates' insistence on the doctrine that wrongdoing is
error, and is therefore not " voluntary." Here he is in intense
earnest, but the device by which he extracts the doctrine from the
text of Simonides by an impossible " punctuation " is itself merely
playful, just as his suggestion that what he well knew to be the
" paradox " of his own theory is so universally admitted by all
thinking men that it is incredible Simonides should not accept it,
is equally playful. He knows that the very proposition he represents as too well known to be ignored by Simonides will be rejected
as an extravagance by his audience when he comes shortly to
defend it. His object in getting it into the otherwise whimsical
exposition of Simonides is simply to bring back the discussion to
the original issues from which it has been allowed to diverge, and
he has the natural delight of a humorist in clothing his thesis in

the most provocative and arresting words he can find. How far he is from expecting his excursus into literature to be taken seriously is shown by his remark that he has now discharged his part of a bargain by allowing Protagoras to deliver a second speech, and would be glad if Protagoras would honour the agreement by returning to the interrupted discussion. For his own part, he thinks it unprofitable to spend our time debating the meaning of the poets, whom we cannot call directly into court ; it is much better to let them alone and try to get at truth by the direct interplay of our own thoughts (347c–348a).

V. THE MAIN ARGUMENT RESUMED.—*The Identity of Goodness with Knowledge, and its Consequences* (348c–360e).—Now that Socrates has succeeded in bringing back the conversation to the point where it had been broken off, he carefully restates the question, with a polite assurance that he is not talking for victory but honestly asking the help of Protagoras towards the clarification of his own thought. The question is whether the names of the great virtues are different names for one and the same thing (349b), or whether to each of these names there answers " a peculiar reality or object with its own special function " (ἴδιος οὐσία καὶ πρᾶγμα ἔχον ἑαυτοῦ δύναμιν, where note that the word οὐσία, exactly as in the *Euthyphro*, implies the whole of the " doctrine of forms," expounded in the *Phaedo*). Protagoras has been so far impressed by the former arguments of Socrates that he now restates his original opinion with a large modification. He admits that most of the " parts of goodness " are " fairly like one another," but holds that ἀνδρεία, valour, courage, has a distinct character of its own. This is a matter of everyday observation, for it is a manifest fact that many men are singularly brave, but have no other virtuous quality ; they have no regard for rights, no religion, no command over their passions, no prudence. (The view is a familiar one ; it is habitually adopted, for example, in the character-sketches of a work like Macaulay's *History*. It implies, of course, that its supporters identify ἀνδρεία with the " popular " courage which the *Phaedo* pronounces to be a counterfeit of true valiancy, mere hardihood in the face of perils.) The first point which has to be made against this position is that it rests on the false conversion of a true proposition. It amounts to identifying " the valiant " with the " confident " or " fearless " (θαρράλεοι). Now it is true that all brave men are fearless, but it is not true that all the " confident " or " fearless " are truly brave, and the two classes, therefore, cannot be identified. In the absence of a logical terminology, this point has to be made by examples. Men who have learned a " dangerous " accomplishment, such as diving, fighting in the cavalry, or the like, will be " fearless " in facing the risks they have learned to deal with, as we also call them " brave " divers or fighters But persons who have never learned to dive or to manage a horse will also sometimes be reckless in throwing themselves into the water or plunging into a charge. But this, Protagoras says, is not valour ; it is simply madness. (He means, of course, that there is no valour in taking a risk simply because you are not alive to its magnitude. True valour involves consciousness of the risk you are facing.) Protagoras accordingly points out that though he had admitted that the valiant are fearless, he had not admitted the converse, and complains that Socrates is treating him unfairly (of course, Socrates' real object was simply to lead up to the making of the distinction). It is true that fearlessness may be the effect of knowledge, but it may also be the effect of high temper ($\theta\nu\mu\delta s$) or mere frenzy ($\mu\alpha\nu\iota a$) ; hence the superior fearlessness of the man who has learned to swim or to use his weapons is no proof that *courage* (as distinct from mere fearlessness) is the same thing as " wisdom " or knowledge ($\sigma\circ\phi\iota a$). In fact, Protagoras holds that the fearlessness which deserves to be called valour is due not to knowledge but to something else, " nature " ($\phi\upsilon\sigma\iota s$) and a " thriving " or " well-fed " state of soul ($\epsilon\upsilon\tau\rho\circ\phi\iota a\ \tau\omega\nu\ \psi\nu\chi\omega\nu$, 351b), just as physical strength is not due to knowledge but to bodily constitution and sound nourishment.[1]

Thus the question whether valour can be shown, as Protagoras now admits that the other leading forms of " goodness " can be, to be knowledge, requires us to raise still more fundamental questions. We admit that one may live well or live ill, and that the man who lives a life of pain and misery is not living well, but the man who lives a pleasant life is. May we say then that the pleasant life is the good life, the unpleasant life the bad ? Protagoras wishes to stipulate that the pleasure must be " pleasure in fine, or noble, things " ($\tau\circ\iota s\ \kappa\alpha\lambda\circ\iota s$, 351c), thus anticipating Mill's " distinction of qualities " of pleasure. But might we not say that things are good just in so far as they are pleasant, and bad in so far as they are unpleasant, so that good and pleasant are synonyms ? Protagoras thinks it due to his character to maintain that this is not true ; there are bad pleasures and good pains, and there are both pleasures and pains which are neither good nor bad. But he is willing to treat the suggestion, in the Socratic manner,[2] as one for further investigation. (It is very important, then, to remark that the Hedonist identification of good with pleasant comes into the conversation, in the first instance, as problematic ; it is to be adopted or rejected according as its implications approve themselves or do not.) And the question about the relation between pleasure

---

[1] The precise position is, and is meant to be, vague. The champion of $\nu\acute{\circ}\mu\circ s$ is clearly conceding more importance to $\phi\upsilon\sigma\iota s$ (" original temperament ") than we might have expected of him from his earlier utterances. This part of the *Protagoras* has directly suggested Aristotle's observations about the " fearlessness " produced by $\epsilon\mu\pi\epsilon\iota\rho\iota a$ or by native $\theta\nu\mu\delta s$ (*E.N.* 1116b 3 ff.).

[2] 351e, $\omega\sigma\pi\epsilon\rho\ \sigma\upsilon\ \lambda\epsilon\gamma\epsilon\iota s,\ \epsilon\phi\eta,\ \epsilon\kappa\alpha\sigma\tau\circ\tau\epsilon,\ \omega\ \Sigma\omega\kappa\rho\alpha\tau\epsilon s,\ \sigma\kappa\circ\pi\omega\mu\epsilon\theta a\ \alpha\upsilon\tau\acute{\circ},\ \kappa\tau\lambda$. Thus Protagoras knows all about the Socratic method of " hypothesis " expounded in the *Phaedo*. We must suppose that he had learned of it on the earlier occasion when he had met Socrates and formed a high opinion of his abilities. Rightly read, the *Protagoras* confirms the *Phaedo* in a way which can hardly be accounted for except by supposing that both are portraits of the same original.

and good directly raises another fundamental issue. The popular opinion is that " knowledge " has not much influence on conduct. It is held that a man often knows quite well that something is good or evil, but acts " against his better knowledge," which is mastered by " temper," or " pleasure," or " pain," or " lust," as the case may be. But may it not be that the popular opinion is wrong, and that if a man knows good and evil, nothing will ever prevail on him to act contrary to his knowledge ? Protagoras thinks that it would only be proper in a professional teacher of goodness, like himself, to take this view, and Socrates expresses his firm conviction of its truth.[1] But, since most men think otherwise, we, who dissent from them, must give a correct analysis of the facts they have in mind when they talk of a man's judgment as " overcome " by pleasure or pain, and satisfy them that the popular analysis of these facts is inaccurate (353*a*). We might, in fact, ask the mass of men, who profess to believe that a man can be seduced by the prospect of pleasure or frightened by that of pain into doing, against his better knowledge, what he recognizes to be evil, the following questions : (*a*) When you talk of something as pleasant but evil, do you not mean simply that the pleasant thing in question leads to painful consequences, and when you call some things good but unpleasant, do you not mean that, though unpleasant for the time being, they lead to pleasurable consequences ? " The many " would readily admit this, and thus would (*b*) commit themselves to the view that good and evil are identical with pleasant and painful. In fact (*c*) they would admit that the end they always pursue is getting the " greatest possible balance of pleasure over pain " (354*c–e*). It follows at once that, on the showing of the " many " themselves, the experience which they *call* " being overcome by pleasure or by pain " is really making a false *estimate* of pleasures and pains. To be " overcome " means " to take a greater amount of evil in exchange for a smaller amount of good " (356*e*), and on the hypothesis we are examining, " good " means " pleasure " and " evil " means " pain." Errors of conduct are thus on the same level as false estimates of number, size, and weight. Now we are preserved from mistakes about number, size, weight, by the arts or sciences (τέχναι) of counting, measuring, and weighing. In the same way we need to be preserved from false estimates in moral choice by a similar art of estimating the relative *magnitudes* of " lots " of prospective goods and evils, that is to say, prospective pleasures and pains, in fact by an " hedonic calculus," which will terminate disputes. And a " calculus," of course, is " knowledge," or " science." An argument of this kind ought to reconcile the " many " themselves to the view that

---

[1] 352*d* 2-4. Note that Socrates definitely commits himself to one of the two premisses of the argument which is to follow, the proposition that no one really acts against his own knowledge of good and evil. He never commits himself to the other premiss, the Hedonistic doctrine that good is pleasure. This remains a suggestion for examination.

wrong choice, the victory of passion over knowledge as they call it, is really nothing but miscalculation, and therefore that wrong action is due to error and is always involuntary (357–358).

It is on this section of the dialogue that the notion of a Platonic " Hedonism " has been erected, with the consequence that one of two equally impossible inferences has to be made, either that there is no consistent ethical doctrine to be found in the dialogues— Plato allows himself at pleasure to argue for or against any view which interests him for the moment (the theory of Grote)—or that the *Protagoras* expresses an " early theory " which is afterwards abandoned when we come to the *Gorgias* and *Phaedo*. Careful reading will show that neither of these conceptions is justified. Neither Protagoras nor Socrates is represented as adopting the Hedonist equation of good with pleasure. The thesis which Socrates is committed to is simply that of the identity of goodness and know-ledge. The further identification of good with pleasure is carefully treated, as we have seen, as one neither to be affirmed nor denied. We are concerned solely with investigating its consequences. One of these consequences would be that what is commonly called " yielding to passion against our better knowledge " is a form of intellectual error and is involuntary, since it means choosing a smaller " lot of pleasure " when you might choose a greater. (These consequences are, in fact, habitually drawn by Hedonists.) Hedon-ism thus is in accord with the doctrines of Socrates on one point, its reduction of wrong choice to involuntary error, and for that reason Socrates says that you can make the apparent paradoxes of his ethics acceptable to mankind at large, if you also adopt the Hedonist equation, good=pleasure. (The " many," in fact, do in *practice* accept this equation, because they are votaries of some form of the βίος φιλοχρήματος.) It does not follow that because Socrates agrees with vulgar Hedonism on the point that wrong choice is involuntary error and arises from lack of knowledge of good, that he identifies knowledge of good, as the Hedonist does, with calculation of the sizes of " lots " of pleasure and pain. All he wants to show is that even from the point of view of the persons who mistake " popular goodness " for genuine goodness, it is no paradox to say that goodness is knowledge of some sort ; the Hedonist is a " rationalist " in his ethics, though his " rational-ism " may not be of the right kind. That this is all that is meant is clear from the way in which Socrates is careful to insist over and over again that the appeal is being made to the standards of " the mass of mankind." We must also not forget that the appeal to the unconscious Hedonism of the average man is being made for a further special purpose. The object of convincing the average man that, on his own assumptions, goodness is a matter of right calcula-tion, is to prepare the way for the further proof that, even on these assumptions, courage can be brought under the same principle as all the rest of " goodness." When we thus take the argument in its proper context, we see that the *Protagoras* no more teaches

Hedonism than the *Phaedo*, which also represents the morality of average men as a business of estimating pleasures and pains against one another. Rightly interpreted, *Gorgias*, *Phaedo*, *Protagoras*, are all in accord on the one doctrine to which Socrates commits himself in the present section of our dialogue, the doctrine that " goodness " is knowledge. The confusion between " knowledge of the good " and computation of pleasures and pains is given, in the *Protagoras* as in the other dialogues, for what it is, a confusion of the " average man," and for nothing more.

To come to the application to the problem about ἀνδρεία. What is it that the courageous face, but the cowardly refuse to face ? The current answer is that it is " dangers " (τὰ δεινά). But " danger " means an anticipated evil, and we have just seen that even the average man, when he comes to theorize about his own practice, holds that no one " goes to face " what he believes to be evil for him. The very fact that he chooses to face the situation shows that he regards it as the " lesser evil " to do so. The real reason, then, why some men face the risks of war but others run away, must be that the former judge that more good, which to them means more pleasure, is to be got by standing your ground than by running away ; the latter think that they will get more good, and again they mean more pleasure, by running. If we praise the one and condemn the others, we are praising a true (and also condemning a false) calculation about the " balance of pleasure over pain." The brave man of everyday life faces the present pain and peril because he has correctly calculated that endurance of it will lead to a greater balance of pleasure than flinching. Thus even the unconscious theory of the average man at bottom implies the view that courage is a matter of *knowing* what is and what is not formidable (σοφία τῶν δεινῶν καὶ μὴ δεινῶν, 360c). This is, in fact, exactly what Socrates says about " popular " courage in the *Phaedo*. (That what the " many " suppose to be knowledge of the good— namely, knowledge of the hedonic consequences of your act—is something very different from what Socrates means by knowledge of the good is true, but irrelevant to the present argument, which only aims at showing that, even if you adopt the working morality of the average man, courage stands on the same footing as the other " virtues." From his standpoint, it resolves itself, like the rest, into calculation of hedonic consequences ; from Socrates' standpoint, it and all the rest issue from knowledge of the true and eternal good.)

VI. Epilogue.—Our discourse has, after all, only ended by bringing us in face of the really fundamental problem, what true " goodness " *is* (360c). (This remark, again, shows that Socrates is not represented as accepting the Hedonism which he finds to be the unconscious assumption of the average man. We have seen clearly enough what " goodness " is, on that theory.) In fact, we have ended by exchanging positions in a very entertaining fashion. Protagoras, who began by being sure that goodness can be taught and that he can teach it, seems now to be equally sure that, whatever goodness is, it is not the one thing which can be taught, knowledge ; Socrates, who began by raising the doubt whether it can be taught, is now doing his best to prove that it must be knowledge and nothing else.   And here the party breaks up, with a last word of graceful compliment on the part of Protagoras.   He has often testified to his admiration of Socrates' parts and rates him far above all other persons of his years ; he would not be surprised if he should yet become famous for his " wisdom."

Of course, the apparent paradox of which Socrates speaks can be very simply explained.   What he doubted was whether the sort of " goodness " of which the public men of Athens are examples can be taught.   Since this " goodness " is just another name for " tactful management " of affairs, it obviously cannot be " taught." A man has to acquire tact by the handling of affairs and men for himself ; you cannot teach the theory of it.   But political tact is something very different from anything Socrates understood by goodness.   There is thus no real confusion or shifting of ground, so far as he is concerned.   Protagoras is in a different position. By his own showing, the " goodness " he aims at teaching is just the secret of political success, and political success really does depend on a " tact " which cannot be taught.   Hence Protagoras really does combine incompatible positions when he asserts both that " goodness " is not knowledge, and also that it can be taught. If by " goodness " we mean what Protagoras defined as " success in managing the affairs of your household and city," he is right in maintaining that goodness is not knowledge, but clearly wrong in holding that it is an " art " which he can teach.[1]

See further :

RITTER, C.—*Platon*, i. 308–342.
RAEDER, H.—*Platons philosophische Entwickelung*, 106–111.
NATORP, P.—*Platons Ideenlehre*, 10–18.
GOMPERZ, TH.—*Griechische Denker*, i. 250–264.
STEWART, J. A.—*The Myths of Plato*, 212–258 (*The Protagoras Myth*).
DITTMAR, H.—*Aeschines von Sphettus*, 186–212 (on Aeschines' dialogue *Callias*, where, however, the author's chronology of the life of Callias is wrong.   Callias had two sons, both in at least their later 'teens in 399.   *Apol.* 20a–c.)

---

[1] Cf. Burnet, *Early Greek Philosophy, Part I.*, 170–179.

CHAPTER XI

THE *REPUBLIC*

THE *Republic* is at once too long a work, and too well known by numerous excellent summaries and commentaries, to require or permit analysis on the scale we have found necessary in dealing with the *Phaedo* or *Protagoras*. We must be content to presume the student's acquaintance with its contents, and to offer some general considerations of the relation of its main theses to one another and to those of dialogues already examined.

To begin with, it is desirable to have a definite conception of the assumed date of the conversation and the character of the historical background presupposed. It should be clear that Athens is supposed to be still, to all appearance at any rate, at the height of her imperial splendour and strength.[1] Also, the time is apparently one of profound peace. No reference is made to military operations ; though the company consists mainly of young men of military age, no explanation of their presence at home is offered. Yet Plato's two elder brothers, Adimantus and Glaucon, who are both young men, have already distinguished themselves in a battle near Megara (368*c*), which can hardly be any other than that of the year 424 (Thuc. iv. 72). We have to add that the sophist Thrasymachus is assumed to be at the height of his fame, and we know that he was already prominent enough to be made the butt of a jest in the first play of Aristophanes, produced in the year 427.[2] Similarly, the tone of Socrates' initial remarks about old age as an unknown road on which he will yet have to travel shows that we are to think of him as still very far from the age (sixty) at which a man officially became a γέρων at Athens. Damonides of Oea is referred to at 400*b* as still alive, and since we have the evidence of Isocrates for the statement that he " educated " Pericles, we cannot suppose him to have been born much, if at all, later than the year 500. All these considerations, taken together, suggest that the supposed date of the conversation must be about the time of the

---

[1] This is made especially clear by the tone of the satire on democracy viii. 557 ff., where it is unmistakably the powerful, opulent, and formidable democracy of the Archidamian war that Socrates is depicting. The year 411, assumed as the dramatic date by some commentators, is about the worst of all possible choices. It is rendered impossible by the fact that in the *Republic*, Cephalus, the father of Polemarchus and Lysias, is still alive, though an old man. The date is thus before his death and the removal of his sons to Thurii, whence they returned, after a good number of years, to Athens in 411 (*Vit. Lysiae*, c. 1).

[2] Aristoph., Fr. 198.

peace of Nicias (421 B.C.) or the preceding truce of 422. It is important to remember that Athens came out of the Archidamian war, though not quite on the terms she might have got, but for the folly of the democratic leaders after Sphacteria (425), far and away the richest and most powerful of the combatant states, with the main of her empire intact. For purposes of illustration the student should read by the side of the *Republic*, the *Wasps* and *Peace* of Aristophanes, as illustrative of the conditions of the time. Socrates must be thought of as being no more than middle-aged, somewhere about fifty years old, and we must bear in mind that it was at most a couple of years before that Aristophanes had brought him on the stage in the *Clouds*. Plato himself would be a mere child of some five to seven years.

There is nothing in the dialogue to support any of the fanciful modern speculations about a possible " earlier edition " without the central books which discuss the character and education of the " philosopher-kings," or the possible existence of the first book by itself as a " dialogue of search." On the contrary, the appearances are all in favour of regarding the whole as having been planned as a whole. It is not until we come to the sixth book that we are in sight of the " goodness " which is one and the same thing with knowledge ; the goodness of the " guardians " of *Republic* ii.–iv. has been carefully marked as remaining all along at the level of " opinion." It rises no higher than loyalty to a sound national tradition taken on trust, and is thus so far on a level with the " popular " goodness of the *Phaedo*, though the tradition in this case is that of a morally sounder society than that of Athens, or of any existing Greek πόλις.[1] Hence it is inconceivable that Plato should ever have composed a *Republic* which ignored the central points of Socratic ethics. The first book, again, serves its present purpose as an introduction to the whole work perfectly. In outline, all the main ideas which underlie the description of the ideal man and the ideal society are there, the conception of the life of measure (in the argument about πλεονεξία), the thought of happiness as dependent on " function " or vocation, and the rest ; but all are stated, as they should be in an Introduction, in their abstract form ; their real significance only becomes apparent as they are clothed with concrete detail in the full-length picture of the good man and the good community. To me it is inconceivable that *Republic* i. should ever have been planned except as the introduction to a work covering the ground of the *Republic* as we have it.[2]

[1] This is why in Book IV. the virtues, as practised in the "reformed" city, are still distinguishable, so that different virtues are most specially prominent in different sections of society, and, again, why we are told at iv. 430c 3 that the account just given of courage is adequate only as a description of " citizen " courage, and may have to be revised later on. The " unity of the virtues " only emerges in *Republic* vi. when we come to discuss the character of the " philosopher-king."

[2] The only specious argument for an earlier *Urstaat* is that, at the beginning of the *Timaeus*, where Socrates is made to recapitulate the contents

It has sometimes been asked whether the *Republic* is to be regarded as a contribution to ethics or to politics. Is its subject " righteousness," or is it the " ideal state " ? The answer is that from the point of view of Socrates and Plato there is no distinction, except one of convenience, between morals and politics. The laws of right are the same for classes and cities as for individual men. But one must add that these laws are primarily laws of personal morality ; politics is founded on ethics, not ethics on politics. The primary question raised in the *Republic* and finally answered at its close is a strictly ethical one, What is the rule of right by which a man ought to regulate his life ? And it should be noted that the first simple answer offered to the question, that of Cephalus and Polemarchus, makes no reference at all to the πόλις and its νόμοι, and this, no doubt, is why it is put into the mouths of speakers who were not Athenian πολῖται but protected aliens. The political reference is brought into the dialogue in the first instance by Thrasymachus, who insists on treating morality as a mere product and reflex of the habit of obedience to a political κρεῖττον or " sovereign." Socrates finds it necessary to keep this political reference in view throughout his own argument, but he is careful to explain that the reason for studying the public life of classes and communities is simply that we see the principles of right and wrong " writ large " in them ; we study the " larger letters " in order to make out the smaller by their aid. All through, the ultimate question is that raised by Glaucon and Adimantus, what right and wrong are " in the soul of the possessor." This comes out most clearly of all in the part of the work which is written with most palpable passion, the accounts of the degenerate types of city and men. Each defective constitution is studied and the tone of public life fostered by it noted, in order that we may learn by this light to read the heart of the individual man. We see the real moral flaw in the outwardly decent man who regards becoming and remaining " well-off " as the finest thing in life, by considering the quality of national life in a merchant-city, like Carthage, where the " merchant-prince " is dominant and gives the tone to the whole community, and so on. The *Republic*, which opens with an old man's remarks about approaching death and apprehension of what may come after death, and ends with a myth of judgment, has all through for its central theme a question more intimate than that of the best form of government or the most eugenic system of propagation ; its question is, How does a man attain or forfeit eternal salvation ? For good or

of the *Republic* (*Tim.* 17a–19a), nothing is said about the philosopher-kings and their education. Nothing, however, is said about the account of the " imperfect " types of men and societies in *Republic* viii.–ix. either. The silence of the *Timaeus* about everything which follows *Republic* v. can be explained conjecturally in more ways than one. The simplest explanation is that the real purpose of the recapitulation is to serve as an introduction to the projected but unfinished *Critias*. Any explanation of the facts must remain conjectural, since Plato wrote only the opening pages of the projected *Critias*, and we do not know how he meant to develop the story.

bad, it is intensely " other-worldly." Man has a soul which can attain everlasting beatitude, and this beatitude it is the great business of life to attain. The social institutions or the education which fit him to attain it are the right institutions or education ; all others are wrong. The " philosopher " is the man who has found the way which leads to this beatitude. At the same time, no man lives to himself, and the man who is advancing to beatitude himself is inevitably animated by the spirit of a missionary to the community at large. Hence the philosopher cannot be true to himself without being a philosopher-king ; he cannot win salvation without bringing it down to his society. That is how the *Republic* views the relation between ethics and statesmanship.

The fundamental issue is raised in the introductory book with great artistic skill. From the simple observations of old Cephalus about the tranquillity with which a man conscious of no undischarged obligations can look forward to whatever the unseen world may have to bring, Socrates takes the opportunity to raise the question what δικαιοσύνη, taken in the sense of the supreme rule of right—" morality " as we might say—is. What is the rule by which a man should order the whole of his life ? Before we can embark on the question seriously, we need to be satisfied that it is not already answered for us by the ordinary current moral maxims of the decent man ; that there really is a problem to be solved. Next we have to see that the theories in vogue among the superficially " enlightened," which pretend to answer the question in a revolutionary way, are hopelessly incoherent. Only when we have seen that neither current convention nor current anti-conventionalism has any solution of the problem are we in a position to raise it and answer it by the true method. Thus there are three points of view to be considered: that of the unphilosophical decent representative of current convention, sustained by Cephalus and his son Polemarchus ; that of the " new morality," represented by Thrasymachus ; and that of sober philosophical thinking, represented by Socrates.

As to the first point of view, that of decent acquiescence in a respectable convention which has never been criticized, we note, and this may serve as a corrective to exaggerations about the extent to which " the Greeks " identified morality with the νόμος of a " city," that Plato has deliberately chosen as the exponent of moral convention a representative who, as a μέτοικος, naturally makes no appeal to the " city " and its usages ; the rule of Cephalus is specially characteristic not of a πόλις but of a profession, and a profession which in all ages has enjoyed the reputation of sound and homely rectitude. The old man's morality is just that which is characteristic of the honourable merchant of all places. " Right," according to him, means " giving to every man his own, and speaking the truth," *i.e.* a man is to honour his business obligations and his word is to " be as good as his bond " ; the man who acts thus has discharged the whole duty of man. The point of the conversation

begun between Socrates and Cephalus, and continued with Polemarchus as respondent, is merely that this simple rule for business
transactions cannot be regarded as a supreme principle of morality
for two reasons. (1) There are cases where to adhere to the letter
of it would be felt at once to be a violation of the spirit of right ;
(2) if you do try to put it into the form of a universal principle by
explaining that " giving a man his own " means " treating him as
he deserves," " giving him his due," however you understand the
words " a man's due," you get again a morally *bad* principle.[1]
Against Polemarchus, who thinks that morality can be reduced to
" giving every one his due " in the sense of being a thoroughly
valuable friend to your friends and a dangerous enemy to your foes
(a working morality expressed in the " gnomic " verses of Solon
and Theognis), it has to be shown that to make such a principle
of conduct acceptable to a decent man's conscience, we must at
least take our " friends " and " foes " to mean " the good " and
" the bad " respectively, and that, even then, the principle is
condemned by the fact that it makes it one half of morality to
" do evil " to some one. The argument equally disposes incidentally
of the " sophistic " conception of " goodness " as a kind of special
accomplishment by showing : (1) that in any definite situation
in life, the " accomplishment " needed to confer the benefit demanded by that situation is some kind of skill other than " goodness " ; and (2) that all these accomplishments can be put to a
morally bad, as well as to a morally good, *use.* Virtue, for example,
will not make a man the best of all advisers about an investment,
and the knowledge which does make a man a good counsellor on
such a matter also makes him a very dangerous adviser, if he
chooses to use it for a fraudulent end. This prepares us to discover
later on that though " goodness " in the end is knowledge and
nothing but knowledge, it is something quite different from the
" arts " or " accomplishments " with which the professional
" teachers of goodness " confound it.

When we come to the anti-conventional " immoralism " of the
" enlightenment," it is important to remark that Thrasymachus
is made to overstate the position ; as Glaucon says, at the opening
of the second book, he has bungled the case. (As we know of no
reason why Plato should misrepresent a prominent man of the
preceding generation, the violence and exaggeration is presumably
a genuine characteristic of the actual Thrasymachus, and it is used

---

[1] The apparent triviality of the examples chosen by Socrates to illustrate
his point is only apparent. He takes simple illustrations, as Professor Burnet
has said, because the issue at stake is most readily seen in such cases. Thus,
e.g., the question whether one should return a weapon to a lunatic because it is
his raises the problem whether it is the duty of a banker to honour all the
cheques of a wealthy senile client, or of a solicitor to take his instructions for
a manifestly insane will without any warning to his family ; and these are
questions of moment, not only for the casuist but for the legislator. Grotius
has to begin with precisely the same kind of elementary example when he
wants to discuss the problems connected with international good faith in the
De iure belli et pacis.

mainly for humorous effect. Thrasymachus, like modern authors whom one could name, must not be taken to mean all he says too seriously. Bluster is a mannerism with him, as it is in fact with some successful advocates. The serious statement of the immoralist case is reserved for Glaucon.) As Thrasymachus states the case, there is really no such thing as moral obligation. What men call " right " is " the interest of the superior." (In this phrase, τὸ κρεῖττον is to be taken as neuter, and what is meant is " the sovereign " in a community.) The theory is that right or morality is a synonym for conformity to νόμος (the institutions and traditions of the community). But these institutions have been originally imposed on the community by the " sovereign " purely with a view to his own benefit, and the *only* reason why they should be respected is that the " sovereign " has the power to make you suffer if you do not respect them. Hence, unlike Hobbes, Thrasymachus feels no need to justify the absolutism of the " sovereign " by appeal to the " social contract " by which he has been invested with his sovereign powers ; since he does not regard " right " as having any meaning, he has not to show that the sovereign has any right to obedience ; it is sufficient to observe that his *power* to enforce obedience is guaranteed by the simple fact that he *is the* sovereign. Like the imaginary prehistoric kings and priests of Rousseau or Shelley, he has succeeded in imposing his will on the community and there is nothing more to be said. In practice this theory would work out exactly like that of Callicles in the *Gorgias*, but there is the important difference that, in theory, the two immoralists start from opposite assumptions. Callicles is a partisan of φύσις who honestly believes that in the " order of things " the strong man has a genuine *right* to take full advantage of his strength ; Thrasymachus is pushing the opposite view of all morality as mere "convention" to an extreme. The evidence for his theory is, in the first instance, simply the fact that all governments make "high treason," the subversion of the sovereign, the gravest crime. The first care of every government is to ensure the constitution, whatever it is, against revolution. By pure confusion of thought the safeguarding of the constitution is then identified with the safeguarding of the private interests of the particular persons who happen at any moment to be exercising the function of sovereignty. Subsequently an appeal is made to the familiar facts about the " seamy side " of political and private life, the unscrupulosity and self-seeking of politicians, and the readiness of private men to cheat one another and the community, to job for their families and the like, when the chance offers. It would be easy to show that the indictment is drawn up with careful reference to features of contemporary Athenian life, but the reasoning of Thrasymachus rests on the further assumption that the seamy side of life is its only side ; life is robbing and being robbed, cheating and being cheated, and nothing else. This is, after all, not an impartial picture even of a society groaning under the rule of a tyrant or a demagogue, and when Socrates comes to reply, he also finds no difficulty in appealing to equally " real " facts of a very different kind, *e.g.* the fact that a politician expects to get some sort of remuneration for his work, which shows that the work itself is not necessarily a " paying " thing. Even in the world as it is, the " strong man's " life is not all getting and no giving.

The fact is that Thrasymachus, like Mr. Shaw or Mr. Chesterton, has the journalist's trick of facile exaggeration. He is too good a journalist to be an *esprit juste*, and the consequence is that he lands himself in a dilemma. If his " sovereign " who has a view only to the interests of " number one " is meant to be an actual person or body of persons, it is obvious, as Socrates says, that he is not infallible. It is not true that the moral code and the institutions of any society are simply adapted to gratify the personal desires of the sovereign who, according to Thrasymachus, devises them, or to further his interests ; judged by that standard, every existing set of νόμοι is full of blunders.[1] But if you assume that the sovereign is always alive to his own interests and always embodies them in his regulations, your sovereign is a creature of theory, an " ideal," and you lay yourself open at once to the line of argument adopted by Socrates to show that his worth depends on fulfilling a social function, independently of the question whether he gets any private advantage from his position or not. The " new morality " of Thrasymachus must therefore stand or fall on its own merits as an ethical theory ; it derives no real support from his speculations about the origin of government in the strong man's " will to power."

On the argument by which Socrates meets the strictly ethical assertion that " conventional " morality is a mere expression of the low intelligence and weakness of the " herd," all I wish to remark here is that he is guided throughout by the Pythagorean analogy between tuned string, healthy body and healthy mind, which is the key to half the best thought of the Greek moralists. The immoralist's case is really disposed of in principle by the often misunderstood argument about πλεονεξία (*Rep.* i. 349*b*–350*c*). The reasoning already contains in germ the whole doctrine of the " right mean " afterwards developed in the *Philebus* and the *Ethics* of Aristotle. The point is that in all applications of intelligence to the conduct of activity of any kind, the supreme wisdom is to know just where to stop, and to stop just there and nowhere else.

---

[1] For example, on Thrasymachus' theory, the δῆμος, which is the κρείττον at Athens, must be supposed to have adopted the institution of ostracism in the interests of the δῆμος, as a safeguard against 'would-be " dictators." But in actual working the institution favours the aspirant to a dictatorship by giving him a chance to remove the natural leaders of a " constitutional opposition." The selection of magistrates by lot, again, must be supposed to have been adopted to equalize the chances of the citizens ; but, as its ancient critics said, it may work the wrong way, since it gives the μισόδημος as good a chance of office as anyone else, whereas he would be handicapped under an elective system by his known or suspected hostility to the constitution.

The "wise man," like the musician or the physician, knows what the fool or the quack never knows, "how much is enough." The mistake common to the fool in the management of life and the bungler tuning a musical instrument or treating a sick man, is that they believe in the adage that you "can't have too much of a good thing." On the strength of this misleading faith, one ruins his instrument, another kills his patient, and the third spoils his own life. There is a "just right" in all the affairs of life, and to go beyond it is to spoil your performance, and consequently to miss "happiness." Once grasped, this point leads on to the other that the "just right" in any performance means the adequate discharge of function, and that happiness, in turn, depends on discharge of function. The introduction to the *Republic* thus leads us up to precisely the teleological conception of the rule of conduct from which Butler starts in the Preface to his *Sermons*. "Happiness" depends on "conformity to *our* nature as active beings." What "active principles" that nature comprises and how they are organized into a "system" we learn in the immediately following books.

With the opening of the second book, we are introduced to the genuine version of the immoralist doctrine of which Thrasymachus had given a mere exaggeration, the theory that regard for moral rules is a *pis aller*, though one which is unfortunately unavoidable by ordinary humanity. The theory is often referred to as that of Glaucon and Adimantus, but it should be noted that Adimantus takes no part in the statement of the theory and that Glaucon, who does explain it fully, is careful to dissociate himself from it; it is given as a speculation widely current in educated circles of the time of the Archidamian war and supported by specious though, as Glaucon holds, unsound arguments. His own position is simply that of an advocate speaking from his brief. He undertakes to make an effective defence of the case which Thrasymachus had mismanaged, in order that it may really be disproved, not merely dismissed without thorough examination of its real merits. The important feature of his argument is not so much the well-known statement of the "social contract" theory of the *origin* of moral codes as the analysis of existing morality to which the historical speculation is meant to lead up. The point is that "men practise the rules of right not because they choose, but because they cannot help themselves." At heart every one is set simply on gratifying his own passions, but you will best succeed in doing this by having the fear of your fellow-men before your eyes and abstaining from aggression on them. If you get the chance to gratify your passions without moral scruples, and can be sure not to be found out and made to suffer, you would be a fool not to benefit by your opportunity. This is the point of the imaginative fiction about the "ring of Gyges." The real fact which gives the sting to the fiction is simply that we all know that there is no human virtue which would not be deteriorated by confidence of immunity from detection. None of us could safely be trusted to come through the ordeal with our characters undepraved. We are all prone to lower our standard when we believe that there is no eye, human or divine, upon us. There can be little doubt that a theory of this kind, which amounts to the view suggested as possible by Kant that no single human act has ever been done simply " from duty," was a current one in the age of Socrates, and we can even name one of the sources upon which Plato is presumably drawing. The theory attempts to combine in one formula the two rival conceptions of " nature " and " convention " as regulative of action. It amounts to saying that there is a morality of unscrupulous egoism which is that of " nature " and is practised by us all when we are safe from detection, and another and very different " morality of convention," a morality of mutual respect for " claims and counter-claims " which we are obliged to conform to, so far as our behaviour is exposed to the inspection of our fellows. This doctrine is taught in so many words in a long fragment, discovered at Oxyrhynchus, of Socrates' contemporary and rival, Antiphon the " sophist." [1] According to Antiphon, the " wise man," who means to make a success of life, will practise " conventional justice " when he believes that his conduct will be observed by others, but will fall back on " natural justice " whenever he can be sure of not being found out. This is exactly the position Glaucon means to urge in his apologue. What he wants Socrates to prove is that the conception of the two rival moralities is a false one ; that mutual respect of rights is the true morality of " nature," as much as of " convention," the course of conduct suitable to " our nature as agents." The proof is supplied in the end by the doctrine of the " parts of the soul " in *Republic* iv., exactly as Butler attempts to supply a similar proof of the same thesis by his account of the hierarchy of the " active principles " in his three *Sermons on Human Nature*.

The contribution of Adimantus to the discussion is that he places the argument for regarding respect for the rights of one's neighbour as a mere cover for self-seeking on a basis independent of all speculations about moral origins. The tone of his speech is carefully differentiated from that of Glaucon. Glaucon, as he himself admits, is simply making the ablest forensic defence he can of his case, and can jest about the gusto with which he has thrown himself into the cause of a dubious client ; Adimantus speaks from the heart in a vein of unmistakable moral indignation. He complains not of the speculations of dashing advanced thinkers, but of the low grounds on which the defence of morality is based by the very parties who might be presumed to have it most at heart. Parents who are sincerely anxious that their sons should grow up to be honest and honourable men regularly recommend virtue simply on the ground of its value as a means to worldly success and enjoyment ; they never dwell on the intrinsic worth of virtue

[margin note] nature (egoism) convention (mutual respect of rights)

[1] *Oxyrhynchus Papyri*, XI, no. 1364.

itself. On the contrary, their habitual insistence on the hardness of the path of virtue and the pleasantness of vicious courses suggests that they think virtue in itself no true good. And the poets all speak the same language. When you come to the representatives of religion, who might be expected to take the highest line, you find that they are worst of all. They terrify the sinner by their stories of judgment to come, but only as a preliminary step to assuring him that they will, for a small consideration, make his peace with Heaven by easy ritual performances and sacraments which involve no change of heart. The whole influence of religion and education seems to be thrown into the scale against a genuine inward morality, and this is a much more serious matter than the speculations of a few clever men about the " original contract " and the motives which prompted it. We need a new religion and a new educational system. (We must, of course, note that the indictment of religion is throughout aimed not at the official cultus of the city, but at the Orphic and similar sects ; the vehemence with which Adimantus speaks seems to indicate an intense personal hostility to these debased " salvationists " which is presumably a real trait of the man's character.)

The effect of the two speeches, taken in conjunction, is to impose on Socrates the task of indicating, by a sound analysis of human nature, the real foundations of morality in the very constitution of man, and of showing how education and religion can be, and ought to be, made allies, not enemies, of a sound morality. This, we may say, is the simple theme of the whole of the rest of the dialogue. Some comments may be offered on the various stages of the demonstration. The theme has already been propounded in the demand of Glaucon that it shall be made clear how "justice " and " injustice " respectively affect the inner life of their possessor, independently of any sanctions, human or divine. It is to the answer to this question that Socrates is really addressing himself in the picture of an ideally good man living in an ideal relation to society, which culminates in the description, given in Books VI.–VII., of the philosopher-king, his functions in society, and the discipline by which he is fitted for their discharge, as well as by the briefer studies, in Books VIII. and IX., of increasing degeneration from the true type of manhood. The answer to Adimantus, so far as his indictment of education is concerned, has to be found in the account of the training of the young into worthy moral character by a right appeal, through literature and art, to the imagination (Books III.–IV.); his attack on immoral religion may be said to be the direct occasioin both of the regulation of early " nursery tales " with which Socrates opens his scheme of reform in Book II., and of the magnificent myth of judgment with which the dialogue closes, itself a specimen of the way in which the religious imagination may be made the most potent reinforcement of a noble rule of life. In dealing with the details of the positive contributions of the dialogue to both politics and religion, it is necessary to observe some caution, if we are to avoid specious misunderstandings. We must remember all through that the political problem of the right organization of a state is avowedly introduced not on its own account, but because we see human virtue and vice " writ large " in the conduct of a state or a political party, and may thus detect in the community the real moral significance of much that would escape our notice if we only studied humanity in the individual.[1] Hence we shall probably be misunderstanding if we imagine, as has sometimes been imagined, that either Socrates or Plato is seriously proposing a detailed new constitution for Athens, and still more if we imagine that either would have approved of the introduction of the new constitution by revolution into a society wholly unprepared to receive it. The most we are entitled to say about any of the detailed proposals of the *Republic* is that Plato presents them as what, according to Socrates, is most in accord with the moral nature of man, and may therefore be expected to be approximately realized in a thoroughly sound condition of society.

(1) In the impressive picture given in Books II.–IV. of the working of the principle of specialization of function according to vocation, which will ultimately turn out to be the foundation of all " justice," there are one or two points which have perhaps not received sufficient attention, and may therefore be briefly noted.

I think it is clear that we must not take the description of the three successive stages through which Socrates' community passes as meant to convey any speculation about the beginnings of civilization. The " first city " is already on the right side of the line which separates civilization from barbarism. Its inhabitants are already agriculturists, permanently cultivating a fixed territory ; they are at home in the working of metals, and in some respects they exhibit an advance in economic organization on the Athens of the Periclean age. (Thus they have their clothes made by a distinct class of artisans, not woven in the house by the women of the family, as was still largely the custom at Athens.) The notion that we are reading a satire on Antisthenes and the " return to nature " is merely ludicrous. What is really described is, in the main, the condition of a normal πόλις where the citizens are farming-folk. To me it seems clear that, so far as Plato has any particular historical development before his mind, he is thinking of what Athens itself had been before the period of victory and expansion which made her an imperial city and the centre of a world-wide sea-borne commerce. (This is suggested almost irresistibly by the assumption that even the " first city," like Athens, requires to import a good many of its necessaries from elsewhere,

---

[1] For example, punctuality is what is commonly considered a " minor social virtue." A man is not thought much the worse of, if he is always late at an appointment. But when we see how the issue of a campaign or even of a war may be affected, if expected reinforcements arrive just a little too late, we are reminded that it is a dangerous thing to call any virtue a " minor " one. The contemplation of the " large letters " teaches us not to despise " minute particulars."

and consequently contains merchants and sailors, and is already producing for the foreign market.) In the description of the steps by which this little society expands and becomes a city with a multitude of artificial wants, and trades which minister to them, thus acquiring a " superfluous population " which must somehow be provided for, we can hardly see anything but a conscious reflection of the actual expansion of Attica under Cimon and Pericles.

(2) We must, of course, note that not all the artificial wants which arise in the city as it becomes " luxurious " are meant to be condemned. Even the demand for delicacies for the table is an indication that the standard of living is rising, and all social students know that a rise in this standard is by no means an entirely unwholesome thing. It is more significant that one of the chief features of the development is the growth of professions like those of the actor and the *impresario*. People are beginning to feel the need of amusement, and this means, of course, that they are becoming conscious that they have minds, which need to be fed no less than their bodies. Presumably the reason why Socrates could not look for " justice " in the community of farmers, but has to wait for the " luxurious city " to come into existence and be reformed, is precisely that the members of the first society would hardly be alive to the fact that they have souls at all ; they could not feel the need for a daily supply of any bread but that which perishes ; they have no " social problem."

(3) It has been asked why, when over-population leads to an acute social problem, aggressive warfare rather than colonization should be assumed as the only way out of the difficulty. The answer, of course, is simple. In the first place, peaceful colonization of derelict territories had never been a feasible procedure for a Greek city. The founders of the ancient and famous cities we call the " Greek colonies " had regularly had to wrest their sites from previous occupants not much inferior to themselves in " culture." There was no America or Australia in the Mediterranean basin. And in the second, Socrates knows his countrymen and is well aware that a Greek " surplus population " would not be likely to transport itself across the seas in quest of a new home so long as there was a fair chance of a successful inroad on its neighbours. He is, as he says, not discussing the morality of the proceeding ; he is merely noting that it is what the city would, in fact, do. (In *theory*, to be sure, it was a commonplace that an aggressive war of expansion is not a *iustum bellum*.) And the point he wishes to insist on is the perfectly sound one, that the experience of having to make common sacrifices and face common dangers in war, just or unjust (but when did any nation throw its soul into the prosecution of a war which it seriously believed to be unjust ?), does more to generate self-devotion in citizens than any other. War gives the social reformer his chance, for the double reason that it produces the temper which is willing to live hard, make sacrifices, and submit to discipline, and, when it is hard contested and

the issue doubtful, it makes the necessity for sacrifice and submission pressing and patent. We who have lived through the events of 1914–1918 should be able to understand this from our own experience.

(4) It is unhappily customary to make two bad mistakes about the nature of the reconstituted social structure which, in Socrates' narrative, emerges from the experience provided by a great war. It is called a " system of caste," and the matter is then made worse by calling the δημιουργοί who form the third of Socrates' social classes, " the working class," or " the industrial class." The immediate consequence is that the social and political theory of the *Republic* suffers a complete travesty, due to the unconscious influence of ideas derived from our experience of modern " industrialism." To guard against misconceptions of this kind, we must, in the first place, be clear on the point that there is no system of " caste " in the *Republic*. The characteristic of " caste " is that one is born into it, and that once born into a caste it is impossible to rise above it. You may forfeit your caste in various ways, as a Brahmin does by crossing the seas, but no one can become a Brahmin if he is not born one. Now Socrates believes, rightly or wrongly, that heredity is a powerful force in the intellectual and moral sphere ; as a general rule, a man will find his natural place in the " class " to which his parents belong (all the more, no doubt, as procreation is to be placed under careful " eugenic " regulations). But the rule has its notable exceptions : there are those who prove quite unfitted for the work of the class into which they are born, and those who show themselves qualified to take their place in a higher class. Hence it is part of Socrates' idea that the early life of the individual shall be under close and constant surveillance, and subjected to repeated tests of character and intelligence. There is to be every opportunity for the discovery and degradation of the unworthy and the promotion of the worthy; no one is to be ensured by the accident of birth in a particular social status, and no one is to be excluded by it from rising to the highest eminence. This qualification of the principle of heredity by the antithetic principle of the " open career " for ability and character is absolutely destructive of " caste." The philosopher-kings or the soldiers of the Socratic state are no more a " caste " than Napoleon's marshals. And, in the second place, the δημιουργοί do not correspond to what we call the " artisan " or " working " class, *i.e.* to wage-earners or persons who maintain themselves by selling their labour. They include our wage-earners, but they also include the great bulk of what we should call the civilian population, independently of economic status. The thought underlying the distinction of the three classes has primarily nothing to do with economic status. It is simply that in any full-grown society, you may distinguish three types of social service. There is a small section which serves the community directly by directing its public life, making rules and regulations and controlling policy. These are the " complete " or " full-grown " guardians. There is necessarily

an executive arm, whose business it is to support the directive action of the first class by the necessary physical force against enemies from without and malcontents and offenders from within, the army and police. It is this body which Socrates calls by the name ἐπίκουροι, and it should be noted that he selects the word not merely for the appropriateness of its literal sense ("helpers," "auxiliaries"), but because it was, as we can see e.g. from Herodotus, the technical name for the trained professional body-guard of monarchs, and therefore indicates the important point that the "executive" of the Socratic State is a carefully trained professional fighting force, not an amateur constabulary or militia. The associations of the word are the same as those of such an English expression as "the Guards," and Socrates does not scruple to apply to his ἐπίκουροι the opprobrious name by which such permanent professional soldiers were called in Greek democracies, which objected on principle to their existence. They *are*, like the Ionian and Carian soldiers of an Amasis, μισθωτοί ("mercenaries"),[1] except for two considerations—that they are citizens, not aliens, and that the only μισθός they get is their "keep." These two classes are distinguished by the fact that they are the only direct "servants of the public." What remains is the whole bulk of the "civilian population," with the exception of the "guardians"— every one who does not directly serve the public either as a states- man or as a soldier or policeman. Thus the δημιουργοί include not only all the so-called "working class," but the whole body of professional men, and the whole class of employers of labour. Since the two superior classes are expressly forbidden to have any kind of property, personally or as classes, it follows that the whole "capital" of the State is in the hands of the δημιουργοί. A "merchant prince," under such a classification, is just as much one of the "industrials" as his clerks and office-boys. Much purely perverse criticism of the scheme would have been obviated if this simple consideration had been duly kept in mind.

(5) An immediate consequence is that, in spite of all that has been said about the "socialism" or "communism" of the *Republic*, there is really neither socialism nor communism to be found in the work. The current confusions on the point are probably due mainly to the mistaken notion that the emphatic demand of Book IV.[2] for the banishment of "wealth" and "penury" from society must be the proposal of a communist, or at least of a socialist. This assumption is, on the face of it, absurd. The point made in Book IV. is simply that a man's character and work in life will be spoiled equally by the possession of irresponsible wealth, with no adequate social duties attached to it, and by a penury which breaks his spirit and forces him to do bad and scamped work in order to keep himself alive. A man may be aware of these dangers without adopting either the socialist or the communist theory of the right economic organization of society. In point of fact,

---

[1] *Rep*. iv. 419a–420a. [2] *Rep*. iv. 421d ff.

nothing much is said in the book about the economic organization of the only class who have any economic function at all, the δημιουργοί, but the implication of what is said is that there are differences of wealth among them, and that the "means of production and distribution" are individually owned and operated. In Book VIII. it is carefully indicated that one of the first signs of the degeneration of the ideal State into a "timocracy" is the acquisition of real and personal property by the two superior classes (they "appropriate lands and houses," (viii. 547*b*)), but nothing is said of the first introduction of private property among the δημιουργοί, who thus must be presumed to have enjoyed it all along. There are other more general considerations which point to the same conclusion. For one thing, both pure communism and "State monopoly" of the means of production are so alien to the system of a Greek πόλις— the "State ownership" of the silver mines at Laurium was an exception at Athens—that Socrates could not be presumed to be contemplating either, unless he expressly explained himself. For another, it is clear that agriculture is the assumed economic foundation of the life of his city, and agriculture is just the pursuit to which a "socialistic" economic system is least easy of application. Collectivism is historically an ideal of the "proletariat" of great towns ; the farmer has always been tenacious of the very different ideal of peasant ownership. And it is noticeable that in the *Laws* Plato declares himself for peasant ownership in its extreme form. The citizens there not merely own their "holdings" but own them as their inalienable patrimonies, and "common cultivation" is expressly forbidden (v. 740*a–b*). We may fairly take it that if he had intended to represent his master as advocating views of a radically different type, he would have made the point unmistakable. Hence, it seems to me that we must recognize that the economic organization of the ideal city of the *Republic* is definitely "individualistic." Yet we must not suppose that Plato is in any sense putting Socrates forward as a conscious "anti-socialist." The real object of the one restriction of ownership on which the dialogue insists as fundamental, the prohibition of all property to the direct servants of the State, is not economic. The purpose is the same as that of the still more emphatic prohibition of family life, the elimination of the conflict between public duty and personal interest. What Socrates wants, as Bosanquet has said, is simply to divorce political power from financial influence. Wealth is to have no political influence in his society ; it is "plutocracy," not individual ownership, which he is determined to suppress. His rulers are much more in the position of a mediaeval military monastic order than in that of a collectivist bureaucracy.

(6) It may not be unnecessary to remark that, as there is no socialism, there is also no "community of women" in the *Republic*. If the reader will take the trouble to work out the consequences of the regulations prescribed for the mating of the guardians, he will find that the impulses of sex and the family affections connected with

them are subjected to much severer restraint than any which has ever been adopted by a Christian society. It is plain that the governing classes, to whom the regulations are meant to apply, are expected to find no gratification for the sexual impulses except on the solemn occasions when they are called on to beget offspring for the State. The extension of the duties of the " guardian " to both sexes of itself carries the consequence that these occasions arise only at long intervals ; and the self-denial implied in the acceptance of such a rule of life might prove to be even severer than that imposed on the monk by his vow of chastity, for the very reason that the inhibition has to be broken through at the time when the State so commands. Indeed, the overwhelming probability is that if any society should attempt to enforce on any part of itself regulations of the kind proposed in the *Republic*, the attempt would fail just because of their intolerable severity. No actual ruling class would be likely to consent to the absolute elimination of the affections of the family circle from its own life, even if it were prepared to reduce the gratification of the physical impulses of sex to the contemplated minimum. The true criticism on the whole treatment of sex in the *Republic* is that, like all non-Christian moralists, rigourist or relaxed, Socrates very much *under*estimates the significance of sex for the whole of the spiritual life. Whatever we may think on this point, it is important to remember that at any rate the general principles which underlie the treatment of the position of women in *Republic* v. are no personal " development " of Plato's ; they belong to the actual Socrates. Aeschines, in the remains of his *Aspasia*, agrees with Plato in representing the philosopher as insisting that " the goodness of a woman is the same as that of a man," and illustrating the thesis by the political abilities of Aspasia and the military achievements of the Persian " Amazon " Rhodogyne.[1] Hence the thought that the duties of statesmanship and warfare should be extended to women must be regarded as strictly Socratic, and the rest of the proposals of *Republic* v. are no more than necessary consequences of this position. If they are to be rejected, we must refute the assumption on which they are based, that the distinction of sex is one which only affects the individual in respect to the part to be played in contributing to procreation and the rearing of a new generation ; we must be prepared to hold that the difference goes deeper and modifies the whole spiritual life profoundly.

(7) There are one or two remarks which may be made about the plan of moral and religious training laid down in Books II. and III., as supplementary to the many excellent studies of this part of the dialogue already in existence. We note that in the proposed purification of the stories by which religious impressions are to be communicated to the very young, it is not merely, nor even mainly, the Homeric mythology to which exception is taken. The crowning offenders are Hesiod and the other theogonists who have related

[1] See the fragments of the *Aspasia* collated in H. Dittmar's *Aeschines von Sphettos*, 275–283.

stories of the violent subversion of older dynasties of gods by younger. This would, of course, include the Orphicists ; Socrates has not forgotten that it was they against whom the denunciation of Adimantus had been more specially directed. It is even more instructive to observe that the attack on tragedy as propagating false religious conceptions is directly aimed at Aeschylus, who has often been mistaken in modern times for an exponent of the religion of simple-minded Athenians. This means two things. It means that to the Periclean age, even as late as the time of the peace of Nicias, Aeschylus was still the great representative of tragedy, in spite of the popularity and renown of Sophocles, who was clearly thought of, as he is thought of in Aristophanes' *Frogs*, as a follower, though a worthy follower, of the great originator of tragedy. If Sophocles had in his own day already been recognized as " the mellow glory of the Attic stage," it would be a mystery why nothing is said of the very unsatisfactory part played by the gods in such a work as the *King Oedipus*. It also means that Socrates is alive to the fact that Aeschylus is no old-fashioned, simple-minded worshipper of Apollo of Delphi, or the Olympians generally. In fact, a " blasphemy " against Apollo is precisely one of the counts brought against him. If it is " atheism " to represent the Olympians as practising a questionable morality, Aeschylus, in spite of Dr. Verrall, is just as much an " atheist " as Euripides, and Socrates rightly makes the point.[1]

(8) Most of the specific criticisms contained in the discussion of the educational employment of poetry and music are, naturally enough, negative. Socrates clearly holds quite strongly that the tendency of the art of his own time is to a love of a relaxed and formless complexity and variety for its own sake, and he thinks it necessary, in the interests of character, as well as of taste, to revert to austerer and more " classical " standards. It is important to remember that these strictures are put into the mouth of Socrates, speaking not later than the peace of Nicias.

We must not, then, suppose that they are aimed at *epigoni* of a later generation. It is not the floridity of Timotheus or Agathon which is the object of attack, but the art of the Periclean age. We are only throwing dust in our own eyes if we suppose that Socrates wants merely to repress the cheap music-hall and the garish melodrama, or the equivalents of freak movements like *Dada*. He is seriously proposing to censure just what we consider the imperishable contributions of Athens to the art and literature of the world, because he holds that they have tendencies which are

[1] It would be singularly unlikely that Aeschylus, who had fought at Marathon, should feel any particular devotion to a god who had " medized " all through the Persian wars. That he felt none is surely proved by the part Apollo is made to play all through the Orestean trilogy. The so-called *naïveté* of Aeschylus, like that of Herodotus, is a product of consummate art. In one important passage where the poet really is expressing personal religious conviction he is at pains to tell us that " popular orthodoxy " is against him (*Agam.* 757, δίχα δ' ἄλλων μονόφρων εἰμί).

unfavourable to the highest development of moral personality.
The magnitude of the sacrifice is the true measure of the value
he ascribes to the end for which he purposes to make it. We shall
not appreciate his position unless we understand quite clearly
that he is in downright earnest with the consideration that the
connexion between aesthetic taste and morality is so close that
whatever tends to ennoble our aesthetic taste directly tends to
elevate our character, and whatever tends to foster a " taste " for
the debased in art tends equally to deprave a man's whole moral
being. Whether we share this conviction or not, the recognition
that Socrates holds it with as little qualification as Ruskin is the
key to the understanding of the whole discussion of early education.
We are allowed also to see incidentally that the suggested reforms
in " musical " education are not meant to be limited to the censure
of what is debased. It is meant that the young " guardian " is to
be subjected from the first to the positive influences of lofty art of
every description. (Painting, embroidery, architecture, and certain
" minor arts "—one naturally thinks of the characteristic Athenian
art of pottery as an example—are expressly specified, *Republic* iii.
401*a* ff.) The growing boy or girl is to live in an environment of
beauty, and the appreciation of the beauty of the environment
is expected to lead insensibly to appreciation of whatever is morally
lovely and of good report in conduct and character. To Socrates'
mind the moral employment of such epithets as " fair," " foul,"
" graceful," " graceless," is no mere metaphor, but a genuine
analogy based on the fact that all sensible beauty is itself the expression and shadow of an inward beauty of character.[1]

(9) Since the whole of the early education contemplated in the
Republic is based on an appeal to taste and imagination, it follows
that, as Socrates is careful to insist, the " goodness " it produces,
though it will be quite sufficient for every class except the statesmen,
is not the true and philosophic goodness of which the *Phaedo* speaks.
As we are carefully reminded, the self-devotion of even the fighting
force of the reformed city is founded on " opinion," not on knowledge ; their virtue is absolute loyalty to a sound tradition which
they have imbibed from their " social environment," not loyalty to
the claims of a *summum bonum* grasped by personal insight. Thus
the virtue described and analysed in Book IV. is still " popular
virtue "; its superiority over the goodness of the average Athenian,
the respectability we have heard Protagoras preaching, is due simply
to the superiority of the " social tradition " of the Socratic city
over that of Periclean democracy. There is thus a double reason

---

[1] Besides painting, embroidery, and architecture, the *Republic* (*l.c.*) mentions weaving, the manufacture of all " vessels " or " furniture " (σκευῶν), and
appears to allude to gardening. There would be plenty of room in Socrates'
city for the arts of design, if there is not much left for the poet and dramatist.
It is an interesting question whether Socrates may not be right in what is his
evident conviction that the greatest art does require a certain austerity and
severe restriction in the matter of its vehicles of expression. I suggest the
question without wishing to answer it.

why we are bound to regard the picture of philosophers and their philosophic virtue drawn in the central books as an essential part of the argument, and to reject any speculations which treat this part of the *Republic* as an afterthought. The account of that supreme goodness which is indistinguishable from knowledge is absolutely necessary in any presentation of Socratic ethics. And again, since the statesmen of the *Republic* have to control and conserve the national traditions, they must have a goodness which is not simply the product of those conditions themselves. There would be no point in subjecting the good soldier to the control of a higher authority if the loyalty to established tradition which is the soldier's point of honour were the highest moral principle attainable. In a *Republic* without the central books, Sparta would have to figure not as an example of the second-best, but as the ideal community itself, whereas the whole point of the description of the " timocracy " in Book VIII. is that a State like Sparta, where the qualities of the mere soldier and sportsman are regarded as a moral ideal, has taken the first fatal step towards complete moral anarchy and, in the ordinary course of things, must be expected to take those which follow in due succession.

Recognition that the whole account of the virtues given in *Republic* iv. is thus provisional should save us from attaching too much importance to the famous doctrine of the "three parts" of the soul. We must be careful to understand that this doctrine does not profess to be original nor to be a piece of scientific psychology. We have already found it presupposed as something known in educated circles in the *Gorgias* and *Phaedo*, and have seen reason to think that it is Pythagorean in origin, as Posidonius is known to have maintained,[1] and directly connected with the theory of the " three lives." This means that we are to take it primarily as a working account of " active principles," or " springs of action," which sufficiently describes the leading types of " goodness," as goodness can be exhibited in any form short of the highest. The scheme will thus be excellently applicable to the goodness of the ἐπίκουροι, for their life is still a form, though the worthiest form, of the φιλότιμος βίος. Loyalty to " honour," " chivalry," " ambition " (though a wholly unselfish ambition), is the utmost we demand of them ; the life of duty remains for the best of them a struggle between a " higher " and a " lower," though a struggle in which the " higher " regularly wins, and this justifies our recognition of a plurality of " parts of the soul " in them. It will be characteristic of their experience that there should be conflicts of " desire " with the tradition of loyalty, and that chivalrous sentiment should be required to act as the reinforcement of loyalty to tradition in the conflict. But the familiar Socratic doctrine is that the " philosopher " who has directly gazed for himself on that supreme good of which the *Symposium* has told us, necessarily desires the good he has beheld ; to him " disobedience to the heavenly vision "

[1] Burnet, *Early Greek Philosophy*[3], 296 n. 2.

would be impossible, exactly as in Christian theology sinful volition is held to be impossible to the saints who actually enjoy the beatific vision of God. Hence it must follow that, as a description of the moral life of the philosopher, the doctrine of the distinct " parts " of the soul becomes increasingly impossible as he makes progress towards the goal at which his activity is consciously directed. This is why the last word of Socrates on the doctrine is to remind us that it may be necessary to revise it when we have grasped the truth of the " divinity " of the soul (*Rep.* x. 611*b* ff.), and why we are told, when it is first introduced, that we must not expect to arrive at exact and certain truth by the line of inquiry we are now pursuing (iv. 435*d*).[1] I do not think it needful to say more about the doctrine here, than to utter a word of warning against two possible misunderstandings. We must avoid every temptation to find a parallel between the " parts " or " figures " in the soul and the modern doctrine of the " three aspects " of a complete " mental process " (cognition, conation, feeling). Plato is not talking about " aspects " of this kind, but about rival springs of action, and the doctrine, as presented in the *Republic*, has no reference to anything but action and " *active* principles," or " determining motives." Also we must not make the blunder of trying to identify the θυμοειδές with " will." From the Socratic point of view, *will* cannot be distinguished from the *judgment* " this is good," and this judgment is always, of course, a deliverance of the λογιστικόν. But the λογιστικόν may pronounce a true judgment, or it may be led into a false one under the influence of present appetite or of anger or ambition, or again, it may only be saved from false judgment because the " sense of honour " comes into collision with the promptings of appetite. To look in the scheme of the *Republic* for some *facultas electiva*, intervening between the formation of a judgment of " practical thinking " and the ensuing action, would be to misunderstand its whole character.

(10) We see then why there can never have been a " first *Republic*," including the " guardians " and the scheme for their early education, but without the philosopher-king and his training in hard scientific thinking. The philosopher-king is doubly demanded as the only adequate embodiment of the Socratic conception of goodness, and also as the authority whose personal insight into good creates the public tradition by which the rest of society is to live. To do full justice to the conception we must not forget that Socrates' statesmen are expected to combine two

---

[1] The suggestion is that in the man who achieves his eternal salvation, the elements of " mettle " and " concupiscence " are, so to say, transubstantiated, swallowed up in intellect. (Of course this " intellect " would not be a " cold, neutral " apprehension of truth, but an intellect on fire with intellectual " passion," a white-hot intelligence.) The same suggestion is made more openly in the *Timaeus* (69*c* ff.). Since we cannot suppose the Pythagorean Timaeus to have learned about the " tripartite soul " for the first time from the conversation of Socrates two days before, the fact that he makes a point of the doctrine indicates that Plato regards it as Pythagorean.

characters which are not often united. They are to be original scientific thinkers of the first order, but equally, they are to be " saints." In the account of the character which will be demanded of them and the natural endowments it presupposes, we hear, indeed, of the qualifications we also should demand of a scientific genius—intellectual quickness, retentive memory and the like—but we hear as much, if not more, of what we should regard as moral qualifications for sainthood, which may be wanting to a man without impairing his eminence in science. How serious Socrates is with this side of the matter is shown by the fact that his philosophers are to be selected exclusively from the best specimens of young people who have come out pre-eminently successful from the hard discipline by which the fighting-force is made. The " auxiliary " himself, as described in the earlier books, is expected to have all the moral elevation of Wordsworth's " Happy Warrior," and the " Happy Warrior " is, in turn, only the raw material out of which years of hard intellectual labour will make the philosophic states-man. If we lose sight of either half of this ideal we shall form a sadly defective notion of what the *Republic* means by a " philo-sopher." By thinking only of the sainthood, we might come to imagine that the philosopher is a kind of Yogi, bent on a selfish absorption into the divine calm of the Absolute ; it would then be a mystery why he is to be trained for his vocation by years of severe mathematical study, and again why, when he has at last descried the vision of the good, he should at once be made to devote all his powers, throughout the prime of his life, to the work of government. If we think only of the science, and say merely that what is aimed at is that the highest intellectual attainments shall be employed in the business of governing the world, we shall be forgetting that many of the most eminent men of science would have been dis-qualified for the supreme position in Socrates' city by defects of character. From the point of view of intellectual eminence we could think, perhaps, of no names so illustrious as those of Galileo and Newton. But it may be taken as certain that both would, by the Socratic standard, be relegated to the class of δημιουργοί. The moral cheapness of the one man's character, the vein of small egotism in the other's, would debar them from being so much as ἐπίκουροι. What we need to understand clearly is that Socrates holds firmly to two positions at once—the position that only a moral hero or saint is fit to be a supreme ruler of men, and the further position that discipline in sheer hard thinking, which can only be won by personal service of science, is the immediate and indis-pensable path to the direct vision of good which makes the saint or hero. We are clearly here on Pythagorean ground. The under-lying thought is just that which seems to have been distinctive of Pythagoras, the thought that " salvation " or " purification " of the soul is to be achieved by science (μαθήματα), not by a ritual of ceremonial holiness ; the philosopher-kings embody the same ideal which had inspired the Pythagorean communities when they set to work to capture the government of the cities of *Magna Graecia*. There is no reason to doubt that the actual Socrates, whose standing complaint against Athenian democracy in the dialogues is that it has no respect, in matters of right and wrong, for the authority of the " man who knows," shared these ideas. They are avowed by Plato himself in his correspondence, where they figure as the true explanation of his apparently Quixotic attempt to make Dionysius II into a possible constitutional monarch by an education in mathematics. No doubt Plato and his friends were expecting from science something more than it has to give, but, as Professor Burnet has said, their proceedings are unintelligible unless we understand that the expectation was passionately sincere.

How preoccupation with science was expected to ennoble character (provided that only the right type of person is allowed to meddle with it), we see most readily by comparing the courage pronounced in Book IV. to be all that is wanted of the ἐπίκουροι with the still higher type of courage declared in Book VI. to be part of the character of the philosopher. The " courage " demanded of the good soldier, in whose make-up θυμός plays the leading part, was defined as steadfast loyalty in the face of perils and seductions to the right *opinions* inculcated in him by education. Its foundation is thus allegiance to a code of honour held with such passion that no fear of pain or death and no bait that can be offered to cupidity is able to overcome it. Clearly a courage like this will carry a man " over the top," make him volunteer for a desperate enterprise, or win him a V.C. But there are situations in life which make a demand for a still higher degree of fortitude. It is matter of experience that a V.C. may not be equal to the task of duty imposed, for example, on a priest whose business it is to tend daily the last hours of the victims of some foul pestilence in a plague-smitten city. Or again a brave soldier, who will face deadly peril when his " blood is up " and the eyes of his comrades and his commander are on him, may not have the nerve of the scientific man who will quietly inoculate himself with some loathsome disorder to study its symptoms, or try the effects of some new and powerful anæsthetic upon himself, in order to decide on its possible utility in medicine. This is the sort of courage of which Socrates speaks as only possible to a man who " knows " the relative insignificance of the duration of any individual personal life from his habitual " contemplation of all time and all existence." We should, probably, prefer, both in the case of the priest and in the case of the man of science, to speak of " faith," but the point is that, in both cases, the agent is inspired by an absolutely assured personal conviction about the universal order and his own place in it. Without this absolute assurance of conviction, one is never wholly free from liability to illusion about one's own personal importance, and so never quite a free man. Because Socrates holds that the sciences form a ladder which leads up in the end to the vision of the

" Good " as the clue to the whole scheme of existence, he looks to science, as its supreme service, to make us thus at last completely free men. From this point of view, clearly in the soul of the man who " knows," the " parts " (μόρια) or " figures " (εἴδη) which have been distinguishable at a lower level of moral development will be finally fused. His life will have only one spring of action or active principle, his vision of the supreme good itself. The forms of virtue, at its highest level, will therefore lose their distinction. It might be possible for the average good civilian, or even for the good soldier of the State, to be characterized by one form of goodness more than by another. This is what is meant by the assignment of different virtues as characteristic to different sections of the community. It is not meant that so long as the shop-keeper or the farmer is " temperate," it does not matter whether he is a coward. He could not be a good man at all, if he were that, and a society in which no one had any courage except the members of the army and police would be morally in a bad way. But fighting is not the civilian's trade. He will be none the less a valuable member of society as a shop-keeper or a farmer because he has not been trained to show all the pluck and presence of mind which would win a D.S.O. or a V.C., though the State would succumb in the hour of peril if its fighting-arm had no more martial courage than the average civilian. But if a man is inspired in all the acts of his life by the vision of the supreme good, he will be equal to all the emergencies of life alike ; in having one virtue, he will necessarily have all. Substitute for " the good " God, and the principle of the unity of the virtues takes on the familiar form *Ama et fac quod vis.*

(11) The conception of science as the road to vision of the good leads us at once to consideration of the central metaphysical doctrine of the *Republic*, the doctrine of the " Form of Good " (ἰδέα τἀγαθοῦ). As is usual when the forms are mentioned in a Platonic dialogue, their reality is neither explained nor proved. It is taken for granted that the company in the house of Polemarchus, or at least Glaucon and Adimantus who conduct the discussion with Socrates, know quite well what the theory means and will not dispute its truth. It is assumed also as known to every one that the mathematical sciences are concerned with forms ; forms are the objects which we get to know from mathematics, though the mathematician leads us up to acquaintance with them by starting from the sensible " figures " which he employs as helps to our imagination. So far, we are told nothing we have not learned from the *Phaedo*. But there are two points of the first importance on which the *Republic* adds to that dialogue. (*a*) We now hear of a certain supreme " form," the " Good " or " Form of Good," which is the supreme object of the philosopher's study. We learn that, over and beyond the recognized mathematical studies, there is a still more ultimate discipline, " dialectic," and that it is the function of " dialectic " to lead directly to this vision of the " good." Further, we are told

that this " good " is something Socrates cannot describe ; it is not
" reality or being," but " on the other side " of both, though it is
the source of all the reality (ἀλήθεια) and being (οὐσία) of everything.   (b) The procedure of the mathematical sciences is criticized
and contrasted with that of " dialectic," with a view to explaining
just why the ideal of science is realized in dialectic and in dialectic
alone.   Both points call for some special consideration.

(a) THE FORMS (ἰδέαι) IN THE REPUBLIC.—From the Phaedo,
among other dialogues, we gather that there is a form corresponding
to each " universal " predicate which can be significantly affirmed
of a variety of logical subjects.   The same thing is explicitly said
in the Republic (vi. 507b, x. 596a) ; in the latter place the " form
of bed (κλίνη) or table " (τράπεζα) is given as an example.   (This
seems at variance with the well-known statement of Aristotle
that " we "—i.e. the Platonists—deny that there are " forms " of
artificial things,[1] but we must remember that Aristotle is speaking
of the doctrine as elaborated in the Academy, not of the position
ascribed to Socrates in the dialogues.)   But in the Republic we
learn that there is a " Form of Good " which is to the objects of
knowledge and to knowing itself what the sun is to visible objects
and to sight.   This is then further explained by saying that the
sun both makes the colours we see and supplies the eye with the
source of all its seeing.   In the same way, the " good " supplies
the objects of scientific knowledge with their being (οὐσία) and
renders them knowable.   And as the sun is neither the colours
we see nor the eye which sees them, so the " good " is something
even more exalted than " being." [2]   Later on, we find that the
sciences form a hierarchy which has its culmination in the actual
apprehension of this transcendent " good." [3]   Now, since it is
assumed in the Republic that scientific knowledge is knowledge of
forms, the objects which are thus said to derive their being from
" the good " must clearly mean the whole body of the forms.
The " good " thus holds a pre-eminence among forms, and strictly
speaking, it might be doubtful whether we ought to call it a " form "
any more than we can call the sun a colour.   At least, all the other
forms must be manifestations or expressions of it.   In the Phaedo
nothing was said which would warrant this treatment of the forms
as a hierarchy or ordered series with a first member of such a unique

---

[1] Metaphysics, A. 991b 6, M. 1080a 6.
[2] Rep. vi. 508b–509b.   For the full understanding of the analogy with the
sun it is necessary to understand the theory of colour-vision implied, which is
fully expounded in the Timaeus.   A colour is itself a kind of " flame "
(Timaeus, 67c ff.), and the immediate organ of the sight by which it is apprehended is also itself a fire, like that of the sun, which is contained in the eye
and issues forth from it in the act of vision (ibid. 45b ff.).   Thus the sun, as the
source of light, actually is also the source both of colour and of colour-vision.
The well-known Neoplatonist formula that νοῦς and τὰ νοητά taken together
as inseparable proceed immediately from the supreme reality " the One " is
a perfectly correct transcript of the doctrine of the Republic into the terminology of technical metaphysics.
[3] Rep. vii. 532a.

character; they appeared rather to be a vast plurality of which all the members stand on the same footing.   Hence it is intelligible that the view should have been taken that the " good " of the *Republic* represents a Platonic development going far beyond anything we can attribute to Socrates himself.   I think, however, that we must be careful not to exaggerate on this point.   There can, at least, be no doubt that the " form of good " is identical with the supreme Beauty, the vision of which is represented in the *Symposium* as the goal of the pilgrimage of the philosophic lover.   Hence, though it is true that the name " form of good " occurs nowhere but in the central section of the *Republic*, it would not be true to say that the object named does not appear in the *Symposium* with much the same character.   Again, though the *Phaedo* does not name the " form of good," the phrase εἶδος τἀγαθοῦ is verbally no more than a periphrase for τὸ ἀγαθόν (" the good "), just as similar periphrases occur constantly with the words φύσις, δύναμις, in Plato.[1] And it is in the *Phaedo* itself that we are told of Socrates' conviction that the ἀγαθὸν καὶ δέον (the " good and the ought ") is the principle which " holds everything together," and thus the cause of all order in the universe.[2]   The statements of the *Republic* merely make the implications of this passage of the *Phaedo* a little more explicit. If the good is the universal cause, it obviously must have just the character the *Republic* ascribes to it.   Hence Professor Burnet seems to be right in holding that what is said of the " form of good " is strictly within the limits of Socratism, and that this explains the point of contact between Socrates and an Eleatic like Euclides of Megara.[3]   That Socrates finds himself unable to speak of this form of good except negatively, and that he can only characterize it positively by an imperfect analogy, is inevitable from the nature of the case.   The same thing may be seen in any philosophy which does not simply deny or ignore the " Absolute " or supreme source of all reality.   Because this source is *ex hypothesi* a *source* of all reality, you are bound to insist that it transcends, and is thus " wholly other " than, every particular real thing ; every predicate you affirm of it belongs properly to some of its effects in contradistinction from others and can therefore only be asserted of the supreme source " analogically " and with the warning that the analogy is imperfect and would mislead if pressed unduly.   At the same time, because it is the source of all *reality*, every predicate which expresses a " positive perfection " must, in its degree, characterize the source of all " perfections " and must be ascribed to it " analogically."   All we gain by knowledge of the " detail " of the universe must add to and enrich our conception

---

[1] To take the first examples which come to hand : *Phaedo*, 98*a* 2, αἰτίας ἄλλο εἶδος=another cause ; *Phaedrus*, 246*d* 6, ἡ πτεροῦ δύναμις=" a wing "; *Timaeus*, 70*d* 8, τὴν τοῦ σώματος φύσιν=the body.

[2] The physicists are accused (*Phaed.* 99*c* 5) of falsely thinking that τὸ ἀγαθὸν καὶ δέον συνδεῖ καὶ συνέχει οὐδέν.   As one might say, " they forget that obligation is the ligature " which connects all things.

[3] *Greek Philosophy, Part I.*, 168–170.

of the source of reality, and yet we can never " comprehend " or completely " rationalize " that source. It remains, when all is said, an unexhausted and surprising " mystery." Hence the necessity Christian theology has always felt itself under of incorporating the profound agnosticism of the " negative way," or " way of remotion," in itself and the grotesque aberrations into which it has always fallen in the hands of second-rate theologians who have attempted to know God as one may know the " general conic." Hence also the tension between the affirmative and the negative moments in a metaphysic like that of Mr. Bradley. Hence equally the inevitable failure of " positive science " to complete its task of explaining everything. To explain everything would mean to get completely rid of all elements of " bare fact," to deduce the whole detail of existence from a body of " laws," perhaps from a single " law," in themselves (or itself) " evident to the intellect," as Descartes tried to deduce physics from geometry, because geometry appeared to him to involve no postulates which are not immediately " evident " as true. In fact, we only " rationalize " nature, in the sense of eliminating " bare fact " for which no explanation is forthcoming, at one point by reintroducing it somewhere else, as M. Meyerson has insisted in his series of illuminating works on the philosophy of the sciences. And it is just because science is under this restriction that its interest is perennial ; if we could ever expect to " complete " it, we should have to anticipate a time when it would no longer interest us. Science is eternally progressive just because it is always tentative.[1]

The language used in the *Republic* of the " Form of Good," as the last paragraph has suggested, at once raises the question whether or not this form can be identified with God, of whom language of the same kind is used by Christian theologians and philosophers. We cannot answer this important question correctly except by making a *distinctio* sometimes forgotten. If the question means " is the Form of Good another name for *the God recognized in the Platonic* philosophy ? " the answer must be definitely No, for the reason given by Burnet, that the good is a form, whereas God is not a form but a " soul," the supremely good soul. When we come to deal with the *Laws*, we shall see the importance for Plato's own thought of this distinction. It is just because his God is not a form that God can play the part the Platonic philosophy assigns to Him. But if we mean " is the Good spoken of in the *Republic* identical with what Christian divines and philosophers have meant

[1] The last word on the question whether the philosophy of the *Republic* and the dialogues generally is " rationalism " or not is briefly this. If we could fully comprehend " the good " we should see directly that it is through and through intelligible, and the *only* object which is wholly and perfectly intelligible ; as we never can comprehend it completely, there is, in fact, always something mysterious, not yet understood, about it. It is free from all self-contradiction, but it always contains " surprises " for us. We can " see into it " to some extent, and it is the philosopher's duty to see further and further into it ; but you will never " see through it."

by God ? " the answer must be modified. In one most important respect it is. The distinguishing characteristic of the " Form of Good " is that it is the transcendent source of all the reality and intelligibility of everything other than itself. Thus it is exactly what is meant in Christian philosophy by the *ens realissimum*, and is rightly regarded as distinct from and transcendent of the whole system of its effects or manifestations. And, as in the *ens realissimum* of Christian philosophers, so in the " Form of Good " the distinction, valid everywhere else, between *essentia* and *esse*, *So-Sein* and *Sein*, falls away. In other language, it transcends the distinction, too often treated as absolute, between value and existence. It is the supreme value and the source of all other value, and at the same time it is, though " beyond being," the source of all existence. This explains why, when a man at last comes in sight of it at the culmination of his studies in " dialectic," it is supposed to be grasped by direct vision, and for that reason is strictly " ineffable." Neither Plato nor anyone else could tell another man what the good is, because it can only be apprehended by the most incommunicable and intimate personal insight. Thus, as it seems to me, metaphysically the Form of Good is what Christian philosophy has meant by God, and nothing else. From the Christian standpoint, the one comment which would suggest itself is that since, on Socrates' own showing, the distinction between *essence* and *existence* falls away in the good, it should not properly be called one of the forms at all, and hence Socrates and Plato are not fully alive to the significance of their own thought when they speak of a " God " who is a $\psi\nu\chi\eta$ and thus on a lower level of " reality " than the good. Their form of theism is only necessitated because, in fact though not in words, they are still haunted by a feeling that the good is, after all, a " value " or an *essentia*, and needs some intermediate link to connect it up with the hierarchy of " realities " or " existents." On this point the last word of Greek constructive thought was said not by Plato but by Plotinus and Proclus. (Of course, also, we must remember that a specifically Christian philosophy is determined in its attitude towards the theistic problem by the fact that Christianity is an *historical* religion. It starts with the *fact* of the " Word made flesh," itself a coalescence of existence and value, and to preserve its Christian character, it is bound to be true to that starting-point in its whole metaphysical construction.)

(*b*) THE CRITICISM OF THE SCIENCES.—In studying the criticism Socrates passes upon the sciences and his theory about their limitations, we must not be misled by the fact that he deals throughout only with the various branches of mathematics as recognized in the fifth century. This was inevitable because he had before him no other examples of systematic and organized knowledge. In principle what he has to say is readily applicable to the whole great body of more " concrete " sciences which has grown up since his own day. If we speak of his comments as a criticism on the mathematical method, we must understand the phrase "mathematical method" in the same wide sense in which it is to be understood in reading Descartes, as meaning simply the method which aims at knowing exactly what its initial assumptions mean, and at deducing their implications exactly and in the right order. This is the method of all genuine science whatsoever ; there is nothing in it, as Descartes rightly insisted, which involves any restriction to the special subject-matter, " number and quantity " (and, in fact, pure mathematics themselves have long ago outgrown the restriction). The point of the criticisms is that the μαθήματα themselves do not and cannot succeed in being absolutely true to the ideal of method they set before themselves. This is why we find that if we are to pursue the path of science to the end, we are driven to recognize the reality of " dialectic " as the crowning science of all sciences, and to demand that the existing μαθήματα shall themselves be reconstituted on a more certain basis by the light of the dialectician's results. The recognition of this necessity may well belong to the actual Socrates, since the most sensational thing in the whole history of fifth-century science had been the demonstration by the dialectician Zeno that the postulates of mathematics, as hitherto prosecuted by the Pythagoreans, contradict one another.[1] To save mathematical science in the face of Zeno's arguments it became necessary in the fourth century to reconstruct the whole system, and the reconstruction is preserved for us in the *Elements* of Euclid. The men by whom the actual reconstruction was done, Eudoxus, Theaetetus, and their companions, so far as they are known to us, were all associates of Plato himself in the Academy, and it is quite certain that this revision of the accepted first principles of mathematics was one of the chief problems to which the school devoted itself. In the *Republic*, which is concerned with the fifth century, we naturally hear nothing about the way in which the difficulty was subsequently met, but we are allowed to hear of the imminent need that the work should be done.

The main thought is quite simple. In all the sciences the objects we are really studying are objects which we have to think but cannot see or perceive by any of our senses. Yet the sciences throughout direct attention to these objects, which are, in fact, forms, by appealing in the first instance to sense. The geometer draws a figure which he calls a " square " and a line which he calls

---

[1] To take one of the simplest examples : you cannot advance a step in elementary geometry without recognizing that any terminated straight line can be bisected, and there is no doubt that the Pythagorean geometers made the assumption. But it is also one of their assumptions that points are " *units* having position." If this is so, since a " unit " cannot be split, when I " bisect *AB* at *C* " ; *C* cannot be a " point of *AB*," and, in fact, cannot be a " point " at all. Thus one at least of the assumptions, " a straight line can be bisected at " a point," " a point is a unit having position," must be false. But the Pythagorean geometer cannot see his way to do without either. All Zeno's " antinomies " are of this type.

its " diagonal." But when he demonstrates a proposition about the square and its diagonal, the objects of which he is speaking are not this visible figure and this visible line but *the* square and *the* diagonal, and these, of course, we do not see except " with the mind's eye " (vi. 510*d–e*). (It would not even be true to say, like Berkeley, that what he is talking about is *this* visible figure *and* an indefinite plurality of others which are " like " it, for the simple reason that we can construct no visible figure at all which exactly answers to his definition of a " square.") Further, all through his reasoning the geometer or arithmetician depends on certain " postulates " (ὑποθέσεις) of which he " gives no account " (λόγος), such as the " postulate " that every number is either odd or even, or that there are just three kinds of angle. It is meant that these postulates are neither immediately self-evident, nor is any proof given of them. They are " synthetic " in Kant's sense of the word, and they are assumed without proof (vi. 510*c–d*). Thus there are two initial restrictions on the thinking of the mathematicians, as represented by the existing state of their science. They depend upon sensible things like diagrams as sources of suggestion, though not as the objects of their demonstrations. What cannot be " illustrated " or " represented " to the eye falls outside the scope of their science. And they make no attempt to reach real self-evidence in their initial postulates. They show that their theorems follow by logical necessity from a group of unproved premisses, but they do not undertake to show that there is any necessity to admit these premisses themselves. Thus the whole body of conclusions is left, so to say, hanging in the air. The geometer's " results " in the end rest on a tacit agreement (ὁμολογία) between himself and his pupil or reader that the question whether his assumptions are justifiable shall not be asked. In strictness we cannot call the results " knowledge " so long as the assumptions from which they have been deduced are thus left unexamined (vii. 533*c*).[1]

This suggests to us at once the possibility and necessity of a higher and more rigorous science, " dialectic." Such a science would differ from the sciences in vogue in two ways : (1) it would treat the initial postulates of the sciences as mere starting-points to be used for the discovery of some more ultimate premisses which are not " postulated," but strictly self-luminous and evident (ἀνυπόθετα), a real " principle of everything," and when it had

---

[1] We may readily supply further examples in illustration of the two points on which Socrates dwells. Thus the notion that the visible diagram is either the object about which the geometer reasons, or at any rate, a necessary source of suggestion, is dispelled by the elementary consideration that *e.g.* a work on Conics commonly begins with propositions about the properties of the " general conic." But you cannot draw even a rough diagram of a " general conic." So the other point is well illustrated by the labour spent for centuries on trying to show that what we now know to be the arbitrary Euclidean postulate of parallels (that non-intersecting straight lines in the same plane are equidistant) is a necessity of thought.

discovered such a principle (or principles), it would then deduce the consequences which follow ; (2) and in this movement no appeal would be made to sensible aids to the imagination, the double process of ascent to the " starting-point of everything " and descent again from it would advance from " forms by means of forms to forms and terminate upon them " (vi. 511b–c). In fact, we may even say that " dialectic " would " destroy " (ἀναιρεῖν) the postulates of the existing sciences (τὰς ὑποθέσεις ἀναιροῦσα, vii. 533c), that is, it would deprive them of the character of ultimate postulates by showing that—so far as they are not actually false, as they may turn out to be—they are consequences of still more ultimate truths.

In this account of the aims of dialectic we recognize at once the method described in the *Phaedo* as that of σκέψις ἐν λόγοις on which Socrates had fallen back after his disillusionment about Anaxagoras. Only here the special emphasis is thrown on just that side of the dialectic method which the immediate purposes of the *Phaedo* permitted us to dismiss in a single sentence. We are contemplating the procedure there said to be necessary if anyone disputes an initial " postulate." In that case, the *Phaedo* told us, our " postulate " will require to be itself deduced as a consequence from one more ultimate, and the process will have to be repeated until we come to a postulate which all parties are content to accept. In the last resort this would, of course, involve deduction from some principle which can be seen to possess unquestionable internal necessity. Thus, so far, the *Republic* agrees exactly with the *Phaedo* about the task of " dialectic," except that it lays special stress on just that part of it which had not to be taken into account in the *Phaedo* because the company there were all willing to admit the doctrine of forms as a " postulate " without demanding any justification of it. It is clear from the *Republic* that *if* a disputant should refuse to make this admission, the theory of forms itself would require to be examined in the same way in which the postulates of the mathematician *von Fach* are to be investigated. In the one passage of the dialogues where any such examination is made, it is not put into the mouth of Socrates but into that of the Pythagorean Timaeus (*Tim.* 51b 7 ff.).

Though Socrates naturally confines himself to criticisms of the sciences which had attained some degree of organization in his own day, it is obvious that they would apply with equal force to any others. Physics, chemistry, biology, economics are all full of undefined " primitive notions " and undemonstrated assumptions, and it is part of the work of the students of these sciences themselves to make a steady effort to ascertain just what their untested presuppositions are, and to consider how far they are really required, and how far they form a consistent system. The progress made by pure mathematics in the last half-century has largely consisted in a more accurate and complete statement of the " primitive notions " and " indemonstrable postulates " of the science and the

elimination of numerous conscious or tacit " postulates " as actually
false. Thus, for example, the process by which the Infinitesimal
Calculus has been purged of bad logic and false assumptions, or
the development of " non-Euclidean geometry," is an excellent
illustration of the self-criticism and self-correction of thought which
Socrates and Plato call " dialectic." Socrates' complaint (vii.
533*c*) about the mathematician who gives the name of science to a
procedure in which the starting-point is something one does not
know, and the conclusion and the intermediate steps " combinations of things one does not know," would be a perfectly correct
description of the contents of any average text-book of the Calculus
in vogue seventy years ago. And it is manifest that the same sort
of scrutiny is required by such notions as " force," " accelera-
tion," " atomicity," " evolution," " price." They are all inevitably in practical use long before the sciences which employ them
have formulated any very precise account of their meaning, and
the progress of science as science (as distinct from its application
to " commerce ") consists very largely in the steady correction of
our first crude attempts to explain what we mean by them. The
physicist of to-day may, like Democritus, make the " atomic
structure of matter " a foundation-stone of his science, but he
means by his " atom " something Democritus would not have
recognized as " atomic " at all. Similarly we all talk of the " evolution " of species, but the view that new species originate by sudden
and considerable " mutations," if established, would change the
whole character of the special " Darwinian " postulate about the
character of the process ; it would involve exactly what Socrates
means by a " destruction " of the postulate. Thus, so far, we may
say that what the *Republic* calls " dialectic " is, in principle, simply
the rigorous and unremitting task of steady scrutiny of the indefinables and indemonstrables of the sciences, and that, in particular, his ideal, so far as the sciences with which he is directly
concerned goes, is just that reduction of mathematics to rigorous
deduction from expressly formulated logical premises by exactly
specified logical methods of which the work of Peano, Frege, Whitehead, and Russell has given us a magnificent example.

But the " reduction of all pure mathematics to logic " is only
a part, and not the most important part, of what the *Republic*
understands by " dialectic." Such a unification of the sciences
as the *Republic* contemplates would require a combination of the
reduction of mathematics to logic with the Cartesian reduction of
the natural sciences to geometry. When the task was finished, no
proposition asserting " matter of fact," devoid of internal necessity,
should appear anywhere among the premises from which our conclusions are ultimately drawn. The first principles to which the
dialectician traces back all our knowledge ought to exhibit a self-
evident *necessity*, so that science would end by transforming all
" truths of fact " into what Leibniz called " truths of reason."
This involves a still more significant extension of the range of

" science." It implies that in a completed philosophy the distinctions between value and fact, *essentia* and *esse*, *So-sein and Sein* are transcended. The man who has attained " wisdom " would see that the reason why anything is, and the reason why it is *what* it is, are both to be found in the character of an *ens realissimum* of which it is self-evident that it is and that it is what it is, a self-explanatory " supreme being." This is why dialectic is said to culminate in direct apprehension of " the good " as the source of both existence and character. The thought is that all science in the end can be transformed into a sort of " algebra," but an algebra which is, as Burnet says, *teleological*. The demand for such a science is, in fact, already contained by implication in the remark of Socrates in the *Phaedo* that he hoped to find in Anaxagoras a solution of the problem of the shape and position of the earth based on proof that " it is best " that it should have just that shape and position and no other (*Phaedo* 97d–e). When a modern biologist explains the structure of an organism by the notion of " adaptation " to its environment he is thus using on a small scale the principle which the *Republic* would make the supreme universal principle of all scientific explanation whatsoever. Only, of course, the biological conception of " adaptation " stops short with a relative best ; the particular environment of a particular species is taken as (relatively) constant and independent ; the " best " realized in the development of the species is adequate adaptation to that given environment. When the principle is made universal, the " best " becomes an *ethical* and absolute best, since no place is left for an " environment " of everything. The " goodness of God," or its equivalent, takes the place of the fixed " environment " as that to which the structure of things is conceived as " adapted."

We need not suppose that Plato imagined this programme for the completion of science as capable of actual execution by human beings. We have learned from the *Symposium* that " philosophy " itself is a life of progress, it is not those who are already in possession of " wisdom," but those who are endeavouring after it, who philosophize. The *Timaeus* reminds us with almost wearisome repetition that, in physical science in particular, all our results are inevitably provisional, the best we can reach with our present lights, and that we must be prepared to see them all superseded or modified. One of the standing contrasts between Plato and his great disciple Aristotle is just that this sense of the provisionality and progressiveness of science is so prominent in the one and so absent from the other. Plato never assumes, as Aristotle was so apt to assume, that he can do the world's scientific thinking for it once for all. This apparent finality, which made Aristotle so attractive to the thinkers of the thirteenth century, who were just recovering the thought of " Nature " as a field for study on her own account, makes the real value of Aristotle's science rather difficult for us to appreciate to-day. Plato was far too true to the Socratic conception of the insignificance of human knowledge by comparison with the vastness of the scientific problem to fall into the vein of cheap and easy dogmatism. But though the final " rationalization " of things may be an unattainable goal, there is no reason why we should not try to get as near to the goal as we can. If we cannot expel the element of " brute fact " for which we can see no reason from science, we may try, and we ought to try, to reduce it to a minimum. We cannot completely " mathematize " human knowledge, but the more we can mathematize it, the better. We shall see, when we come to speak of Plato's oral teaching in the Academy, how earnestly he set himself to carry out the programme by getting behind the mere assumption of the forms as the last word in philosophy, and deducing the forms themselves from the " good."

(c) It should be unnecessary to dwell on the point that, with all his devotion to this demand for a critical metaphysic of the sciences, Plato is no champion of a mere *vita contemplativa* divorced from practical social activity. One could not even say that he, like Kant, conceives of " speculative " and " practical " reason as active in two distinct spheres of which one is subordinated to the other. To his mind, the two spheres are inseparable. The uni-fication of science is only possible to one who is illuminated by the vision of the Good which is the principle of the unification, and the Good is only seen by the man who *lives* it. Hence the demand that the " philosopher " shall devote the best years of his working life to the arduous practice of governing, in all its details great or small, is only the other side of the conviction that without the " heroic " character no one will ever rise to the supreme rank in science itself. The " philosopher " is necessarily a missionary and a sort of lesser Providence to mankind because, on Socratic principles, the " Good " cannot be seen without drawing all who see it into its service. The " philosophers' " social activity is all the more effective that it is not pursued directly for its own sake, in the spirit of the well-meaning but tiresome persons of our own day who take up " social work " as they might take up typewriting or civil engineering, but issues naturally and inevitably, as a sort of " by-product," from their aspiration after something else, just as the " great inventions " of modern times regularly issue from the discoveries of men who were not thinking at all of the applications of science to convenience and commerce, or as art, literature, social life have all owed an incalculable debt to St. Francis and his " little brethren," who never gave a thought to any of them.

(12) This desultory chapter may be brought to an end by a few remarks on the impressive picture of *Republic* viii.–ix. about the stages of progressive degeneration through which personal and national character pass as the true ideal of life falls more completely out of view. It should be obvious that the primary interest of these sketches is throughout ethical, not political. The " imperfect " constitutions are examined in order to throw light on the different phases of personal human sinfulness, not in the interests of a theory

of political institutions. We see the sinfulness of even " honour-able " ambition or " business principles," when they are made the mainspring of a man's life, more clearly by considering the type of national character exhibited by a community in which these motives determine the character of national life. Socrates is still adhering to his declared purpose of using the " larger letters " to decipher the smaller. In the sketches themselves, Socrates is all through " drawing with his eye on the object." We are told in so many words that Sparta has furnished the model for the picture of the second-best society, where education is neglected and the highest moral ideal is to display the character of a good fighting-man and sportsman, *i.e.* the society in which " honourable ambition," the pursuit of the *cursus honorum,* is thought the supreme virtue. As mankind go, a community of this kind is not a bad one ; it is morally in a much healthier state than a society where every one regards " getting rich " as the great aim in life, and the " merchant prince " is the national hero. Rome, in its better days, would be an example of the kind of society intended, no less than Sparta. The point of Socrates' criticism is that when " ambition " becomes master instead of servant, it is not likely to remain " honourable " ambition, ambition to " serve." From the first, the ambition of the " timocratic " State has not been aspiration to be pre-eminent in the best things ; at their best, the Spartans made a very poor contribution to the positive pursuit of the highest life. When they were not at their best, their " ambition " took the form of mere devotion to military success ; and at their worst, they were mere aspirants to the exercise of power and the accumulation of the wealth to be got by " empire," as the " timocratic man," in his old age, degenerates into the kind of character who is greedy of the power money will give him. It ought to have been im-possible to find any idealization of Sparta in the picture. As I have written elsewhere, it would be truer to say that in the *Republic* we discern the shadows of the third-century ephors and of Nabis behind the " respectable " figure of Agesilaus.

It is generally admitted that the picture of the " democratic " city where every one does as he pleases, and the most typical of citizens is the gifted amateur who plays, as the mood takes him, at every kind of life from that of the voluptuary to that of the ascetic—a sort of Goethe, in fact—is a humorous satire on Athenian life and manners. Of course we should be alive to the further point that the satire would be wholly beside the mark if directed against the drab and decent *bourgeois* Athens of Plato's manhood. The burlesque is aimed directly against the Imperial democracy of the spacious days of Pericles when Athens was a busy home of world-commerce and the " new learning." If we read the description side by side with the famous Funeral Oration in Thucydides, we shall see at once that the very notes of Athenian life which Pericles there selects as evidence of its superiority are carefully dwelt upon by Socrates for the opposite purpose of proving that, for all its surface brilliancy, such a life is at bottom so diseased that society is on the verge of complete collapse. I, at least, cannot avoid the conviction that Socrates sees in just what must have been the great charm of Athens for men like Sophocles, Protagoras, Herodotus—its apparently inexhaustible variety and freshness—the unmistakable " symptoms of the end." [1] (Perhaps he was not very far wrong. What would probably have been the issue of the Periclean age if Alcibiades, the incarnation of its energy and versatility, had returned triumphant from the subjugation of Sicily ? One may " hazard a wide solution.")

We are given no hint of the source from which the picture of the intermediate society, where wealth is the great title to admiration and " merchant princes " control the national destiny, is taken. But I do not doubt that we can name the State which Plato has in mind. When we remember that, as we see from allusions in the *Laws* and in Aristotle's *Politics*,[2] there were just three cities whose constitutions impressed Greek thinkers by their appearance of being framed on definite principles—Sparta, Crete, and Carthage. I think it may safely be assumed that Carthage has supplied the hints for the Venice or Amsterdam of the *Republic*, just as we may presume that Socrates has the Carthaginians more than anyone else in mind in the earlier passage where he remarks on the exceptional aptitude of " Phoenicians " for commerce. The subsequent history of Carthage during the first two Punic wars affords an interesting commentary on what is said about the internal dissensions which paralyse the " oligarchical city." On the concluding argument, by which the life of respect for right is pronounced far superior in happiness to the life of sating one's cupidities and ambitions,[3] there is no need to say much. The reasoning is that we have already met in the *Gorgias*, and turns on the application of the medical formula of " depletion and recovery from depletion " to the moral life. The " passions," like the physical appetites of hunger and thirst, are capable of no permanent and progressive satisfaction. You feed full to-day, but to-morrow finds you as hungry again as though to-day had never been. What you mistake for happiness has been only the temporary arrest of a " depletion." On the other hand, what you gain in knowledge

---

[1] Cf. V. Soloviev's saying that " visible and accelerated progress is a symptom of the end."

[2] Arist. *Politics*, B 11 (1272b 24 ff. ; note that Aristotle too comments on the "plutocracy " of the Carthaginian scheme, and plutocracy is what is meant by " oligarchy " in the *Republic*). For a reference to Carthage in the *Laws*, see *Laws*, 674a, written, no doubt, after Plato's association with affairs in Sicily had made Carthage very much of an actuality to him. Commerce made Carthage an object of interest to Athens in the Periclean age (Aristoph. *Knights*, 174), and it has been plausibly suggested that the great plague of the third year of the Archidamian war was brought to Athens from Carthage by infected merchandise.

[3] *Republic*, ix. 583b ff. Cf.
" ' Mete unto wombe and wombe eek unto mete,'
Shall God destroyen bothe,' as Paulus seith."

and goodness is not won to-day to be " excreted " by the time to-morrow is upon you. It is permanently acquired. It is not with character and intellect as it is with bodily health, which is a mere balance between antithetic processes of waste and repair ; character and intellect are κτήματα ἐς αἰεί. This is the reason for the distinction between the " false " pleasures of sensuality and ambition and the "true" pleasures of the philosophic life. The former are "false," not in the sense that they are not really felt, but in the sense that they are not what they promise to be. " Alle Lust will Ewigkeit," but no *Ewigkeit* is to be got out of the βίος φιλοσώματος or the βίος φιλότιμος, a truth which no special pleading for Hedonism can explain away. I will add one final caution against possible misinterpretation. Plato credits the " three lives " with distinctive pleasures, much as Mill talks of a distinction of " higher " and " lower " in pleasure.[1] But he gives a rational reason for his preference of the " philosopher's " pleasure where Mill gives an absurd one. Mill tries to persuade his readers that a jury of pleasure-tasters devoid of all moral principle would be unanimous in preferring the philosopher's pleasures, or, alternatively, that the dissentients may be disabled as no genuine connoisseurs.[2] Plato gives the right reason for the preference, that the issue is one which must be decided by " intelligence," and it is just intelligence which the philosopher has and his rivals have not. This is what John Grote also meant when he said that Mill's argument is based on a misconception of our reason for attaching weight to the philosopher's verdict. We go to him, not as Mill assumes, for *evidence*, but for *authority*.[3]

See further :

NETTLESHIP, R. L.—" Lectures on the *Republic* of Plato " (vol. ii. of *Philosophical Remains*) ; *Plato's Conception of Goodness and the Good* ; *The Theory of Education in Plato's Republic* in *Hellenica* [2], 61–165.

NATORP, P.—*Platons Ideenlehre*, 175–215.

RITTER, C.—*Platon*, ii. 3–39, 554–641 *al.* ; *Platons Staat, Darstellung des Inhalts.* (Stuttgart, 1909.)

RAEDER, H.—*Platons philosophische Entwickelung*, 181–245.

BARKER, E.—*Greek Political Theory : Plato and his Predecessors*, 145–268.

STEWART, J. A.—*Myths of Plato*, 133–172 (*Myth of Er*), 471–474 (*Myth of the Earth-born*) ; *Plato's Doctrine of Ideas*, 47–62.

SHOREY, P.—*Plato's Republic.* (London and New York, Vol. I. 1930, Vol. II. 1935.)

DIÈS, A.—*Introduction* to the edition of the dialogue in the *Collection des Universités de France.* (Paris, 1932.)

---

[1] *Republic*, 582a–e.

[2] Mill's plea is a perfect example of the kind of argument the Greeks called a λόγος ἀντιστρέφων, i.e. one which makes for neither party, because it can be equally well applied by the other. If the sage disables the judgment of the profligate on the plea that he must have lost the taste for the " higher pleasures " before he can prefer the lower, the profligate can equally retort on the sage with the adage about sour grapes. " You have taken to philosophy," he may say, " because you are physically too old to enjoy debauchery."

[3] *Examination of the Utilitarian Philosophy*, p. 47.

CHAPTER XII

THE *PHAEDRUS*[1]

THE *Phaedrus* presents a double difficulty to the student of Plato's work as a whole. What is its proper place in the series of the dialogues? And what is its purpose? Is it, as it professes to be, a discussion of the principles upon which "rhetoric" (prose style) may be made into a "science," or is its real subject Eros? Is Plato primarily concerned with the question of the use and abuse of sexual passion, or are the speeches Socrates delivers on this topic merely examples of the right and the wrong use of persuasive eloquence?

The first question, on examination, proves capable of being narrowed down to one which we may regard as of minor importance. No serious student of Platonic style now defends the singular theory of some critics in classical antiquity that the prominence of Eros in the dialogue and the loaded rhetoric of Socrates' encomium on him prove the work to be a youthful writing, perhaps the earliest of all the dialogues.[2] It is matter of common agreement that, on stylistic grounds, the dialogue cannot be placed earlier than those works of Plato's maturity as a writer with which we have been dealing in the last four chapters; it cannot be far removed from the great quadrilateral in point of date. But there still remains the question whether it may be earlier than some of these four, or whether it is later than all of them. In particular, we have to ask whether the *Phaedrus* is earlier or later than the *Republic*. Arguments from stylometry cannot be wholly trusted in this case, since it is manifest that many of the peculiarities of language are due to deliberate imitation. On the whole, the stylometrists appear to be satisfied that the *Phaedrus* is the later of the two works, and this view is plausibly supported by the contention urged by H. Raeder, that some of the details of the mythical part of the dialogue are hardly intelligible except on the assumption that its readers would be familiar with *Republic* v. and the concluding myth of *Republic* x. I do not myself find the argument conclusive.[3] On the other hand,

[1] On the problems connected with the dialogue, see *inter cetera* Thompson, *Phaedrus*, Introduction; C. Ritter, *Platon*, i. 256; H. Raeder, *Platons philosophische Entwickelung*, 245 ff.

[2] Diogenes Laertius (iii, 25) mentions the theory; Olympiodorus repeats the story as a fact.

[3] Raeder sees in the mention of the "journey of a thousand years" on which the soul enters after each incarnation (*Phaedrus*, 249a) a reference to the fuller explanation in the *Republic* (615a). This is inconclusive, since the

as we shall see in the next chapter, there is convincing reason for thinking that the *Theaetetus*, which pretty certainly opens the group of dialogues of Plato's later life, was not written until about twenty years after the *Republic* and its immediate fellows, and it is perhaps hard to believe that so great a writer as Plato was absolutely silent through so long a period. Hence I have nothing to set against the conclusions of recent eminent scholars on the point, and would merely remark that the priority of the *Republic* is not absolutely demonstrable, and also that, in view of the difference in spirit between *Republic* and *Theaetetus*, we must fairly suppose the *Phaedrus*, if the composition falls in the interval between those two dialogues, to have been written early rather than late in the interval.

The other problem is more difficult, and I would recommend the reader to suspend his judgment on it until he has followed our analysis of the dialogue. My own opinion is on the side of those who regard the right use of "rhetoric" as the main topic, for the following simple reason. In Socrates, with whom the "tendance of the soul" was the great business of life, it is quite intelligible that a discussion of the use of rhetoric or anything else should be found to lead up to the great issues of conduct. If the real subject of the *Phaedrus* were sexual love, it is hard to see how its elaborate discussion of the possibility of applying a scientific psychology of the emotions to the creation of a genuine art of persuasion, or its examination of the defects of Lysias as a writer, can be anything but the purest irrelevance.

In structure the dialogue is of the simplest type. Socrates falls in with Phaedrus who is, under medical advice, taking a constitutional in the country outside the city walls, and, for the sake of his company, joins him, departing for once from his preference for the streets of the town. He soon persuades Phaedrus to sit down by the bank of the Ilissus under the shade of a plane tree ; the conversation which ensues takes place here and is strictly *tête-à-tête*. As for the supposed date of the conversation, it can be approximately fixed by the opening sentences. Lysias, who figures as a mere lad in the *Republic*, is now at the height of his fame as a writer of λόγοι (228a), and is living at Athens (227b). We may add the further detail that Polemarchus is also alive and, according to Socrates, "has betaken himself to philosophy" (257b), also that Isocrates, though still young, is already rivalling Lysias in his profession ; Socrates anticipates that he may either throw Lysias and all former professors of it into the shade, or even aspire to a still higher calling,

period seems in both cases to be taken over from current Orphic mythology. So the reference to the "lots" which play a part in assigning a new body to the soul (*Phaedrus*,249b) need not be to *Republic* 617d, since the κλῆροι appear to be Orphic (Burnet, *Early Greek Philosophy³*, 190 n. 3). Still less convincing is the argument that the *Phaedrus* tacitly presupposes the doctrine of the " parts of the soul " expounded in *Republic* iv., since this is equally true of the *Gorgias*, as we have seen, and the doctrine appears to be a piece of fifth-century Pythagoreanism. Raeder's other arguments are complicated by the assumption that the dialogue contains a polemic against Isocrates. On this *vide infra*.

for " there really is philosophy in him " (279a). The conversation thus falls at some date between 411, when Polemarchus and Lysias returned to Athens from Thurii, and the year of anarchy, 404–3, when Polemarchus fell a victim to the " Thirty." The tradition was that Isocrates was some seven years older than Plato, so that his birth would fall about 435 B.C. ; as he survived the battle of Chaeronea (338 B.C.), he cannot well have been born much if any earlier ; hence he would be about twenty-four in 411 and thirty-one in the " year of anarchy." A date intermediate between 411 and 404 is thus required by the supposed facts. We note then that Phaedrus must now be between five and twelve years older than when we met him in the *Symposium* ; no lad (for he figured in the *Protagoras*), but a man at least approaching forty[1] ; Socrates is a γέρων, a man of at least sixty and perhaps more.

When Socrates falls in with Phaedrus, the time of day is already close on noon (this explains why the pair so soon take rest under the plane-tree). Phaedrus has spent the early morning listening to a brilliant and paradoxical λόγος—we should call it an essay—by Lysias in defence of the thesis that a lad should be kinder to a wooer who is not " in love " than to one who is. He has the written text with him, and Socrates professes to believe that he is taking his solitary stroll for the express purpose of getting it by heart. The main point of the short and playful conversation between Socrates and Phaedrus as they make their way to the place they have chosen for their *siesta* (227–230) is to pitch the ethical key for what is to follow. Socrates is not interested in the " rationaliza-tion of myths," like that of Boreas and Orithyia, because he is pre-occupied with a graver problem, that of learning to " know him-self " ; he is indifferent to the charms of the country, because the trees, unlike the men he meets in the streets, can " teach him nothing " that bears on this supreme topic, the moral being of man. These remarks prepare us for the moral earnestness with which the merits of Lysias's essay and the possibilities of rhetoric are to be treated in the body of the dialogue.

THE ESSAY OF LYSIAS (230e–234c).—It has been disputed whether the discourse Phaedrus proceeds to read is an authentic composition of Lysias or a brilliant imitation of his style by Plato himself. There is no evidence either way, but for my own part, I feel that we must agree with those scholars, including Lysias' latest editor, Hude, who regard the essay as genuine. No one doubts Plato's ability to compose a λόγος for Lysias with perfect fidelity to the style of the supposed author. But, since the dialogue ends with severe and formal censure of Lysias, founded on a search-ing criticism of the λόγος, I find it difficult to believe that the document is an invention. It would be self-stultifying to publish a severe criticism of a well-known author based on an imitation of him which the critic had composed for his own purposes and could

[1] The same point is taken by Parmentier, *Bulletin de l'association Guillaume Budé*, No. 10, p. 4.

not expect readers to take as authentic. One might as well suppose that Berkeley could have made the point he wants to make in *Alciphron* about the false glitter and shallowness of Shaftesbury by composing an imitation of the *Characteristics*. Plato's purpose, like Berkeley's, demands that the attack should be made on work which is both genuine and admired by the circles whose literary and moral false taste is to be exposed. Hude seems to me fully justified in printing the discourse as part of his text of *Lysias*.

The thesis of Lysias, we must remember, would be an offensive paradox even to the section of Athenian society which practised " unnatural " aberrations. The fashionable theory was that the relations in question are ennobled when they are inspired by genuine " romantic " attachment, but not otherwise, as is taken for granted by the encomiasts of them in the *Symposium*. To suffer the advances of an ἐραστής from calculations of advantage was regarded as the basest thing a Greek lad could do. For a modern parallel to the paradox we might imagine a clever essay written to show that Tom Jones's conduct towards Lady Bellaston is morally more innocent than his affair with Molly Seagrim. We must not suppose that Lysias intends his argument to be taken seriously. He simply means to exhibit his cleverness by showing how good a case he can make out for the worst conduct, much as a clever writer to-day might amuse himself and his readers by an essay on the moral elevation of a bomb-throwing " Communist." But there are theses which cannot be defended and arguments which cannot be employed, even in jest, without revealing deep-seated moral depravity or insensibility ; the kind of cleverness which sustains such theses by the use of such arguments is a real moral danger to the community and requires to be countered, as it is by Socrates, with better morality and superior wit.

The discourse may be summarized very briefly ; it is throughout an appeal to considerations of " utility " in the most sordid sense of the word. One is likely to make one's price much more effectively out of a suitor who is a cold sensualist. Romantic love has its fits of repentance and its lovers' quarrels ; it changes its object, and when it does so, it passes into hate and scorn. It imperils reputation, since the romantic suitor " blabs " of his success, while the business-like sensualist knows how to hold his tongue. The " lover " is notoriously jealous and tries to monopolize his beloved ; the cool sensualist does not object to going shares with rivals recommended by their wealth or other qualities.[1] The " lover " is attracted by physical charm before he has considered the suitability of the connexion in other respects ; the man who is not " in love " chooses carefully. The lover's judgment is blinded by his passion, and this makes him the worst of confidants and advisers. He flatters one's weaknesses and quarrels with one's better qualities. On all these grounds it is absurd to expect solid and lasting advantage from one's complaisances towards him. (Manifestly such a

[1] Like our own Charles II, to take an actual example.

discourse, apart from the moral turpitude which pervades it, is really a failure, considered merely as a defence of its thesis. Lysias gives a number of excellent reasons for thinking that it is bad to " grant favours to a lover " ; he has given no reason for thinking that it may not be as bad, or worse, to grant them to a sensual " man of the world."   The speech is thus, judged by any reasonable standard, bad rhetoric, as well as bad ethics, a point which Socrates will not be slow to make.)

Socrates professes at first to have paid no attention to the matter of the discourse. He was attending wholly to its stylistic qualities, and these even Lysias himself could hardly approve, since it was full of empty repetition and tautology.   The mere recollection of what poets like Sappho and Anacreon have said about love would enable a man to make a much better speech on the same theme.   Lysias has in fact shown no " invention " in his essay ; he has merely dwelt on one obvious point, the " blindness " and irrationality of the lover's passion," a point no one could miss.   The whole merit of his performance, if it has any, must be looked for in the arrangement (διάθεσις) of this commonplace material. Phaedrus himself admits this (236a–b), but challenges Socrates, if he can, to treat the same theme (ὑπόθεσις), the admitted " madness " of the lover's passion, better than Lysias has done. Socrates accepts the challenge, with a prayer to the Muses to make up for his well-known ignorance by the aid of their " inspiration."   With this preface he makes a rival speech on the theme, only carefully introducing one slight but significant modification. The supposed speaker, in his discourse, is to be not a cold-blooded sensualist making a disgraceful " business proposition," but a " lover " astute enough to cloak his passion under an *appearance* of indifference. (This gives Socrates a double advantage over Lysias. He safeguards his own character by abstaining from even a playful defence of a morally disgraceful thesis, and he leaves himself free, if he pleases, to urge subsequently that the apparent reasonability of the speech is only the simulated rationality of a madman, since the client into whose mouth it is put is really inspired all the time by " romantic " unreason.)

FIRST SPEECH OF SOCRATES.—Thesis : *It is Bad to Listen to the Blandishments of a " Lover "* (237b–241d).—The first requisite for all sound deliberation is to *know* the real character of the object about which we are deliberating. Since the question is whether one should yield to a lover, we must start by understanding what " love " is, and what it aims at, and whether it is for our good or for our harm.   " Love " is, of course, a desire or craving for something.   Now there are two principal types of desire—the " inborn " craving for the *pleasant*, and the desire for the " best," which is not inborn, but has to be acquired, and is based on judgment (δόξα)— and there is often a clash between the two.   The victory of judgment (δόξα) in this conflict over appetitive craving is what we call *sophrosyne*; the victory of appetite over our judgment of good we call " lust " or " passion " (ὕβρις). " Love " (ἔρως, sexual passion) is one special variety of ὕβρις or " lust." It is the prevalence of violent desire for the pleasant uninformed by rational judgment of good, when aroused by physical beauty (238c). The question before us, then, is whether it is for the benefit or for the hurt of the party who has aroused such a passion to gratify it. And here, Socrates says, he will give the rein to an almost " poetical " eloquence with which he feels himself inspired beyond his ordinary, perhaps by the surroundings in which he is speaking. (The artificial graces of Lysias are to be met by the " unstudied eloquence " of the " heart.")

The " lover," being a slave to his pleasures, will, of course, desire his beloved to be the pliant minister to them, and will hate everything which makes him less subservient, and gives him any kind of personal independence. Now wisdom, valour, even ready wit and eloquence themselves, tend to give one an independent personality, and for that reason a " lover " will object to them in the object of his passion. His jealousy will prompt him to exclude the beloved from all intercourse which would " make a man " of him, and above all from " divine philosophy." The last thing he will desire is that his " minion's " charm for himself should be endangered by the acquisition of intelligent and manly qualities of soul. In the next place, he will resent the acquisition of hardy and manly physical qualities such as make one of worth in " war and other necessities " ; he will deliberately, for his own pleasure, try to keep the ἐρώμενος to a soft and effeminate course of life. Finally, he will be anxious to isolate his victim from all the influences of family affections ; he will object to his having any financial independence, or to his marrying and forming a family of his own, since he resents whatever tends to emancipate the victim from the position of mere minister to his own selfish pleasure. Thus the " lover " is an enemy to the good alike of the victim's soul, of his body, and of his estate. (We see that Socrates' pretence of being carried out of himself on a flood of " inspired " eloquence must not be taken too seriously. He is deliberately observing the rules of arrangement which Lysias had neglected. His theme is nominally that of Lysias, the jealous and petulant selfishness of the "lover." But he has carefully articulated his argument and avoided vain repetition by grouping the effects of the lover's jealousy on his victim under the heads of mind, body, estate. This has given him further the opening for lifting the whole argument to a worthier moral level by insisting on the supreme importance of the moral goods which are jeopardized by complaisance. Considered simply as an example of effective pleading, Socrates' speech has thus stylistic advantages over that of Lysias which far outweigh his neglect of the verbal graces and prettinesses of the other.)

The speech ends with a further consideration. Connexion with an ἐραστής has been shown to be productive of evil to mind, body, and fortune. We may add, as a minor point, that besides being " harmful," it is also not even pleasant. Association with a flatterer or a kept mistress is also hurtful, but the palliative can be urged that, at any rate, these are " pleasant vices." But in the connexion of the ἐραστής with his victim, the victim does not even get the pleasure ; such as it is, it is all on the side of the other party ; the victim's position is intolerable, and he only sustains it on the strength of promises of solid advantages, which the " lover " will not implement, when once he has had his wicked will and sated himself. The " love " of the ἐραστής is thus the proverbial love of the wolf for the lamb.

Even Phaedrus can see that this discourse, though it gives good reasons against bestowing favours on a " lover," does nothing to advance the plea of the suitor who is not " in love." Socrates, who, of course, did not mean to act as advocate for such a client, suggests that it would be enough to add that such a person is in all respects the very opposite of the lover whose faults we have exposed. He is about to take his leave of Phaedrus with this remark, when " the divine sign " checks him. He professes to understand this as a warning that, since Eros is a god, he has committed an impiety by denouncing him and must purge himself of his contempt by a palinode, as Stesichorus did when he had blasphemed Helen. If a real gentleman had overheard either the speech of Lysias or that which Socrates has just delivered, he would have imagined that he was listening to persons brought up among " common sailors," incapable of understanding what a free man means by " love." Thus the point of the " palinode " is to be that it is a recantation of the identification of ἔρως with a brutal physical appetite (241d–243e).[1]

SECOND SPEECH OF SOCRATES (244a–256e).—*The True Psychology of Love*.—The ground on which we have so far maintained that it is better to associate with one who is not in love than with a " lover " is that the lover is " beside himself " (μαίνεται), but the man who is not in love retains his sanity, and sanity is better than " madness." This is the proposition we are now to recant. It would be true if there were only one kind of frenzy, common madness. But there is an inspired " frenzy " which is productive of good we could not equally obtain in a state of sanity and control of ourselves. One of its forms is *prophecy* ; the priestess of Delphi, who predicts in a state of " exaltation," is far superior as a prophet to diviners who predict the future by calculations based on the flight of birds and similar omens ; a second form is the " exaltation " of the authors of " purifications " and " initiations," " founders of

---

[1] The definition of ἔρως from which the speech of Socrates started was correct in the sense that it is a true definition of what Lysias had called ἔρως in formulating his thesis. Hence it was rightly adopted also by Socrates for the immediate purpose of showing how the same thesis might have been treated with less superficiality and without idle repetition. But, as we shall see, it is not in fact an adequate account of even guilty and degraded *human* " love," to call it a craving for a certain physical " exoneration." (Even an unholy love—if it is " love " at all—is the pollution of a high sacrament.)

religions " as we should say ; a third is the inspiration of the poet. No one who attempts to compose poetry in a state of " sanity " by rules of art ever achieves anything great (244a–245e). The madness of the lover, as we shall find, is a fourth form of this divine " frenzy " which is so much wiser than the wisdom of the world.[1] We intend to show, that, if the lover is mad, his madness is an inspiration from heaven and may be a great blessing. To prove this we must lay down the principles of a sound psychology ; we must see what is the nature, and what the actions and passions of the soul.

In the first place, the soul is immortal (245c), a statement which means to a Greek that it is divine. The proof of this is that whatever is always in motion is immortal, and the soul is always in motion. The minor premiss of this syllogism is again proved thus. The soul is the source and initiator of its own motions ; its motions are not communicated from without, but spontaneously originated from within. Thus they were never started by anything else, and, as the soul itself is the first fountain of them, they can never come to an end. If the soul could come to an end, there would be an end of nature and becoming universally (245e)—a statement which implies that souls are the *only* things which can move from within, and so the only possible sources of movement. The soul may thus be rigorously defined as " that which moves itself " (246a).[2] But

[1] To appreciate this doctrine aright, we must neither forget the habitual " irony " of Socrates nor exaggerate it. The key to his meaning is given by his well-known theory about the poets. He found the poets unable to explain in bald prose what they meant by their finest passages, or how they came by them. Hence he classes them among the persons who think they have a knowledge which they really have not. They are not alive, whatever they may suppose, to the full significance of their best work. He does not, of course, mean to suggest either that the great things in Sophocles or Euripides are not really great, or that great poetry may be nonsense. It means more than the poet himself in his " uninspired " hours could tell you, and this shows that some influence which the poet cannot wholly control has been speaking through him. In the same way, though it is part of his irony to dwell on the alleged benefits conferred on men by the trance-utterances of the Pythia or the " purifications " devised by abnormal and eccentric " religious geniuses," it is quite consistent with his habitual attitude to " things divine " that he should suppose a higher power to use such vehicles for revealing the future, and admit the real healing effects of some " initiations " and " purifications " on the body and mind. The great defect he finds in poetry as in μαντική is just that the spirits of the prophets are *not* subject to the prophets. Hence you cannot depend on the Pythia's predictions, and hence also the great poet is apt to decline into bathos or nonsense as much as the Shadwell to deviate (occasionally) into sense.

[2] This argument, in an expanded form, is reproduced in the *Laws*, as we shall see, and treated there as the sufficient proof both of the existence of God and of the immortality of the soul. Unlike the arguments of the *Phaedo* it has no special connexion with the theory of the forms. But it would be rash to say that its introduction shows that we are dealing with a post-Socratic development of Plato's own thought, since in principle the argument is that of Alcmaeon of Crotona that the soul is immortal because it " is like immortal things, and is like them in the point that it is always in motion " (Aristot. *de Anima*, 405a 30). Hence the argument must have been well known to

what is the character of this " self-moving " source of all movement ? For our purposes, we may content ourselves with an
analogy. It is like a charioteer with a pair of winged steeds,
forming a single living whole.[1] In the case of the gods, driver and
horses are all as good as they can possibly be ; in the human soul,
the driver has to manage two horses of different strain, and this is
what makes his task so difficult. While the horses keep their wings,
they travel round the circuit of heaven and the soul " administers "
the Cosmos. But they may lose their wings and fall to earth ; the
soul then acquires an earthly body which seems to be able to move
itself (though it is really moved by the soul within it), and it is this
complex of body and soul which we call the mortal " animal."
By analogy we come commonly to think of God (falsely) as a being
with a soul and body which are never separated by death (246d).
(We see at once that we are dealing in a parable with the " three
parts " of the soul ; the driver is judgment, the two horses are
" honour " or " mettle " and " appetite." If we press the details,
they imply that all three " parts " are present not only in the soul
which has not yet put on the garment of the flesh, but in the gods,
who are never embodied at all. This would be quite at variance
with the hints of the *Republic* and the express teaching of the
Timaeus. But it is not really permissible to extract metaphysics
from mythical details which are necessitated by simple regard
for the coherency of the pictorial representation.)
The myth proceeds to describe the life of all souls under the
image of a great festal procession. The souls progress, under the
leadership of the gods, round the whole compass of the heavens,
maintaining the universal order of things. The goal of the whole
pilgrimage is reached by an ascent to a region outside the whole
heaven, " the plain of reality," where the procession pauses and
enjoys a Sabbath rest in the contemplation of " bodiless reality,
without figure, colour, or tangible quality " (in other words the
forms) ; this is the true home of souls, and the source of their
spiritual food. Thus the thought is that it is in the strength of this
pure contemplation that gods and men alike execute the practical
task of establishing and maintaining natural and moral order in the
realm of mutability and becoming. Like Moses they make everything after the pattern they have seen " in the mount." The gods,
of course, achieve this " steep ascent of heaven " with complete
success ; they actually conduct their living chariots out of the
whole region of " nature " to the goal outside it. With men it is
otherwise. The best of them only succeed for a time in getting
their heads above the visible region, and attaining a glimpse of

Socrates, who alludes to the views of Alcmaeon about the brain as familiar to
himself in the autobiographical narrative of the *Phaedo*.

[1] *Phaedrus* 246a, ἐοικέτω δὴ συμφύτῳ δυνάμει ὑποπτέρου ζεύγους τε καὶ ἡνιόχου.
συμφύτῳ here should mean, as the word regularly does in Plato, literally *con-
cretae*, " grown together into one." It is inserted in order to insist on the
unity of the individual mind. We are to think of the driver and his horses as
a single organism.

what lies wholly beyond it, and then redescend. The worse are thrown into complete confusion by the restiveness of the horse of inferior strain and the unskilfulness of the horseman. Their horses lose their wings, and horses and horseman sink to earth, not to regain their old place until the wings of the soul have grown afresh. The magnitude of the fall is shown by the kind of life which the now incarnate soul leads in the body. Those who have " seen most " become philosophers, lovers of beauty, musical men or lovers ; then follow in descending order, law-abiding kings and soldiers, men of affairs and business, athletes and physicians, prophets and " initiators," poets and artists, mechanics and farmers, professional sophists and demagogues, tyrants. The rule which applies to all is that after each life a man receives the rewards of the deeds done in the body. None may recover his wings and return to the place from which he fell until ten thousand years are over, except one who chooses to live the life of the " philosopher or philosophic lover " three times in succession. For such a man the ten thousand years are reduced to three thousand.[1] For others the scheme includes, like that of the *Republic*, reincarnations in animal as well as in human bodies, but no soul can finally recover its wings after such a degradation until it has once more been reincarnated in human form, for the recovery of the soul's wings is only effected by *recollection* of the things of which the soul caught a glimpse when it was following the great procession of the gods, and it is only man to whom the experiences of sense suggest these recollections. A man in whom these recollections are being awakened is popularly thought " distracted," from his loss of interest in the things other men take seriously, but he is really " inspired " ($\dot{\epsilon}\nu\theta ov\sigma\iota\acute{a}\zeta\omega\nu$).[2]

Now our sensible experiences only suggest few and faint images of righteousness and temperance and the other forms, but beauty is much more impressively adumbrated in sense-experience, and the effect of the experience in awakening " recollection " is therefore exceptionally startling. In the soul which has all but lost the impression of heavenly beauty, the effect of its earthly adumbration is to provoke " brutal " appetite ($\tau\epsilon\tau\rho\acute{a}\pi o\delta os$ $\nu\acute{o}\mu o\nu$, 250e) for intercourse with the beautiful body. But in a soul fresh from deep contemplation of spiritual beauty, the sight of earthly beauty

---

[1] Thus the scheme is the same as that of the myth of Er in the *Republic*. The assumption is that the normal extreme limit of human life is a hundred years. Reincarnations take place once in a thousand years in order that the rewards and punishments at the end of each incarnation may be on a tenfold scale. The privilege of escape from the wheel after three incarnations and the hope that in general it will be achieved after ten, are not mentioned in the *Republic*, but I suspect Orphic origin for part at any rate of this. Empedocles fixes the soul's period of exile from heaven at 30,000 " seasons " (Fr. 115, R.P., 181), and we may suspect that he is reckoning three $\tilde{\omega}\rho\alpha\iota$ to the year, $\tilde{\epsilon}\alpha\rho$, $\theta\acute{\epsilon}\rho os$, $\chi\epsilon\iota\mu\acute{\omega}\nu$. On the details of the *Phaedrus* myth the student should consult the full commentary in Stewart's *Myths of Plato*.

[2] Cf. Browning's *Epistle of Karshish* with its treatment of Lazarus as " the madman," or St. Paul's language about the " foolishness " of the Cross.

arouses religious awe and worship ; the soul's wings begin to sprout, and this process, like the getting of teeth, is a mingled one of uneasiness with intervals of relief, pain in the absence of the beloved, rest and pleasure in his company. Hence the lover gladly forsakes all other society, neglects his property, and throws convention to the wind, so long as he can win the society in which he is getting his heart's desire. Men call this " being in love " ; it is really growing one's spiritual wings again (250*d*–252*c*). What sort of person will provoke this passion is a matter of the lover's peculiar temperament. In the best type of man the qualities which awaken it are " love of wisdom " and a " commanding personality " (252*e*) ; others are attracted by different gifts. In every case the " lover " aims at moulding the being he " idolizes " into the more and more perfect image of the " god " whom both serve, and the affection between them grows with every fresh step of the process (252*c*–253*c*).

But we must remember what we said about the difference in strain between the horses of the human soul. The better horse is modest and chivalrous, a " thorough-bred " ; the worse horse is a " bolter." So when the charioteer is wrapt in the contemplation of the beloved, the better horse modestly holds himself in, but the worse " bolts," in spite of rein and whip, from lust after carnal delight. The worse horse may be often " pulled to his haunches," but he persists in his struggles, and the time of really fierce temptation comes when the passion which began on one side is reciprocated on the other. If the temptation is successfully resisted, the pair have won one out of the three " Olympic victories " necessary to release them from incarnation in the flesh. Henceforward they have mastered the evil in themselves and won their freedom. But if their lives are directed only to the second-best, " honour," in the place of the first-best, " wisdom," the evil horse may get his way in an unguarded moment, and then there will be other such moments in their lives, though not many, as their conduct has not commended itself to their " whole souls." Their attachment will be real, but not so real as that of the pair who have won the mastery over themselves. At death, they are still " wingless " though " desirous to be winged," and even this is a gain. It is at least a beginning of the journey heavenwords, and the rest will come (253*a*–256*d*).[1]

This, then, is what association with a true lover may bestow ; intimate relations with the man who is " not in love " lead to a meanness of soul, falsely taken for a virtue, and a nine-thousand-years' period of " folly," spent on and under the earth. May Eros accept this recantation, grant Socrates not to lose his " skill in matters of love," and punish Lysias by converting him, as his

---

[1] The power and insight with which this account of the conflict between the spirit and the flesh is written should not mislead us into supposing that it must be concealed autobiography. Comparison with what Alcibiades says in the *Symposium* about the relations between himself as a boy and Socrates suggests that the model for Plato's picture of the lover who has come through the severest temptation unsmirched is to be found in Socrates and his behaviour to the beautiful and petulant boy.

brother Polemarchus has already been converted, to philosophy [1] (256e–257b).

Phaedrus is delighted with the fine speech to which he has just listened. Lysias himself could hardly match it. Perhaps he would not try ; he is a touchy man and was recently gravely offended by a politician who had called him a mere " writer of speeches " in depreciation. But, says Socrates, politicians who affect to despise " discourse-writing " are only disguising envy under the mask of contempt. They are vain enough of the decrees they propose and carry, and what is a decree but the record of a " discourse " to which the author has prefixed the names of its admirers, " the council " or " the people " ? And how much vainer a man is when his " discourses " are preserved in perpetuity as the " laws " of a State. Clearly, if there is any discredit it is not in composing discourses, but in composing them ill. And this raises the whole question, what is *good* writing ? (258d). This is the sort of problem which it gives an educated man real pleasure to discuss. If we neglect it and prefer to sleep out the warm noon-tide, the cicadae over our heads may carry our bad report to their patrons the Muses.[2] Accordingly, we now find ourselves launched on a serious inquiry into the problem of *style*. What is a good style ?

The Principles of Style (259e–278b).—(Nominally the question under discussion is that of the canons of a sound *rhetoric*, but we shall see that it rapidly expands into a consideration of the character of " style " in literature in general. A speaker or writer has a case of which he wishes to convince his hearer or reader. The question is what principles may be laid down for the presentation of this case in the way which will be most effective. Thus the considerations urged by Socrates bear as much on the written exposition of a subject in an essay or a treatise as upon the spoken presentation of it to an audience. The reason for approaching the topic primarily from the side of spoken discourse is simply that, in the age of Socrates, there was no serious prose literature in existence. The one still extant prose work of importance of an earlier date than the supposed conversation between Socrates and Phaedrus was the book of Herodotus. The " pre-Socratic philosophers " had, indeed, attempted to state their views about φύσις in a sort of prose ; the Periclean age saw the first written manuals of " rhetoric " and medicine, and the first written discussions of ethical and political problems. But the writers of τέχναι made no pretensions to style, and their compositions were not regarded as " literature." Literary prose, as a vehicle for the artistic expression of reflection upon life, was the creation of Isocrates,

---

[1] The point of the remark about Polemarchus is unknown. Had he, as would be quite possible, fallen in with some belated survivor of the downfall of the Pythagoreans during his years in Italy ? *E.g.* with Philolaus ?

[2] Note the allusion in 259d to the saying familiar from the *Phaedo* that philosophy is the μεγίστη μουσική. It is assumed that the saying is already current ; hence we cannot be far wrong in supposing that its origin was Pythagorean.

and at the assumed date of the conversation, Isocrates is still simply a composer of speeches to be delivered in the law-courts.)

It would seem obvious that the first prerequisite of a really good " discourse " is that the deliverer of it should know the truth about his subject. Yet the accepted view is that this is unnecessary. To compose a telling speech you need not know what are the δίκαια, the " rights and wrongs of the case " ; you need only know what the audience who are to decide the issue *think* right and wrong. You win your case by appeal to the " prejudices of your hearers." But this view will not bear examination. It would be a comic situation if Phaedrus, being under the impression that the word " horse " means a donkey, should be persuaded by a discourse on the usefulness of the horse in war to provide himself with a donkey [1] against his next campaign. It would be worse than comical if a public man with a persuasive tongue confused evil with good and led the community to embark on a policy based on the confusion. This would not be statesmanship, but the reverse of it. Possibly, however, the professors of rhetoric might reply that they do not claim for their art that it can teach us the principles of good and evil, but simply that even if you know these principles, you will not be able to turn your knowledge to account in practice unless you also follow their precepts.[2] Thus sound knowledge of good and evil would be an indispensable prerequisite for statesmanship, but mastery of the technical rules of rhetoric would be necessary for the statesman who needs to convince the public. So far as it goes this is a fair defence of rhetoric,—on one condition. The condition is that the rules in question form a real τέχνη or " art," the application of real scientific knowledge to practice. But there is a view that they are nothing of the kind ; " persuasion " is a mere empirical " knack " (τριβή) for which no rules can be laid down, and there is no " art of speaking " distinct from the knowledge of the true facts about the subject-matter of the discourses. This view demands consideration (259e–261a).

May we not define rhetoric as verbal " sorcery " (ψυχαγωγία) [3] whether practised in the courts, in other public gatherings, or in private life, and whether the issues on which it is employed are grave or trivial ? The writers on the subject, it is true, generally confine the sphere of the art to public discourses before law-courts and popular assemblies ; but they forget that such a restriction would amount to excluding Zeno and his paradoxes from considera-

---

[1] The implication is that Phaedrus is still a rich man ; he would have to serve in the cavalry, if called out, and thus belongs to the class of πεντακοσιο-μέδιμνοι or that of ἱππῆς.

[2] This, we may remind ourselves, is actually the view taken by Gorgias in the dialogue called after him. He disclaims any pretence to be able to " teach goodness."

[3] The word should be understood in its literal sense of " spirit-raising." The eloquent speaker deals with the ψυχαί of the audience as the sorcerer does with the ghosts he raises and lays ; he puts a " spell " on you. So we hear in our modern slang of " wizards " and " spell-binders " in public life.

tion. This would be a bad mistake. Zeno, like the speakers in the courts or the *ecclesia*, is a controversialist. Just as a skilled political or forensic pleader can make us think the same course or the same case just or unjust at his pleasure, Zeno makes us accept or deny the same proposition in the mathematics as he pleases. Rhetoric is thus universally skill in controversy. Success in it depends on ability to establish resemblances or similarities and to expose resemblances which have been tacitly presupposed by the antagonist [1] (261e). Now we are most readily led astray in cases where the dissimilarity between two things is apparently slight, and therefore a man who wants to confuse others but avoid being misled himself, as the controversialist does, needs to *know* what are the real similarities and dissimilarities between things, and this makes it ridiculous to talk of an " art of discourse " which can be divorced from " knowledge of the real " (262c). We may illustrate the point from the discourse of Lysias with which we have been concerned. Lysias is discussing the question whether a " lover " is a blessing or a curse. Now " love " is not, like " iron " or " silver," a word with a definite and undisputed meaning. Different persons understand very different things by the name. It is idle to ask whether a " lover " is a blessing or not, unless we begin by defining " love." Lysias never explains what he means ; in his opening sentence he introduces the word " lover " without any explanation. The ambiguity thus introduced into his speech is definitely an offence against art, a violation of a law of good style. He begins where he ought to have ended.[2] Socrates was better inspired by the local deities, since he opened his speech by the required definition.

A second grave fault in style is that there is no recognizable order in the discourse of Lysias. It is not the consistent development of a theme and has no organic structure. There is no discoverable reason why the various points of the speech might not have been made in a wholly different order. But a good discourse ought to have a definite organic structure, just like a living creature. There should be a definite plan underlying it which would be ruined if you inverted the order of its paragraphs.[3] Here again the discourse with which the Nymphs inspired Socrates presents an instructive contrast. It began by saying what " love " is, a kind of " madness " or " frenzy." Next it distinguished two main types of

---

[1] Cf. the appeals to " precedents " which are so common a feature of both forensic and political oratory. The παράδειγμα which Aristotle calls a " rhetorician's form of induction " (*Analyt. Post.* A, 71a 9) is just the " appeal to precedent."

[2] The right order of thought would be to say first what the passion " love " is, then to consider how it will affect the man who is dominated by it, and last of all to ask whether these effects will make him a better influence in a lad's life than the man who is not " in love." Lysias *begins* with this last question, and never raises the others.

[3] Socrates puts his finger on the defect which, above all others, is the most glaring fault of the bad stylist, neglect of the logical sequence of the parts of his essay or the chapters of his book.

madness, that due to human disease and that due to divinely
sent " exaltation " above everyday " conventionalities." Then
it went on to make a further subdivision of divine " exaltation "
itself, and so to distinguish the " exaltation " of the lover from that
of the " seer," the " poet," and the founder of a religion, and ended
with an imaginative hymn in praise of Eros (264b–265c). Much of
what we said was, perhaps, sportive, but there are two points about
the method we followed which are of serious importance. When
any subject is to be expounded, it is vitally important to define it,
and to define it one must be able to " collect " its *disiecta membra*
into a single " pattern " (ἰδέα), as we did when we reduced all the
manifestations of " love " under the one head of " distraction "
(παράνοια). But it is no less important, when we have got our
single " pattern," to " divide " it again rightly into sub-patterns,
like a skilful carver who disjoints an animal at the proper articula-
tions. This was what we tried to do when we went on to distinguish a " sinister," or left-hand and a " right-hand " distraction,
and then carefully subdivided both again along the proper lines,
so that we were left with a " sinister " love which we were entitled
to denounce and a clearly discriminated " right-hand " or " divine "
love which was eulogized as the source of the greatest blessings.
(It was just this process of first " collecting " the definition and then
making a scientific subdivision of the *definitum* on a proper *funda-
mentum divisionis* which enabled us to give a rational justification
for our answer and our approbation.) Socrates is devoted to this
method of combined " composition " and " division," and is ready
to follow the steps of the " dialectician " who possesses it, as those of
a god. Thus we are brought to the conclusion that " dialectic is
philosophy " in the wide sense in which that word means the
capacity for seeing the real affinities in things, and so grouping
them in well-defined *genera*; and detecting the differences which
mark off different *species* within the *genus*, is the first requisite
of a masterly style. To be a true stylist, you must have a clear
view of your subject as a whole, and be able to articulate it aright
(265c–266a).

Phaedrus agrees that this is a good account of " dialectic,"
and that Socrates has a correct conception of a " scientific style."
But Thrasymachus and the other teachers of prose style have not
the qualities we have described. What they mean by " rhetorical
style " is something different. They mean, in fact, the arrangement
of the parts of a " discourse " on a certain model which they prescribe, but which has nothing to do with the kind of logical structure
just described. To use technical terms, they say, *e.g.*, that a good
speech must have its *exordium* (προοίμιον); then you must go
on to the *narration* (διήγησις), which relates what you allege to
be the facts of the case; next to the production of the *depositions*
(μαρτυρίαι) of witnesses; then to a consideration of the *presumptions*
(τεκμήρια) and plausibilities (εἰκότα); and there are many other
subdivisions. (The precise meaning of the technical terms is in

many cases uncertain, since some of them were not preserved in the later manuals of the art, and even of those which are preserved, we cannot be certain that they already had their later meanings as early as the fifth century. The reader may consult the notes in Thompson's edition of the dialogue.) Gorgias and his master Tisias insist on the importance of a dexterous art of exaggeration and extenuation ; Polus and Protagoras before him on grace and appropriateness of verbal phrasing. We need not follow them into all these details, but we must test the worth of their theory of style as a whole ; perhaps its texture will look very loose if we view it in a clear light (266c–268a).

Suppose a man claimed to be a physician on the ground that he knew recipes for raising and lowering the body's temperature, producing a vomit and an evacuation and the like, would specialists like our friend Eryximachus admit his claim ? If he did not know also in what patients, when, and with what violence to produce these effects, they would say at once that he did not know medicine. So Sophocles or Euripides would say to anyone who knew how to make single speeches effectively but not how to construct an artistic whole out of them, " You may understand the preliminaries to play-making, but you don't know how to make a *play*." So Pericles, we may be sure, would have told us urbanely that a man who has learned the devices of the textbooks has only learned the pre-liminaries to " rhetoric." The art consists in knowing how and when to use the various devices to effect ($\pi\iota\theta\alpha\nu\hat{\omega}s$) and to make your discourse into a real *whole* (268a–269c).[1]

Admittedly *this* cannot be learned from any of the law-books : how then should a man set himself to acquire a really persuasive style ? To begin with, he must have a natural *gift* of expression, or he will be wasting time in trying to cultivate a barren soil. If he has the natural gift, its cultivation demands both knowledge and practice ($\mu\epsilon\lambda\acute{\epsilon}\tau\eta$), and is thus not wholly a matter of " art." In so far as it does depend on knowledge and thus is an " art," Lysias and Thrasymachus have misconceived the kind of knowledge required. What it is may be suggested to us by the facts about Pericles, the most effective of all our great orators. Over and above his natural gift of speech ($\pi\rho\grave{o}s \tau\hat{\omega}$ $\epsilon\mathring{v}\phi v\grave{\eta}s$ $\epsilon\mathring{l}\nu\alpha\iota$, 270a), Pericles had the advantage of early association with Anaxagoras. This gave him a certain largeness of mental outlook which makes itself felt in his political oratory.[2] The great stylist, in fact, needs

---

[1] Note that Euripides is definitely associated here with Sophocles (268c). Both are assumed to be living and accessible. Hence we should date the conversation before the final departure of Euripides from Athens (408 or 407). The reference to Eryximachus and his father (268a) shows that if they are the persons of the same names who were implicated in the scandal of 415, it had not such serious consequences for them as it had for some of their circle.

[2] Of course, the allusion is half playful. The suggestion is that Pericles turned to account in practical statesmanship the Anaxagorean physical speculations about the sovereignty of $\nu o\hat{v}s$; he made *mens agitat molem* into a political principle (270a 5).

to build on the same foundations as the great physician. If a man is to be more than a mere empiric in medicine, as we may see from the teaching of Hippocrates, he needs a scientific knowledge of the body, which can hardly be acquired without a knowledge of " nature " as a whole. He must know whether the human body is composed of one single ingredient or of many, and, in either case, he must further know how the substance or substances composing the human body are affected by each and all of the substances which medicine employs in its pharmacopoeia. Without this scientific basis, medicine would be a mere " fumbling in the dark."[1] The same thing is true of the " orator." He is trying to produce healthy convictions in the minds of his audience by discourses exactly as the physician produces healthy conditions in their bodies by his prescriptions. Hence anyone who undertakes to teach the art of persuasion needs first of all to have a thoroughly scientific knowledge of the *mind*. He must know what are *its* components and exactly how each type of discourse will affect them. In a word, he must have a sound psychology of human nature. Thus he must understand what different temperaments there are among his auditors, what different types of " discourses " there are, and why such and such a type of " discourse " appeals to such and such a temperament. And this is not all. The effective speaker, like the successful physician, must have skill in diagnosis. He must be able in practice to judge rapidly and surely of the temperament of an actual audience and the type of appeal which will go home to them. Only when he has thus diagnosed his hearers' temperaments and decided on the right kind of appeal to make will he be in a position to apply the rules given in the hand-books for producing the kind of effect which will be opportune (269*d*–272*b*).

The road to oratorical success we have described is, no doubt, a long and difficult one ; but can the writers of the handbooks really show us an easier short cut ? We know that, as has been already mentioned, they often say the " speaker " or " stylist " need not concern himself with realities or " truths " ; he need only aim at being plausible, and, indeed, should often prefer plausibility to truth. Thus if he is employed in a case where a plucky little man has beaten a stronger but cowardly man, he would, speaking

---

[1] Plato is thinking mainly of the doctrine of the four fundamental " humours " (blood, phlegm, red bile, black bile) on which the Coan school of medicine built up its humoral pathology, and is arguing that the physician must have a scientific knowledge of the action of each substance in the pharmacopoeia on each of these " humours." The counterpart would be a scientific knowledge of the " active principles," as Butler calls them, in the human mind and the way in which each may be stimulated or inhibited by the appropriate type of verbal appeal. The particular Hippocratean work alluded to is, perhaps, the περὶ φύσιος ἀνθρώπου, where the humoral pathology is expressly expounded. But see the discussion of Diés, *Autour de Platon*, 30 ff. The sure and rapid gauging of the temper of the audience, on which he rightly insists as all-important, is just the sort of thing of which there can be no τέχνη. No rules can be given for it ; it is a matter of αἴσθησις (271*e*).

for the defence, dwell on the improbability that the small man should have attacked a bigger man, or, if he spoke for the prosecution, he would try to suggest that there had been a concerted assault by several assailants. In either case, the real facts of the situation are just what the clever advocate would take care to keep dark. But we must retort once more that one can only judge of the " plausibilities " in proportion as one knows the real facts. (The advocate may rely on distortion of the facts, but he must know what they are if he is to distort them in a really plausible way.) So we adhere to our view that it is a long and a hard task to acquire the art of a persuasive style. The time and labour required would be disproportionate if one's object were merely to make an impression on one's fellow-mortals, and not, as it ought to be, to make our words, like our deeds, acceptable to God. (That would, of course, be the aim of a true statesman, who employs his knowledge of human temperaments and the way in which they may be appealed to, to enlist his fellow-citizens in the prosecution of good and the avoidance of evil.) This is, in substance, all we have to say about the principles of an *art* of style. It must be based on a masterly knowledge of the subject-matter dealt with and an equally masterly knowledge of the psychology of the hearers (or readers) addressed, combined wtih a natural gift of language (272c–274b).

We may now turn to the question, suggested by the sneer of the unnamed politician about Lysias (257c), whether it is a proper thing to perpetuate one's discourses in writing. Socrates professes to have heard a story—Phaedrus prefers to think that he is inventing it—that, in the old days when Egypt was governed by gods, the god Thoth invented the art of writing and recommended it to Amon,[1] who then ruled at Thebes, as a device which would make the Egyptians wiser and improve their memories. Amon reproved him, on the ground that written records tend to make us neglect the cultivation of memory by making it unnecessary, and to fill men with an empty conceit of their own wisdom. They think they know a great deal which they have merely read without understanding and without any abiding effect on their minds. The art of writing does not act as a substitute for memory ; it merely provides us with *memoranda*—convenient means of *refreshing* our memory from time to time. A book is like a picture. The figures of the picture may actually " look alive," but they cannot speak. So the words and sentences in a written book look full of wisdom, but if you question the book about its meaning, you can get no reply. A " discourse," once written down, comes into the hands of the unintelligent, as well as of the intelligent, and is exposed to misinterpretation. If it is to be rightly understood, it needs the living voice of the author to explain and defend it. Thus the written discourse is at best a lifeless image of the living thought which is

---

[1] Plato calls him Thamus, but the mention of Thebes shows what Egyptian god he has in mind. Is the name Thamus, which has perplexed the commentators, due to a presumably wilful confusion with the Syrian Thammuz ?

written " in the soul of him who understands it." A gardener may, for amusement, force flowers in a " garden of Adonis," [1] but he takes care to sow the seeds of crops about which he is in earnest in the appropriate soil and to wait months for their maturing. So the man who is in earnest about raising the fruit of righteousness and goodness will not trust to forcing it by writing his deepest convictions in ink ; he will trust to the slow and steady cultivation of them in his own soul, and in those of others with whom he is in constant personal contact. When he commits his thoughts to writing, it will be partly as a *memorandum* against the " forgetfulness of his old age," partly because such literature affords a worthy form of entertainment in our hours of relaxation. So we may tell Lysias—and we might say the same thing to Homer and the poets, or to Solon and the " composers " of laws—that if any of them has really understood what his " works " can effect and what they cannot, and how secondary a place they hold by comparison with his living thought—such a man has a claim to a very different name from that of λογογράφος ; he is a true " philosopher." But if he really has nothing better to give mankind than the painfully elaborated phrases and clauses of his writings, he deserves to be called a mere poet or speech-writer or " law-writer." [2] The man ought always to be greater than his book or poem or code (274*b*–278*e*).

This conviction that a man's personality ought to be greater than his literary " work," and, in particular, that the true philosopher is a great personality whose very deepest thoughts are those which he cannot set down " in black and white," was one Plato held strongly and retained to the end of his life.[3] It explains why he never attempted to put in writing any of his own profoundest metaphysical speculations. They were the fruit of a " way of life," and, to be understood, pre-supposed the living of the same life on the part of the recipient. To record them for the world at large would have been merely to court dangerous misunderstanding. Even so, Carlyle, as the jest has it, wrote thirty-seven volumes to persuade the world that silence is golden. Naturally he could not tell us the secret of the " golden silence." That could only be told to a man with the soul of a second Carlyle, and such a man would discover the secret without needing to read the thirty-seven volumes.

---

[1] As we should say, " in a hot-house." The *horti Adonidis* were pots in which flowers were rapidly forced, to die again equally rapidly.

[2] νομογράφον (278*e* 2) cannot mean " writer of music." The word appears to be used nowhere else in literature. Here it obviously means a " code-maker," and the point is that if a man like Solon really exhausted all his wisdom in the mere excogitation of the clauses of a code of laws, so that in personal intercourse he merely talked his own code, as some writers are said to talk their own books, he deserves to be spoken of with disparagement. The word is invented to convey the same sort of depreciation as λογογράφος.

[3] Compare the insistence on the point in *Ep.* vii. 341*c*–342*a*, 343*e*–344*d*, where the imagery and language seem directly reminiscent of our dialogue.

Epilogue (278c–279c).—Has Socrates any message for his friend Isocrates, the younger rival of Lysias ? He can only conjecture what the young man's development will be, but he believes that Isocrates has better natural endowments and a nobler temper of soul than Lysias. Probably, if he continues in his present profession, he will out-distance all rivals and competitors, and it may be that he will be led " by a diviner impulse " to still higher things, for there really is a " strain of philosophy " in him.

Nothing remains now but that Socrates should take leave of the spot where he has spent his hour of *siesta* with a brief prayer to Pan and its other tutelary spirits. His prayer is that " he may become fair in the inward man, and that the outer man may be conformable to the inward ; that he may regard wisdom as the true riches and that his wealth may be such as none but the temperate can carry." Thus the prayer is for good of mind, body, and fortune, and is worded in a way to remind us of the Socratic estimate of the relative importance of the three.

There is no real need to enter into the idle questions which have been raised about the significance of the allusions to Isocrates. What is said is strictly true and appropriate to the assumed situation. Isocrates certainly had greater parts than Lysias and stood on a higher intellectual and moral level. He showed his superiority in parts by becoming the real creator of literary prose style, and his superiority in character by deserting " speech-writing " for the foundation of a school for the training of the young for public life. However defective Plato may have thought the training he gave, the simple fact that it was based on a generous Pan-Hellenism, and that Isocrates was the recognized mouthpiece of this Pan-Hellenism among the publicists of his age, fully explains Plato's ascribing to Socrates the remark, quite likely enough to have been actually made, that there was a strain of philosophy in the man. There can be no doubt about the historical fact of the influence of Socrates on Isocrates.[1] As to the alleged " feud " between Isocrates and Plato, of which much has been made by some modern writers, there is really no evidence for it. The frequent expressions in Isocrates' writings depreciatory of " science " and " eristic " as a propaedeutic for the statesman are, indeed, pretty clearly meant specially for the Academy, but the attempts to find sarcastic rejoinders in Plato to these little acerbities have not really been successful, and the ingenuity devoted to these attempts seems to me to have been simply wasted. After all, Plato and Isocrates had a good deal in common in their views on practical politics, and they were neither Alexandrian *literati* nor German Professors. We in this country can quite understand how two eminent men can differ in their

[1] On this see Burnet, *Greek Philosophy, Part I.*, 215–219 ; " Socratic Doctrine of the Soul," in *Proceedings of the British Academy*, 1915–16, p. 235 ff. So the point of Isocrates' comments on the attack on Socrates by Polycrates is that Socrates was as absurd a theme for invective as Busiris for eulogy. Polycrates showed his silliness by denouncing a man of exemplary virtue no less than by eulogizing a monster (Isocr. xi. 4).

philosophical programmes without becoming personal enemies, or how the bigger man of the two can afford to take an occasional " rap over the knuckles " from the lesser in good part. (No one supposes, for example, that Shakespeare's relations with Ben Jonson were disturbed by Ben's occasional quips.) Hence I cannot but agree with Professor Burnet in thinking that the tradition followed by Cicero, which represents Plato and Isocrates as being on personally friendly terms, is likely to be the true one.[1]

In taking leave of the *Phaedrus*, we may note that while it supplements the *Gorgias* in its conclusions about the value of " style," it modifies nothing that was said in the earlier dialogue. The moral condemnation pronounced on the use of eloquent speech to pervert facts and produce false impressions remains the same. So does the verdict that the sort of thing the professional teachers from Tisias to Thrasymachus profess to expound is not a science but a mere " trick " or " knack " (and therefore cannot be conveyed, as they professed to convey it, by " lessons "). In adding that a thorough knowledge of a subject-matter and a sound knowledge of the psychology of the public addressed furnish a really scientific basis for a worthy and effective style, Plato is saying nothing inconsistent with the results of the *Gorgias*. There is thus no sufficient ground for thinking that the teaching of the *Phaedrus* represents a later " development " from the more " Socratic " position of the *Gorgias*. Socrates cannot have lived in the Athens of the Archidamian war and the subsequent twenty years without having had occasion to turn his thoughts to the problem of the value of " rhetorical " style, and there is no reason why he should not actually have reached the conclusions of the *Phaedrus*, though naturally we cannot *prove* that he had.

See further :

THOMPSON, W. H.—Plato's *Phaedrus*.
ROBIN, L.—*Phèdre (Collection des Universités de France*, Paris, 1933).
RITTER, C.—*Platon*, ii. 39–62 ; *Platons Dialog Phaidros* [2], pp. 1–28a.
RAEDER, H.—*Platons philosophische Entwickelung*, 245–279.
NATORP.—*Platons Ideenlehre*, 52–87.
STEWART, J. A.—*Myths of Plato*, 306–396 (*Phaedrus Myth*) ; *Plato's Doctrine of Ideas*, 62–65 and Part II.
DIÈS, A.—*Autour de Platon II*, 400–449.

[1] Cicero, *Orator*, xiii. 42, " me autem qui Isocratem non diligunt una cum Socrate et Platone errare patiantur." Cf. Diogenes Laert. III., 8, where we are told that the Peripatetic Praxiphanes wrote a dialogue in which Isocrates figured as the guest of Plato. The theory of a rivalry has no ancient tradition behind it. This is the more significant that the rivalry between Aristotle and the school of Isocrates is quite well attested (Cicero, *de Oratore*, iii. 35, 141, *Orator*, xix. 62). I should suppose that Plato's purpose in ending the dialogue with a marked compliment to Isocrates is to show that it is *not* meant as a polemic against him.

CHAPTER XIII

THE *THEAETETUS*

IT seems possible to date the composition of the *Theaetetus* more precisely than that of any other Platonic dialogue. For the main discussion is introduced by a short preliminary conversation between the Megarians, Euclides and Terpsion, whom we met in the *Phaedo* as members of the inner Socratic circle. Terpsion relates that he has just met Theaetetus of Athens, who is being conveyed home from the Athenian camp at Corinth after a battle, wounded and suffering severely from dysentery. The thought of the loss such a man will be to the world reminds Euclides that Socrates had once met Theaetetus, just before his own death, and had prophesied a distinguished future for the lad. Euclides professes to have heard all about this from Socrates himself ; he was so struck that he at once wrote out *memoranda* of what Socrates had told him, and afterwards corrected and enlarged them with the help of Socrates himself.

Since much stress is laid on the point that Theaetetus, who is called a distinguished " man " by Terpsion (142*b*) was a mere " lad " in the year 399, it is clear that the battle from which Theaetetus, as the whole tone of the Prologue implies, was carried home to die, must fall a good while later. As Dr. Eva Sachs has shown,[1] the known engagement which best satisfies the implied conditions is that of the year 369, in which Epaminondas broke through the Athenian and Spartan lines on Mt. Oneion.[2] Manifestly the dialogue was written as a tribute to the memory of Theaetetus, shortly after his death, which Euclides and Terpsion regard as certainly impending. This brings us to 368 or the beginning of 367 as the date of its completion. Thus, as Burnet points out, it must have been finished on the very eve of Plato's departure from Athens to throw himself into his great political adventure at Syracuse, and probably with full consciousness that he was, for the time, about to abandon the studious life for that of affairs.

Several points in the introduction call for remark. (1) When Euclides explains that, to avoid tediousness, he has adopted the

---

[1] In her dissertation *de Theaeteto Atheniensi* (Berlin, 1914), which finally disposes of Natorp's singular theory that the dialogue is a juvenile work.

[2] Xenophon, *Hellenica*, vii. 1, 41 ; Bury, *History of Greece*, p. 608. The engagement appears to have been a trivial one, but even trivial engagements involve casualties. Theaetetus apparently owed his death more to dysentery than to his wounds (142*b*)

directly dramatic form of narration (143*b*–*c*), we must, of course understand that this is really Plato's explanation of his abandonment of the method adopted in all the great dialogues of his literary prime (except the *Phaedrus*). Henceforth, with a possible exception for the *Parmenides*, we shall find him returning to the simply dramatic method of his earliest writings.[1] This is, no doubt, because in these later works the old interest in reproducing a living picture of Socrates and his contemporaries has at last yielded pretty completely to the more philosophical interest of developing the subject-matter. The *Theaetetus* is the latest dialogue in which the personality of Socrates is made prominent. (2) The stress laid on the prophetic insight shown by Socrates in his estimate of the lad Theaetetus seems unintelligible, unless we are to take the meeting of the lad and the old philosopher, and the forecast made by the latter, as genuine historical facts. They are just the sort of facts which might properly be made the most of in a work meant as a " tribute " to the memory of Theaetetus. (3) Euclides' account of the way in which he worked up his narrative, with the help of Socrates himself, may be a fiction, but Plato evidently thought it a natural fiction. We may fairly infer that admirers of Socrates actually took down such notes of striking conversations, and that Plato himself may have used such records, made by himself or others, as material for his Socratic dialogues. In the present case, by appealing to the record of Euclides he contrives to let us know that he was not himself actually present when Socrates met Theaetetus, though we might otherwise have expected him to be there. Possibly this is explained by the illness which also kept him away from the death-scene of the Master a few weeks later. (4) The introduction of Euclides and Terpsion into the narrative, like the preoccupation with the personality of Parmenides and Zeno in the *Parmenides*, and the appearance of a " visitor from Elea " as chief speaker in the two later dialogues, which are made to continue the conversation of the *Theaetetus*, shows that we have reached a period in Plato's life when his special interest is to define his attitude towards the Megarian developments of Eleaticism. This is a matter which will call for consideration more particularly when we go on to deal with the *Parmenides* and *Sophistes*. We shall find Plato in these dialogues taking up an attitude of decided hostility to the one-sided intellectualism of the school as tending to pervert philosophy into a mere barren sporting with " abstractions." The same attitude is shown in our dialogue by the emphatic recognition of the contribution of sensation to real knowledge. By virtually dedicating the dialogue to his old friend Euclides,[2]

---

[1] On the question whether the *Parmenides* is earlier or later than the *Theaetetus*, see the next chapter. In any case, they must be nearly contemporary. Probably the difficulty of keeping up the indirect method in the *Parmenides* was the immediate occasion for its abandonment.

[2] Euclides can hardly be assumed to have died in the interval between 369 and 367. That would be too much of a coincidence.

Plato gives us to understand that his growing dissatisfaction with the contemporary "Megarians" implies no change in his sentiments towards the founder of the school, an old and faithful member of the group who had been lifelong admirers of Socrates.

The main conversation is dated very shortly before the famous trial of 399, as we see from the concluding sentence (210*d*), where Socrates explains that he has to attend at the offce of the "king," to put in his answer to the indictment of Meletus. The parties present, besides Socrates, are the Pythagorean geometer Theodorus, the lad Theaetetus, his companion the younger Socrates (147*d*), who is a "mute personage," and possibly one or two other unnamed lads. The scene is an unnamed *palaestra* (144*c*), possibly that in the Lyceum. We learn in the course of the dialogue that Theodorus comes from Cyrene, and that he is a friend and admirer of the now deceased Protagoras, though he professes to be strictly a mathematiciαn, wholly unversed in the methods and terminology of contemporary Athenian "philosophy" (146*b*, 165*a*). That he belonged to the Pythagorean order is indicated by the appearance of his name in the list of Pythagoreans given by Iamblichus (*Vit. Pythag.* xxxvi. 267). A notice preserved by Proclus in his commentary on the First Book of Euclid's *Elements* (Friedlein, p. 66) shows that Eudemus in his History of Mathematics ranked Theodorus with Hippocrates of Chios as one of the greatest of fifth-century geometers. Xenophon (*Mem.* iv. 2, 10) mentions him in a way which implies that Socrates knew him, though this may be only Xenophon's inference from our dialogue. Theaetetus, it is important to remember, was a member of Plato's Academy and one of the very first mathematicians of the fourth century. Eudemus, as we see from Proclus (*loc. cit.*), named him along with Archytas and Leodamas as one of the three prominent geometers of the fourth century. From notices in the Scholia to Euclid's *Elements* and elsewhere, we gather that he was one of the first mathematicians to begin the systematic study of the types of "quadratic surd" worked out to its completion in Euclid's Tenth Book, and he is still more often referred to as the geometer who completed the theory of the "regular solids," by adding to the three known to the Pythagoreans (tetrahedron, cube, dodecahedron) the remaining two (octahedron, icosahedron).[1]

Though the dramatic power of the *Theaetetus* is still remarkable, it has features which show that we are near the point at which

[1] There is a little difficulty here. The meaning of the statement must be that the fifth-century geometers already knew the constructions for the inscription of three of the figures in the sphere: Theaetetus added the constructions for the remaining two and thus completed the doctrine of Euclid, *Elements*, xiii. But Plato definitely attributes to the Pythagorean Timaeus a knowledge of all five regular solids (and this is why these solids were known in antiquity as the "figures of Plato"). Careful reading, however, will show that Timaeus is never allowed to *mention* the inscribing of the octahedron and icosahedron in the sphere, as he does that of the tetrahedron and dodecahedron. This seems to me confirmation of the tradition that these constructions were unknown in the fifth century.

dialogue will become a mere conventional form for what is in reality an essay on a set theme. The theme is propounded at the beginning of the discussion and is then pursued, except for one remarkable digression, owned to be such by the author himself, with a system and strictness we have not yet met in any of the major dialogues. The Socratic cross-questioning is becoming a conscious pursuit of the " critical " method, brought to bear on a single determinate problem. This makes the analysis of the dialogue unusually easy to follow.

INTRODUCTION (143*d*–151*e*)

The problem to be discussed is still made to arise, in the fashion of the *Protagoras* or *Republic*, apparently almost by accident. In the old way, Socrates is made to speak of his interest in the young and to ask Theodorus whether any of the lads of Athens have struck him as showing remarkable promise. Theodorus says that there is one whose remarkable combination of quick intelligence, perseverance, and modesty afford grounds for hoping very great things of him, Theaetetus. It is curious that this remarkable boy has a quaint physical resemblance to Socrates himself. This gives Socrates his opening. He calls Theaetetus out of the group of lads who are anointing themselves after their exercises and begins a conversation with him. Theodorus, he says, has just made a remark about our facial resemblance. As Theodorus is not a portrait-painter, such a remark from him is not very important. But as he is an eminent man of science, his opinion about our mental endowments carries weight. Hence Socrates would be glad to discover whether the lad's mental gifts really bear out the very high commendation they have just received. He will put this to the test by asking a question. Theaetetus is learning geometry and other things from Theodorus. Now to learn means to be acquiring knowledge. But what exactly is knowledge ? Can Theaetetus offer any answer to this question, one which has often perplexed Socrates himself ? The lad begins, as Plato so often makes an interlocutor do, by an enumeration. Geometry and the other things taught by Theodorus are knowledge ; so is shoe-making or carpentry.

Of course, as Socrates points out, this is no answer to the question. To answer the question what knowledge is by saying that shoemaking is knowledge only amounts to saying that *knowing* how to make shoes is knowledge. Knowing how to make furniture is also knowledge. Our problem is to say what we mean by the " knowing " which appears as a " determinable " in both these statements. Theaetetus seizes the point at once, since it makes the problem under consideration the same in type with a mathematical one which he and the younger Socrates have just solved. That problem was to find a common formula for what we call, in our modern terminology, " quadratic surds," or " irrational square roots." As stated by Theaetetus, the question is treated, exactly as it is in Euclid, as one about " lines " (γραμμαί). You cannot construct a straight line commensurable with your unit of length, such that the square upon it is 3 or 5 or 7 or 11 or 13 or 17 times the area of the square on the unit line. But you can devise a general formula for all these cases as follows. We may divide the integers into two classes : those which are the product of two equal factors (4, 9, 16, etc.), and those which are not (e.g. 6, 8). We may then call the first class " square " and the second " oblong " numbers. This enables us to make a correlated division of all terminated straight lines. If the area of the square described on such a straight line can be represented, in terms of the area of the square on a unit line by a number which is the product of two equal factors, we call the line in question a " length " (μῆκος) ; if this area is represented by a number which is not the product of two equal factors, we call the corresponding line a " power." Lines of the first class are all commensurable with one another, since they are all " measured " by our standard unit of length ; lines of the second class have no common measure, but the areas of the squares on them have (e.g. $\sqrt{3}$ and $\sqrt{5}$ have no common measure, but an area of 3 square feet and one of 5 square feet have one, namely, the square on a line 1 foot long). This is why the lines of the second class are called " powers " ; they are not themselves commensurable with one another but their " second powers " are commensurable.[1] Thus, since every terminated straight line under consideration belongs to one and only one of these two classes, Theaetetus has succeeded, by the use of dichotomy, in strictly defining the class which we should call " quadratic surds " (148b).

Socrates is delighted with this achievement, and only wishes Theaetetus to apply the same ability to determining the class of " sciences " or " knowledges," by bringing them all under one common determinable (148d). Theaetetus is eager to solve the problem, but does not feel equal to the task, though he cannot persuade himself to let it drop from his mind. This shows that Theaetetus is " pregnant " with a thought which he cannot successfully bring to the birth. Now Socrates, like his mother, practises the obstetric art, not, like her, on the bodies of women, but on the souls of men. He has no spiritual offspring of his own to bear, as midwives are no longer fruitful when they enter on their profession.[2] But he has great skill in assisting at the birth of a younger man's thoughts, and in discerning whether they are healthy and well formed or

[1] The use of the word δύναμις in this sense of " quadratic surd " was presumably an experiment in language which did not perpetuate itself. The name for the " quadratic surds " which became technical in the Academy and has passed thence into Euclid and later mathematics generally, is εὐθεῖαι δυνάμει σύμμετροι, straight lines whose squares have a common measure (Eucl. Elements, x. Def. 3).

[2] Note that it is implied in the comparison that Socrates had not always been spiritually " past procreation," any more than his own mother had always been barren.

sickly and misshapen. This discernment is the more necessary that the offspring of the mind, unlike that of the body, are sometimes mere fantastic " ghosts " (εἴδωλα) of thoughts.¹ Socrates is like his mother in another respect. Midwives are excellent match-makers, since their professional skill makes them good judges of the physical suitability of a couple to one another. So Socrates has often judged shrewdly that some of the young men who have frequented his company are not really " pregnant " with thoughts at present, and in such cases he has found mates for them in whose society they have ceased to be barren, such as Prodicus.² He has now an occasion for the practice of his gift. He will help Theaetetus' spiritual first-born into the world, and then we will try it, to see whether it is a genuine thought or a mere " changeling " (149e–151d).

FIRST DEFINITION OF KNOWLEDGE (151e–186e)

KNOWLEDGE AND SENSATION : THE THEORY STATED (151e–160d).—With this encouragement Theaetetus attempts a first definition. A man who knows a thing " perceives " the thing he knows (as our own proverb says, " seeing is believing "). So we may say, as a first suggestion, that " knowledge (ἐπιστήμη) is just perception " (αἴσθησις).³ This would seem to be only another way of saying what Protagoras expressed by the formula that " man is the measure." Theaetetus, who has often read Protagoras (152a), agrees with Socrates that Protagoras meant by this that " what *appears* to me, *is* to me ; what *appears* to you, *is* to you." In fact, " I perceive this " = " this appears to me " = " this *is* so to me " (152b). " Sense " (αἴσθησις) is thus always apprehension

¹ The suggestion is that if—as is not the case—a woman sometimes gave birth to a real child and sometimes to a " changeling," the midwife's task would become even more responsible than it is. She would have to decide in a given case whether the offspring should be cast away. The passage lends no support to the erroneous popular theory of infanticide as a feature of Athenian life.

² The transparent irony of this passage has actually been missed by some of the zealots for the " sophists." It is the minds which Socrates judges to be barren, the persons on whom his own endeavours would be thrown away, *i.e.* the second-rate, whom he hands over to Prodicus and his likes. That the conception of the obstetrics of the soul is a genuine Socratic fancy is shown by the allusion in Aristophanes' *Clouds*, 137 ff.

³ I render αἴσθησις in this statement by " perception," rather than by " sensation," since it is not clear to me that Theaetetus is at first using the word with the specific meaning of discernment by *sense*. Until Socrates leads him to make his statement more precise, he seems to me to be employing αἰσθάνεσθαι, in the fashion of the pre-Socratics, for direct apprehension of any kind, whether sensuous or not. What a man is directly apprehending he is sure of (ἐπίσταται). For this sense of ἐπίστασθαι cf. Heraclit. Fr. 35 (By-water), τούτων ἐπίστανται πλεῖστα εἰδέναι, " they feel sure he—sc. Hesiod—was so wise." That αἴσθησις is meant at first to include *all* immediate conviction is shown by the introduction of the argument about numerical propositions, 154c ff.

of something which *is* ($\tau o\hat{v}$ ὄντος), and is infallible, and therefore is the same thing as *certain* knowledge (ἐπιστήμη) (152c).

We should note very carefully exactly what is the theory here ascribed to Protagoras. (That the interpretation of his *dictum* is the correct interpretation, or at least that supposed by his readers at large to be correct, is clear, since it is assumed that all the parties to the conversation are quite familiar with the context of the saying, and not one of them suggests that there can be any mistake about its meaning.) The view Plato ascribes to Protagoras is *not* " subjectivism." It is not suggested that " what appears to me " is a " mental modification " of myself. The theory is strictly realistic ; it is assumed that " what appears to me " is never a " mere appearance," but always " that which is," " reality." But Protagoras denies that there is a *common* real world which can be known by two percipients. Reality itself is individual in the sense that I live in a private world known only to me, you in another private world known only to you. Thus if I say the wind is unpleasantly hot and you that it is disagreeably chilly, we both speak the truth, for each of us is speaking of a " real " wind, but of a " real " wind which belongs to that private world to which he, and only he, has access. No two of these private worlds have a single constituent in common, and that is precisely why it can be held that each of us is infallible about his own private world. Protagoras is not denying the genuine " objectivity " of each man's private world ; his equation of " appears to me " with " *is, is real*, to me " is meant to insist on this objectivity. But he denies the reality of the " common environment " presupposed by " intra-subjective intercourse." His thesis is strictly metaphysical, not psychological.

But now, how if Protagoras really meant something more elaborate than this, and explained his meaning more fully to his intimates " in secret," though he gave the world at large only this one hint of it ? There is a " far from contemptible " (οὐ φαῦλος) view which we might regard as implied by the Protagorean dictum, and it is as follows.[1] *All* truth is strictly relative. Nothing, *e.g.*, is big or hot " absolutely," but only " big " or " hot " relatively to some *standard* of comparison. If you selected your standard differently, the same thing could truly be said to be " small " or " cold," relatively to the new standard. This applies even to existential propositions. You cannot say absolutely " this *is*," any more than you can say " this is so." You can only say " this is, is real " relatively to something else. For the very word " is " is a misnomer. The things we speak of as " existing " are really events which " *happen* " as a consequence of movements ; movement is the only thing which is ultimately real in the universe, as

---

[1] *Theaet.* 152c–d. Since Socrates suggests that this doctrine was only told by Protagoras to his followers "in a mystery," *sub sigillo* (ἐν ἀπορρήτῳ), clearly nothing of the kind can have been found in his book. The suggestion is that if you think out all that is really implied in the *Homo mensura* formula, you will be led to the metaphysical theory now to be expounded.

all the " wise," with the solitary exception of Parmenides, seem to have held from time immemorial. All life, bodily or mental, is movement and activity ; cessation of movement is lethargy, stagnation, death (152c–153d). Now apply this to the case of anything we perceive by sense, *e.g.* a white expanse. We must not say that the white we see is " in " a body outside our own, nor yet that it is " in " our own eye. It is not anywhere. The truth is that what we call our " eye " and what we call the " outside world " are simply two sets of motions. When they come into contact and interfere with one another, something " happens " (γίγνεται) momentarily as a consequence of this interference, and this something is the colour, which is thus neither " within " us nor " without " us, but is just the joint product of *two* factors, the system of motions which are outside the organism and the system of motions which are the eye [1] (153e). This explains at once why each of us lives in a strictly private world. Any change in either of the causal factors, the " motions " in the larger world and the " motions " in the organism, may affect their joint product, and therefore a man and a dog will not see the same colours, nor a man in health the same colours as a man out of health. If the perceived quality, " hot," " white," or what not, were simply an affection of " that by which we measure or apprehend," *i.e.* of our own organism or " sensibility," it ought not to be modified by changes in anything else (as, in fact, it is by, *e.g.*, variations in illumination) ; [2] if it were simply a character of " that which is measured or apprehended " (the external object), it should similarly be unaffected by changes internal to the organism (but, in fact, it is affected by them). The facts thus show that the perceived world is a function of two variables, *my* special organism and its environment ; hence it is *necessarily* a " private " world (154b).

Before we can judge such a theory on its merits we need a further clarification of our thoughts. On the " private-world " theory, six dice will not only " appear " but " be " at once " many " and " few ": " many," if a group of four is my standard of comparison, " few " if my standard is a dozen. Reflection on such cases leads us irresistibly to make three affirmations which seem to be self-evident and yet not all mutually compatible : (1) nothing can become greater in bulk or number except by being augmented

---

[1] We shall see later on that this is not a complete account of the matter. The " product " of the two motions is itself a motion, and this motion has *two* aspects. The " seeing eye " is as much a momentary event as the seen colour. As to the terminology of 153e, the *active* motion (τὸ προσβάλλον) must be conceived as that of the eye's own " visual ray " issuing out of the eyeball ; the *passive* (τὸ προσβαλλόμενον) is what we commonly call the " external " object on which this supposed visual ray impinges. *We* should think more naturally of reflected light striking on the retina as the προσβάλλον, but Plato always presupposes the Empedoclean conception of seeing as effected by a " search-light " thrown out by the eye into the world around us.

[2] In 154b, τὸ παραμετρούμενον is simply a paraphrase for αἴσθησις. Socrates inserts the παραμετρούμενον simply to echo the curious use of the word μέτρον in the formula of Protagoras.

($αὐξηθέν$); (2) that to which nothing has been added and from which nothing has been subtracted has been neither augmented nor diminished; (3) what once *was* not but now *is* must have " come to be " in the interval (*i.e.* there has been a transitional process of " coming into being," 155*b*).[1]

Yet the case of the dice, or the case in which Socrates is one year taller than Theaetetus but the next shorter, seems to create a difficulty. In this last case, Theaetetus has grown, but Socrates has neither grown nor shrunk. He *is* now, what he was *not* last year, " shorter," and yet there has been no process of " coming to be shorter." How are we to explain the paradox? We cannot explain it at all to a corporealist who denies the reality of acts and processes and the invisible generally. But it might be explained by the theory of certain more refined ($κομψότεροι$) persons, whose secret Socrates offers to disclose (156*a*). Their theory is this. As has been already suggested, the only reality is motion. There are two types of motion, the active and the passive. The mutual friction or interference ($τρῖψις$) of an active and a passive motion regularly gives rise to a *twin* product, " sense "+" sensible quality," and neither of these is ever to be found without its " twin." And this twin product is itself, again, a pair of movements, though of movements more rapid than those which gave rise to it. Thus, to apply the theory to the case of vision, you have first two " slower " causative " movements " (the " active " movement *here* is supposed to be the " event " which is the visual apparatus, the " passive " is the event we call the environment); when there is an " interference " of these two motions, in that very process there emerge two correlated " quicker " movements, neither of which ever exists without the other,[2] " vision in act " and " seen colour." Thus the couple " seeing eye " and " colour seen " are themselves a dual more " rapid " event produced as an effect by the mutual interference of the two " slower " causal movements. It follows that all predication is strictly relative. The " causal " motions themselves are strictly relative to one another, each is " active " or " passive " only in relation to its correlate; and similarly in the " effect," the seen colour is seen only by *this* " seeing eye," and this " seeing eye " sees only *this* colour. " Being " is thus a strictly relative term. To speak accurately, we ought never to say " *x* is," but " *x* is, relatively to *y* "; if we omit the qualification, it is only because of an inveterate linguistic bad habit. Socrates does not

---

[1] Note that we have here in outline the fundamental thought of the Aristotelian doctrine about " generation " and " corruption." The $ἀπορίαι$ connected with the problem are one of the topics of the *Parmenides* (155*e*–157*b*).

[2] Thus the theory is closely analogous to Aristotle's doctrine that in actual perception the $αἴσθησις$ and the $αἰσθητόν$ are, while the perception lasts, one and the same. The important difference is that in the account given here, *both* the $αἰσθητόν$ and the $αἰσθανόμενον$ only exist actually during the process of perception; apart from the process, " eye " and " colour " only are " potentially." On Aristotle's theory, this is true of the " seeing eye," but not of the seen colour.

commit himself to this theory of " absolute becoming," any more than to any other, but he has stated it because we cannot dispose of the assertion that " is " = " appears to me " without deciding this still more fundamental question (158*d*).

We note that the difference between the Protagorean formula and the doctrine now given as that of certain unnamed " fine wits " is that the first is a piece of " epistemology," the second is ontology, and professes to give the grounds for the individualistic or " solipsist ' epistemology. The proposition that *my* perceived world only exists *for* me, and that it is meaningless to ask whether your " world " and " mine " can contain one and the same object, is only one special consequence of the much more far-reaching doctrine that " is " itself has no meaning unless one adds the qualification " relatively to." It is now being asserted not merely that perceived qualities only exist " for " the percipient who is aware of them, and he is only " percipient " of just these qualities, but that the correlated active and passive " slower " movements, thing and environment, only *are* relatively to one another. (Thus, *e.g.*, the statement that a particle *A* exists would actually *mean* that *A* interacts in a certain way with *B* and *C*, and so on for *B* and *C* themselves.) This is why the doctrine described here cannot be disposed of in the summary way in which Mr. Bradley has disposed of the " phenomenalism " of many modern scientific men in *Appearance and Reality*. The persons of whom Mr. Bradley is thinking have really not got behind the restricted doctrine of the " relativity " of perceived quality to percipient. At the back of their minds there is still the notion that both percipient and per- ceived quality are effects of something which, though not itself perceived, *is*, or is real in an absolute sense, and thus they are easily convicted of inconsistency with themselves. But the theory we are now dealing with asserts that the " slower motions," assumed by the victims of Mr. Bradley's dialectic to be simply " real," are *themselves* purely relative, each such " active " motion being relative to a specific " passive " motion and *vice versa*. It is thus not open to the criticism that it regards anything whatever, per- ceptible or imperceptible, as simply real ; " this is real " is, on this view, always an incomplete statement which, as it stands, is strictly devoid of significance.

It is not clear from what quarter Socrates is supposed to have learned the theory. He is clearly not inventing it, since he repre- sents it as the " secret " of certain refined wits. Nor do I think it likely that Plato has devised the whole thing for himself simply as a metaphysic which might be urged, and in fact would have to be urged, by a far-seeing defender of the Protagorean formula. The insistence on motion as the only reality at once suggests a Heraclitean influence, and the elaborate kinematic working out of the thought further suggests that the κομψοί of whom Socrates is thinking are persons with a strong mathematical interest. If we had more information than we have about the curious blend of

Heracliteanism and Pythagorean mathematics represented in our tradition by the stories told of the mysterious Hippasus, we might be able to say something more definite. From Plato's own point of view, the theory would be perfectly acceptable as an account of " pure " sensation ; but we must remember that, as it is part of the object of the dialogue to show, no piece of knowledge, not even the crudest statement about present fact, ever is a *mere* deliverance of sensation.

With this general metaphysical theory as a presupposition, we could now dispose of the superficial objection to Protagoras that some " appearances "—those of dreams, delirium, fever—are deceptive. The world of the sleeper or the fever-patient is as real to him, while his dream or fever lasts, as the world of the man awake and in health is to him. And it is not true to say that there is any conflict between the way in which the world appears *to one and the same percipient*, according as he is awake or asleep, ill or well. On the theory, the " twin-product," sensation + sensed quality is a function of the complex, organism + environment. But it is an immediate consequence that, since a sleeping or delirious organism is different from a waking or healthy organism, the result of interaction with environment must be different. Socrates asleep is different from Socrates awake in important organic respects, and, on the theory we are considering there is no " self " or " percipient " but the organism as it is at the moment. Thus the *sensa* of Socrates asleep are real relatively to Socrates asleep, exactly as those of Socrates awake are real relatively to Socrates awake, and it would be abandoning the whole theory of the relativity of " being " to judge of the reality of the *sensa* of Socrates asleep by reference to those of Socrates awake (157e–160c). The *sensa* of any percipient organism at any moment are relative to the state of that organism at that moment, and to nothing else, just as that organism at that moment is relative to those *sensa* and to nothing else. (The *esse* of the organism at the moment *t*, we may say, is to perceive the *sensa* it perceives at that moment ; the *esse* of those *sensa* is to be perceived by it at that moment ; neither organism nor *sensa* have any further reality.) Consequently the " world " of any percipient at any moment is private to *that* percipient and that moment. " My perception is inerrant, for it is relative to my world ($\dot{\epsilon}\mu\dot{\eta}$ $o\dot{v}\sigma\dot{\iota}a$) at that moment." [1] Thus the theory we have stated justifies the Heracliteans in saying that all is motion, Protagoras in saying that " man " is the measure," and Theaetetus in saying that sense is knowledge (160d–e).

---

[1] 160c, $\dot{a}\lambda\eta\theta\dot{\eta}s$ $\ddot{a}\rho a$ $\dot{\epsilon}\mu o\dot{\iota}$ $\dot{\eta}$ $\dot{\epsilon}\mu\dot{\eta}$ $a\ddot{\iota}\sigma\theta\eta\sigma\iota s$—$\tau\dot{\eta}s$ $\gamma\dot{a}\rho$ $\dot{\epsilon}\mu\dot{\eta}s$ $o\dot{v}\sigma\dot{\iota}as$ $\dot{a}\epsilon\dot{\iota}$ $\dot{\epsilon}\sigma\tau\iota\nu$, where note (*a*) that $\dot{a}\epsilon\dot{\iota}$ means not " always " but " at each moment," " at a given moment," and (*b*) that $\dot{\eta}$ $\dot{\epsilon}\mu\dot{\eta}$ $o\dot{v}\sigma\dot{\iota}a$ does not mean " my own being," as though the thought were that what I perceive is a " subjective " $\pi\dot{a}\theta os$ or state of my own body or mind, but " the reality which is mine," a real world of objects which is my own *private* world. The crux of the whole theory is that it is an attempt to insist at once on the *objectivity* of the world I perceive and on its purely private character.

THE THEORY EXAMINED.—*First Criticism* (160e–165e).—The
thought of which Theaetetus was in labour has now been fairly
brought into the world, Our next task is to consider whether
it is a genuine piece of thinking or only a " changeling." To give
the lad breathing-time for recollection, Theodorus partially takes
his place as respondent while Socrates raises a number of critical
doubts. (*a*) How does Protagoras justify his selection of man in
particular as the " measure " ? The theory would equally warrant
the statement that any creature—a pig, a baboon, or a tadpole—is
the " measure," provided only that it is sentient. (*b*) If each of
us is the " measure " of reality and unreality in his own world,
where has Protagoras any advantage over his pupils ? How can he
claim to correct a pupil's views about the reality of a world which,
on the theory, is private to the pupil and relative to the pupil as its
" measure " ? (The very attempt implies, contrary to the theory,
that there is a " world " of some kind common to Protagoras and
the pupil, and that Protagoras is a better " measure " of it than the
other.) Was the professional career of Protagoras a prolonged
practical joke ? Protagoras might, however, fairly say that this
sort of " criticism " is mere caricature.[1] We must examine the
proposed identification of sense-perception with knowledge in dead
earnest. So we go on to ask (*c*) whether when we *hear* foreigners
speaking their own language we also *know* " what they are saying,"
or whether when a person who cannot read *sees* a written page he
knows what is written on it. The only possible answer is that in
such a case one does know what one actually hears or sees, the
pitch of the syllables or the shape and colour of the letters, but one
does not know the *meaning* of the foreign vocables or the written
words. (Thus the formula knowing = perceiving by the senses
will not cover the case of knowing the meaning of such symbols ;
their meaning can neither be heard nor seen.) (*d*) Suppose a
man has seen something and then shuts his eyes, but still remembers
what he saw. He no longer sees it, but can we say that he does not
know what he has seen and still remembers ? There is real point
in these questions, but we must take care not to " crow " over
Protagoras and his theory prematurely. If he were alive, he would
probably have known how to make a telling rejoinder to such cavils.
As he is dead and has no one to represent him, we must try to act
as his advocates ourselves, and to plead the cause as effectively as
we can (164e–165a).[2] If we are to press mere verbal points, any

---

[1] *Theaet.* 162d–e. This might be, but need not be, a hint that there had been
attempts to discredit the formula of Protagoras by caricatures of this kind.
But I think it very rash to indulge in conjectures about Antisthenes—to whom
I can discover no certain allusions in Plato—as the author of the arguments.
The ἀντιλογικοί were a fairly numerous class, and we may suppose that many of
them exercised their wit on so tempting a theme. Protagoras would have an
easy retort to the first of the four objections. A tadpole is quite a good
" measure " of the " world " with which the tadpole has to concern itself.

[2] The personification of the " discourse " of Protagoras as an " orphan "
whose natural guardians are neglecting their duties lends no colour to the silly

ἀντιλογικός could quite easily make many more formidable than those we have made ourselves, without ever coming to close quarters with Protagoras' real thought.

SOCRATES' PROPOSED DEFENCE OF PROTAGORAS (166a–168c).— Protagoras might fairly say that he would not have been affected by the question about memory which puzzled a lad like Theaetetus. He would have exposed the absurdity of talking about memory as if it meant the " persistence " of the state of the organism in which it was at the moment of stimulation. He would have insisted on the point that, according to his theory, each of us is not one percipient but a different percipient with every change in the state of his organism. And he would have urged that it is for his opponent to refute him directly by proving *either that a man's " senses "* (αἰσθήσεις) *are not private to himself, or, alternatively, that, granting this position, the sense-object which " appears " or " is " need not be private.*[1]

Meanwhile, the thesis of Protagoras remains untouched. Each percipient has his own strictly personal and private world ; it is not merely his " apparent " world, but a real, though private, world. And yet there is a difference between the wise man and his neighbours, a *practical* difference. The wise man is one who can influence another so that the other man's private world, which appears and really is bad, is made to appear and be good (166d). Thus the abnormal perceptions of the diseased organism are as much a disclosure of reality as the normal perceptions of the healthy. The physician does not attempt to argue the patient into denying their reality. He subjects the patient to a regimen which brings his perceptions into accord with those of his fellow-men, and thus makes them " wholesome " or " useful," whereas they were, before treatment, dangerous and unwholesome. So the " sophist," who is the physician of the soul, aims not at giving a pupil " truer views " —that would be impossible, if the pupil is the " measure " of his own real world—but at giving him " better " and more wholesome views of life (166d–167c). The defence made by Socrates for Protagoras thus amounts to crediting him with a " pragmatist " view. Any one belief, actually held, is as " true " as any other, but some sensations and some ways of thinking are " better," that is, " more useful in practice " than others. It is implied, though not actually said, that the " useful " way of perceiving and thinking is that

legend about the prosecution of Protagoras and the destruction of his book. Socrates is merely jesting over the reluctance of Theodorus to commit himself to a "non-professional" controversy. Theodorus is called the natural guardian of the orphan simply because he professes to be an old friend and admirer of its author. The image, of course, implies that the book of Protagoras had *not* been destroyed, but had survived its " father." Only, no one will venture on an " official " defence of it.

[1] *Theaet.* 166c. In this alternative, the first position, that each man's αἰσθήσεις are " private," cannot be contested. I see with my own eyes, and no other man can see with them, any more than I can see with his eyes. Thus the issue between realism and " absolute phenomenalism " is rightly made to be just whether two men, each using his own private senses, can perceive an object which is " common " to both of them.

which agrees with the perception and thought of your " social environment," since it is only such agreement which makes concerted action possible. To be gravely " eccentric " in your perceptions or your moral convictions puts you into the class of the insane and makes practical co-operation with your neighbours impossible. The root of the matter is that, though the notion of a " common " natural or moral world is, strictly speaking, a fiction, it is a fiction which is necessary to life. The practical urgencies of life require that my private world and your private world should not be very dissimilar. If they are sufficiently alike, by a useful fiction we can act " as if " we had a common world ; where the divergence is too great to admit of this fiction, when I call black what you call white, one of us needs a physician for the body or the soul. By altering the state of the percipient, the physician, according to the Protagorean theory itself, necessarily also alters the character of his " world."

Since Socrates offers this interpretation as a substitute for an " official " exegesis, it is clear that it cannot have been given by Protagoras himself ; since it is welcomed by Protagoras' old admirer Theodorus, we may infer that it is offered as a fair and honest attempt to explain what Protagoras meant, on the assumption that he was a man of intelligence and that his doctrine was intended to be compatible with his claims for himself as a practical teacher. So far as I can see, it is not only offered in good faith, but is about the best defence which can be made for the view that the " common " world is strictly the *creation* of the " intersubjective intercourse " on which all practical co-operation depends. Against modern statements of pragmatism it has the advantage that it does not attempt the task of equating " true " with " practically useful " ; it simply sets aside the distinction between " true " and " false " as irrelevant to human life, and *replaces* it by the obviously relevant distinction between " useful " and " harmful." Our attention is thus concentrated on the fundamental question whether the abolition of the distinction of true from false really leaves this all-important practical distinction between useful and harmful standing or not. This ultimate issue is so serious that we cannot allow the case for the pragmatist to be prejudiced by being left to the championship of a boy, even if he is, like Theaetetus, a boy of genius ; Theodorus must take the defence on himself (168c–169e).[1]

---

[1] It may be advisable to warn some readers again against the really wanton attempt to find a hidden attack on Antisthenes in the pleasantries interchanged between Socrates and Theodorus at 169b. Theodorus compares Socrates with Antaeus, who compelled every one to wrestle with him, merely because Socrates is so insistent on dragging Theodorus himself into a philosophical argument he would rather decline. This leads naturally to the mention of Heracles as the person who finally vanquished Antaeus. It is needless to look for any more recondite reason for the allusion. And it is still more needless to suppose that when Socrates speaks of the numerous Heracleses with whom he has had stiff " bouts," he is thinking of his own friend and companion. It is to be hoped that we shall hear less in the future of the imaginary " feud " of Plato with Antisthenes since Wilamowitz has uttered his timely protest against this *Antisthenes-Legende.*

SECOND EXAMINATION OF THE PROTAGOREAN THESIS (169*d*–172*c*, 176*c*–179*b*).—The task now before us is to examine the " pragmatist " philosophy on its own merits. The examination falls into two sections, between which the famous panegyric on the life of devotion to " useless science " is inserted, admittedly as a digression. It strikes us at once, as a common experience, that every one knows there are some things about which he thinks himself wiser than others and other things about which he thinks others wiser than himself (170*a*–*b*). Every one admits that there are things about which he is ignorant and incompetent and needs to be taught or directed. And by " wisdom " and " ignorance " men suppose themselves to mean true and false belief (δόξα) respectively. According to the thesis of Protagoras, this belief that some of my beliefs are true and others false, being one of my beliefs, must be true. It must be true, since it is a belief, that there are things of which a given man is *not* the " measure." This is a direct consequence of Protagoras' own principle, and yet it contradicts that principle. And the worst of it is that if there is one point on which every one, even those who would most readily concede that any one man's sensations are just as veridical as any other's, is agreed, it is that when you come to the question what is wholesome or hurtful, each of us is not equally the " measure " for himself. That is just why we need the expert physician (171*e*). So in moral matters, even those who hold that there is no common standard of right and wrong, but that " right " means simply for any community what that community agrees in approving, never think that " expediency " is a purely relative matter. No one holds that the expedient is what a given community thinks expedient, though many persons hold that right is just whatever the community happens to think right. Every one holds that there is a *common* standard of expediency (172*b*). These considerations are meant to lead up to the conclusion that the plausible " pragmatist " substitution of the " useful " for the " true " as the criterion of value in beliefs fails at its central point. It refutes itself by presupposing that the value of the belief " this is useful " itself must be estimated by reference to a standard of " truth." " It is true that this practice is useful " cannot simply mean " it is useful to believe that this practice is useful." The full development of the thought is postponed for a moment by the introduction of the eulogy of the contemplative life.

DIGRESSION.—*The Contemplative Life* (172*c*–176*c*).—How far the pragmatist criterion is from being self-evident or universally accepted we may see by contrasting the whole attitude towards life of the philosopher or true man of science with that of the " man of affairs," and the man of law. The former is free where the latter is a slave,[1] as we can see by comparing the style of their " discourses."

---

[1] *Theaet.* 172*d*. The distinctive mark of the " free man " is that all his time is σχολή, " leisure," " free time," " his own time." The " life of business " is not " free " because in business a man's time is not " his own "; it is engrossed

The one can follow up his thoughts wherever they lead ; time is no object to him, and the length of an argument no obstacle, so long as it leads him to the " reality." The other has to plead with a time-limit and under a double control. He must speak " to his brief "—his opponent will take care of that—and he must adapt himself to the prejudices of his "lord and master," the court, or he may have to pay dear for it, and thus cannot afford to have a single-minded eye to simple truth. The other is free, as we are at this moment, to follow up any line of thought which seems promising ; he is the master, not the slave, of his " case." Hence the violent contrast between the whole characters of the typical thinker and the typical " practical man." The former, in an extreme case, barely knows where the law-courts and places of public assembly are, or what is being done in them ; he belongs to no political "club," and cares as little about the social as about the serious side of such institutions. He knows nothing of the current political and social gossip, and is not even alive to his own deficiency. You might say that, while his body is here in Athens, his mind freely roams over the universe as its domain. When he is dragged down into the world of petty local affairs, proceeded against in the courts for example, he is lost in such a strange situation, and the practical man sets him down as an absent-minded fool. He cannot make a telling invective because he is quite unaware of the personal scandals which furnish the appropriate matter. He is equally ineffective in eulogy, since the topics of the ordinary eulogy, the subject's illustrious descent and splendid wealth, are unimpressive to him. The biggest estate seems a little thing to one who is accustomed to think in terms of the spaces of astronomy, and the finest pedigree laughable to one who knows how many kings and how many beggars there must be in every genealogy, if we could only trace it back through unrecorded generations. Hence the popular contempt of him as a man who is so wrapt up in his star-gazing that he cannot see what is under his nose.

But from the philosopher's point of view, the brilliant practical man is equally absurd. Take him away from the field of small personal concerns and set him to think about the ultimate issues of life, what are right and wrong, what are human happiness and misery, and how is the one to be found and the other shunned—in a word, take him out of the realm of the temporal into the eternal, and he is helpless in " discourse," for all his forensic " acumen."

This conflict between opposing standards of valuation is inherent in " mortality," and that is the very reason why the man who means to be happy must make it his supreme aim to " escape " from mortality. The only way of escape is " to become assimilated

by the demands of those whom he serves—his customers, patrons, clients, "the public." The thought reappears in Aristotle's *Ethics* and *Politics*, where the best life for man is .identified with the " noble use of leisure," and the standard in education is made fitness to prepare the recipient to make this right use of his " leisure."

to God as wholly as may be," to exchange temporality for eternity. And " assimilation " means becoming " righteous and pious and wise." The difficulty is to convince men that the real reason for this pursuit of goodness is not the advantage of a reputation for goodness, but the fact that goodness and wisdom make us like God and therefore constitute real " manhood," and confer the only real happiness.

The whole passage recalls, and is obviously meant to recall, the spiritual mood and even the phraseology of the *Gorgias* and *Phaedo*. But its connexion with the present argument is loose, and hardly amounts to more than this, that the worldly man's estimate of the philosopher and the philosopher's estimate of him furnish the best proof that there is no single accepted standard of valuation. The most natural way of accounting for the presence of the digression is that of Burnet, that it is an expression of the mood in which Plato is contemplating his own coming absorption in the necessarily largely uncongenial mundane life of the Syracusan court. The ideal of the world-renouncing pure " scientist " had never been his own; his early ambitions had been definitely political, and his mature conviction was that the gifts of the philosopher ought to be consecrated to the work of practical administration, but we can readily understand that he would have a keen sense of the sacrifice he was making to public duty and the pettiness of the personalities and problems with which he was now called to mix himself up.[1] It would be a bad mistake, though the mistake has been made, to find in so splendid a passage a polemic against the aims of his older rival Isocrates. Whatever the limitations of Isocrates were, Plato must have sympathized with his attempt to give his pupils at least a broader and nobler outlook on the problems of public life than that of the mere party-man of a little Greek πόλις ; the whole picture of the " man of affairs " who is pitted against the philosopher suggests in its details an admirer of Antiphon or Thrasymachus rather than a figure from the school of Isocrates, the last place where the cult of " successful unrighteousness " would be likely to be in favour.

Second Criticism of the Protagorean Thesis concluded (176c–179b).—To return. We had just said that though the thinkers who identify reality with change and those who teach that " what appears to anyone is for him the reality," are ready enough to extend these formulae to right and wrong, no one seriously contends that what a city agrees to regard as *good* or *useful* must really be so, so long as the agreement continues. Every one recognizes that what is really good or profitable is so independently of the beliefs which may be entertained about it. Now this suggests a generalization of the problem raised by the saying of Protagoras. When a city makes regulations to ensure good or advantage, it is acting with a view to the *future*. So we may ask, granting that the *Homo mensura* formula is valid for convictions about the present,

[1] *Greek Philosophy, Part I*. pp. 244–5.

is it also valid for convictions about the future? If a man feels
hot, he *is* hot. *Soit;* but if a man believes that he is going to have
a fever with a " temperature," while his physician denies it, what
then ? In such a case the physician's forecast is certainly a better
" measure " of what is going to be the layman's " reality " than the
layman's opinion. So the best " measure " of the sweetness or
dryness of next autumn's vintage is the husbandman ; a skilled cook's
judgment about the enjoyment a company will receive from the
dishes he has prepared is sounder than their own. Protagoras
would be a better judge than one of us about the effect of a speech
one of us was going to deliver. Generally, whenever a future issue
is in question, the specialist will be the best " measure " of other
men's experiences as well as his own. The *Homo mensura* formula
thus is invalid in all cases where there is a reference to *future* experiences. And this rids us of the doctrine that any and every
belief is true, which is, moreover, self-refuting, since it implies its
own contradictory. But we have still to examine the metaphysical
theory which is the foundation of the dictum that *actual present*
sensation and the judgments (δόξαι) based on it are always true.

*Final Refutation of the Identification of Knowledge with Sense-
perception* (179*d*–186*e*).—The complete examination of the theory
that actual present sense-perception is knowledge demands a
consideration of the already mentioned metaphysical theory that
nothing is real but movement. We cannot get any coherent statement of the grounds for this theory from its official representatives,
the Heracliteans, who disdain connected exposition and affect to
speak in cryptic aphorisms ; we must try what we can make of the
doctrine for ourselves (179*e*–180*c*). We must remember, too, that
Melissus and Parmenides maintain the very opposite—that what is
is one and unmoving. A complete examination would involve
studying the views both of the " men of flux " (the ῥέοντες) and of
the " faction of the one-and-all " (the τοῦ ὅλου στασιῶται) ; it might
end by carrying us over into one of the camps, or by leaving us in
the comically persumptuous position of standing alone against both
parties. Still we must make the venture, and we will begin by
considering the Heraclitean view (180*c*–181*b*).

Everything is always in motion : what is the precise sense of
this ? There are two easily distinguishable types of " motion " :
(*a*) one which includes translation and rotation, which we will call
locomotion (φορά) ; (*b*) another illustrated by the transition from
youth to age, from black to white, from hard to soft ; we will call it
alteration (ἀλλοίωσις). Is it meant, then, that everything is at every
moment changing both its position and its quality, or only that
each thing is at every moment exhibiting one or other of these
changes ? If the statement that there is *no* rest or stability in
the world at all is meant strictly, we must take the former interpretation. Nothing ever keeps the same quality for the tiniest
interval, any more than it retains the same position (181*e*). Otherwise there would be some sort of stability about things.

Let us bear this in mind and remember also the further details, which are part of this same theory, of the way in which the mutual interference of two of the " slower " motions gives rise to the twin effect sensation + sensible quality. The theory was that when two such " slower " motions meet, the result is a *definite* process of sensation + a definite sensible quality, *e.g.* a " seeing of white "+ " white seen." But if nothing has any permanency, there is no such definite process of seeing white, and no such definite white seen. The process of seeing white itself is at any moment turning into some other process, and the white seen is turning into some other quality. We must not even speak of " colour-vision " and " colour," since both process and quality are always turning into something else. It will be no more true to say at any moment that a man is seeing or having sensation of some other kind than that he is not having it, and therefore, if sensing is knowing, it will never be more true to say that a man is knowing than to say that he is not knowing. The safest answer to any question would be to say, " It is so and it is not so," but even this is more than we should be really warranted in saying, since the very word " so " implies a determination which, on the theory, never exists (183*b*). These considerations dispose finally of both statements : that every one is the " measure," and that knowledge is sensation. Both must be false, if the theory of absolute " fluidity " on which they themselves rest is to be upheld. Theaetetus would like to proceed now to consider the rival Eleatic theory that " nothing happens," there is no " fluidity " at all. But his wishes must not be indulged. Socrates met Parmenides, who was then an old man, in his own youth and was powerfully impressed by his " noble depth."[1] If we discussed his view, we should very likely misunderstand it, the examination would have to be very long and searching, and we should be diverted from our present task, which is to practise " spiritual obstetrics " on Theaetetus (184*b*).

Socrates now enters on a line of thought which is by far the most important contribution the dialogue has as yet made to the solution of its problem. He calls attention to the, so far neglected, distinction between sensation and thought, or judgment. We can point out the bodily instruments which a man uses in seeing, hearing, touching. He sees with his eyes, hears with his ears, and so forth. Or to be still more accurate, since it is always the man, that is his ψυχή, which sees and hears, we should do well to say rather that he sees and hears *through* his eyes and ears (184*d*).[2]

---

[1] *Theaet.* 183*e*. There is a similar reference to this encounter at *Soph.* 217*c*, and the *Parmenides* professes to be a third-hand report of it. It seems to me that the emphatic way in which the impression made on the youthful Socrates is insisted on in both references shows us that Plato wishes us to regard the meeting as a real fact, and there is no reason why it should not be one (see Burnet, *E.G.Ph.*[3], p. 168, n. 3).

[2] The point of the distinction here made between that *with* which (ᾧ) and that *through* which (δι' οὗ) we see and hear can be better expressed in English differently. It might be made by objecting to the accuracy of the expressions

Eyes, ears, and the rest of the body are not the agents in perception but the *implements* (ὄργανα) of it—the first appearance of the word " organ " in this sense. For each " implement " there is what Aristotle was later to call its " proper " (ἴδιον) sensible. None can do the work of another. Colour can only be taken in by the channel of the eye, sound through the ear. But if a man is *thinking* about two such sensibles of different senses, comparing and discriminating them, or counting them as " two," pronouncing them like or unlike, asserting that they are " really there," the soul is considering the matter " by herself " (αὐτὴ δι' αὐτῆς) without the employment of a bodily " implement " (185d).[1] If we try to make a list of the determinations of an object which are thus made " without any bodily organ," we have to reckon among them not only " reality " (οὐσία), number, sameness, difference, likeness and unlikeness, but good and bad, right and wrong (186a). Thus the ultimate categories of value, like those of " fact," are apprehended by thought, not by sense. In fact, they are asserted as the result of reflection, comparison, and discrimination : this explains why animals are as capable of sensation as men, and babies as adults (186c), but sound convictions about " reality and value " (οὐσία and ὠφέλεια) are only attained by us with time and pains and education. Now we cannot have knowledge without apprehension of a " reality " (οὐσία) which is known. Hence it follows that " knowledge " is not to be sought for in the affections of our sensibility (τοῖς παθήμασι) but in the mind's reflection upon them (ἐν τῷ περὶ ἐκείνων συλλογισμῷ, 186d). And this finally proves that knowledge is *not* the same thing as sensation (*ibid. b*).

SECOND DEFINITION. KNOWLEDGE IS TRUE JUDGMENT
(187b–200c)

The common name for the process of reflection, comparison, and discrimination to which the occurrence of our sensations gives rise is " belief " or " judgment " (δόξα, τὸ δοξάζειν). The word δόξα is being used here in a way characteristic of Plato's later dialogues. In his earlier writing δόξα had commonly been thought of as contrasted with ἐπιστήμη ; it had meant " belief," with the implication that the belief is a mistaken one, or at any rate a doubtful one ; in our dialogue, and henceforward, the meaning is judgment, intellectual conviction in general, without any suggestion of disparagement. This is one of the many indications that a chief

----

" the eye sees," " the ear hears," and the like, on the ground that they obscure the point that both seeing and hearing are functions of a unitary central consciousness. This is what Socrates means by saying that there are not a group of αἰσθήσεις seated inside a man, like the warriors in the fabled " wooden horse " of Troy.

[1] It does not occur to Socrates to consider the view, afterwards taken by Aristotle, that some at any rate of the functions enumerated here might be discharged by a " common sensorium " (κοινὸν αἰσθητήριον), placed by Aristotle in the heart.

difference between mature Platonism and the Socraticism out of which it developed is that the former attributes a decidedly higher value to beliefs which do not reach the level of demonstrated " science," that is, to our " empirical knowledge " of the sensible world. We must not suggest that judgment is knowledge, since there are such things as false judgments. But we may take it as an amended definition that knowledge is *true* judgment (187*b*).

If we are to examine the truth of this statement, we must begin by considering the difficulty suggested by the old arguments which have been used to show that a false judgment is impossible. The old argument, which we have met in the *Euthydemus*, was that either you know what you are judging about or you do not. If you do know, you cannot judge falsely ; and if you do not, you cannot make any judgment at all, because your mind is a mere blank about that of which you " know nothing." The point has now to be considered elaborately with a view to discovering the specific character of *true* judgments. If a man knows *both A* and *B*, it would seem that he cannot mistake one for the other ; if he knows *A* but not *B*, how can he compare *A* with the merely unknown ? If *both A* and *B* are unknown, is not the impossibility of a confusion even greater (188*a–c*). Perhaps we may avoid these difficulties if we say that a false judgment is a belief in " what is not " (188*d*), thus avoiding all reference to " knowing " in our definition.[1] But the " unreal " (τὸ μὴ ὄν), it may be said, is just nothing at all, and you can no more think and yet think nothing than you can see and yet see nothing. To think or believe is always to think or believe *something* ; to think nothing is all one with not thinking at all. (Just as Parmenides had long ago declared that " what is not " can neither be thought nor spoken of.) This consideration leads us to try a third explanation of what we mean by a false judgment. We mean thinking that one reality (one ὄν) is some *other* reality, thinking that something is *other* than it is (ἀλλοδοξία) ; false thinking is thus the mental confusion of one reality with another (189*c*), *e.g.* thinking that " fair is foul and foul is fair." In the *Sophistes* we shall find that this is the true account of the matter and can be successfully defended against the Eleatic dialectic. But the defence will depend on recognizing that the Eleatic metaphysic itself requires a grave modification ; there is a sense in which " the unreal " can be both thought and spoken of. In our dialogue Socrates is not allowed to probe the question to the bottom ; he has already explained that he is not prepared at present to examine Eleaticism as a metaphysical theory. He contents himself therefore with raising the question within what limits the " confusion " of one reality with another would seem to be possible.

[1] The difficulty it is intended to avoid by the new formulation arises from the ambiguity of the word εἰδέναι, which may mean either " to be acquainted with " or " to know *about*." It is suggested in effect that we may eliminate the ambiguity by recourse to metaphysics ; we will say that false belief is belief in something " unreal " (in a μὴ ὄν). But, as we shall see, this at once raises the Eleatic problem how it is possible to think the " unreal " at all.

To understand the very possibility of such a confusion, we must begin by recognizing that thinking is a kind of argument (λόγος) in which the mind carries on a debate within itself, asking itself a question and answering its own query. The judgment, once formulated, is the verdict or conclusion which puts an end to this internal dispute (190*a*). In what conditions is it possible for this verdict to involve "confusion" of one thing with another? At first sight, the old dilemma about the impossibility of confusing a thing you "know" either with something else which you "know" or with something you do not "know" appears equally formidable when you substitute the word "believe" or "think" for "know" (190*b*–191*a*). But we seem to have been wrong in admitting the premisses of the dilemma. Clearly a man who "knows" Socrates might mistake an "unknown" stranger for Socrates, if he saw the stranger in the distance. The hard and fast distinction between "what I know" and "what I do not know" is false to fact and rests on the deliberate ignoring of the consideration that there is such a thing as "learning," "getting to know" something one did not know before (191*c*). Let us consider the nature of this process.

We may represent the process figuratively thus. There is something in each of us like a wax block prepared to receive the "impressions" of signets of all kinds; the quality of the wax is very different in different persons. We may regard sensation as a process in which an object stamps an impression of itself on the wax (the whole of the traditional language about "impressions" and "ideas" is ultimately derived from this passage).[1] How definite this impress is and how long it will remain undeformed depends on the original quality of the wax. So long as the impress remains, we may say that a man has memory and knowledge (191*d*). Now consider the case of a man who "knows" the impresses left on the block, and at the same time is attending to his present sensations. We may say that the confusion with which we have identified error can only arise in one specific way. If I "know" both Theodorus and Theaetetus and am simply thinking about one of them, I cannot confuse him with the other. If I "know" only one of them, I cannot confuse him in thought with the other, who is wholly unknown to me. If I neither "know" nor am

---

[1] In particular, the Aristotelian description of perception as a process in which the soul "receives the forms of *sensibilia* without their matter, as the wax receives the shape of the iron signet-ring without the metal," is seen at once to be directly based on the simile of the wax block, which is consequently the far-away source of the whole mediaeval doctrine of "sensible" and "intelligible *species*. Note that the suggested theory is a psychologizing version of the doctrine that "knowledge is recollection." The first stamping of the wax with a wholly novel pattern gives "acquaintance"; ἐπιστήμη arises when the wax is stamped with the pattern a second time and the pattern is "recognized" as already familiar. The whole argument would have been easier to follow if Attic, like Ionic, had possessed the word εἴδησις, which might then have been specialized to mean "acquaintance." Plato can discriminate οἶδα from ἐπίσταμαι, but he has no verbal noun which stands to οἶδα as ἐπιστήμη to ἐπίσταμαι.

actually seeing either, confusion of thought is impossible. It can only come in in one case ; when I " know " both parties, and so have the " impressions " made by past perception of both still remaining in the waxen block, but also am actually seeing both or one of the two, I may try to " fit " the new " impression " or " impressions " into the old " imprints," and may fit them into the wrong ones. That is, I may make an error in *recognition*, like that of the man who tries to put his foot into the wrong shoe. Thus " false judgment " will depend on mistaken *recognition*, and consequently will only be possible when there is a misinterpretation of an actually present sensation. Such misinterpretation may be caused by any of the defects of memory symbolized by the various defects which make a given block of wax unsuitable to receive a clear-cut impression, or to retain it permanently, or to receive many such distinct impressions without crowding and superposition of one on another. The result is that error cannot arise in sensation taken by itself, nor in thought taken by itself, but only " in the conjunction of sensation with thought " (195d). *I.e.* a false judgment is always a misinterpretation of present sensation, from which it would seem that true judgment, which the definition under consideration identifies with knowledge, is always the correct interpretation of present sensation by thought.

On reflection, however, this theory proves to be unsatisfactory in spite of its attractiveness. For it is not the fact that all error is misinterpretation of present sensation. A man may falsely think that $7+5 = 11$, and most men do make arithmetical errors of this kind in operating with big numbers. And they do not make such mistakes only when they are counting things present to their senses, but when they are simply thinking of numbers and numerical relations. Thus error (and by consequence true judgment) cannot be restricted to the interpretation of present sensations. There may be false (and also true) judgments where the " sensible " does not figure as a constituent of the judgment at all (195d–196b). Thus our simile of the waxen block has not done what we hoped it would for us. (It has the merit of taking into account the *facts* of learning and forgetting, ignored in the crude old argument against the possibility of " false beliefs," but it leaves the possibility of sheer *intellectual* error where it found it.[1])

To cover the case of purely intellectual error we must amend our account of ἀλλοδοξία, and this may be done if we borrow a hint from a current statement about knowledge. (It is true that a mere " disputant for victory " would deny our right to use any such statement while we are still in quest of a definition of knowledge, but the fault, if it is one, is inevitable, and we have committed

---

[1] The one criticism I should feel inclined to pass on Burnet's analysis of the dialogue (*Greek Philosophy, Part I.*, 237-253) is that he seems to make Plato into a Kantian by ascribing to him the view that all knowledge contains as a *constituent* a factor supplied by the " manifold of sense." This seems to me to miss the point of the illustration from false judgments in arithmetic.

it already every time we have used such phrases as " we know that . . .," " we understand that . . .," and the like.) Knowing is commonly said to be the " having " of knowledge (197*b*). But we might improve on this statement by distinguishing " possession " and " having." A man may " possess " or " own " a cloak without actually " having it on." So possibly a man may " possess " knowledge without " having " it. In fact, we may distinguish " possession " from " having in *use*." A man who has caught and caged a multitude of wild birds " possesses " them all, but may not actually have any one of them in hand, though he can " put his hand " on one when he wants it (197*c*). Let us then introduce a new simile. The mind is like an aviary ; when we are babies the aviary is empty (Locke's " empty cabinet ") ; each new piece of knowledge we acquire is like a wild bird caught and caged. But actual knowing is like putting our hand on the bird we want and taking it out of the cage. Now a man may put his hand on the wrong bird instead of the one he wants, since the captured birds are alive and can fly about in the cage. So we may " possess " a certain knowledge, and yet when we want to use it, we may not be able to recapture it, we may capture the wrong piece of knowledge, and this will be the case of the man who makes a false judgment (197*d*–199*c*).

Clearly the new suggestion has advanced the argument. As Socrates says, the distinction between knowledge in possession and knowledge in use has relieved us of the old difficulty that false judgment seems to involve both knowing and not knowing the same thing ; there is no difficulty in admitting that a man " possesses " what he cannot lay his hand on. We may add (1) that a comparison of " beliefs " with living creatures is psychologically much sounder than the old comparison with " impresses " made once for all on a block of wax ; judgment is a living process, not the mere retention of a stamp left on the mind once for all ; (2) that the distinction made here is the starting-point for the more extended antithesis of " potentiality " and " actuality "[1] in which Aristotle was to find the universal explanation of movement and becoming ; (3) that the formula no longer requires us to confine the possibility of error to the interpretation of present sensation.

But there is still a grave unsolved difficulty. Error is now said to be due to a wrong " use " of knowledge which we already have in possession. If this is so, a man's knowledge is the direct source of his false judgments ; he only confuses *A* with *B* because he possesses " knowledge " of them both. At this rate, might we not equally say that error may be the cause of knowledge, or blindness of vision ? (This difficulty is perhaps not meant to be taken wholly

[1] That the distinction between the actual and the potential is primarily due to the Academy seems to be further indicated by its appearance as something needing no explanation in Aristotle's *Protrepticus* (Fr. 52, Rose), which is shown by the considerable remaining fragments of it to have been an eloquent exposition of Platonism and was probably written during Plato s lifetime (Jaeger, *Aristoteles*, c. 4).

seriously. It is true that the more you " know," in the sense of
" having the knowledge in possession," the graver are the errors
to which you are exposed. As Mr. Chesterton says somewhere,
" a man must know a great deal to be always wrong." Really
grave error is regularly due to the misuse of wide knowledge. But
the point is not really examined. Socrates' object is simply to
prelude to a much more real difficulty.)

Theaetetus suggests that we might elude this difficulty by
modifying our image. We might say that there are " ignorances "
as well as " pieces of knowledge " in the aviary, and that the man
who makes a false judgment is putting his hand on an "ignorance."
But if that is so, since he really believes his false judgment, he must
suppose the " ignorance " to be a piece of knowledge. And this
gives an opening to the eristic for raising the old problem once more.
Can a man who knows what knowledge and ignorance are confuse
one with the other ? And if he does not know what both are, how
can he confuse something he knows with something of which he is
quite unaware, or one thing of which he is unaware with another of
which he is equally unaware ? If we try to meet our opponent
by suggesting that there is a " knowledge of the difference between
knowledge and ignorance " which is a sort of knowledge of the
second order, and that false judgment arises from inability to
put one's hand on *this* knowledge, we shall clearly be involved in
an impossible " infinite regress " (200*c*). Thus the point which
Socrates is labouring is the sound one that it is impossible to have a
psychological *criterion* of true and false beliefs.

Independently of this impossibility of a criterion, there is an
obvious objection to the identification of knowledge with a " true
belief." A man may be induced to hold a belief which in fact is
true not by *proof* but by *persuasive* dexterous special pleading.[1]
Thus the court which is led by clever advocacy to find a man guilty
of an act of dishonesty cannot be said to know that he has committed the crime ; to know that, they would require to have seen
the act committed. But if the man had really committed the act,
the court has a " true belief " about him. This proves beyond all
dispute that there is true belief which is not knowledge. The importance of the point may become plainer if we put it in a rather
more modern way, What the illustration shows is that there is
a real and significant difference between " historical " and " scientific " truths. History is not, and never can be, a department of
" demonstrative science."

Third Definition. Knowledge is " True Judgment accompanied by Discourse " (201*d*–210*d*)

Possibly the difficulty just raised may be turned. As Theaetetus
says, he had forgotten to specify that a true judgment, to be

[1] The same point reappears at *Timaeus* 51*e*, where it is put into the
mouth of Timaeus of Locri. Presumably it is not specially Socratic nor
Platonic.

knowledge, must be accompanied by " discourse " (λόγος). If
there are any objects of which there is no " discourse," they
will not be objects of *knowledge*, though we may have true
judgment about them. At least, so Theaetetus has heard from
some one whom he does not name. The point of the correction
is to distinguish between " *simple* apprehension " and apprehension attended by " discourse," and to deny the name " knowledge " to simple apprehension. Thus the passage is the source
of the familiar Aristotelian and mediaeval doctrine that the
" complex enunciation," or proposition, is the unit of knowledge, as well as of the notion of " thought " as " discursive."
We note also, at once, that the theory suggested has a remarkable *prima facie* resemblance to that put forward by Socrates himself in the *Meno*, where it was said that " beliefs " are converted
into knowledge when they are " secured " αἰτίας λογισμῷ, by a
" computation of the grounds " for them. In our dialogue, Socrates
says that he too has a dream to tell. He seems to have heard
" in a dream " that there are certain *elementa* (στοιχεῖα) which
are the ABC of nature, all other things being " syllables," complexes
of these " letters." The " letters " can be simply apprehended and
named, but we can *say* nothing about them, can predicate nothing
of them, since to attribute any predicate to them would be admitting complexity in them (contrary to the hypothesis). The
complexes composed of these letters have a λόγος, since you can
analyse the complex back into its simple constituents, just as you
can spell a syllable. The complexes then are " knowable and
rational " (ῥητά), but their elements are not ; they have to be
seized by direct simple apprehension (are αἰσθητά). Knowledge,
" *grounded* belief," is always of the complex. Probably this theory
is the same as that of which Theaetetus had heard (201*d*–202*c*). We
are not told anything of the authorship of this interesting theory,
which has its counterparts in our own day, though it is plain that
it is not being invented by Plato. Where it comes from we can
only guess. The atomists have been thought of, but without
much probability. The question which Socrates goes on to raise,
whether a " syllable " is nothing but its components or a new unity,
would have no significance for persons who disbelieved in the reality
of all " composition," and is not a natural criticism to address to
them. It would be more reasonable to think of the doctrine of
Empedocles, which admits of genuine " chemical " composition.
From his point of view, the " four roots " correspond exactly to
the ABC of the book of Nature, bone, flesh, and other tissues to
" syllables," and organisms composed of these tissues to complete
words. But the employment of the epithet ῥηταί (" expressible ") to
describe the " syllables " of Nature's language suggests also mathematical connexions of some kind. Thus I should be inclined to
attribute the theory to some Pythagorean of the type who were
trying in the later part of the fifth century to find room within
their own doctrine for the " four roots " and the Empedoclean

biology.[1] But why is Socrates said only to have heard of the theory " in a dream " ?   Possibly because the person who is responsible for it had only produced it after the death of Socrates, or because it only became known at Athens after that date, and therefore some apology has to be offered for making Socrates speak of it. Hence, when we remember the precisely parallel doctrine attributed by Theophrastus to the Pythagorean Ecphantus of Syracuse, it is natural to suspect with Burnet that the reference is to him.[2]

The analogy from letters and syllables is specious, but we must examine it more closely.   It is true that the first syllable of Socrates' name, the syllable *So*, has a certain λόγος.   You can say that it is *S* and *o*—the letter *S* has no such λόγος.   You can make statements about it, *e.g.* that it is a "hissing" sound, but you cannot explain the sound by analysing it into components.   But now arises a difficult question.   Is the syllable *So* simply the sounds or signs *S* and *o*, taken in that order, or is it a new unity of a type different from that of its "component" sounds or symbols ?   If you take the first view, that *So is* just "*S* and *o*," then it seems ridiculous to say that a man can "know" "*S* and *o*," and yet neither know *S* nor know *o*.   On the second view, *So* is itself a unity, and has not really *S* and *o* as "constituent" parts.   Hence the syllable should, like the single letter, be an object of simple apprehension, and therefore, on the proposed definition, not an object of knowledge (202*d*–205*e*).   Besides, the experience of our own early schooldays seems to show that we learned to recognize syllables simply by learning to recognize the letters of which they are composed; this tells forcibly against the view that "syllables" can be known when their component "letters" are not known (206*a–c*).

Apart from the question of the soundness of this analogy from letters and syllables, what may we suppose to be meant by λόγος (" discourse ") in the statement that knowledge is "a true judgment accompanied by discourse " ?   Three, and only three, possible meanings occur to us.   (*a*) " Discourse " may mean actual uttered speech made up of nouns and verbs.   This, however, cannot be the meaning intended, for *any* true judgment can be expressed in speech, even if it is not entitled to rank as knowledge (206*d*).   (*b*) Or the meaning might be a complete enumeration of the component "parts" of the thing thought about.   Hesiod says that a hundred planks go to a waggon.   You and I cannot name more than a few of them : is it meant, then, that we have only a "true judgment" about a waggon, but should *know* what a waggon is, if we could name all the hundred ?   The objection to this interpretation is that we cannot say that a man really knows a complex unless he can recognize its components not merely as components of that

---

[1] Philolaus is now known to have been a Pythagorean of this type (Burnet, *E.G.Ph.*[3], 277 ff.), and it is just this combination of Pythagorean mathematics with the biology and medicine of Empedocles which is expounded at length in Plato's *Timaeus*.

[2] For the doctrine of Ecphantus see Diels, *Fr. d. Vors.*[3], i. 340–341.   The historical reality of E. is, as Diels says, guaranteed by the fact that our notices of him come from Theophrastus, who could not well have been mistaken on the point.   Whether he belongs to the fifth or the fourth century is not clear.

complex, but when they recur in another setting. *E.g.*, we should not say that a man " knew " how to spell the syllable *The*, if he wrote it correctly in spelling the name of Theaetetus but wrongly when he had to spell the name Theodorus. And a man *might* be liable to make the same sort of blunder about each of the remaining syllables, and yet might spell the one name Theaetetus right. Thus he would have enumerated all its letters correctly and yet would have mere " right judgment," not knowledge (208*b*). (*c*) Or was it meant that a true judgment about a thing becomes knowledge when you add to it the discourse which indicates the character which distinguishes that thing from every other thing ? Is knowledge a true judgment accompanied by a statement of the *differentia* (διαφορά, διαφορότης) of the subject of the judgment ? [1] This account looks as though it ought to be true, but when you examine it closely it is as perplexing as theatrical stage-paintings seen from close quarters. How can I have a " true judgment " about Theaetetus at all, if I am not alive to the distinctive individual characters which mark off Theaetetus from every one else ? If I am unaware of them, how can my judgment be said to be about Theaetetus rather than about Theodorus or any man you please ? Thus it would seem that to make a true judgment about Theaetetus, I must already have the *differentia* of Theaetetus in mind. Then what is added when this true judgment is converted into knowledge by the addition of the " discourse " of the *differentia* ? It cannot be meant that we are to add a " true judgment " of the *differentia* to our existing true judgment, for we must clearly have possessed that in order to make a true judgment about Theaetetus. And to say that what is meant is that we reach knowledge when we not merely think but actually *know* the *differentia* amounts to the circular definition that " knowledge is true judgment *plus* knowledge of the *differentia* " (208*c*–210*e*).

Thus our dialogue of search ends formally with a negative conclusion. Three suggestions have been made and all found untenable. Theaetetus has no further suggestion of which to be delivered. If he should ever find himself pregnant with any further suggestions in future, we must examine them in the same fashion. It is not the function of Socrates to make any positive contribution to knowledge, and besides it is time that he went to the " king's " office to make his formal reply to the indictment preferred by Meletus (210*b*–*d*).

The *Theaetetus* has thus been true to type as a Socratic dialogue in ending with no avowed results. But negatively we have reached a series of results of the highest importance. We have disposed of the identification of knowledge with sensation or any form of simple apprehension. We have also seen that pure relativism is untenable alike in the theory of knowledge and in metaphysics. It may be added that it has been at least forcibly suggested by the tenour of the whole argument that all the proposed definitions have failed precisely because each of them has attempted to provide a *psychological* criterion of knowledge, and no such psychological criterion is possible. The most important positive

[1] The first occurrence of the word in the sense which Aristotle was to stereotype as a technicality of logic.

result of the discussion is probably the recognition that the discovery of the great categories both of existence and value is the work of thought, " the soul by herself without any instrument." We may note also the appearance for the first time of a whole series of technical terms of the first importance : " quality " (ποιότης), " organ " of perception (ὄργανον), " criterion " (κριτήριον), " differentia " (διαφαρά, διαφορότης). Also we see the very fundamental problems connected with the notion of " simple apprehension " and the difference between " acquaintance " and " knowledge about " coming into prominence and receiving illustration, though without the formulation of a definite result.

Possibly the most striking feature of the whole dialogue is its silence on a matter about which we should have expected to hear something. Plato has written a long and elaborate discussion of knowledge without making a single reference to the doctrine of forms, though we might have thought it almost impossible for him to keep it out of the argument against relativism. A similar silence may be said to occur in all the dialogues we still have to examine. The forms are mentioned only in two of them : the *Parmenides*, where the doctrine is said to be that of Socrates in his early years and is criticized by Parmenides and Zeno, and the *Timaeus*, where it is put into the mouth of a fifth-century Pythagorean. I do not see how to account for these facts on the view that Plato had himself originated the doctrine and regarded it as his special contribution to philosophy. If we trust his own accounts of the matter, we shall find it most natural to suppose that in the earlier dialogues, which speak of the forms, Plato has not yet developed a doctrine which he feels to be specifically his own ; he is reproducing the common inheritance of Socratic men. If that is so, the silence about the forms in the *Theaetetus* may mean either that when he wrote that dialogue he was feeling the necessity for a " Platonic " doctrine which had not yet been definitely worked out, or else that he *had* already arrived at the results Aristotle always assumes to be the Platonic teaching, and felt that they were so definitely his own that dramatic versimilitude would be outraged by putting them into the mouth of Socrates.

See further :

BURNET.—*Greek Philosophy, Part I.*, 234–253.
CAMPBELL, L.—*The Theaetetus of Plato* [2]. (Oxford, 1883.)
RITTER, C.—*Platon*, ii. 96–120 ; *Gedankengang und Grundanschauungen von Platos Theätet* in appendix to *Untersuch-. ungen ueber Platon.* (Stuttgart, 1888.)
RAEDER, H.—*Platons philosophische Entwickelung*, 279–297.
DIELS, H.—*Elementum.* (Leipzig, 1899.)
DIÈS, A.—*Autour de Platon*, 450–452.
STEWART, J. A.—*Plato's Doctrine of Ideas*, 65–68.
NATORP, P.—*Platons Ideenlehre*, 88–116.
SACHS, E.—*de Theaeteto Atheniensi* (1914).

CHAPTER XIV

THE *PARMENIDES*

IT is most probable that the *Parmenides* and the *Theaetetus* were composed almost simultaneously. The *Parmenides* cannot well be a decidedly earlier work than the other, since it exhibits the same interest in Eleaticism and its great founder Parmenides ; it cannot well be later, since it is the best example in Plato of that cumbrousness of the indirectly reported dialogue form which is mentioned in the *Theaetetus* as the reason for return to the simpler type of the earliest dialogues. Indeed, it may well be that it was just the difficulty of keeping up in the *Parmenides* the fiction that the whole is recited by a speaker to whom it had been formerly recited by a second person, who in his turn had heard it from a third, which led Plato to renounce this type of composition for the future. It had been useful so long as his purpose had been largely dramatic, but was found to be worse than useless for works in which the main interest lies in the analysis and criticism of ideas.

The dialogue has always been regarded as an exceptionally puzzling one, and the most divergent views have been held about its main purpose. Yet if we attend to certain plain hints, given by Plato himself, we may find that his object is indicated with unusual clearness. The general scheme of the dialogue is this. It falls into two parts of unequal length. In the first and briefer part (126*a*–135*c*) Socrates is represented as a very young man expounding his newly formulated theory of the " participation " of sensible things in forms to the great Parmenides and his famous scholar Zeno ; Parmenides subjects the theory to a series of criticisms which look annihilating and to which Socrates offers no reply. Still he maintains that philosophy cannot dispense with the conception of the forms. The weakness of Socrates is that, being very young, he is attempting to philosophize without a sufficient logical discipline in considering all the consequences which follow from the acceptance or denial of a fundamental " hypothesis." In the second part of the dialogue (136*a*–166*c*), Parmenides illustrates the kind of logical discipline he has in mind by taking for examination his own thesis that " Reality is One " or that " Things are a Unity." He apparently shows in a series of antithetical " antinomies " that whether this thesis is affirmed or denied, the consequence is that a host of pairs of contradictory statements may *either* be simultaneously affirmed *or* simultaneously denied. In either case, of course, the principle of Contradiction has been violated. The dialogue ends without a word of comment on this portentous result.

Now it is quite certain that Plato never dreamed of denying the law of Contradiction ; Aristotle would certainly have said something on the point if that had been so.[1] We get a clue to Plato's real drift when he makes Parmenides say (135*d*) that the method of which he is about to give an example is that of Zeno, the inventor of " antinomies." This remark is clearly meant to send us back to the earlier sentences (128 *c–d*) in which Zeno has been made to explain the real intention of his own famous puzzles. His purpose, he says, was simply to retort on opponents who said that the Parmenidean doctrine " reality is one " leads to paradoxical conclusions by showing that their rival " hypothesis " that " reality is many " leads to still worse paradoxes. If we interpret the *Parmenides*, as we clearly ought to do, in the light of these broad hints, we shall see that it is constructed on the same pattern as the paradoxes of Zeno. A series of attempts to show that the Socratic " hypothesis " of forms leads to impossible results is retorted upon by an elaborate attempt to show that the Eleatic hypothesis is in still worse case. It is not safe even to mention it, for whether you assert it or deny it, in either case a clever formal logician can compel you to admit either that all assertions whatsoever are true or alternatively that they are all false.

It follows then that the objections urged against the doctrine of sensible things as " partaking of " forms are not Plato's own, and are not meant as a serious criticism by himself either of Socrates or of his own earlier theories. They correspond to the objections against Parmenides which Zeno had in view in composing his own work. In other words, we are directed to regard these criticisms as coming from opponents of the theory of " participation." And since Plato's imitation of the Zenonian method takes the form of raising still worse puzzles about the consequences of the Eleatic doctrine, it is clear who these opponents must be. We must look for them among the formal logicians of the school of Megara who were the continuators of Eleaticism. It is in strict keeping with this interpretation that the main point of the objections made by Parmenides to Socrates is not to raise difficulties about the reality of the forms. *That* he seems to concede. What he criticizes is

[1] Cf. Aristot. *Met.* 1005*b* 25, where it is mentioned that " some persons " suppose Heraclitus to deny the principle of contradiction, " but it does not follow necessarily that a man means what he says." *Ibid.* 1007*b* 22, the " argument of Protagoras " would lead to the denial of the principle, as is argued at length at 1009*a* 6 ff. Heraclitus and Protagoras are the only eminent men named in the course of the argument, and of them Aristotle only says that by pressing, in one case, the thinker's mere words and, in the other, the consequence of his thesis, you could reach this result. He means that neither really intended to reject this " most certain of all principles." If he supposed the antinomies of the *Parmenides* to be meant seriously, he would have been bound to refer to the point in this context.

the view of Socrates that sensible things " partake " of the forms, and so have a kind of secondary reality. This is exactly as it should be if the critics Plato has in view are the Eleatics of Megara. From their point of view, the great fault of the doctrine expounded in the *Phaedo*, *Republic*, and other dialogues is that it allows any kind of reality at all to the objects of sense. Plato does not, in the dialogue, offer any answer to these extreme " idealists " ; he simply sets himself to show that two can play at the game of abstract formal logic, and that he can, if he pleases, play the game better than its professed champions. Their own methods may be applied to their own fundamental doctrine ; let them see how they will like the result.

If this is the right way to understand the dialogue, and Plato seems to tell us that it is, it follows that the *Parmenides* is, all through, an elaborate *jeu d'esprit*, and that all interpretations based on taking it for anything else (including an earlier one by the present writer), are mistaken in principle. It equally follows that the ironical spirit of the work must not be forgotten in dealing with isolated passages. *E.g.*, when Parmenides gravely censures Soc- rates for refusing to believe in forms of mud and dirt, and says that he will get the better of such a prejudice when he grows older and more philosophical (130e), we must understand the remark to be a piece of polite irony. In Parmenides' mouth, it can only mean that a man who is going to admit any kind of reality in sensible things ought to be prepared to " go the whole hog," and nothing more. Presumably the remark is a reproduction of actual Megarian criticism. It tells us nothing of *Plato's* own thought. More than any other Platonic work of any considerable compass, the *Parmenides* bears throughout the stamp of being an " occasional' composition. Its purpose is to " have some fun " with Monists who regard the sensible as illusion, and very little more.

There are several interesting points to be noted in connexion with the introductory narrative. The otherwise unknown speaker, Cephalus, who recites the dialogue, is a citizen of Clazomenae, the native town of Anaxagoras. It is not said where he is speaking or to whom, but apparently the scene is in one of the Ionian cities. The assumption is that he had gone to Athens expressly to learn the true story of the meeting between Socrates and the great Eleatics from the only surviving person who could relate it, Plato's own half-brother Antiphon, son of Perictione by her second husband, the well-known statesman Pyrilampes. Antiphon could tell the tale accurately because he had often heard it when he was younger, from Pythodorus. (The person meant is the well-known Pytho- dorus, son of Isolochus, prominent in the Archidamian war, whom the writer of the *Alcibiades I* names as an actual pupil of Zeno.) Pythodorus had been the host of Parmenides and Zeno on their visit to Athens at the time of the great Panathenaea in a year when Socrates was still " very young." It follows from all this that we are to suppose the meeting of Socrates with the Eleatic philosophers to have taken place about 450 B.C., nearly a quarter of a century before Plato's own birth. The visit of Cephalus and his friends to Antiphon must be supposed, as Proclus said, to be after the death of Socrates. The recital of Antiphon was needed precisely because all the persons who had been present at the original meeting were dead.

Why does Plato make this unparalleled assumption that a conversation of Socrates is being repeated outside Athens, after Socrates' death and a good half-century after the holding of the conversation ? Clearly, by insisting on the early date of the conversation, and the fact that no one is living who could check the third-hand report of what passed, he frees himself from responsibility for the strict accuracy of his narrative. If we find the conversation so *à propos* to present-day Megarianism, well, we only know what Socrates and Parmenides said from a second-hand story told by Antiphon, a younger man than Plato himself, and who will go bail for Antiphon ? I think it ought also to be said that the tale of the anxiety of the Ionian philosophers to hear Antiphon's story justifies an inference. Why the Ionians of Asia Minor should feel this interest is obvious. They would be members of the school founded in Ionia by Anaxagoras on his removal from Athens ; Socrates, the favourite pupil of Anaxagoras' successor Archelaus, would in any case be an object of interest to such a group. That Plato thinks it a plausible fiction that their interest should lead them to visit Athens in order to gather a true account of events fifty years old seems only explicable on the supposition that the encounter of Socrates with the great Eleatics was a real historical fact and, for philosophical circles, a memorable one, as an encounter between two great chess-players or gamblers is memorable for persons interested in chess or gaming.

The situation at the opening of the conversation is this. Zeno has just been reading aloud his famous work containing the antinomies for which he is still remembered. Socrates fastens on one of them, an argument which has not survived and of which the precise sense is uncertain, to the effect that " if things are many, they must be like and must also be unlike, but this is absurd," as an example of the rest. He proposes to regard the whole work as intended to establish the thesis of Parmenides by disproving its contradictory. Parmenides says " reality is one," Zeno that "reality is not many." Zeno accepts the statement with the minor correction that his object was not to prove the Parmenidean thesis, but simply to silence its critics by showing that their own rival " hypothesis " has even more impossible consequences than those they urge against Parmenides (127*d*–128*e*). Socrates then suggests that if we will only accept the doctrine of forms and the participation of things in forms, there is really no paradox in saying that the same " things " may " partake " at once of the form of likeness and of that of unlikeness, and so be at once like and unlike. But it would be a real and intolerable paradox ($\tau\acute{\epsilon}\rho\alpha\varsigma$) to hold that unlikeness can be predicated of the form of likeness or likeness of the form of unlike. So it is intelligible enough that a sensible thing, my body, for example, should be *one* body out of the six or seven human bodies present in this room and also have *many* members. But it would be quite another thing to hold that *Unity* is many or *Plurality* one (129a–130a). Parmenides and Zeno are both impressed by the ability of Socrates, and Parmenides at once asks him whether the theory is original. "Did you make this distinction between forms and things which partake of them αὐτός ? "—"for yourself," "out of your own head" (130b) ? Parmenides asks the question, as Proclus says, because it might be that Socrates had "heard of" some such distinction from some one else. The noticeable thing is that it is not the doctrine that there are "intelligible" forms which strikes Parmenides as novel ; the original point which impresses him is that Socrates holds that the things we see and handle "participate in" the forms. None of the difficulties he intends to raise arises from the belief that there are forms ; the difficulties all concern the relation of "participation" by which the sensible thing is connected with a form. It is the reality of the "phenomenal" world which he, as an Eleatic, finds a stumbling-block. The conclusion to which his criticism is meant to conduct us is the double one (a) that unless we admit the reality of the forms, there is an end of all philosophy; if we do admit it, the form cannot be "present in" sensible things, and these must therefore be simply unreal (135a–c).[1] This is precisely the position of Euclides and his friends, who taught that "reality is one ; the 'other' is unreal" (Aristocles *ap.* Euseb. *P.E.* xiv. 17, R.P. 289). Hence we shall expect to find that the arguments urged against Socrates by Parmenides are theirs also.

I may summarize these arguments the more briefly that they are admirably dealt with by Professor Burnet in *Greek Philosophy, Part I.*, 253–264, and other writers on the philosophy of Plato. I have attempted a complete discussion of their weight and derivation elsewhere in "Parmenides, Zeno, and Socrates," *Philosophical Studies*, pp. 28–90, whither I may refer a reader desirous of further information.

Parmenides begins by raising the question what precisely is the content of the world of forms. Socrates professes himself certain that there are forms corresponding to the fundamental notions of *ethics*—Right (δίκαιον), Good (αγαθόν), Noble (καλόν) ; he is doubtful about forms of organisms and physical things (Man, Fire, Water) ; in the case of such things as mud, dirt, hair—*i.e.*

---

[1] This is, ın fact, the position of the historical Parmenides himself. His "one" is, no doubt, corporeal; it is a solid homogeneous sphere. But our eyes and ears do not show us anything of the kind. Hence the apparent "things" which they disclose to us must be pure illusion. Though the "one" is corporeal, we only apprehend it by *thinking*. Its sole reality is deduced by Parmenides from what he regards as the postulates of coherent thought.

sensible things which do not appear to have a recognizable type of structure—he is inclined to think that there are no forms. In these cases there is no reality beyond " what we see." But he is not quite sure that consistency would not demand forms of these too, though he is afraid the admission might lead him into " abysmal nonsense " (130 b–d). What he means by this " nonsense " we can see, as Burnet suggests, by the notices preserved to us of the arbitrary fashion in which the Pythagorean Eurytus attempted to assign " numbers " to man, horse, and other things. The main point is, that though Socrates is not certain about the contents of the system of forms, the forms of which he is most certain are those which correspond to our ethical ideals. (Since we can define these as the mathematician defines his " figures," they must have the same kind of reality as that the geometer ascribes to his figures.)

The theory then is that all the " particulars " of which a common predicate is affirmed owe their possession of that predicate to their " participation " in the corresponding form, and Parmenides sets himself to show that, however we understand this relation of " participation," we are led to consequences which are logically absurd. This is exactly the line of reasoning adopted by Zeno for the confutation of the Pythagorean mathematicians who assume that " reality is many." The argument may be analysed as follows : (a) If a form is " in " each of a number of things, either the whole of it is " in " each of them, or only part of it is " in " each. In the first case the form itself being as a whole " in " each of several separate things is " outside " itself (i.e. it is, after all, many and not one, contrary to the Socratic thesis of its unity). In the second case, the form is divisible ($\mu\epsilon\rho\iota\sigma\tau\acute{o}\nu$), and thus becomes many by division just as, on the alternative view, it becomes many by multiplication ; the whole form is thus " in " no one of the things called after it, and thus they are not really entitled to the " common name " (131a–e). Thus we have an apparent *reductio ad absurdum* of the " hypothesis " of " participation " ; it permits of only two alternative interpretations and you are led, by a slightly different route, to the same denial of the hypothesis itself, whichever alternative you adopt. The hypothesis is thus " self-refuting." (The precise meaning of the reasoning by which the second of the alternatives is refuted in the special case of the form " magnitude " is obscure, but seems to be this. If you say that one thing is bigger than another in virtue of the presence in it of a " part " of the form of " magnitude," less than the whole of the form, you are maintaining in effect that there is such a relation as " not quite bigger than." Thus you are committed to holding that, e.g., if A and B are segments of a straight line, the relation between them may be that A is " not quite longer " than, or " nearly longer " than B, and this is manifestly nonsense. So, in the case of the form of " smallness," you are committed to the view that it would be significant to say that " A is nearly smaller than B, but not quite smaller." But this is senseless. Either *A* is quite smaller than *B* or it is not smaller at all. If there is *any* departure from strict equality, either *A* is definitely greater than *B* or it is definitely less than *B*, a perfectly valid argument against the notion of strictly " infinitesimal " differences, which is exactly on a par with the argument of Zeno against the view of the point as a " vanishing " magnitude.) We note, of course, that the reasoning is not directed against the reality of forms, but against the assumption that a form can be " in " or " present to " something which is not a form.

(*b*) The reason and the only reason for Socrates' doctrine is the assumption that when several things have a common predicate, it is assumed that there is a single determinate reality (the form) denoted by this predicate. But it ought to follow that, since the common predicate can be affirmed of the form itself, there must be a second form " present " alike to the first form and the things which " participate " in it, and similarly, by the same reason, a third, and so on *in indefinitum*. Thus there must be no one single form of, *e.g.*, magnitude, but a simply infinite series of forms of magnitude ; thus, once more, the Socratic theory is shown to be self-refuting, and again it is the asserted " presence " of forms to things which has created the difficulty (132*a–b*).

In strict logic this reasoning is not conclusive, since it turns on a confusion between a predication and the assertion of an identity. *E.g.* David and Jonathan are a *pair* of friends, Orestes and Pylades are another pair. Both pairs have something in common, the cardinal number 2, which is *the* number of the members of each. But the number 2 is not itself a pair ; it *is* a number, and cannot be said to *have* a number. Since Plato's object is merely to rehearse the objections of Eleatics to the Socratic doctrine in order to over-trump them by showing that their own methods can be turned with even more effect against their own theories, we need not suppose that he was unaware of this logical flaw, though he has no occasion to expose it. He had already made Socrates himself in the *Republic* (597*c*) remark in passing that if you once surrender the absolute unity of the form by admitting that there can be two forms of the same thing, you are committed to the " infinite regress." We may reasonably infer that this kind of reasoning was already current in Socrates' own lifetime, not invented for the first time after his death by Eleatic critics of the positions ascribed to him in the Platonic dialogues. Hence I think it unlikely that this particular difficulty has anything to do with the difficulty urged, as Alexander of Aphrodisias tells us, by Polyxenus the Megarian against the doctrine of " participation." As I understand the state-ments of Alexander, the point of Polyxenus was that on the Platonic theory there ought to be not only visible men, like Socrates and Plato, and a form of man, but also a " third " man, intermediate between the two, exactly as, on the Platonic theory itself, there are certain " mathematical objects " intermediate between the form of

circularity and the visible diagram drawn on a black-board.[1] I think also that when Aristotle talks of the "third man" as a difficulty to which the doctrine of forms leads us,[2] he is always intending to refer to this last-mentioned argument and not, as is commonly supposed, to the "indefinite regress." I have tried to argue the point fully in the essay already referred to (*Philosophical Studies*, pp. 52–69).
Zeno, and Socrates, pp. 255–270).

(*c*) At this point Socrates suggests a way of escape from the difficulty about the unity of the form. How if a form is really a "thought" (νόημα) and therefore is not "in" things at all, but "in our minds" (ἐν ψυχαῖς)? We could then maintain its unity without exposing ourselves to either of the lines of argument (*a*) and (*b*). Parmenides, however, has a reply based on the principle which is employed in his own poem as the foundation of his criticism of all his precursors. You cannot think without thinking of *something*—that is, of something *real* (to think of nothing would be equivalent to not thinking at all); this something is some *one determinate* thing which "that thought thinks, as being there in all the instances." In other words, what the thought thinks is always a form. (*E.g.*, when you think of Socrates, Plato, and Aristotle, you think some *definite* predicate about them, such as, *e.g.*, that they are all *men*, and thus we are back at our old position. You are thinking of *man* as a form " present " to the three.) What then, on this view that a form is a thought, can the " presence " of the form to the thing mean? Does it mean that a thing is a complex of thoughts and that everything thinks? Or would you admit that there are " thoughts which do not think " ? (132*b–c*).

Once more, the difficulty is one not about the reality of the form but about the possibility of the " presence " of it to something

[1] Thus we can distinguish (1) *the* circle of which we give the equation in analytical geometry, (2) the terrestrial equator, (3) the black line on a terrestrial globe which stands for the equator.   (1) is the form, (2) is an invisible perfect " instance " of the form, (3) a visible and imperfect embodiment of the form. On Polyxenus see *Early Greek Philosophy, Part I.*, pp. 254, 259–260. It has been suggested that the difficulties urged by Parmenides were originally raised against Plato himself by his pupil Aristotle, and that it is in acknowledgment of this that the Aristotle who was afterwards one of the " Thirty " figures as a character in the dialogue and is made the respondent throughout the second part.   The fancy must be rejected for the following reasons : (1) Aristotle only entered the Academy in the year 367, the very year of Plato's departure for Syracuse, as a mere lad.   It may even be doubted whether he can have held any personal intercourse with Plato until after the end of Plato's first visit to Dionysius II ; (2) the one real point of contact between the Aristotelian criticism of Plato and the *Parmenides* is the supposed identity of the τρίτος ἄνθρωπος with the argument from the " regress."   If the two are not identical, this point of contact disappears.   Even if they are, the very fact that Aristotle refers to the argument by such a nickname indicates that it was something already familiar.   (3) As has been finally established by Jaeger in his *Aristoteles*, Aristotle's divergence from the Academy on the doctrine of forms was first indicated in the work περὶ φιλοσοφίας shortly after Plato's death.   His earlier works, so far as we know them (*Eudemus, Protrepticus*), are wholly Platonic in spirit.

[2] *Met.* 990*b* 15 ff. = 1079*a* 11 ff., 1039*a* 2 ff., 1059*b* 8 ff. ; *S.E.* 178*b* 36.

which is not a form. Socrates has just suggested that the form or universal may be just a "thought in our minds," a *way of looking at* things. The theory is, in fact, that historically known to us as Nominalism, though Conceptualism would be a better name for it. It treats a "significant universal" simply as a point of view from which the mind contrives to look at a plurality of things with a single glance. We find it convenient, as making for "economy of mental effort," to look at Socrates, Plato, Aristotle, all together as "instances of the universal *man* "; according to the theory, the employment of this common name "man" only expresses the fact that we have effected this economy and nothing more ; what is common to Socrates, Plato, Aristotle, is simply that we have succeeded in viewing them together and have therefore given them the common name. Parmenides' objection is, in principle, that the name remains insignificant unless there really is a "common nature" which justifies the common name. But if the common "nature" is a "thought in our minds," then the things which are said to have this common nature must be just complexes of thoughts, and we shall have to say that everything whatever thinks, or, alternatively, since in any case a thing is assumed to be a complex of forms, and forms have been declared to be thoughts, that there are "thoughts which do not think" (ἀνόητα νοήματα). The suggested Conceptualism, it should be noted, would be just as fatal to Aristotelianism as to Platonism. On the Aristotelian view, though there are no universals *ante res*, there are universals *in rebus*, and it is only because there are universals *in rebus* that there are also universals in the *intellectus* of the scientific thinker. As against the Conceptualism which, like that of Mach or Karl Pearson, denies that universals exist at all except *in intellectu*, where they are merely labour-saving devices, "conceptual shorthand," the rejoinder of Parmenides seems decisive. As to the source of this Conceptualism, it is not easy to say anything with confidence. The best suggestion known to me is that made *ad loc.* by Grote,[1] who calls attention to a statement of Simplicius (commenting on Arist. *Cat.* 8*b* 25) that the "school of Eretria" maintained that "qualities" are ψιλαὶ ἔννοιαι, "mere thoughts," "mere notions." Since Menedemus of Eretria and his followers were famous formal logicians and agreed with the Eleatics of Megara in objecting to negative predication (Diog. Laert. ii. 135), it seems to me that Grote is probably on the right track, and that we are still dealing with a criticism on the theory of forms derived from Eleatic sources.

(*d*) Socrates next falls back on what Aristotle regarded as the Pythagorean formula for the relation between form and thing. The form is an archetype or model (παράδειγμα), the other things called by its name are likenesses (ὁμοιώματα) of it, so that the relation between sensible thing and form is that the "thing" is a

[1] Grote, *Plato and the other Companions of Socrates* (ed. 1885), vol. iii. 74 n. 2.

" copy " of the form.   (This would, apparently, save the unity of the form by suggesting that there may be many " imitations " of one form just as there may be many copies of the same original.) Parmenides again argues that the theory refutes itself.   For " resemblance " is a symmetrical relation.   If A is like B, B is also like A.   It follows that the form must be like the things which " resemble it."   And, since the theory itself explains the likeness of one thing to another by the existence of a common archetype of both, we must account for the likeness of form to " thing " by postulating a more ultimate archetype of both, and so on *in indefinitum* (132*d*–133*a*).

As before, the difficulty really arises from a fallacy.   As Proclus rightly says, the relation of copy to original is not simply one of likeness.   (It is in fact a relation of resemblance+derivation, and this relation is not symmetrical.   My reflection in the glass is a reflection of my face, but my face is not a reflection of it.)   It should be specially remarked that the suggestion that the relation between form and " thing " is one of " likeness " is not offered as an alternative to the doctrine of " participation," but as a further specification of its precise meaning (132*d* 3, ἡ μέθεξις αὕτη . . . τῶν εἰδῶν οὐκ ἄλλη τις ἢ εἰκασθῆναι αὐτοῖς), and that Parmenides meets both formulae with precisely the same objection that they appear to involve the " indefinite regress."

(*e*) The gravest difficulty of all has yet to be faced.   It is that the recognition of two " worlds," presupposed by Socrates, a world of forms and an " other " world of " things " which somehow " partake " of the forms, leads direct to complete scepticism (133*a*– 135*c*).   For the world of which each of us is a member is *ex hypothesi* not the world of forms, but the " other " world (since it had been observed at the outset that each of us is *a man*, none of us is the " form of man ").   Consequently the relations between forms will belong exclusively to the world or system of related forms ; corresponding relations of which " we " are terms will belong to " our world " and will have their correlates within " our world." There will be a relation between " master " as such and " servant " as such, and the terms of this will be the form of master and the form of servant.   But each of us will be master or servant to another man, and the relation between this pair will fall outside the world of forms ; it will connect one man with another man, not with a form.   So the correlate of the form of knowledge will be Reality as such.   But the correlate of our knowledge will be such reality as the objects of our world possess.   And it is admitted that " our " knowledge is not the form of knowledge (that is, the knowledge we have is partial and imperfect).   Its counterpart therefore is not the completely real.   We are precluded from knowing what real good is, for the counterpart of a merely relative and partial knowledge must be a relative and partial reality.   And we may invert the argument with even more startling results.   God, at any rate, might be supposed to possess " absolute " or " perfect " knowledge. But, by our previous reasoning, it follows that God knows nothing of our imperfectly real world. And in the same way, we may deny the rule of God over us, on the ground that the correlate of human subject is human superior. In a word, the consequence of a theory of two distinct " worlds " or " orders " will be that every relation falls wholly within one of the two ; there can be no relation connecting a member of the one world with a member of the other. (In the mouth of an Eleatic, of course, this means that one of the two " worlds " is an illusion, and that one is the supposed " sensible world." Parmenides, who wrote the words ταὐτὸ γὰρ ἔστι νοεῖν τε καὶ εἶναι (" it is the same thing which can be thought of and can be "), has no intention of surrendering the " intelligible " world, and any interpretation of the *Parmenides* which assumes that its object is to discredit the reality of the intelligible is necessarily false).

Yet to deny the reality of forms is destructive of thought itself, since it amounts to a denial of the possibility of definite knowledge. If Socrates has been badly perplexed by the discussion which has just been closed, it is because, in his zeal, he has attempted to enunciate his doctrine about forms without a sufficient preparatory discipline in arid and apparently " useless " formal logic. The kind of discipline required may be exemplified by Zeno's famous antinomies, but needs to go even beyond them. Zeno had attempted to prove the thesis that " reality is many " self-refuting by showing that it can be made to lead to pairs of contradictory conclusions. For a really searching investigation it is not enough to ask what follows from the assertion of a thesis, but also what follows from the denial of it. *E.g.* Zeno should have asked not merely, " If things are many, what can be asserted about the many things, and what about the unit, and about the relation of the two ? " but also, " If things are not many, what follows about plurality, the unit, and their relations ? " (It was not enough to argue that the consequences of Pluralism are self-contradictory ; the same issue should have been raised about the consequences of denying Pluralism.) Complete investigation of any proposed philosophical principle demands this twofold consideration of the implications both of its assertion and of its denial (135*b*–136*c*).

In these remarks, which effect a transition to the second half of the dialogue, there are two interesting implications. If Parmenides ascribes the helplessness of the young Socrates in face of the difficulties just raised to want of training in formal logic, we may infer that the suggestion is that the apparently formidable arguments are themselves fallacious and would be seen to be so by a more practised logician. That is, the fault of Plato's Megarian critics is not that they are logicians, but that they are not logical enough. If we are only thorough enough with our logic, the alleged logical objections to the metaphysic of forms will vanish of themselves. It seems further to be meant that the particular fault of these logicians is one-sidedness. They scrutinize the consequences of the

Socratic and Platonic assertion of the " participation " of sensible things in forms, but they forget to consider whether the denial of the assertion may not involve worse antinomies than those they have detected in the Platonic dialogues. Plato is, in fact, suggesting that he knows how to play the game of formal logic according to the rules even better than the famous professionals themselves. Beyond these significant hints that what we need is not less but more logic, the dialogue provides no solution of the problem it has raised.

In the second part of the dialogue Parmenides consents to give an elaborate example of the kind of logical method he has been recommending, choosing as the respondent to his questions the youngest member of the party, Aristoteles, on the ground that his very youth will be a guarantee that his answers will be given without *finesse* of any kind. The thesis selected for examination is, naturally enough, Parmenides' own principle that "reality is one." (136c–137c. It is significant that he speaks of the whole proceeding as an elaborate " game " (παιδιά), a plain hint that the antinomies now to follow are not to be taken quite seriously, and that we must not be surprised if there is a touch of conscious " sophistry " about some of them. In fact, it is incredible that Plato should not have known that some of them are pure fallacies. But, as his purpose is simply to show that the methods of his critics can be made to recoil on themselves, it is strictly fair that he should play their game by their own rules. Any kind of reasoning they permit themselves is equally permissible in a " skit " upon them.)

According to the programme already laid down by Parmenides, we should expect to find him raising four problems : (1) if the real is one, what can be asserted about this one real ? (2) if the real is one, what can be said about " the many "? (3) if the real is not one, what can be said about the one ? (4) if the real is not one, what can be said about the many ? But by a further refinement, each of these questions is raised twice over, the purpose being to show that on either assumption (that the real is one or that it is not one) you can make it appear at pleasure either that contradictory predicates can be both affirmed or both denied alike of the one and of the many. Thus we get altogether eight arguments forming four " antinomies "—two in which the subject of both thesis and antithesis is the one, and two in which it is the many. The issue is that the apparent dilemma to which Socrates had been reduced at the end of the first part of the dialogue, that knowledge of the real is equally impossible with or without his theory about forms and " participation," is more than matched by the dilemma offered to the Eleatics, and maliciously offered through the mouth of their own founder Parmenides professing to be applying their own peculiar method, that, whether you accept or reject their Monism, you must either simultaneously assert or simultaneously deny both members of an indefinite series of contradictory pairs of propositions.

The formal arrangement of the eight " hypotheses " is this:

A {
   I. *If the real is one*, nothing whatever can be asserted of it (137*c*–142*a*).
   II. *If the real is one*, everything can be asserted of it (142*b*–157*c*).[1]

B {
   III. *If the real is one*, everything can be asserted of " things other than the one " (157*b*–159*b*).
   IV. *If the real is one* nothing can be asserted of " things other than the one " (159*b*–160*b*).

C {
   V. *If the one is unreal*, everything can be asserted of it (160*b*–163*b*).
   VI *If the one is unreal*, nothing at all can be asserted of it (163*b*–164*b*).

D {
   VII. *If the one is unreal*, everything can be asserted about " things other than the one " (164*b*–165*e*).
   VIII. *If the one is unreal*, nothing can be asserted about anything (165*e*–166*c*).

It would be taking Plato's metaphysical jest too gravely to make a minute examination of all the details of these bewildering arguments. It will be sufficient to point out the peculiar character of the dialectical method employed and to summarize the results. The peculiarities of the method are dictated by the consideration that it is avowedly a parody of that of Zeno. Now Zeno's special trick of fence, a perfectly legitimate one, was to turn one-half of the assumed " postulates " of his opponents against the other half. This is the secret, for example, of the famous " paradoxes " about motion. The double assumption of the geometers whom Zeno is criticizing is that (*a*) any finite segment of a straight line can be bisected, (*b*) such a segment is a path between two end-points which are finite minima of magnitude. The geometers cannot give up (*a*) without ruining their whole scientific edifice; they cannot give up (*b*) without destroying the parallelism between geometry and arithmetic which is part of their system. Zeno turns (*a*) against (*b*). From (*a*) it follows at once that there must be an endless series of points intermediate between any two given " end-points," and this is fatal to the view that the point has a finite magnitude. His reasoning silences his opponents because they are not prepared to surrender (*a*) by admitting the existence of " indivisible lines," nor yet to give up (*b*) by regarding the point as a geometrical zero. In exactly the same way, the " hypothesis " of the Eleatics—" if It is one " or " if there is One "—as *they* understand it, really covers two assumptions—(*a*) unity is real, (*b*) reality is unity; Plato's trick is to play off one of these assumptions against the other. This will come out more clearly if we compare the main positions of the antithetical members of each " antinomy."

A. I. " It is one; " therefore, " it " is not many, and therefore is not a whole and has no parts. *Ergo* it has neither beginning,

---

[1] The main argument ends at 155*e* 3. What follows down to 157*b* 5 is an appended special development which would, in a modern writing, be relegated to a note.

middle, nor last part. *Ergo* it is unbounded (ἄπειρον) and has no figure (σχῆμα). " It " has no place, since it cannot be " in " anything. *Ergo* " it " cannot *change* its place, nor can it change its quality without ceasing to be one. Thus " it " cannot move. Nor yet can it be " at rest," since we have seen that it cannot be " in " any place at all, and therefore not " in the same place where it was." It cannot be identical with or other than anything. For it cannot be identical with anything but itself, nor yet different from itself. Nor can it be different from something " other " than itself. If it were, it would be different from the other in virtue of some point of difference ; thus it would have two characters at once : it would be one and also " different " from something in some specific way. That is, it would " be " two things at once, whereas, by hypothesis, it is one and only one. So again, it cannot be identical with itself. For " to be one " and " to be identical with " are not the same. Once more, if " it " were "identical with itself," it would have two characters, unity and identity, and so would be two and not one. For similar reasons, " it " can neither be like nor unlike itself or anything else. Again, it can be neither equal nor unequal to itself or to anything else. For terms are equal when they are of "the same measures" (τῶν αὐτῶν μέτρων, 140*b*). And " it," as we have seen, cannot be " the same " with anything in any respect and yet remain one. Nor can it be unequal to anything. That would mean that it has " more " or " fewer " measures than something, and therefore that it has parts.

So it can have no temporal predicates. It cannot be contemporary with, nor more nor less ancient than itself or anything else (the reasoning being exactly like that just used about equality and inequality). It cannot, then, be in time at all. For we may say of whatever occupies time, but of nothing else, that (*a*) it is at any moment " becoming older " than itself and also " becoming younger " than itself ; and (*b*) that its existence fills just the duration it does, and neither more nor less, and so it is " simultaneous with," " of the same age as " itself. Since neither statement can be made about the one, it cannot be " in time." Therefore, we must not say of it, " it was," " it became," " it will be," " it will come to be," since all these expressions involve reference to past or future, that is, to time. But the very word " is " or " comes to be " also involves a reference to time, to present time. And therefore we may not say of " it " that " it is " or " it becomes," since " it " is not in time at all. But if we cannot say " is " of the one, we cannot ascribe being to it. It must be non-existent. And if it is non-existent, it cannot even be one, for to be one, it would have to be. But what is nothing at all can neither be named, spoken of, thought of, known, nor perceived by the senses. Thus we actually deduce from the proposition " it is one " the conclusion that nothing whatsoever can be thought or said about " it."

It has been asked what the " it " presupposed as the subject of the thesis " it is one " is. The answer, as the character of the reasoning shows, is " anything whatever which is conceived to be a mere undifferentiated unity admitting no plurality whatsoever." The argument is that *all* affirmation implies plurality of some kind possibility of distinguishing. If there is anything which is such a mere undifferentiated unity that there are no distinctions within it, you cannot even affirm of it that it is one. It is the " hypothesis " of the Eleatics that their " One," which is the only thing there is, is just such a bare unit, and this hypothesis is self-refuting. We note then, that in I., in the hypothesis " if there is one," the emphasis falls on the unity of reality, not on the reality of unity. The assumption is that " what is is one," not that " something which is one is." The work of turning that part of the Eleatic "hypothesis" against the other is undertaken in II.

II. If the one *is* ($\text{\ae}\nu \ \epsilon\iota \ \text{\ae}\sigma\tau\iota\nu$), it "partakes of " being. It has *two* distinct characters; it *is*, and it is *one*. Thus it has "parts " (or, as we should say, distinct "aspects "). Unity and existence are *parts*, or constituents of " the existing one," which is therefore a *whole*. And each of these " parts," on inspection, is found to have itself the same two " parts." Each *is* a constituent of the " existing one " and each is *one* such constituent. The " existing " one " is thus an infinite manifold ($\text{\ae}\pi\epsilon\iota\rho\nu \ \pi\lambda\hat{\eta}\theta\sigma$). Again, unity is different from existence, and difference is itself something different from both existence and unity. Here then are several terms—unity, existence, difference—which can be grouped into pairs. Each pair has a number—the number 2. We have thus established the existence of the numbers 1 and 2, and the addition of 1 and 2 establishes the existence of 3. We can then go on, by addition and multiplication, to establish the existence of the whole integer-series as a direct consequence of the existence of " the one." Being thus has an infinite plurality of parts, and each of these parts is *one* part ; there are as many units as there are " parts " of being. Thus not only " being " but " unity " itself turns out to be infinitely many.

Since parts are parts of a *whole*, they are contained by the whole and thus have a bound ($\pi\text{\ae}\rho\alpha$s). The "existing one," then, is not only indefinitely many or boundless, but is also bounded, and therefore has first, last, and intermediate parts—beginning, middle, and end. Thus it has a *shape* or *form* ($\sigma\chi\hat{\eta}\mu\alpha$) of some kind. It is " in " itself, for all the parts are in the whole, and "the one " is at once " all the parts " and " the whole." But equally the whole is not *in* the parts, either singly or taken together. To be in them all, it would have to be in each singly, and that is impossible. But it must be somewhere, if it is anything, and, as it cannot be " in itself," it must be " in " something else. Thus, considered as " all the parts," it is in itself ; considered as " the whole," it is in something not itself. Since it is " in itself " and so in *one* place ($\text{\ae}\nu \ \text{\ae}\nu\text{\ae}$) it is at rest ; but since it is "always in something else," it cannot be at rest, and so is moving. The one is neither a part of

itself nor related to itself as whole to part, nor different from itself ;
hence it is *identical* with itself.   But, as we said, it is also outside
itself, and therefore *different* from itself.   Of course, also it is
different from the things which are other than itself.   But it is also
identical with these other things.   For there can be no difference
in what is " the same."   Hence " difference " can never be " in "
anything, for, if it were so for the smallest fraction of a moment, it
would be, for that time, " in the same thing."   Hence the things
which are not the one are not different from the one.   Nor do they
" partake " of it ; for then they would not be " not one," but,
" in a sense, one."   So they are not a whole of which the one is a
part.   And they are not parts of the one.   The only possibility
left is that they are *identical* with the one.

The one is different from other things, and they are neither
more nor less different from it, but to a " like " degree.   Thus
the one and other things are *alike* because different.   But if difference implies likeness, identity will imply unlikeness, and the one
and other things have just been shown to be identical.   Therefore,
because identical, they are *unlike*.   And yet again, in so far as two
terms have the same predicate they are alike, and in so far as they
have different predicates they are unlike.   So the one and other
things will be alike because identical, and unlike because different.
And since the one has been shown to be both identical with and
different from itself, it must be both like and unlike itself.

Since the one is both " in " itself and " in " other things, it
will have *contact* with itself and with them.   But things which are
in contact must occupy adjoining regions (ἐφεξῆς κεῖσθαι), and
that which is *one* cannot occupy two adjoining regions.   Hence the
one is not in contact with itself.   But once more, nothing has
contact with itself, and if there are to be *n* contacts, there must be
n+1 things in contact.   Now the " things other than the one "
cannot have any number, since what has a number " partakes of
unity."   There can therefore be no contact between the one and
other things, since contact implies number.

Again, the one is at once equal to and unequal to itself and to
" other things."   (*a*) If *a* is > *b*, this means that the form of μέγεθος
is in *a* relatively to *b*, and the form of σμικρότης in *b* relatively to *a* ;
if *a* is to be absolutely small or large, this means that the form
σμικρότης or μέγεθος is " in " *a*.   But neither μέγεθος nor σμικρότης can
be " in " the one as a whole or in any part of it.   For if σμικρότης is
in the one as a whole it is equal with the one, and if it " envelops "
it it is greater than the one ; in either case the form σμικρότης
would be " doing the function " of the different form ἰσότης or
μέγεθος.   And the same reasoning applies if we suppose σμικρότης
to be in any one part of the one.   We may argue in the same
way, *mutatis mutandis*, about μέγεθος.   Thus σμικρότης and μέγεθος
cannot be " in " anything whatever, and it follows that nothing,
except the form of μέγεθος, can be " greater than " anything, and
nothing except the form of σμικρότης " less than " anything.

Hence neither the one nor what is other than the one can be greater or smaller than the other, and therefore they must be equal. For the same reason, the one can be neither greater nor smaller than itself, and is therefore equal to itself. (*b*) Since the one is " in " itself, it contains and is contained by itself, and thus must be, as container greater, as contained less than, itself. Further, there is nothing outside the one and things other than the one. And whatever is must be somewhere, and consequently the one and " the others " must be in each other reciprocally, and therefore each of these terms is at once greater and less than the other. And therefore also the one will be metrically of " equal," " more numerous," " fewer " measures, and so numerically equal with, higher and lower than, itself and " the others."

Once more, " if there is one," the one *is*. And *is* expresses *present* participation of being. Hence the one is " in time." And time " goes on " ($\pi o \rho \epsilon \acute{v} \epsilon \tau a \iota$). Hence the one is always *getting* older than itself as time goes on, and therefore, since " older " always has " younger " as its correlate, it is always *getting* younger than itself also. And at any moment in this process, it *is* both older and younger than itself. And yet it fills the same duration as itself, neither more nor less, and so neither is nor grows older nor younger than itself. Again, before there can be several things, there must be one to start with. Hence the " one " must have come to be before " the others " ; it must be more ancient than " the other things." Yet we proved that the one has " parts," beginning, middle, end. Its beginning must have come to be before itself ; the one itself will not be there until its end also comes to be. Thus the one is the last thing to come to be ; everything else is more ancient than the one. But, after all, each " part " of the one is *one* part, and thus whenever anything comes to be, the one comes to be, and the one thus comes to be contemporaneously with everything else. Next, if one thing is older or younger than another, the interval in age between the two never grows greater or less. So we may say that the one *is* more ancient or more recent than other things, but never *grows* more ancient or more recent. And yet, though the one has been " in being " ($\gamma \acute{\epsilon} \gamma o \nu \epsilon$) longer than " the others," the difference between their respective ages is steadily being relatively diminished as time goes on, and we may therefore say that, in so far as the one is more ancient than " the others," it steadily becomes less ancient relatively to them, and they more ancient relatively to it. But, in so far as it is less ancient than " the others," it is steadily growing, relatively to them, older, and they, relatively to it, younger. And finally, in so far as a time-interval remains the interval it is, the one is neither becoming more nor becoming less ancient than anything else.

In conclusion, the one, " partaking of time," has past, present, future. It was, is, will be, was becoming, is becoming, will become. It stands, has stood, will stand, in various relations. There can be knowledge of it, belief about it, perception of it, and therefore it can be named, described, and, generally, everything which was denied in I. must be affirmed.

Appendix (155e–157b).—The one, then, both is and is not, and its being is " in time." It is during some intervals, during others it is not, since it cannot be said to be and not to be *at once*. It must pass through transitions from being to not-being and from not-being to being. It undergoes aggregation and disgregation, assimilation and dissimilation, augmentation and diminution. It begins to move and ceases to move. So these reversals of the sense of a process must also be " in time." And yet they cannot be " in time " ; the reversal must be strictly *instantaneous*, occupying no time, however paradoxical we may find the conception of an instant (τὸ ἐξαίφνης) which is strictly without duration. *At* the instant of the reversal of sense, *both* members of a pair of antithetic processes must be denied of the one. At such an instant, it is not " coming to be " nor yet " passing away," neither being aggregated nor being disgregated, neither being assimilated nor dissimilated. As with states, so with processes ; both members of an antithesis must be asserted of the one and both must be denied.

Perhaps the most striking feature of this argument to our own minds is this introduction at its close of the notion of an unextended " instant." Plato is plainly stating exactly the paradoxes which beset the founders of the Calculus when they took the notion of the " infinitesimal " seriously and mistakenly supposed that the Calculus really deals either with infinitesimal increments or with ratios between infinitesimals. But the subtlety of some parts of the long development must not blind us to the fact that most of the reasoning throughout II. is purely sophistical and much of it clearly consciously sophistical, and that the fallacies committed are mostly of a very obvious kind, such as equivocation between " each " and " all collectively." Plato can and does, in this very dialogue, when it suits his purpose, expose the very confusions in question and therefore must not be supposed to be serious when he commits them. It is enough for his purpose to perplex the " eristics " by availing himself of fallacies of the kind which they habitually commit in their own argumentation. His parody of their *elenchus* is also an exposure of it. The one important point to keep in mind is that the conclusions to which he is led by his application of the Eleatic methods to the Eleatic " hypothesis " are not meant to be asserted as his own. They are simply what happens to the " hypothesis " if you make the Eleatic criticize himself by his own methods. If we wish to know what Plato himself thought of the Eleatic thesis, we must turn from the *Parmenides* to the *Sophistes*, where he is really criticizing it by the rules of a logic which is his own. For the present it is enough to remark that, just as in I., the emphasis was laid on the *unity* of " what is," with the consequence that being itself has to be denied of it, so in II. the emphasis is laid on its reality, with the consequence that the unity of the one has to be simultaneously affirmed and denied. So far, and no further, the paradoxes of the *Parmenides* prelude to the positive results of the *Sophistes*.

III. If the one is, what of "other things"? Since they are "other" things, they are not the one; yet they must "partake of" it. For they must have parts (if they had not, they would be just "the one"), and therefore parts of *one* complete whole. And each of these parts must again be itself *one* definite part of the *one* whole. The "other things" are therefore a manifold or aggregate (πλείω). They must be a numerically *infinite* manifold, since each "part" *participates* in unity and therefore is not itself, in its own nature, one. And yet, in the act of participating in unity, each part is "bounded" or "limited" or "determinate" relatively to the whole and to any other part; "something arises in it" which constitutes a bound (πέρας). The "other things" are thus at once infinitely numerous and also bounded. In so far as all are "unlimited," each is *like* every other, and again each is like every other in exhibiting "limit." But in so far as each is at once unlimited and limited, each is *unlike* itself and the rest, and by similar reasoning we may show that all the antithetical pairs of predicates canvassed in I. and II. may be both affirmed and denied of the "other" things.

IV. But let us consider the same question once more. "The one" and "the others" form a complete disjunction. Neither is the other, and there is no *tertium quid*. They are thus completely "separated" (χωρίς). And what is strictly one can have no "parts." From these two premisses it follows that neither the one as a whole, nor a "part" of it, can be in "the others." They cannot participate in it in any sense. There is no unity in them, and therefore they are not even a manifold (πολλά), and have no number. They are, after all, not "both like and unlike" one another; if they were, each of them would have in it *two* opposed forms, and would thus "partake of two," whereas we have just seen that none of them can even "partake of one," and therefore we must also deny that *either* member of the alternative "like-unlike" can be asserted of "the others." The same kind of reasoning will show that no predicates at all can be asserted of them.

III. and IV. thus answer in inverted order to I. and II. In III., as in II., the emphasis falls on the reality of the Eleatic ὂν ἕν, in IV. as in I., on its unity. III. proves for τὰ ἄλλα what II. had proved for τὸ ἕν. IV. undertakes to prove of them what I. had established for τὸ ἕν. The total result of I.–IV. is summed up for us at 160*b* 2: "If the one is, the one is everything and is nothing at all, relatively alike to itself and to 'the others.'"

V. We come to the second half of the complete dialectical investigation proposed at 136*a–b*. *If the one is not, what follows?* When a man says "if the one is not," or "if magnitude is not," or generally "if *x* is not," he is making an intelligible supposition. Whether we say that "the one" is or that it is not, we mean the same thing by " one " in both cases, and we mean something definite. So we may put our question in the form, " If the one *is* not, what must be true of it ? " (τί χρὴ εἶναι). It must be knowable, or the statement " there is no one," " the one does not exist," would have no sense. " The others " must be *different* from it, and it from them. Thus we must be able to call the one " that " or " this " and to ascribe *relations* to it. We must not say that it *is*, but we are bound to say that it " partakes of " many things (has many predicates). It is *unlike* anything else, but *like itself*. It is not *equal* to τὰ ἄλλα, for then it would be *like* them ; hence it is *unequal* to them, and therefore has magnitude, is greater and less. But whatever is greater than *x* and less than *y* is equal to something. Thus the *one* must, after all, be *equal* to something. It must also have *being* of some kind (μετέχειν πῃ οὐσίας), because we can ascribe *true* predicates to it, just as " what is " must partake of not-being, since it " is not " whatever can be truly denied of it, so " what is not " must in a sense be, since " it is " whatever can be significantly predicated of it. And since the " non-existent one " thus both is and is not, it must pass from one of these conditions to the other and so change. It must exhibit motion. But again, it is nowhere, and thus cannot change its place, nor rotate, nor suffer change in quality (for if it did, it could no longer be " the one "). Thus it has no motion, and so is at rest. But it is also moving and therefore does change in quality, for whatever has moved " is no longer *as* it was but otherwise." The one, then, alters and does not alter, and so at once " comes to be " and " passes away " and does neither. Everything can be affirmed of it and everything denied. (Thus V. corresponds to II. ; all that had been proved of the one in II. on the assumption that the one *is*, is proved of it in V. on the assumption that it is *not*.)

VI. And yet again, " if the one is not," that means that being is wholly denied of it. The denial is absolute and must be understood without qualification. If the one is not, it cannot come to *be*, nor pass out of *being*, since it can neither get nor lose what is, *ex hypothesi*, wholly foreign to it. Neither can it *alter* in any way, for the same reason, and therefore it cannot *move*. Nor can it be at rest, for to be at rest is to *be* " in the same place " at successive times. It can have no predicates or relations, for if it had any, it would *be* whatever you truly assert of it. Hence it cannot be known, thought of, perceived, spoken of, or named. (Thus what was proved about the one in I. on the assumption that it exists, is now proved on the assumption that it does not exist. In either case nothing can be affirmed or denied of it.)

VII. " *If the one is not*," *what must be said of* " *the others* " ?— They must be " other than " and therefore *different* (ἕτερα) from something or we could not call them " the others." As there is no " one " from which they could differ, they must be different from one another. They must also be different infinite *assemblages* (ὄγκοι), not different *units*, since, *ex hypothesi*, there is no unit.

Each of them must be an infinite assemblage, different from the rest of these assemblages, which falsely *seems* on a distant view to be one single thing. Since each such assemblage *seems* to be one thing, there will seem to be a definite number of them, and there will *seem* to be a *least* among them, though this again will seem to be many and numerous by comparison with its own components. Each assemblage will be bounded by others (will have a πέρας), but will have in itself neither first term, middle, nor last term (*i.e.* each assemblage will be an infinite series without end-terms, and every component of it will be another assemblage of the same type). Thus each will *seem* to be both bounded and unbounded, to be like or unlike any other, according as we take a distant or a near view of it. (In general, all that III. had said of τὰ ἄλλα will *appear* to be true of them.)

VIII. And yet, to go over the ground for a last time, " if there is no one," τὰ ἄλλα obviously cannot be one. And they cannot be many, for then each of the many would be one. They must be zeros, and no multitude can be constructed out of zeros. And they do not even *seem* to be one or to be many. By hypothesis, "the unit " is just nothing at all, and hence nothing can even seem to be a unit ; *a fortiori* nothing can seem to be *many*, a collection of units. By carrying the thought out it would follow that τὰ ἄλλα have none of the positive or negative determinations we have ascribed to them, and do not even seem to have any. *Nothing* can be thought or said of them, (a conclusion which answers to that drawn in IV.). Thus we may summarize the result of our whole series of antinomies by saying that " whether the one is or is not, it and ' the others ' alike, are and seem to be, and also are not and do not seem to be, all sorts of things (πάντα), relatively both to themselves and to one another " (166c 2).

In the four discussions which take for their point of departure the non-existence of the " one " or " unit," even more obviously than in those which have preceded, the ultimate source of our perplexities is the ambiguity of the word " is." We get contradictory results according as " is " is taken to be the symbol of predication (Peano's ε), or that of *existence* (Peano's ∃).[1] Many of the inferences turn simply on this confusion of a predication with what we now call an " existential proposition." It is legitimate parody to employ this fallacy, because, as we can see from the remains of the poem of Parmenides, the whole point of Eleaticism lies in ignoring the distinction. To make it clear, and to show that Eleaticism had ignored it, is, in fact, the main purpose of Plato's *Sophistes*. So long as he is merely undertaking to show that the Eleatic logic would be even more damaging to the Eleatic " postulate " than to the Socratic postulate of μέθεξις, he is fully entitled

---

[1] There is, of course, a further confusion of both with the symbol of *identity* (=). The poposition *A is an a* is treated on occasion as implying both *A exists* and *A is identical with a*. (Not to mention the further refinement that *existence* also appears to be itself a *vox equivoca*.)

to avail himself of the double-edged tools of his opponents. It does not follow that Plato himself was not alive to the ambiguity when he wrote the *Parmenides* and only discovered it in the interval between the composition of that dialogue and of the *Sophistes*. The presumption from the skilful way in which he makes or ignores the distinction in the *Parmenides* just as it suits his immediate purpose is that his own logical doctrine is already complete in his own mind ; the parody of Megarian dialectic probably serves a double purpose. It provides a highly enjoyable philosophical jest, and also provokes the thoughtful mind, by the manifest impossibility of the conclusions reached, to reflections which may prompt the reader to discover the sources of the trouble for himself, without waiting to have them explained to him by Plato. More than any other dialogue the *Parmenides* has the appearance of being written for a rather circumscribed group of readers ; it was presumably meant to amuse the literary circles but to fructify in the students of the Academy.

See further :

BURNET.—*Greek Philosophy, Part I.*, 253–272.
RITTER, C.—*Platon*, ii. 63–96 ; *Platons Dialoge*, 1–24. (Stuttgart, 1903.)
RAEDER, H.—*Platons philosophische Entwickelung*, 297–317.
NATORP, P.—*Platons Ideenlehre*, 215–217.
APELT, O.—*Beiträge zur Geschichte der griechischen Philosophie*, 3–66. (Leipzig, 1891.)
STEWART, J. A.—*Plato's Doctrine of Ideas*, 68–84.
STALLBAUM, G.—*Platonis Parmenides*. (Leipzig, 1848.)
WADDELL, W.—*The " Parmenides " of Plato*. (Glasgow, 1894.)
WAHL, J.—*Étude sur le Parménide de Platon*. (Paris 1926.)
DIÈS, A.—*Platon, Parmenide*, vi.–xix., 1–53. (Paris, 1923.)
ROBIN, L.—*Platon*, 119–140.
HARDIE, W. F. R.—*A Study in Plato*. (Oxford, 1936.)
TAYLOR, A. E.—*Parmenides Zeno and Socrates* (*Philosophical Studies*, London, 1934, pp. 28–90).
TAYLOR, A. E.—*Plato's Parmenides*. (Oxford, 1934.)
LEE, H. P. D.—*Zeno of Elea*. (Cambridge, 1936.)
TANNERY, P.—*Pour l'Histoire de la Sciènce Hellène* (ed. 2, by A. Diès, Paris, 1930, c. x. *Zénon d'Elée*).

CHAPTER XV

SOPHISTES–POLITICUS

THE dialogues which we have still to consider all reveal themselves, by steady approximation to the style characteristic of the *Laws*, as belonging to the latest period of Plato's activity as a writer. In particular they all agree linguistically in the adoption of a number of the stylistic graces of Isocrates, particularly the artificial avoidance of *hiatus*, a thing quite new in the prose of Plato. They also agree, as regards their form, in two important respects. All of them are formal expositions of doctrine by a leading character speaking with authority ; the part of the other speakers is merely to assent, and there is no longer any thoroughly dramatic eliciting of truth from the clash of mind with mind ; in every case, except that of the *Philebus* where there is a good reason for the exception, Socrates is allowed to fall into the background, and in the *Laws* he is absent. To account for so marked a change in manner even from the *Theaetetus* and *Parmenides*, it seems necessary to suppose a reasonably long interval of interruption in Plato's literary activity, and if, as we have seen reason to think, the *Theaetetus* was composed just before Plato's visit to Syracuse in the year 367, we can account for the interruption by the known facts of his life. From 367 down to at least 361–360, the year of Plato's second and longer sojourn with Dionysius II and his final resolution to take no further direct part in the affairs of Syracuse, he must have been too fully occupied in other ways to have much time for composition. We must probably, therefore, think of this whole group of latest dialogues as written in the thirteen last years of Plato's life, 360–348/7. Since the *Sophistes* and *Politicus* attach themselves outwardly to the *Theaetetus*, and the former, in fact, contains the critical examination of Eleatic principles which that dialogue had half promised, it is reasonable to hold, as most recent critics do, that the *Sophistes* opens the series. The curious state of the text of the *Laws*—it is not permissible to account for it by the arbitrary assumption that our MSS. are less trustworthy for the *Laws* than for other works—seems to show that the work had never received the author's final revision. Thus Plato's activity as a writer has no assignable *terminus ad quem* earlier than his death. Beyond this, we have no special evidence by which to date the composition of the individual dialogues. The main thing which is clear about the whole group is that Plato felt that the logical, cosmological, and juristic matter with which they deal could not be handled by Socrates without a gross violation of historical truth ; hence the selection of other characters to play the principal part, except in the *Philebus*, which deals with the same ethical problems we have already met in the *Gorgias* and *Republic* as the " speciality " of Socrates.[1]

In a biography of Plato it would be necessary to dwell at some length on the precise character of his experiences at Syracuse, as illustrated by his extant correspondence with Dionysius and Dion. I must be content to refer the reader for all details to the excellent accounts of Grote [2] and E. Meyer,[3] and the shorter narrative of Professor Burnet.[4] The chief points which have to be borne in mind are these. Plato's interposition in Syracusan affairs had from the first a very practical object. The immediate political necessity was to secure the future of Greek civilization in Sicily and the West against the double peril that the work of Dionysius I might be undone by the aggressions of Carthage, or that, under a successor unequal to the position, the Oscans or Samnites whom that vigorous ruler had employed might usurp the sovereignty of Syracuse for themselves. The project of Dion and Plato was clearly that Dionysius II should first be educated into statesmanship himself, and should then use his position to convert the real though informal " tyranny " at Syracuse into a constitutional monarchy embracing the cities which Dionysius I had subdued, and strong enough to hold both the Carthaginians and the Italians at bay. The hope of making a scientific statesman out of Dionysius II appears not to have survived Plato's experiences of 367/6, and, indeed, had always, according to *Epistle* vii., been a very remote hope ; the more modest anticipation that the personal feud between Dionysius and Dion might be accommodated and that constitutional monarchy might at least get its chance, though an imperfect chance, took Plato back once more to Syracuse in 361. It even outlasted his final disillusionment about Dionysius, as we see from the fact that most of the correspondence with that monarch belongs to the time after Plato's last departure from Syracuse. For the years between 367/6 and 361/360 we have only one contemporary document (*Epistle* xiii.). The suspicions which have been felt about the letter have been based entirely on its contents ; linguistically it is above suspicion. One or two of the objections commonly raised are curiously captious. It is said, absurdly enough, that the reference to Plato's mother as still living, and to the existence of four

[1] The *Sophistes* and *Politicus* would have to be dated earlier if E. Meyer and others were justified in identifying them with the διαιρέσεις spoken of in *Ep.* xiii. as sent with that letter to Dionysius (*i.e.* in 366 or at latest 365). But the way in which these διαιρέσεις are mentioned (*op. cit.* 360b) should show that the reference is not to works of Plato, but to *specimens* or *samples* of " divisions " (πέμπω σοι τῶν διαρεσέων—partitive genitive).

[2] *History of Greece*, chapters lxxxiv.–lxxxv.

[3] *Geschichte des Altertums*, v. 497–528.

[4] *Greek Philosophy, Part I.*, 294–301.

great-nieces whom he, as their most well-to-do kinsman, may be legally required to portion, are ludicrous. Yet it is a fact that old ladies do sometimes live to be centenarians, especially when they belong to families of marked longevity, and that elderly men sometimes have a number of young nieces. Plato has even been thought incapable of estimating the expense of his mother's anticipated death and funeral at ten minae, on the ground that in the *Laws* he limits such expenses to one mina ; as though Plato and his mother were living in the Cretan colony for which the *Laws* professes to legislate.

Read without misconceptions of this kind, the document is a natural one enough, and highly creditable to the writer. Apart from references to certain small commissions undertaken by Plato at the request of Dionysius, and from an introduction to him of Helicon, who had studied under Eudoxus and Polyxenus as well as in the school of Isocrates, as a man who could be serviceable to him in his studies,[1] the writer is chiefly concerned with a friendly settling of accounts, such as was inevitable in the situation. Plato must have been put to considerable expense and inconvenience in removing himself for months to Syracuse ; he is anxious to be as little beholden to Dionysius in return as possible, but thinks it reasonable that he should receive what assistance he may need in meeting the impending expense of burying his mother and portioning the eldest of his grand-nieces, who is on the point of marrying her uncle Speusippus.[2] Dionysius had also undertaken to defray the expenses of his voyage to Syracuse.

Apart from this settlement of accounts between the parties, the letter deals with two other matters. Dionysius had employed Plato's offices in attempting to obtain a credit on the Aeginetan banker Andromedes, who declined to make any advance, on the ground that he had found it difficult to recover advances made to Dionysius I. Application in another quarter was more successful, and Plato takes the opportunity to administer a courteous homily to the young king on the importance of prompt discharge of money obligations and attention to one's accounts. The details of the transaction in question are only hinted at, but it can hardly have been concerned simply with the personal settlement between Dionysius and Plato. More probably Dionysius wanted a credit for his own purposes, and found it difficult to obtain one from bankers who had known his father as an unsatisfactory customer. This would explain the emphasis laid in the letter on the necessity to a monarch of a good financial reputation.

---

[1] Helicon would thus represent at once the political ideas of Isocrates, the mathematics of Eudoxus and the formal logic of Megara.

[2] The request is not, as often supposed, for portions for all the nieces. Plato asks to be helped, if necessary, to portion the eldest niece, now on the point of marrying. He mentions the portioning of the others, one of whom is an infant, simply as possible future contingencies. The dowry he thinks necessary, thirty minae, is not, as some have supposed, a large one, but, as the letter says, a " moderate " or " middle-class " portion, as will be seen by reference to contemporary speeches for the courts which deal with these matters.

There is also a cryptic reference to the relations between Dionysius and Dion, who was at the moment living in a sort of real, but not technical, banishment at Athens. The writer says that he has not actually approached Dion about a certain matter, but his judgment is that he would take the business very ill, if it were proposed ; in general, Dion's attitude to Dionysius is reasonably amicable. Probably the matter, about which Dionysius had clearly asked for a confidential opinion, may be his own desire that Dion should dissolve his marriage with Arete, aunt of Dionysius. This would be a way of showing that he had no sinister designs on the " tyranny " of Syracuse, and, in fact, when Dionysius became more suspicious, the marriage was forcibly dissolved without Dion's consent. We may fairly take it that Dionysius would have preferred a " parting by mutual consent " and had asked Plato's opinion on the matter. If so, Plato's reply amounts to a tactful disapproval of the project. There is nothing discreditable to him either in his being consulted or in the response that the suggestion of such an arrangement would gravely embitter Dion's feelings.[1]

Sophistes-Politicus

Though the main interest of the *Sophistes* is logical, that of the *Politicus* political, outwardly the two form a single whole, and both are externally linked more loosely with the *Theaetetus*. The assumption is that we are still in the spring of the year 399. The personages of the *Theaetetus* have reassembled, as had been suggested in the last words of that dialogue (210*d* 3), but Theodorus has brought a friend with him, an Eleatic pupil of Parmenides and Zeno, who is—the words imply that one would not have expected it —a really profound " philosopher." After a brief initial conversation this Eleatic visitor takes the conduct of the conversation into his own hands ; Socrates and Theodorus relapse into what is all but unbroken silence. The Eleatic remains throughout anonymous, and in this respect stands alone among the characters in Plato, but for the other example of the Athenian who plays the leading part in the *Laws*. We could hardly be told more plainly that these two personages are purely fictitious ; the object of the fiction seems to be that, as they have no historical character to sustain, they may be used freely as simple mouthpieces for the views of their creator. No one doubts that this is the case with the Athenian of the *Laws*. We are not entitled to say that he is meant precisely as a portrait of Plato by himself, but he is certainly meant to represent the ethics and politics of the Academy. Our Eleatic, too, turns out to be a respectful but exceedingly outspoken critic of the main thesis of his nominal teacher, Parmenides. The suggestion plainly

---

[1] There is no question of a private plot between Plato and Dionysius against Dion's family happiness. The dissolution of a " royal " marriage, if that is really the matter in question, is an " affair of state," and it would be quite proper in a young monarch to ask confidential advice on such a point. Plato's answer is plainly meant as a strong dissuasive.

is that, in spite of all divergences, it is Plato, and not the professed Eleatics of Megara, who is the true spiritual heir of Parmenides. One of the objects of the *Sophistes* in particular is to justify this claim.

Formally there is a further link between the *Sophistes* and the *Politicus*. The question propounded at the opening of the *Sophistes* is whether sophist, statesman, philosopher, are three different names for the same person, or three names for two types of person, or names for three different types.[1] The answer of the " Eleatic " is that the three characters are all distinct. The object of the two dialogues is ostensibly to prove this by defining first the sophist and then the statesman ; both definitions are obtained by elaborate and repeated use of the characteristically Academic method of subdivision of a genus (εἶδος) into its constituent species. The method itself has consequently to be explained and illustrated by simple and half-playful examples. Incidentally this explains what might at first seem a strange feature of the *Politicus*. We can understand the silence of Socrates in the *Sophistes*, where the logical matter of the discussion takes us far away from the circle of ideas commonly represented by Plato as familiar to him. But the problems of politics are precisely those in which the Socrates of the *Gorgias* and *Republic* had been peculiarly interested, and we might have expected that here he would be given his old part of chief speaker. What makes this impossible is not so much the particular character of the results arrived at, though they do depart to a marked degree from the uncompromising " idealism " of the *Republic*, but the necessity of employing the precisely formulated " method of division." The peculiarity of both dialogues is that each has thus a double function. Each has certain definite results to be arrived at ; each is meant, at the same time, independently of its special conclusions, to be an elaborate exercise in the careful employment of logical method. As far as " results " go, we might say that the object of the one is to explain the true character of a significant negative proposition, of the other to justify " constitutionalism " in politics. But we must not allow ourselves to forget that both have further the common purpose of presenting us with an " essay in philosophical and scientific method." Hence the chief speaker in both must be a logician ; it is because the speaker is a " formal logician," with a sounder logic than that of the Eleatics of Megara, that he is represented as the true continuator of Parmenides and

[1] Thus the question arises, Did Plato intend to devote a further dialogue to the character of the " philosopher," and if he did, must we suppose that he abandoned his design, or are we to identify the *Philosopher* with some existing dialogue ? In antiquity some persons thought of the *Epinomis* (D.L. *Vit. Plat.* 60; so, doubtfully, Raeder, *Platons philosophische Entwickelung*, 354). Moderns have thought of the *Parmenides* (Stallbaum, at one time, Zeller), *Phaedo* (Schleiermacher), *Republic* vi.–vii. (Spengel), *Symposium* (Schleiermacher). Chronological reasons, even if there were no others, make all these suggestions impossible except the first. This also seems excluded by the impossibility of regarding the *Epinomis* as anything but a part of the *Laws*.

Zeno. The true cure for the "antinomies" of the "eristic" is not to desert logic for some method more "varied and flexible," but to be *more* in earnest with it.

1. THE *SOPHISTES*.—The opening words of the dialogue show us how keenly Plato feels that the Megarian formal logic is a departure from the genuine Socratic spirit of pursuit of real truth. He is greatly relieved to learn that the Eleatic friend of Theodorus is a "truly philosophic soul"; from his antecedents he had expected rather to find in him a θεὸς ἐλεγκτικός, a "fiend" in constructing dilemmas, (like those of the *Parmenides*). But the true philosopher is not always easy to recognize; he is taken sometimes for a sophist, sometimes for a statesman, and sometimes for a downright madman. Now this raises the question whether the philosopher, the sophist, the statesman, are three distinct characters, or two, or possibly are all the same. The genuine Eleatic tradition is that they are three distinct types, though it is hard to define the precise differences between them (217b). The Eleatic undertakes, if Theaetetus will act as respondent, to attempt a precise delineation of one of the three types, the sophist, though he warns his audience that the discussion will be long and tedious, a distinct hint that the name "sophist" will be found to stand for something less readily recognizable than the familiar type of the fifth-century teacher of "goodness." We discover, as the dialogue proceeds, that the persons meant are, in fact, the Megarian pedants of an uncritical formal logic. They are "sophists," not genuine philosophers, precisely because they have never subjected the principles on which their own logic rests to a thorough critical scrutiny. (In fact, they are "dogmatists" in Kant's sense of the word.) This special use of the word σοφιστής is a real innovation in terminology, though its adoption by Aristotle, who regarded his Megarian opponents as conscious tricksters, has given rise to the modern conception of sophistry as the deliberate abuse of logic. The length of the discussion is due to the difficulty of analysing so elusive a thing as the spirit of uncritical logical formalism.

Illustration of Method (218d–221c).—Our problem, then, is to frame a satisfactory definition, and it is to be solved by a method characteristic of Plato and the Academy, the method of accurate logical *division* of a genus into its constituent species. As this method was definitely a creation of Plato and his immediate followers, it is necessary to explain and illustrate it for the reader by applying it to a simple and familiar case; Plato chooses that of the *angler*. Of course, as Burnet has said, the example is half-playful; the very baldness of the illustration chosen is an advantage since the simplest and most obvious illustrations are the best for the purpose of setting the principle of the procedure in the clearest light. In practice the use of the method in the Academy led to results of great importance. Thus the tenth book of Euclid's *Elements*, that great repertory of demonstrated propositions about "quadratic surds," is at bottom concerned with the attempt to make a systematic classification of such expressions. The vast zoological work of Aristotle, again, belongs mainly to the years before he had finally separated himself from the Academy, and thus has to be taken in connexion with the similar, though no doubt inferior, work in the same field of Speusippus and other Academics, and their starting-point, as we can see from the remaining fragments of the book of Speusippus on *Homologies*, was the search for a satisfactory classificatory system. The *Laws* again offers us repeated examples of the importance of the same problem in the field of jurisprudence and political theory. The services rendered to science by Plato's elaboration of the method of division have to be measured by results of this kind, not by the easy examples furnished to the " general reader " in the *Sophistes* and *Politicus*.

In principle the procedure is this. If we wish to define a species *x*, we begin by taking some wider and familiar class *a* of which *x* is clearly one subdivision. We then devise a division of the whole class *a* into two mutually exclusive sub-classes *b* and *c*, distinguished by the fact that *b* possesses, while *c* lacks, some characteristic *β* which we know to be found in *x*. We call *b* the right-hand, *c* the left-hand, division of *a*. We now leave the left-hand division *c* out of consideration, and proceed to subdivide the right-hand division *b* on the same principle as before, and this process is repeated until we come to a right-hand " division " which we see on inspection to coincide with *x*. If we now assign the original wider class *a* and enumerate in order the successive characters by which each of the successive right-hand divisions has been marked off, we have a complete characterization of *x* ; *x* has been defined. The Aristotelian rule of definition by " genus and difference, or differences " is simply the condensation of this Academic method into a formula ; a still more exact reproduction of it has been given in our own times in W. E. Johnson's account of the progressive determination of a " determinable " (*Logic*, i. xi). It is, of course, presupposed that we are already adequately acquainted with the " determinable " or " genus " *a* itself, and that, at each step in its further determination, we have the " gumption " to select as the character constitutive of the new " right-hand " division one which is *relevant* to the specification of *x* and also itself admits of further " division " ; finally that we recognize the point at which the process can stop because *x* has now been sufficiently specified. The satisfaction of these conditions depends on our native acumen and our acquaintance with the subject-matter, and no rules can be given for it, precisely as no rules can be given for the discovery of a promising explanatory hypothesis. The method, like all scientific methods, will not work *in vacuo*. This is what Aristotle seems to ignore in his depreciatory remarks about the " method of divisions " (*Analyt. Prior.* A 46a 31 ff.). He complains that the method involves a *petitio principii*. From *man is an animal, an animal either is mortal or is immortal*, it does not follow that *man is mortal*, but only that *man either is mortal or is immortal*; and so with the other successive steps of the division, so that nothing is really *proved* when the division has reached its end.   As a criticism of Plato, the complaint misses its mark.   When we are told in the *Sophistes* that hunters capture their prey either by snaring or by wounding, and that the angler is a hunter who makes his capture by wounding, we are presumed to know from our acquaintance with the facts of life that a rod and line are not a snare ; there is no intention to *prove* the point by making the division.   We are as much entitled to draw on our general stock of information for guidance as we are to go to the same source for our information that the Duke of Wellington is a man when we infer his mortality from the admitted mortality of men.   Neither the syllogism nor any other formal logical device can enable us to dispense with first-hand acquaintance with facts.   Possibly some members of the Academy may have overlooked this limitation in their enthusiasm for their own method, but Aristotle seems equally to be forgetting for the moment that his own method of syllogism is subject to precisely the same conditions.

DEFINITION OF THE SOPHIST (221c–237a)

The actual " division " by which the definition of angling is obtained need not detain us long.   So far as it is anything more than a simple illustration of the method to be adopted in characterizing the sophist, its further point lies in the playful suggestion of certain unpleasing features which we shall rediscover in the sophist himself, who is also, among other things, a kind of " angler."   The division itself may be graphically represented by the following tree :

```
    Arts
         Λ
of making   of acquiring
           Λ
  of acquiring   of capture
  by consent
              Λ
     of open   of stealthy capture
     capture      = hunting
                 Λ
        of lifeless   of living
          things       things
                     Λ
           of terrestrial   of animals which
             animals         live in a fluid
                           Λ
                 of birds   of fishes
                          Λ
           fishing by nets   fishing by striking
                            Λ
                 by night   by daylight
                           Λ
                 by a stroke   by a stroke
                 from above    from below
                               = angling.
```

By a summing up of the " differences " constitutive of the successive " right-hand " divisions we get the definition that angling is an art of acquiring by stealthy capture creatures which inhabit the water, the capture being made by daylight, by a stroke delivered from below. We might, of course, have carried the division further, but our acquaintance with the facts makes this superfluous. It is a linguistic fact that we give the name *angling* to every procedure which has the characteristics enumerated and to no other.

We now proceed to apply this method several times over to the sophist. (Thus Plato is fully alive to the point that the same species may be determined by the division of different *genera*, the same term may have more than one adequate definition ; relevancy to the purpose in hand will be the principle which guides us in the selection of a *genus* to be divided. Each of the successive divisions is meant to throw some one characteristic of the sophist into strong relief.)

(*a*) We might follow the precise example we have just chosen down to the point where we divided the art of hunting living things, and then turn our attention to the left-hand division of this. For the sophist is a hunter of " civilized living beings," that is, of men. He hunts them, not like kings, pirates, and kidnappers, by violence, but by the arts of persuasion. Persuasion may be practised in public, or, as the sophist practises it, on individuals. And the persuading may be done by one who *gives* a present (the lover), or by one who *takes* a fee. And the fee may be taken for making one's self agreeable and amusing (as in the case of the κόλαξ or " parasite ") or got by promising to impart " goodness." This gives us a possible definition of the sophist as a professional of the art of hunting rich young men individually for a cash payment, on the pretence of educating them (223*b*). Thus the points brought out are the sophist's commercialism, the unreality of his " wisdom," and his suspicious family likeness to the " parasite."

(*b*) The sophist, however, has more guises than one. We might detect him again if we started by dividing the left-hand branch of the art of acquisition, namely, acquisition by exchange, and then subdivided exchange into exchange of presents and exchange of commodities (ἀλλακτική). Exchange of commodities again includes the transactions of the man who sells his own produce and those of the middleman who sells that of others. And middlemen may be engaged either in the home retail traffic (καπηλική) or in inter-state trade (ἐμπορική). One branch of such inter-state trade is traffic in mental wares (ψυχεμπορική), serious or trifling. Under this head falls inter-state traffic in sciences (μαθήματα), and one form of this traffic is the selling of scientific knowledge of " goodness." This enables us to define the sophist again as a retail exporter of the knowledge of goodness (224*d*), though we must add that he sometimes retails his merchandise in the home market, and occasionally even manufactures some of it himself. As before, stress is laid on the commercialism of this peddling of spiritual wares for a living, and a new point is introduced by the suggestion that the " ideas " which the sophist sells are usually not his own, but come to him " second-hand."

(c) Yet again, we might diverge from our original division at a different point. We spoke of an art of acquisition by open capture. We may, if we please, divide this into two branches, competition and combat. (Plato is thinking of competition for prizes in the great games, at the Dionysia, and the like.)   And combat may be physical or mental; the latter being contention, of which " discourses " (λόγοι) are the weapons.   When the " discourses " employed are question and answer, we call this sort of contention disputation, and disputation about right and wrong (περὶ δικαίων αὐτῶν καὶ ἀδίκων) carried on under regular rules of the game is what we call eristic.   When eristic is practised for gain, it is sophistry.   Thus the sophist now appears as a man who makes a paying business of contentious disputation about right and wrong (226a). He invents insincere paradoxes about morality for gain.

(d) We have not done with him even now.   Making an entirely new start, we observe that there are a host of familiar occupations which are all alike in being ways of *separating* different materials from one another.   Now some of these separate like from like, others aim at separating a better from a worse, and all these we may group together under the common rubric of purifying or refining. Purification or refining, again, may be either of the body or of the soul.   And purification of the soul itself may be of two kinds, since there are two " vices " which affect the soul: spiritual disease and spiritual deformity (αἶσχος), villainy, " wickedness " as it is commonly called, and mere ignorance (ἄγνοια).   The soul is purified from wickedness by justice, " the art of discipline " ; from ignorance by teaching (διδασκαλική).   But there are different kinds of ignorance and correspondingly different kinds of teaching. The worst form of ignorance is the self-conceit which believes itself to know what it does not know ; the teaching which purifies from this is what we mean by παιδεία, " education," " culture," and all other teaching is merely subservient to it (229d).   There are, again, two forms of παιδεία.   There is the old-fashioned method of the *père de famille* who relies for success on rebuke, mingled with exhortation ; this we may call *admonition* (νουθετητική).   But some of us are convinced by reflection that all error is involuntary, and that no one can be expected to " learn better " until he has been convinced that as yet he does not know.   They adopt the milder method of trying to convince the man who has a false conceit of his wisdom by asking questions which lead him to discover his ignorance for himself and to feel the longing for knowledge (230b–e).   We cannot well give the name sophist to those who practise this kind of teaching (which is, in fact, the familiar " obstetric " of Socrates) ; the title would perhaps be too high an honour for them.[1] There is a certain resemblance between the eristic and these dialecticians, but it is such a resemblance as that of the wolf to the high-bred dog. Still, for the sake of argument, let us waive this scruple and define the sophist once more as a professional of the art of purifying the soul from its false conceit of wisdom (231b). (Here, of course, it at last becomes clear what quarry Plato is hunting. The definitions already suggested would cover Protagoras and his rivals ; the specialization of the sophists' method to " contention by question and answer " definitely indicates that the persons meant are inferior imitators of the Socratic dialectic who abuse its resources for a purpose which Plato regards as at bottom commercial.)

(e) We have still not gone quite to the root of the matter. The sophist has exhibited the guises successively of : (1) a paid hunter of rich youths ; (2) an exporter of spiritual lore ; (3) a retailer of such lore in the home market ; (4) a small manufacturer of it ; (5) an " athlete " of controversy ; (6) a " refiner " of convictions which are hostile to knowledge (though his title to this last distinction is not uncontested). To penetrate deeper we must ask what one calling there is which can masquerade in all these guises (233a). The answer is suggested by the consideration that, as we have seen, the sophist is, among other things, an ἀντιλογικός, a pitter of discourse against discourse, a contradiction-monger. He undertakes to discover antinomies everywhere—in divinity, in nature, in morals and politics—and writes books explaining how the specialist in all these departments can be reduced to silence. Now obviously one man cannot really be an " expert " in all knowledge. The secret or miracle (θαῦμα) of sophistry lies in contriving to *appear* to be such a universal expert. A clever illusionist might delude children into the belief that he can *make* anything and everything by showing them *pictures* of all sorts of things at a sufficient distance. (If a child were young enough, it would, *e.g.*, take the men and horses in a cinema picture for real animals.) Why then should there not be an analogous art of illusion by means of discourses which imposes " imitations " of truth on the youthful mind ? May we not say that at bottom the sophist is an " imitator " and

[1] 231a 3, μὴ μεῖζον αὐτοῖς προσάπτωμεν γέρας. Ostensibly the remark is ironical. Socrates, for example, who made it a point in his defence that he had never professed to be able to " educate men," would say that he had never aspired to so fine a name as σοφιστής. But the suggestion is intended that the practitioner of the Socratic method is the " philosopher " whom it is the nominal purpose of the dialogue to distinguish from the sophist. φιλόσοφος, as we have learned from the *Symposium*, is a less assuming *designation* than σοφός (or its equivalent σοφιστής), but the character is the loftier. (Campbell's interpretation *in loc. cit.* that " the sophist seems scarce worthy of so high a dignity " seems to me to miss the irony and to be grammatically impossible.) The connexion of 231a with what follows in 231b is simply that the speaker proposes, for the time being, to disregard the scruple he has just raised and to define the sophist in terms which are really applicable only to the true dialectician. This is, as we are to see, irony. He professes for the moment to take the eristic at his own valuation. The expression ἡ γένει γενναία σοφιστική (231b 7), which has been oddly misunderstood, is meant merely to point the irony.

"illusionist " (γόης) or " wizard " (θαυματοποιός, 235b). This yields us a new " division." The sophist's " illusionism " is clearly a branch of εἰδωλοποική, the art of making images. But there are two kinds of " images." Some are " likenesses " (εἰκόνες), exact reproductions of an original in all its proportions and colouring. But in some cases, as in that of the makers of " colossal " figures, the artist has to distort the real proportions to get a result which will look right when seen from below ; [1] we may call his product a " phantasm " (a deceptive reproduction), to distinguish it from an exact likeness. The question then arises whether the sophist's product is a " likeness " or a " phantasm " of truth. If we say that it is a " phantasm," a distorted reproduction of a reality, we commit ourselves to the view that there are such things as *false* appearances, *false* discourses, *false* beliefs. We are assuming that there can be an " *unreal* something," that " what is not " can be.[2] This has always been felt to be a paradox, ever since Parmenides called attention to the difficulty, and we must therefore examine the question to the bottom (237a–b). This leads us straight up to what, though formally a digression, is materially the main topic of the dialogue.

Criticism of Eleaticism (237b–249d).—The difficulty must first be fairly stated. If we say seriously " *x* is not," it seems clear that the subject of the statement *x* cannot be anything that *is* (an ὄν), and therefore cannot be a " somewhat " (τὶ), since " somewhat " always means a " being," *an* " existent." Hence he who speaks of " what is not " seems to be speaking about " nothing." Yet can we say that he is " saying nothing " (making an " unmeaning noise," 237e) ? This is bad, but there is worse behind. If we are to talk about " non-entity " at all, we must do so either in the singular (μὴ ὄν) or in the plural (μὴ ὄντα). But mere non-entity can have no predicates, and so neither unity nor plurality can be significantly asserted of it. Hence it seems we can neither think nor speak of it at all (238c). Yet in the very act of saying that " *it* is unthinkable," by using the word " it " we are talking of non-entity as though it were *one* thing (239a). It seems then that we must say nothing whatever about " what is not," and this ruins our attempt to characterize the sophist as an artist in illusion. He would argue that an illusion is " what is not," and therefore that " maker of an illusion " is a meaningless sound. Unless the sophist really " takes us in " by producing a false belief in us, there is no illusion, and if he succeeds for a moment in producing the illusion, a false belief must be *something* real ; but, as we have just seen, that is what the sophist will not admit. He will say that

---

[1] Plato's example (235e) is that in the case of the colossal work of art, the upper parts (the head of the statue, the capital of the column, etc.) must be made larger in proportion than it really should be if it is to look duly proportioned when seen from the ground.

[2] And if you try to get over the difficulty by saying that the illusion is really something, it *is* a " real illusion," he will merely reply that " real illusion" = " real unreality " (240b).

in calling a belief "false" we are involving ourselves in the contradictions we have just exposed. If we are to defend ourselves against this attack, we shall have, with all respect, to correct the fundamental principle of the great Parmenides, to say that "what is not in a way *is*, and what is, also, in a sense is *not* (241*d*)." If the Eleatic principle " what is is, what is not is not " is maintained in all its rigour, there can be no such thing as a "likeness" or "image," and no "false beliefs."

We may say that Parmenides and all the early thinkers have dealt with the problem too light-heartedly, almost as though they were merely "telling a fairy-tale " (μῦθον, 242*c*). Some of them have said that what is is three things (?Pherecydes); another (?Archelaus),[1] that it is two, *e.g.* the hot and the cold, or the moist and the dry; Xenophanes, and our own school of Elea, that it is one. Heraclitus and Empedocles say that it is both one and many: the "austerer" Heraclitus that it is both at once, the "laxer" Empedocles that it is each by turns. Every one of them is too anxious to get on with his story to trouble himself about our ability to follow him (242*c*–243*a*). But if we look into the matter, these different statements about what is are just as puzzling as we have found the current statements about what is not. We have to ask what these thinkers really meant by *being* (243*d*). When a man says, *e.g.*, that "the hot and the cold are " and are all that there is, he says of each of them that *it is*, and thus he means by "being" something, and one something, which is different both from "being hot" and from "being cold" (243*d*–*e*) (he is making a "synthetic" judgment). So the Eleatic who says that "there is just *one* thing," can hardly mean that "one" and "being" are just two equivalent names for the same thing; if he means what he says, he cannot well admit that there are names, since no name is a name for itself (244*b*–*d*). Parmenides complicates matters still more when he talks of "what is " as a *whole*. He implies that it has parts, but how can this be if it is "just one"? If "wholeness" is a character of the one, then there are two significant terms, "one" and "whole," and not merely one; if "wholeness" is a significant term but "what is " is *not* a whole, it is *not* something, and so there *is* something wanting in "what is." If "wholeness" means nothing at all, there is the additional complication that "what.is" cannot even come to be, for "whatever has come to be in every case has come to be as a *whole*." [2] Thus we see that the theory of those who

---

[1] Or is the reference to some Pythagorean cosmology? In any case, the "opposites" are those which play the chief part in the various Ionian cosmologies.

[2] τὸ γενόμενον ἀεὶ γέγονεν ὅλον, 245*d* 4. The meaning is that a γένεσις or process of "being evolved " is, at any moment of its duration, unfinished, a process to a goal not yet reached. So long as the process is still going on, that of which it is the "evolution " is not yet there. When it is there, the process is over and complete. That process is *finished*. This is the principle used by Aristotle in *N.E.* x. to prove that a feeling of pleasure is not a γένεσις. Note the way in which this short section of the *Sophistes* assumes and recapitulates the difficulties already developed in the second part of the *Parmenides*.

draw this precise and fine line of distinction between " what is " and " what is not " involves difficulties about being quite as serious as any of those raised by the Eleatics about " what is not " (245*e*).

To complete our survey of the difficulties about being, let us consider what " the other side " [1] have to say about it. This " other side " falls into two main sections who are at loggerheads with one another, like the giants with the gods in the old tale. The " giants " insist that nothing is but what can be laid hold of and felt ; " being " and " body " are the same thing. The other party maintain that real being consists of " intelligible bodiless forms," and that the bodies which their opponents regard as the only being are " becoming," not " being." We need not say much about the thesis of the " materialists," but we may imagine them to be at any rate so far better than they actually are as to deign to answer our questions civilly. We will then ask them whether there *is* not such a thing as a soul ; whether some souls are not righteous and wise, others wicked and foolish. If they say Yes, as they must, we shall ask whether this does not imply that wisdom and the other " virtues " are something, and whether they are anything that can be seen or handled. Even if they try to save themselves by saying that the soul is a kind of body, they will hardly venture to say that wisdom is a body, nor yet to say that it is nothing at all, though a genuine and persistent materialist would have to take this second alternative. We shall have gained our point with any of them who will admit that anything whatever can be and yet not be a body. To put it most simply, we shall ask them to admit no more than this, that anything which has any " power," however slight, of acting or being acted upon, certainly is—in fact, that " what is " is δύναμις (" force "), active or passive (245*e*–247*e*).

It is not clear precisely what persons are meant by the " giants " of materialism. They are certainly not atomists, as has sometimes been fancied. The atomists who insisted on the reality of the ἀναφὴς φύσις (*vacuum*) cannot be classed among persons who say that only what can be seen and felt is. Nor could Theaetetus say, as he does (246*b*), that he has met " lots " of these men ; he would not meet many disciples of Leucippus, to say nothing of Democritus, in the Athens of 399 B.C. It seems to me most probable that Plato has in view the crass unthinking corporealism of the " average man," rather than the doctrine of any particular " school." We must also be careful not to make the mistake of taking the proposed definition of " being " as " force " for one seriously intended by Plato. It is given simply as one which the materialist could be led to concede if he were willing to reflect, and we are warned that, on further consideration, we might think better of it.

<hr />

[1] τοὺς ἄλλως λέγοντας, 245*e* 8. Since they are opposed to the διακριβολογούμενοι ὄντος τε πέρι καὶ μή, *i.e.* the Eleatics, this " other side " must be pluralists of various kinds ; the men of Megara cannot be included among them, as they were always regarded in antiquity as Eleatics of a kind, and are, of course, among the διακριβολογούμενοι περὶ ὄντος. This point is important.

The point is simply that the " materialist " who uses the notion of a " force " has already surrendered his materialism.

We have now to consider the view of the " friends of forms," the immaterialists already referred to. They hold that " becoming " and " being " are sharply contra-distinguished. Our body is in touch with " becoming " through sense-perception ; our mind in touch with real and unchanging " being " through thought (248a). We have to ask them what they mean by " being in touch with " (τὸ κοινωνεῖν). Do they mean " acting or being acted on by a force " ? Theaetetus may not be able to say, but the Eleatic speaker is familiar with the persons who are being criticized, and consequently knows that they would reject the statement. So far from accepting the identification of being with " the power to act or be acted on," they would say that both action and passion belong to the realm of " becoming " ; " being " neither acts nor is acted on.[1] But we shall then ask them whether they do not admit that " being " is known by the mind, and whether " being known " is not " being acted on " and knowing, acting. To be consistent, they will have to deny both statements. If " being " is acted on in being known, it πάσχει (" has something done to it "), and therefore is " moved," and it is not true that being is simply " quiescent " (ἠρεμοῦν, 248e).

We cannot seriously think that " what utterly is," the perfectly real, neither thinks nor lives, or that it thinks but does not live. If it thinks and is alive, it must have a soul, and if it has a soul, it cannot stand everlastingly still ; it must have movement. If mind is to be real, there must be both motion and variety and also rest and uniformity in things (248e–249d).

It has been a much-discussed question who are the thinkers to whom the dialogue ascribes the doctrine just criticized. From the statement of their theory, it is clear that they are extreme dualists, who regard " being " and " becoming " as absolutely sundered. They then identify " becoming " with the sensible world, and consequently hold that the sensible world has no real existence. To put the same thing from the epistemological standpoint, they deny that sensation has *any* cognitive value, or plays any part in the apprehension of truth. This shows that the reference cannot be to the type of theory ascribed to Socrates in the *Phaedo* and *Republic*. The whole point of the doctrine of " participation " of sensible things in forms was just to break down the absolute severance between a real world of " being " and an illusory world of " becoming," by ascribing a partial and secondary reality to the sensible. So the doctrine of " recollection " was intended to assign sensation a genuine, if a humble, part in the process of reaching truth ; sensation is, on that theory, just what " suggests " or " calls into our minds " the thought of the forms. *A fortiori*,

[1] 248c 7–9. The view suggested is that acting and being acted on, both involve process and change : hence neither can be found in the realm of eternal and changeless being.

if the criticism is not aimed at Socrates, it is not directed against Plato's " earlier self " or disciples, if there were any, who retained a doctrine which Plato had once held, but had outgrown. Nor, again, can the persons meant be Euclides and his friends at Megara. They were strict rationalistic monists who did not admit the existence of even an " illusory " world of " becoming," and regarded themselves as Eleatics, whereas the " friends of forms " are one of two groups who have both been carefully distinguished at 245e from the Eleatic monists. The one hint of their identity is given by the Eleatic visitor when he says (248b) that Theaetetus probably will not know their views, but he is acquainted with them himself διὰ συνήθειαν, because he has lived with the men in question. As the speaker is certainly an Italian Eleatic—he refers to his own personal recollections of Parmenides (237a)—we must plainly look to Italy for these rationalistic dualists. Hence Proclus is pretty likely to be right when he says that the persons meant are " wise men in Italy " whom he also calls Pythagoreans, especially, as Burnet remarks, since he makes the statement without any discussion as though it were the recognized traditional interpretation.[1] The Pythagorean formula that " things *are* numbers " would readily lend itself to development along these lines.

The Meaning of Significant Denial.—The Platonic Categories (249e–259e).—So far we have reached the result that though movement and rest are contraries, both of them certainly *are.* There *is* movement and there *is* rest, and when I say " rest *is,*" I do not mean that rest is motion, nor when I say that " motion *is,*" do I mean that motion is rest. Motion, rest, being, are all distinct, and being embraces both of the others ; though it is neither of them. It thus seems as difficult to say what " being " is the name for, as we found it to say what " what is not " is the name for. If we can answer the one question we shall probably find that we have learned how to answer the other [2] (250e–251a).

Every one knows that we are always making assertions about, *e.g.*, a man, in which we do not confine ourselves to the statement that " a man is a man," but say something further about his complexion, his shape, size, good or bad qualities, and the like, and in all these cases we are saying that a man is not one thing only, but at the same time many (not merely a man, but ruddy, tall, lanky, patient, etc.). Raw lads and men who have begun their thinking too late in life [3] fasten eagerly on such " synthetic " propositions,

[1] Proclus in *Parmen.*, p. 562 Stallbaum (Cousin, iv. 149) ; *Greek Philosophy, Part I.*, 91 n. 1, 280.

[2] This means, to use language more familiar to ourselves, that if we can solve the question, What is implied by an affirmative " synthetic " proposition ? the answer will also solve the problem about significant denial. The upshot of the whole discussion is to be a general theory of the conditions of significant non-identical assertion.

[3] I can see no allusion to Antisthenes in the use of the adjective ὀψιμαθής (251b 6). There is no reason why he should be dragged into the discussion, and, as he had been a pupil of Gorgias (D. L. vi. 1), the epithet ὀψιμαθής is really not quite applicable to him.

and declare them to be absurd, on the ground that they all imply that one can be many and many one. They plume themselves on the discovery that only identical propositions can be true. This is the thesis we have really to combat (251c–d).

If we consider the three concepts being, rest, motion, there are just three logical possibilities : (a) that they all " partake in " one another, i.e. any one can be predicated of any other ; (b) that none of them can be conjoined with any other, i.e. none can be predicated of another ; (c) that some of them can be predicated of (" partake in ") others. We can reject (b) at once, since it would forbid us to say both that there is motion and that there is rest. This would make an end of the views alike of Heracliteans, Eleatics, " friends of forms," as well as of all the physicists who account for things as due to the aggregation and disgregation of " elements," whether infinite in number (Anaxagoras) or finite (Empedocles). The theory is actually self-refuting, since you cannot state it without using such words and phrases as " is," " apart from everything else," " by itself," and the like (252c). You cannot even deny the possibility of " synthetic judgments " except by making such a judgment. The proposition " only identical propositions are true " is not itself an identity ; (a) is an even more absurd theory, since it would require us to affirm that rest is motion and motion rest (252d). Thus the only possible alternative is (c) that some " concepts " will " combine " and others will not (252e), just as some letters can be combined to form syllables, others cannot.

This illustration suggests a further point of supreme importance. Vowels hold a " favoured position " among the elementary sounds of language. Every syllable must contain a vowel, and the vowels are thus the " connecting links " which make syllabic composition possible. There is a special art (τέχνη), that of the " teacher of letters," which considers what combinations of consonants by the help of a vowel are possible and what are not, just as another art, music, considers what combinations of notes of different pitch will make a tune and what will not.[1] So there clearly must be a science which considers what " concepts " will " blend " so as to give rise to " discourses " (λόγοι) and what will not, and again whether there is a class of concepts which, like the vowels in spelling, make all combinations possible, and another class which gives rise to distinctions (253c). Thus logic is here, for the first time in literature, contemplated as an autonomous science with the task of ascertaining the supreme principles of affirmative and negative propositions (the combinations and " separations "). But this task of dividing things rightly according to their " kinds," detecting one " form " (ἰδέα) where it is disguised by complication with others, and distinguishing several which form a single complex, is precisely that of " dialectic." Thus we have unexpectedly identified the true philosopher before

---

[1] The reference is, of course, to permissible and unpermitted melodic intervals, not to the construction of " chords." Thus the parallel between γραμματική and μουσική is kept exact.

we have come to an end with our identification of the sophist. The philosopher is the dialectician who knows how to find the many in the one and the one in the many (253a–e). We had already been told much the same thing by Socrates in the *Phaedrus*, but there is an important point in which the problem now under discussion marks a great advance on the theories ascribed to Socrates in the earlier dialogues. In them, the combinations or complications considered seem always to be the " things " of the everyday world of sense. The sensible " thing " had been treated in the *Phaedo* and *Republic* as a sort of complex " partaking " at once in a plurality of forms—in fact, as a bundle of " universals." Each form had been spoken of as something independent of every other, and the only " combination " of several forms contemplated had been their simultaneous " presence " in the same αἰσθητόν. Or, to put the same thing from the opposite point of view, the question had never been raised, what constitutes the *particularity* of the particular thing. Plato is now raising a different issue. We are to see that forms *as such* can " combine," so that you can predicate one " universal " of another, and it is the special function of the new science Plato is contemplating to specify the lines on which such combination is possible. The doctrine of forms as known to us from the " Socratic " dialogues throws no light on this problem, and this, no doubt, is why it is never referred to in our dialogue. It is not that it is disavowed, or even called in question, but that it is simply not relevant to the issues which Plato now finds himself called on to face. We might, perhaps, say that the language of the *Phaedrus* about the dialectician's task of seeing the one in the many and the many in the one, if followed up, raises precisely the same question. But the *Phaedrus* is, to all appearance, one of the very latest " Socratic " dialogues, and Plato is probably there on the verge of straining the limits of historical accuracy.

We cannot now work out the whole inquiry into the " communion " between forms, but we may deal with it for the special case of a few of the most important and all-pervading. As we have said, " being," " motion," " rest," are three of these *universalissima* or μέγιστα γένη. Two of them—rest and motion—refuse to combine. But the third will combine with both of the two, since both motion and rest *are*. Moreover, each of the three is distinct or different (ἕτερον) from the other two, but identical with itself. And difference and identity, again, are neither motion nor rest. Nor is either of them the same as " being." We ascribe being alike to motion and to rest, but this is not to assert that motion is identical with rest. For " different from " is always a relative term, whereas *being* has an absolute sense.[1] Thus we have five, not merely

---

[1] 255*d* 3–7. The meaning is, that I cannot intelligibly say " *x* is different " without specifying some *y* from which *x* differs. But I can intelligibly say not only that " *x* is a *z*," but that " *x* is," " there is an *x*." To this absolute sense of " is " there is no corresponding sense of " is different." See Campbell's note, *loc. cit.*

three, Forms (εἴδη, γένη, both words are used interchangeably) to consider — being, motion, rest, identity, difference. *Difference* manifestly pervades all the others, for each of them is different from the rest, and so "partakes of the form of different" (254*b*–255*e*). Let us now consider the relations between these five all-pervading forms. (It is never said that the list of the *universalia universalissima* is complete, though later Platonists, like Plotinus in *Ennead* vi. 1–3, treat them as a complete list of Platonic "highest universals," or categories.) Motion is not rest, nor rest motion. But both *are* and are identical with themselves, and thus "partake" (μετέχει) of being and identity, and also, since each is different from the other, of difference. Thus we can say, *e.g.*, that motion is— it is *motion*; but also is *not*—it is *not* rest. But in just the same way we can say that motion "partakes of" being and so *is*— there is such a thing as motion; but motion is not identical with being, and in that sense we may say that it is *not, i.e.* it is not-being. The same line of thought shows that "not-being" may be asserted of all the five forms already enumerated, even of being itself, since each of them is different from any of the others, and thus is *not* any of the others (255*e*–257*a*).

Now these considerations enable us to dismiss the difficulties which have been raised about "not-being." When we say that something "is not so-and-so," by the not-being here asserted we do not mean the "opposite" (ἐναντίον) of what is but only something different from what is. "*A* is not *x*" does not mean that *A* is nothing at all, but only that it is something other than anything which is *x* (257*b*–*c*). Not-beautiful, for example, is the name not of nothing but of all the things other than the things which are beautiful. And the things which are not-beautiful *are* just as truly as those which are beautiful. The "not-large" *is*, every whit as much as the "large," the "not-right" as much as the "right." In making a denial we are not asserting an antithesis between nothing and something, but an opposition of something and something else different from it (258*b*). We may say, then, that "not-being" is as real and has as definite a character as being. This is our answer to Parmenides. We have not merely succeeded in doing what he forbade, asserting significantly that "what is not, is "; we have actually discovered *what* it is. It is "the different" (τὸ θάτερον), and since everything is different from all other things, we may say boldly that "not-being" is thoroughly real (ὄντως ὄν, 257*b*–258*e*). Henceforth we shall not give ourselves any further concern about the alleged paradox that "what is not" is that unthinkable thing "the absurd," the "opposite" of what is. It is childishly easy to see that any thing is different from other things and so may be said to be "what is not "; the true difficulty is to determine the precise limits of the identity and difference to be found among things (259*d*).

Application of our Result to the Problem of "False Opinion" : *Final Definition of the Sophist* (260*a*–268*c*).—Our identification of

" not-being " with difference shows that " not-being " itself is a pervasive and categorial feature in things. We have now to consider whether this pervasive characteristic can " combine " with discourse and belief (δόξα). If it cannot, if we cannot say or think " what is not," falsehood of speech or thought will not be possible, and consequently there will be no such thing as error or illusory belief, and no " resemblances," " likenesses," or " phantasms," all of which *seem* to be what they are not. The sophist's last retreat will be to the position that at any rate discourse and belief will not " blend " with " what is not " : there is no such " complex " as utterance of or belief in what is not, and therefore no such art as the fabrication of " phantasms." This is the position from which we have now to dislodge him (261*a*). Let us begin by an analysis of discourse. Just as not all combinations of letters yield a syllable, not all complexes of forms a concept, so not all combinations of words yield a significant discourse. The words of a language fall in the main into two great classes : nouns (ὀνόματα) and verbs (ῥήματα). The verbs are vocal symbols of actions (πράξεις), the nouns are the names of the agents in these actions. A string of verbs, *e.g.* " walks, runs, sleeps," is not a λόγος or significant statement, neither is a string of nouns, *e.g.* " lion, deer, horse." The simplest discourse, the unit in discourse, is the complex of a noun and a verb, *e.g.* " a man learns." Here not only is something *named*, but something is signified (262*d*). Further, a discourse or statement must be " of " or " about " something and it must have a certain " quality," must be ποιός τις. Thus, take the two statements, " Theaetetus is sitting down," " Theaetetus, to whom I am now speaking, is flying." The " quality " of the first statement is that it is *true*, of the second that it is *false*, for Theaetetus is not at this moment flying but sitting [1] (263*b*). And both the statements are *about* Theaetetus, the false statement no less than the true. A statement which was not about (or " of ") some subject would not be a statement at all (263*c*). Thus some complexes of nouns and verbs are false. Now thinking is an internal conversation in which the mind asks itself a question ; belief or judgment (δόξα) is the statement, affirmative or negative, in which the mind answers its own question, without audible words. Sometimes the internal conversation is accompanied by sensation, and then we call it " fantasy " (*i.e.* when the debate of the mind is started by the attempt to interpret a present sensation). Hence, from the possibility of false statement or discourse follows the equal possibility of false belief or judgment and false " phantasy " (erroneous interpretation of sensation,

---

[1] I cannot agree here with Burnet (*Greek Philosophy, Part I.*, 287 n.) that what is meant by the *quality* of propositions is *tense*. It is clear from 263*b* 2–3 that the speaker means " truth-value," as has usually been supposed. His point is that the two statements about Theaetetus have *opposed* " quality " ; but both of them have the *same* tense. For a similar reference to " true " and " false" as the " qualities " of propositions, which Burnet has overlooked, see *Philebus*, 37*b* 10–*c*2.

264a–b). A false belief that Theaetetus is now flying is not a belief about nothing at all but a belief about Theaetetus which asserts of him that he is performing a definite πρᾶξις different from that which he is in fact performing. This disposes of the old objection to our assumption that there are " images " and " phantasms," and so we may go back to our attempt to define sophistry as a branch of the art of making images (264c). We now proceed to divide the making of images more carefully.

We said that we could divide it into the making of accurate likenesses (εἰκόνες) and the making of inaccurate images (φαντάσματα), both of which are forms of " imitation." Let us reconsider this more in detail. The making of imitations is a branch of creative art, as distinguished from the arts of acquisition, as we said long ago. We may now divide creative art into divine creative art and human creative art. The difference is that God (not, as the thoughtless say, unintelligent " nature ") creates all real things without any pre-existing material (πρότερον οὐκ ὄντα, 265c) [1]; man's " creating " only originates fresh combinations of materials thus created by God. Next we may take a new principle of division, and subdivide both divine and human creation into creation of actualities and creation of images.[2] The images created by God are such things as dreams, shadows thrown by a light, reflections in a polished surface ; those created by man are pictures of things made by man (houses, etc.), and the like. Here we bring in again our former and now justified subdivision of images. Man-made " images " are either accurate *likenesses* or phantasms. Phantasms again are of two kinds : those produced by tools of some kind (like the painter's brush), and those for which the producer acts as his own tool, as when another man (*e.g.* an actor) imitates the physical bearing or the tone of voice of Theaetetus by his own facial gestures and his own voice, and this kind of imitation is what we call *mimicry* (μίμησις). Mimicry, again, is twofold. A man may know what he is mimicking or he may not know it. Many persons who have no knowledge of the true figure (σχῆμα) of justice or goodness generally try to make their speech and action exhibit the appearance of what they fancy to be goodness and justice, and some of them succeed in conveying the impression they are aiming at. This is a plain case of mimicry by a man who does not know (267d). There is no recognized name for this specific " mimicry by the man who does not know," so we coin one for the moment and call it δοξομιμητική

---

[1] The language, perhaps, must not be unduly pressed, but it proves at least that the idea of " creation *ex nihilo* " was quite intelligible to Plato.

[2] The language of 266a 1 about the division in πλάτος presupposes this diagram :

Divine creation of actualities.	Human creation of actualities.
Divine creation of images.	Human creation of images.

("counterfeiting"). But there are also two varieties of the art of counterfeiting. The maker of the sham may honestly believe that he knows the reality which, in fact, he does not know. Or he may have an uneasy suspicion all the time that he does not really know what he poses as knowing (268a). In the second case he is an " ironical imitator," a conscious " humbug," as well as a mere counterfeiter—in fact, an impostor. The professional sophist has had too much practice in " discourse " to be a mere honest pretender ; he must have his suspicions of the unsoundness of his own " discourse," and thus his " art " falls under the head of conscious counterfeiting—imposture or charlatanism. Only one further distinction remains. The charlatan may practise his imposture in lengthy discourses before a public audience, or he may employ brief discourses with an individual in which he tries to make his interlocutor contradict himself. The one type of impostor is the δημολογικός, the dishonest " spell-binder " passing himself off for a statesman ; the other is the sophist who counterfeits the " wise man," more than half knowing himself to be a fraud (268c).

One closing remark may be made on the main result of the whole dialogue. Plato's solution of the old puzzle about " what is not " and the later paradox, grafted on it, of the impossibility of error, turns, as we see, on distinguishing what we should call the use of " is " as the logical *copula*, or sign of assertion, from the existential sense of " is." To us the distinction may seem almost trivial, but it only seems so because the work of making it has been done so thoroughly, once for all, in the *Sophistes*. Though Plato lets us see that he thought the ordinary Megarian a good deal of a conscious impostor, the difficulty about the possibility of error and of significant denial was a perfectly serious one with its originators and remained so until the ambiguity had been thoroughly cleared up. It is impossible to overestimate the service to both logic and metaphysics rendered by Plato's painstaking and searching examination. We shall realize the magnitude of the issue better if we are careful to remember that, as Plato himself knew, the problem is at bottom one which affects *all* assertion. His point is that *all* significant propositions are " synthetic," in the sense that they are more than assertions of the equivalence of two sets of verbal symbols, and that they are all " functions " of an " argument " which is " not null." This would be a mere paradox if there were no other sense of " is " than the existential. We can see that a completed logic would have to carry the work of distinction further than it is carried in the dialogue. Notably the " is " which asserts the identity of the object denoted by two different descriptions (*e.g.* " the victor at Pharsalia is the consul of the year 59 B.C.") needs to be distinguished both from the " copula " and the existential " is." But the first step and the hardest to take is the recognition of the " copula " and its functions for what they are. Since the *Sophistes* takes this step for the first time, it is not too much to say that it definitely originates scientific logic.

2. THE *POLITICUS*.—We must deal much more briefly with the application of the method of division to the definition of the statesman. We may be content, now that we have grasped the principle of the method, to concentrate our attention in the main on the solid result it is used to establish. Plato's real purpose in the dialogue is much less merely to continue his lesson in logical method than to deal with a fundamental problem in the theory of government on which men's minds even now continue to be divided. The issue is whether, as the actual world goes, " personal rule " or impersonal " constitutionalism " is the better for mankind, and Plato means to decide definitely for constitutionalism and, in particular, to commend " limited monarchy." His reading of the facts of the political situation is that monarchy has to be revived, as it was in fact revived by Philip, Alexander, and their successors, but that whether it is to be a great blessing or a great curse will depend on the question whether it is revived as constitutional monarchy or as irresponsible autocracy. Democracy, with all the defects it has shown at Athens, is the most tolerable form of government where there is no fixed " law of the constitution," autocracy the most intolerable ; where there is such a fixed law, a monarch is a better head of the executive and administrative than either a select " oligarchy " or a " town's meeting."

In form, the dialogue is a continuation of the *Sophistes*, with one change in *personnel*. Theaetetus is present as a silent character, but, to save him from undue fatigue, his place as respondent is taken by his companion, a lad named Socrates, who has been present without speaking through the *Theaetetus* and *Sophistes*. (The great Socrates, as in the *Sophistes*, is completely silent but for one or two opening remarks.) The " younger " Socrates has been introduced by one phrase in the *Theaetetus* (147*d* 1) as studying mathematics in company with Theodorus and Theaetetus. He is known to have been an original member of the Academy. There is one further reference to him in a letter belonging to the later years of Plato's life, usually condemned by the editors as spurious, though for no obvious reasons (*Ep.* x. 358*e*). We learn there only that he is in poor health at the time of writing. Aristotle mentions him once (*Met. B* 1036*b* 25) in a way which shows that he belonged to the Academic group reproached elsewhere by Aristotle for their " pam-mathematicism." [1] I think it all but certain that it is he, not the

---

[1] The statement of Aristotle is that " the younger Socrates " used to regard the " material " constituent in the human organism as falling completely outside the definition of man, exactly as the bronze of which a disc is made falls outside the definition of circle. Aristotle's own view is that there is a difference in this respect between a " physical " and a mathematical definition. It is indispensable to mention in the " physical" definition the fact that the material constituents in which the formula is embodied are such-and-such. (Just as it would be no adequate definition of water to say that it is " two units of something with one of another " : you must specify that the two units are units of *hydrogen*, and the one a unit of *oxygen*.)

great philosopher, to whom Aristotle's practice has given a spurious immortality as a " logical example." [1]

The dialogue begins (257a–267c) with an attempt to characterize the science or art (τέχνη, ἐπιστήμη) of the king or statesman (πολιτική, βασιλική) by assigning it a place in the classification of the sciences. Some " sciences " merely provide us with knowledge, others, including all the industrial arts, produce results embodied in material objects (σώματα). So we begin by dividing sciences into the practical (πρακτικαί) and the purely cognitive (γνωστικαί). The science of the statesman involves little or nothing in the way of manual activity ; it consists wholly or mainly in mental insight. Thus we class it as *cognitive* (259c). But there are two kinds of cognitive sciences. Some of them are concerned merely with apprehending truths, and may be called *critical* (arithmetic is an example) ; others issue directions or orders for the right performance of actions, and may be called *directive* (ἐπιτακτικαί), and the science of the statesman is of this kind (260c). Again, some of the arts which direct merely pass on instructions which do not originate with the practitioner (as a " herald " communicates the directions of his commander), others give *sovereign* directions, are sovereignly directive (αὐτεπιτακτικαί, 260e). Among these we may distinguish those which have the sovereign direction of the production of living beings from those which are concerned with the production of lifeless things (like the science of the master-builder). This puts the king, or statesman, in the class of persons exercising sovereign control over the production and nurture (τροφή) of animals. Next, there is a distinction between the groom, who exercises this calling on a single animal, and the herdsman who practises it upon a whole herd or flock ; the statesman, like the latter, has a flock or herd to deal with (261d.).

We are thus on the point of identifying the ruler with the shepherd of a human flock (a metaphor as familiar to the Greeks from their recollections of Homer as it is to us from the language of Old Testament prophecy). But it would be a violation of the rules of method to divide " herds " at once into herds of men and herds of other animals. We must observe the rule that a division must proceed in regular order from the highest to the lowest classes, not make sudden leaps. It is unscientific to single out mankind as one class and to throw all the rest of the animal world, irrespective of all differences of structure, into the one ill-constituted group " other animals," just as it would be unscientific to divide mankind into Greeks and " barbarians " (262d) or integers into " the number 10,000 " and " all other numbers." A reflective crane might be

---

[1] This seems to be proved by the illustration of *Topics* 160b 28 ff., where it is supposed that " if Socrates is sitting, he is writing." Obviously the allusion is to a scene in the lecture-room ; Socrates is one of the audience and it is wrongly inferred that he must be taking notes of the lecture. So the common examples, " S. is λευκός (pale)," " is μουσικός," are not naturally understood of the famous Socrates. He is not likely to have been " pallid " ; it is impossible to see an allusion to the *Phaedo* in his " sitting " and his " music."

supposed just as reasonably to divide animals into " cranes " and " brutes " (263*d*). We must take care to avoid constituting *infimae species* so long as our division permits of being continued. Animals may be divided into the " wild " and the " domesticated " (τιθασόν, 264*a*), domesticated animals into the aquatic and the terrestrial (the tame fishes of Egypt belong to the one class; our familiar domestic quadrupeds, domesticated geese, and the like to the other). The terrestrial, again, are either birds which fly or beasts which walk. From this point we may proceed by either of two alternative routes, a longer or a shorter, to the same result. The longer route is to divide " gregarious domesticated beasts " into the horned and the hornless, the hornless once more into those which can be " crossed " and those which cannot, and the last group into quadruped and biped (266*b*) (or, alternatively, we might have divided the hornless class into those with undivided and those with divided hoof). A division like this has a comic side to it ; it ranks that most dignified of beings, a king, much on a level with a swine-herd. But science has no concern with our conventions about dignity, and is anxious only to get at the true facts (266*d*). The shorter procedure would be to divide " gregarious domestic animals " into quadrupeds and bipeds. Since observation teaches us that man is the only wingless biped, we might then divide the bipeds into winged and wingless, with the same result as before (266*e*).

The effect of our division then is to define the statesman as a kind of herdsman of gregarious animals, with a trade of the same kind as the cow-keeper or the pig-drover, except that his herd consists of unusually " kittle " beasts. But there is a difficulty of which such a definition takes no account. In the case of the statesman there are a goodly number of rivals who might challenge this description. Farmers, corn-dealers, physicians, professors of " gymnastic," might all urge that the definition " raiser of the human herd " applies to themselves as much as to the ruler. This difficulty does not arise in the other analogous cases of the shepherd, ox-herd, swine-herd, because every one of them is at once breeder, feeder, and physician of his herd. As this is not the case with the ruler of men, there must be something faulty about the classification we have followed ; our business is next to see where the error has come in. We may get a hint from a tale we all heard as children, the story that the sun reversed his daily path in horror when Thyestes started the series of crimes which disgraced the line of Pelops by stealing the " golden lamb " (268*e*).

The imaginative myth which now follows (268*e*–274*e*) is built up on the basis of ideas of which we may find traces in the early cosmogonists, combined with fancies known to have been specially affected by the Pythagoreans. From the cosmogonists we have the notion of a past " golden age " before Zeus had dethroned Cronus ; many of the details about this age of gold seem to be " Hesiodic." The conception of the life of the universe as an alternation of half-cycles with opposite senses is most familiar to us from the fragments of Empedocles ; the thought of the world as a ship sailing over the stormy waters of the ἄπειρον is specifically Pythagorean,[1] though, no doubt, both Empedocles and the Pythagoreans were availing themselves of the suggestions of pre-scientific cosmologists. Thus dramatic propriety is observed by making the Eleatic visitor utilize for his story precisely the materials which would be specially familiar to a native of Magna Graecia. The tale is told simply to make an immediate point. It is wrong on principle to take any part of it as scientific cosmology meant seriously by Plato, and to attempt, like Adam, the impossible task of fitting the story into that of the *Timaeus*. In outline the story runs as follows. The tale of the sun's return on his track, like much of the existing mythology, is a fragment of a very ancient tradition about the transition from the age of Cronus to the age of Zeus. The whole may be reconstructed thus. Only God has complete immortality. The universe as a whole, being corporeal, cannot be quite immutable, but makes the nearest approximation it can to immutability by alternately revolving round the same axis in opposite senses. There are periods when God himself is at the helm of the world-ship with his hand on the rudder, and there are alternate periods when he " retires " to his look-out (περιωπή, 272e) and leaves the ship to follow its own course. The immediate result is a complete reversal of sense of all biological as well as cosmological processes. Life runs backward, in " looking-glass " fashion. The reversal of sense is attended by gigantic cosmic catastrophes, but when the first confusion is over, the ship settles down once more to a uniform course, though with a reversed sense ; at first the regularity of its processes is almost as complete as when God was steering. But as time goes on, the world " forgets God its Maker," and the irregularities due to the " lusts " inherent in its bodily frame accumulate ; all regularity is on the point of vanishing, the ship nearly founders in the " sea " of the " infinite," when God puts his hand to the tiller again, and once more reverses the sense of the cosmic movements.

The stories of the golden age, when men lived peacefully, without agriculture, clothes, or laws, are reminiscences of the condition of the world " under Cronus," when God was actually steering the ship, and acting literally as the " shepherd " of mankind, with departmental gods under him as " deputy shepherds." Our own age, that of Zeus, belongs to the period when the world is left to itself,

---

[1] For the "world-ship " see *E.G.Ph.*[3] 294, with notes *in loc. cit.* On the whole " myth " cf. Stewart, *The Myths of Plato*, 173–211 ; Adam, *Republic of Plato*, ii. 295 ff. As to the " sea," see *Politicus*, 273e 1, where the true reading is not τόπον, as given by MSS. and editors, but πόντον. This is not a conjecture of Stallbaum, but the best authenticated text, as it is the only reading recognized by Proclus, who frequently refers to the passage. The variant τόπον is senseless, but may be ancient, since it appears at Plotinus, *Enn.* i. 8, 13, ἐν τῷ τῆς ἀνομοιότητος τόπῳ—a passage where the metaphor of the ship is missing. Unless, indeed, Plotinus also wrote πόντῳ, as is just possible.

and is separated from the " golden age " by the catastrophic reversal of all motions. At this reversal the gods withdrew from their immediate direction of the human flock. Mankind were left naked, needy, uncontrolled ; all *our* arts of industry and government have been slowly acquired in the gradual conquest of nature. (The " noble savage " is thus not a figure in *our* history ; he belongs to a world where men are born as full-grown out of the earth and " live backwards.") [1]

Were the men of the golden age really happier than ourselves who belong to the " iron time " ? It depends on the use they made of their immunity from the struggle with nature for physical existence. If they used their freedom from the cares of life to glean wisdom from the beasts and one another, no doubt they were happier. If they used it merely to fill themselves with meat and drink, and to tell idle stories to the beasts and one another, we know what to think about that kind of life (272c).

The moral of the story is that our attempt to define the statesman as the " shepherd of men " has involved two errors—one serious, the other comparatively light. The serious error is that we have confused the work of a statesman in our historical world with that of one of the gods of the "age of Cronus." They actually " fed " their flock ; the statesman of the historical world does not. The minor fault was that we said truly that the statesman is a *ruler*, but made no attempt to specify the kind of " rule " he exercises. We ought to have reserved the work of " feeding and breeding " the flock for a god ; of the statesman, who is a man among men, we should have said more modestly that his business is the " tendance " (ἐπιμέλεια, θεραπεία) of the flock (275b–276b). (The object of the remark is to eliminate the " superman " from serious political theory, and so to strike at the root of the worship of the " man who can," the autocrat or dictator paternally managing the rest of mankind without the need of direction or control by law.) If we had made this clear, we should not have found the provision-dealers and others claiming that our description was as applicable to them as to the statesman. As to the other fault, it arises from overlooking an important step in our division. We forgot that the " feeding," or, as we now propose to say, the " tendance," may be either forced on the flock (βίαιον) or freely accepted by them (ἑκούσιον). This is what makes all the difference between the true " king " and the " tyrant " or " usurper." The " tyrant "

---

[1] The humorous zest of the description of life in the days when it began with old age and ended with babyhood ought of itself to prevent us from taking the story seriously. The cosmological story of Timaeus is given, not indeed as science, but as a " *likely* story," and Plato is careful, for that reason, to allow no such extravagances in it. We may reasonably infer that Plato regards the whole conception of the happiness of the alleged " state of nature " as a mere unhistorical fancy. In the real world to which we belong, man has painfully fought his way up out of hunger, nakedness, and savagery. The " state of nature " dreamed of by sentimentalists belongs to the unhistorical world where animals talk. Adam (*loc. cit.*) is an example of the danger of reading Plato without a sense of humour.

forces his tendance on his subjects ; the "king" is the freely accepted ruler of freemen, a " free tender of free bipeds " (276e).

Yet we must not be too much in a hurry to accept this as an adequate account of statesmanship. We have, it may be, drawn the outline of our portrait of the statesman correctly, but we still have to get the colouring of the picture right (277a–c). To explain what we mean by this, we shall do well to illustrate our point by a familiar example. And before we do this, we may even illustrate the use of examples by a preliminary example. This preliminary example shall be taken from the way in which small children are taught their letters. At first they may be given a set of very simple syllables which they soon read off exactly. But they still make mistakes in recognizing these very same combinations when they meet with them elsewhere. We correct their mistakes by making them compare the combinations they have misread with the standard alphabet or syllabary they have already mastered. This is their exemplar ; the purpose of repeatedly referring them back to it is to make them able to detect unerringly any combination given them when they meet with it again in a new setting. This is the function of every example (277c–278d).

Now for our example of the kind of discrimination which will be necessary, if we are to distinguish the statesman's " tendance " of the community from all cognate or analogous occupations. We may take it from the humble industry of weaving woollen garments. If we set to work to distinguish the weaver's industry from every other, a series of obvious " divisions "—we need not repeat them, though Plato gives them—soon leads us to the result that it is the industry of fashioning defences against climate and weather by the intertexture of wools (279b–280d). But this statement, though true, is not sufficiently precise. If we described the weaver as occupied with the " tendance " of clothes, wool-carders, fullers, stitchers, and others, to say nothing of the makers of the implements they all use, might put in a claim to be called " weavers." If we are to avoid this difficulty, we must, in the first place, distinguish carefully between the art which actually makes a thing, and those which only contribute in a subsidiary way to its production —the principal and the subordinate arts (281d–e). Next, among principal " arts " concerned with clothes, we must set aside those which have to do with cleansing, repairing, and adorning the material ; this is " tendance of clothes," but not the kind of tendance exercised by the weaver (282c). Next, if we consider the work of actually making the clothes, which we will call " working in wool " (ταλασιουργική), we can divide it into two kinds, each of which may be subdivided again. Part of the work consists in separation of the composite (the carding of the wool is an illustration) ; part consists in combining the separate into one. And this work of combining may take either of two forms, twisting or interlacing (282d). Both the warp and the woof of the intended web are made by twisting (or spinning), the one being spun closer and the other less close ; the weaving is the subsequent interlacing of the threads of warp and woof to make the web (283a). We might, of course, have made so simple a statement without going through the tedious series of divisions which have led up to it. They might be thought superfluous and unduly prolix. This leads us into a digression on the true standard of proportion in discourse generally (283c).

We may distinguish two kinds of measurement (μετρητική) and two standards of measure—one extrinsic and relative, the other intrinsic and absolute (the actual names are mine, not Plato's). We may measure things as great and small simply by reference to one another, or by reference to the standard of τὸ μέτριον, the *right* amount, or, as it is also expressed, in words meant to sound paradoxical, κατὰ τὴν τῆς γενέσεως ἀναγκαίαν οὐσίαν (" by the standard of the being which is indispensable to the production," 283d). (The meaning is, to take a simple example, that a tea-spoonful of a liquid may be " very little " by comparison with a bucketful ; but it is dreadfully "too much," a dreadful "over-dose," if the liquid contains a concentrated poison, medicinal in minute doses.) The arts and their products, for example both statesmanship and the art of weaving, of which we have just spoken, are constantly employing this standard of the " just proportionate " in estimating excess and defect ; it is by adhering to it that " all good things " are produced and preserved. To demonstrate the reality of this intrinsic standard of measurement might prove as long a business as we found it to demonstrate the reality of " what is not," and, as we do not wish to be led too far away from our immediate topic, it is sufficient for our purpose to point out that unless we recognize it we shall have to deny the very possibility of applying science to the regulation of action (284a–d). (This thought of a " just right mean " and its significance for action will meet us again still more prominently in the *Philebus*. From the use made of it in the *Ethics* it has come to be spoken of familiarly as the Aristotelian principle of the Mean. In justice to both Aristotle and Plato it is necessary to point out that the whole doctrine is Platonic, and that Aristotle never makes any claim to its author-ship, though he is careful to call attention, throughout the *Ethics*, to the points on which he believes himself to be correcting Plato and the Academy.)

Thus the sciences generally fell into two classes—those which measure numbers, lengths, areas, velocities, etc., against one another, and those which take as the standard of their measure-ments the right mean (μέτριον), the appropriate (πρέπον), the seasonable (καιρός), the *morally* necessary (δέον). The saying that " all science is measurement " is only true on the condition that we remember this distinction between two kinds of measure-ment. (Thus Plato combines the view that " science is measure-ment " with strict adherence to the principle of the absoluteness of moral and aesthetic *values*.) As an illustration of the point, we cannot answer the question whether the disquisitions of the present conversation or of yesterday's are " excessively long " except by considering that our *primary* object has not been to define the weaver's work or even the statesman's, but to train our souls in the accurate apprehension of the most important realities—those which are incorporeal and unseen. If this purpose could not have been equally effected by a quicker method, our longest digressions cannot be said to have been " too long " (284e–287b).

We now return to the main argument. The example has impressed it on us that in defining a science it is indispensable to discriminate it from others which are (a) subsidiary to it ; (b) analogous, but not identical with it. We must try to make this double discrimination for the case of the statesman (287b–305d).

Arts or callings subsidiary to a principal " art " will, with a little forcing, come under one of the following heads :

1. Those which make the *instruments* used by the principal art as its implements ;
2. Those which make *vessels* for the safe keeping of products of all kinds ;
3. Those which make stands and vehicles (ὀχήματα) ;
4. Those which make coverings and defences of all kinds ;
5. Those which ornament and embellish a product, and make it tasteful—arts of " play " ;
6. Those which fabricate what the principal art uses as its " raw material " ;
7. Those which provide nutriment of all kinds (287c–289c).

If we add one other branch of art, " the rearing of herds," already often mentioned, this classification will cover all our " property " (κτήματα), except slaves and personal servants (*i.e.* except those human " chattels " who directly assist a man, in a subordinate way, in the actual *living* of his life). (The thought is that the only piece of " property " which cannot be reckoned, roughly speaking, under the head of " implements " or " provisions," is the " chattel " who is also your *assistant* in the work of living. You could not well apply to the services of your confidential clerk— who at Athens would have been your " property "—the formula that his business is to make, or to take care of, that which you *use*. He really is, in his degree, contributing to the actual " tendance " of your soul.) Thus there is the same sort of analogy between the work of the king and that of a personal servant or slave as between the work of the weaver and that of the carder or spinner. The person whom it would be most excusable to mistake for the king— the irony is characteristically Platonic—is the " menial " (289c). For all his pomp and circumstance, the king really is very much like a " menial servant."

We should expect, then, that the most plausible false pretender to the functions of the king would be some class of menials. On inspection we find, however, that most menials never dream of advancing such pretensions. If we extend the range of the term to include all who render " personal services," we may bring seers (μάντεις) and priests under it ; both seer and priest are " messengers " or " errand-runners " of a sort (290c–d). Now we are getting on the track of the pretender we wish to detect. Seers and priests are persons of self-importance and " prestige," as we see from many examples, particularly from that of Egypt, where it is a rule that the king *must* be a priest. But the pretender whom it is hardest to distinguish from the true statesman or king is a rather different creature, who, like the sophist, has many disguises, and may, in fact, be said to be the greatest " wizard " (γόης) and sophist of all (291c). What he really is we may discover from the following considerations.

There are three well-known types of government : monarchy (the rule of a single person), oligarchy (rule by a small select group), democracy (rule by the general citizen body). But we may add that the first two have two forms, so that the whole number of types should be reckoned as five. The single person may rule in accord with law and with the consent of the ruled,[1] or he may rule by mere force, without law ; in the first case we call him a monarch, in the second a " tyrant " (dictator, usurper). So the rule of the few, based on law, is aristocracy ; the lawless rule of the few by mere force is oligarchy. Democracy commonly retains the name whether it is based on law or on mere force (291d–292a). This is the current popular classification of forms of government. (It is, in fact, that regularly insisted on by Isocrates, a good representative of " popular culture.") But is the classification really scientific ? We have already seen that kingship or ruling is a directive science. The one relevant distinction between claimants to be rulers is therefore their possession or want of this science, not the distinctions between rule by the rich and rule by the poor, rule by fewer or more persons, on which the current classification is founded (292c). Now real knowledge of the science of ruling men is a very rare thing —rarer even than first-rate knowledge of draughts, though even that is rare enough. The number of genuine statesmen must be exceedingly few (293a). Those few, because they have scientific knowledge of principles, will be true kings or statesmen, whether they exercise their profession with the popular consent or not, with a written law as a control or not, just as the man who knows the science of medicine is the true physician whether his patients like his treatment, whether he follows the prescriptions of a textbook, or not (293a–b). In any case, he, and only he, does the work of the physician, preserves the bodily health of the patients he " tends." So the one ideally right form of statesmanship is rule by the man who has true scientific knowledge about the " tendance of the soul,"

---

[1] It is assumed that government resting on a law of the constitution is the same thing as government by consent of the governed. This is in accord with the current view that νόμος is συνθήκη πολιτῶν (" the convention of the citizens "). It is not meant that anything like the original formal " social compact " has ever passed.

and makes the souls of the citizens healthy, be his methods what they may (293e).

Yet it is a hard saying that it is indifferent whether government is carried on by law or without it, and our position requires further examination.   Legislation is, in a sense, part of the work of a states-man, and yet the ideally best thing would be the supremacy not of the laws but of the embodied wisdom of the true king.   For no law can be trusted to produce the best effects in every case ; this is impossible, since the law cannot take account of the infinite variations of individual character, situation, and circumstance. Any law will give rise to "hard cases" (294b–c).   Why, then, is legislation indispensable ?   Because it is impossible for the ruler, who is a man with the limitations of humanity, to give in-dividual direction in each of the countless cases which have to be considered.   He has to fall back on giving general directions which will suit the " average " man and the " average " situation (295a).

Now suppose that, over and beyond this, any practitioner of a directive science, e.g. a physician, were compelled to absent himself from his patients for long and frequent intervals, how would he meet the risk of their forgetting his directions ?   He would provide them with written memoranda of the regimen they were to follow in his absence ; but if he came back sooner than he had expected, he would have no scruple about changing these written regulations if the case demanded it.   So the true statesman, if he could return after an absence, would have no scruple in modifying his institutions and regulations for similar reasons, nor a second true statesman in changing those of a first (295e).   It is popularly said that an in-novation in the laws is permissible if the proposer can *persuade* the city to adopt it, but not otherwise.   Yet we should not say that a medical man who insisted on breaking through a written rule of treatment when he thought it necessary to do so had committed a fault in medical treatment because the patient had objected to the departure from the " books " ; so if a statesman makes the citizens better men by forcing them to innovate on their written and in-herited laws, we must not say that he has committed a fault in *his* science, a " crime " or a " wrong " (296c).   Nor does a man's claim to make such innovations depend on superior wealth ; the one and only relevant qualification is his wisdom and goodness.   If he has these qualifications, he is entitled to save the " vessel of the State " as his goodness and wisdom direct, just as an actual pilot shapes his course by his living " art," not by a written rule.   The wise ruler has only one rule which is inviolable, the rule of doing what is wise and right (τὸ μετὰ νοῦ καὶ τέχνης δικαιότατον, 297b).   The one perfect " form of government " would be government by the living insight of such an ideal ruler ; all others are mere imperfect " imitations," of varying degrees of merit.

In the absence of such an ideal ruler, that is, in the actual circumstances of human life, the best course is the very one we have just pronounced absurd where the ideal ruler is presupposed.   The laws ought to be absolutely sovereign, and violation of them should be a capital crime in a public man (297e). We may illustrate the point by recurring to the examples of the navigator and the physician. It is quite true that the competent navigator or physician frequently puts us to grave inconvenience and discomfort, and actually expects to be paid for doing so. But if this led us to make a rule that no one should practise these callings αὐτοκράτωρ (with full authority), but that anyone who pleased might follow them on the condition of always adhering to regulations approved by a public assembly of laymen, we should get very strange results, and still stranger, if we further went on to appoint our practitioners annually by lot or by a property qualification, and required them, at the end of the year, under heavy penalties, to satisfy a court that they had infringed none of the regulations (298a–299b). If we went the further length of enacting that anyone who made a new discovery in these or any other of the practical sciences might be prosecuted as a traitor and " corrupter of youth," and put to death if convicted, there would soon be an end of science and of life itself (299b–e). But the case would be even worse if the courts entrusted with the enforcement of the supposed regulations were not expected to follow any regulations themselves, but were free to give their verdicts as personal considerations prompted (300a). After all, there was some experience (πεῖρα) which suggested these rules, and some intelligence employed in getting them generally accepted ; they were not the expression of mere individual greed or vanity or caprice.

The laws are at least an approximate " imitation " of the principles on which the living ideal " king " would act. As we said, such a man would refuse to be bound by formulae when they do not really apply. In this one respect of departing from formula and precedent, the politicians who disregard the law are like the true statesman. But, since they are by hypothesis ignorant of the principles of statesmanship, they imitate his " innovations " badly they depart from law and precedent in the wrong cases and for wrong reasons. In any community where the ruler is not the ideal scientific statesman, and that means in every society where the " sovereign " is a body of several men, and most, if not all, when he is one man, the law ought to be absolutely paramount (301a). (This means that we must eliminate from " practical politics " the " rule of the saints " at which the Pythagorean brotherhood had aimed in the cities of Magna Graecia. The infallible ruler would be a god or a superman. Supermen are not found in the historical world ; there, the sovereignty of law is the *succedaneum* for an actual theocracy, as is further explained in the fourth book of the *Laws*.)

These considerations explain why in actual fact we find five, not merely three, distinguishable forms of government. When the " well-to-do " govern with strict regard for law we have aristocracy ; when they disregard law, oligarchy. One person ruling with reverence for law is so near an imitation of the ideal statesman that we give him the same name of king. When he " pretends to act, like the true statesman, always for the best, unhampered by regulations," but is really inspired by ignorance and lust, we call him a tyrant. Democracy receives one and the same name, whether it rests on a fundamental law or not. Since the perfect scientific statesman is not met in actual life, and his place has to be taken by very imperfect laws which must not be contravened, it is not surprising that the public life of states should be as unsatisfactory as it is ; the real marvel is that some of them exhibit as much vitality and permanence as they do (302*a*).

It is an important, if not strictly relevant, question which of these various constitutions is least unsatisfactory. We may say at once that monarchy, the rule of a single person, is the best of all, if it is strictly subject to good fundamental laws ; in the form of sheer personal rule without laws, "tyranny," it is worst of all. As for the " rule of a few," it is " middling " ; the rule of the multitude, from the inevitable subdivision of the sovereign power, is weakest of all for good or evil. Thus, where there is a fundamental law, monarchy is the best constitution, aristocracy the second, democracy the worst ; where caprice rules instead of law, democracy is least bad, oligarchy worse, despotism worst of all. (There is likely to be more " fundamental decency " in a big crowd than in a little " ring," and least of all in an uncontrolled autocrat, 302*b*–303*b*.)

We can now at last say who are the serious pretenders to the name of the statesman or king, from whom it is so important to discriminate him. They are the men of affairs in the imperfect constitutions, who delude themselves and their admirers into false belief in their practical wisdom ; they call themselves πολιτικοί (statesmen), but are really στασιαστικοί (party politicians). These are the supreme " wizards " and " sophists " of the world (303*c*).

We have now, so to say, purged away all the dross from our concept of statesmanship ; only good ore is left. But as " adamant," itself a precious thing, is separated from gold in the last stages of the process of refining, so we have still to distinguish statesmanship from the tasks of the soldier, the judge, the preacher of righteousness who " persuades men " into goodness by the noble use of eloquence. Reflection satisfies us that the business of the statesman is not to persuade or to win battles, but to decide whether persuasion or enforcement shall be adopted, whether war shall be made or not. So his business is not to administer the laws but to make the laws which the courts then administer. Each of the callings just mentioned has charge of one action, the proper performance of which is its contribution to the " tendance " of the city ; the statesman's superior function is to control and co-ordinate all these inferior activities (303*d*–305*e*). His task is to weave together all classes in the State into the one fabric of the life of the whole.

Just as a web is made by the intertexture of the stiffer threads of the warp and the softer of the woof, so the garment of national life or character has corresponding components : there are the harder and sturdier and the softer and gentler temperaments, as material. Speaking generally, there are two main types of temperament—the adventurous, keen, and masculine, and the quiet and gentle. The very " virtues " of the two are, in a way, opposed ; that of the one is valour, that of the other modesty and orderliness ($\sigma\omega\phi\rho\sigma\sigma\acute{v}\nu\eta$). And either, carried to the extreme and untempered by the other, degenerates, the one into harshness, violence, and fury, the other into softness and sloth. If the life of a society permanently takes its tone from the predominance of the softer type, it begins by being unambitious, peaceful, and neighbourly, but there is the risk that, for sheer want of grit and backbone, the city will end by being enslaved ; where the adventurous, ambitious type prevail, the same result is likely to follow from the hostilities in which such a society is sure to be entangled by its aggressiveness (308a). The task of true statesmanship is just to weave these two contrasted strains well and deftly together. The true statesman would begin by a careful testing of the temperaments in the State ; he would then demand that the educator should train the characters of the young, so as to make them into the right kind of material from which to weave the fabric of a sound public life, as the weaver of cloth looks to the carder and others to provide him with properly prepared yarn (308d). Thoroughly intractable temperaments would be excluded by death and banishment, or at least reduced to the status of slavery (309a).

The statesman then proceeds to give instruction for the interweaving of the threads he has selected, the characters who can be trained into the combination of valour with *sophrosyne*. He will regard as the threads of his warp the temperaments in which the original bias is to action and adventure, as the threads of the woof the tamer and quieter. The actual weaving of the two together is a double process ; the " everlasting " in the souls of the citizens will be knit by a " divine " bond, the merely " animal " by a " human." The " divine " bond is constituted by " true and assured beliefs " about good and right, bad and wrong. These the statesman will look to the educator to provide. The effect of such an education is to make the naturally daring soul gentler by teaching it respect for the rights of others, and to develop the natural orderliness of the quiet and unambitious into *sophrosyne* and wisdom. This education, which corrects the bias of each type, is the " divine " bond which most effectively produces unity of life and character, but it will only produce its full effect in the finest souls. The " human " and inferior way of producing unity in the society is to take care that marriages are contracted on the right principles.

At present, to say nothing of marriages based on equality in fortune or rank, the tendency is for persons of the same type of temperament to mate with one another, the adventurous with the adventurous, the quiet with the quiet. But this is a false principle, and militates against real unity of spirit in the community. The right principle would be that persons in whom either bias is present should be mated with partners of the other bias. This would not only prevent the society from falling outwardly into two groups without close relations, but would lead to a cancelling out of one-sided bias in the children of the marriage, and so make for the permanent continuance of the type of citizen whom we must have if the community is to endure. The main necessity is to provide by the right kind of education that both " temperamental " types shall have the same convictions about good and evil ; if this is once attained, the further unification of the community by proper regulations about marriage and the like is an easy task (309b–311a). When the fabric has been thus duly woven, it only remains for the statesman to constitute the officials necessary for the administration. Where a single official is required, he will take care to select one who exhibits the union of the two strains of temperament of which we have spoken. Where a board has to be constituted, he will see that both types are properly represented, so that the energy and vigour of one part of its members tempers and is tempered by the gentleness and caution of the other part (311a–b). This is how the science of the statesman directs and controls the construction of the most glorious of all fabrics, the garment of a righteous and happy national life.

It will be observed that the dialogue is peculiarly rich, apart from its immediate political teaching, in ideas which have passed over into the substance of Aristotelian ethics. Thus, in addition to the conception of the " intrinsic " standard of the Right Mean, we may mention the distinction between Cognitive and Practical Science, which corresponds to Aristotle's fundamental distinction between Theoretical and Practical Philosophy ; [1] the conception of the relation of a " directive," or, as Aristotle says, " architectonic " science to its subordinate disciplines, together with the specification of the two marks of the " directive " science—that it *uses* what its subordinate disciplines *make*, and that it superintends and regulates their practitioners ; the conception of the science of the statesman—Politics—as being, in virtue of its concern with the production of the good life for the community, *the* single supreme directive practical science ; the insistence upon education, which provides the statesman with his proximate raw material, men and women with the right type of character, as the most important of all the disciplines subservient to statesmanship. All these conceptions happen to be more familiar to us from the *Ethics* and *Politics* than from the *Politicus*, but it is from the *Politicus* that

[1] There is the difference that Aristotle, unlike Plato, insists that Politics is a *practical* science. This is a mere verbal difference. Plato's reason for calling it cognitive is that, though it deals with πράξεις, its work is not *manipulative*, but the giving of *directions*, an intellectual task. Aristotle's real reason for denying Politics the name of " theoretical" science is that he is preoccupied, in a way in which Plato is not, by his distinction between necessary and contingent subject-matter.

Aristotle took them, as is shown by the frequency with which he echoes his master's phraseology and repeats his illustrations.

See further :

BURNET.—*Greek Philosophy, Part I.,* 273–301 ; *Platonism* (1928), c.5.

RITTER, C.—*Platon,* ii. 120–165, 185–258, 642–657 ; *Platons Dialoge,* 25–67 ; *Neue Untersuchungen ueber Platon,* 1–94.

RAEDER, H.—*Platons philosophische Entwickelung,* 317–354.

NATORP, P.—*Platons Ideenlehre,* 271–296, 331–338.

APELT, O.—*Platonische Aufsätze,* 238–290. (1912.)

APELT, O.—*Platonis Sophista.* (Leipzig, 1897.)

STEWART, J. A.—*Plato's Doctrine of Ideas,* 84–91 ; *Myths of Plato,* 173–211 (*The Politicus Myth*).

DIÈS, A.—*Autour de Platon,* ii., 352–399, 450–522.

BARKER, E.—*Greek Political Theory : Plato and his Predecessors,* 276–291.

CAMPBELL, L.—*Sophistes and Politicus of Plato.* (Oxford, 1867.)

DIÈS, A.—*Platon, Le Sophiste* (Paris, 1925) and *Platon, Politique* (Paris, 1935).

CORNFORD, F. H.—*Plato's Theory of Knowledge.* (Translation of *Theactetus* and *Sophistes* with Commentary, London, 1935.)

STENZEL, J.—*Zahl und Gestalt bei Platon und Aristoteles,* 10–23, 126–133. (Leipzig, 1924.)

And for the history of Plato's relations with Dion and Dionysius II, the full treatment in

MEYER, E.—*Geschichte des Altertums,* v. 497–528.

CHAPTER XVI

THE *PHILEBUS*

IN the *Philebus* we are once more dealing with "practice," and more specifically with "individual" morality. The dialogue is a straightforward discussion of the question whether the "good for man" can be identified either with pleasure or with the life of thought. Socrates once more takes the part of chief speaker, a place given him in no other dialogue later than the *Theaetetus*. The explanation of this is no doubt, as Burnet has said, that the subject-matter, the application of Pythagorean "categories" to problems of conduct, is precisely that which Plato represents as having always been his chief interest. I think it significant that, as we shall see, all through the discussion the "categories" with which Socrates works are the Pythagorean concepts of the Unbounded, the Limit, and their synthesis. We know from Aristotle that one of the characteristic divergences of Plato from the Pythagoreans was that he substituted for their antithesis of the Boundless and the Limit that of the Boundless, conceived as "unbounded in both directions" (the Great-and-Small), and the *One*.[1] (On the Pythagorean view, the One, or Unit, was the simplest synthesis of the Boundless with Limit.) It is clear, since Aristotle never hints at any change in Plato's teaching, that the doctrine he calls Platonic must have been taught in the Academy as early as his own arrival there in 367 ; the *Philebus* is certainly one of the latest works of Plato's life, and must have been written years after 367, but it still uses the Pythagorean, not the Platonic, antithesis. I can see no explanation except the simple one that for the purposes of the discussion the Pythagorean categories are satisfactory, and that Plato is unwilling to make Socrates expound what he knows to be a novelty of his own.

There are no data for determining the relative dates of composition of *Philebus*, *Timaeus*, *Laws*. Presumably the composition of the *Laws* was going on when the other two were written. The dramatic date of the conversation cannot be fixed, except that from *Philebus* 58a 7 we see that it is later than the first visit of Gorgias to Athens ; the scene is also left unspecified, though it is, no doubt, "somewhere in (or about)" Athens. The two young men who figure as interlocutors, Protarchus and Philebus, are entirely

[1] *Met.* A 987b 25, τὸ δ' ἀντὶ τοῦ ἀπείρου ὡς ἑνὸς δυάδα ποιῆσαι καὶ τὸ ἄπειρον ἐκ μεγάλου καὶ μικροῦ, τοῦτ' ἴδιον.

unknown to us.[1] Socrates addresses the former as " son of Callias," but the name Callias was a common one, and we cannot say what Callias is meant, except that it cannot be Socrates' acquaintance Callias the " millionaire," whose children were mere boys at the time of Socrates' trial (*Apol.* 20a).

If we know so little about the date of the dialogue, we seem able to say much more definitely than for most of the dialogues what were the circumstances which occasioned its composition. The object of the discussion is to examine two rival theses about the " good " : (*a*) that it is pleasure (ἡδονή), (*b*) that it is " thinking " τὸ φρονεῖν, τὸ νοεῖν. The way in which the theses are formulated at the outset (11*b*) suggests at once that we are dealing with a *quaestio disputata* within a regular philosophical school. When we find that the purpose of the dialogue is to criticize both, to dismiss both as inadequate, and to suggest a *via media*, the impression naturally arises that Plato, as head of the Academy, is acting as " moderator " in a dispute within his own school. The evidence of Aristotle's *Nicomachean Ethics* seems to convert the possibility into a certainty. As is well known, Aristotle there deals twice over with the problem of the relation between good and pleasure. In the discussion of the seventh book, he starts with an anti-Hedonist thesis that pleasure is not good at all, examines the arguments adduced by its defenders, and urges that they are so inconclusive that they do not even prove that pleasure is not the supreme good. The arguments are all taken from Platonic dialogues, including the *Philebus* itself, but employed to prove something different from the conclusions drawn in Plato. Since one of these is that " pleasure must be bad, because it hinders thought "—a misrepresentation of the argument of *Phaedo* 66*a* ff.—the persons who advanced them clearly held that the good is " thinking " (τὸ φρονεῖν), the thesis pitted against the identification of good with pleasure at the opening of our dialogue. Aristotle incidentally mentions among their arguments the contention that pleasure cannot be the good because pleasure and pain are both bad things which a wise man avoids, and names the author of the doctrine, Speusippus.[2] In the second discussion of the subject, he also tells us who the person who identified " the good " with pleasure was ; it was the famous

---

[1] It is assumed that there is also a considerable number of young men who form a silent audience (16*a* 4). Socrates is even said to be granting the party a συνουσία (19*c* 5), a word which has the suggestion of a formal "lecture " or *conférence*. It is clear, in spite of the opposite view of some editors, that Philebus, who is almost silent throughout the dialogue, is a mere lad, much more immature in mind than Protarchus. This explains the touch of petulance about his declaration (12*a*) that nothing will ever persuade him out of his Hedonism. His worship of ἡδονή is just a boy's zest for the *joie de vivre*.

[2] *E.N.* 1153*b* 5. Speusippus argued that the badness of pain does not prove the goodness of pleasure ; both are opposed to the " good," as " the greater " and " the less " are both opposed to " the equal." *I.e.* the good condition is absence of both pleasurable and painful excitement. Hence the point that " the good man pursues not the pleasant but the painless " (*E.N.* 1152*b* 15) will be part of his argument.

mathematician Eudoxus, and his argument was precisely that which is hinted at in the opening words of the *Philebus* (11*b* 5) and alluded to again at its close (67*b* 1), that pleasure is the one end which *all* living things instinctively and spontaneously pursue.[1] These references seem to make it certain that the issue discussed in the dialogue is one which had actually divided the members of the Academy, the question what is really meant by the Platonic "Form of Good." One party thinks that it means pleasure, the other that it means thought.[2] The attitude taken by Plato in the dialogue to this discussion is, to all intents and purposes, precisely that of the "moderator" in the schools of the Middle Ages "determining" a *quaestio disputata*. The arguments produced by both parties are reviewed and weighed, and the balance is struck between the disputants. It is decided that the issue shall be narrowed down to a consideration of the "good for *man*" in particular. When the question has thus been delimited, it is "determined" by the answer that neither pleasure alone nor thought alone is the "good" or best life for men; the best life must include both thought and grateful feeling; but of the two, thought is the "predominant partner." This is, in fact, the conclusion to which the discussion is made to lead; it is also the verdict given on the same issue in Aristotle's *Ethics*, which owe more of their inspiration to the *Philebus* than to any other Platonic dialogue.

THE QUESTION PROPOUNDED (11*a*–20*b*).—What is "the good"? Philebus has an answer to this question: "pleasure, joy, delight," this is the good for all living creatures. Socrates disputes this: "thought, intelligence, memory, true judgment," are better than pleasure "for all who can share in them" (11*b*). Thus Philebus originally makes an assertion not simply about the good for *man* in particular, but about good universal, "the" good. Socrates commits himself to no assertion about good universal, but asserts that for an intelligent being, like man, there is something better than pleasure, namely, the exercise of intelligence. If we are to decide between those conflicting views, we must at least agree on the sense to be put on the phrase, "the good for man." We may take it that both of us mean by this phrase "a condition and state (ἕξις καὶ διάθεσις) of soul which can make any man's life *happy*" (11*d*).[3] The question is whether pleasure, or again, thought, or possibly something better than either, is that "state and condition."

---

[1] *E.N.* 1172*b* 9–15.

[2] Few scholars would now make the old mistake, which unfortunately persists in some of the best expositions of the dialogue, of supposing the Hedonists and anti-Hedonists aimed at to be Cyrenaics and Cynics respectively.

[3] This is the definition of Aristotle also, except that Aristotle holds that the true genus of happiness is not ἕξις (state) but ἐνέργεια (activity). This is a valuable correction of the language of the Academy, but no more than a correction of their language. Aristotle never suggests that Plato, or any member of the Academy, *meant* that the "good" is a mere passive state. He blames their *terminology* for not marking the difference between such a "state" and an "activity."

In this last case, we should have to say that neither pleasant feeling nor thought is, by itself, the good for man, but we should still have to say that whichever of the two is most akin to the complete good for man is the better of them (11e). (These remarks foreshadow the coming conclusion that the " good for man " includes both components, but that thought is the more valuable of the two.)

Now " pleasure " is a word with many shades of meaning. A " life of pleasure " often means a vicious life, yet we say that the continent man finds his very continence pleasant ; we talk of the " pleasures " of folly and extravagant day-dreams, but we also say that the " thinking man " finds his thinking pleasant. Thus there may be pleasures of many kinds, and we have no right to assume that *all* must be good (12d). You may say, as the Hedonist does, that the difference of which Socrates speaks is a difference in the *sources* from which pleasure is derived, not in the pleasure yielded, but this would be evading the real issue. All pleasant experiences agree in being pleasant, just as all coloured surfaces agree in being coloured. But there are more or less marked colour-contrasts also. Why then may there not be pleasure-contrasts within the *genus* pleasure ? If there are, this will be a reason for hesitating to ascribe the predicate *good* to all pleasures.

" Pleasure is good " is, in fact, a synthetic proposition (13a), and therefore we cannot assume the impossibility of regarding some pleasures as good, but others as bad. They are all, of course, pleasant, but pleasantness might be present both in good and in bad experiences. Similarly, if we consider the rival thesis, that thought is " the good," we can see that it is one thing to make the analytic propositions " science is science," " knowledge is knowledge," another to say that " science (or knowledge) is *good*." If there are a plurality of " sciences," or other activities of intellect, some of them may conceivably be good, others bad (14a). Thus we see that our present discussion raises the old and eternally recurring problem of the one and the many (14c).

One form of this problem may now be regarded as long ago disposed of, the ancient difficulty of the possession of many qualities or parts by the same individual (14d–e). This was the form in which the problem had arisen, *e.g.* in the *Phaedo* ; presumably Plato means that the solution given there is sufficient to dispose of the question. The case which still needs investigation is that in which the " one " is not a thing which comes into or passes out of being, but belongs to the non-phenomenal order. This case gives rise to three questions : (a) whether there really are such non-phenomenal " units " ; (b) how we are to reconcile their *unity* with their reality or *being* ;[1] (c) how we can think of such units as being at

[1] *Phileb.* 15b 2–4. The wording of this second question is a little obscure, but the meaning seems to be made plain if we read the words in the light of the " antinomies " of the *Parmenides*. When we try to think of an ὃν ἕν, a *real* unit, we seem driven either to deny its unity in order to maintain its reality, or to deny its reality in order to save its unity. This is also how Burnet takes the words (*Greek Philosophy, Part I.*, 326, n. 2).

once one and many. (This last question is manifestly the same which has met us in the *Sophistes*, the problem of the " communion " of a form itself with other forms.) These are the problems which still give rise to vehement discussion (15*a–c*).

We certainly cannot evade these problems ; they are perpetually turning up in all our " discourses," and we must meet them as best we can (15*d*–16*b*). There is no better way of dealing with them than that of which Socrates has always been a lover. (Compare the way in which he speaks in the *Phaedrus* of his reverence for the true dialectician who knows how to " divide " a subject rightly.) There was long ago a Prometheus—Pythagoras is the person meant —who revealed the art by which such problems may be treated. His followers have handed down to us the tradition that " whatever is at any time said to be " is composed of the constituents limit and the unlimited. No matter what subject we study, we can find these elements in it. We can always find a single form (the allusion is to the Pythagorean doctrine that the " unit " is the first combination of limit and unlimited)—and on inspection we shall, with care, be able to discover two, or three, or some other number of definite further forms included in it. We should next take each of these forms and look for a definite number of forms included in them, and continue this process as long as fresh forms are to be found. It is only when we can no longer repeat the process that we should let things " go to infinity." In this way, the only way worthy of a dialectician, we shall discover not only that every form is at once one and infinitely many, but also *how* many it is (16*c*–17*a*). (That is, we must not be content to say, for example, that animal, or anything else, is one kind and also that there are an indefinite number of animals ; we must attempt to make a logical division which will show us exactly what and how many *species* of animals we can distinguish. It is only when we have reached an *infima species* incapable of further logical subdivision that we may consider the indefinite multiplicity of individuals. So long as you can go on with the logical division, each genus has not an indefinite plurality but a determinate number of constituents.) Thus the grammarian must not say that articulate sound is in a sense one, and yet that there are " any number " of different articulate sounds ; he must know how many distinct sounds his alphabet has to represent. To do this he has to divide articulate sounds into vowels and consonants, and the consonants again into " stops " and " sonants." It is only if he finds that these classes cannot be subdivided into sub-classes that he may then *enumerate* the individual vowels, stops, or sonants. Thus definite number (the number of the constituent species and sub-species) is everywhere the intermediate link between the one genus and its indefinitely numerous members (17*b*–18*d*).

We must apply this consideration of method to our special moral problem. Before we can decide whether *all* pleasure or *all* thinking is good or not, we must know not only that pleasure is one and knowledge one, and again that there are " ever so many " pleasures and forms of knowledge, but also *how* many there are. The question is, in fact, whether we can discover distinct " forms " or " kinds " (εἴδη) of pleasure or of thinking, and how many (19*b*). But this is a long and perplexing inquiry, and Protarchus would be glad if Socrates could find some way of deciding the immediate question whether thinking is better than pleasure without raising this more fundamental issue (20*a–b*).

PRELIMINARY DELIMITATION OF THE PROBLEM.—*Neither Pleasure nor Thought alone is the Good for Man* (20*c–*22*c*).—Socrates, as we shall see, has no serious intention of allowing the question whether there are " kinds " of pleasure to be shirked. But we can get rid of one of the issues raised without going so deep into the matter. He seems to remember hearing—perhaps in a dream—that " the good " is neither pleasure nor thought, but something better than both. If that should be true, we can, at any rate, dispose of the doctrine that pleasure is *the* good, and we can deal with this point without going into the question about " kinds " of pleasure (20*c*), if we can agree on certain " notes " [1] characteristic of the supreme good and find that pleasures do not exhibit these notes. Obviously it is a note of *the* good that it is something " finished " or " complete " (τέλεον), and consequently that it is " sufficient " (ἱκανόν), and finally, therefore, that it is the one thing and the whole of the thing at which any creature which apprehends it ever aims, the whole and complete fulfilment of desire (20*d*).[2] We may thus make it a criterion of the good for man that it is what any one of us who knows what it is would choose in preference to anything else, and would be completely satisfied by. Judged by this criterion, neither pleasure nor " thought " can be that good. Even a professed Hedonist would not choose by preference a life simply made up of moments of intense pleasurable feeling and nothing else. He would want to be aware that he *is* feeling pleasure in the present, to remember that he has felt it in the past, and to anticipate that he will feel it in the future. Thus he would demand intellectual activity as well as feeling to make him happy ; a life all feeling would be that of an oyster rather than of a man. The same thing is true about a life which is all thinking and no feeling. No *man* would choose a life of mere intellectual activity entirely neutral in feeling-tone. Any man would prefer a " mixed " life, which contains both " thought " and pleasant feeling. The " mixed life " is thus better for *man* than the unmixed. A life of " unmixed " feeling would only be " complete " and " sufficient " for a brute, or perhaps a plant ; a life of " unmixed " intellect may perhaps be suitable to

---

[1] I use the word much as Newman uses it when he talks of the " notes " of the true Church.

[2] These same notes are adopted by Aristotle from the dialogue as the characters which must be exhibited by the " good for man " (*N.E.* 1097*a* 25 ff.). The λόγος of which it is there said that it " comes to the same thing " as Aristotle's own is the Academic theory of the " good for man," as given in the *Philebus*.

God, but not to man. The good for man must exhibit both factors. But the real problem of our dialogue still remains. Does the " mixed life " owe its goodness primarily to the presence of thought in it, or to the presence of pleasant feeling ? Which is preponderantly the *cause* of its goodness? Socrates must not expect to be " let off " this discussion, and to deal with it we shall require to follow a long and difficult line of thought. This brings us to the main argument of the dialogue.

THE RELATIVE SIGNIFICANCE AND PLACE OF PLEASURE AND THOUGHT IN THE GOOD FOR MAN (23c–66d).—*Formal Character of Each* (23c–30e).—Anything which is actual can be placed in one of four classes : (a) infinite or unbounded (τὸ ἄπειρον) ; (b) limit (πέρας) ; (c) the " mixture " or combination of both these constituents ; (d) the *cause* which brings them together (23c–e). To explain a little more precisely : " temperature," or, in the Greek phrase, " hotter and colder," is an example of what we mean by (a). We can call it " infinite " or " boundless " because anything can always be made hotter or colder than it is ; there is no temperature which is the maximum or minimum conceivable, and again, if you have two different degrees of temperature, you can insert between them an endless number of intermediate temperatures different from both. Since temperature may be increased or diminished, we may also call it a " great and small " or " a less and more " (a μέγα καὶ μικρόν), and this, as we know from Aristotle, was Plato's own name for what the Pythagoreans, whose language Socrates is using in our dialogue, called the ἄπειρον. And what we can say about temperature, we can equally say about everything which allows of indefinite variation in magnitude or in degree, admits of " more and less," or such qualifications as " intense," " slight." We may thus class together all that admits of such variation under one single head as the " infinite " (24e). The " infinite " is thus what we should call quality with a continuous range.

By the " limit," again, as a single " form " we mean whatever does not admit " the more and the less," but admits such predicates as " the equal," " the double," in a word, whatever is " as an integer to an integer or a measure to a measure " (25b). The limit (πέρας) means thus precise mathematical determination, number, ratio, measure. (The last is added to cover the case of " surd " ratios, like that of 1 : √2 or side of square : diagonal.)

The " mixed " class, or " mixture of the two," means a precise and definitely determined magnitude or intensity of any quality. (Thus, *e.g.*, temperature is an ἄπειρον, 20° is a πέρας, a temperature *of* 20° C. is an instance of the " mixture "; rainfall is an ἄπειρον, 6 is a πέρας, but a rainfall *of* 6 inches is a μεικτόν, and so on.) The introduction of determination into a " more and less " is precisely what we call a γένεσις, or process of becoming (25e). (*E.g.*, to raise water to a temperature of 100° C. is the " process " of making it boil, it is also the introduction of the " limit " 100° into the ἄπειρον, temperature.)

Now we note that health in the body, proper attunement in music, beauty and proportion in a body or a face, good climate, and the like, all depend on the production of definite " limit " or ratio in an ἄπειρον of some kind ; departure from this proper ratio produces disease, false intervals in music, ugliness, bad climate. And the same thing holds about goodness in the soul (26*b* 6). The point to be made is thus that the right or sound or good state of anything is marked by definite proportion and " limit " ; there may be infinitely numerous divergences from this one right proportion or equilibrium, but they are all in varying degrees bad. This is what is meant by calling the development which leads up to and stops at the production of the right proportion a γένεσις εἰς οὐσίαν, a development leading to a stable *being* (26*d*). The point is that the physician producing health in his patient, for example, may do so by steadily increasing the proportion of the " dry," or again of the " moist," in the invalid, but he does not aim at increasing this beyond limits. There is a definite ratio of the " hot " to the " cold," or of the " moist " to the " dry," which is characteristic of health. When the γένεσις set up by the physician's treatment has secured this ratio, he dismisses the patient. Health once attained, you don't make the man healthier *in indefinitum* by passing further and further beyond the " limit " ; you would only give him a new disease instead of the old one. This explains why we shall be told directly that all the good things in life belong to this class of the " mixed."

As for the " cause," we mean by it the agent which sets up such a process as we have described, τὸ ποιοῦν (26*e*). We have therefore to distinguish it both from that which it produces, the process or γένεσις, and that which " subserves it for the process," the " matter " of the process. The process we have already referred to our third class ; the " matter " of the process is just the factors which are brought into combination, the unlimited and limit. This is why we had to add the fourth class to the other three. We note here that the account of the " mixed " class is the direct source of the " right mean " in Aristotle's *Ethics*. " Moral " goodness, according to Aristotle's familiar account in *E.N.* ii., is a fixed and habitual right " mean " or proportion in our appetitions and tempers, and the process of becoming good is one of " qualifying " them, *i.e.* training them to exhibit just the proportion demanded by the " right rule " (ὀρθὸς λόγος).[1] Thus it is just such a process of γένεσις εἰς οὐσίαν as has just been described, the ἄπειρον in the case being the indefinite degrees of frequency and intensity which tempers and appetitions admit, and the πέρας the *exact* degree demanded by the " right rule."

---

[1] The ὀρθὸς λόγος itself is Platonic too, and appears to come from *Laws*, 659*d*, where education is said to be the " drawing and attracting of children to the right discourse (ὀρθὸς λόγος) uttered by the law." That Aristotle was influenced by this passage is shown by his allusion to it as excellently said by Plato at *E.N.* 1104*b* 12.

Now let us apply what we have just said to our particular problem. We see that the " mixed life," including both intellectual activity and agreeable feeling, on the face of it, falls in our third class, because it has these two distinct factors. (It is intended to hint at the result to be established later, that the two factors need to be combined according to definite law and proportion.) But what about the life of pleasure recommended by Philebus, which consisted in having as much pleasure and as intense pleasure as you can get ? Pleasure, and again pain, clearly belong to the class of the " infinite," since neither, in its own nature, has a minimum or a maximum ($27e$). Philebus thinks that it is this impossibility of ever exhausting the possibilities of pleasure which makes it so good. But you might also say that it is the same impossibility of exhausting those of pain which makes pain so bad ($28a$). Hence it is clear that the mere indefinite range of pleasure is no proof of its goodness. What, again, about the " intelligence " ($\nu o\hat{v}s$), knowledge, wisdom, preferred by Socrates ? Into what class does this fall ? ($28a$). We are agreed to reject the theory that the course of the universe is random ($\epsilon i\kappa\hat{\eta}$, $28d$), and to agree with the traditional belief that it is directed by a supreme wisdom ($\phi\rho\acute{o}\nu\eta\sigma\iota s$) and intelligence ($\nu o\hat{v}s$) in every particular. Now when we look at our own constitution, we see that the materials of which our body is made are only small parcels of the great cosmic masses of similar materials, and that these constituents are found in a much higher degree of purity from other ingredients elsewhere in the universe than in our bodies. The " fire " in us [1] is small in bulk and " impure " in substance by comparison with the fire in the sun. And again the " fire " or " water " in us is fed and kept up by that in the larger world ($29c$). And generally our little body is fed by the mass of body without us ($29e$). By analogy, we may infer that since there is soul in us, it too comes from a greater and brighter soul in the universe. Also, we see in our own case that when things are amiss with the body, it is the intelligence, resident in the soul, which re-establishes order by means of the medical art. So we may reasonably hold that in the universe at large, the same holds good. The order in it is due to intelligence ($\nu o\hat{v}s$), and intelligence is only found in souls. So we may hold that there are superhuman souls, and that it is their intelligence which is the cause of cosmic order ($30d$). And we may answer the question now before us by saying that $\nu o\hat{v}s$ (intelligence) belongs to the fourth of our classes, the class of " the cause of the mixture " ($30e$).[2]

---

[1] Plato may be thinking, *e.g.*, of the " animal heat " of the organism and its dependence on a proper supply of solar warmth, but more probably his allusion is to the theory, adopted in the *Republic* and *Timaeus*, that the immediate organ of vision is itself a ray of light issuing from the eye, and is itself derived from the sun's light.

[2] I have given the general sense of the passage from $30a$ 8 to $30e$ 3 without going into the question of precise reading and interpretation of particular phrases. I think Plato clearly means to *identify* $\nu o\hat{v}s$ with the " cause of the mixture." This is not inconsistent with his view that the good for man is not

There has been a great deal of discussion on the point of the place to be assigned to the forms, as we know them from earlier dialogues, in the classification of the *Philebus*.[1] No one has imagined that they could be reckoned as examples of the ἄπειρον, but different scholars have placed them in each of the other three classes. I do not propose to spend much time on the problem, since it seems plain that the fourfold classification has been devised with a view to a problem where the forms are not specially relevant, and the true solution is thus that they find *no* place in this classification. We must not look for them in the class of the " cause," since *cause* has been explicitly equated with *agent*, and it is quite certain that the forms of the *Phaedo* and *Republic* are not agents. (At least, we could only ascribe agency to the " Form of Good," and that, as Socrates' difficulty in speaking of it shows, holds a unique place in the scheme.) Limit, again, has been defined in a way which shows that it means specifically mathematical ratio. Hence, though, in a way, the forms may be said, as defining and determining the character of the sensibles which " partake " them, to function as " limits," they must not be identified with the πέρας of this dialogue. Again, though this is a matter which must not be discussed until we reach our final chapter, it is plain from Aristotle's allusions [2] that, according to the doctrine taught in the Academy as early as 367–6, the forms, " man," " animal," and the rest actually contain two factors, a " great-and-small " and a limiting factor, " the one " or " unit." So far they resemble the " mixed class " of our dialogue, and Professor H. Jackson did right to call attention to this. But all the examples of the " mixed " class in the *Philebus* are taken from the world of " events," and the forms clearly are not " mixtures " of that kind. Not to dwell on the further point that the πέρας of the *Philebus* stands for *any* definite ratio, whereas the πέρας element in the forms, according to Aristotle, was the " one," and the " one " in the *Philebus* is only spoken of as equivalent to any *genus* regarded as a single whole. It is clear that the line of thought which leads to the classification in the *Philebus* brings us nearer to what Aristotle knew as the central doctrine of Platonism than anything else in Plato's writings. But it seems equally clear that Plato's final thought is not disclosed even here. From his own language in *Epistle* vii. we may infer that he never intended the reading of a written work to do more than supply hints which might put a really original mind in the position to discover his thought after a great deal of hard personal thinking, and that he did not expect even as much as this apart

νοῦς. It is clear from the *Republic* (506b) that the general question whether the good can be knowledge or pleasure is older than the speculations of Speusippus and Eudoxus. What is distinctive in the *Philebus* is the appeal to psychology as relevant to the issue.

[1] See Burnet, *Greek Philosophy, Part I.*, 332 ; R. G. Bury, *Philebus*, pp. lxiv–lxxiv ; H. Jackson, *Journal of Philology*, **x.** 253 ff. ; Raeder, *Platons philosophische Entwickelung*, 370 ff.

[2] Cf., *e.g.*, Aristot. *Met.* 987b 18–27

from the actual daily contact of the student's living mind with his own.[1] Hence I shall defer anything I have to say about the central mystery of the Platonic philosophy for consideration in a final chapter. Provisionally, I will merely say what is quite obvious, that, viewed in their relation to the things which " partake " of them, the forms, as we have so far met with them, act as an element of " limit " and determination, but that, as the recognition in the *Sophistes* of a "communion " of forms, as such, with one another shows, this is quite consistent with the view that a form which functions as a " limit " should itself also be analysable into a combination of an " unlimited " and a " limit."

THE PSYCHOLOGY OF PLEASURE AND PAIN (31a–53c).—We have seen to what class pleasure and pain themselves belong ; they are ἄπειρα. We must next consider " that in which they arise " (the subject of them), and the πάθος, or state of things, which gives rise to them, in other words, the actual conditions of their occurrence. To begin with pleasure. " That in which pleasure (or pain) arises " is always a living creature, the creature which feels the pleasure (or pain), and as such it belongs to the " class of the mixture," since its organism is a complex of a plurality of ingredients (31c). The way in which they arise, the πάθη which occasion them, are that " when the attunement (that is, the proper balance between the ingredients of the organism) in an animal is disturbed, pain is felt, and when it is restored after disturbance, pleasure is felt." Disturbance of organic equilibrium is attended by pain, restoration of the equilibrium by pleasure (31d–e). Thus when the body is unduly heated or chilled, we have a λύσις τῆς φύσεως or disturbance of the normal organic equilibrium, and it is painful ; the antithetic process of recovering the normal temperature, which is a return to the οὐσία (the " natural state "), is pleasant. This defines for us one kind or form (εἶδος) of pleasure, namely, the agreeable processes of return to the normal condition of the organism after disturbance, or, as the defenders of the same type of theory in modern times usually say, the process of recovery from organic waste (22a–b).[2] Next, there is a second " form " or " kind " of pleasure which depends on processes purely mental, and is not attended by either disturbance or recovery of the balance in the organism. A simple example is that the mental anticipation of a painful disturbance of the organic balance is itself painful, the expectation of the agreeable antithetic recovery from disturbance is itself pleasant, and in these cases there is no actual accompanying organic process, the pleasure and pain belong in a special way to " the soul by herself " (32c). These are the two distinct εἴδη of pleasure and pain it is necessary to begin by discriminating, if

[1] *Ep.* vii. 340c–e, 341c–e, 343e–344d.
[2] Like Aristotle, Plato confines the waste-and-repair, or depletion-repletion theory of pain and pleasure to the case of pains and pleasures connected with the body and its needs. He does not regard it as applicable to pain and pleasure generally. For a criticism of this type of theory, when extended to all pains and pleasures, see Stout's *Analytic Psychology*, ii. c. 12.

we are to judge soundly on the question whether all pleasures are good.

Next, if there are antithetic processes of disturbance and recovery of the organic balance, and these are respectively painful and pleasant, there must also be an intermediate case, that in which the balance is maintained without deflection in either direction, and this, on our theory, must be neutral in respect of feeling-tone, neither pleasant nor painful (32*e*). This would be the condition, so far as feeling-tone is concerned, of the life of thought unmixed with pleasure or pain already spoken of, and there is no impossibility in the notion that there might be such a life, a life of permanent maintenance of equilibrium. Very possibly it is the life appropriate to a god (33*b*) and so the best of all. But we are discussing a different matter, the part which thought and pleasant feeling should play in the life of men like ourselves (for whom such an existence without any rhythmic alternation is out of the question). For our purposes, we must pursue the psychology of the second class of pleasures and pains further. They are all dependent on *memory* (since, of course, without memory we could have no anticipations), and this makes it necessary to explain briefly what memory is and what sensation itself is. We may say that some bodily processes die away before they can reach the soul, but others penetrate to the soul : the first we may call unconscious ; the second are conscious. This enables us to define sensation as a movement (κίνησις) which affects the body and soul together (κοινῇ, 34*a*). Memory (*i.e.* *primary* memory) is the retention (σωτηρία) of sensation as thus defined (*ibid.*) ; and, finally, recollection (ἀνάμνησις) is the recovery (reproduction) by the soul " by herself " of a lost memory or sensation (34*b–c*). These considerations will make it clearer what we mean by a " purely mental " pleasure, and also throw light on the nature of desire (ἐπιθυμία, 34*e*). To understand what desire is, we may consider it in its simplest form, such as hunger or thirst. A thirsty man desires, or lusts after drink. To speak more precisely, the thirsty man is in a state of depletion, his organism has been depleted of its normal supply of liquid, What he really desires is not simply " drink," but to be " filled up " with the liquid he will drink. (He desires not the water, but the drinking of it.) Thus he actually is in one state (a state of depletion), but desires the antithetic state (the corresponding repletion). To desire to drink the thirsty man must " apprehend " (ἐφάπτεσθαι) repletion. He does not " apprehend " it with his body. That is just what is undergoing the unnatural depletion, and it cannot be passing through two antithetic processes at once. Thus it must be with his soul that he " apprehends " the repletion he lusts after. The importance of the example is that it shows that (in spite of popular language), there is really no such state as a " bodily " desire or lust. All desiring is a state of soul (35*c*), since desire is endeavour towards the opposite of the present state of the organism, and it is in virtue of memory that this " opposite " is apprehended.

These considerations show that all impulse and desire belong to the soul.

They also suggest an important problem. When a man is actually in a state of pain due to organic " depletion," but re-members and thinks of the pleasant experiences which would remove the depletion, can we say that his condition is either purely painful or wholly pleasant ? If he despaired of ever realizing the anticipation of " filling up," no doubt, he would be doubly wretched, but suppose he is feeling the painful depletion but expecting the repletion (like a really hungry man who expects to be fed) ? The anticipation that his want will be removed is pleasant, but the felt want must surely be painful, and thus it appears that we must say that, in the case assumed, the experience is a mixed one, pleasurable and painful at once (36b).

(The conception of " mixed " states which are half pleasant, half painful, is so characteristic of Plato and so important in itself that it cannot be passed over without some comment. Hedonists naturally refuse to accept it, since it is quite inconsistent with the treatment of pain as equivalent to subtraction of pleasure which lies at the root of the Hedonic calculus. They have, accordingly, to explain the facts to which Plato appeals in one or other of two ways. They have to hold that the total feeling-tone of any moment of life is either simply pleasant or simply painful. It is then open to them either to interpret the facts about still unsatisfied craving by holding that the experience is one of rapid alternation between pleasure and pain, or by holding that it is, according to circumstances, one of a low degree of pleasure, or one of pain, though of a moderate degree of pain. Neither view seems to me to be in accord with fact. When I am genuinely and acutely thirsty, e.g. in the course of a long tramp in hot weather, but confidently anticipating arrival at a place of refreshment in an hour's time, it is not the fact that I oscillate rapidly between pure misery and pure delight according as my attention is directed to my present condition or to the con-dition I anticipate ; nor yet is it true that I am continuously feeling a qualified pleasure or a qualified pain. I certainly feel the tension between the pleasant anticipation and the actual pang of thirst in a single pulse of experience. And there is no real difficulty in understanding why this is so, if we remember that the physical correlate of my mental condition is made up of a great complex of neural excitations. No one of the constituent neural excitations can have two antithetic senses at once, but the complex may perfectly well contain elements with opposite senses. Hence it seems to me that Plato's doctrine of " mixed states," which coincides with the standing thought of great poets about the " unrest which men miscall delight," is strictly true to the facts of common experience, and that the criticisms levelled against it are all based on false simplification of the facts.)

TRUE AND FALSE PLEASURE (36c–53c).—We have thus dis-tinguished two " kinds " of pleasures: (a) those directly due to an

actual organic process of recovery of equilibrium or repair of waste;
(*b*) those dependent on mental anticipation, where no such actual
organic process is taking place. The recognition of this second
class at once suggests a further question of first-rate ethical importance : Can we admit of a second and different distinction of
pleasures (and pains) as true and false, real and merely apparent ?
(36*c*). In other words, when we come to the *valuation* of pleasures
as ingredients in the good for man, must we make any deduction
for the " illusoriness " of some of them ? This is the vital distinction for the Platonic ethics ; it is to lead up to and justify it
that the whole psychological discussion has been introduced.
Protarchus denies the validity of the distinction. Beliefs or judgments can be true or false, but not feelings (36*d*). Hedonists, like
Grote, have naturally taken his side and argued that Socrates is
merely in the wrong in making the distinction. For, it is argued,
a pleasure or a pain is exactly what it is felt to be ; its *esse* is simply
the fact of its being felt. If I feel pleased or pained, I am having
pleasure or pain ; if I feel greatly pleased, I am having a great
pleasure ; the pleasure always exists when it is felt, and it is
always just as great as it is felt to be. This reasoning, however,
is irrelevant to Socrates' contention. He is not asking whether I
am pleased when I *feel* pleased, or greatly pleased when I *feel* greatly
pleased ; he is asking whether I am always pleased when I *think*
I am pleased, or intensely pleased when I *think* I am intensely
pleased, and this is a perfectly reasonable question, and, as he
says, one which needs careful examination. To put it simply,
the issue is this : Is the excitement in an exciting experience a
true measure of its pleasantness ?[1] May not the excitingness of
an experience lead to an over-estimate of its pleasantness ? To
answer this question, we need to make a considerable apparent
digression.

There is such a process as judging, and such a process as feeling
pleased. When we judge, we make a judgment about something,
and when we feel pleased, we are pleased with something. And a
judgment does not cease to be an actual judgment because it is
false ; similarly a false feeling of pleasure would still be an actual
feeling of pleasure (37*b*). (This last remark, of itself, shows that
Plato has no intention of denying that a " false " pleasure is a
pleasure ; it is its worth, not its actuality, which is in question.)
The question is whether pleasure and pain, like judgment, permit
of the qualifications true and false. They certainly permit of some
qualifications, such as " great," " small," " intense"; and Protarchus

---

[1] The question is vital, since the " intensity " regarded by all Hedonists
as a dimension of pleasure or pain is primarily a character of the situation by
which we are pleased or pained. We can only measure the intensity of the
pleasantness or painfulness by measuring the intensity of an objective feature
of the situation, and this makes it all-important to know whether such
a measurement can be implicitly trusted. For example, the satisfaction of
the impulses of sex is normally an intense organic excitement, but is its
pleasantness equally intense ?

allows that they may permit of the further qualification " bad."
But he denies that a pleasure can be said, like a judgment, to be
" erroneous " or false (37e) ; if, as often happens, a false belief
yields us pleasure, the falsity belongs to the belief, not to the
pleasure.

Let us look at the facts. Pleasure and pain sometimes accompany true beliefs or judgments, sometimes false. Now these beliefs
may be regarded as answers given by the soul to questions which
she has put to herself ; sometimes the answer is right, sometimes
it is wrong. We have, so to say, a scribe and a painter within our
souls. The interpretation of present sensation by the aid of
memory involved in all perception is the work of the scribe writing
" discourses " in the soul ; the painter (imagination) designs
illustrations (εἰκόνες) to the scribe's text (39a–c), and his pictures
may be called true or false " imaginings " according to the truth or
falsity of the " discourse " they illustrate. These discourses and
pictures concern the future as well as the present or the past ; we
are all through life full of "fancies" (ἐλπίδες) about the future, and
when we anticipate pleasure or pain to come, we take an " antici-
patory " pleasure or pain, which has already been classed as strictly
" mental " in entertaining such expectations (39d–e). This is
true of good and bad men alike, but, since the good are " dear to
God," their pleasant anticipations are commonly fulfilled, those of
the bad are not (40a–b). (The good man gets pleasure in anticipating
sequences which are in accord with the order God maintains in the
world ; the bad man gets his pleasure from day-dreams of sudden
enrichment and other events which do not come about in the
" world as God made it.") Thus the bad man's pleasure in his
anticipations is as actual as the good man's, but the good man, as a
rule, gets the pleasure which he anticipates, the bad man does not.
This affords one sense in which the bad man may be said to have
false, or unreal, pleasures ; he derives present pleasure from anticipations which will not be realized, and this pleasure may rightly be
said to be deceptive, a *caricature* of true pleasure, and the same
argument will apply to pains due to anticipation (40c) as well as
to emotions—fear, anger, and the like—generally (40e). Like beliefs,
all these states may have a foundation in reality or may have none.
Now the goodness of a belief lies in its truth, and its badness in its
falsity ; only true beliefs are good, and only false beliefs are bad.
(For, of course, the *raison d'être* of a belief is that it should be true ;
that is what every belief aims at being.) May we not say then
that the badness of bad pleasures—Protarchus has allowed that
there are such states—is simply falsity and nothing else ? a bad
pleasure means a " false " or " deceptive " pleasure.

Protarchus is unconvinced. There may be "wicked" (πονηραί)
pleasures or pains, but pleasures and pains are not made wicked
by being " false." We will, however, reserve the consideration
of wicked or sinful pleasures for a moment, and call attention to
a second sense in which it might be possible to speak of many

pleasures as " false " (41*a–b*). Consider once more the case already mentioned of unsatisfied appetite, where the soul is craving for the removal of a state of painful organic want now present in the body. In this case we simultaneously apprehend the present painful want and the pleasant anticipated reaction against it. " The body supplies us with a certain feeling, and the soul desires the opposite condition " (41*c*). And both pleasure and pain admit of " the more and the less." Hence the problem constantly arises how to estimate the painfulness of the present state against the pleasurableness of the desired " opposite condition " (or, again, the pleasureableness of the present state against the painfulness of the " opposite "). In making such estimates we are always liable to errors of perspective ; the anticipated " opposite " is overestimated by contrast. We expect the coming pleasure to be greater than it will really prove to be, by contrast with the present pain, and an expected pain is over-estimated in the same way by contrast with present pleasure (41*e–42c*). There is thus an element of illusion in all such cases, which must be allowed for before our estimate of anticipated pleasure or pain can be admitted as correct.

The illusion is still more marked in other cases. As we said before, disturbance of the organic balance is painful, restoration of the balance is pleasant. But suppose the organism is undergoing neither process. It is true that many of the wise deny that this case actually occurs ; they say that " everything is always flowing either up or down," or, in Leibniz's phrase, that the " pendulum never is at rest." But they must concede at least that we are not always *conscious* of its oscillations. Small oscillations either way are " infinitesimal." It is only considerable oscillations which are attended by pleasure and pain (43*c*). Thus we have to admit the possibility of a life which is neither pleasant nor painful, but just painless. There are persons who actually say that this painless life is the " most pleasant " of all (44*a*). But this statement cannot be strictly true. To feel no pain is manifestly not the same thing as to feel pleasure, though this is the thesis of the real " enemies of Philebus," the downright anti-Hedonists. These anti-Hedonists are eminent scientific persons, who maintain that there really is no such thing as a pleasure and that the experience Philebus and his friends call pleasure is merely " relief from pain " (44*c*).[1] Though we cannot accept this doctrine, which is really due to the scorn of fastidious souls for vulgar pleasures, it will yield us a useful hint towards the discovery of the kind of pleasures which deserve to be called " true " (44*d*). Their thought is this. If we want to

[1] *Phileb.* 44*b* 9, καὶ μάλα δεινοὺς λεγομένους τὰ περὶ φύσιν. The words are enough to prove that neither Antisthenes nor Diogenes is meant. They could not be called δεινοὶ περὶ φύσιν. But the phrase exactly fits the anti-Hedonists of the Academy—Speusippus, Xenocrates, and their followers. The reference is probably rather to their views about forms and numbers, discussed in Aristotle's *Metaphysics*, than to such things as the works of Speusippus on zoological classification. It is meant that they are διαλεκτικοί.

understand any " form " or quality, we do well to study it in its extreme and most marked manifestations. So, if we want to know what pleasure really is, we ought to start by considering the most vehement and violent pleasures. But these—this is given as the reasoning of the anti-Hedonists—are the pleasures connected with the body (45a). Now such pleasures are found in their most exciting degree not in health, but in disease. The delight of refreshing thirst with a cool draught, for example, is much more intense when one is suffering the heat of a raging fever than at another time, because the preceding want (ἔνδεια) or craving is so much more violent. We are not arguing, of course, that pleasures are more *numerous* in disease than in health ; our point is that they are more violent and exciting (45c). And so the life of " sin " (ὕβρις) is marked by violent and exciting pleasures which make a man " beside himself " ; the life of virtue by moderate pleasures, regulated by the rule of " nothing too much " (45d–e). The most exciting and violent pleasures, as well as the most violent pains, are to be found in the diseased or bad body or soul.

Now let us consider one or two examples of these exciting experiences. A man who has an itching spot on his body gets great enjoyment from scratching or chafing it ; but, of course, he is only stimulated to do so by the irritation of the itching. This is typical of a host of experiences which language calls " bitter-sweet." They depend on a tension between antithetic processes ; these processes may be both bodily, or one may be bodily and the other purely mental, or both may be mental. In all cases the violently exciting character of the experience depends on the tension. There must be a highly painful factor in order that the rebound may be intensely pleasant (46b–c). (Thus the difference between this case and that of the " illusions of perspective " already mentioned is that the element of contrast and antithetical tension is now an ingredient in the actual concrete single experience.) The point, then, is that in such a " mixed " experience, there may be an exact balance of pleasurable and painful ingredients, so that, exciting as it is, its " net pleasure value " would be *nil*, or pleasure may predominate, or pain may predominate. But in no case is the " pleasure value " simply measured by the intensity of the excitement, and the " ticklish " person, for example, who gets so excited when he is tickled that he says he is " dying with pleasure," is not really getting anything like the " quantity of pleasure " he supposes. For the intensity of the excitement is due to the simultaneous contrast between the fully stimulated region of the skin and a neighbouring region which is uneasily aching for similar stimulation, 46d–47b). Here is a plain case where a man's own estimate of the pleasure he is getting is erroneous. The cases of tension already mentioned, where the antithesis is between the actual condition of the body and a mentally anticipated " opposite " condition, may, of course, give rise to the same " mixture " of pleasure with pain and the same errors in estimation (47c).

There is still a third case where both factors in the tension belong to the soul. There are a whole range of painfully toned emotions—anger, fear, malice, and others—and we know, and the poets constantly tell us that, though they are painfully toned, to give them full expression may be pleasant. To let yourself go, when you are angry, Homer says, is sweeter than honey ($47d$–e), and it is possible to revel in lamentation. So people in the theatre enjoy a sensational tragedy which sets them crying for the distresses of the hero ($48a$). Our feelings, when we see a comedy, are a still subtler example of a "mixed" state, half painful, half pleasant. This leads Plato to indulge in an acute psychological analysis of the emotion aroused by comedy. We have just spoken of φθόνος (*malice*) as an unpleasantly toned emotion, and yet by malice we mean " being *pleased* by the misfortunes of our neighbour " ($48b$). Now ignorance and folly are certainly misfortunes. But what is it which amuses us in a " comic situation "? A certain kind of badness (πονηρία) in the comic character, namely, want of " self-knowledge." (It is the discrepancy between his real character or situation and his own estimate of them which makes him " comic.") "Ignorance of self " may be : (1) ignorance of one's financial position, as when a man fancies himself richer than he is ; (2) ignorance of one's physical defects, as when a man has an empty conceit of his beauty or strength ; (3) ignorance of the state of one's soul, especially a false conceit of one's own wisdom ($49a$). All these states are bad, but we may make a distinction. They may be accompanied with feebleness or they may not. In the former case a man's vain conceit of self does not lead to any serious harm to anyone, and is merely " funny " ; in the latter it is not funny, but dangerous. It is the " harmless self-conceit " of the hero which we find comic and laugh at ($49a$–c).

Now to explain why the feeling this spectacle rouses in the audience is "mixed." It might seem that it is wrong to enjoy the misfortunes of our friends ; yet we do find self-conceit in persons we like " funny," when, as has just been explained, it is quite harmless. (The connexion with comedy, I take it, is that, if we are to enjoy a comedy, we must feel that we " like " the person who is being exposed, for all his failings. If we could not find him likeable, the comedy would cease to be comic, as *Tartuffe* does, for the simple reason that we detest Tartuffe seriously.) Thus our sense of the " comic " is a kind of *malice* (φθόνος), and this is, in its nature, a painful emotion ; yet our laughter shows that we are enjoying the experience, which must therefore be a " mixed " one ($49e$–$50a$). (The observation appears true and subtle ; when, for example, we see Malvolio on the stage, there is an element of the painful in our mirth. It is, in a way, humiliating to see another man " make such a fool of himself." If the absurdity were carried a little further, or the exhibition of it a little more prolonged, the painful would distinctly predominate. Even as it is, we can detect its presence by a careful examination of our feelings.) Now this is true also of the "tragedy and comedy" of actual life; the situations of real life are constantly provoking emotional reactions in which the painful and the pleasing are blended, no less than the situations in a stage-play. We may take it as certain then that the fusing of the pleasant and the painful in a single experience occurs where the sources of both factors lie in the soul, no less than where the source of one or both is in the body (50b–e).

We may now consider the question what experiences are purely pleasant without any admixture of painfulness. On our general theory of the connexion of feeling-tone with organic process, we can see at once that in any case where a "subliminal" or unconscious process of "depletion" is followed by a conscious process of "repletion," there will be an experience which is wholly pleasant. This may explain the case of the pure aesthetic pleasure we get from the contemplation of pattern (σχήματα), colour (χρώματα), tone (φθόγγοι), and the great majority of odours (51a–b).[1] These pleasures are not preceded by a painful sense of craving, like those of the satisfaction of hunger or thirst, and do not owe any part of their apparent intensity to contrast; they are "pure," in the sense of being pleasant through and through, without any admixture of painfulness. We may suppose that they correspond to processes of organic repletion after depletion, but that the depletion has been insensible.[2] We must note, however, that we are not referring here to pleasure got by seeing "patterns" which are likenesses of animals or the like, where the pleasure arises from our perception of the resemblance of the copy to the original, but strictly to the pleasure we take in geometrical form as such, and the same remark applies to the pleasantness of colours and sounds, and still more to odours (51c–e).[3]

Again the "intellectual pleasure" which we get from the "sciences" (μαθήματα) is of this "unmixed" kind. There is no felt pain antecedent to it; merely not to possess geometrical knowledge, for example, is not painful as hunger is painful; and again, the process of forgetting something we have learned is not attended by pain. Of course it may be disagreeable to find that we have forgotten something which it would now be advantageous to know, but the process of forgetting itself is not painful, as the process of growing hungry again, after we have eaten, is (52a–b).

---

[1] He says "most" odours, of course, to exclude the case of those, e.g., of articles of food, or those which indicate to the male animal the proximity of a female. The pleasantness of these would depend on a previous sense of unsatisfied want.

[2] Timaeus expressly teaches that this is the case (Tim. 64a–65b).

[3] I do not take this to mean that Plato regards the pleasure we get from seeing the "faithfulness" of a picture to its original as aesthetically illegitimate. His purpose is simply to exclude from the list of unmixed pleasures any which depend on a previous sense of want for their existence or their intensity. Thus the degree of pleasure got from contemplating a "nude" clearly may be affected by unsatisfied sexual desire in the beholder; the pleasure with which we hear the sound of a beloved voice will often depend for its intensity on a pre-existing longing to hear that voice again.

By comparison of these now discriminated types of pleasures, we can see that the " mixed " type, which depend on antecedent painful craving, are marked by violence and " want of measure," and exhibit the fluctuations of the " more and less " ; the " unmixed " type, on the other hand, exhibit " restriction by measure," are " moderate in intensity " (52c). But we may make a further distinction between the two types. They differ in " truth " or " genuineness " (ἀλήθεια). Just as a small expanse of white colour, for example, if it is a pure white, with no admixture, is more truly white than a vast expanse which is not equally pure, so even a " small " pleasure which is pleasure through and through, is more truly pleasure, deserves that name better, than a " big " pleasure which is mixed throughout with its opposite, pain (52d–53c). *I.e.* the highly exciting experiences which are commonly reckoned the " greatest pleasures," since their exciting character actually depends on tension and contrast with a painful factor equally indispensable to the effect, are not the " truest to type." It is the " moderate " pleasures, preceded by no painful craving and independent of internal tension, which are pleasant through and through, and thus deserve the name of pleasures most completely. It is in this sense that Plato speaks of this class as " true," of the others as " false " or " deceptive " pleasures. The first are what they are taken to be ; the others are, to a large extent, something different from what men take them to be.

THE METAPHYSICS OF PLEASURE.—*Can it be an End?* (53c–55c).— We may remind ourselves of a second doctrine of the " wits " (κομψοί), which we shall find suggestive. They say that pleasure is always a " process of becoming " (γένεσις) ; that it has *no* stable and determinate *being* (οὐσία, 53c). That is, the theory is that pleasure is an accompaniment of transitions, incompleted developments. It is felt while the development is going on, but falls away when the definite and permanent goal of the " evolution " is reached. We must not be misled into identifying the " wits " of this passage with the third-century Cyrenaics who called pleasure a " gentle motion," nor have we any right to ascribe their doctrine by anticipation to the elder Aristippus. We meet it again in Aristotle's *Ethics*, where one of the string of arguments against the goodness of pleasure, all taken from recognizable passages in Plato, is said (1152b 13) to be that " every pleasure is a sensible transition (or development) into a natural condition " (γένεσις εἰς φύσιν αἰσθητή), an obvious allusion to the section of the *Philebus* we are now considering. We may take this as an indication that the κομψοί to whom the doctrine is due are the anti-Hedonist party in the Academy, a view which, as we shall see, is borne out by the language of Aristotle in dismissing their doctrine. The thought arises by a natural, though illegitimate, extension of the depletion-repletion formula to cover all cases of pleasures. On this theory, the good, healthy, or normal state is, of course, that of balance or equilibrium ; pain and pleasure are both felt only when there is a departure from this ideal condition—pain while the process of depletion is going on, pleasure while that of repletion, restoration of the balance, is happening. The natural end or goal of this " repletion " is the establishment of an equilibrium, and the best that could befall a man is that the equilibrium, once restored, should be permanent. But, on this theory, pleasure is only felt during the " filling-up " by which we approach this best condition. When we have reached it and are steadily persisting in it, there is no longer any process of " filling-up," and consequently no pleasure. Pleasure attends our progress to the " good," but not our fruition of it; that will be the " neutral condition," painless but not pleasurable. This is what is meant by the view that pleasure is always " becoming," never is " being."

We can now express this thought in a general formula. The end or goal is always of more worth and dignity than the means or road to it. The means is " for the sake of " the end, not the end for the sake of the means. And a process which culminates in the establishment of a permanent condition is to that condition as means to end. Thus the processes of shipbuilding and all the appliances and raw material they employ are " for the sake of " what comes out of them, the vessel. (E.g. the naval architect's skill, his implements, the timbers of which he makes the vessel, all of them only have worth because the vessel itself has worth—in this case, an " economic " worth (54c).[1]) If pleasure is a " becoming," then it must be relative to an end in which it culminates, must be the coming-to-be of *something*. That something will be in the μοῖρα or category of the *good*, *i.e.* will have " intrinsic value." But the end and the process by which it is reached are never in the same category, and therefore, on the hypothesis, pleasure will not be a good. The " wits " from whom we have borrowed this suggestion will therefore think it ridiculous to say that life is not worth having without pleasure. This would amount to saying that life is worth having when it is an alternation of aspiring after a good we have not yet attained and losing one we have attained, but not when it is the fruition of present good (54c–55a).

We note that Socrates is not made to accept the doctrine that pleasure is only felt in the *transition* from an " unnatural " to the " normal state " as his own. He clearly does not accept it without reserve (as Spinoza does in his definitions of *laetitia* and *tristitia*, *Ethics*, iii. Appendix, def. 2, 3). He cannot do so because he holds, as we shall see, that some pleasures, the " pure " or " unmixed " class, are themselves good, whereas the theory under criticism, as he is careful to point out, compels us to hold that *no* pleasure is good, since no pleasure, according to it, can be an end. The criticism of Aristotle on the theory is based on the same conviction of the

---

[1] The φάρμακα of 54c 1 are, of course, the paints employed for coating the sides of the vessel, etc. So the ὕλη mentioned along with the " tools " does not mean " raw material " in general, but the " timber " from which the planks of the ship are made.

goodness of these unmixed pleasures, and is one of the most valuable things in the *Ethics*. As he points out, even the pleasures of " repletion " cannot be proved not to be good, or even *the* good, by this line of reasoning. For what gives rise to the feeling of pleasure which accompanies return to the " normal state " after disturbance, is not the process of return itself, but the successful reassertion of the activities of the organism which were not affected by the disturbance. The " filling-up " only gives rise to the pleasure *accidentally* because it is attended with removal of an inhibition. The thought is that the feeling-tone of normal organic life is itself pleasant. A disturbance of the " balance " partially inhibits function. Recovery from the inhibition is pleasant because it is the successful reassertion of a normal activity which has persisted, though under inhibition, all through the antecedent " depletion." Hence we need to correct the proposed definition of pleasure as " sensible transition to a natural state " into " unimpeded exercise of a natural activity." The pleasure-giving process is not a " coming-to-be " (γένεσις) but the discharge in act (ἐνέργεια) of an already developed function.[1] The insistence on the difference between the two kinds of process, "coming-to-be " and "activity," is a correction of first-rate importance in the Academic terminology. We need not suppose that Aristotle is correcting Plato's views about the worth of pleasures, which, in fact, agree with his own. It is Speusippus and Xenocrates, not Plato, whose anti-Hedonism he is criticizing, though he rightly notes that the want of a word like his own ἐνέργεια makes it easy for the Academic to employ this unconvincing argument against the goodness of pleasures.

We may add the further consideration that it is a paradox to hold that all goods are mental, that pleasant feeling is the only mental good, and, by consequence, that, *e.g.*, beauty and strength, valour, temperance, intelligence, have no inherent value, and that a man's intrinsic worth depends on the question how much pleasure he is feeling (55*b*). This, we see, is a valid argument against the Hedonist, independently of the worth of the contention that all pleasure is a γένεσις.

THE INTELLECTUAL VALUES (55*c*–59*d*).—We have seen that there are two types of pleasures, the "pure " and the "mixed," and we shall expect to find that they have different values for human life. We must now consider intellectual activities and their worth in the same way. As with pleasures, so with forms of knowledge, we have to discover which are " truest to type," most fully deserving to be called knowledge. We may begin by dividing " knowledges " or " sciences " into those which have to do with *making* things, the " industrial " arts (χειροτεχνικαὶ ἐπιστῆμαι), and those which are περὶ παιδείαν καὶ τροφήν, have to do with the cultivation of the soul itself, the " cultural " arts and sciences. (This is, in effect, the Aristotelian distinction between " theory " and " practice.") We may begin by considering the " industrial,"

---

[1] *E.N.* 1153*a* 7–14

manual, or operative arts themselves, and ask whether some of them do not contain more, others less, of genuine knowledge, so that we can introduce again the distinction between " purer " and " more mixed " forms of knowledge. We see at once that if we eliminated from the industrial arts all that they derive from the exact knowledge of number, measure, weight, very little which we can call knowledge would be left. What these arts contain beyond the application of number, weight, and measure is little more than empirical guess-work. We see the presence of this empirical factor in such callings as those of the musician (who has largely to depend on his " ear "), the practising physician, the soldier ; we might fairly say that there is more genuine science in the builder's business than in any of these professions, because he is so much more concerned with the exact processes of measuring, so dependent at every point on his implements of precision, plumb-line, compass, and the rest. So we will divide these crafts into a more exact and scientific class of which building is the type, and a less exact, of which music is typical (55c–56c). (The notion of " exact " science seems to be definitely formulated here for the first time in literature ; the thought is that of Kant, that every branch of knowledge contains just as much science as it contains mathematics.)

Again, if we consider the " exact " sciences themselves, we have to make a similar distinction. There are two "arithmetics ": that of the "many," and the much more scientific arithmetic of the " philosopher." The former operates with " concrete " and very unequal units, such as one man, one army, one ox, and disregards the fact that the men, oxen, armies, counted may be unequal ; the other operates with units which are absolutely and in every way equal—in fact, with *numbers*, not with numbered *things*. So there are two forms of " mensuration " : the loose measurement of the architect or the retail trader, and the accurate measurement of the geometer and calculator.[1] Thus one " knowledge," no less than one pleasure, may be " purer," truer to type, than another. The " exact " forms of knowledge which are concerned with number, measure, weight, are much more exact and " truer " than all others, and the " philosopher's " or " theorist's " arithmetic and geometry are much more exact and true than those of the mechanician or engineer (56d–57e). And we cannot, without blushing, deny that dialectic, whose business it is to study the absolutely real and the eternal, must insist on a still more rigid standard of exactness and truth than any other kind of knowledge. It must be still more intolerant of mere approximation than any other science. Gorgias, to be sure, used to claim the first place among the sciences for rhetoric, on the ground that it can secure

---

[1] The simple man who undertook to settle the value of π by fitting a string round a disc, unrolling it, and measuring it with a measuring-stick was confusing the " tradesman's " mensuration, which is always rough approximation, with the geometer's, which must be accurate within a known and very precise " standard of approximation."

the voluntary services of the professionals of all the rest. We need not quarrel with him about this. Our question is not what " art " has the highest prestige or the greatest utility-value, but simply which sets up the most severe standard of truth and accuracy, and there can be no doubt about the claims of dialectic in this particular. Most of the " arts " are content to build on δόξαι, contested beliefs, and even the cosmologists confine their attention to " actual fact," what " happens "; absolutely *exact* knowledge of actual fact is never to be had ; there is always an element of the incalculable and contingent about it. The knowledge which is through and through knowledge must therefore be " abstract "; that is the price it pays for its exactness. It must be concerned with the non-temporal (57*d*–59*d*).

THE FORMAL STRUCTURE OF THE GOOD LIFE (59*e*–66*d*).—The best life for men, we saw, must be a blend of two constituents— intelligent activity and pleasant feeling. We have now examined each genus of the two apart, and distinguished in each a variety which is truer, and one which is less true, to type. We have now to consider on what principle the two ingredients should be blended. What will be the formula which appears as the πέρας in this " mixture " ? Our task is like that of the man who mixes the ingredients of a sweet drink ; pleasure is the honey for our mixture, intelligent thought the water ; the problem is to mingle them in just the right proportion (61*c*). It would be rash to assume that we shall succeed in doing this by simply blending every form of pleasure with every form of " thought "; we need to proceed more cautiously. It will be prudent to begin by considering first those pleasures and those forms of knowledge which we have found to be most genuine, most true to type (ἀληθέστατα) ; if we find that the blend does not completely satisfy our original condition that the " good " must be " sufficient," *all* a man's life requires, we can then consider admitting the inferior pleasures and arts into the mixture (61*e*). There can be no dispute about stipulating that the good is to include all knowledge of the " truer " type, the exact knowledge of the timeless things ; we shall certainly require for the best life a knowledge of " righteousness itself " and the intelligence to use the knowledge, and the same considerations will apply to all such knowledge of the " absolute." But will this be enough for the purposes of life ? If a man is to live a life among men, he must have some at least of the inferior knowledge which is inexact. A man who knew only the " absolute " and exact lines and circles of the geometer, but knew nothing of the rough approximations to them with which life presents us, would not even know how to find his way home. (As we might say, a chemical balance is a beautiful thing, but it won't do to weigh your butter and cheese in.) So the intervals we make on our musical instruments are only approximations, they are not " true "; but a man must be conversant with them, as well as with the mathematical theory of harmonics, unless he is to go through life with none but the " unheard " melodies for his companions. In fact, we may reasonably let in the whole crowd of second-class knowledges; some of them we really need if we are to live as men among men, and none of them will do us any harm, if we have the superior knowledge too, and so are not in danger of mistaking the rough approximation for something better (62a–d).

Thus we have let all the " water " go into the bowl in which the draught of " happiness " is to be brewed. We must now consider what we are to do with the " honey." Here, again, it will be safer to consider the " unmixed " pleasures first and the " mixed," which, as we have seen, are not wholly true to type, afterwards. It is clear that we shall not be able to let in all this second class without reflection. If there are any of them which are " unavoidable " (ἀναγκαῖαι, sc. such as arise directly from the functions of sound and healthy life themselves), they must, of course, be admitted. But whether we can admit all the rest depends on the question whether all pleasures, like all knowledges, are profitable, or, at worst, harmless (63a). To decide this question we may ask the pleasures themselves whether they would prefer to keep house with all wisdom and knowledge, or by themselves. We may be sure (since we have seen that the best life is the " mixed " one) that the pleasures would reply that it is not good to live alone, and that the best companion with whom to keep house would be " knowledge of all things and in especial of ourselves " (63c).

Now we put the same question to the various knowledges. " Do you need the company of pleasure ? " " In particular, do you need, over and above our class of true pleasures, the company of the intense and violent pleasures ? " Knowledge would say that, so far from desiring these exciting pleasures, she finds them a perpetual hindrance ; they vex the souls in which she has taken up her abode with mad frenzies, and destroy her offspring by producing forgetfulness and neglect. She would claim kinship with Socrates' class of " true " and " unmixed " pleasures ; of the rest—those which are " mixed " satisfactions—she would accept such as accompany health and a sober mind and any form of goodness, but reject those of " folly and badness " in general, as obviously unfit to find a place in such a " blend " as we are contemplating (63d–64a).[1] There is only one further ingredient for which we must stipulate—ἀλήθεια, " truth," " reality," " genuineness." If this is left out, the result of the blending itself will not be real or genuine. (The bearing of this remark is a little obscure, but it is probably meant to lead up to the next stage of the argument, the consideration of the relative importance to be laid on the different constituents of the " mixed life " for man and the assigning of the first place in it to its rational structure, the last, to the " harmless " pleasures.)

We have now tracked down the good, so to say, to its very

---

[1] Thus a place would be found in the " good for man " for all the pleasure which attends the healthy and morally virtuous satisfactions of " bodily appetite." It is not expected that the best man shall not enjoy his dinner when he is hungry. But dinners are not things he cares supremely about.

doors. It only remains to discriminate the relative values of its various ingredients and so to answer the question we have been considering so long, whether intelligence or pleasure is more akin to the principle or cause which makes the good life so satisfactory to us all (64c). We may say at once that what makes any mixture or blend a good one is *measure* and *proportion* (μέτρον, ἡ τοῦ συμμέτρου φύσις). Neglect of the rule of due proportion makes a "mixture" unstable and vitiates the components. Where the rule is neglected, you get not a genuine "mixture" but a mere "mess." The good is thus a form of the beautiful (καλόν), for measure and proportion are the secret of all beauty (64c–e). We may thus take measure or proportion (συμμετρία), beauty, and truth (or reality, ἀλήθεια) as three "forms" (ἰδέαι) or "notes" found in the good and say that the goodness of our "mixture" is due to the presence of this trinity in unity (65c). Our business is now to confront first intelligence and then pleasure successively with these three distinguishable but inseparable notes of the good. Let us begin with the note of ἀλήθεια (truth, genuineness). Pleasure is the "hollowest" (ἀλαζονίστατον) of all things, *i.e.* it promises to be so much more satisfactory than it proves to be ; the illusoriness of the "pleasures of sex" is a notorious case in point. Intelligence (νοῦς) is either the same thing as ἀλήθεια, or, at any rate, it is the most "genuine" thing in the world (the least illusory, 65c–d). Next, as to the note of "measure" : pleasure notoriously tends to wild excess; there is nothing more "measured" than intelligence and science (65d). And finally, as to beauty. There is no uncomeliness (οὐδὲν αἰσχρόν) in wisdom and intelligence, but the intensest pleasures are so unseemly that we think the spectacle of a man who is indulging in them is either ridiculous or disgraceful. We are actually ashamed to see such a sight, and think that it ought to be covered by darkness (66a).

We may now draw our conclusion. Pleasure is neither the best nor the second-best thing. We must give the first place to "measure, the measured, that which is 'in place'" (τὸ καίριον) ;[1] the second to proportion, beauty, completeness (τὸ σύμμετρον καὶ καλὸν καὶ τὸ τέλεον καὶ ἱκανόν) ; the third to intelligence and wisdom (νοῦς καὶ φρόνησις) ; the fourth to "sciences and arts and true convictions" (ἐπιστῆμαι καὶ τέχναι καὶ δόξαι ὀρθαί) ; the fifth to the class of pleasures, whether involving actual sensation or not, which have no pain mixed with them (the "pure" pleasures of the discussion) : we stop short, like Orpheus, with the sixth "generation" (66a–d).[2]

---

[1] The concluding words of 66a 8 are the worst textual crux in Plato. The mischief is in the αἴδιον. Burnet's suggestion τὴν ἃ (=πρώτην) ἰδέαν is highly attractive, or conceivably we might read αἰτίαν, rendering, "you may say that . . . the cause has been hunted down in the region of μέτρον, M. Diès holds that W supports a variant ὁπόσα τοιαῦτα, χρὴ νομίζειν τινὰ ἥδιον ᾑρῆσθαι. But is ἥδιον quite in place *here* ?

[2] This might mean that the moderate satisfactions of appetite, which we expect to find in the sixth place, are excluded from the "good" (on the

(For the precise meaning of this enumeration I would refer the reader to Appendix B in Mr. R. G. Bury's edition of the dialogue. I understand the passage in a way which is, I suppose, much the same as Mr. Bury's. Measure, proportion, rational structure are mentioned first because they have a cosmic significance ; they are found in the " great world " without, no less than in the lesser world of man's soul, and they are the " notes " of good, wherever found. Then ἐπιστῆμαι and " pure " pleasures are mentioned, in that order, because they are the two aspects in which rational structure and law show themselves in *human* mental life, and ἐπιστῆμαι are put first, because we have just seen that intelligence is " more akin to " rational structure, reveals it more manifestly and clearly than feeling. There is no question of introducing into the good for man any *constituents* beyond the two which have been contemplated all along, intellectual activity and grateful feeling.)

FORMAL EPILOGUE TO THE DISCUSSION (66*d*–67*b*).—Philebus had originally said that the good for us is the plenitude of pleasure (ἡδονὴ πᾶσα καὶ παντελής), Socrates that " intelligence " (νοῦς) is at any rate (γε) a far better thing for man's life than pleasure. We long ago convinced ourselves that neither can be the whole of human good, since neither would be " all-satisfying," apart from the other. But our investigation has shown us that " intelligence " is at any rate infinitely (μυρίῳ) more closely related to the " victor " (the " mixed life " which proved to be the best of all for a man) than pleasure. (The point is that though the best life includes both elements, it is the element of rationality which gives it its specific character. A man is not a creature who uses an intellect to contrive ingenious devices for getting pleasures, but a creature who finds it pleasant to practise intellectual activities. Hume's view that in action reason " is and ought to be the slave of the passions " just inverts the true relation. *Human* " passions " should be the servants of intelligence.) Pleasure is not the good, even though all the horses and oxen of the world should say it is, with the assent of the " many " who think the " lusts of beasts " better evidence than the discourses of philosophers (67*b*).

The last sentence obviously alludes, in its reference to the θηρίων ἔρωτας, to the argument of Eudoxus, afterwards adopted by Epicurus, that pleasure must be " the good " because it is that which " all living creatures " pursue when left to themselves (*E.N.* x. 1172*b* 9 ff.). The supposed unmannerly reference to Aristippus in the remark about the " horses " (ἵπποι) is a mere unhistorical fancy. Even if Aristippus had ·been aimed at in the criticism of Hedonism, such an allusion would be impossible, for the simple reason that the leading anti-Hedonist of the Academy, Speusippus,

ground that they are not actually good but merely harmless). As they were admitted at 63*e*, however, the meaning may be that the " sixth degree " is actually counted in as the lowest and last. This makes the allusion to " Orpheus " (Fr. 14, Kern) more apt. The theogonic poet quoted must have described his " sixth generation " of deities as well as the preceding five.

whose views we have found Plato expressly reproducing in two places, had a " horse " in his name too.

See further :

BURNET.—*Greek Philosophy, Part I.*, 324–332.
RITTER, C.—*Platon*, ii. 165–258, 497–554 ; *Platons Dialoge*, 68–97 ; *Neue Untersuchungen ueber Platon*, 95–173.
RAEDER, H.—*Platons philosophische Entwickelung*, 357–374.
NATORP, P.—*Platons Ideenlehre*, 296–331.
NETTLESHIP, R. L.—*Plato's Conception of Goodness and the Good.* (Works, i. 307–336.)
BAEUMKER, C.—*Das Problem der Materie in der griechischen Philosophie*, 193–196. (1890.)
POSTE, E.—*The " Philebus " of Plato.* (Oxford, 1860.)
BURY, R. G.—*The " Philebus " of Plato.* (Cambridge, 1897.)
DIÈS, A.—*Autour de Platon*, ii., 385–399.
STEWART, J. A.—*Plato's Doctrine of Ideas*, 92–100.
ROBIN, L.—*Platon*, c. iv.

CHAPTER XVII

TIMAEUS AND CRITIAS

THE *Timaeus* stands alone among the Platonic dialogues in being devoted to cosmology and natural science. Owing to the fact that the first two-thirds of it were continuously preserved through the " dark ages " in the Latin version and with the commentary of Chalcidius, it was the one Greek philosophical work of the best age with which the west of Europe was well acquainted before the recovery of Aristotle's metaphysical and physical writings in the thirteenth century ; it thus furnished the earlier Middle Ages with their standing general scheme of the natural world. In the present volume it is impossible to deal with the contents of the dialogue in any detail ; I have tried to perform the task in my *Commentary on Plato's Timaeus* (Oxford, 1928), with which the later commentary of Professor Cornford (*Plato's Cosmology*, London, 1937) should be compared.

The date of composition cannot be precisely determined. There is no external evidence, and the internal evidence of style only serves to show that the dialogue belongs to the last period of Plato's authorship ; thus we must place the composition at some time after the *Sophistes*, *i.e.* within the years 360–347. It is quite uncertain, so far as I can see, whether we should regard the *Timaeus* or the *Philebus* as the later work. As to the date of the imagined conversation I think it is possible to be more precise. We have to consider (*a*) the internal evidence of the *Timaeus* itself, (*b*) the evidence supplied by the *Republic*. (*a*) The interlocutors in the dialogue are Socrates, Timaeus, Critias, and Hermocrates. Of Timaeus nothing is known except what we learn from Plato, that he is a Locrian from South Italy, with a career of eminence in both science and politics behind him (*20a*). From the fact that the doctrine he is made to expound is recognizably a version of Pythagoreanism in which the biology and medicine of Empedocles is grafted on the original Pythagorean mathematics, we can really have no doubt that he is meant to be a Pythagorean of the same type as the more famous Philolaus. This suggests that he is at least as old a man as Socrates, and that we may perhaps connect what we are told of the magistracies he has filled with the facts about Pythagorean political ascendancy in Magna Graecia in the first half of the fifth century.[1] Hermocrates is plainly the famous

[1] I cannot agree with those who dispute Plato's intention to represent Timaeus as a Pythagorean. Everything in his doctrine can be traced back

Syracusan best known by the prominent part he played in the defence of Syracuse against the Athenian Armada of 415. Socrates implies (20a) that Hermocrates is still a man with his career before him, and bases his estimate of him on the general report. This shows that Hermocrates is a stranger at Athens and indicates that the conversation is presumably to be dated not too long after the " pan-Sicilian Congress " at Gela in 425, where Hermocrates seems to have first made his reputation (Thuc. iv. 58).[1] Critias is certainly not, as all writers before Professor Burnet have assumed, Critias the so-called " oligarch " who figured in the usurping government of 404–3. He has already distinguished himself in science and politics (20a), and he refers pointedly to his own extreme old age and the way in which he remembers the distant events of his childhood, though he can hardly recollect what he has been told yesterday (26b). He also says that his great-grandfather was a friend and connexion of Solon (20e), and that he himself, as a boy of ten years old, used to sing the verses of Solon, which were then a " novelty " (21b). All this shows that the Critias meant is the grandfather of the " oligarch," Plato's own great-grandfather. Even so we have to suppose him, at the date of the dialogue, to be extremely old. (b) The *Timaeus* unmistakably announces itself as in a way a continuation of the *Republic*. Socrates opens the dialogue by recalling the main heads of what he had said " yesterday " to the present company (17a–19a), and the recapitulation coincides exactly with the contents of *Republic* i.–v. Thus we seem directed to date the discourse of Timaeus two days after the conversation in the house of Polemarchus.[2] If we were right in our view of the dramatic date of the *Republic*, this brings us to the time of the peace of Nicias or very shortly before it, the year 422 or 421. Such a date fits all the indications of the *Timaeus* itself. It enables

to Pythagorean sources except the use of the four Empedoclean " roots " and the equally Empedoclean sense-physiology and medicine, a point which I have tried to establish in detail elsewhere. For the evidence that Philolaus similarly combined Pythagorean mathematics with Empedoclean biology, see Burnet, *E.G.Ph.*[3] 278–279, *Greek Philosophy, Part I.*, 88–89. I have tried to add something to the evidence elsewhere. The name is not given as that of a Locrian by Iamblichus in his catalogue, but he mentions a Timaeus among the Crotoniates, and again (unless it is the same man) among the Parians, who precede the Locrians immediately in his list. This looks as though the name had been displaced by a copyist. Plato's avoidance of the name of Pythagoras is a standing habit ; it, no doubt, has to do with the disrepute into which the word was brought by the more superstitious members of the order.

[1] It is impossible to imagine the meeting as taking place *after* the dispatch of the Athenian fleet to Syracuse. As we know from Xenophon and Diodorus, Hermocrates was serving against Athens in the East from 413 until his descent on Sicily in 409 or 408. We cannot suppose that he would be likely to choose Athens as a place to visit in this interval, or that he could meet Socrates there on friendly terms, still less that Socrates would contrast him, at that date, as a man with a career to make, with Timaeus and Critias as men whose distinction has been already achieved.

[2] It is, however, suggested that the present discourse is held during the Panathenaea, which do not fall even within two months of the day mentioned in the *Republic* (the feast of Bendis). This secures us against connecting the two dialogues too closely.

us to understand that the boyhood of old Critias would fall immediately after the expulsion of the Pisistratidae from Athens, and we can guess why the poems of Solon would be likely to be popular and " novel " at that date.   (Pisistratus and his sons are not likely to have encouraged the singing of them.)   It also gives us a reason for the presence of a distinguished public man from Locri and another from Syracuse.   Only a year or two before the peace the Athenians had sent envoys on a tour of the South Italian cities, including Locri, for the express purpose of forming a league to keep the power of Syracuse in check.   A general pacification would, of course, leave a good deal to be " redd up " in the western Mediterranean. We may be sure that Timaeus did not come to Athens expressly to talk to Socrates about the creation of the world.   We see also why Hermocrates is known to Socrates only by reports of his abilities and education.   And it is significant that, if we are right, the date at which Socrates is represented as listening with keen interest to a cosmological lecture is only a year or two after the burlesque of him in the *Clouds*.   This is a much more appropriate dramatic date than one later in his life.   Hence I feel little doubt that it is right.

The dialogue falls into three distinct parts: (*a*) introductory recapitulation of the contents of *Republic* i.–v. by Socrates (17*a*–19*b*), with expression of a strong desire to see the doctrine there laid down embodied in a dramatic story of concrete achievements (19*b*–20*c*) ; (*b*) relation by Critias of the alleged heroic exploit of Athens in resisting and defeating the kings of Atlantis (20*c*–26*d*) ; (*c*) the cosmological discourse of Timaeus, which extends unbroken, but for an occasional word of assent from Socrates, to the end of the dialogue (27*c*–92*c*).   We may consider these divisions in their order.

(*a*) *Introduction* (17*a*–20*c*).—There is not much on which we need make any comment.   It is useless to speculate on the identity of the unnamed person who has been kept away from the conversation by indisposition and whom Timaeus agrees to replace as speaker. As Timaeus takes his place, we are no doubt to understand that he belongs to the same group of " Italian " philosophers.   Philolaus, as Burnet suggests, would suit the part, or we might perhaps even think of Empedocles.   Plato is merely intending a graceful expression of the debt of his dialogue to fifth-century " Italians." The most striking feature of the recapitulation of the *Republic* is that it covers only the ground of Books I.–V.   Nothing is said of the philosopher-kings and their education in mathematics and dialectic, of the Form of Good, or of the contents of *Republic* viii.–x. I suggest that the most likely explanation of this silence is that which is also the simplest.   Just so much of the *Republic*, and no more, is recalled as will be an appropriate basis for the story of the Athenian victory over Atlantis.   Plato is quite alive to the fact that the philosopher-king is an " ideal " which has never been realized, and therefore abstains from an attempt to exhibit a society of philosopher-kings in action. It is more credible that there should be an actual society at the level of that described in *Republic* i.–v., and he feels himself equal to the vivid imaginative delineation of its performances.

The remarks with which Socrates closes his recapitulation are interesting as showing that Plato fully understood that his own hero had his definite limitations. Socrates, as he says, can give us a picture of the really healthy society, but he cannot " make the figures move." He cannot tell an actual story of the behaviour of such a society in a life-like way, and the reason is that he has not enough personal experience of the work of the active statesman. He remains, after all, something of the theorist and *doctrinaire* (19*b*–*e*). This was, in fact, true of Socrates, and it helps to explain the fact that his influence on many of his associates was not wholly beneficial. Association with him in early life was not an unmixed good for the average lad ; so far, there was just a slight basis of foundation for the distrust with which practical workers of the democratic constitution, like Anytus, regarded him.

(*b*) *The Story of Atlantis* (20*c*–25*d*).—The story told by Critias is to the effect that nine thousand years before the time of Solon Athens had enjoyed just such institutions as those described in *Republic* i.–v. Her soil was then wonderfully rich and fertile, as it had not suffered from the denudation which has since reduced the district of Attica to a rocky skeleton. The prehistoric Athenians, strong only in public spirit and sound *moral*, encountered and defeated the federated kings of Atlantis, an island lying in the Atlantic outside the Straits of Gibraltar, who had already successfully overrun all Europe as far as Italy, and all Africa as far as the Egyptian border. Afterwards both the prehistoric Athenian victors and the island Atlantis were overwhelmed in a single day and night of earthquake and inundation. The story only survived in the records of Egypt, where Solon heard it when on his travels.

It should be clear that this whole tale is Plato's own invention. He could not tell us so much more plainly than he does in the *Critias* (113*b*), when he makes Critias appeal to the testimony of " family papers " as his sole evidence for the narrative. Not only the existence of the island-kingdom, but the statement that Solon had ever contemplated a poem on the subject is represented as a " family tradition " ; in other words, nothing was ever really known of any such intention. It is not hard to see what the materials for the tale are. The alleged shallowness of the sea just outside the " pillars of Heracles," and perhaps tales of Carthaginian sailors about islands in the Atlantic, are the foundation for the story of the lost island ; the account of its destruction is manifestly based on the facts of the great earthquake and tidal wave of the year 373 which ravaged the Achaean coast. The main conception of the successful conflict of a small and patriotic nation in arms against an invader with vast material resources and immense superiority in the art of military engineering—a point on which the *Critias* lays great stress—is clearly suggested by the actual facts of the Athenian resistance to Darius and Xerxes. Plato has projected the events of the Persian wars backwards, magnified their scale, and thus made the moral, that numbers, wealth, and engineering skill are no match for the national spirit of a free people, the more obvious to the dull. Strictly speaking, the whole narrative has no logical connexion with the special theme of the *Timaeus*. Its real function is to serve as a prelude to the *Critias*, where the narrative now briefly summarized was to be told with full detail. As Critias puts it, at the end of his story ($27a–b$), the division of labour between speakers is to be that Timaeus shall now describe the formation of the world and of man, as its closing " work," Socrates is then to be understood to have explained how man is educated, and it is left for Critias to describe the heroic achievements of the men whose production has been dealt with by Timaeus and their education discussed by Socrates. Thus the *logical* order of the three dialogues would have been *Timaeus, Republic, Critias.* The express allusion in this passage to the contribution of Socrates seems to show that this definitely means the *Republic*, the only Platonic work where Socrates expressly discusses the question of educational method. From the absence of any reference to a discourse of Hermocrates, and the difficulty of seeing what has been left for him to discourse upon, I should infer that it was never Plato's intention to carry the scheme beyond the *Critias*. Hermocrates, the youngest member of the group, was probably to be a listener, not a speaker.

(*c*) *The Discourse of Timaeus* ($27c–92c$).—The lecture which Timaeus now delivers covers the whole ground of natural knowledge from astronomy to pathology and psychophysics. It will be impossible to deal with more than its most outstanding features. It starts with two fundamental positions : (*a*) that the sensible world, being sensible, " becomes," or, as we might say, is a world of " happenings " or " events " ; (*b*) that whatever " becomes " has a cause, by which Timaeus means that it is the product of an *agent* ($28a–c$). The " artisan " or " craftsman " ($\delta\eta\mu\iota\upsilon\rho\gamma\delta s$) who makes the world thus comes into the story, and it is assumed that this maker is God. Now a craftsman always works with a model or archetype before him, and so we must ask whether the model on which the world has been made is itself something that has " become " or something eternal. Since the maker is the best of all causes and the thing he makes the best of all effects, clearly the model of which the sensible world is a " copy " or " likeness " ($\epsilon\iota\kappa\omega\nu$) is eternal ($29a$). (In more modern language, it is meant that the natural world is not constituted by " events " only, but by events and the objects (in Professor Whitehead's sense) situated in the events, and this is why it is intelligible and can be known.) This leads us to lay down an important canon of the degree of truth to be expected in natural science. Discourse about the fixed and unchanging archetype, or model, can be exact and final ; it has the definiteness of its object : discourse about its sensible copy, which is continually varying and changing, can only be approximate. Hence in natural science, we have no right to demand more than " likely stories," *i.e.* in metaphysics and mathematics there can be finality ; in the natural sciences we have to be content with approximate and tentative results, though our business is to make our approximations as accurate as we can (29*b–d*). In other words, physical science is progressive in a sense in which metaphysics and mathematics are not. (Newton's gravitation formula may be a "first approximation" on which later physicists can improve ; such a formula as $\cos\theta = \frac{1}{2}(e^{\theta i} + e^{-\theta i})$ is no "first approximation" and there is no improving on it.) This principle, that a proposition of physics is always "approximate," and that none is therefore beyond the possibility of correction, is one so important that Timaeus is careful to call repeated attention to it in connexion with the special scientific hypotheses he propounds to explain special groups of facts. A simple modern illustration would be the consideration that all actual measurements of physical magnitudes are approximate, and that no determination of such a magnitude by experimental methods can be trusted, unless it is accompanied by a statement of the "probable error." When we are told that all our natural knowledge is only a "likely story," it is not meant that we may substitute fairy tales for science ; what is meant is that while we must make our results as precise as we can, we must remember that they are all liable to improvement. Our best measurements may be superseded ; our most satisfactory explanatory hypotheses may always have to be modified in the light of overlooked or freshly discovered facts. What Timaeus is really trying to formulate is no fairy tale, but, as we shall see, a geometrical science of nature.

Next we may ask ourselves *why* the Maker produced a world at all. He was perfectly good, and for that very reason did not want to keep his goodness to himself, but to make something like himself. So he took over the whole of the "visible," which was in a condition of chaotic disorder, and made it into an ordered system, since order is *better* than chaos. For the same reason, he put *mind* (νοῦς) into it, and, as mind can only exist in a soul (ψυχή), he gave it a soul, and thus the sensible world became "by the providence of God, a living being with soul and mind" (30*b*). The model in the likeness of which he made it was, of course, a νοητόν or "intelligible," something complete and whole (τέλεον), and something living. The sensible world, then, is the sensible embodiment of a living creature or organism (ζῷον) of which all other living creatures are parts. And there is only one "world" of sense (as against the Milesian tradition of the "innumerable" worlds). For the model is one, and a *perfect* copy of it will reproduce its uniqueness (30*c–31b*).

Thus, in the scheme of Timaeus, we see that the "efficient cause" of the world is thought of definitely as a "personal" God, and this "creator" or "maker" is, strictly speaking, the only God, in our sense of the word, the dialogue recognizes. Later on we shall find the *name* θεός given both to the world itself as a whole and to certain parts or denizens of it, but this must not mislead us. These θεοί are all " created " ; their *raison d'être* is the will of the δημιουργός (29*e*, 41*b*), who is thus distinguished from them as God is from " creatures " in Christian theology. The *formal* cause of the world, however, is not God but the " intelligible living creature," the αὐτὸ ὃ ἔστι ζῷον, which God contemplates as the model for his work. The language used about this model shows that we are to think of it as a form, the " form " of an organism of which all other organisms are parts. It thus has the peculiarity that there is only *one* unique " sensible " which " partakes " of it.

It may naturally be asked how much of this can be conceived to be serious Platonic teaching and how much is mere imaginative symbolism ? No one, of course, could answer the question precisely ; possibly Plato himself could not have made a hard-and-fast distinction between philosophical content and mythical form. But one or two points are important. It would stultify the whole story to follow the example of some interpreters, who wish to find something like the philosophy of Spinoza in Plato, by making the " artisan " a mythical symbol of his " model," the νοητὸν ζῷον. This may or may not be good philosophy and theology, but it is not the thought of Plato, as we shall see more clearly when we come to deal with the doctrine of God in the *Laws*. God and the forms have to be kept distinct in Plato for the reason that the activity of God as producing a world " like " the forms is the one explanation Plato ever offers of the way in which the " participation " of things in forms is effected. If " God " simply meant the same thing as the forms, or as a supreme form, it would remain a mystery why there should be anything but the forms, why there should be any " becoming " at all. How far the explanation that God " makes " a world on the model of the forms was taken by Plato to be a literal statement of truth is a question that may be left to anyone who is bold enough to pronounce exactly how literally Leibniz intended his similar language about God's " choice of the best " as the reason why the actual world is actual. The one thing which is clear from the *Laws* is that God, in Plato, is a " soul," not a form.

A more legitimate question is whether God in the *Timaeus* is quite all we mean by a " creator." Are we to take seriously the representation, which runs through the dialogue, of God's action as the imposing of order on a pre-existing chaos ? Does Plato mean that the world was formed out of pre-existing materials ? On this point we find a discrepancy of interpretation springing up in the first generation of the Academy itself. Aristotle, as is well known, insists on finding in the *Timaeus* the doctrine that the world is γεννητός (" had a beginning "), and is severely critical of this error, as he regards it. On the other hand, the Platonists for the most part — the Neoplatonists unanimously — adopt the view, originally propounded by Xenocrates, that the representation of the world as having a beginning is adopted simply " for convenience of exposition " (διδασκαλίας χάριν), as a geometer talks of "drawing" a line, when all that he does is to point out that the existence of the line is *already* implied by our initial postulates.[1] Thus, on their view, the account of the world, or rather its constituents, as they were before God began his work, is merely a picture of the sort of thing you would have left on your hands if you tried to do what you never can do successfully, to think away all traces of the order and structure in which God's authorship of things reveals itself. The only two Platonists who are known to have taken Aristotle's view on this question are Plutarch and Atticus, a writer of the Antonine age. It is significant that their attempt to take the words of Timaeus literally gets them into very grave difficulties. Since the undoubted Platonic doctrine, expounded most fully in the *Laws*, is that " soul " is the cause of all movements, Plutarch finds himself bound to discover in the *Laws* the doctrine that there is an " evil " world-soul, which he supposes to have animated the original chaos. Though this discovery has been followed in modern times by such scholars as Zeller, it is certainly a mere "mare's nest." The words of the *Laws* say no more than that, since there is disorder in the world as well as order, there must be some soul or souls other than God to cause the disorder.[2] And we may be sure that Aristotle would never have been silent about a doctrine which would be, to him, sheer blasphemy, if he had known of it as a Platonic theory.

If we look at the text of the *Timaeus*, we shall see that at any rate Plato does not mean to say that there ever was a *time* before God constructed the world, since he tells us, as Aristotle allows,[3] that time and the world "began" together, God, in fact, making both of them. Thus the language which seems to imply a primitive state of pure chaos cannot be meant seriously, and so far Xenocrates seems to be right in his interpretation. (This would leave it a logical possibility that the series of events had a first member, and that the interval between the first member and the event which is my writing of these words, is a finite number of years, but I do not think any scholar acquainted with Greek thought is likely to suppose Plato to be contemplating this alternative.) Again, as will be clearer from what we shall have to say later on about the use of the notion of "necessity," it seems plain that the

---

[1] For Aristotle's interpretation, see *Physics*, 251b 17, *de Caelo*, 280a 30, *Metaph.* 1072a 1. Since he comments on the fact that the dialogue makes time and the world begin together, he is presumably alive to the point that Timaeus does not ascribe a beginning to nature in the usual sense of that phrase. For the explanation of Xenocrates, see Plutarch, *de Animae Procreatione in Timaeo*, 1013a–b, where it is admitted that on this point the Academy in general followed Xenocrates.

[2] *Laws*, x. 896e, where all that is said is that, since there is disorder and " dysteleology " in the world, the perfectly good soul cannot be the only soul there is ; there must be *one or more* faulty souls. Neither Plutarch nor Zeller had any right to manufacture an " evil world-soul " out of this straightforward rejection of Pantheism.

[3] *Physics*, 251b 17, *Metaph.* 1072a 1.

Timaeus knows of no external limitation imposed on God's will by conditions independent of God himself. The " maker's " goodness is the whole and complete explanation of the very existence of the natural world. This should justify us in saying that the " Demiurge " really is thought of as a Creator in the full sense of the word. Probably Xenocrates may also have been right in taking the dialogue to imply the " eternity of the world " in the sense in which that phrase is commonly, but inaccurately, used, that the order of events never had a first member. It still remains true that, in Plato's own more accurate terminology, the world is a γεγονός, "something that has become," not ἀΐδιον, eternal. Even if there never was a first event, everything sensible has " emerged " as the result of a process ; in the Platonic conception the world is always " in evolution," even if the evolution never began and will never come to an end. This is why the world, unlike God, has a *history*. It is always getting itself made ; there is never a point at which it is full-made.

The story of the making we cannot here follow far into its details. Since natural things can be seen and grasped, fire (light) and earth must be among their constituents. To combine two such terms in a stable way, there must be a " mean " between them. But fire and earth are volumes and have three dimensions. Hence you cannot insert a single mean proportional between them, but need two.[1] This need is met by air and water. Fire is to air what air is to water and water to earth. This playful application of the doctrine of the geometrical mean effects a transition from Pythagorean mathematics to the four " roots " of Empedocles. We shall see shortly that for Timaeus they are not " elements " (31*b*–32*c*). God used up the whole of these materials in making the world. It excretes nothing and assimilates nothing, and this secures it against age or disease. Its form was appropriately made spherical, since the sphere has the greatest volume of all bodies with the same perimeter, and is therefore the right figure for that which is to contain everything. It was given no sense-organs, since there is nothing outside itself to be apprehended, no digestive organs, as there is nothing it can take in as food, and no organs of loco-motion, for it has nowhere to travel. It needed no hands, for there is nothing for it to grasp or repel. Being alive, however, it moves with the most uniform of all motions, uniform rotation on its own axis. Finally, we must add that it was animated all through with a ψυχή, and this was the generation of a " blessed god " (32*c*–34*b*).

We have begun, however, at the wrong end. We should have described first the fashioning of the world's soul, since soul takes precedence of body in order of " production " as well as of worth

---

[1] The allusion is to the famous problem of the " duplication of the cube," connected by later anecdote with Plato's own name. The meaning of Timaeus is clearly that no one rational " mean " can be inserted between two integers, when each is the product of three *prime* factors and no more.

(since, on Plato's view, soul initiates all movements). The world's soul has three constituents : (*a*) a *Being* which is intermediate between that which is *always* " self-same " and that which " becomes and is divisible " in bodies ; (*b*) a similarly " intermediate " kind of *Sameness*, and (*c*) of *Otherness*. God thus makes the soul as a *tertium quid* between the eternal and the temporal.[1] Next he " divided " the result in accord with the intervals of a musical scale which Timaeus describes.[2] (Apparently we are to imagine a long ribbon with intervals marked on it at distances corresponding to the numbers indicated by the directions for making the notes of the scale.) Next, the ribbon was split longitudinally into two halves, which were laid cross-wise, thus +. Then each ribbon was bent into a circle so as to give two circles, in planes at right angles to one another, with double contact, like the equator and a meridian on a sphere. The outermost of these circles was called that of the Same, the innermost that of the Other. The circle of the Same was made to revolve " to the right," that of the " Other " was subdivided into seven concentric circles at unequal distances from one another, which were made to revolve with unequal velocities " to the left " (34*c*–36*d*). We learn a little later that the inclination of the two circles was made oblique (39*a*), so that they turn out in the end to stand for the sidereal equator and the ecliptic, their revolutions being the (apparent) diurnal revolution of the " starry heavens " and the orbits of the sun and the planets in the Zodiac respectively. It must be carefully noted that nothing is said of " spheres," and, again, that as usual in the classical period, the *orbit* of a heavenly body is thought of as itself revolving, like a cart-wheel, and carrying round the body which is set in it. We have heard now of the orbits of the whole and of the seven planets, but so far nothing has been said about any *bodies* which, as we should say, " revolve in " these orbits. We are now at last (36*e*) told that the creator finally constructed the body of the world " within " its soul and adapted the two ; this begins the " unceasing and reasonable life " of the κόσμος as an organism. The circle of the Same and the Other, being circles primarily " in the soul " of the world, have an epistemological as well as an astronomical significance. Their absolutely uniform revolutions symbolize—perhaps *Timaeus* means that they actually embody—

---

[1] I have adopted the exegesis given by Mr. Cornford in *Plato's Cosmology* as convincing, and modified these sentences accordingly.

[2] For the construction of this scale—its compass is four octaves and a sixth —see *Tim.* 35*b*–36*b*. Modern editors and translators in general have, in my opinion all been led into errors by exaggerated deference to Boeckh, who, in his turn, has been misled by an erroneous statement in *Timaeus Locrus* about the sum of the terms of the progression. That Boeckh and his followers, at least, must be wrong seems to be shown by their twice introducing into *their* scale the interval called the ἀποτομή or major semitone. As Proclus says, the silence of Timaeus shows that he does not intend to admit this interval, but only the minor semitone, or λεῖμμα, which he is careful to describe.

in the one case, science of the eternal and unchanging, in the other true conviction (δόξα) about the temporal (37a–c). (We must remember that the cosmic animal is a rational animal.)

The creator next proposed to make his work even more like the model on which he had designed it. He could not make it, like its model, eternal (ἀΐδιος) (since nothing sensible can be so), but he made it as nearly eternal as he could. He devised a " moving image of eternity," which he called *time*. Time is to eternity as number is to unity ; its absolutely uniform flow is an imperfect mirroring of the self-sameness of eternity, and time is the character- istic form of the sensible. We try to speak of the eternal as that which " was and is and is to be." But strictly, what is eternal simply " is " ; we must not say that it " was " or " will be," for such language can only be used properly of what " happens." So again we say that the past *is* past, the future *is* to come, the non-existent *is* non-existent. But all such language, which ascribes *being* to what is mere " becoming " and even to " what is not," is un- scientific [1] (37c–38b). The true state of the case is that the model eternally is, its sensible embodiment has been going on and will be going on all through time (38c). If there is to be time, there must be perceptible bodies with uniform movements to serve as measures of it, and so God devised the sun and the other " planets " and put them into the orbits provided for them by the splitting of the circle of the Other. Their order, reckoning outwards from the earth, is Moon, Sun, Hesperus, the " star of Hermes," then the three " outer" planets, for which no names are given here. The sun, Hesperus, and the " star of Hermes " have the same " period," but the two latter are in an unexplained way opposed to the sun, so that they are always catching him up and being caught up by him. The details about the apparent behaviour of the others would require more time than we can spare for their description. The important points to remember are that their velocities are different, that each of them has two motions, one communicated to it by the outermost circle, that of the Same (which revolves from E. to W. with a period of twenty-four hours), another, oblique to this, and with a longer period (the planet's " year "), from W. to E. The result is that the actual visible movements are complicated " cork- screws " (ἕλικες). Men ought to understand, as they do not, that the components of the movements of all are perpetually uniform and regular, and are " time " just as much as a lunar month, or a solar year. There is a great period, the longest of all, at the completion of which all the planets are once more, relatively to the sidereal heavens and to one another, in the same positions. " To enable them to see their way " round these circuits, a great

[1] Timaeus, we see, is not allowed to show any consciousness of the important logical results Plato had reached in the *Sophistes*. This is presumably because his discourse must be kept within limits imposed by the assumption that he is a fifth-century Pythagorean. All through the dialogue we need to remember that the speaker is not Plato, and that Plato need not be supposed to regard his utterances as a complete exposition of his own convictions.

light (the sun) was kindled in the circle next but one to the earth (37c–39d).[1]

God had now to make the various lesser animals which were to inhabit the different regions of the universe. This was done by reproducing the various forms of organism mind discovers in the form of " living being." Of these there are four, each inhabiting its own region : gods who live in the sky, winged creatures who inhabit the air, aquatic creatures, and land-animals. The " gods " were made approximately of pure fire, given spherical form, distributed over the heaven which revolves with the circle of the Same, and given a double movement—motion with the circle of the Same (*i.e.* a diurnal revolution), and an axial revolution of their own. (Thus the " gods " of Timaeus are simply the stars. We gather that they are self-luminous, since they are made of fire, and from comparison of the mention of their axial rotations, with the absence of any corresponding statement about the planets, we may (perhaps ?) infer that the *planets* are not supposed to have any such rotations.) As for the earth, our mother, God made it for " a guardian and artificer of night and day, swinging (ἰλλομένην) on the path about the axis of the universe " (τὴν περὶ τὸν διὰ παντὸς πόλον τεταμένον, 40b). To describe the system further would be impossible without an actual visible model, and is irrelevant (39e–40d).

Full discussion of this astronomical passage is impossible here, but the following points should be noted. (*a*) There is no reference to the famous theory devised by Eudoxus within the Academy itself, which analyses the apparent movements of the heavenly bodies into combinations of axial rotations of imaginary " spheres," with a common centre at the centre of the earth. Timaeus never speaks of " spheres," but, in the language originated by Anaximander, of " circles," conceived to turn round like a wheel spun about its centre. And though one of the motions of each true " star " is said to be " controlled by " the circle of the Same (40b), this motion is expressly ascribed to the star itself, not to an outermost " sphere." Presumably the mere fact that Timaeus is a fifth-century astronomer, speaking many years before the origination of Eudoxus' hypothesis, sufficiently explains this. (*b*) The stars are not thought of, after Aristotle's fashion, as made of a superior and " celestial " stuff. They are made of " fire," the finest quality of fire, but still the same fire to be found in ourselves and bodies round us. We cannot too carefully remember that the fateful distinction between " celestial matter " and " elementary matter " was unknown to Greek science until Aristotle introduced it as a direct consequence of his hypostatization of the purely mathematical spheres of Eudoxus into physical globes. (*c*) It is worth while also to observe the complete freedom of the whole theory from any traces of the planetary astrology which was, later on, to infest the minds of the Hellenistic age. The position of

---

[1] *I.e.*, *all* the planets shine by reflected solar light, as Empedocles had taught for the case of the moon.

the planets in the theory is a very humble one. They are not called " gods," as the stars are, and the natural interpretation of Timaeus' language is that they are not supposed to have any " souls " of their own, but merely to be directed by the soul of the κόσμος. They serve as timepieces, and that, so far, is all. The remark of Timaeus (40d) that though their movements are all calculable, their occultations, reappearances, and conjunctions frighten " those who cannot do a sum," and are supposed to be portents, is probably meant to deride the astrological superstitions of the East, and it is amusing to note that the negative in the phrase " who cannot do a sum," preserved in A, and guaranteed by the version of Cicero, has been dropped in our other best MSS. and marked for deletion by the *diorthotes* of A. In the age of our copyists, it was assumed that it is just the astronomer, who can do the sum, who is frightened by the appearances he foresees ! (d) As to the astronomical theory itself, it agrees with that of Eudoxus in being one of a " double " planetary motion. Each planet is assumed to have a " proper motion " through the zodiac from W. to E., and, over and above this, to be affected by the diurnal revolution from E. to W., with the result that it is brought daily back almost, but not quite, to the position it had twenty-four hours earlier. Thus, in this view, the moon, which most successfully resists the " diurnal revolution," is the swiftest of the planets, Saturn the slowest, since the moon succeeds in getting round the zodiac in a month, Saturn takes about thirty years. Both theories thus contradict the older view, traceable back to Anaximander, that *all* revolutions are in the same sense. If this were so, we should have to say that the moon is left farthest behind, Saturn lags least behind the diurnal revolution.[1] Since the double revolution theory is expressly employed in the myth of Er (*Rep.* 617a), it is pretty clearly of Pythagorean origin, and may be as old as Pythagoras himself, though this is uncertain.

(e) A much more important question is suggested by the remarks about the earth. Does Timaeus mean to ascribe a motion to the earth, or does he not ? In the middle of the last century there was a sharp controversy on the point between Grote, who found the motion of the earth in the dialogue, and Boeckh, who denied it. On one point Boeckh was clearly right. Timaeus cannot mean, as Grote thought, to give the earth an axial rotation with a period of twenty-four hours, since this would conflict with his own express attribution of this period to the " circle of the Same " at 39c. If the stars were revolving round us once in twenty-four hours and the earth rotating in the opposite sense with the same period, manifestly the interval between two successive transits of the same star over the meridian would not be twenty-four hours but twelve, and we cannot suppose, as Grote suggested, that Plato may have forgotten so obvious a point. On the other hand, though nearly all later editors have followed Boeckh, it is equally plain that he must be wrong in making the earth of Timaeus motionless. His inter-

[1] On all this see Burnet, *E.G.Ph.*[3] 110–111.

pretation is overthrown at once by restoration of the correct text of the passage (τὴν περὶ τὸν διὰ παντός, κτλ). The τήν here can only mean τὴν ὁδόν or τὴν περίοδον, and is an accusative of the path traversed. Also the verb used, ἰλλομένην, is notoriously a verb of motion, and we have to add that Aristotle twice over, commenting on the passage, expressly interprets it as asserting a movement of some kind. He does not even produce any argument to show that this is what is meant, but assumes that no one will dispute the point. Hence I think we may feel fairly sure that it was the accepted exegesis of the first generation of the Academy.[1] It follows that Timaeus regards the centre of the universe as empty and ascribes to the earth a " to-and-fro " movement about it. This oscillatory motion we must pretty certainly take to be recti-linear, not circular or cycloidal like the movement of a pendulum-bob. This will explain why Aristotle, discussing the motion of the earth in *de Caelo*, B 13, distinguishes the view of Pythagoreans and certain unnamed other persons, that the earth revolves " *round* the centre," from that of the *Timaeus*, that it moves " *at* the centre."

The interpretation just given follows Professor Burnet, who is at least certainly right in insisting that the word used by Timaeus of the earth (ἰλλομένην) must stand, as Aristotle said, for a notion of some sort. Mr. Cornford has since developed a very different, and attractive explanation, according to which the meaning is that the earth, situated at the centre of the universe, has a diurnal rotation in the opposite sense to that of the " circle of the same " and thus exactly compensating it (*op. cit.*, pp. 120–124). Attrac-tive as this view is, I still doubt whether it could have been ex-pected to be divined by a reader with nothing before him but the bare statement that the earth ἴλλεται, " winds " or " curls," and have therefore hesitated to adapt my text to it, though I am not confident that it may not be right after all. But it is conceivable that Timaeus may be supposed to hold that some sort of " slide " of the earth would explain one or both of two " appearances," (*a*) the inequality of the " seasons " into which the year is divided by the equinoxes and solstices, (*b*) the notorious fact that though the sun and moon are " in conjunction " every lunar month, a solar eclipse is not regularly observed at each conjunction. But I give this avowedly as a guess.[2]

[1] For Aristotle's interpretation, see *de Caelo*, B 293*b* 30 ff., and cf. *ibid*. 296*a* 26. The important point is that the grammar of the passage in the *Timaeus* demands a verb of motion, and that Aristotle expressly explains the word by adding καὶ κινεῖσθαι. That he should be mistaken, or speaking with *mala fides*, on such a point seems incredible. Cf. Burnet, *Greek Philosophy, Part I.*, 348 and notes. The summary to D.L. (iii., 75) also ascribes a motion to the earth, though wrong about its nature (κινεῖσθαι περὶ τὸ μέσον).

[2] On the anomaly of the seasons, see Theo Smyrnaeus, p. 153 (Hiller), and on the Metonic cycle the passages quoted in Diels, *Fragmente der Vorsok-ratiker*[3], i. 29, 9 (*s.v.* Oinopides). For the problem raised by the comparative rarity of visible eclipses of the sun, see *Placita*, ii. 29 (the explanation ascribed to the Pythagoreans and to Anaxagoras). I suspect that Timaeus may intend his sliding motion to explain why we do not see an eclipse of the sun

It is, in any case, improbable that the vague expression put into the mouth of Timaeus is meant to disclose Plato's full doctrine. Theophrastus, as Plutarch has told us, related that "in his old age" Plato repented of having placed the earth at the "centre," which should have been reserved for a "worthier body."[1] In the chapter of the *de Caelo* already referred to, Aristotle, after mentioning that some of the Pythagoreans held that the earth is a planet revolving round a central luminary, adds that "many others too might accept the view that the centre should not be assigned to the earth, for they think (οἴονται) that the most honourable region should belong to the most honourable body, and that fire is more honourable than earth, and the boundary than the intermediate. Now circumference and centre are boundaries ; so on the strength of these considerations they *think* that not the earth, but rather fire, is situated at the centre of the sphere" (*op. cit.* 293a 27–35). Aristotle does not say who these persons are, except that they are not the Pythagoreans of whom he had begun by speaking. Yet he must be speaking of actual persons, since he twice uses the phrase "they think." From what Plutarch has told us on the authority of Theophrastus, it seems to me certain that the unnamed "some" mean here, as so often in Aristotle, Plato and his followers. In that case, we have the evidence not only of Theophrastus, though that would be sufficient, but of Aristotle, that Plato "in his old age" regarded the earth as a planet revolving along with the rest round a central luminary, a view quite unlike that expounded by Timaeus. This is borne out by the evidence of an important passage in the *Laws* (821e–822c) where the Athenian speaker speaks of it as a truth which he has only recently learned that every planet has one and *only* one path (οὐ πολλὰς ἀλλὰ μίαν ἀεί). This can have only one meaning, that the speaker intends to deny the doctrine of the double or composite motion on which Timaeus insists. He must mean that the diurnal revolution is not communicated to the planets, and so is not a component of their motions ; each planet has only its "proper" movement through the Zodiac. Since the appearances which prompted the double motion theory still have to be accounted for, we are driven to suppose that the "diurnal revolution" must be intended to be regarded as only apparent, being really due to a motion of the earth. The implication is that the earth is a planet revolving round an invisible central luminary in a period of twenty-four hours, as the moon is supposed to revolve round the same body in a lunar month, or the sun in a year. A little more light is thrown on the matter by a sentence of the *Epinomis*, a dialogue which is generally "athetized" on extremely inadequate grounds, but admitted to have been at any

at every new moon, nor an eclipse of the moon at every full moon, by suggesting that on most of these occasions the earth happens to be a little "out of the centre."

[1] Plutarch, *Quaest. Platon.* 1006c, *Vit. Numae*, c. 11.   See on this evidence Burnet, *Greek Philosophy, Part I.*, 347.

rate composed immediately after Plato's death by a disciple for circulation along with the *Laws*, and is therefore, in any case, likely to be faithful to the master's teaching. We are there told (*Epin.* 987*b*) that the various planets revolve in one sense and with different periods; the outermost circle revolves—we are not told with what period—in the opposite sense, " carrying the others with it, as it might seem to men who know little of such things." [1] This is, of course, only an urbane way of saying that it does not " carry the others " with it, another denial of the double motion theory of Timaeus. Presumably the reason why the period of this revolution is not stated is that, now that the twenty-four hours' period has been given to the earth, there is no reason to suppose that we know what the period of revolution of the " outermost circle " is. It must have a movement, because the world has a ψυχή ; that Plato supposes its revolution to explain any particular appearance is very unlikely. We can only say that, since the periods of the planets become steadily longer as we advance farther from the " centre," the period of the outermost circle is presumably a very long one.[2]

Plato's own doctrine would seem, thus, to be neither that of the motionless earth, nor that of Timaeus, nor the full-blown Copernicanism which some modern admirers have read into him. He appears to attribute one motion only to the earth, a motion of revolution round an invisible centre (not round the sun), with a period of twenty-four hours. The important point is not that he has a well-worked-out hypothesis, but that his scientific instinct has seized the fundamental point that a true mechanic of the heavens must start with a revolving earth ; this, no doubt, is his reason for dissatisfaction with the scheme of Eudoxus, beautiful as it is. Another inference of first-rate importance is this. We clearly have no right to assume that the view ascribed to Plato by Theophrastus and apparently presupposed in the *Laws* was arrived at after the completion of the *Timaeus*. We have seen that the *Timaeus* and the *Laws* must have been in progress simultaneously. And it is hardly credible that if Plato had suddenly made so

---

[1] *Epin., l.c.*, ἄγων τοὺς ἄλλους, ὥς γε ἀνθρώποις φαίνοιτ' ἂν ὀλίγα τούτων εἰδόσιν. If it only " appears so " to the " beginner," of course it is not so. Burnet's insertion of οὐκ before ἄγων only makes the meaning needlessly plain at the expense of Plato's little jest at the blunder of disciples like Aristotle, who had committed themselves to the Eudoxian view. There seems to be a deliberate rejoinder in Aristot. *Met.* 1073*b* 8, ὅτι μὲν οὖν πλείους τῶν φερομένων αἱ φοραὶ φανερὸν τοῖς καὶ μετρίως ἡμμένοις· πλείους γὰρ ἕκαστον φέρεται μιᾶς τῶν πλανωμένων ἄστρων—just what the *Laws* denies.

[2] This interpretation of the testimony of Theophrastus is that of Schiaparelli, C. Ritter, and Burnet. However we understand his evidence, it is far too weighty to be simply set aside, nor do I think Mr. Cornford's ingenious attempt to minimize its significance (*Plato's Cosmology*, p. 128) happy. I think it more likely that Plato has deliberately chosen for his fifth-century astronomer phraseology which, except that it ascribes movement of some kind to the earth, is left studiously vague.

startling a change in his doctrine during the time when Aristotle was a member of the Academy, Aristotle should have told us nothing about the fact. It would have been " grist to his mill " if he could have urged against the doctrine of a moving earth that Plato had been forced to hold two inconsistent theories about its motion in the course of a few years. Presumably, then, Plato held astronomical views more developed than those which he has ascribed to Timaeus at the very time he was writing the dialogue. This should help us to appreciate Plato's real regard for historical verisimilitude and make us on our guard against over-readiness to suppose that all the theories of his Pythagorean are such as he would find himself satisfied with.

Timaeus next adds that the Creator further made a number of created gods who, unlike the stars, only show themselves when they choose, Oceanus, Tethys, Phorcys, Cronus, Rhea, and their offspring. We have no evidence for the existence of these beings except that of persons who claim to be their descendants, but we may fairly suppose these persons to know their own pedigrees (40d–e). This is, of course, satire, not, as has been sometimes supposed, a concession for safety's sake to the religion of the State. Most of the figures named belong to the cosmogonies of poets like Orpheus and Hesiod, not to the Attic cultus, and the ironical remark that a man must always be believed about his own family-tree is aimed at poets like Orpheus and Musaeus. Timaeus, as a scientific Pythagorean, has his own reasons for not wishing to be confounded with the Orphics. The Creator now addresses the created gods, explaining that whatever is his own immediate work is imperishable. Hence for the making of creatures which are to be perishable, he will employ these created gods as his intermediaries (41a–d). He then himself makes immortal souls, in the same number as the stars, of the " seconds " and " thirds " of the mixture from which he has made the souls of the world and the stars. Each soul is conducted to its star and made to take a perspective view of the universe and its structure. It is then explained to the souls that in due process of time they are all to be born as men in the various " instruments of time " (i.e. the planets).[1] If they live well in the body, they will return to their native stars ; if less well, they will have to be reincarnated in the bodies of women ; if that lesson is insufficient, they will be reborn as various brutes, and will never return to their " star " until they have first climbed up the scale from brute to man again.[2] The souls are then sown, like seeds, in the various planets, while the created gods fashion bodies

[1] The souls sown in the planets are not, of course, to be future inhabitants of the earth. They are to inhabit the planets where they are " sown." Timaeus is alluding to the Pythagorean belief that there are men and animals in the planets as well as on earth.

[2] The connexion of a soul with its " star " has nothing to do with either planetary or zodiacal astrology. The thought is simply that there is a correspondence one-to-one between the " gods " and the human denizens of the universe.

for them and any additions to their souls which may be required for their life in the body (41e–42d).

We are next told something of the way in which this work was done, but the story is only given in outline, with the necessary warning that, since it has to do with the mutable, it can only be tentative (42e–47e). In making the human body, the gods first constructed the head as a suitable dwelling-place for the immortal soul, which, of course, like the soul of the κόσμος, contains the two circles of the Same and the Other. (This means that Timaeus rightly accepts the discovery of Alcmaeon of Crotona that the brain is the central organ in the sensory-motor system.) The skull was therefore made spherical, as the body of the κόσμος is spherical. The trunk and the limbs were added for the safety and convenience of the head (44c–45b). The organ of sight was then constructed. It is literally a ray of sunlight dwelling within the body and issuing out through the pupil. We thus see by an actual long-distance contact of this ray, which is a real, though temporary, member of the body, with the visible object—the theory explained by Empedocles in verses cited by Aristotle. To this account of vision Timaeus appends an explanation of sleep as produced by an equable diffusion of this internal " fire " when darkness prevents its issuing out to join its kindred fire outside us, and a brief account of mirror-vision (45b–46c). His main points at present are, however, of a different kind. He dwells on the thought that the effect of the conjunction of the soul with a body which is always " flowing," giving off waste material and taking in fresh, is to throw the movements of the " circles " in the soul into complete disorder. The movement of the circle of the Same is temporarily arrested, and that of the circle of the Other rendered irregular. Hence the thoughtlessness and confused perception and fancy of our infancy and childhood. It is only when the " flow " of the body becomes less turbid, as waste and repair come to balance one another in adult life, that the movements of the " circles " recover from the init al disturbance of birth, and men come to discretion and intelligence, and then only with the aid of " right education " (43a–44c). Also, we must be careful to remember the distinction between true causes and mere subsidiary causes (συναίτια). Any account we give of the mechanism of vision, or any other function, is a mere statement about the subsidiary or instrumental cause. The true cause, in every case, is to be sought in the good or end a function subserves. Thus the real end for which we have been given eyes, is that the spectacle of the heavenly motions may lead us to note the uniformity and regularity of days, nights, months, and years, and that reflection on this uniformity may lead us to science and philosophy, and so make the revolutions of the " circles in the head " themselves regular and uniform. And the same thing is true of hearing ; its real purpose is not that we may learn to tune the strings of a lyre, but that we may learn to make our own thinking and living a spiritual melody (46c–47e).

We next come to one of the most important and character-istic sections of the discourse—an outline of the principles of a geometrical science of nature. So far we have been talking about the work done by Intelligence in the construction of the sensible world. But this world is a " mixed " product, born of Intelligence (νοῦς) and Necessity (ἀνάγκη), and we must now describe the con-tribution of Necessity to the whole. The relation between In-telligence and Necessity, which is also called the " errant " or " irregular " cause (πλανωμένη αἰτία), is that " for the most part " Intelligence is superior (ἄρχων, 48a), Necessity is servant, or slave, but a willing slave ; Intelligence " persuades " (πείθει) Necessity. The special reason given for now studying the working of Necessity is that, unless we do so, we can give no account of the origin of the " four roots " of Empedocles, the " stuff " we have so far been assuming as there for God to form a world of. Hitherto no one has explained the structure of these bodies ; they have been treated as the ABC (στοιχεῖα, elementa, 48b) of things, though, as we shall see, they do not even deserve to be called syllables. We are now to analyse them back into something very much more primitive, and we are carefully reminded again that, from the nature of the case, our analysis can at best be tentative and " likely."

The sections which are now to follow are marked by Timaeus as the most original and important part of his whole cosmology. We shall see that they serve to connect the two main currents of scientific thought, the biological and the mathematical, by providing a geometrical construction for the " corpuscles " of the four " elements " which the biologist Empedocles had treated as the " simples " of his system. The four types of body thus con-structed are then, in the Empedoclean fashion, treated as the immediate units from which the various tissues and secretions of the living body are formed by chemical composition. The result is thus that Timaeus, in the spirit of Descartes, offers us an anatomy and physiology in which the organism appears as an elaborate kinematical system ; natural science is thus reduced in principle, as Descartes and Spinoza held it ought to be, to geometry. Plato is not, of course, very strictly committed by the details of speculations which he repeatedly says are provisional, but it is clear that he is in sympathy with the general attitude known to-day in biology as mechanistic. The human organism, as he conceives it, is a machine directed and controlled by mind or intelligence, but the machine itself is made of the same ultimate constituents as other machines and the workings of it follow the same laws as those of the rest.

It is important, if we are to approach the exposition in the right spirit, to understand what is meant by the initial distinction between the part of Intelligence and that of Necessity in the cosmic system. We must be careful not to confuse the " necessity " of which Plato is speaking with the principle of order and law. Law and order are precisely the features of the world which he assigns to intelligence as their source ; we are carefully told that necessity is something disorderly and irregular, the πλανωμένη αἰτία, a name probably derived, as Burnet has suggested,[1] from the use of the disrespectful name πλανῆται, " tramps," " vagabonds," for the heavenly bodies which seem at first sight to roam about the sky with no settled abode. Thus the Necessity of the *Timaeus* is something quite different from the Necessity of the myth of Er, or of the Stoics, which are personifications of the principle of rational law and order. On the other hand, Necessity is plainly not meant to be an independent, evil principle, for it is plastic to intelligence ; mind " for the most part " is said to " persuade it " ; its function is to be instrumental to the purposes of νοῦς.[2] The reason for introducing it into the story seems to be simply that it is impossible in science to resolve physical reality into a complex of rational laws without remainder. In the real world there is always, over and above " law," a factor of the " simply given " or " brute fact," not accounted for and to be accepted simply as given. It is the business of science never to acquiesce in the merely given, to seek to " explain " it as the consequence, in virtue of rational law, of some simpler initial " given." But, however far science may carry this procedure, it is always forced to retain *some* element of brute fact, the merely given, in its account of things. It is the presence in nature of this element of the given, this surd or irrational as it has sometimes been called, which Timaeus appears to be personifying in his language about Necessity. That " mind persuades necessity " is just an imaginative way of saying that by the analysis of the given datum we always can rationalize it further ; we never come to a point at which the possibility of " explanation " actually ceases. But the " irrational " is always there, in the sense that explanation always leaves behind it a remainder which is the " not yet explained." When we have followed the exposition a little further, we shall discover that in the last resort this element of the irreducible and given turns out to be exactly what Professor Alexander has called the " restlessness of space-time." But, unlike Professor Alexander, Plato does not believe that the restlessness of space-time is enough to account for its elaboration into more and more rationally articulated systems ; left to itself, it would be

---

[1] *Greek Philosophy, Part I.*, 341–346. The " necessity " of the *Timaeus* is not " uniform sequence." So far as sequences are " uniform," the uniformity is due to the " persuasion " of necessity by νοῦς ; that is, the uniformity is an effect and sign of the presence of rational purpose. It is the exceptional departures, the " sports " in nature, which we are to account for by the presence of a πλανωμένη αἰτία. More generally, " necessity " explains why the course of actual fact only conforms *approximately* to the formulae of kinematics. The " necessity " of the dialogue is thus precisely what Aristotle has taught us to call " contingency."

[2] This excludes the superficial identification of " necessity " with an evil " material principle." The doctrine that " matter " is the source of evil is wholly un-Platonic. Historically, of course, the ἀνάγκη of Timaeus connects directly with the ἄπειρον of early Pythagoreanism. It is the element of indetermination in events, the element which a Spinozistic conception of the universe persists in ignoring.

merely restless ; order and structure are the work of the mind of God, in whose hands necessity is plastic.

We find, then, that we need to revise our first account of the sensible world. We had already spoken of two things which need to be carefully discriminated, the intelligible archetype and its visible copy. We have now to take into account a third concept which we shall find obscure enough, that of the " receptacle " (ὑποδοχή) or "matrix" (ἐκμαγεῖον) in which "becoming" goes on. This receptacle or matrix of process cannot be fire or water or any of the things which the earliest philosophers had selected as the primary "boundless." Experience shows that these are constantly passing into one another ; there is now fire where there was water, or water where there was fire. The various bodies are mutable and impermanent ; what remains permanent under all the variations is the region or room or place where they arise and vanish. This is there and self-same under all the processes of change, and has no form or structure of its own, precisely because it is its indifference to all which makes the appearance of all within it possible. We find it hard to apprehend, because it cannot be discerned by sense ; it must be thought of, but can only be thought of by a sort of " bastard reflection " (λογισμῷ τινι νόθῳ, 52b), i.e. by systematic negation, the denying of one definite determination after another. It is, in fact, "place" (χώρα). We may, incidentally, remind ourselves that each of our three principles is apprehended in a special way. We can satisfy ourselves of the reality of the forms by considering that if there were only sensible objects, science and true belief would be the same ; whereas it is clear they are not. Science can only be acquired by learning (διδαχή) a true belief may be produced by "persuasion," appeal to our emotions ; what we know can always be justified to the intellect (τὸ μὲν ἀεὶ μετ' ἀληθοῦς λόγου), a true belief not always ; we cannot be argued out of the one, we can be persuaded out of the other. Since science and true belief thus differ, their objects must be different.[1] (Thus Timaeus has nothing to say in the one passage in which he discusses the forms which differs from the presentation of them in the *Phaedo*.) Sensible things we apprehend, of course, by sight and the rest of our senses ; " place," as we have just said, by a curious kind of thinking (48e–52c).

If we try to picture the condition of things " before " the introduction of ordered structure, we have to think of the " receptacle "

---

[1] There is an almost absolute equivalence of Timaeus' analysis with that of Whitehead in his *Principles of Natural Knowledge*, and *Concept of Nature*. Whitehead's " objects " have exactly the formal character of the ἰδέαι; his account of the " ingredience of objects into events " corresponds almost verbally with that given by Timaeus of the determination of the various regions of the " receptacle " by the " ingress " and " egress " of the impresses of the forms. The " receptacle " itself only differs from " passage " in being called " space " and not " space-time." If we try to picture " passage " as it would be if there were only " events " and no " objects " ingredient in them, we get precisely the sort of account Timaeus gives of the condition of the " receptacle " before God introduced order and structure into it.

or *matrix* just described as *place* as agitated everywhere by irregular disturbances, random vibratory movements, and exhibiting in various regions mere rude incipient "traces" (ἴχνη) of the definite structure we know as characteristic of the various forms of body. (Thus its general character is exactly that of the "boundless" of Anaximander, agitated by the "eternal motion," before the "opposites" have been "sifted out" and a κόσμος formed. This is, in fact, pretty clearly the historical starting-point from which Pythagorean cosmology had taken its departure).[1] The first step God takes towards introducing determination and order into this indeterminate "happening" is the construction of bodies of definite geometrical structure. This brings us to the doctrine of the geometrical structure of the "corpuscles" of the "four roots" which Empedoclean biology wrongly treats as simple ultimates. The construction is effected by making a correspondence between the "four roots" and the originally Pythagorean doctrine of the regular solids which can be inscribed in the sphere (53c–56c). There are five and only five distinct types of regular solid, and four of them can be built up geometrically by starting with two ultimate simple types of triangle, which are the most beautiful, and therefore the most appropriate, of all. These two triangles are the ultimate "elements" of the *Timaeus*. One of them is the isosceles right-angled triangle, called by the Pythagoreans the "half-square"; the other is the triangle which can be obtained by dividing the equilateral triangle into six smaller triangles by drawing the perpendiculars from the angular points on the opposite sides, or less symmetrically, by dividing the equilateral triangle into two by a single such perpendicular. (Hence the Pythagorean name for it, the "half-triangle.") Timaeus does not explain what the peculiar beauty of these triangles is, but we know independently that it lies in the fact that the ratios of the angles of the two triangles are the simplest possible. Those of the "half-square" have the ratios $1 : 1 : 2$, those of the "half-triangle" the ratios $1 : 2 : 3$. From the former, by a symmetrical arrangement of four such triangles about a centre of position we get the square, and from a proper arrangement of six square faces, the *cube*. A similar symmetrical arrangement of six triangles of the second type gives us the equilateral triangle, and there are three regular solids which can be made with equilateral triangles as their faces—the *tetrahedron*, the *octahedron*, the *icosahedron*. For physical reasons, we take the cube as the form appropriate to a corpuscle of earth, the tetrahedron as that of a particle of fire, the other two as the forms of the particles of air and water respectively. There is still a fifth regular solid, the dodecahedron, which has twelve pentagons as its faces; but this can be constructed from neither of the elementary triangles, and has a different part to play. God employed it (55*b*) "for the whole, adorning it with constellations." (This

[1] For the historical connexion of Pythagorean cosmology with the scheme of Anaximander see *E.G.Ph.*[3] 108 ff., *Greek Philosophy, Part I.*, c. 2.

out the celestial sphere for purposes of astronomical description by dividing it into twelve pentagonal regions, exactly as a leather ball is made by stitching together twelve pentagonal pieces of leather.[1]) It follows from the theory that a corpuscle of one of the " roots " can only be broken up along the edges of the triangles from which it has been built up. Hence, since earth is formed from a special type of triangle, it cannot be " transmutable " with any of the other three, but they are all transmutable with one another. Timaeus then proceeds to give a number of equations which determine the equivalences between the corpuscles of these "roots." Into the physical difficulties created by this table of equivalences we cannot enter here. It must be enough to have seen that the general programme contemplated is precisely that reduction of all physics to applied geometry and nothing else which is equally characteristic of Descartes.

We next have an attempt to specify the most important " varieties " of each of the four types of body and the " chemical compounds " they form with one another, and to account for the sensible qualities of all these bodies by reference to their geometrical structure, which must be passed over here ($58c$–$68d$). Its most interesting feature is a long psycho-physical account of the conditions of pleasure-pain ($64a$–$65b$), in terms of the depletion-repletion formula. The " unmixed " pleasures of sense are brought under the formula by the hypothesis that they are sudden and appreciable " repletions " of a " depletion " which has been too gentle and gradual to be propagated to the " seat of consciousness."

With the next section of the dialogue we pass definitely from physics to anatomy, physiology, and medicine ($69a$–$87b$). Again, it must be sufficient in this volume to pass over the details lightly. The main point is that the organism has been constructed throughout to minister to the soul. To fit the soul for its embodied life it had to receive two temporary and inferior additions, the " spirited " and " concupiscent " " parts " or " forms " already familiar to us from the *Republic*. Each of these has a central " organ " or " seat," just as the " rational " part has its seat in the brain ; " spirit " is lodged in the thorax, " appetite " in the lower region of the trunk, beneath the diaphragm ($69a$–$70e$). In connexion with this least orderly and disciplined element in the soul, the liver has a specially important part to play. It is the source of visions and bad dreams

---

[1] The whole of this construction is Pythagorean in origin, as we see by comparison with the valuable fragment preserved at the end of the *Theologumena Arithmetica* from the work of Speusippus on *Pythagorean Numbers* (Speusippus, Fr. 4; Diels, *Fragmente d. Vorsokr.*[3] i. p. 303 ff.), where the relations silently presupposed by Timaeus between the angles of the " half-square " and " half-triangle " are explained in full. The one point where Timaeus may be going beyond results reached by the Pythagoreans is in his tacit assumption that all his five solids and no others can be inscribed in the sphere. Note that he makes a point of it that Socrates and the others are *mathematicians*, and so will follow him easily ($53c$ 1).

of all kinds, and the utterances of the " possessed," " seers," and the like are really due to a disordered liver. They can be interpreted by spokesmen (προφῆται), who are themselves not in the state of " possession," and thus given a salutary moral influence (71a–72b). The details of the anatomy and physiology have more interest for the historian of these sciences than for the student of philosophy, especially since they are all given as tentative and liable to revision. The most prominent feature of the section is the elaborate attempt (77b–79e, 80d–81e) to account (of course in a fanciful way) for respiration, the systole and diastole of the heart, digestion, all together as one vast rhythmical mechanical process with the double purpose of maintaining the vital heat of the organism and distributing nourishment through the blood to the various tissues.

The physiology is followed up by a section on pathology which makes a curious attempt at a classification of the various known diseases (82a–86a). The theory could only be properly discussed in connexion with what we know of other fifth- and fourth-century speculations on the same subject from the Hippocratean *corpus* and other sources. Its most outstanding feature is that it departs wholly from the lines of the Hippocratean " humoral pathology " by treating " phlegm " and " bile " not as ingredients of the organism in its normal state but as unwholesome morbid secretions. I have tried elsewhere to show reasons for supposing that Plato is deriving the doctrine from Philistion of Locri, with whom, as we see from the *Epistles*, he had made acquaintance at Syracuse, and that in its main outlines it is in general accord with what we know to have been the medical theory of Philolaus, though there are points of difference. If this is so, we can understand why this particular medical theory should be expounded by the Locrian Timaeus. In any case, we must not suppose that Plato has invented an amateur pathology of his own and is teaching it dogmatically. He will simply be following what he regards as respectable specialist authority.

The pathology of the body leads up to the pathology of the soul (86b–87b), and this to some regulations of physical and mental hygiene (87e–90d). Undesirable moral propensities are due very largely to physical constitutional defects ; *e.g.* undue propensity to sexual irregularities is largely of physiological origin. The other chief cause of " badness " is education in bad social traditions. Hence Timaeus infers—not quite consistently with his own earlier insistence on personal responsibility—that those who begot and educated the transgressor are really more to blame than the transgressor himself. We must remember that he is, among other things, a medical man, and that " the profession " are prone to views of this kind. Plato may well be treating his speaker with a certain touch of irony when he makes the moral theory of Timaeus a little inconsistent with his mental pathology.

In laying down rules of hygiene, the supreme object we should aim at is the correction of any disproportion between the body and the soul which animates it. This disproportion is dangerous to both body and soul. The soul which is too big for its " pigmy body " actually wears the body out, as we see in the case of so many keen political and scientific controversialists ; when the body is too robust for its soul, a man too often makes the soul dull and slow by ministering to the body's clamant appetites. The rule should be that neither body nor soul should be exercised exclusively. The student must take care to attend to his physical condition, or he will suffer for it in soul as well as body. The best kind of " motion " by which to exercise the body is active muscular exertion, and the next best easy rhythmical passive motion, like swinging, riding in a carriage, being rowed on the water. The worst kind, which may only be resorted to in case of absolute necessity, is the violent production of intestinal motions by drugs and purges (87c–89d).

A still more important topic is the hygiene of the mind which is to rule and direct the movements of the body. Timaeus cannot relevantly enter on a systematic discussion of the principles of education, but he lays down the general principle that our intelligence is the divine thing in us, and the real " guardian spirit " (δαίμων) of each of us. It has been truly said that man, whose divine part resides in the head, is like a tree with its root not in the earth, but in the sky (90a). The rule of healthy living for the soul is that this divine thing in us should " think thoughts immortal and divine," and that the merely human " parts " of the soul should " worship " and " tend " it. The true " tendance " of any creature consists in providing it with its appropriate food and " exercise " (κινήσεις, 90c), and the " exercise " appropriate to the rational soul is thus " the thoughts and revolutions of the whole." The end of life is to correct the " revolutions in the head " and bring them once more into correspondence with the " tunes and revolutions " of the world-soul, in whose image they were made at first (90a–d).

The story closes with a development which should not be taken as seriously as has been done by some interpreters. Timaeus, we remember, had incorporated in his narrative the old fancy that the first men were directly sprung from the soil. Hence his physiology has taken no account of the reproductive system. This, we are now told, was only wanted in the second generation, when the second-best of the original " men " came to be reborn as women. He gives an unmistakably playful account of the modifications which had to be introduced into the physiological scheme to suit the new situation (90e–91d), and then adds more briefly that the lower animals in general were also derived by degeneration from the original human pattern, the deformation being greater or less as the souls which were to tenant the various bodies had fallen more or less short of virtue and wisdom in their first life (91d–92b). Nothing is said here of the hell and purgatory of the eschatological myths of the *Gorgias, Phaedo, Republic.* Presumably the scientific Pythagoreans of the middle of the fifth century regarded them as no more than edifying mythology, exactly as the author of the so-called *Timaeus Locrus* regards Timaeus' own statements about metamorphosis. We should pretty certainly be wrong if we took this part of the discourse as a serious speculation on the part of Plato about a possible evolution *à rebours.* Timaeus himself is probably meant to be less than half in earnest ; as in the tale of Aristophanes in the *Symposium,* we are really dealing with a playful imitation of the speculation of Empedocles about the " whole-natured " and double-sexed forms with which evolution in the " period of strife " began. What Plato himself thinks of all this is sufficiently indicated when we are told in the *Politicus* that the " earth-born " men and the " age of Cronus " do not belong to our " half of the cycle," *i.e.* they belong to fairy-tale, not to history.

Here our story comes at last to an end. We have now told the whole tale of the birth of this sensible world, " a visible living creature, modelled on that which is intelligible, a god displayed to sense " (92c).[1]

The *Critias* calls for no special consideration. Its declared purpose is to relate in detail the story of the defeat of the Atlantid kings, of which Critias had given the bare outline in the *Timaeus.* It remains, however, a bare fragment. Critias describes the topography of Attica and Athens as they were before the process of denudation which has reduced the country to a mere rocky skeleton (109b–111d), and the happy condition of the inhabitants (111e–112e). He then gives a much longer account of the island of Atlantis and its kings, the descendants of the god Posidon, their institutions, and their wonderful engineering works (118a–120d), and is about to relate how their hearts were lifted up with pride in their wealth and power, and how Zeus resolved to bring them into judgment, when the fragment breaks off, just as Zeus is about to declare his purpose to the assembled gods. The chief things which call for notice are the clear-headed way in which Plato has grasped the effects of gradual geological denudation on Attica,[2] and the special stress he lays on the marvellous skill of the Atlantids in naval engineering. The description may have been inspired by a re-collection of what had actually been effected at Syracuse,[3] but the

---

[1] εἰκὼν τοῦ νοητοῦ, θεὸς αἰσθητός. In this sentence νοητοῦ must not be taken, against all the rules of grammar, as masculine agreeing with an " understood " θεοῦ, since the word θεός has not yet occurred in the sentence. νοητοῦ is neuter, and we must either understand ζῷον from the preceding ζῷον, or possibly take τὸ νοητόν substantivally. The *v.l.* ποιητοῦ found in A is inferior to tne vulgate, which is also the better supported reading, as it occurs in both F and Y.

[2] But it is said (Rivaud, *Timée*, p. 239) that much of the denudation of Attica ascribed by Plato to the natural cataclysm mentioned at *Timaeus* 25d and *Critias* 112a is actually the work of man.

[3] Plato is thinking also, perhaps, of the conversion of the Piraeus into a great naval harbour, but the immediate source of the description is probably what he had seen himself at Syracuse.

works ascribed to the mythical kings more than sustain comparison with the greatest achievements of Roman architects and engineers. The whole account illustrates Plato's exceptional knowledge of the technical arts and his high estimate of their possibilities. We may be sure that, if the story had been completed, one of its main points would have been the triumph of patriotism and sound *moral* over technical skill.

The conception of the " purpose of Zeus " seems to be an echo from epic poetry. It is hardly a mere accident that the last complete sentence of the fragment recalls the version of the Trojan story given in the *Cypria*, where the origin of the great war is traced to the plan of Zeus for the prevention of over-population. There may be some significance in the fact that Zeus is said to summon the divine council to his " most honourable abode " in the centre of the universe.[1] Since one of the names given by those Pythagoreans who believed in a " central fire " to this luminary was Διὸς φυλακή, this looks as though Critias meant to hint at that astronomical doctrine. Timaeus, as we have seen, makes the " centre " empty.

See further :

BURNET.—*Greek Philosophy, Part I.*, 335–349 ; *Platonism* (1928), c.7.

RITTER, C.—*Platon*, ii., 258–287 al. ; *Platons Dialoge*, 98–158 ; *Neue Untersuchungen über Platon*, 174–182.

LEVI, A.—*Il Concetto del Tempo nella Filosofia di Platone*. (Turin, N.D.)

STEWART, J. A.—*Plato's Doctrine of Ideas*, 101–105 ; *Myths of Plato*, 259–297 (*The Timaeus*), 457–469.

DIÈS, A.—*Autour de Platon*, ii., 522–603.

TAYLOR, A. E.—*A Commentary on Plato's Timaeus*. (Oxford, 1928) ; *Plato, Timaeus and Critias* (translated) (1929).

RIVAUD, A.—*Platon, Timée, Critias*. (Paris, 1925.)

FRIEDLANDER, P.—*Platon ; Eidos, Paideia, Dialogos* (1928). *Excursus II*. (on the city of Atlantis).

RAEDER, H.—*Platons philosophische Entwickelung*, 374–394.

NATORP, P.—*Platons Ideenlehre*, 338–358.

BAEUMKER, C.—*Das Problem der Materie in der griechischen Philosophie*, 115–188.

MARTIN, T. H.—*Études sur le Timée de Platon*. (Paris, 1841.)

ROBIN, L.—*Études sur la signification et la place de la physique dans la philosophie de Platon*. (Paris, 1919.)

ROBIN, L.—*Platon*, c. v.

CORNFORD, F. M.—*Plato's Cosmology* (*Timaeus* translated with commentary, Cambridge, 1937).

---

[1] *Critias* 121c 2–4. The sentence adds to the case for my view that the astronomy of Timaeus is not Plato's own.

CHAPTER XVIII

THE *LAWS* AND *EPINOMIS*

THE *Laws* is not only the longest of all Plato's writings ; it also contains his latest and ripest thought on the subjects which he had all through his life most at heart—ethics, education, and jurisprudence. Plato's services to the theory of education, in particular, have usually been grossly underrated, from an inexcusable neglect of the very thorough treatment given to it in what he probably himself regarded as his most important work. His theology, again, has often been misconceived in modern times, because the tenth book of the *Laws* is the only place in his works where it is systematically expounded. This neglect of so noble a work is perhaps to be explained by two considerations. In one respect the *Laws* makes a greater demand on the reader than any other Platonic writing. The dramatic element is reduced to a minimum ; if one does not care for the subject-matter of the book, there is little in its manner to attract. To all intents and purposes, the work is a monologue, interrupted only by formulae of assent or requests for further explanation. Further, the purpose of the whole is severely practical, and will not appeal to a reader who cares more for metaphysics and science than for morals and politics. More than any other work of Plato, the *Laws* stands in direct relation to the political life of the age in which it was composed and is meant to satisfy a pressing felt need.

In the last twenty years of Plato's life it was becoming more and more obvious that the old city-states which had been the centres of Hellenic spiritual life had had their day. Athens herself had become a second-rate power ever since the collapse of the great Syracusan expedition, as Plato knew only too well. Sparta, to whom the hegemony had passed at the end of the Decelean war, had proved wholly unfitted for such a post, and had been crushed, in a way from which she never recovered, by the brilliant successes of Epaminondas, which made Thebes for a few years a power of the first order. Meanwhile the very existence of Hellenic civilization was endangered by the encroachments of Persia in the East and Carthage in the West. It was clear that if civilization of the Hellenic type was to hold its own, none of the older city-states was in a condition to become its centre. We know now that the historical solution of the problem was to be provided by the rise of the Macedonian monarchy and the achievements of Philip and Alexander.

But the work of Philip was only in the beginning in Plato's last years; his appearance south of Thermopylae as the ally of Thebes against Phocis, the first manifest sign that a new power had succeeded to the hegemony of the Hellenic states, did not take place until the year after Plato's death. In the meantime, the most striking feature of the situation was the founding of new cities or the revival of old ones. Epaminondas' foundation of Megalopolis as a centre for Arcadia is a good example of the one process, his restoration of Messene an equally good example of the other; and it is pertinent to remember that, according to Greek ideas, the first thing to be done in such a situation was to provide the new or revived community with a complete constitution and fundamental law. It was naturally the practice to call in the aid of experts in " politics " as advisers in the task. In the fifth century, Pericles had employed Protagoras in this way, to give advice on the laws to be made for Thurii; in the fourth, the Academy was constantly being asked, as a recognized society of experts in jurisprudence, to do the same sort of work. Plato himself is said to have been requested to legislate for Megalopolis, and, though he declined, work of the same kind was done by his associates for many foundations.[1] Hence it was eminently desirable that men contemplating the probability of being called on to " legislate," should be provided with an example of the way in which the work should be gone about, and the *Laws* is meant to furnish just such an example. The assumed situation is that a new city is to be founded, and that an Athenian is invited to lend his assistance in the work. The particular situation assumed, of a city to be founded in Crete on the site of a prehistoric town, is presumably fictitious, especially if, as Wilamowitz has asserted, the topographical details show that Plato was not really acquainted with actual Cretan conditions; a fictitious situation will serve as well as a real one to illustrate the principles which have to be enforced.

The date of composition of the work cannot be very precisely fixed. But we may readily fix a *terminus a quo*. One of the chief principles on which Plato insists is that the legislator has not really done his work when he has merely enunciated an enactment and provided it with a " sanction " in the form of a penalty for non-observance. This is like the method of an empiric " slave " doctor, treating other slaves; he merely orders a prescription to be followed under the threat of consequences if it is neglected. A great physician treating an intelligent freeman tries to enlist his patient in the work of the cure by explaining to him the principles on which the treatment rests. In the same way, a legislator should try to enlist

[1] See the list of active " law-givers " among Plato's pupils in Plutarch (*Adv. Colotem,* 1126c–d). " Plato sent Aristonymus to the Arcadians, Phormio to Elis, Menedemus to Pyrrha. Eudoxus and Aristotle wrote laws for Cnidus and Stagirus. Alexander asked Xenocrates for advice about kingship; the man who was sent to Alexander by the Greek inhabitants of Asia and did most to incite him to undertake his war on the barbarians was Delius of Ephesus, an associate of Plato." Cf. D.L. iii., 23, for the request from Megalopolis.

the sympathies of decent men on the side of the law by prefixing
to his whole legislation and to the several main divisions of it
"proems" or "preambles" explaining the aims of the legislation
and the reasons why its enactments are what they are, and why the
penalties for transgression are what they are (*Laws* 719e–722a). Now
in *Epistle* iii. 316a, Plato refers to himself as having been occupied
with Dionysius at Syracuse upon "preludes" or "preambles" to
the laws to be given to the cities they were proposing to form into a
constitutional monarchy. Thus we may reasonably infer that the
conception of legislation characteristic of the *Laws* was suggested
by Plato's personal experience of the Syracusan situation. The
occasion to which *Epistle* iii. refers is probably that of Plato's last
visit to Syracuse in 361/60, though it may conceivably be that of
the visit of 367/6. In either case, it is unlikely that Plato would
have the leisure to plan a work of the scope of our *Laws* before 360,
when his direct connexion with the affairs of Syracuse was over.
Such a work would necessarily involve a great deal of thought and
time and may well have occupied Plato more or less continuously
for the remaining years of his life, though the one actual allusion to
a dateable event seems to be the mention (638b) of a victory of
Dionysius II over the Locrians, probably to be assigned to the
year 356.

The *personnel* of the dialogue, if we can call it one, is exceedingly
simple. There are three characters—an Athenian, left anonymous,
who is the main speaker, and two minor characters, Megillus, a
Spartan, and Clinias, a Cretan. All of them are old men ; of the
Athenian we learn that he has astronomical and mathematical
knowledge, is regarded by the others as a highly suitable person
to give advice on matters of jurisprudence and political science, and
that he has had personal experience of association with a "tyrant"
(711a). Thus his intellectual qualifications are those of a member
of the Academy, and his personal experiences are modelled on
Plato's own, and to that extent we may fairly take him as standing
for Plato, though we have no reason to suppose that he is drawn
with any deliberate intention of self-portraiture. All we learn of
the others is that the Spartan belongs to a family in which the office
of *proxenus* of Athens is hereditary, and that the Cretan is connected
by blood with the famous medicine-man Epimenides (642b, d).
This is meant to account for the unusual readiness of both to learn
from an Athenian. When the work opens we find the three old
men engaged in a general conversation about the merits and purpose
of the institutions of the traditional legislators of Sparta and
Cnossus, Lycurgus and Minos. They propose to continue their
conversation as they walk to the cave of Dicte, the legendary birth-
place of Zeus. The full situation is only disclosed at the end of the
third book (702b–d). It then appears that the Cretans have resolved to resettle the site of a decayed city ; the making of the
necessary arrangements has been left to the citizens of Cnossus,
who have devolved it upon a commission of ten. Clinias, the head

of this commission, proposes to take the Athenian and Spartan into consultation as advisers about the legislation and the constitution generally. We have already incidentally heard that the time of the year is midsummer, so that the long day will suffice for a full discussion.

The argument of the first three books may be regarded as introductory. Plato winds his way very gradually into his subject, advancing almost imperceptibly from a problem of ethics, through educational theory, to the consideration of strictly political and juristic matter, and does not reveal his full purpose until the preparatory positions have been thoroughly secured. This method is very characteristic, and it is unfortunate that some modern readers should have appreciated it so little as to speculate about the possibility that the whole arrangement is due to the piecing together of disconnected papers by an editor. I trust that the brief analysis which follows will reveal the real march of the argument as far too carefully studied to be the result of a well-meant blunder.

(Book I.) What is the central purpose of the institutions of Lycurgus and Minos ? The Spartan and Cretan agree that their law-givers have discovered the fundamental truth that, under all disguises, the brute hard fact about the life of a city is that it is a " war to the knife " with all rivals ; almost in Hobbes's phrase, independent cities are in a state of nature towards one another, and the state of nature is a state of real but undeclared war (πόλεμος ἀκήρυκτός). Hence the supreme good for a city is victory in this unremitting warfare, and the business of a citizen is to be, before everything, a combatant. All the institutions of Sparta and Crete are therefore rightly directed towards producing the one great virtue, efficiency in warfare, ἀνδρεία, valour. The Athenian dissents entirely from this ethic of warfare. The supreme victory for any community or any man is not victory over the foe without, but victory over self, that is, the conquest of the worser elements in the community or the individual soul by the better. And this victory is not complete when the better elements coerce or expel the worse ; it is only complete when subjugation is followed by reconciliation and harmony. Peace, not war, between the components of community or individual soul is the best state ; it is with a view to peace that a good legislator must make his enactments. From this point of view, wisdom, *sophrosyne*, justice, are the supreme virtues ; mere martial valour will rank only fourth (631c). Now when we consider the Spartan system of training we see that all its peculiarities—the common meals of coarse fare, the bodily exercises and hunting, and the rough discipline in general —aim only at fostering the one virtue we have just ranked lowest among the four of the familiar quadrilateral. And, what is more, they aim at teaching only the easier and less valuable half of the one virtue.

True " manliness " or valour does not consist simply in the power to face danger, pain, and weariness ; it means also being able to face the seductions of pleasure without giving in to them, and this is the finer half of the virtue and the harder to learn. But Megillus himself cannot point to any training provided by the Spartan system in this part of valour (634*b*). The explanation is that the only way to learn to get the better of temptation is to be made to face it and overcome it. The Spartans act on this principle when they teach the young to face peril and pain bravely by exposing them to them. They avoid making them learn to face and overcome the seductions of pleasure. Indeed, the perverse sexual practices which are fostered by the " barrack-room " life of Sparta have given her a universal bad name (636*b*) no less than the relaxed manners of her women (637*c*).

A chance remark of Megillus in reply to these criticisms provides the material for the rest of the discussion of Book I. He regards it as highly creditable to Sparta that its pleasures are so few ; a wine-party, for example, is an unheard-of thing (637*a*). This leads the Athenian into a long discussion of the practice of μέθη, the *convivial* use of wine. (As a mere drink with meals wine was used sparingly at Sparta, as everywhere else in Greece, for the simple reason that the water is bad.) Some communities wholly prohibit the practice, others allow anyone who pleases to indulge in it as much as he pleases and whenever he likes. Both, the Athenian thinks, are mistaken. A Spartan may urge that the Spartans beat the " wet " forces in the field whenever they meet them, but we cannot generalize by enumeration from a few instances. The issue of numberless engagements goes unrecorded, and we can point to examples on the other side, such as the victory of the toping Syracusans over the abstemious Locrians. If we are to judge of wine-drinking or any other practice we must see what can be made of it under proper regulation. Now under two important conditions—(*a*) that the party is presided over by a sober man who is not himself giving way to the merriment, and (*b*) that this president is a man of more years and experience than the rest of the party—such a gathering might have valuable social uses. *In vino veritas* is true in the sense that when a man is warmed with wine, he shows himself for what he is without disguise. He blurts out thoughts which he would normally keep to himself, and exhibits tempers he would normally hide. If there were a drug which would gradually produce groundless fear and apprehension, as there is not, it would enable us to make a very safe and easy test of a man's courage. We could make him take deeper and deeper draughts of it, and watch his success in mastering his pathological alarms. We should thus be able to do without risk what, in fact, we can only do by exposing a man to actual risk, distinguish the more from the less valiant. Wine does give us such a test of a man's *sophrosyne*. We can see who forgets himself least and keeps his modesty best under the artificial removal of restraints produced by the wine-cup, and, if the party is rightly conducted, there is no danger that the application of the test will have serious consequences ; the subject will be a little noisy and silly for the time, and that is all.   It is much better to learn a man's weakness from such a slight exposure than to have to discover it from his exposure to a grave temptation to unlawful love or the like. The practice might thus be of great value to the magistrate who wants to know what citizens he can safely trust to come well out of positions where there is opportunity for gratifying the desire for unrighteous pleasures.   And to the members of the party, of course, learning to " drink their wine like gentlemen " does afford a very real drill in learning to say " no " at the right time.   On these grounds the Athenian advocates the strictly regulated permission to drink wine convivially.   If there is to be no regulation of such parties, he would like to see wine absolutely prohibited to the young of both sexes, soldiers in the field, servants, magistrates during their tenure of office, sea-captains, jurymen and counsellors when acting in that capacity, and " any person immediately contemplating the procreation of children " (674a–b).   No doubt the main reason for the discussion is that it serves to illustrate the great principles that the better half of valour is mastery over one's desires, and that the true way to master temptation is to stand up to it, not to make its occurrence artificially impossible.

(Book II.)   The sentence just quoted does not occur until the end of the second book, but before we reach it, Plato has ingeniously made the problem of the right use of wine lead up to that of the use of music and poetry as a vehicle of early moral education.   There is still a further valuable social service which may be derived from a proper use of wine, but before we can say what this service is, we must ask the question what right education is.   To answer this, we reflect that a child's first experience in life is acquaintance with pleasure and pain (653a), and that an education in character begins with learning to feel pleasure and pain about the right things (*ibid. b*).   To understand how this education is to be got, we consider that a young creature cannot keep still ; it is always jumping and shouting (*ibid. d*).   In man, by the gift of God, these boundings and shoutings can be transformed into tuneful and rhythmical singing and dancing, and it is with this transformation that education begins (654a).   Thus, by a liberal interpretation, the whole of the early moral training of the young, which is to begin as soon as they are sensible to melody and rhythm, can be brought under the rubric of education in the " choric " art, the art of song accompanied by the lyre and by the movements of an appropriate *ballet d'action*. The connexion of the discussion with the previous problem of the right use of wine is effected by a playful artifice very characteristic of Plato.   It is at first assumed that, since the community as a whole must take its part in the worship of the Muses, there will be three choirs at our musical festivals—one of the boys and girls, a second of the younger, and a third of the older, men.   But old men who are " stiff in the joints " and past the feelings of frolic will naturally not find it easy to recapture the youthful spirit of gaiety which will make it natural for them to sing and dance before a public audience. If they do not enter thoroughly into the spirit of the thing, there will be an awkwardness and constraint about their contribution which is specially out of place in a festival of the deities of graceful achievement. The concession to them of a proper use of wine would provide just the requisite means of recovering for the time the *abandon* of youth, and would be appropriate, when we remember that Dionysus, one of the gods who are patrons of song and dance, is also the giver of wine. As the argument develops, we discover that we are not to take the description of the functions of this " choir of Dionysus " quite literally. What they are really to do is to select the words and music for the songs of younger persons. They are, in fact, to be compilers of the official anthology, and the use of wine is to assist them in this task. The besetting fault of compilers of anthologies for the young is that they make their selections much too " grown-up." The middle-aged compiler's taste is not a safe guide. Plato thinks that if he came to his work warmed with a few glasses of a generous wine, he would be more likely to escape this commonly recognized danger and to make a wiser selection.

The details of the book cannot be discussed here, but it should be noted that while the treatment proceeds on the same main principles as those laid down for the employment of music in the schoolroom in *Republic* iii., the whole discussion is much richer in psychological insight ; no account of Plato's views about the moral influence of music on character can possibly afford to neglect *Laws* ii., though many professed accounts commit the fault. For the general theory of moral education, the most significant utterances are the declaration, emphatically commended by Aristotle, that the whole problem is to teach the young to " feel pleasure and pain " rightly (653*b*) and that " rightly " means " in accord with the rightly uttered discourse of the law " (659*d*, πρὸς τὸν ὑπὸ τοῦ νόμου λόγον ὀρθὸν εἰρημένον),[1] a sentence which seems to be the source from which the expression ὀρθὸς λόγος has got into the *Ethics* of Aristotle. We may also note the vigour of the protest against the view that " the tastes of the audience " are the standard of excellence in art (658*e*–659*c*), and the allusion to the example of Egypt as proof that it is possible to establish permanent canons of aesthetic taste (656*d*, *e*).[2]

With Book III., we enter on the main problem of political science, what a " city " is, and how it arises. To illustrate the way in

[1] The whole sentence should be familiar to every one who wants to appreciate Plato's educational theory ; " education (παιδεία) is the drawing and guiding (ὀλκή τε καὶ ἀγωγή) of children towards the discourse rightly uttered by the law and assented to as truly right by the best and oldest men, on the strength of their experience." The *immediate* point is that sound musical education must accustom the young from the first to *enjoy* what is really good, so that " young and old alike " have the *same* tastes in music.

[2] Note that Plato does not, as is often said, express any approval of the actual " stereotyped " Egyptian art. He merely appeals to the fact that Egyptian art has remained stationary as a proof that permanent standards are possible.

which historical development of institutions is conditioned, we imagine what would happen if a natural cataclysm destroyed the whole of a community with the exception of a few shepherds and goat-herds who escaped by the very fact that they occupied a remote and inaccessible position. They would be the rudest members of their society, and thus all the arts of civilization would be temporarily lost. It would be only very gradually that the chief industrial arts and the arts of letters would be recovered. The survivors would at first live in isolated family groups in out-of-the-way places, with little or no means of intercommunication, and hardly any implements of industry. In the main, when they began to recover communication with one another, they would live, after the fashion of nomads, on the produce of their herds, without accumulating " portable property," and hence without strife and greed (679*a–e*). Their rule of life would be " patriarchal," each head of a house making regulations for his own household, as Homer has correctly assumed in his account of the pastoral Cyclopes (680*b*).

In course of time, men would pass from this " nomad life " to agriculture, and the inhabiting of some sort of " city." These settlements would naturally be made first of all in the uplands, and agriculture would bring along with it the first rude attempts at " enclosures " (681*a*). For defence against dangers, families would coalesce in large " houses " (like the " long houses " of the North American Indians). This would, in time, lead to an *Ausgleich* of rules of life. The " large house " would develop a rule of life out of the various rules each family group brought with it into the settlement, and we might call this the first rude beginning of legislation (*ibid. b–c*). So we should find the first beginnings of sovereignty at the same stage in the appearance of a sort of " aristocracy " of headmen, who see that the rule of life is duly observed (681*d*). When the memory of the cataclysm had sufficiently died out, a further step would be taken. Men would venture to come down into the plains and build cities on a larger scale, like Homer's Ilios (682*a*). With this development we find ourselves in an age of rich and powerful monarchs who can engage in serious hostilities. (It will be noted with how sure an eye Plato discerns the general character of the Greek " Middle Ages," as they are depicted for us in the *Iliad*, which he rightly regards as historical in its representation of the old days of " chivalry.")

The traditional story of the disasters of the return from Troy and of the Dorian conquest of the Peloponnese also has a lesson for us. The narrative of the conflicts between the returning warriors and the new generation, and of the Dorian invasion, throw light on the way in which a " world-war " changes the face of history (682*d* ff.). The main point, made at considerable length, is that the Dorian invaders, if they had only been wise in their generation, had the opportunity of establishing a State which could have held its own against all the Oriental monarchies, since they found themselves in occupation of a new territory, had no ancient traditions or vested interests to hamper them, and so had a free hand for legislation. They must have misused their opportunity, for, though tradition says that they set up a federation of three States—Sparta, Argos, Messene—pledged to mutual support, two of the three were in course of time reduced to subjection or impotence by the third, and it is only in part, and in the one city of Sparta, that the old rule of life, which dates from the conquest and was, in fact, dictated by the position of the Dorians as invaders in the midst of an alien and hostile population, has lasted on. The great mistake made at the conquest was that, though the three kingdoms tried to ensure the permanency of their institutions by a compact that if any attempt at innovation was made in any one of the three States, the other two would help to suppress it, they did not understand the all-important principle that (691c–d) the permanent well-being of any State demands the *division* of the sovereign power between several parties. Concentration of the plenitude of sovereignty in the same hands is fatal. If Sparta has retained much of the old institutions it is because the " division of power " has preserved her. Providence gave an opening for this, when circumstances led to the division of the kingship between two houses ; the wisdom of an ancient statesman—this certainly means Lycurgus—carried the principle further, by dividing sovereignty between the kings and the γερουσία ; the process was afterwards completed by the institution of the ephors. Hence the Spartan constitution is, as Plato holds that a stable constitution always ought to be, a mixed one (691e–692c).

We learn the same lesson from the history of Persia and that of Athens. The principle is that, in the last resort, there are two " matrices " of constitutions—personal rule (monarchy), and democracy (popular rule, 693d). In a sound constitution both need to be blended. This was the case with the Persians under Cyrus, as well as with the Athenians of the same time. But in Persia, the element of popular control has disappeared, and government has become capricious autocracy, with the result that Persia is now only formidable on " paper," since there is no real loyalty in the subject. At Athens, respect for personal character and authority has been lost in a complete reign of the mob. The cause, in both cases, has been the same, ignorance of the true principles of education. Since the great Darius, every Persian prince has been " born in the purple " and brought up by women and eunuchs, who ruin him by gratifying all his caprices. At Athens, the mischief began when the uneducated learned to think their own opinion about music and drama as good as that of the educated, and the same delusion soon spread to political matters ; the Athens of to-day is not really a " democracy " but a " theatrocracy " of ignorant sensation-lovers (694a–701d). In Persia, no one is taught how to command, and in Athens no one learns how to obey. The lesson of history for the intending legislator is thus that every wholesome government must rest on a " division of sovereignty " ; it must combine the " popular " element with " something of personal authority," or, as Plato puts it, must unite " monarchy " and " freedom." There must be somewhere a seat of authority, but authority must not degenerate into regimentation ; there must be ἐλευθερία, the freedom of the individual, but not a freedom which is anarchical.

It is a good corrective to some popular misconceptions of Plato, to note the judicious way in which he employs poetry and tradition as the basis for his tentative reconstruction of pre-history, and the moderation and sobriety of the lessons he draws from history. In the main, his conception of the stages by which men pass through the nomad to the agricultural state, and from the life of the family group to that of the " city," agrees with Aristotle's, and I might suggest that the well-known account of the " household " and " village " as the precursors of the " city " in the *Politics* is consciously inspired by the more detailed picture of *Laws* iii. In one respect, Plato is more " modern " than Aristotle or any other ancient ; he, like ourselves, has a vivid sense of the enormous lapses of time and the numerous changes which must have gone to the making of society before our records begin. Alone among the Greeks, he has a genuine sense of the recency of the "historical" period of human life, and the importance of pre-history. For the theory of politics, the great feature of the book is the clear and definite enunciation of the principle of the " division of sovereign power." Lord Acton once wrote, improving on Dr. Johnson, that the first Whig was not the devil, but St. Thomas. It might be even truer to say, neither St. Thomas nor the devil, but Plato.

The third book of the *Laws* ends with the statement that Clinias and his friend are actually engaged in a visit to the site of the proposed new city, and an invitation to the Athenian to assist them by continuing his discourse on legislation as they walk. In Book IV. Plato proceeds at once to give us a lesson in practical constitution-making. The very first requisite is to be well informed about the topography, climate, economic resources of the State for which we are to legislate, and the character of its inhabitants. The constitution and legislation must, of course, be adapted to all these conditions ; Plato is no builder of Utopias, but an extremely practical thinker. In the present case, he assumes that the territory of the imagined city is varied : it contains arable, pasture, woodland, and the like, in reasonable quantity, but it is not extremely fertile. In situation, the city is some miles from the sea, though there is a spot in its territory which would make a good harbour. It has no very near neighbours. These conditions are assumed, because without them some of the features Plato regards as most desirable in national life could not be secured. He wants his territory to be varied in order that it may be as nearly as possible self-supporting and independent of imports ; he wants it not to be over-fertile, mainly in order to exclude the rise of production for the foreign market, and for much the same reasons he is glad that it should not have easy access to

the sea, the great highway of commerce. His objection is to the
influx of large bodies of aliens engaged in trade, whose presence
would be a menace to the stability of national traditions of life.
(There is to be no Peiraeeus.) And he wants to exclude a big export
trade also, because he does not wish the spirit of the community to
be commercialized. A further danger is that, as in the case of
Athens herself, the development of a sea-borne commerce will lead
to the growth of a navy, and with it to the growth of aggressive
"imperialism." This explains the motive for the long passage in
which it is argued that, contrary to the general opinion, the rise
of Athens as a sea-power has been her chief misfortune (705d–707d).
This was also the opinion of Isocrates, and seems to be true, in spite
of the customary glorification of Themistocles and Pericles. It was
the spirit of commercialistic imperialism which led directly to the
attempt of Alcibiades and his admirers to create an Athenian
empire in the western Mediterranean, and it was this adventure
which irretrievably ruined the Periclean democracy.[1] The history
of Athens explains why Plato wishes a morally healthy society to
be agrarian rather than industrial, just as Ruskin, Carlyle, and
Morris all wished the same thing for England. The composition
of the prospective inhabitants by invitation of settlers from all
over Crete and from the Peloponnese is intended to provide another
advantage. As the citizens come from different quarters, they
will have different original traditions, and this will mean that a
legislator will not have the same dead weight of unintelligent
conservatism to contend against (708d).

Now what would be the most favourable opportunity for the
creation of a thoroughly sound system of laws and institutions?
Though the remark seems paradoxical, the best chance would be
offered by the co-operation of a thoroughly wise statesman with a
"tyrant," but the tyrant would have to be young, intelligent, and
endowed with unusual moral nobility (709e). The thought is that
in this case the statesman would have the freest hand. He would
need only to convert the autocrat to his plans, and the rest of
society would follow suit, partly from loyalty, partly because the
autocrat has the requisite force to constrain the malcontent. He
must be young as well as intelligent, of course, if he is to be won to
such an undertaking: an older man would be less easily impressed.
He must have moral nobility, because he will be called on to sacrifice his own position as autocrat, if the combination of authority
with "freedom" is to be effected. It is improbable that there
should ever be such a conjuncture as the association in one age and
place of a supreme statesman with a young autocrat of such unusual
qualifications, but we cannot say that the thing is impossible (711d).
So we may imagine that the condition has been realized and proceed

[1] Of course it was not the fault of the Athenians that they were a naval
power. They had to be one, just because, like ourselves, they needed to import
their wheat. But the necessity of possessing a powerful fleet inevitably led
to the temptation to use it for purposes of selfish aggrandizement.

to consider what institutions the statesman with such a force at his disposal would be likely to recommend.[1]

If a man with a genius for statesmanship ever got this favourable opportunity of carrying his conceptions out in practice, he would, in accord with the principles already laid down, take care not to establish an " unmixed " constitution of any of the three types familiar in the Greek world. That would be to create a sovereignty of a favoured person or class over a subject class or classes. In a true " constitution " the sovereign is not class-interest, but God, and the voice by which God makes His commands known is the law. Hence the fundamental principle of good government is that the sovereign shall be not a person or a class, but impersonal law (713*e*). In such a society the posts of authority will be awarded for superiority not in birth, or wealth, or strength, but in whole-hearted service to law. Its point of honour will be loyalty to the laws. The Athenian accordingly imagines himself to be in the position of a legislator speaking in the presence of the whole body of intending citizens, and proceeds to begin an address to them on the majesty of law (715*e*–718*a*) ; the opening words of this speech are, perhaps, the one " text " quoted more frequently than any other by the Platonists of later antiquity. God eternally pursues the " even tenour of his way," and Justice attends Him ; he who would be happy must follow in their train with a " humbled and disciplined " spirit ($\tau a\pi\epsilon\iota\nu\grave{o}s$ $\kappa a\grave{\iota}$ $\kappa\epsilon\kappa o\sigma\mu\eta\mu\acute{e}\nu o s$). To follow God means to be like God, who is the true " measure of all things " (716*c*). We are like God so far as we follow the life of right measure.

In the life of measure reverence ($\tau\iota\mu\acute{\eta}$) must be meted out to its various recipients in the right order, first to the gods of the upper world and our city, next to those of the underworld, then to " spirits and heroes," then to ancestors and dead parents, and last to our living parents ; in honouring these last, we must remember that to support them with our substance is the least office, to minister to them with our bodies something more, to give them the affection and devotion of the soul the great thing. We cannot do too much for them while we have them with us ; when they die, the most modest funeral is the most decent and honourable. At this point the discourse on the duties of life breaks off, to be resumed again in the following book. The reason for the interruption is that the speaker recollects that there are two possible types of law, a brief one and a longer. The brief type of law is that in common vogue. It consists of a command or prohibition accompanied by a " sanction " in the form of a penalty threatened for non-compliance.

[1] Why does not Plato suggest that the supremely wise statesman should himself be born heir to the throne ? Presumably because wisdom in states-manship only comes with years and experience. But an experienced monarch of advanced years would have neither the enthusiasm nor the entire freedom from self-interest demanded of the autocrat who is to employ his position to suppress himself. Hence the wisdom must be that of a man who has not to struggle with the insidious temptations of self-interest, the enthusiasm that of a man who has not lost the first flush of youth.

The wise legislator will not, however, wish to overawe the subject into obedience by mere threats. He would prefer to enlist the feelings of the subjects in favour of his regulations as far as he can, leaving only the worst kind of citizen to be merely coerced. If we look at the practice of physicians of the body, we shall see that there are two types among them. There are the mere empirics, usually themselves slaves with slaves for their patients, who give a prescription magisterially with a threat that things will go ill with the patient if he disregards it. There are the eminent physicians, educated men with educated men for their patients ; they explain to the patient the nature of their treatment and the purpose of their regulations and do all they can to get him to help in effecting the cure. It is their method the legislator should adopt. He should therefore prefix to his whole legislation and to the principal sections of it " preambles " explaining the purpose of his regulations and the reasons why such-and-such penalties are proper for neglect of them, and so win the sympathies of the society for whom he legislates (719e–720e). Thus, in enacting that a man shall marry before he reaches a given age or be subject to fine or loss of civil rights (ἀτιμία), he would dwell on the reason for the law, namely, that it aims at securing such immortality as is possible for the race,[1] and the reason for selecting just this " sanction," namely, that the man who shirks the duty to save himself expense shall be visited in his pocket, and that the man who has done nothing to leave a younger generation behind him shall not share in the honours we expect to be shown by the younger generation to their parents (721a–d). We may therefore regard the interrupted discourse on the beings entitled to reverence and the respective degrees in which they are entitled to it, as the opening of a general preamble to our whole legislation.

Book V. in its opening pages contains the continuation of the great preamble (726–734d). From reverence to parents, we proceed to the reverence or respect due to ourselves and our fellows. The rule of self-reverence is that the soul is more than the body and the body than possessions. A man must prize his soul more than his body and his body more than his " goods." We dishonour our own soul when we put bodily vigour and health or power or riches before wisdom and virtue, or when we gratify unworthy caprice or passion. We dishonour the body when we prefer wealth to health. Plato's view is that extraordinary beauty or robustness or wealth are bad for the soul, generally speaking, no less than extraordinary ugliness, deformity, ill-health, penury. The first breeds vanity, the second gross lusts, the third idleness and luxury. In respect of advantages both of body and of fortune,

---

[1] This thought, which had already appeared in the *Symposium*, has no bearing on the doctrine of the immortality of the *soul*. It is the *man*—the complex of soul and body—of whom Plato says that survival in his descendants is the nearest approximation he can make to deathlessness. The ψυχή divorced from the body is not ἄνθρωπος but just ψυχή, a " spirit."

the middle condition is preferable to an extreme. The main rules for right relations with others are that (1) in our relations with friends and fellow-citizens, we should rate the benefits we receive from them at a higher rate than they themselves do, the services we render them at a lower ; (2) in relations to the alien, especially to the suppliant, we ought to be specially careful to be on our best behaviour, for nothing is so odious to man and God as taking advantage of those who are defenceless (726–730a).

Next follows an exhortation as to the spirit in which a man should conduct himself in matters where the law can lay down no specific commands or prohibitions. The supreme demand on a man is for ἀλήθεια (" genuineness ") in all the relations of life—in fact, for " loyalty." A man who is not " true and loyal " is wholly untrustworthy ; want of loyalty makes friendship and all the happiness of life impossible. We must lay it down that in this, and in all points of virtue, it is good to practise them yourself, better to go further and to bring the misdeeds of others to the knowledge of the authorities, best of all, actually to assist them in chastising the misdoer. We must add that rivalry in goodness of all kinds is the one form of emulation we should encourage in all our citizens, as it is the one kind of rivalry which aims not at engrossing a good to one's self, but at communicating it as widely as possible. To the faults of others a good man should be merciful, whenever they are remediable, since he knows that " no one is bad on purpose " ; he will only let his anger have its course with the incorrigible. A man must beware, too, of the deadly fault of improper partiality to one's self. And he must repress all tendency to unrestrained emotionalism (726b–732d).

We must not forget that it is men, not gods, whom we are trying to enlist on the side of virtue. We must therefore make allowance for the universal human desire for a pleasant existence. We cannot expect men regularly to choose the noble life unless they are persuaded that it is also the pleasant. Its nobility has already been argued ; Plato now proceeds to contend that, even by the rules of a Hedonic calculus, if you only state the rules correctly and work the sum right, the morally best life will be found to be also the pleasantest. The rules are that we wish to have pleasure, and not to have pain ; we do not wish for a neutral condition, but we prefer it to pain. We choose a pain attended by an overbalance of pleasure, and refuse a pleasure attended by an overbalance of pain ; to an exact balance of pleasure and pain we are indifferent. We have to take into account as " dimensions " of pleasure and pain " number " and " size "—i.e. frequency and duration and intensity. We wish to have a life in which, when attention has been given to all these " dimensions," the balance works out on the side of pleasure ; not to have one in which the balance is on the side of pain. The life in which the balance is zero is preferable to that in which there is a balance of pain. If we consider four pairs of lives, corresponding to the four currently recognized virtues and their contrary

vices—the life of the temperate and that of the profligate, the life
of the wise man and that of the fool, the life of the brave man and
that of the coward, the morally " healthy " and the morally
" morbid " life—we find that in the first member of each pair there
is less excitement than in the second ; the pleasures and pains are
both less intense, but at the same time these pleasures are more
frequent and more lasting than the pains, whereas, in the second
members of the pairs, the pains are more numerous and lasting
than the pleasures. Thus, in each case, the balance is on the side
of pleasure in the first member of the pair, on the side of pain in the
second. This is Plato's proof that, if the calculation is fairly
worked, the better life proves to be also the pleasanter. Its moral
superiority, we must remember, is not identified with nor inferred
from its greater pleasantness, but is taken to have been already
established independently (732*e*–734*e*). This brings us to the end
of our general prelude to the legislation.

There is still one more matter to be dealt with before proceeding
to the legislation in detail—the creation of the necessary magistracies. The magistrates are, so to say, the warp, the rest of the
citizens the woof, of the fabric we have to weave. The warp must
have the stronger and tougher constitution, must be made of
those elements of the population who have most strength of character and are least pliable. We begin by laying it down (737*c*)
that the size of the community, the number of households, must be
kept permanent. (We want to exclude the social revolutions which
would be produced by either marked decline or marked increase
in population.) We require to have just such a population as
our territory will support in industry and sobriety, neither more
nor fewer. If the population grows beyond this limit, it will begin
to expand at the cost of wrong to its neighbours ; if it falls
below it, it will not be adequate to its own defence. The actual
number of households will depend on the size of the territory, but,
for purposes of illustration (737*e*), we may imagine it fixed at 5040,
a number which recommends itself by the fact that it is divisible
by all the integers up to 10. This is convenient, since there may
be practical reasons for wishing to divide the inhabitants into
administrative groups for various purposes.[1]

We may say at once that the very best and happiest of all
societies would be one where there was no " private " interest,
where even wives and children were " common," and the word
" my own " never heard (739*c*). What we are describing now is a

---

[1] 5040 = 7 ! (the continued product of the integers from 1 to 7). Plato has
chosen it because, since 7 is the highest prime number less than 10, and the
numbers 8, 9, 10 are each products of a pair of factors of which each is less
than 7, 7 ! will obviously be divisible by every integer up to 10. It will also
be divisible by 12 (2 × 6) ; and this is a great convenience, since 12 is the number
of months in the year. Ritter's note on the passage rightly points out that
the reason for choosing such a number is strictly practical ; it prevents any
difficulty in determining the precise quota a particular subdivision of the
population ought to contribute to the revenue or the defences.

society which is to come nearest to this ideal, an ideal only possible perhaps to beings who are more than men (θεοὶ ἢ παῖδες θεῶν, 739d).[1] For this " second city " we must lay it down that the land is not to be cultivated in common ; there are to be private estates and houses, as a concession to human weakness, but the owner of a patrimony must always regard it as belonging to the " city " as much as to himself. It will be an obligation of religion that the number of " hearths " is always to be the same. A patrimony is always to descend undivided to one son, chosen by his father, who will keep up the household worship. Daughters are to be provided for by marriage, and, to ensure their marriage, there will be a law against giving or receiving dowries (742c). A man's remaining sons will be provided for by encouraging adoption on the part of the childless or those who have been bereaved of their sons. Plato is thus aware that his scheme demands that the normal family shall be one of two children. Tendency to over-population will be counteracted by " moral suasion " (740d), or, in the last resort, by sending out colonies. (Apparently no " artificial " methods of birth-control are contemplated.) Unavoidable depopulation by epidemics and the like can be met, though reluctantly, by inviting new settlers.

It will, unfortunately, be impossible to prevent economic inequalities altogether, but they may be kept within bounds, and both penury and irresponsible wealth excluded by the following regulations. The patrimonies should be, as nearly as possible, of equal value (737c) ; to secure that they remain inalienable in the same family, a careful survey of the whole territory will be made and preserved in the public archives (741c). To keep out the taint of commercialism, the State will have its own currency, value-less outside its own territory, and it will be a crime in a citizen to own the coined money of a foreign city (742a).[2] There shall be no lending of money on interest, and no credit (742c). The reason for this is simply that we do not wish to encourage a man to live on the automatic return of investments ; we want him to be a farmer living by the labour of his own hands. Accumulation will be checked by the establishment of four economic classes, the poorest possessing nothing beyond their patrimony, the richest being allowed to possess no more than four times the yield of the patri-mony. Any further increase of wealth will be escheated to the State (744d–745a). Thus wealth will have some weight, as well as character and birth, in the distribution of offices. This is re-grettable, but it is a condition we cannot wholly exclude (744b).

[1] Plato still adheres to the moral ideal of the *Republic*, though he seems definitely to be saying that it cannot be actually embodied in flesh and blood. It may be doubted whether he had ever thought otherwise. At any rate, he now regards a system of peasant-proprietorship with inalienable patrimonies as the society in which ordinary men and women will be likely to show most of the spirit of devotion to the " common " good.

[2] A regulation based on the Spartan practice, which is proposed also by Fichte in his *Geschlossener Handelsstaat*.

The community will be divided into twelve "tribes," [1] care being taken that the total property of the tribes is approximately equal and that their holdings are equalized. Each patrimony will be divided into a half situated nearer to and one situated farther from the town, which must have a central position, and we should be careful to see that this division is fairly made, so that, *e.g.*, a man who has the advantage of having half his estate close to the town shall have the other half on the outskirts of the State (745*b–e*). In connexion with the topic of subdivisions and measurements, Plato shows his practical interest in small matters by expressly insisting on the importance of a rigid standardization of the currency and of all weights and measures (746*e*),[2] the object being, of course, to suppress the possibility of small dishonest gains. It is an unphilosophical prejudice to suppose that the eye of the law should be blind to such things. Arithmetic is of the highest value, provided it is pursued in a spirit untainted by the commercialism of Phoenicians and Egyptians (747*a–c*).

Book VI. brings us at last to the appointment of the various magistrates and administrative boards. We must be content here to describe the most important of these and the method by which they are constituted, as illustrative of Plato's insight into the practical business of " representation." The most important ordinary magistracy is that of the νομοφύλακες or guardians of the constitution, a body of thirty-seven men of approved character and intelligence, who must be at least 50 years old at appointment, and must retire at the age of 70. Their functions are to watch over the interests of the laws in general and, in particular, to take charge of the register of properties, and penalize and " blacklist " any citizen guilty of fraudulent concealment of income. They figure also as the presiding magistrates in connexion with the trial of grave offences of various kinds. They are to be elected by votes given in writing and signed with the voter's name (as a precaution against an irresponsible vote), and the election has several stages, by which the three hundred names first selected are finally reduced to thirty-seven (three for each " tribe " with an odd man to prevent an equal division of opinions).

The ordinary great council, the " representative chamber " of the society, is elected on a plan ingeniously contrived to eliminate extreme " class-consciousness " and to make wire-pulling and cabal impossible. It is ultimately to consist of 360 members, ninety from each of the four property-classes, but the selection has several stages and is spread over a week. In the first instance 360 representatives of each class are chosen, the voting covering four days.

---

[1] The number is selected for the practical convenience that it makes it easy for an office or duty to rotate through all the tribes in the course of a year. The official year is to have 365, not 360, days—a reform never adopted by any actual Greek " city " until a later date (828*b*).

[2] Ritter, *ad loc.*, rightly calls attention to the point that Plato is here, for the first time, pointing out the necessity of regulations of this kind, which were unknown in Hellenic practice.

Citizens of the two richest classes are obliged under a penalty to vote for the representatives of all four classes. The citizens of the third and fourth classes are compelled only to vote on the first two days, and may or may not vote on the second two, as they please. (The thought is that they would mostly abstain, since they have already lost two days from their working week, and will not wish to lose two more. Thus, as the poorer citizens will be the most numerous, the representatives of the two richer classes will be elected by a vote in which the poorer classes will have most influence ; those of the poorer classes will mainly be chosen by the votes of the richer. This means that the names selected will be those of moderate men from all classes ; neither a Coriolanus nor a Cade will stand much chance of election. This secures that the whole body shall be public-spirited, fair-minded, and likely to co-operate harmoniously.) In the second stage of the process, the number of names is reduced to one-half by a vote which must be compulsorily exercised by all citizens. (An extremist who might slip through the first election would thus very probably be eliminated at this stage, and, as the voting is compulsory for every one, the danger that the richer classes might make the representation of the poorer a farce by inducing their poorer fellow-citizens to abstain from voting for the members of their own class is also reduced to a minimum.) Finally, the numbers are again reduced to one-half by the use of the lot. (This would be a final precaution against electioneering jobbery.) The council thus appointed holds office for the year, one-twelfth of it forming a committee which exercises the main functions of sovereignty for each month.

The chief criticism a modern thinker would be likely to pass on the scheme would probably be that it runs the risk of making the extremist all the more dangerous by leaving him no chance of airing his grievances in the " council of the nation." But it might be said that we are learning by experience how hard it is for the same body to combine the functions of a " safety-valve " and a really effective national council.

The most important office in a Platonic community is, as we should expect, that of the Minister of Education. The well-being of the community depends directly on the character of the education given to successive generations, and the overseer of education should therefore be the best and most illustrious man in the community, as holding its most responsible post. He must be a man of over fifty, with children of his own, and should be elected for a period of five years out of the body of the νομοφύλακες by the votes of the other magistrates ($765d$–$766b$). The " President of the Board of Education " is thus the " premier " in Plato's commonwealth.

If the life of the society is to be thoroughly sound from a moral point of view, we must first ensure that the tone of family life itself is sound. Marriage must be regarded as a solemn duty to society ; selfish neglect to discharge that duty, as we have already learned, will be penalized. Extravagant expenditure on wedding festivities must be discountenanced. The peace of the household also demands that we lay down a right rule for the treatment of servants. A master must, for his own sake as well as for his servant's, make it a rule to be even more scrupulously fair in his treatment of his slaves than he is in his behaviour to his equals (777*d*). But he should be strictly just, without compromising his position as master by improper familiarities. His word must be law to his slave, and he must punish all disobedience. When our young people have been married, we must see to it that they begin their married life on the right lines. We must not let them think they can spend these early days, before children have yet come, just as they please, as a sort of honeymoon. The young husband must, for example, take his place at the public table with his fellow-citizens, exactly as he has been used to do (780*b*). And, though this is a thing which has not been attempted even at Sparta, women, no less than men, must be taught to live under the eye of the society to which they belong. They are frailer than men, and need even more to be safeguarded by the knowledge that their conduct is open to public censure. They, too, must have their common table, and we should not listen to the complaints always raised against the moral reformer who claims the right to regulate " private affairs " (780*d*–781*d*). The three keenest of human appetites are those of hunger, thirst, sex, and the rudiments of civilized existence are only made possible by the proper regulation of all three (782*d*–783*b*). When man and woman have been married, they must think it their bounden duty to present the city with worthy offspring. There should be a board of ladies, appointed by the authorities, to supervise the behaviour of married couples in this respect and advise them. This committee will have a general control over married people for ten years after marriage, and it will treat its duties from both a eugenic and a moral point of view. If a marriage remains childless, they will arrange for its dissolution on equitable terms after the ten years. They and the νομοφύλακες will act as conciliators in conjugal disputes, and there will be penalties for parties who are intractable to their remonstrances. They will also see that violations of conjugal fidelity are chastised, where they are too grave to be winked at. It need not be said that a careful register of births and deaths must be kept ; without it we could not secure observance of the regulations about the proper age qualifications for marriage, public office, or military service. Men must marry between 30 and 35, girls between 16 and 20.[1] A man may not be appointed to an office under 30, nor a woman under 40. The period of liability for military service will be for a man from 20 to 60 (the Athenian rule) : if women are given any " war work," it should be after they have borne their children and before they have reached 50 (783*d*–785*b*)

[1] Later on (833*d*) the minimum age of the girls at marriage is reckoned at 18 ; we must remember that the *Laws* has not received its final revision by the author.

The seventh book of the *Laws* contains Plato's most important and detailed scheme for a universal education. The principles are at bottom those already familiar to us from the *Republic*, but the treatment is much more detailed, and in some respects the level of the demands has risen. There must be systematic organization from the first, since if we leave anything to the caprice of the individual householder, we shall not secure the community of spirit and character we need in the State. And we cannot take the matter in hand too early. It is just when the child's body and mind are most plastic that most enduring harm can be done by wrong treatment. We ought, therefore, to begin the task even before a child's birth, An expectant mother must take such exercise as is required in the interests of her unborn child (789*d*). When the child is born, we must see that, even before it can walk, its nurse gives it the exercise and air which is good for it, and particularly, that it is not allowed to injure itself by walking too early (789*e*). A baby should live, as nearly as possible, as though it were always at sea ; it should be dandled and danced about and sung to (790*c–e*) to keep it from being frightened. This is a first preparation for the development of a brave and steadfast character. And care must be taken to keep the baby in a placid mood ; it is a bad moral beginning for it to be allowed to become fretful or passionate (791*d*–793*d*). When the child is 3 or older, we can begin to correct it judiciously, and it will take to playing games. It is best to leave children to invent their own games, but from the age of 3 to 6 they should be brought together daily in the various temples to play under the supervision of ladies appointed by the authorities, who will thus have the opportunity of seeing that the nurses really bring up their charges in the way the State expects of them (793*d*–794*c*). At the age of 6, lessons will begin in earnest, and with them the segregation of the girls from the boys. The boys should be taught to ride and use bow, sling, and dart, and it would be well for the girls to learn the same things, or at any rate, the use of these weapons (794*c–d*). Care should be taken to train the children to be ambidextrous. That this is possible we see from the indifference with which the Scythians use either hand to hold the bow, and it is of great practical importance to have two " right hands " (794*d*–795*d*). Taking "gymnastic" and "music" as the names for the training of body and mind respectively, we may divide the former into two branches, dancing and wrestling. For educational purposes, " trick " wrestling is useless ; only the stand-up sort which is also good training for warfare is to be practised (796*a–b*) [1]; the dancing to be specially commended is similarly the dance in armour, which affords a good preliminary training against the years of military education (796*b–d*).

" Music " requires a fuller treatment. We must remind our-

---

[1] Plato has no use for fancy wrestling and boxing, and would clearly have thought ju-jitsu unseemly. He condemns in so many words the art of Antaeus, who was fabled to vanquish an opponent by sinking to the ground.

selves once more of the great practical importance of the subject.
It is important that there should be no needless innovations in the
" play " of a society, for innovations in play lead on to innovations
in what is supposed to be earnest, and all departure from an established " regimen " is attended with risk to the health of a society,
just as it is dangerous for an organism (797a–798d). Music,
as we have so often said, " imitates " or " reproduces " types of
moods and characters, and, since we wish the national ideal of
character to be kept constant, we shall need to keep the standards
of this imitation constant too. The Egyptians set us an example
in this ; each type of permitted musical form is consecrated by them
to the cultus of a god, and innovation thus becomes sacrilege, and
we ought to require that the example shall be followed in our city,
singular as it seems to a Greek. To see that it is observed should
be one of the functions of our board of νομοφύλακες (799a–800b).
They will not allow the festivals of the gods to be polluted by
choruses declaiming blasphemies and wailing in a way only seemly
for the performer of a dirge (800c–e). (This is meant to exclude
tragic " choruses " and tragedy itself along with them.) Our
poets must feel that their work is prayer, and that the first rule for
it is that of εὐφημία, reverent reticency; the second that they do
not know themselves how to " ask aright " and must learn from the
law what are the true blessings for which men should pray (801a–c).
The poets, then, must submit to a censure and circulate no composition which has not the *imprimatur* of the νομοφύλακες (801d).
It will be the business of the State to compile a suitable anthology
of verse which meets our requirements ; the compilers, besides
being men of sound taste, must have reached the mature age of 50.
In this way we may hope to imbue our young people from the first
with the right taste for high austere art (802a–d). There should,
of course, be a distinction between the songs learned by boys and
by girls ; the tone of the former must be lofty and manly, of the
latter, sedate and pure (802e).

We proceed with the details of the education to be reared on this
basis of a sound taste which is at once aesthetic and moral. We
have, so to say, laid the keel of the vessel and have now to design
the ribs. We may feel, perhaps, that the voyage of life is not so
serious an affair as it seems. Perhaps we are only playthings for
God, but even if that is so, we must " play the game " well, not
in the inverted fashion of mankind at large, who fancy that war is
the business of life, peace only the play. The truth is that it is
peace which is " real " and " earnest," for it is only in peace that
we can pursue *education*, the most serious affair of life (803a–804c).

To return to our subject. We shall need schools for the teaching of the things we have spoken of, with proper buildings and
grounds. And the teachers in these schools will have to receive
salaries, and therefore must be foreigners. All the children must
attend school (φοιτᾶν) daily ; this must not be left to parental
caprice. This applies to girls as well as to boys ; they must even

learn to ride and shoot, or the State will be deprived of the services it has a right to expect at need from the one-half of its citizens (804e–805b).

It is important to note the magnitude of the proposal made here. As Professor Burnet points out, what is being conceived for the first time is the " secondary school," a permanent establishment for the higher education of boys and girls by specially competent teachers duly organized and paid. (The impossibility of maintaining such an institution without salaries is the reason why, in accord with Hellenic sentiment, it is assumed that they must all be non-citizens.) The " grammar school " meets us as an actual institution in the Macedonian age ; it is presumable that it owes its existence to the influence exerted in that age by members of the Academy as the recognized experts in education and jurisprudence. The old practice of the Periclean age had been that " higher education " of all kinds was got from attending the lectures of sophists, each with his speciality. Plato's new idea is the systematization of secondary education by co-ordinating the specialists in single institutions.

We need not be afraid of the criticism that our views on the education of women are paradoxical. We see that women can share the labours of men by the example of Thrace and other districts where they do agricultural work, though at Athens they are expected to do nothing but sit indoors, mind the store-closet, and spin and weave. At Sparta a middle course is followed ; the girls learn to wrestle, and they do no house-work, but they are not expected to be capable of doing anything for the national defence. With all courtesy to a Spartan hearer, we must confess that we cannot be satisfied with such a compromise ; the women should at least be able, in case of need, to scare away raiders from the city (806b).[1]

The scheme we have adopted for our community makes it certain that our citizens will not have to labour long hours for the means of existence ; they will have abundant leisure, and they must not waste it in fattening themselves like cattle, but use it in setting themselves to live the most strenuous of all lives, that which aims at goodness of mind and body. They will have to be up betimes, before all the servants, and to prevent waste of the precious hours in sleep, it will be enjoined that public as well as household business shall be transacted in the early morning. Sleeping long and late is as bad for the body as for the mind (806d–808c). It follows that the boys must be taken to school at daybreak, and both the servants who conduct them there and the schoolmasters must pay the closest attention to their *moral*, for a boy, just because he has a " spring of intelligence " in him, which does not as yet run clear, is the most unruly of all animals. As to the subjects of

---

[1] There is a clear allusion to the fact dwelt on by Aristotle (*Pol.* B 1269b 37), that the panicky behaviour of the Spartan women when Epaminondas was threatening an assault on the city proved that the famous training in rough exercises had no effect in making them braver than women anywhere else.

education at school, we have already spoken of the principles on which songs and poems should be selected, but it will be more difficult to select suitable prose. Of course enough arithmetic must be learned for the purposes of daily life, enough elementary astronomy to understand the Calendar (809c–d), and enough of music to know how to tune one's lyre. This will suffice until a boy is 16 years old, if we allow three years (from 10 to 13) for reading and writing and three more for the study of the lyre, taking care that the sharp boys are not permitted to push on too fast nor the dull to lag behind (810a). The one serious problem at this stage is the selection of prose reading. We may certainly let the boys read sound works on morals and law (811c–e), but there is a difficulty about other kinds of prose, and too wide reading would not be good for boys (811b).[1] The supervision of the whole system will be in the hands of the Minister of Education, assisted by the advice of experts chosen by himself (813c). It must be understood that there will be paid expert teachers of all the exercises we have prescribed for the training of the body ; there will be women as well as men among these teachers, and girls as well as boys will receive the training, so that they may be capable of defending themselves in necessity (814a).

There are still three " branches of knowledge " ($\mu\alpha\theta\acute{\eta}\mu\alpha\tau\alpha$) which any free man should possess—arithmetic, geometry, astronomy (817e). Only a few young people are capable of high proficiency in them, but all must study them " so far as is truly necessary " (818b). But how far is that ? At least as far as the Egyptians succeed in carrying large classes of young people. They have a method of teaching them to deal with fractions and to find the divisors of numbers by means of games in which garlands and other objects have to be divided among a given number of persons,[2] or boxers to be paired. The study of this sort of problem can readily be made to lead up to the recognition that there are " incommensurable " lengths, areas, and volumes, a subject on which Greeks, even Greeks who dabble in mathematics, are disgracefully ignorant (820b), but we must not let our young people share such ignorance. Similarly our secondary education in astronomy must correct the really " impious " mistake of current Greek astronomy, which ascribes irregular movements to the heavenly bodies, and leads to calling the swiftest of them the slowest. We must make it clear that every so-called " planet " has a strictly regular motion and only *one* such motion (822a).[3]

---

[1] The point of this is that what prose literature there was in Plato's time consisted for the most part of the works of the Ionian men of science and of technical works on medicine and rhetoric. For reasons which will become apparent when we speak of Plato's theology, he regards books on science as dangerous reading for the boys and girls.

[2] Two problems seem to be contemplated, the discovery of the factors of composite numbers and the handling of fractions. On the Egyptian problems in question see Burnet, *E.G.Ph.*[3] 18–19.

[3] $\tau\grave{\eta}\nu$ $\alpha\mathring{v}\tau\grave{\eta}\nu$ $\gamma\grave{\alpha}\rho$ $\alpha\mathring{v}\tau\hat{\omega}\nu$ $\acute{o}\delta\grave{o}\nu$ $\emph{\'e}\kappa\alpha\sigma\tau o\nu$ $\kappa\alpha\grave{\iota}$ $o\mathring{v}$ $\pi o\lambda\lambda\grave{\alpha}s$ $\mu\acute{\iota}\alpha\nu$ $\mathring{\alpha}\epsilon\grave{\iota}$ $\kappa\acute{v}\kappa\lambda\dot{\wp}$ $\delta\iota\epsilon\xi\acute{\epsilon}\rho\chi\epsilon\tau\alpha\iota.$ This clearly means not only that the real motion of a planet is regular, but that it

It might seem in place here to add something about the value of hunting as a pursuit for the young. But we must lay it down once for all that we cannot be expected to deal with the whole of such problems in a law. The details must be left to the really competent Minister of Education to regulate by his personal judgment (822*d*–823*d*). For us it is enough to say that we mean only to encourage the sort of hunting which contributes to make good men. We do not wish our citizens to take to the sea, so we shall discourage sea-fishing ; for stronger reasons, we object to raiding and capturing men, and to any kind of chase which depends on mere cunning. Hence we should discourage the mere netting and snaring of any kind of creature, retaining only " the hunting of quadrupeds with horses and dogs and one's own body," as a training in endurance and courage (824*a*).

The contents of Books VIII. and IX. must be dealt with very summarily. Provision is made, as would be the case in any actual Greek " legislation," first of all for the cultus of the State, every month of the year and every day of the month being provided with its appropriate worship ; the object is simply to place the whole daily life of the whole community under the " religious sanction " (828). Since there will be " gymnastic " and musical " contests " as part of this regular worship, Plato then goes on to lay down regulations for the regular monthly exercises of the citizen militia, as well as for the " contests " which will mark special festivals. The latter are meant to correspond to the pan-Hellenic games of actual life, but the programme of " events " is revised. Competition is to be in exercises of strength and endurance which have a real military value, particularly in rapid evolutions in complete accoutrement, and the mimic warfare is to reproduce its model as closely as possible ; there must be a spice of real danger about it. The girls and women must share in all this, so far as their physique permits, but we cannot make detailed regulations on this point in advance (829–835*d*).

This raises an important ethical question. Is there not a real danger that the very free association of young people of both sexes in pursuits of this kind, and their abundant leisure from " work," may lead to a relaxed sexual morality ? Plato thinks not, if we can only establish the right social tradition in such matters, which is that " homo-sexual " relations of all kinds must be reprobated as unnatural and that the normal sexual appetite is to find no gratification outside the bounds of lawful matrimony. This demand may strike most persons as Utopian, and as an attempt to suppress " love." But we must not be misled by equivocal terms. " Love of good-will " is one thing, love of carnal appetite quite another ; the suppression of the second in no way militates against

is not composite. The object is thus to deny all theories, like that of Eudoxus, which ascribe to a planet a double motion in opposite senses. I still think that this must be meant, in spite of the dissent of Professor Storey and Professor Cornford.

the cultivation of the first.[1] That the standard of continence proposed can be attained is proved by the lifelong abstinence of well-known athletes, and surely our citizens can do to obtain a spiritual crown what boxers will do for an Olympic garland.[2] That carnal appetite can be effectually restrained by moral and religious sanctions we see from the complete suppression of incestuous desire in the lives of civilized societies, which is effected simply by the tradition that incest is shameful. So our standard will be found practicable when once it has been consecrated by the sanctions of a social tradition (835*d*–842*a*). If we should find it beyond our power to secure absolute conformity to this rule, we shall at least demand that " unnatural " passion shall be wholly suppressed and that more normal irregularities shall be visited by disgrace if detected.

The speaker now turns to a consideration of regulations necessary for the pursuit of agriculture, the economic foundation of his contemplated society. Under this caption we have proposals for dealing with such matters as encroachments on boundaries, diversion of watercourses, ownership of stray animals, regulation of the market,[3] and the like. In matters like these, there are many already existing good rules which we shall do well to follow (843*e*), a significant hint that many of the regulations proposed are simply based on the actual code of Attica. The student of Plato's political philosophy need not delay over such details, though they have a double interest for the historian of law and custom. They throw a great deal of light on questions of Attic law, and they provide the starting-point for the casuistry by which Roman lawyers and, in modern times, publicists like Grotius and Pufendorf have laboured to arrive at the principles of a satisfactory law of property. It is not surprising that Plato's actual examples recur, for example, in the *Institutes* of Justinian and the *de Jure Belli et Pacis*. The discussion of the regulation of the market leads naturally to consideration of the conditions on which aliens may be allowed to enter the society and practise industry (850*b*–*d*). They are to be subjected to no poll-tax, but they must have an industry by which to support themselves, must conform to the rules of the

---

[1] *Loc. cit.* 837*b*–*d*. This is a criticism of the current theory of many Greek societies—not of Athens—according to which " unnatural " attachments are of great value for military purposes because of the mutual devotion they inspire, the theory presupposed by the institution, *e.g.*, of the Theban ἱερὸς λόχος. The *Phaedrus* had already denied the fact of the " devotion " ; the *Laws* exposes the verbal equivocation by which the practice is defended. (For such a defence, cf. the speech of Phaedrus in the *Symposium*, 178*e*.)

[2] *Loc. cit.* 839*e*–840*c*. The reasoning is familiar to us from the Pauline parallel, 1 Cor. ix. 23–27. The standard here set up is no novelty of Plato's last years ; the demands made on the guardians of the *Republic* would be even more rigorous.

[3] The important points in connexion with the market are that (1) all transactions must be on the basis of immediate payment, (2) there is to be no " higgling " about prices. The seller must have a fixed price and must take neither more nor less. Like Ruskin, Plato is not so anxious to prevent a seller from asking too much as to keep him from palming off bad wares at a pretended " sacrifice " (*loc. cit.* 849*a*–850*a*).

State, and should normally be expected to depart again after twenty years' residence (*i.e.* they are not to acquire a "right of settlement ").

We come now to criminal jurisprudence, with an apology for the necessity of admitting that there will be any crime to be legislated against in a rightly constituted society. The crimes first considered are, in the order of their gravity, sacrilege, treason, parricide. These are "capital" crimes, and it is best for a citizen who commits them that he should be allowed to live no longer, but we must lay it down once for all that the capital sentence must not include the penalizing of his innocent family by the confiscation of property, and that they are not to be regarded as tainted in their honour by his offence. Similar crimes in an alien or a slave will be more mildly visited by whipping and expulsion from the country. In general, Plato allows himself a freer use of corporeal chastisements than modern legislators, since he does not accept the "humanitarian" estimate of physical pain nor the view that its infliction is peculiarly degrading. These capital crimes are to be tried before a court composed of the νομοφύλακες and a number of the magistrates of the preceding year,[1] and the proceedings must be spread over three days.

We must insist, however, that in our State criminal jurisprudence takes a scientific account of the psychology of the offender (857c–d). Current opinion on this matter, as shown by the practice of existing societies, is in a state of confusion. Justice is held to be a "fine" thing (καλόν), but the just chastisement inflicted on a criminal is regarded as a disgrace to him (859d–860b). Yet to be consistent, we ought to hold that if it is "fine" to do what is just, it is also "fine" to get what is just done to you.[2] The secret of the current confusion is that actual jurisprudence assumes that men are bad and do wrong "voluntarily," hence the one great distinction recognized by actual law is the distinction between voluntary and involuntary transgression. But we must adhere to the philosophical principle so familiar to us from earlier dialogues that "all wrongdoing is involuntary" (860d), and therefore we cannot make the distinction between voluntary and involuntary the basis of our penal code (861d). The distinction we really need is a different one, that of βλάβη, the causing of hurt or loss, from ἀδικία, the violation of a right. In inflicting penalties, the proper question is not whether the act committed was voluntary or not, but whether the person on whom it was inflicted received mere loss or hurt, or was further injured in his rights. The proper thing to say about a man who has caused an unintended loss or hurt to another is not,

---

[1] 855c ff. The constitution of the court is thus suggested by that of the Attic Areopagus. Plato is careful to avoid the miscarriage of justice attending on the Athenian practice of allowing a capital case to come before an irresponsible body of ordinary citizens chosen by lot, from whom there was no appeal.

[2] The thought is the old one of the *Gorgias*. It is good for the offender's soul to receive the penalty, and since the suffering is good for him it cannot be αἰσχρόν. The "disgrace" lies not in the punishment but in the crime.

as current jurisprudence says, that he has done an " involuntary wrong," but that he has not committed a wrong at all, but only caused a loss or hurt (861e–862c). It is this distinction between causing loss and infringing a right which we really need to make fundamental in assessing penalties. Thus the important distinction between the causing of detriment and the infraction of a right, with the consequent distinction between an action for damages and a criminal prosecution, is introduced into legal theory for the first time in *Laws* ix. The courts can make mere damage good by the award of *compensation* for it, but contravention of a right must further be met by the imposition of a *penalty* intended to make the offender's soul better (862c–e). If we doubt whether wrongdoing is really involuntary, we need only remember what its causes are—temper, (θυμός), lust for pleasure, ignorance (863a–864b).

Plato now applies these principles to the construction of a penal code. We have to distinguish violation of rights from the mere causation of damage, and in the case of the former, we must distinguish between violence and craft. Regulations are then laid down for the cases of homicide, suicide, maiming, wounding with intent to kill, minor assaults, the object being to give a specimen of a logically constructed criminal code. The penalties will depend not only on the main distinction already laid down, but on the status of the parties, whether citizens, aliens, or slaves. The details must be passed over here. What inevitably impresses a modern reader most unfavourably is the special severity with which injuries committed by a slave on free persons are treated. This is, however, a direct consequence of the recognition of the servile status, which gives these crimes something of the character of mutiny.

Book X. introduces us to one of the most important developments of Platonism, its theology. Plato appears as at once the creator of natural theology and the first thinker to propose that false theological belief—as distinguished from insults to an established worship—should be treated as a crime against the State and repressed by the civil magistrate. He is convinced that there are certain truths about God which can be strictly demonstrated, and that the denial of these leads directly to practical bad living. Hence the denial of these truths is a grave offence against the social order and must be punished as such, the principle upon which the Roman Church still maintains that it is the duty of the magistrate to suppress heretical pravity. Historically we have here the foundation of natural or philosophical theology, The name we owe to the famous Roman antiquarian, M. Terentius Varro, who distinguished three kinds of theology, or " discourses about gods,"— the poetical, consisting simply of the myths related by the poets; the civil, which means knowledge of the Calendar of the State's cultus and is the creation of the " legislator " ; and the natural or philosophic, the doctrine about things divine taught by philosophers as an integral part of their account of φύσις, *natura*, reality. The first, according to a view as old as Herodotus, is the mere invention of poets who aim only at interesting and amusing; the second has been manufactured by the authorities with a view to social utility; the third, and only the third, claims to be part of the truth about things.[1] We must, of course, be careful to remember that the epithet "natural," as originally applied to this kind of theology, conveys no contrast with a "revealed" or "historical" theology; it means neither more nor less than "scientific."

The three heresies Plato regards as morally pernicious are, in the order of their moral turpitude : (*a*) atheism, the belief that there are no gods at all, the least offensive of the three ; (*b*) Epicureanism, as we may call it by a convenient anachronism, the doctrine that God, or the gods, are indifferent to human conduct ; (*c*) worst of all, the doctrine that an impenitent offender can escape God's judgment by gifts and offerings. It is morally less harmful to believe that there is no God than to believe in a careless God, and it is better to believe in a careless God than in a venal one. Against these three heresies Plato holds that he can prove the existence of a God or gods, the reality of providential and moral government of the world and man, and the impossibility of bribing the divine justice.

(*a*) *Atheism.*—Atheism is treated by Plato as identical with the doctrine that the world and its contents, souls included, are the product of unintelligent motions of corporeal elements. Against this theory, he undertakes to demonstrate that all corporeal movements are, in the last resort, causally dependent on "motions" of soul, wishes, plans, purposes, and that the world is therefore the work of a soul or souls, and further that these souls are good, and that there is one ἀρίστη ψυχή, "perfectly good soul," at their head. Thus the demonstration of the being of God serves also, in principle, as a proof of the indestructibility of the soul, a doctrine which has to be introduced in refuting the two graver heresies. He indicates that atheism as an opinion has two chief sources—the corporealism of the early Ionian men of science, who account for the order of nature on purely "mechanical" principles without ascribing anything to conscious plan or design (889*a–d*), and the sophistic theory of the purely conventional and relative character of moral distinctions (889*e*–890*a*). If these two doctrines are combined, atheism is the result. It has to be shown, as against this atheism, that the motions of body are actually all caused by prior "movements" of soul, so that τέχνη, conscious design, purpose, is the parent of τύχη, not τύχη of τέχνη, as the proverb says (892*b*). Or, more briefly, mind, not bodies, is "what is there to begin with " (892*c*).[2]

---

[1] See for Varro's doctrine on this point Augustine, *de Civitate Dei*, vi. 5.

[2] 892*c*, γένεσιν τὴν περὶ τὰ πρῶτα = τὴν τῶν πρώτων γενέσιν = τὸ τῶν πρώτων γένος = τὸ πρῶτον. That γένεσις here is equivalent to γένος is clear from the context,

The proof turns on an analysis of the notion of κίνησις, motion or process (893*b*–894*e*). Ten senses of the word are enumerated. The first five are different forms of actual physical motion : (1) revolution in a circular orbit, (2) rectilinear motion, (3) rolling, (4) aggregation, (5) disgregation. Then follow three " ideal " motions : (6) the " fluxion " of a point which " generates " a line, (7) the fluxion of the line which generates a surface, (8) the fluxion of a surface which generates a solid. These distinctions are merely preliminary to that which is essential for the purposes of our proof. All motions belong to one of two classes : (9) *communicated* motion, " the movement which can only move other things," or (10) spontaneous motion, the " movement which can move itself " (894*b*). And it is argued that causally communicated motion always presupposes spontaneous motion as its source (894*c*–895*b*). Now when we see anything which exhibits spontaneous, or internally initiated, motion, we call it *alive*, ἔμψυχον ; we say that there is ψυχή in the thing. ψυχή, in fact, is the *name* which language gives to " the motion which can move itself." Thus, " soul " is the name, or *definiendum*, of which the " discourse " (λόγος), " movement which can move itself," is the *definition*. The name and the discourse are therefore equivalent, and it follows that the movements of soul, " tempers and wishes and calculations, true beliefs, interests (ἐπιμέλειαι), and memories," are actually the source and cause of all physical movement, since no physical movement is spontaneous (896*d*). This constitutes the proof that soul or mind is the cause of cosmic movement. So far the argument is an elaboration of that which has been given more briefly in the *Phaedrus* for the immortality of the soul.

Next, there must be more than one soul which is the cause of cosmic movements (*i.e.* Plato's theology is theistic, not pantheistic). There *must* be at least two such souls and there *may* be more. For there is disorder and irregularity in nature as well as order and regularity, hence the " best soul " clearly cannot be the only source of motion in the universe ; since order has the upper hand, God, the " best soul," is clearly the supreme cause, but there must be other souls which are not wholly good (896*e*–898*d*). (It must be carefully noted that there is no trace in the language of the doctrine of a " bad world-soul " read into the *Laws* in ancient times by Plutarch and Atticus, and in modern times by Zeller and others. The point is not that there are *two* souls responsible for the universe, but that there are at least two ; the " best soul " is not the only soul there is, but we are at liberty to suppose as many inferior souls as the appearances seem to require.)

If we are not to misunderstand Plato's whole conception we must note the following points carefully. (1) Evil, no less than

since the criticism made on the old physicists is that they regard such things as " fire " and " air," *i.e.* their primary bodies, as the γένεσις περὶ τὰ πρῶτα. For this use of γένεσις see Ast, *Lexicon Platonicum*, s.v., who, however, wrongly places the passage under a different heading.

good, is expressly said to be due to " soul," being identified with disorderly motion. Hence the doctrine of " matter " as intrinsically evil, and the source of evil, which figures in the popular Platonism of later times, is wholly un-Platonic. (2) God (or the gods) is quite definitely declared to be a ψυχή, and we are told that this means that the universe is a result of τέχνη, design. Plato thus definitely believes in a divine purposive activity—in other words, in what is really meant by the " personality " of God. " Pantheism," which repudiates the notion of conscious creative design, would be only another form of the very doctrine Plato identifies with atheism. (3) God is a soul, not a form. The movement which can move itself is the highest type of agent known to Plato, and the fundamental difference in theology between Plato and Aristotle is just that Aristotle insists on getting behind it to a still more divine source of movement, an " unmoved " mover. We have to think of Plato's God as contemplating the forms and reproducing them in the order of the sensible world. Plato's last word on the old question of the *Phaedo*, " what is the cause of the presence of a form to a sensible thing ? " is that God is the cause. Being perfectly wise and good, God makes the sensible order after the pattern of the forms he contemplates. (4) The argument disregards the question, never felt by a Greek to be very important, whether there is only one God or many. But the very phrase " best soul " shows that there is one such soul which is supreme. This, no doubt, is the soul responsible for the one movement which, from the point of view of Plato's astronomy, presents no irregularity or anomaly at all, the movement of the " outermost heaven." This soul would be God in a special sense. How it is related to that which it moves Plato does not tell us, though he suggests alternative views (899a). (5) What are the irregularities which, to his mind, prove that not all cosmic motions are due to a single divine soul ? We may reasonably conjecture that they are, in the first place, the various apparent anomalies in the motions of the planets. These anomalies are not ultimate, but they at least require us to analyse the appearances into combinations of several movements, and this would suggest, as it does to Aristotle, the plurality of " movers." But I think something further is meant. The course of nature on the whole, by its regular periodicities, favours the development of intellectual and moral civilization. Yet there are natural " catastrophes " which are adverse to this development, inundations, successions of barren or pestilential seasons, volcanic eruptions, and the like, and these exceptions to the rule have to be referred to the agency of souls of some kind ; clearly these souls must be thought of as at least partly irrational and evil. Whatever we may think of a Theism of this kind, it seems to me plain that we can find no other doctrine in Plato without doing violence to his language, and we should take note that, though religious faith in God was, of course, no novelty, Theism as a doctrine professing to be capable of scientific demonstration is introduced into philosophy for the first time in this section of the *Laws*. Plato is the creator of " philosophical Theism."

The refutation of the two other heresies now becomes a simple matter.

(*b*) *Epicureanism* (899*d*–905*d*).—The belief that though there are gods they are indifferent to our conduct is suggested by the spectacle of successful lifelong iniquity, but it is really no more than a nightmare or bad dream (900*b*). If the gods pay no attention to our conduct, the reason must be either that they are unable to regulate everything or that they regard man and man's doings as trifles, and neglect the control of these small matters either because they think them insignificant or because they are " too fine " to attend to them. We may dismiss the suggestion of lack of power at once ; it is easier in action to handle small affairs than to handle great, though it is the minute things which it is hardest to perceive accurately. As to the other suggestions, all competent practitioners of medicine, engineering, and the other arts, especially that of the statesman, know that no one ever succeeds in the main of any enterprise if he neglects what appear to be " small details," and we cannot suppose that the " best " soul is more ignorant than a human practitioner, even if it were certain, as it is not, that human conduct is a " trifle " from God's point of view. To suppose that God neglects us because He is too indolent or fastidious to attend to us, would amount to saying that the " best soul " is cowardly or " work-shy," and this is no better than blasphemy. Nor is it true that the regulation of human destiny in accord with moral law would involve endless " interference " with the machinery of things. The result is secured from the first by a law of singular simplicity, the law that " like finds its like," souls, like liquids, " find their level." A man " gravitates " towards the society of his mental and moral likes, and thus, through the endless succession of lives, he always " does and has done to him " what it is fitting that such a man should do or have done to him (904*e*). That is the " justice of God " from which no man can escape in life or death.

We may dispose of (*c*) the doctrine that God can be bribed to wink at sin even more summarily (905*e*–907*d*). For our argument has justified the old belief that we are the " chattels " or " flock " (κτήματα) of the gods. If they wink at the conduct of human " beasts of prey," they are behaving like shepherds or watch-dogs who allow the wolf to rend the flock on condition of sharing in the plunder. A blasphemy like this is more fittingly met by honest indignation than by argument or gentle remonstrance.

We now come to the penalties for the publication of these various heresies. The overt maintenance of any of them ought to be brought at once to the notice of the magistrates, who are to bring the case before the proper court. If a magistrate neglects to act, he must himself become liable to prosecution for "impiety." In the case of each class of offenders we must distinguish between two degrees of guilt—that of the heretic who is otherwise morally blameless, and that of the worse offender who adds practical evil-living to his heresy. For the morally inoffensive heretic the penalty, on conviction, will in every case include at least five years of imprisonment in the " House of Correction," where he will see no one but members of the " nocturnal council," who are to visit him from time to time and to reason with him on the error of his ways (909a). A second conviction is to be followed by death.[1] The worst offenders are those who add to the speculative belief that the gods are indifferent or venal the still graver crime of trading on the superstition of their neighbours for their own profit or aggrandisement, by founding immoral cults. They are to be imprisoned for life in " penal servitude " in the most desolate region of the country, visited by no citizen whatever, and cast out unburied at death, in fact, treated as " dead in law " from the moment of conviction. But their innocent families must not suffer for their offence, and should be treated as wards of the State [2] (909c).

Plato is so much in earnest with this horror of immoral superstition that he ends by proposing to suppress all shrines and sacrifices except those belonging to the public worship of the city. No one may be permitted to have a private " chapel " or " oratory " or to sacrifice except at the public altars and with the established ritual. His motive is not so much the economic one of preventing the locking-up of wealth in the " dead hand," as the moral one of protecting society against the insidious lowering of the ethical and religious standard.

The discourse now proceeds to deal with legislation for the security of private property and trade, particularly with the regulations necessary to prevent dishonesty in buying and selling, and in executing or paying for " piece-work." Then follow regulations about wills, the guardianship of orphans, the conditions on which a son may be disinherited, and the enforcement of the claims of parents on their children. Penalties are enjoined for vendors of philtres and sorcerers, with the remark that the last-named offence

---

[1] We may suppose that the term of imprisonment would be longer for the two graver heresies. The length of the term and the rule of seclusion are meant, of course, to give full opportunity for a genuine conversion and to prevent the contamination of the rest of the community. Death is the penalty for a second conviction, because the offender is presumed to have shown himself " incurable," and death is better for such a man. On the composition of the " nocturnal council " see below.

[2] The simple atheist apparently runs no risk of this severer penalty, since his heresy is not one on which an hypocritical " priestcraft " can be grafted. It may be remarked here that by demanding a grading of prisons into (1) a house of detention for persons awaiting trial, (2) a house of correction for the reclaimable, (3) a house of punishment for the irreclaimable, Plato has anticipated an important reform never fully carried out in our own administration until quite recent times.

might be ignored in a society of perfectly rational persons, but must be treated as serious in a community where the current belief in the sorcerer's powers makes him mischievous (933*b*). We then have a paragraph dealing with larceny and robbery and another on the necessity of enforcing proper supervision of the insane and mentally deficient. Begging must be strictly suppressed, but it will be the duty of the State to see that no one, not even a slave, who is unemployed through no fault of his own is allowed to starve (936*b*). Rules are laid down about the admission of evidence in courts of law and the penalties of perjury. Litigiousness, a common Athenian failing, should be checked by penalizing the vexatious prosecutor ; if his motive was gain, the penalty should be death.[1] The abuse of the profession of λογογράφος is to be met by making the σύνδικος in a vexatious suit liable to the same penalties as his principal (938*a–c*).

These matters of private law must not detain us here, though Plato's treatment of them has the double interest of being founded largely on Attic practice, which he is trying to amend where it seems defective, and of having exercised a considerable indirect influence on the development of Roman law.[2] With Book XII. we return to the sphere of public law and the law of the constitution. Peculation or embezzlement of the public funds, an offence regularly charged on every Attic politician by his enemies, is unpardonable and in a citizen must always be visited with death, irrespective of the magnitude of his defalcation (942*a*). In military matters everything depends on discipline and strict fidelity to orders ; this must therefore be enforced in all the exercises which have been enjoined as the standing military training. Cowardice in the face of the enemy is to be punished by loss of all citizen-rights as well as by a heavy fine (944*e*–945*a*).

To ensure that the magistrates do their duty, Plato adopts the Attic practice of requiring every magistrate at the end of his term of office to submit to a εὔθυνα or audit, and gives special care to the appointment of the board of *corregidors* (εὔθυνοι) charged with the holding of the audit. The members of the board must be over 50 years old, and are to be chosen by the following method. There is a vote by universal suffrage, each citizen voting for only one candidate. This process is to be repeated until the number of names not eliminated is reduced to three. Twelve such officials are to be appointed in the first instance. As soon as the three oldest members of the board reach the age of 75 they retire, and in future there will be an annual election of three new

---

[1] The severe penalty is due to the heinousness of the attempt to make the court of justice itself accessory to the infliction of a wrong. The abuses Plato has in view are specifically Athenian, and would not be likely to be common in the sort of society for which he is ostensibly legislating.

[2] See Burnet, *Greek Philosophy, Part I.*, p. 304. The Academy was the first permanent and organized school of law as well as of mathematics. The two studies are really connected by the importance for both of " clear and distinct ideas."

members (946c).[1] Arrangements are made, however, for an appeal against the findings of the board, and any member whose action is quashed is to lose his post (948a). This board of *corregidors* is the highest ordinary court of justice, and it is interesting to see that Plato provides for appeals from its verdicts.

It would be inconsistent with the whole spirit of the legislation to permit citizens to withdraw themselves from the life of the State at their choice. Travel abroad must therefore always receive the sanction of the authorities, and this sanction will only be given in the case of persons over 40 (950d). It is desirable that older men of sound character should visit other States with a view to learning how the customs of our own society may be improved by judicious imitation of those of others. The traveller should, on his return, make a report on his observations to the " nocturnal council," a sort of extraordinary Committee of Public Safety, which is to be in perpetual session and is charged with a general super-vision over the public welfare. We have heard of this body before in connexion with the proceedings against heresy, and are now told how it is constituted. Its members are the εὔθυνοι,[2] the ten senior νομοφύλακες, the minister and ex-ministers of Education, and ten co-opted younger men between the ages of 30 and 40. It gets its name from the regulation that its daily sessions are to be held before daybreak. One of its chief functions is to foster sound scientific research (952a). There will be a similar careful control of the temporary admission of foreign visitors to our own community. Special encouragement will be given to responsible persons from abroad whose object is to impart or acquire lessons in true states-manship. They will be honoured " guests of the nation " (953d).

It is not enough to have made a good constitution and code for our society ; there is need for constant vigilance to preserve our institutions from degeneration (960d). This vigilance will be exercised by the " nocturnal council," which may fairly be called the " brain " of our whole system (961.d). To discharge its functions it will need to have a thorough understanding of the end to which social life is directed, the development of " goodness " in all its four great forms. This means that its members will require very much more in the way of education than anything we have yet provided (965b). If they are really to understand what goodness is, they must be able to " see the one in the many " (965c), to appreciate and realize the great truth of the unity of all virtues (*ibid. d–e*). In fact, they must have a genuine knowledge of God and the ways of

---

[1] It is clear that the details of the plan would need more adjustment before it would work in practice. Perhaps it is tacitly assumed that most of the original twelve εὔθυνοι would be nearer 75 than 50, and that the three oldest retire in each subsequent year.

[2] The actual words are (951d) τῶν ἱερέων τῶν τὰ ἀριστεῖα εἰληφότων ; that this means the εὔθυνοι is shown by comparison with 947a. In the recapitulation at 961a–b the composition of the council is apparently slightly different. The two passages would, no doubt, have been better adjusted on a final revision of the text.

God (966c) ; they must not be content, as the average citizen may be, with a mere faith based on the tradition of the society (*ib.*). (In other words, they must thoroughly understand the natural theology already laid down in Book X.). We have seen that scientific astronomy, with its doctrine of the regularity and order of the celestial motions, is a chief foundation of the whole Platonic *apologia* for an ethical Theism. Hence a thorough knowledge of astronomy will be indispensable for the men who are the intellect of the State. It is a common, but wholly mistaken, opinion that such science makes men " infidels." When astronomical knowledge is combined with insight into the true nature of the soul as the one source of movement, it leads direct to piety. Hence no one will be qualified to serve on the nocturnal council unless he is a trained mathematician and astronomer and has also rightly grasped the principle of the causal priority of soul in the scheme of things. There remains the task of determining what other studies are implicitly demanded by our programme (966c–969d).

It is sometimes said that in the *Laws* astronomy has taken the place formerly given to dialectic as the supreme science, and that this indicates a growing uncertainty in Plato's own mind about the possibility of metaphysics. This is a complete misinterpretation of the concluding section of the *Laws*. The intellectual quality demanded in the members of the supreme council, that they should be able to see the " one in the many " is precisely the character always ascribed in the dialogues to the dialectician. And we note that astronomical science is only one-half of the qualification laid down. It must be accompanied by a right understanding of the doctrine of the place of ψυχή in the universe, the doctrine which, more than any other, lies at the root of Platonic metaphysics. Though the name " dialectic " is not used, the demand for the thing remains unabated.[1]

THE *EPINOMIS*.—There is no real division between the *Epinomis* and the *Laws*, and the former is sometimes actually quoted by later writers as the " thirteenth " book of the *Laws*, though the *Epinomis* was already reckoned as a distinct work by Aristophanes of Byzantium.[2] There is no real ancient evidence against the authenticity of the dialogue. Diogenes Laertius (iii. 1, 37) says that " some " ascribed it to the Academic Philippus of Opus, but, as he has just told the story that Philippus " transcribed " the *Laws* " from the wax," he presumably only means that he was said to have done the same for the *Epinomis*. Proclus, who disliked the work, wished to reject it, but, as he merely offers two very bad arguments for his view, he presumably knew of no Academic tradition

[1] The *name* is avoided, presumably, as specially characteristic of Socrates, who is absent from the dialogue. The word is carefully avoided also in the *Timaeus* for the same reason.
[2] He made the (spurious) *Minos*, the *Laws*, and the *Epinomis* one of his " trilogies " (Diog. Laert. iii. 1, 62).

in its favour.¹ I can detect no linguistic difference whatever between the style of *Epinomis* and *Laws*, and the very fact that the *Laws* have manifestly not received even the trifling editorial revision which would have removed small verbal inaccuracies and contradictions makes it incredible to me that Plato's immediate disciples should have issued as his the work of one of themselves. Hence I am confident that the current suspicion of the dialogue is no more than a prejudice really due to the now exploded early nineteenth-century attacks on the genuineness of the *Laws* themselves.² In any case, we have to recognize that the work was known to Aristotle, who has a curious allusion to it at *Metaphysics* 1073*b* 9.³ I feel justified, therefore, in regarding the *Epinomis* as Plato's, and holding that it was intended as an integral part of the *magnum opus* of his last years.

The immediate purpose of the dialogue is to discuss the question left unanswered in *Laws* xii., of the complete scientific curriculum necessary for the members of the " nocturnal council ": What studies will lead to σοφία (973*b*) ? We must recognize that σοφία, in any case, is only attainable by a select few, and with difficulty (973*c* ff.), and that most of the so-called ἐπιστῆμαι do not help us to it (974*d*). Thus we may exclude all the arts and sciences which simply contribute to material civilization or to amusement (974*e*–975*d*), as well as those of war, medicine, navigation, and rhetoric, and still more unhesitatingly the mere art of acquiring and retaining multifarious information, which many confuse with σοφία (975*e*–976*c*). We ought to give the name σοφία only to studies which make a man a wise and good citizen, capable of exercising or obeying righteous rule. Now there is a branch of science which, more than any others, has this tendency and may be said to be a gift of a god to man, being in fact the gift of Heaven (οὐρανός) itself. This gift is the knowledge of *number*, which brings all other good things

---

¹ His arguments are given in the *Prolegomena to the Philosophy of Plato*, apparently by Olympiodorus (*Platonis Opera*, C. F. Hermann, vi. 218). They are (1) that Plato would not have gone on to write another dialogue, leaving the *Laws* unrevised, (2) that motion from W. to E. is called in the *Epinomis* " to the right " (*Epin.* 987*b*), whereas in the dialogues (*Timaeus*, 36*c*) it is called " to the left." But (1) assumes that the *Epinomis* is really meant to be " another dialogue," and (2) overlooks the point that the *Laws* use the same language as the *Epinomis* (760*d* 2). The really significant thing is that Proclus makes no appeal to testimony.

² See the good defence of the *Epinomis* in Raeder, *Platons philosophische Entwickelung*, 413 ff. Stenzel (*Zahl und Gestalt*, 103 n. 4) rightly declines to commit himself to rejection. The " demonstration " of the spuriousness of the *Epinomis* by F. Müller (*Stilistische Untersuchung der Epinomis des Philippos von Opus*, 1927) leaves me still unconvinced.

³ It is said there that it is obvious τοῖς καὶ μετρίως ἠμμένοις, that the motions of the planets are composite, a fairly clear retort to *Epin.* 987*b* 9, where the theory that the " diurnal revolution " is a component of the planetary orbits is said to be " what might seem true " ἀνθρώποις ὀλίγα τούτων εἰδόσιν. Jaeger (*Aristoteles*, 146, 153 ff.) has called attention to the connexion between the *Epinomis* and Aristotle's περὶ φιλοσοφίας, but regards the former as an Academic rejoinder to the latter.

along with itself (977b).¹ Without knowledge of number we should
be unintelligent and unmoral (977c–e). How divine a thing it is
we see from the consideration that where there is number there is
order ; where there is no number, there is nothing but confusion,
formlessness, disorder (977e–978b). To be able to count is the
prerogative which marks men off from the animals. We learn to
count up to fifteen by simply studying the daily changes in the face
of the moon as she rounds to the full ; a much bigger problem is set
us when we go on to compare the period of the moon with that of the
sun, as the agriculturist must. In our own recent discussion it was
easy enough to see that a man ought to have goodness of soul, as
well as of body, and that to have this he must be " wise." The
difficult question was what kind of knowledge this all-important
" wisdom " is. What we have just said suggests the answer
(978b–979d).

Perhaps we may not discover a single " wisdom " which covers
the whole ground. In that case, we must try to enumerate the
various branches of wisdom and say what they are (980a). We may
go back to our thought that the best way a man can spend his life
is to spend it in praising and honouring God. Let us then, to the
praise of God, construct an improved " theogony," holding fast
to the natural theology we have laid down, and particularly to the
principle of the causal priority of soul over body (980b–981b). An
" animal," we know, is a soul conjoined with a body. There are
five regular solids, and we may recognize five corresponding forms
of body—earth, water, air, fire, and aether ²—and five corresponding
kinds of animal, each with its special habitat. The body of each
kind of animal is a compound in which the " element " that forms
its habitat is predominant. Hence the two most conspicuously
visible classes of living beings are those which live on the earth,
of whom man specially interests us, and those which have bodies
made chiefly of fire and are gods, the stars and planets. Their
bodies are more beautiful than ours, and more lasting, being either
deathless or of age-long vitality. A comparison of the restless and
disorderly movements of man with the majestically orderly movements of the heavenly bodies is enough to show that their souls
equally surpass man's in intelligence. If they, unlike us, never
deviate from one path, it is because their motion exhibits the
necessity imposed by rational pursuit of the best (982b). Their
real bulk, as science can demonstrate, is enormous, and there is

¹ Number is the gift of " Uranus," because, as Plato holds, the science of
it has been developed in the interest of learning to number and compute
days, months, and years. Cf. *Timaeus*, 38c, 39b.
² The corpuscular theory of the *Timaeus* is here implied, with the addition
that, to get something to correspond with the dodecahedron, the αἰθήρ, the
clear blue of the upper air, is recognized as a fifth " body." This πεμπτὸν σῶμα
(whence the name *quinta essentia*) is identical with Aristotle's πρῶτον σῶμα, or
" celestial matter." But, unlike Aristotle, Plato does not regard it as the
" matter " of the heavenly bodies ; they are made mainly of fire, as Timaeus
had taught.

only one answer to the question how such masses can be made to revolve endlessly in the same orbits ; it is that the masses are alive, and that it is God who has conjoined their ψυχαί with these vast bodies (983*b–e*). Either they are themselves gods, or they are images of gods wrought by the gods themselves (984*a*), and therefore more to be held in honour than any images of man's making. We may suppose that the intervening regions of aether, air, water, are also inhabited by appropriate denizens. A man may give what account he pleases of Zeus and Hera and the rest of the traditional pantheon, but we must insist on the superior dignity of the visible gods, the heavenly bodies. Air and aether will have denizens with transparent bodies and therefore invisible to us ; we may suppose that they are a hierarchy of " spirits " (δαίμονες), who act as unseen intermediaries between gods and men, favouring the good and warring against the bad (984*d*–985*b*). There may be similar semi-divine denizens of the water of whom men get occasional glimpses. The current worships have been largely prompted by real or imagined appearances of such beings, and a wise law-giver will not wantonly interfere with them. Men cannot have real knowledge about such things (985*d*). But the neglect of Greeks to pay proper honour to the heavenly bodies, the gods whom we all do see, is quite inexcusable. They should be honoured not merely by feasts of the Calendar, but by setting ourselves to get a scientific knowledge of their motions and periods (985*e*).[1]

This means that we must master the science of the revolutions of the stars and planets. At present we have not so much as names for the planets, though they are called the stars of several gods, a nomenclature which has come to us from Syria (986*e*–987*d*).[2] It is the general rule that whatever Greeks borrow from barbarians they improve upon (987*e*). Every man who is a Greek should therefore recognize the duty of prosecuting astronomy in a scientific spirit, and cast off the superstitious fear of prying into divine matters. God knows our ignorance and desires to teach us (987*d*–988*e*).

The study we need to lead us to true piety, the greatest of the virtues, is thus astronomy, knowledge of the true orbits and periods of the heavenly bodies, pursued in the spirit of pure science, not in that of Hesiod's farmer's calendar (990*a*). But since such a study is concerned with the difficult task of the computation of the relative periods of sun, moon, and planets (and thus has to reckon with

[1] The irony of the whole passage about the supposed denizens of aether, air, and water and the popular cults of such beings must not be overlooked. We have been told (980*c*) that the whole account is a " theogony," though, as is added at 988*c*, a less objectionable one than those of the old poets, and that knowledge on such matters is impossible. All that is really serious is the insistence on the necessity of giving the first place in the popular cult to the heavenly bodies and recognizing the study of astronomy as the right way to worship them. The rest is a concession to the maxim that harmless popular rites are not to be disturbed. Timaeus had taken the same line (*supra*, p. 452).

[2] The names " star of Aphrodite," " of Ares," " of Zeus," " of Cronus," from which our designations are derived, appear for the first time in literature in this passage. " Star of Hermes " is first found in *Timaeus*, 38*d*.

highly complicated arithmetical problems), it must have as its foundation a thoroughly scientific theory of number. This includes not only a scientific doctrine of whole numbers ("the odd and even," 990c), but two other studies, commonly called by the misleading names geometry and stereometry. Geometry is really arithmetic, a study of *numbers* "which are in themselves dissimilar, but are assimilated by reference to surfaces," and stereometry is similarly the study of another class of numbers which become similar when raised to the third power. Also we need to study for its physical importance the theory of progressions. The geometrical series 1, 2, 4, 8 reveals to us the principle on which the magnitude of length, area, and volume are interconnected ; in the arithmetical progression 6, 9, 12 and the harmonic progression 6, 8, 12 we have the secret of music, since the two means 9 and 8 correspond to the two great intervals within the octave, the fifth and the fourth. Thus we might say that consideration of the ratio 2 : 1, its powers, and the means between its terms, discloses the supreme secret of nature (990a–991b). And besides we must add to this study of a scientific arithmetic which has been extended to cover geometry plane and solid, as the completion of the whole curriculum, insight into the absolute unity of principle which runs through the whole of exact science and makes it one (991c–e).[1] (Thus once more dialectic, the synoptic apprehension of the principles which pervade all science and the whole of the *scibile*, reappears as the foundation of statesmanship.)

Without this scientific knowledge, a city will never be governed with true statesmanship, and human life will never be truly happy. The wisest man is the man who has attained all this knowledge ; we may feel confident that when death translates him from the sensible region, he will finally achieve the complete unification of the self, and his lot, wherever it may be cast, will be truly blessed. As we said before, the attainment is only possible for the few, but we must insist that our supreme governors at least shall devote themselves to it (992a–d). Thus the *Epinomis* ends by the unqualified reassertion of the old demand that statesmanship and science shall be combined in the same persons.

[1] The text of 990c 5–991b 4, the most important mathematical passage in the Platonic *corpus*, is unfortunately uncertain, in part probably corrupted, in part also possibly never reduced to grammatical form by the writer, but the sense is clear. The point of chief significance is the revolutionary demand that quadratic and cubic " surds " shall be recognized as *numbers* in opposition to the traditional view that there are " irrational " magnitudes (lengths, areas, volumes), but no " irrational " numbers. The meaning of the rest is that the succession of the " powers " 2^1, 2^2, 2^3, is the most elementary example of the principle that similar areas have the duplicate and similar volumes the triplicate ratios of the corresponding " sides," and that the ratios corresponding to the fourth and fifth in the scale respectively, the ἐπίτριτος and ἡμιόλιος λόγος, are also the harmonic and arithmetic means between 1 and 2. (Plato selects 6 and 12 as surrogates for 1 and 2 in this illustration because he wishes the two " means " to be whole numbers.) Stenzel comes near explaining the passage correctly (*Zahl u. Gestalt*, 98 ff.).

See further :

BURNET.—*Greek Philosophy, Part I.*, 301–312 *al.*
RITTER, C.—*Platon*, ii. 657–796 *al.* ;   *Platons Gesetze, Kommentar zum griechischen Text* (Leipzig, 1896) ;   *Platos Gesetze, Darstellung des Inhalts* (Leipzig, 1896).
A. E. TAYLOR.—*The Laws of Plato translated into English.* (London, 1934.)
RAEDER, H.—*Platons philosophische Entwickelung*, 395–419.
NATORP, P.—*Platons Ideenlehre*, 358–365.
BARKER, E.—*Greek Political Theory : Plato and his Predecessors*, 292–380.
JAEGER, W.—*Aristoteles*, 125–170.
MÜLLER, F.—*Statistische Untersuchung der Epinomis des Philippos von Opus* (1927).
HARWARD, J.—*The Epinomis of Plato.*   Translated with *Introduction and Notes.*   (Oxford, 1928.)
And for the problems presented by the *Epistles :*
FRIEDLÄNDER, P.—*Platon : Eidos, Paideia, Dialogos* (1928).
EGERMANN, FR.—*Die platonischen Briefe VII und VIII*, (Vienna, 1928.)
SOUILHÉ, J.—*Platon, Lettres.*   (Paris, 1926.)
NOVOTNY, F.—*Platonis Epistulae.*   (Brno, 1930.)
HARWARD, J.—*The Platonic Epistles.*   (Cambridge, 1932.)

CHAPTER XIX

PLATO IN THE ACADEMY—FORMS AND NUMBERS

TO us Plato is first and foremost a great writer, but from his own point of view, books and the study of them are a secondary interest with the "philosopher"; what counts as supreme is a life spent in the organized prosecution of discovery (τὸ συζῆν). There can be no doubt that Plato thought his work as the organizer of the Academy much more important than the writing of dialogues. Since Aristotle commonly refers to the teaching given in the Academy as Plato's "unwritten doctrine" (ἄγραφα δόγματα), we may be reasonably sure that Plato did not even prepare a MS. of his discourses. This explains why there were several different versions in the next generation of the famous lecture on "the Good," which seems to have contained Plato's most explicit account of his own philosophy. We are told that several of the hearers, including Aristotle, Xenocrates, and Heraclides of Pontus, all published their notes of it, and the obvious implication is that there was no "author's MS." to publish. Consequently we have to discover Plato's ultimate metaphysical positions indirectly from references to them in Aristotle, supplemented by occasional brief excerpts, preserved by later Aristotelian commentators, from the statements of Academic contemporaries of Aristotle, like Xenocrates and Hermodorus. This creates a serious difficulty. When it is a mere question of what Plato *said*, the testimony of Aristotle is surely unimpeachable; but when we go on to ask what Plato *meant*, the case is different. Aristotle's references are all polemical, and Aristotle is a controversialist who is not unduly anxious to be "sympathetic." Unfortunately, too, mathematics, the science specially important for its influence on Plato's thought, is the one science where Aristotle shows himself least at home. Thus there is always the possibility that his criticisms may rest on misunderstanding. And the misunderstandings may not even originate with him. The criticism of Plato all through the *Metaphysics* seems to be subsidiary to Aristotle's standing polemic against Xenocrates, the contemporary head of the Academy. Hence it is possible that much of the criticism of *Metaphysics* M–N, the most sustained anti-Academic polemic in Aristotle, may be directed rather against Academic misinterpretation of Plato than against Plato himself.

In a necessarily brief statement our safest course is to deal only with views expressly attributed by Aristotle to Plato, and with them only so far as their meaning seems to be beyond reasonable doubt. This is, at any rate, all I can attempt in the space at my disposal. But we must carefully avoid the nineteenth-century mistake of treating the statements described by Aristotle under the name of the " doctrine " ($\pi\rho\alpha\gamma\mu\alpha\tau\epsilon\iota\alpha$) of Plato as a sort of senile dotage. Aristotle definitely identifies Platonism with these doctrines and never even hints that he knew of any other Platonism, though he does occasionally remark that the dialogues differ from the " unwritten " discourses. It seems to follow that the theories called Plato's by Aristotle must have been formulated as early as 367 B.C., the year of Aristotle's entry into the Academy, and, quite possibly, even earlier.

When we turn to these Aristotelian statements we find that, for the most part, they amount to a version of the theory of forms with a very individual character, and of a much more developed type than anything the dialogues have ascribed to Socrates. There are also one or two other notices of specific peculiarities of Plato's doctrines, all concerned with points of mathematics, and it is with some of these I propose to begin, as they may help us to understand the point of view from which the doctrine of forms as known to Aristotle was formulated.

We must remember that though mathematics was by no means the only science cultivated in the Academy, it was that which appealed most to Plato himself, and that in which the Academy exercised the most thoroughgoing influence on later developments. All the chief writers of geometrical textbooks known to us between the foundation of the Academy and the rise of the scientific schools of Alexandria belong to the Academy. In Plato's own lifetime, Theaetetus had completed the edifice of elementary solid geometry, by discovering the inscription of the octahedron and icosahedron in the sphere. He and Eudoxus and others had laid the foundations of the doctrine of quadratic surds as worked out in the tenth book of Euclid's *Elements* ; Eudoxus had invented the method of approximating to the lengths and areas of curves by exhaustion (the ancient equivalent of the Integral Calculus), and had recast the whole doctrine of ratio and proportion in the form in which we now have it in Euclid's fifth book, for the purpose of making it applicable to " incommensurables." We naturally expect to find traces in Plato's doctrine of this special preoccupation with the philosophy of mathematics which is characteristic of the work of the school.[1]

To understand the motives which were prompting the Academy to a reconstruction of the philosophy of mathematics, we must go

[1] For an account of the Academic work in mathematics I may refer the reader to any of the standard works on the history of mathematics, *e.g.* Zeuthen, *Histoire des mathématiques dans l'antiquité et le moyen âge* (Fr. tr., Paris, 1902), or, for a still briefer account, Heiberg, *Mathematics in Classical Antiquity* (Eng. tr., Oxford, 1922). The ancient notices are chiefly preserved in the second prologue to Proclus' *Commentary on Euclid* i., and in the scholia to Euclid.

back to the age of Zeno. In the Pythagorean mathematics of the fifth century there were two serious logical flaws. One was that in treating geometry as an application of arithmetic, the Pythagoreans had made the point correspond to the number 1, as is indicated in the traditional definition of the point, often mentioned by Aristotle, that it is μονὰς ἔχουσα θέσιν, "a 1 with position." The identification implies the view that a point is a minimum volume, and was ruined by Zeno's acute argumentation from the possibility of unending bisection of the straight line and the impossibility of making a line longer or a volume bigger by adding a point to it. There are just two ways of meeting the difficulty : one is to evade it, by severing geometry from its dependence on arithmetic, as Euclid does; the other is that actually hinted at by Zeno's own language and definitely adopted by modern philosophical mathematicians, of making the point correspond to 0 and regarding 0, not 1, as the first of the integers.[1] It was towards this view that Plato was feeling his way, as we shall see immediately. The other great trouble was the discovery that there are "incommensurables" or "surds," e.g. that the ratio of the length of the side of a square to its diagonal is not that of "integer to integer." Here, again, two ways of meeting a difficulty fatal to the old philosophy of mathematics as it stood are possible. One is again to surrender the parallelism between geometry and arithmetic by admitting the existence of surd geometrical magnitudes, but denying that there are "surd" numbers. This is the position taken by Aristotle in express words and tacitly by later mathematicians like Euclid, who always represents an "incommensurable" by a line or an area. The other is that of modern rationalistic mathematics, to revise the conception of number itself, so that it becomes possible to define "irrational" numbers of various kinds and to formulate laws for their addition and multiplication in terms of the already known arithmetic of integers. The problem has only been satisfactorily solved in the work of the last half-century, but, as we saw in dealing with the *Epinomis*, this was the line which already commended itself to Plato. Geometry and "stereometry" are, according to him, really the arithmetic of the quadratic and cubic "surds," as plane geometry has been said in our own time to be simply the "algebra of complex numbers." In this way the parallelism of geometry with arithmetic is preserved by a revised and enlarged conception of arithmetic itself.[2]

With these considerations in mind, we can readily understand certain statements which Aristotle makes about mathematical views of Plato. There are three such statements which we may at once elucidate. (a) Plato stated that the "point" was a

[1] Cf. the definition of the integer-series in Frege's *Grundgesetze der Arithmetik* which is, put into words, "the integers are the successors of 0."

[2] For a real comprehension of Plato's thought it is indispensable to have a grasp of the modern logic of arithmetic. I would recommend as sufficient (but also necessary) such an exposition as that given in chap. i. (Real Variables) of Professor G. H. Hardy's *Pure Mathematics*.

" fiction of the geometers," and spoke, instead, of the " starting-point of the line " (*Met.* A 992*a* 20). This means, of course, that Plato rejected the conception of a point as a minimum of volume, or " unit." It has no magnitude of its own but is " the beginning " of the straight line which has such a magnitude (its length). In other words, what corresponds in arithmetic to the point is not 1 but 0, if only Greek arithmeticians had possessed a word or symbol for 0. The underlying thought is that which reappears in later Greek Platonists when they speak of a line as the " fluxion " (ῥύσις) of a point, in the very terminology Newton was later to introduce into English. We are on the track of the ideas and terminology of the inventors of what we call the Differential Calculus. It is true, of course, that this notion of an " infinitesimal " which is not quite nothing nor quite something, but a nothing in the act of turning into something, involves a logical paradox and that it has only been finally disposed of by the purification of mathematical logic, which has eliminated " infinitesimals " from the so-called Infinitesimal Calculus. But the Calculus had to be there first before its purification from bad logic could be possible, and it is hard to see how it could ever have been originated without this defective but useful conception. (*b*) (*Met. ibid.* 22) Plato " often used to assume his indivisible lines " (πολλάκις ἐτίθει τὰς ἀτόμους γραμμάς). Aristotle, who apparently distinguishes this point from the one he has just mentioned, does not explain its meaning. In the textually badly corrupt Peripatetic tract *de Lineis insecabilibus*, which appears to be a polemic of an Aristotelian of the first genera-tion against Xenocrates, the " indivisible line " is regarded as a minimum length, and it is urged that there are insuperable geo-metrical difficulties about such a conception, as, in fact, there are. What Plato may have meant by the expression we can only con-jecture. As a conjecture I offer the suggestion that his intention is precisely to deny the conception attributed to some Academic, apparently Xenocrates, by the Peripatetic tract. A line, however short, is " indivisible " in the sense that you cannot divide it into elements which are not themselves lines—in other words, it is a " continuum." The point makes a straight or curved line not by addition or summation, but by " flowing " ; a straight or other line is not made of points in the way in which a wall is made of bricks laid end to end.[1] (*c*) Plato said that " there is a first 2 and a first 3, and the numbers are not addible to one another " (*Met.* M 1083*a* 32, the one statement about numbers which is definitely attributed to Plato by name in the last two books of the *Metaphysics*). A similar point is made about the Academy gener-ally in the *Ethics* (*E.N.* 1096*a* 17 ff.), where we are told that they held that there is no form (ἰδέα) of number, because " in numbers

[1] Cf. the observations of Stenzel, *Zahl u. Gestalt*, 89 ff. The technical expressions ῥεῖν, ῥύσις, the source of Newton's language about " fluents " and their " fluxions," come from the accounts of the doctrine in the Aristo-telian commentators and were presumably coined by the Academy.

there is a before and an after," *i.e.* because numbers form a *series*.
The meaning of these statements seems not to have been clear to
Aristotle, but is manifest to anyone who has learned to think of
number *en mathématicien*. The sense is that the series of numbers is
not made by adding " units " together. *E.g.* we say that $3+1=4$,
but we do not mean that 3 is three " units " or that 4 is 3 *and* 1 ;
4 is not four 1's, or a 3 and a 1, it is *one* 4. What we really *add*
together is not numbers but aggregates or collections. Thus it is
true that if you have a group of *n* things and another group of *m*
things, and form the two into one group, the new group contains
$m+n$ things, but it is not true that the *number* $m+n$ contains a
number *m* and a number *n*. The importance of this view is that it
leads to revision of the whole conception of number. The fifth-
century theory, still represented by Euclid's definition of ἀριθμός
(*Elements* vii. def. 2) is that a " number " is πλῆθος μονάδων, a
" collection of 1's." On the new view, the only really sound one,
no number is a " collection " ; the statement that $3=2+1$, which
is the definition of 3, does not mean that 3 is " a 2 and a 1," but that
3 is the term of the integer-series which comes " next after " 2.

This explains why there is no form of number. The reason is
that each " number " is itself a form, as was really implied in the
Phaedo itself when Socrates spoke of " the number 2 " and " the
number 3 " as instances of what he meant by a form. Hence the
ordered series of integers is not *a* form, it is a series of forms.
The point may be grasped if we remember that in our own philosophy of mathematics we do not find it possible to define " number "
or even " integer " ; all that we can do is to define the *series* of
integers or the series, *e.g.*, of " real " numbers, and to define individual numbers. I can define " the integer series " as a series of
a certain type with a certain first term, and I can define " the
integer " $n+1$ by saying that it is the number of that series which
is next after *n*, but I cannot really define " integer." Aristotle
is never tired of arguing against Plato that there is no number
except what Aristotle calls " mathematical " number, or alternatively " number made of 1's " (μοναδικὸς ἀριθμός) ; but the
simple truth is that *no* " number " is " made of 1's," and that it is
precisely what Aristotle calls " mathematical " number which has
no existence except in his imagination. Plato may well have
been led to this denial that numbers are " addible " by his recognition that " surds " like $\sqrt{2}$, $\sqrt[3]{2}$, must be admitted into arithmetic
as numbers, since it is evident that no process of " adding 1 to 1 "
could ever yield such numbers as these.[1] Thus this doctrine, also,
may well be connected with the fact that the " real " numbers form
a *continuum*. But it is important to be clear on the point that the
principle that number is not really generated by addition of 1's

[1] This is the consideration made prominent in the treatment of the doctrine
by M. Milhaud in *Les Philosophes-géomètres de la Grèce*, a work really indispensable to the student of Plato. But, as we shall see immediately, it is not
the whole, nor the most important part, of Plato's doctrine.

applies equally to the numbers of the integer-series, which is not a continuum.

This brings us to the consideration of Aristotle's account of Plato's theory of forms. According to the *Metaphysics*,[1] Plato actually called the forms numbers, and maintained that each form or number has two constituents, the One, which Aristotle regards as the formal constituent, and something called the " great-and-small " or " the indeterminate duality " (ἀόριστος δυάς), which Aristotle treats as a material constituent. In other words, a number is something which arises from the determination of a determinable, (the great-and-small), by the One. Since the forms are the causes of all other things, these constituents of the forms are the ultimate constituents of everything, and this is what is meant by the statement that other things " participate " in the forms.[2] Aristotle remarks on the theory that it is of the same type as the Pythagorean doctrine that " things are numbers," or are " imitations of numbers," but differs from that view by substituting the " duality " of the " great-and-small " for the " indefinite " (ἄπειρον) as one constituent of numbers, and also by maintaining that " mathematicals " (τὰ μαθηματικά) are intermediate between numbers and sensible things, whereas the Pythagoreans said that the numbers *are* the things.[3] He seems also to connect this theory with the special point in respect of which he holds Plato and the Pythagoreans inferior to Socrates, namely, that they " separated " (ἐχώρισαν) the " universals " or forms from " things " as Socrates had not done.[4]

It is plain from the explanations attempted by the later commentators on Aristotle that the chief source from which the doctrine alluded to in the *Metaphysics* was known in antiquity was the reports of the auditors of Plato's famous lecture on " the Good." As we do not possess these reports and cannot be sure how far the statements of Peripatetic commentators on Aristotle about them can be trusted, we need to be cautious in our interpretation. But there are certain points on which we can be reasonably certain. It is quite clear from the whole character of Aristotle's polemic against " ideal numbers," that the numbers which Plato declared

---

[1] *Met.* A 987b 18–25.

[2] The simple meaning of this is that, as we have been told by Timaeus, all the characters of " things " depend on the geometrical structure of their particles, and thus, in the end, on the structure of the " triangles " into which the faces of these particles can be resolved. And a triangle is determined again by three " numbers," those which give the lengths of its sides.

[3] *Met.* A 987b 25–28. Oddly enough, he does not mention the much more important point that the One is made by Plato the formal constituent in a number, whereas the Pythagoreans taught that " the unit " is the first *product* of the combination of *their* two constituent factors, πέρας and ἄπειρον, though he had correctly stated this doctrine just before, *Met.* A 986a 19.

[4] *Met.* M 1078b 30. Plato is not named in this passage, but a comparison of the criticism passed immediately below (1078b 34 ff.) with that made on Plato at A 990b 2 ff., shows that Aristotle regards the charge of making the " separation " as applicable to him.

to be forms are just the integers and nothing else, and also that the doctrine does not mean that it is denied that " man," " horse," and the like are forms, but that " the form of man " and the like are now held to be themselves in some sense " numbers." Hence Aristotle can raise the difficulty whether the " units " which make up the number which is the form of man or horse are the same as those which are found in the form of animal, or those of the form of man the same as those of the form of horse (*Met.* 1081*a* 9, 1082*a* 18, 1084*a* 13). It also looks as though Aristotle meant to ascribe to Plato, as well as to the Pythagoreans, the view that the integer-series is a succession of repetitions of the numbers up to 10, so that the Form-numbers would be, in a special sense, the first ten natural numbers. (*E.g. Met.* 1084*a* 12, though the allusion there might be rather to a theory of the Pythagoreans and Speusippus than to a personal view of Plato.) It seems clear, at any rate, that the key to the doctrine, if we could recover it, would be found in a theory of the character of the series of integers up to 10.

To some extent, at least, it seems possible to recover this key. We have to begin by understanding what is meant by speaking of one constituent of a number as the " great-and-small " and by calling this an " indeterminate duality." Even without the help of the commentators on Aristotle, the *Philebus* would enable us to give a reasonable answer to this question. We saw there that " that which admits of more and less indefinitely " was Plato's description of what we call a " continuum," though the number-series itself does not figure among the examples of continua given in the dialogue. This enables us to see at once why Plato spoke of what the Pythagoreans had called the " unlimited " (ἄπειρον) as a " great-and-small " or a " duality." It is a duality because it can be varied indefinitely in either of two directions. Probably the commentators are right in connecting this with the more specific view that you can equally reach plurality, starting from unity, by multiplication or by division, *e.g.* when you divide a given class regarded as a whole into sub-classes, you have two or more more determinate forms within the original γένος. This indicates a direct connexion between the theory of number ascribed to Plato by Aristotle and the preoccupation with the problem of the subdivision of forms in the later dialogues on which Stenzel has done well to insist, though he has allowed himself to neglect too much the specifically mathematical problem. We can also see, I think, why the other constituent of a number should be said to be " the one," and why the " unit " is no longer regarded, in Pythagorean fashion, as a " blend " of " limit " with the " unlimited," but as itself the " limit." Here, again, we have a point of contact with the theory of logical " division." As the *Philebus* had taught us, we may arrive at a " form " in either of two ways ; we may start with several different εἴδη as many and seek to reduce them to unity by showing that they are all special determinations of a more general " form," or again we may start with the more general " form " and discover more specific "forms" within it; whichever route we follow, we presuppose as already familiar the notions of *a* form and of forms in the plural. "A" and "some" will be ultimate indefinables.[1]

In the case of numbers it is easy to see how the conception, already implied in the *Epinomis*, of a "continuum" of "real" numbers leads to the Platonic formulas. If we wish to discover a number whose product by itself is 2, it is easy to show that we can make steady approximation to such a number by constructing the endless "continued fraction":

$$1 + \cfrac{1}{2 + \cfrac{1}{2 + \cfrac{1}{2 + \cfrac{1}{2 + \cdots}}}}$$

By stopping off the fraction at successive stages, we get a number of values 1, $1 + \frac{1}{2}$, $1 + \cfrac{1}{2 + \frac{1}{2}}$, etc., with the following peculiarities. The values are alternatively less and greater than $\sqrt{2}$, and each value differs from $\sqrt{2}$ less than the preceding value; by carrying the fraction far enough, we can get a fraction a/b such that a^2/b^2 differs from 2 by less than any magnitude we please to assign. This is what we mean by saying that $\sqrt{2}$ is the limiting value to which the fraction "converges" when it is continued "to infinity." Now in forming the successive approximate values, or "convergents," we are making closer and closer approximation to the precise determination of an "infinite great-and-small." It is "infinite" because however many steps you have taken, you never reach a fraction which, when multiplied by itself, gives exactly 2 as the product, though you are getting nearer to such a result at each step. It is "great-and-small," because the successive approximations are alternatively too small and too large. $\sqrt{2}$ is, so to say, gradually pegged down between a "too much" and a "too little," which are coming closer together all the time. I choose this particular example because this method of finding the value of what we call $\sqrt{2}$ was pretty certainly known to Plato.[2]

---

[1] We must, of course, distinguish carefully between the notion of "a" and that of "the integer 1." The latter is definable exactly as any other integer is. 1 is the number of any group x which satisfies the conditions that (a) there is an a which is an x; (b) "b is an x" implies "b is identical with a." This distinction is not yet clearly recognized in the Platonic formula.

[2] The denominators and numerators of the successive "convergents" are the series called in Greek respectively the πλευρικοί and the διαμετρικοί ἀριθμοί. The rule for finding any number of them is given by Theon of Smyrna (p. 43–44, Hiller). The geometrical construction by which the rule was discovered is given by Proclus (*Comm. in Rempubl.* ii. 24, 27–29, Kroll). The source of both Theon and Proclus appears to be the Peripatetic Adrastus in his commentary on the *Timaeus* (Kroll, *op. cit.* ii. 393 ff.). Plato himself alludes to the πλευρικοί and διαμετρικοί ἀριθμοί at *Rep.* 546c 5.

The same point might be similarly illustrated by the definitions given by modern mathematicians of the "real numbers." The definitions are to a certain point arbitrary, but they all turn on the notion of a "section." *E.g.* we cannot find a rational fraction the "square" of which is exactly 2. But we *can* divide all rational fractions into two classes; those of which the "squares" are less than 2 and those of which the "squares" are not less than 2. We see at once that the first of these sets has no highest term, the second no lowest, and that no fraction can belong either to both sets or to neither set; thus our "section" is unambiguous, *i.e.* every fraction falls into one and only one of the two sets thus constituted. We may then define the "square root of 2" either as this "section" itself, or, if we prefer it, as the set of "fractions whose squares are less (or, if we like, greater) than 2." Here again, the notion of a "section" of the rational fractions exhibits the Platonic characters. It involves a "duality," or "great-and-small," the two sets, one of which has all its terms less than, the other all greater than, a specified value, and the duality is "indefinite" because one of the sets has no highest term, the other no lowest. The section is a determination of the "great-and-small" of the fractions by the "one" precisely because it makes an unambiguous "cut" just where it does. Other cuts can be made at other places in the series, and each will define a different "real number."[1]

It is clear, however, that we have not yet exhausted the meaning of Plato's doctrine. From Aristotle's polemic we see that the Platonic analysis was not meant to apply simply to the case of the "irrationals" which Plato was the first to recognize as *numbers*. The theory also involves a doctrine of the structure of the integer-series itself, since it is clear that the numbers with which the forms are identified are, as Aristotle always assumes, the integers. The integers themselves, then, have the "great-and-small" and the "one" as their constituents. How is this to be understood?

[1] Cf. G. H. Hardy, *Pure Mathematics*[2], p. 14. The "rational fractions" are, to be sure, not a continuum, but they satisfy the only condition for a continuum known in Plato's time, that between any two a third can always be inserted. Stenzel rightly dwells on the connexion of the "duality" with "convergence," but misses the illustration from the πλευρικοί and διαμετρικοί ἀριθμοί (*Zahl u. Gestalt*, 59). The endlessness of the "continued fraction" makes it clear why the "great-and-small" was identified with the "non-being" of which we read in the *Sophistes* (Aristot. *Physics*, A 192a 6 ff.). The meaning of what is said about geometry, plane and solid, in the *Epinomis* will thus be, that the real scientific problem is to obtain a series of "approximations," within a "standard" which we can make as narrow as we please, to the various quadratic and cubic surds. In doing so, we are discovering the ratios of the "sides" or "edges" of the various regular polygons and solids to one another. We discover, *e.g.*, exactly how long—within a known "standard"—a line must be if the area of the square or volume of the cube on it is to be 2, 3, 5 . . . times a given area and volume; and since all rectilinear areas and volumes can be expressed as those of squares and cubes, this solves the question of the surveyor and the "stereometer." It is precisely with such metrical problems, relating to the "regular solids," that Euclid's Book XIII. is concerned, a safe indication of its Academic *provenance*.

The difficulty is that the integers do not form a continuum, even in the sense in which continuity means no more than infinite divisibility, *i.e.* the possibility of inserting a third term between any two given terms of the series. For each integer is "next after" another.

How, then, does Plato suppose the series of integers to be constructed? I doubt if the notices preserved to us enable us to answer the question finally. What is clear is that Plato rightly rejects the view retained by Aristotle, that an integer is a collection of "1's," and that the series is thus constructed by additions of 1 to itself. 2 is not "1 and 1" but "the number next after 1." (This ought to be plain from the simple consideration of the way in which we learn to count. We do not count, "one, one, one, one, . . ." but "one, two, three . . .") But when we ask in what way the "duality" comes in in constructing the series of integers, we are puzzled by the confusion which seems to run through Aristotle and his commentators between the "indeterminate duality" or "great-and-small" and the *number* 2. If it were only in the polemic of Aristotle that this confusion were found, we might conceivably dismiss it as a mere misunderstanding, but it appears to have occurred also in the Academic reports of Plato's doctrine. The complete study of the problem would require a long discussion of the mass of material collected and examined by M. Robin in his volume *La Théorie platonicienne*. Here it must be enough to remark that the following points seem to be quite certain. (1) The "dyad" was called δυοποιός, because it "doubles" everything it "lays hold of." There is no doubt that the "dyad" meant is the "great-and-small," but "it also seems clear that there is a confusion, perhaps from the very first, with the αὐτὸ ὃ ἔστι δυάς, the number 2, and that the function of the "dyad" within the integer-series is thought of as being to produce the series of "powers" of 2 by repeated multiplication, 1×2, $1 \times 2 \times 2$, $1 \times 2 \times 2 \times 2$, and so forth (cf. *Epinomis* 991a 1–4).[1] (2) The "one," we are told, puts a stop to the "indeterminateness" of the "great-and-small" by "equalizing" or "stabilizing" it (τῷ ἰσάζειν).[2] This, I suggest, as my conjectural explanation of an obscure expression, means that each odd number is the arithmetical mean between the preceding and following even numbers, and so "halves their difference." Each odd number will be got by halving "the sum of two even" numbers. Thus the order of the "decade" will be, 1, 2, 4, 8 ; 3 (which equalizes 2 and 4) ; 6 (double of 3) ; 5, 7 (which "equalize" 4 and 6, and 6 and 8) ; 10 (double of 5) ; 9 (which equalizes 8 and 10).[3] Cp. Aristotle's

[1] Cf. Aristot. *Met.* 1084a 5, 1091a 12, 1082a 14, 987b 33.

[2] Plutarch, *de Anim. procreat.* 1012d, reporting the explanation of Xenocrates, ἐκ δὲ τούτων γενέσθαι τὸν ἀριθμὸν τοῦ ἑνὸς ὁρίζοντος τὸ πλῆθος, Aristot. *Met. M.* 1083b 23, 29, where the "unit" is said to arise from the "equalizing" of the "dyad" of the great-and-small.

[3] See Robin, *La Théorie platonicienne*, p. 449. The mathematical reader will see at once a certain analogy between this procedure and the "quadrilateral construction" of von Staudt.

use of the "arithmetical mean" as an "equalizer," *E.N.* 1132*a* 1 ff. If this was the construction, it must be pronounced very faulty. Not only does it involve the confusions of "a" with 1 and of "plurality" with 2, but it involves obtaining the terms of the series in an unnatural order and using more than one principle of construction where one is sufficient. (The one really satisfactory way of defining the integers is to proceed by "mathematical induction," *i.e.* to define each in terms of its immediate precursor. This is readily done in the following way. When we have defined the integer n, we can go on to define $n + 1$ by the statement that $n + 1$ is the number of members of a group satisfying the conditions (*a*) that it contains a group with n members, (*b*) that it contains a member *a* which is not a member of this group; (*c*) that it does not contain any member which is neither *a* nor a member of the group of n members already mentioned.)

If, as seems probable, Plato's conception has these defects, we must not be surprised. He probably started with the right conviction that what we should call the notion of a "section" is necessary for the definition of the "irrationals," and went on to extend the conception to cover the case of the integers. What could not be expected of the first thinker who had formed the notion of a "real" number is the recognition that integers, rational fractions, real numbers, do not form a single series, in other words that the "integer," 2, the "rational number" 2/1, and the "real number 2" are all distinct. In the logical construction of the types of number, we need three distinct steps: the rules for defining the successive integers, the derivation of the rational numbers from the integers, and the derivation of the "continuum" of the real numbers from the series of rational numbers. These, however, are matters on which mathematical philosophers have only reached clear comprehension in very recent times. The important point is that Plato should have grasped the necessity of enlarging the traditional conception of number and of strictly defining numbers of all kinds.[1]

What are the "mathematicals" which Plato distinguished from his numbers or forms? Aristotle tells us that they differ from forms in the fact that they are many, whereas the form is one, and from sensible things by being eternal (*Met.* A 987*b* 15). It is to be noted that he does not call them "mathematical numbers,"

---

[1] Stenzel, *Zahl u. Gestalt*, 31, gives a different construction, but without justifying it. I venture to think he has been misled by an anxiety to discover Plato's number theory directly in the *Philebus*, where it could not have been introduced without the dramatic absurdity of putting it into the mouth of Socrates. In the main, I hope I am in accord with Burnet, *Greek Philosophy, Part I.*, 320 ff. But I should say that I can make nothing of n. 2 to p. 320, which manifestly is a *non-sens*. It appears to be a *partially* correct explanation of something Aristotle tells us about the Pythagoreans, which has got into its present place by some inadvertence. How *can* "the one" be the terms of the series $\sqrt{2}$, $\sqrt{6}$, $\sqrt{12}$ . . . ?

but τὰ μαθηματικά, and that he never appears to ascribe to *Plato* the recognition of " mathematical *number*." The meaning seems to me to be best shown by two passages in the Aristotelian *corpus*. At *Metaphysics* K 1059*b* 2 ff., it is made an objection to the theory of forms that just as the μαθηματικά are intermediate between the form and sensible things, so there ought to be—on the theory—something intermediate between such a form as man or horse and visible men and horses (though we see that there is not). This implies that the " mathematicals " are something quite familiar. I would couple with this *de Anima* A 404*b* 19, where we are told that in τὰ περὶ φιλοσοφίας λεγόμενα Plato said that the form of animal is composed of the one and " the first length, breadth, and depth." The form of animal is, according to the *Timaeus*, the archetype on which the sensible world is constructed, that is, it is the *res extensa*, the subject-matter of geometry, and Aristotle's meaning is thus that this *res extensa* is constituted by the three dimensions of length, breadth, and depth. These *correspond*, as the context of the passage in the *de Anima* makes clear, to the numbers 2, 3, 4 (the line being determined by two points, the plane by three, three-dimensional space by four). Thus Plato's construction recalls the Pythagorean tetractys of the numbers 1, 2, 3, 4. But he spoke not of numbers, but of the first " length, breadth, depth." This seems to mean that though, as the *Epinomis* says, plane and solid geometry may be identified with the study of certain kinds of number, lengths, areas, volumes are not identical with numbers. The study of number provides the key to all these relations, and yet they are not themselves numbers, and the significance of number is not exhausted by its geometrical applications.

So we, too, are familiar with analytical geometry in which we study the properties of curves and surfaces by means of numerical equations. All the properties of the curves and surfaces can be discovered from these equations, but the application of equations is not confined to geometry or geometrical physics ; the same methods, for example, play a prominent part in the study of economics, as when we plot out curves to show the effects of modifications of duties on the " volume " of foreign trade. In a word, I take it, the " mathematicals " are what the geometer studies.

We may now perhaps be in a position to see what is meant by the statement that the constituents of the forms are the constituents of everything. The things of the sensible world, as we have learned from the *Philebus*, are one and all in " becoming " ; they are events or processes tending to the realization of a definite law and this law, Plato thinks, can be expressed in numerical form. Because these things are always " in the making," they do not exhibit permanent and absolute conformity to law of structure ; if once they were " made " and finished, they would be the perfect embodiment of law of structure. And because the stuff of things is extension itself, the law thus realized would be geometrical and therefore, as we should say, be expressible in the form of an equation or equations. This is what Plato means at bottom in his own philosophy by the " participation " of the sensible in forms and by the doctrine that the στοιχεῖα of number are the στοιχεῖα of everything. (I abstain from commenting on the further numerous passages in Aristotle where the question of the relation of the ἀρχαί of geometry to those of arithmetic is raised, since these seem to form part of the polemic against Speusippus and Xenocrates, and it is not clear to me how far any of the views canvassed are meant to be directly ascribed to Plato.)

Aristotle seems, as I said, to connect his complaint about the Academic " separation " (χωρισμός) between forms and sensible things specially with the doctrine we have just been discussing. He is commonly taken to mean no more than that the Platonic form is a sort of " double " of the sensible thing, supposed to be in some " intelligible world," wholly sundered from the real world of actual life. It is hard to suppose that he could put such an interpretation on a theory which according to himself makes the στοιχεῖα of number the στοιχεῖα of everything. Hence I think Stenzel[1] is on the right track in looking for a more definite meaning in the Aristotelian criticism, and that he has rightly indicated the direction in which we should look. As he points out, one of Aristotle's chief difficulties about the " numbers " is that he holds that if " animal " is one number and " man " is another, we have to face the question whether the " units " in " animal " are part of the " units " which constitute " man " or not ; (e.g. if you said " animal " is 2, " man " is 4, since 2 × 2 = 4, " man " would seem to be the same thing as " animal " taken twice over). The complaint, as Stenzel says, is not that an εἶδος is treated as something distinct from a sensible individual, but that the more universal εἴδη, the γένη as Aristotle calls them, are thought of as though they had a being distinct from that of the ἄτομον εἶδος or *infima species*. Aristotle's point is that " animal," for example, has no being except as " horse," " man," " dog," or one of the other species which can no longer be divided into sub-species. This would be, in effect, a criticism on the method of division as practised in the *Sophistes*, where it is made a rule that in summing up the result of the division into a definition, all the intermediate *differentiae* which have been employed must be recapitulated. This is a procedure condemned by Aristotle's own doctrine that a definition need only state genus and specific difference ; the specific difference includes in itself all the intermediate differences. Hence, according to Stenzel, the χωρισμός of which Aristotle complains is that the Platonic account of " division " as

[1] See Stenzel, *Zahl u. Gestalt*, 133 ff., with the Aristotelian texts discussed there. The all-important passage is *Met.* Z 1037b 8-1038a 35. Aristotle urges that if, *e.g.*, you first divide animals into footed animals and animals without feet, and then divide the former into bipeds and others, the Platonic rule would require you to say that man is a " two-footed footed animal." But the determination " footed " only exists actually as contained in the more specific determinations " two-footed," " four-footed." The same problem recurs in *Met.* H 6, 1045a 7 ff.

the instrument of definition is fatal to the unity of the *definiendum*,[1] and, since the process is a direct outcome of the doctrine of μέθεξις, the defect is one which requires the doctrine of μέθεξις itself to be revised.   (Thus Aristotle's rejection of the Platonic doctrine of forms would at bottom be based on rejection of the logical tenet that the relation of species to genus is identical with that of individual to species.)   Whether this interesting interpretation is sound is, however, a question for the student of Aristotelianism rather than for an expositor of Plato.[2]

See further :

> BURNET.—*Greek Philosophy, Part I.*, 312–324 ; *Platonism*, c. 5, 2, 7.
>
> NATORP, P.—*Platons Ideenlehre*, 366–436.
>
> BAEUMKER, C.—*Das Problem der Materie in der griechischen Philosophie*, 196–209.
>
> STENZEL, J.—*Zahl und Gestalt bei Platon und Aristoteles.*   (1924.)
>
> ROBIN, L.—*La Théorie platonicienne des idées et des nombres après Aristote.*   (Paris, 1908.)
>
> MILHAUD, G.—*Les Philosophes-géomètres de la Grèce, Platon et ses prédécesseurs.*   (Paris, 1900.)
>
> TAYLOR, A. E.—*Philosophical Studies*, pp. 91–150.
>
> THOMPSON, D'ARCY W.—" Excess and Defect " in MIND, N.S., 149.

---

[1] *Zahl u. Gestalt*, 126 ff.

[2] It seems clear that a definitive interpretation of Plato's main thought must start with a thorough study of the material collected in M. Robin's great work *La Théorie platonicienne*.   It is time that we should make an end of the pretence of understanding Plato by ignoring the evidence or by arbitrarily reading into him the views of our own favourite modern metaphysicians.   In this brief chapter I have only been able to hint at the interpretation the material suggests to myself.   These hints I have tried to develop briefly in a notice of Stenzel's book in *Gnomon*, ii. 7 (July 1926), and more fully in an essay in MIND, " Forms and Numbers," with reference to the Aristotelian evidence.   (See the reference given above.)

ADDENDA

P. 21, l. 18 ff.   It seems necessary, in view of some criticisms, to say expressly that I regard the date 387 B.C. as a mere convenient " approximation," not as the known precise date of the founding of the Academy.   And, of course, my language about the long interruption in Plato's literary activity must be understood with the qualifications (1) that I expressly decline to commit myself to an opinion about the relative order of composition of *Republic, Phaedo, Symposium*, and (2) that I never meant to exclude the possibility of a minor " occasional " violation of silence.   On my own view the *Menexenus* would have to be dated c. 380–379.   Understood in this " common-sense " way, the view that " roughly speaking " the dialogues earlier than the *Parmenides* and *Theaetetus* were written before the foundation of the Academy still seems to me as probable as it did to Burnet.

P. 207, l. 26 ff.   The reality of Plato's own personal faith in immortality is surely put beyond doubt by the words of Ep. vii. 335a, " one must put genuine faith in the ancient sacred sayings which indicate that our soul is immortal, has to face a judge, and pays the gravest penalties when one has left the body," etc. (πείθεσθ ι δὲ ὄντως ἀεὶ χρὴ τοῖς παλαιοῖς τε καὶ ἱεροῖς λόγοις, οἳ δὴ μηνύουσιν ἡμῖν ἀθάνατον ψυχὴν εἶναι δικαστάς τε ἴσχειν καὶ τίνειν τὰς μεγίστας τιμωρίας ὅταν τις ἀπαλλαχθῇ τοῦ σώματος).

P. 263, par. 2.   It should be noted that the Glaucon of the *Symposium* is not Plato's brother, who figures in the *Republic*, since (*Symp.* 173a) he, like Plato himself, was a mere παῖς at the date of Agathon's party.

P. 263, par. 2.   Professor Burnet, in the posthumous volume of lectures on *Platonism* delivered at the University of California, expresses the opinion that the *Republic* and consequently the *Timaeus* are to be given a dramatic date anterior to the Archidamian War (*Platonism*, pp. 25–26).   This would, so far as I can see, be *possible* but for one consideration.   It would compel us to hold that Perictione, since she was the mother of two sons who are young men before 431, was *at the very least* over a hundred years old in 366, when *Ep.* xiii refers to her as still living.   This is just possible, but hardly likely, and since I am as convinced as Burnet himself of the genuineness of *Ep.* xiii., I would rather not follow him on this point.

P. 278, n. 1.   Xenophon also (*Symp.* ii. 9) ascribes to Socrates the thesis that " woman's *nature* is not inferior to man's " (ἡ γυναικεία φύσις οὐδὲν χείρων τῆς τοῦ ἀνδρὸς οὖσα τυγχάνει), though she is not his equal in physical strength and intelligence (γνώμης τε καὶ ἰσχύος δεῖται).   But he may be dependent on Plato or Aeschines, or on both.

P. 309, n. 1.   Aeschines also in his *Alcibiades* ascribed the " erotic " temperament to Socrates, with special reference to his affection for Alcibiades. (ἐγὼ δὲ διὰ τὸν ἔρωτα ὃν ἐτύγχανον ἐρῶν ᾿Αλκιβιάδου οὐδὲν διάφορον τῶν Βακχῶν ἐπεπόνθειν. Fr. 11, Dittmar. This evidence seems to me to make nonsense of all the inferences about the personality of Plato which have been drawn from the *Phaedrus* and *Symposium*.

P. 450. In *Platonism* (1928), p. 106, Burnet now says that " it can be proved " that Plato " discovered the heliocentric system " in astronomy. The evidence offered is simply the statement of Theophrastus discussed in our text. I do not understand how Burnet reconciles this view with his own defence of the *Epinomis*, in which the sun is still expressly treated as a " planet " (986*b*–987*d*). I am wholly in accord with Burnet about the genuineness of the *Epinomis* and *therefore* am compelled to dissent from his attribution of " Copernicanism " to Plato.

P. 472, l. 20. But it should be remembered, as Mr. Lorimer reminds me, that Aristotle does once observe (*Pol.* 1329*b* 25) that the various arts of civilized life must have been discovered " often, or rather an indefinite number of times in the course of ages," and " Ocellus Lucanus " (c. 3) that " Hellas has often been barbarian, and will often be so again."

P. 516, l. 4. That is, Aristotle's great difficulty with the theory of " forms," as it seems to me, is not so much that there should be a " form " of *man*, " besides " Socrates and Coriscus, as that there should be a " form " of *animal*, " besides " horse, and dog and man. *That* is what he is specially anxious to deny.

CHRONOLOGICAL TABLE

404. End of Peloponnesian War; Athens surrenders to Lysander. Appointment of the "Thirty"; murder of Polemarchus. Affair of Leon of Salamis (404–3).

403. Fall of "Thirty"; deaths of Critias and Charmides. Restoration of democracy at Athens.

401. Expedition of Cyrus and battle of Cunaxa.

399. Trials of Andocides and Socrates for impiety and death of Socrates in archonship of Laches.

395–87. Corinthian War. Rebuilding of Athenian Long Walls (395–393). Pamphlet of Polycrates against Socrates (c. 392–390). *Ecclesiazusae* of Aristophanes. Destruction of Spartan *mora* by Iphicrates (?392 or 390).

c. 388. First visit of Plato to Sicily and Italy at age of 40. Traditional date of capture of Rome by Gauls.

387. Corinthian War ended by "King's Peace." *Approximate* date of foundation of Academy.

385. Birth of Aristotle at Stagirus.

382. Spartan seizure of citadel of Thebes and political murder of Ismenias.

380. *Panegyricus* of Isocrates.

379–8. Spartan garrison expelled at Thebes by Pelopidas and his associates. Raid of Spartan Sphodrias on Piraeus.

378. Alliance of Athens and Thebes. Second Athenian League founded.

373. Great tidal wave and earthquake on the Achaean coast.

371. "Peace of Callias" between Sparta and Athens. Spartan power broken by Epaminondas at Leuctra. Liberation of Messene and foundation of Megalopolis follow in the next year or two.

369. Spartan lines on Mt. Oneion broken by Epaminondas. (Theaetetus probably wounded in this campaign.)

367. Death of Dionysius I. Plato summoned to Syracuse by Dion. Aristotle enters Academy. Traditional date of "Licinian rogations" and defeat of Gauls by Camillus at Alba.

362. Battle of Mantinea; Epaminondas killed.

361–60. Third visit of Plato to Sicily. Traditional date of penetration of Gauls into Campania.

357. Capture of Syracuse by Dion.

c. 356. Birth of Alexander the Great at Pella.

354. Murder of Dion by Callippus. Plato's VII *Epistle*. Earliest extant speech of Demosthenes (on the *Symmories*.)

353. Overthrow of Callippus. Plato's VIII *Epistle*.

351. *First Philippic* of Demosthenes.

349–8. *Olynthiacs* of Demosthenes. Capture of Olynthus by Philip (348).

347. Death of Plato.

346. Peace of Philocrates. Philip acts as general in the "Sacred War" against the Phocians, becomes a member of the Amphictionic Council and presides at the Pythian games. Temporary restoration of Dionysius II at Syracuse.

344–3. Dionysius finally overthrown by Timoleon. Aristotle (343–2) at Pella as tutor to Alexander.

APPENDIX

THE PLATONIC APOCRYPHA

In using the name *Apocrypha* as a convenient collective designation for those items contained in our Plato MSS. of which it is reasonably certain that they have no real claim to Platonic authorship, I make no gratuitous assumption of fraudulence in their writers or worthlessness in their contents. Apart from the collection of *Definitions*, which has its own special character, the *Apocrypha* seem to be undiguised imitations of Platonic "discourses of Socrates," and most of them to be the work of the early Academy ; the attribution to Plato has arisen naturally and by accident. The works in question fall into three classes : (*A*) items actually included in the canon of Thrasylus ; (*B*) the collection of ὅροι or definitions, which falls outside the division into "tetralogies"; (*C*) νοθευόμενοι, dialogues recognized in antiquity as spurious.

A. Dialogues included in the "tetralogies," but certainly, or all but certainly, spurious.

Of these there are seven: *Alcibiades I, Alcibiades II, Hipparchus, Amatores* (the whole of the fourth "tetralogy"), *Theages* (" tetralogy " V), *Clitophon* ("tetralogy" VIII), *Minos* (" tetralogy " IX). All were clearly regarded as genuine by Dercylides and Thrasylus. The only fact known about their earlier history is that Aristophanes of Byzantium had included the *Minos* in one of his " trilogies " along with the *Laws* and *Epinomis* (D.L. iii. 62). Since we never hear of Dercylides or Thrasylus as *introducing* any items into the Platonic canon, it seems reasonable to infer that the whole group were already accepted by the Alexandrian scholars of the third century B.C. and that the composition of all must therefore be dated earlier still. None of the group is certainly quoted by Aristotle, or even Cicero,[1] but this proves nothing since none contains anything which makes any difference to the interpretation of Plato's thought. As I shall try to show, the linguistic evidence is also decidedly against a late date in almost every case ; the Greek with which these dialogues present us is recognizably that of the fourth century.[2] It follows that we should assign their composition,

[1] The allusion of Cicero, *Tusculans*, iii. xxxiv. 77, is certainly, that of *de Oratore*, ii. 8 almost certainly, not to *Alcibiades I*, but to the *Alcibiades* of Aeschines of Sphettus.

[2] The statement perhaps needs a little qualification in the case of *Alcibiades II*, as will be pointed out later.

speaking roughly, to the half-century between Plato's death and
the opening of the third century, while one or two may quite
possibly have been written even within Plato's lifetime. I shall
also try to show that the thought is quite Platonic, though the
way in which it is presented is not altogether that of the Master.
My own conclusion is that the whole group is the work of Platonists
of the first two or three generations, intending to expound Academic ideas by " discourses of Socrates." This thesis cannot be
formally demonstrated, but seems more probable than either the
extreme view of Grote, who accepted the whole group as Platonic,
or the rival extreme view which would bring some of the items well
within the Alexandrian period.

Alcibiades I. This is in compass and worth the most important
member of the group, as it contains an excellent general summary of the Socratic-Platonic doctrines of the scale of goods and
the " tendance " of the soul. The Platonic authorship has been
defended by Grote, Stallbaum, C. F. Hermann, J. Adam and
recently M. Croiset and P. Friedländer ; Jowett included a version
in his English translation of Plato. For my own part I feel reluctantly forced to decide for rejection on the following grounds.
(1) Close verbal study seems to show that in language the manner
is that of the later Plato,[1] whereas the thought is that of Plato's
earliest ethical dialogues, and the exposition, at points, so unskilled
that a resolute defender is almost bound to regard the dialogue as
one of the earliest of all. (2) It seems incredible that Plato, who has
given us such vivid portraits of Alcibiades in the *Protagoras* and
Symposium, should ever have treated his personality in the colourless
fashion of this dialogue. (3) It should be still more incredible
that Plato, with his known views on the worth of " text-books,"
should have composed what is, to all intents, a kind of hand-book
to ethics. The work has the qualities of an excellent manual,
and this is the strongest reason for denying its authenticity. I
agree, then, with those who hold that *Alcibiades I* is a careful
exposition of ethics by an early Academic, written well before
300 B.C., and possibly, though perhaps not very probably, even
before the death of Plato. I should say with Stallbaum that it
contains nothing actually *unworthy* of Plato, but I am equally
satisfied that it contains echoes of Plato which are not in the manner

---

[1] On this question see C. Ritter, *Untersuchungen über Plato*, 89–90 ;
Raeder, *Platons philosophische Entwickelung*, 24–25 ; Lutoslawski, *Origin
and Growth of Plato's Logic*, 197–198. I would add that comparison with
the remains of the *Alcibiades* of Aeschines and that of Antisthenes shows
that our dialogue is almost certainly dependent on the former, and possibly
also on the latter. Use of these sources in this way is barely credible in
Plato. Also, Socrates is represented (103c) as posing as the tongue-tied
" lover " of Alcibiades, whereas according to Plato in the *Symposium* it was
rather Alcibiades who posed as the " beloved " of Socrates. For further
discussion, and for evidence that *Alcibiades I* depends also on Xenophon,
see H. Dittmar, *Aeschines von Sphettos*, 163–177.

of a writer who is echoing himself. In particular, the closing words
(135e) [1] can hardly be anything but an allusion to Plato's description
(*Rep.* 491 ff.) of the corruption of the young man of genius by the
blandishments of that supreme sophist, the " public," a passage
itself perhaps inspired by the tragic career of Alcibiades. There
are other similar disguised quotations, as we shall see.

The writer's purpose is to expound the thoughts that the one
thing needful for true success in life is self-knowledge, that this
means knowledge of what is good and bad for our *souls*, and that
such knowledge is different in kind from all specialism. Alcibiades
is drawn as a young man of boundless ambition just about to enter
on public life. (The date assumed is the end of his " ephebate,"
before the outbreak of the Archidamian War. Pericles is at the
head of affairs, 104*b*.) Socrates, who has long admired the wonderful
boy from a distance, is now allowed by his " sign " to express his
admiration for the first time.[2] He knows that A. is ambitious to
become the first statesman of Europe and Asia, and can help him
to realize the dream if A. will only answer his questions (103*a*–106*b*).[3]
To succeed as a statesman, A. must be a good adviser and so must
have knowledge which his neighbours have not, and this knowledge
must come to him either as a personal discovery or by learning
from others. But none of the things A. has " learned " are matters
considered by sovereign assemblies, and in the matters which such
an assembly does consider there are experts who would be much
better counsellors than A. His boasted " advantages " of person,
rank, wealth, are irrelevant. On what topics, then, would he be
a competent adviser of the public ? He says, " On the conduct
of their own affairs, *e.g.* the making of war and peace." Yet it
is the *expert* we need to advise us whether it is *better* to make war,
on whom, and for how long. Our standard of the " better " is
supplied by the expert's τέχνη. Now, what τέχνη is the relevant
one in these questions of state ? When we declare war, we always
do so on the plea that our *rights* have been infringed. Has A., then,
ever learned " justice," the knowledge of rights and wrongs ? He
has never received instruction in it, nor can he have discovered it
for himself. To do that he would need first to look for it, and to
look for it he must be first awake to his ignorance of it. But from
his childhood he has always been wrangling with his companions

---

[1] ὀρρωδῶ δέ, οὔ τι τῇ σῇ φύσει ἀπιστῶν ἀλλὰ τὴν τῆς πόλεως ὁρῶν ῥώμην, μὴ
ἐμοῦ τε καὶ σοῦ κρατήσῃ.

[2] 103*a*. The representation that S. has not spoken a word to the lad for
years seems an un-Platonic exaggeration. Contrast the representation in
the *Protagoras* which depicts a scene from the same period of the philosopher's
life.

[3] This self-confidence, again, is not in keeping with Plato's conception
of Socrates ; it looks to be borrowed from the Socrates of Xenophon. It is
definitely " un-Platonic " that Socrates boasts (124*c*) of having God for
his " guardian," with reference, as we see by a comparison with 103*a* 5, to
the " divine sign." God and the " sign " are never confused in this way
in any certainly genuine work of Plato.

about his " rights," as if he already knew what they are (106*c*–110*d*). And he certainly cannot have " picked up " knowledge of right and wrong from the " many " at large, as he has done the use of his mother-tongue.[1] The " many " all *agree* about the meaning of vernacular words, and this is why one can learn the language from them. Where their views are at hopeless variance, they cannot be our teachers, and there is nothing about which they are more at variance than their " rights " and " wrongs." A. then is proposing to teach others what it is not possible that he knows himself (110*e*–113*a*).

But, says A., the politician need not know what is right ; he need only know what is *expedient*. Well, if A. thinks he knows what the expedient is, let him answer one question : Is the expedient always the same as the right or is it not ? A. thinks not, but Socrates is confident that he can prove the contradictory (114*d*). The proof turns on establishing the equations καλόν = ἀγαθόν, αἰσχρόν = κακόν (114*d*–116*b*).[2] He who acts " finely " also " does well," *i.e.* is in possession of *good*,[3] and the good for us = the expedient for us. He then who advises as expedient what is wrong is a bad adviser. If A. hesitates whether to admit or to deny this, his very hesitation is a sign that he is becoming conscious of his ignorance about the most important of all subjects (117*a*). He is suffering from virulent ἀμαθία, the common malady of " public men " (118*b*). Pericles, indeed, is said to have " learned " wisdom from Anaxagoras and Damon. But since he never imparted " wisdom " to anyone, we may fairly doubt whether he had it.[4] A. might reply that if all our public men are " laymen," he need not be more than a layman himself to compete with them. But the real antagonists for whom an Athenian statesman needs to be more than a match are foreign powers, the Spartan and Persian kings. Both have the advantage of A. alike in descent, in careful preparatory training for their office,[5] in wealth and resources.[6]

[1] An echo of *Protagoras*, 327*e* ?
[2] Cf. *Gorgias*, 474*c*.
[3] Cf. *Rep.*, 353*e* ff.
[4] Cf. *Protagoras*, 319*e*, *Meno*, 94*b* (both echoed by *Alc. I*, 118*e*).
[5] The starting-point for the long and over-coloured picture of the education of a Persian king (which must be meant ironically) seems to be Aeschines, Fr. 8 (Dittmar), where Socrates ironically argues that Themistocles must have practised " tendance of himself " before venturing to match himself with Xerxes. The development of this hint in our dialogue seems to reflect Xenophon's romance of the *Education of Cyrus* (itself possibly influenced by the *Cyrus* of Antisthenes). Plato's view (*Laws*, 684) is that no Persian prince ever receives any " education " at all. So far I should accept the conclusions of H. Dittmar, but I am wholly sceptical of his further theory that the real object of *Alc. I* is to discountenance the preference of Eastern theosophy, represented by Zoroaster, to Hellenic philosophy.
[6] Note that the statements of the dialogue about the wealth of Sparta would only be true for the period between the surrender of Athens to Lysander and the battle of Leuctra. They are not true for the supposed date of the conversation.

If one is to compete with such rivals, the first lesson to be learned must be " knowledge of self " (the lesson of not underrating your opponent.)

How, then, must we set to work on the " care " (ἐπιμέλεια) of ourselves? We wish to be as good as possible at the goodness of a καλὸς κἀγαθός, that is, of a φρόνιμος, a man of sound judgement in all things. About *what* things do the καλοὶ κἀγαθοί, the " virtuous ", show this sound judgment? A. says, in capacity to command " men who associate with one another to transact the business of civic life " (125c), or more briefly, " men sharing in the constitutional rights and functions of citizenship " (125d). The statesman's τέχνη is εὐβουλία, " excellence in counsel respecting the conduct and safety of the State." This safety depends on the existence of φιλία, or more precisely, ὁμόνοια, " oneness of mind " between the citizens; not the " oneness of mind " secured by the arts of number, weight and measure, but the kind of " oneness of mind " which makes men agree " in a house " and is the basis of family affection. Such agreement implies that both parties to it *have* a " mind of their own," and so differs from any arrangement by which one party leaves a matter of which he is himself wholly ignorant to the sole discretion of the other. *That* is not what is meant when justice is said to be " minding your own business and leaving others to mind theirs " (127d). (The exposition at this point shows traces of a confusion one would not expect in Plato.)

Again (the transition is oddly abrupt), what is " care for a man's self "? With some needless elaboration, we reach the result that to care for a thing means to make it better, and that we cannot tell what will make a thing better unless we know what the thing *is*. So our question becomes " What *is* the self? " (128a). It is argued at length that an *agent* is never identical with the tools he *uses*. All of us are constantly using our hands, eyes, members generally, as tools. The body is thus an *instrument* used, and therefore cannot be the *agent* who uses the instrument. The real self, the agent which " uses " and " commands " the body, must be the ψυχή, and the true definition of man is that he is a " soul *using* a body "[1] (130c.) " Know thyself," then, means " know thy ψυχή "; *sophrosyne*, the true self-knowledge, must be different from any of the " arts " which " tend " our bodies or our possessions. And to be in love with another's body is not to be in love with *him*. (His body is not really his " person.")

The great business of life is " self-knowledge," the " care " of ourselves (132c).[2] Now the eye can see itself only by looking at its reflection. So the soul can " see itself " only by either gazing at another man's soul, particularly at " that region of it where the

---

[1] In refutation of the allegation that this definition, always insisted on by the Neo-Platonists, is " not platonic," Raeder properly refers to *Phaedo*, 115c–d.

[2] Cf. the reference to ἐπιμέλεια of the self in Aeschines, Fr. 8.

goodness of a soul is to be found," or contemplating God, a mirror of perfection brighter than any human soul.[1] We get to know ourselves truly by knowing God (133*c*). Until we know ourselves, we cannot know what is good for ourselves, for other men, for the State. Without such knowledge, a man's career will be disastrous to himself and the public (134*a*). Thus, the true prosperity of a city depends not on its navy, but on its virtue (134*b*).[2] The statesman must impart *goodness* to his countrymen, and he cannot impart what he has not. It must be his first concern to get goodness by "looking to God." Freedom, the power to make one's will supreme, is a bad thing for the ignorant ; it leads them to disease, shipwreck, moral ruin. Until one has acquired goodness, servitude to a better, not being " one's own master," is the condition which befits one.

Alcibiades II. A poor production, stamped as not Plato's by its style, by manifest imitations of *Alcibiades I*, and, as has generally been admitted since Boeckh, by a definite allusion to one of the Stoic " paradoxes."[3]

The subject is *Prayer.* The writer seems to take his cue either from the passage of the *Memorabilia* where Xenophon, who *may* himself be thinking of the closing words of the *Phaedrus*, says that Socrates " used to ask the gods simply to give him good things, since they know best what things are good," and thought it perverse to pray " for gold or silver, or a tyranny, and things of that kind,"[4] or possibly from *Laws*, 689*c*–*e*, where the speaker expresses the same view. A. is about to pray. Now, some prayers are granted, others are not. So a man should be careful not to ask what is bad for him ; his god might happen to be in a giving mood and take him at his word, as happened to Oedipus.[5] A. says, Oedipus was notoriously " a mere lunatic." This raises a problem. " Lunatic " is the contrary of " sane." But mankind may be divided into two classes which allow of no *tertium quid*, the φρόνιμοι, men of sound judgement, and the ἄφρονες, men of unsound judgement. On the

---

[1] The argument presupposes the doctrine of the *Laws* which identifies God with the ἀρίστη ψυχή.

[2] A plain allusion to the language of *Gorgias*, 519*a*, a passage which seems to be in the writer's mind all through his own account of " *sophrosyne* and justice."

[3] On these points see Stallbaum's *Introduction* to his Commentary on the dialogue, and for remarks on the language, C. Ritter (*Untersuchungen*, 88–89), who accepts Stallbaum's objections to several words and phrases, but owns that the dialogue would not be condemned by his own stylometric tests— a significant confession.

[4] Xenophon, *Mem.* i. iii. 2, ηὔχετο δὲ πρὸς τοὺς θεοὺς ἁπλῶς τἀγαθὰ διδόναι, ὡς τοὺς θεοὺς κάλλιστα εἰδότας ὁποῖα ἀγαθά ἐστι. This perhaps explains why the dialogue was attributed by some persons to Xenophon (Athenaeus, 506*e*), with whose manner it has no affinity.

[5] Who prayed that his sons might divide their inheritance by the sword. The writer follows the version of the story which accounts for the imprecation as due to mere insanity. Cf. Frs. 2 and 3 of the *Thebais*, often regarded in antiquity as " Homeric."

principle that "one term has one, and only one, opposite," it looks as though this means that *all* men, except the few φρόνιμοι, are lunatics. But this thesis can hardly be sound ; if all men were lunatics, we could not mix with them, as we do, with safety to life and limb. (Thus the writer knows, and goes out of his way to attack, the Stoic tenet that πᾶς ἄφρων μαίνεται, every one but the ideal "sage " is out of his wits.) We may urge that there are many bodily ailments, many trades ; but no invalid has all the diseases, no tradesman follows all the trades, at once. So there are many degrees of " want of sense," from mere dullness to stark lunacy, and so lack of judgement must not be equated with lunacy (138*a*–140*d*).

The φρόνιμοι are those who know " what is proper to do and say." The ἄφρονες do not know this, and so unintentionally do and say what they should not. Oedipus does not stand alone in this. If a god appeared to Alcibiades himself and offered to make him autocrat of Athens, or Hellas, or Europe, A. would probably think he was offered a great boon. Yet the power and splendour of the position would be no true boon to one who had not the *knowledge* how to use it. A tyranny may prove fatal to the recipient, as was the case with the murderer of Archelaus ; he was himself murdered after a reign of three days.[1] Many Athenian citizens have been undone by attaining high office ; children may prove a curse to those who have prayed for them. The poet who asks Zeus simply to give him what is good and withhold what is bad, even if he asks it, speaks like a wise man (140*e*–143*a*). *What* ignorance is thus shown to be so bad for us ? Some ignorance may be better for us than knowledge. If A.—the example is un-Platonic in its bad taste—formed a murderous design on his guardian Pericles, it would be *better* that he should lose the power of recognizing Pericles when he meets him. Knowledge of other things, not accompanied by knowledge of good, is most often harmful. It is better not to know *how* to do a thing, unless you also know whether it is *good* to do that thing. Mere professional skill does not make men φρόνιμοι ; the national life of a society of " professional experts " destitute of the knowledge of *good* would not be admirable (143*b*–146*b*). Most men have not the knowledge which would tell them whether what they do " skilfully " (προχείρως) is really beneficial. So it is better that the " many " should neither have nor fancy themselves to have a professional skill which they would be sure to misuse. Hence the importance of knowledge of good in private and public life. If it is wanting, the fresher the breezes of fortune blow, the graver the peril. Homer hinted at this when he said of Margites that he " knew a lot of things, but knew them all *badly* " (143*b*–147*e*).[2]

---

[1] This is a bad anachronism, since Archelaus was killed in 399, some years after the death of Alcibiades, who is a mere boy in the dialogue.

[2] πόλλ' ἠπίστατο ἔργα, κακῶς δ' ἠπίστατο πάντα. The forced interpretation of κακῶς as " to his own hurt " looks like an imitation of the whimsicalities of Socrates' exposition of Simonides in the *Protagoras*.

A. now thinks that he would not jump blindly at the offer of a "tyranny," and approves the wisdom of the unnamed poet whom Socrates had quoted. The Spartans, Socrates adds, show a like wisdom. Their only public prayer is a brief petition for καλὰ ἐπ' ἀγαθοῖς, the *honestum et bonum*. There is a tale that the Athenians once asked the oracle of Ammon why Heaven favours the Spartans who, in spite of their wealth, are niggardly with sacrifices, more than the liberal Athenians.[1] The oracle answered that the Spartan εὐφημία—by which it presumably meant the decency of the prayer just mentioned—is more pleasing than all burnt-offerings. In the same spirit the gods rejected the costly offerings of Priam. They are not to be bribed, and they look at our souls, not our gifts (148e–150b).

A. would do well, then, to postpone his prayer until he has learned to pray aright. But who will teach him ? " Your sincere well-wisher," says Socrates, " but there is a mist which must first be removed from your soul." A. rewards these words of encouragement by " crowning " Socrates with the garland he had meant to wear while praying, and Socrates fatuously accepts the compliment. (A tasteless reminiscence of the Platonic playful " crowning " of Socrates by the drunken Alcibiades, *Sympos*. 213d–e.)

The very poor dialogue is dependent on, and therefore later than, *Alcibiades I*. Besides the echoes already mentioned, we note that the μαινόμενον ἄνθρωπον of 138a 6, said of Oedipus, is a verbal imitation of the use of the same phrase, "a mere lunatic," with reference to Alcibiades' own brother at *Alc. I*, 118e 4. The ill-managed fiction of the god who offers A. the " tyranny " of Athens, Hellas, or Europe, is founded on what is said more naturally of A.'s own day-dreams at *Alc. I*, 105b–c.

It is still more significant that the discussion of the Stoic " paradox " is forcibly dragged into the argument at its very opening. Oedipus is mentioned merely to give an opening for the remark that he was " crazy," and the nominal main argument is kept standing still while Socrates goes off at a tangent to discuss the irrelevant question whether all unwise persons are " crazy " too. The writer thus betrays the fact that his real concern is to attack the Stoics. This shows that he is not writing before some date when Stoicism was already in existence, *i.e.* not before the early decades of the third century. In the time of Arcesilaus, president of the Academy from 276 to 241 B.C., anti-Stoic polemic became the main business of the school. It does not *necessarily* follow that the polemic may not have begun rather earlier.

Linguistic considerations do not take us far. Stallbaum produces a respectable " haul " of alleged non-Platonic words and phrases, but forgets that many of these may only go to show that the writer was a poor stylist, without throwing any light on his

[1] The reference to Spartan wealth is another anachronism, taken pretty obviously from *Alc. I*.

date, while, in one or two cases, the text is not certainly sound. No great weight can be attached to his point that the use of the word μεγαλόψυχος at 140c for a " megalomaniac " is singular. This might well be a polite euphemism—it is given as one—in any age. It is urged that the plural οὐδένες is found twice (148c, e). But the same *form* occurs also in Plato (*Euthydemus*, 305d, *Timaeus*, 20b, Ep. vii. 344a) and in Isocrates, and I take its double appearance in a single half-page of *Alc. II* to be due to conscious imitation. The forms ἀποκριθῆναι (149a), οἴδαμεν (141e, 142d) are definitely not classical Attic,[1] but the majority of the Academy were never Athenians. Aristotle, for example, was an Ionian and constantly betrays the fact by his vocabulary. Too much has been made of the employment (140a, 150c) of τυχόν in the adverbial sense of " perhaps." This is not usual in good classical Attic, but there is at least one example in Isocrates.[2] By comparison with such early specimens of the κοινή as the extant remains of Epicurus, *Alc. II* might almost be called Attic. Hence I think it should not be confidently dated too late in the third century. It may belong to any time soon after the first rise of Stoicism.

Amatores (or *Rivales*. The title is Ἐρασταί in the famous MSS. BT, Ἀντερασταί in the margin of B).

The scena is the school of the reading-master Dionysius, said by Diogenes and others (D.L. iii. 5) to have been Plato's own first teacher. Two boys are disputing, apparently on a point of geometry. Socrates is told by the " lover " of one of them that they are " chattering philosophy " about "things on high " (τὰ μετέωρα). The tone of the remark leads him to ask whether philosophy is a thing to be ashamed of. The " lover's " rival is surprised that Socrates should act so much out of character as to put this question to a man who leads the life of a voracious and sleepy athlete. This new speaker is a votary of " music," as the other is of " gymnastic." His opinion is that philosophy is so divine a thing that a man must be less than human if he disprizes it. But what *is* this " philosophy " ? " What Solon meant when he spoke of ' learning something fresh every day of one's life '." [3] Yet, is it so clear that philosophy is simply identical with multifarious learning ? [4] We are used to think that philosophy is for the soul what exercise is for the body. If so, " polymathy " must be the mental counterpart of πολυπονία, excessive exertion, and it may be doubted whether this latter is a good thing. The cultivated "lover " feels bound,

---

[1] The first may be a vulgarism, the second is Ionic. Yet before the time of the New Comedy οἶδας is found once in Euripides, once (probably) in Xenophon ; οἴδαμεν once in Antiphon (the orator), once (probably) in Xenophon.

[2] *Isocr.* iv. 171, τυχὸν μὲν γὰρ ἄν τι συνεπέραναν. Cf. Xenoph., *Anab.* vi. 1, 20, νομίζων . . . τυχὸν δὲ καὶ ἀγαθοῦ τινος ἂν αἴτιος τῇ στρατιᾷ γενέσθαι.

[3] Solon, Fr. 2, γηράσκω δ' αἰεὶ πολλὰ διδασκόμενος.

[4] πολυμαθία (133c). The allusion is to Heraclitus, Fr. 16 (Bywater), πολυμαθίη νόον οὐ διδάσκει.

as a fair-minded man, to allow that πολυπονία may be good, though
the admission goes against his personal bias. His "athletic"
rival takes a different view. As all experts know, it is "moderate"
exertion which keeps the body fit ; even a hog has the sense to
understand that. In that case, may we not argue by analogy that
it is not excessive but moderate "studies" (μαθήματα) that are
good for the soul ? This question leads straight up to another :
Who is the expert who determines what is the right measure in the
matter of studies ?

Again, what studies would a true lover of wisdom regard as
most important ? The "musician" says, "Those which will win
you the highest reputation." A philosopher should be at home in
the "theorick" of *all* the professions, or at least, of those which
are in high consideration, though he should not stoop to meddle
with their manual part. He should know them as the "master-
builder" [1] knows his business (135b–c). But can a man be really
proficient in the theory of two professions at once ? Only if we
concede that the philosopher need not have the "finished" knowledge of a great specialist, but such an amateur's knowledge as will
enable him to follow the discourse of the specialist intelligently
and form a sound judgement on it. That means, says Socrates,
the philosopher is to the great specialist what a "pentathlist" is
to a first-rate boxer or wrestler. He is not supreme in any one
speciality, but a good second-rate man in several (136a). As he is
not subdued to any speciality, he is not circumscribed by any.[2]
But what is the *good* of his philosophy ? We do not want to trust
a second-rate physician when we are ill, nor a second-rate navigator
when we are in danger on the sea. If the philosopher is first-rate
at nothing, life has no place for him ; this seems fatal to the conception of him as an all-round "intelligent amateur" (137b).

Let us make a fresh start. In the case of our domestic animals,
there are two sides to the professions which "tend" them. The
expert *knows* a good horse or dog from a bad one better than other
men ; he also "disciplines," or "corrects" (κολάζει), the animals
under his care. What "art" similarly "corrects" human beings ?
Justice, the "art" of the dicast ; hence we should presume that
the practitioners of this art also *know* a good man from a bad one.
The layman in the art is ignorant even of himself, does not know
the true state of his own soul. This is why we say that he has not
sophrosyne ; by consequence, to have *sophrosyne* will mean to be a
practitioner of the art we have just called justice, the art of true
self-knowledge. We call this art *sophrosyne* because it teaches us
to *know* ourselves, and also justice, because it teaches us to "correct" what we discover to be amiss (138b). Since the life of society

---

[1] A tell-tale allusion to *Politicus*, 259e ff. ?

[2] This reminds one of the unnamed person described at the end of the
Euthydemus as being on the border-line between politics and philosophy (see
supra, p. 101). I suspect the writer means to recall that passage.

is kept sound by the employment of this " correction," we may also call this same self-knowledge " politics," the art of the statesman, or, when it is practised by one man for the whole community, the art of the king, or even of the autocrat (τύραννος). It is the same art which is exercised on a smaller scale in regulating a household. So we may say that the " master," the householder, the statesman, the king, the autocrat are all specialists in an " art " whose true name is indifferently *sophrosyne* or justice. The expert in this art is the person whose discourse a philosopher must be able to follow, and on whose results he must be able to pass a sound judgement (138d). What is more, the philosopher ought to be himself a first-rate practitioner of it (ib. *e*), and this disposes of the attempt to identify the philosopher with the all-round connoisseur.

The purpose of the little work is clearly to set the Platonic conception of philosophy as the knowledge of the good, with its corollary, the identification of the true philosopher and the true king, in sharp contrast with the shallower conception of philosophy as " general culture." The great representative of *this* view of philosophy in Attic literature is Isocrates,[1] and I think the Ἐρασταί may fairly be described as a pleasing essay on the superiority of the philosophy of the Academy to the thing called by the same name in the school of Isocrates. This may have some bearing on the date of the composition. The tension between Isocrates and the Academy seems to have reached its maximum in the last years of Plato's life, when Aristotle was coming into prominence as a rival teacher of " rhetoric." It is natural to regard our dialogue as a contribution to the Academic side of the controversy, a view borne out by the complete absence of all linguistic traces of later date. The explicit recognition of the " tyrant " as a practitioner of " *sophrosyne* and justice " indicates a more favourable view of " personal rule " than anything to be found in Plato. Unless it is to be taken as mere irony, it seems to imply that the writer regards an autocracy as a *fait accompli* of which he definitely approves. He also retains the demand that the philosopher ought to be himself a " ruler," disregarding the modified view of the *Laws*, where the philosopher acts as the sovereign's adviser and coadjutor. May we infer that he is unacquainted with the *Laws* and therefore presumably writing before their circulation ?[2] The facts would,

---

[1] Burnet, *Greek Philosophy, Part I*, 215.

[2] See the remarks of Jaeger, *Aristoteles*, 53–60, on the relation between Aristotle's *Protrepticus* and [Isocr.] I. The *Panathenaicus* of Isocrates is a contribution to the controversy ; the " sophists " of whom he complains there as rivals and critics are unmistakably the Academy. I suggest that the Ἐρασταί belongs somehow to the same " war of pamphlets." There is a remark ascribed (D.L. ix. 37) to Thrasylus that εἴπερ οἱ Ἀντερασταί Πλάτωνός εἰσι, the " lover " to whom Socrates makes the suggestion that the philosopher is a kind of " pentathlist," must be Democritus. This, as it stands, is nonsense. Perhaps Thrasylus really said, what is true, that Democritus was the kind of " all-round man " whom Socrates has in view. I think with

I think, fall into line if we supposed the writer to be connected with the Academic group formed, at the end of Plato's life, at Assos under the protection of the converted " tyrant " Hermias of Atarneus.   I offer this suggestion for whatever it may be worth.

Theages.   The main object of the work seems to be to relate a number of anecdotes about Socrates' " sign." Theages, son of Demodocus (perhaps the general of the year 425–4 mentioned at Thuc. iv. 75), is twice named in Plato (*Apol.* 33*d*, *Rep.* 496*b*). From these references we learn that he suffered from delicate health and was dead in 399.   According to the *Republic*, he might have been lost to philosophy but for the invalidism which kept him out of public life.   In the *Theages* he is a mere lad whose future destination is giving his father some anxiety.   There is no indication of dramatic date except that in 127*e*, apparently verbally echoed from *Apol.* 19*e*. Prodicus, Polus and Gorgias are all assumed to be present in Athens.   The piece can hardly be said to have an argument.   Demodocus thinks that nothing would prepare his son for a great career so well as association with Socrates. But, says S., my young friends do not always benefit by my society ; everything depends on the " divinity." My " sign " sometimes interferes, and it is always lost labour to disregard it.   Charmides neglected my advice not to train for the foot-race at Nemea and had reason to be sorry for it.   Timarchus insisted on leaving a dinner-party to keep an engagement in defiance of the " sign." The " engagement " was, in fact, to assist in an assassination, and Timarchus afterwards confessed, on the way to execution, that he had done wrong to disregard my warnings.   The " sign " also predicted the great public disaster at Syracuse.   Aristides, grandson of the great Aristides, made famous progress while he was with me, but, in a short absence, forgot all he had learned, though Thucydides (the grandson of Pericles' opponent) was associating with me to his great advantage.   Aristides explained that he had never directly learned anything from me, but found his own intelligence mysteriously aided by being in the same room with me.

All through this conversation there are recognizable borrowings from the Platonic dialogues.   The " sign " is described (128*d*) in the actual words of *Apol.* 31*d* ; the statement that it warned S. that some lads would not benefit by his company is taken from *Theaetet.* 151*a*, and the anecdote about the boys Aristides and Thucydides has been constructed by combining that passage with the *Laches*, where these two lads are introduced to S. by their fathers.   There is an allusion to the usurpation of Archelaus (124*d*) which verbally reproduces *Gorg.* 470*d*.   Theages, like the young

Grote that the words εἴπερ κτλ. need not indicate any doubt of the genuineness of the dialogue.   They may quite well mean, " Since, as every one knows, the work is Plato's." The object may be to argue that Plato has made Socrates allude to Democritus.   This would be a retort to the charge that Plato ignores Democritus out of envy (D.L. iii. 25).

Alcibiades of *Alc. I*, would like to be a τύραννος, " and so, I am sure," he says, " would you, or any one else " (125*e*). All these passages are ultimately borrowings from *Gorg.* 469*c*. There is one glaring anachronism, a reference to the mission of Thrasylus to Ionia in the year 409.[1] Since the *Republic* manifestly speaks of Theages as a grown man, the reference to the Sicilian disaster is probably a second. The curious theory of 129*e* ff. that the " sign " could infect the associates of S. with intelligence is unlike anything in Plato, but we may take it as indicating Academic authorship that, in spite of its wonderful stories, the *Theages* agrees with Plato against Xenophon that the " sign " gave no positive recommendations (128*d*).

Stallbaum[2] had a theory which would bring the *Theages* down to a very late date. He argues that the opening for its composition was provided by the words of *Theaetet.* 150*d*, where Socrates says that those of his young friends " to whom God permits it " (οἷσπερ ἄν ὁ θεὸς παρείκῃ) make great progress. Our writer wrongly supposed that " God " here means the " sign," which has nothing to do with the matter. This shows that he was influenced by the Stoic faith in prophecies, divination and omens. We know from Cicero[3] that Antipater of Sidon, a Stoic of *c.* 150 B.C., related curious tales about the " divination " of Socrates, and may infer that the stories of the *Theages* come from him. Hence the work is not earlier than 150 B.C. Stallbaum reinforces this argument by producing a longish list of suspicious words and phrases.

I see no force in this reasoning, which starts with a bad blunder. Stallbaum has forgotten the statement of the *Theaetetus* (151*a*) about the warnings of the " sign " which is our author's real starting-point. There is no misunderstanding of the *Theaetetus* in the *Theages*. Also it is antecedently just as likely that the *Theages* is one of the sources from which Antipater " collected " his tales as that it is drawing on him. In fact, a Stoic would not be likely to be satisfied with Plato's account of the merely inhibitory character of the " sign." Xenophon's version of the matter, which makes the " sign " give positive guidance, is much more in keeping with Stoic theories about " the divinity." Hence I hold that the fidelity of the *Theages* to Plato on this point is definite evidence *against* the presence of Stoic influence. The linguistic arguments are also nugatory. Some of the expressions to which Stallbaum took objection are actually Platonic, others are mere examples of a slightly turgid diction.[4] On the evidence I think it

---

[1] For this mission see Xenoph., *Hellenica*, i. 2, 1.

[2] See his *Introduction* and *Commentary*.

[3] Cicero, *de Divinatione*, I. liv. 123, permulta collecta sunt ab Antipatro quae mirabiliter a Socrate divinata sunt.

[4] He objects to βιῶναι, though Plato has ἐβίωσαν, βιῷ, βιῴη, and even βιώσας; to τεκμαίρεσθαι ἀπό τινος εἰς τι (a phrase directly imitated from *Theaetet.* 206*b* 7); to ποιοῦμαι δεινὸς εἶναι, an odd expression but paralleled, perhaps, *Rep.* 581*d* 10 (where the τι οἰώμεθα of editors is a correction of the MSS. ποιώμεθα.)

most probable that the dialogue is the work of an Academic of the last third of the fourth century, a man of the type of Xenocrates, (president of the Academy 339–314 B.C.). Xenocrates was notoriously interested in " daemons " and seems to have been the original authority, or one of them, for the later Platonist lore on the subject. The *Theages* is the very sort of thing we might expect from his circle.[1] Its chief interest for us lies in the probability that some of its anecdotes *may* have come down from men who had actually seen Socrates, and thus *may* reflect the impression his oddities made on contemporaries. Perhaps it is un-Platonic that the *Theages* represents the δαιμόνιον σημεῖον as leading Socrates to check the acts of other persons. There is no parallel for this in any certainly genuine dialogue.

Hipparchus. By general admission the language and diction of the dialogue are excellent fourth-century Attic, not to be really discriminated from the authentic work of Plato. This should put Stallbaum's view that it is a clever late imitation out of court. That might have been *possible* after the rise of " Atticism," but not earlier. I shall discuss Boeckh's unlucky speculation on the authorship later on.

Socrates and an unnamed friend [2] are considering the question what avarice (or greed, τὸ φιλοκερδές) is and who is the avaricious or greedy man (the φιλοκερδής). The first and obvious answer is " A greedy man is one who is not above making a profit from an unworthy source " (ἀπὸ τῶν μηδενὸς ἀξίων). But a man who expects to make a profit from what he *knows* to be worthless must surely be silly, whereas we think of the greedy not as silly, but as " cunning knaves," " slaves of gain " who know the baseness of the source and yet are not ashamed to make the profit. Here there is a difficulty. He who knows when and where it is " worth while " to plant a tree, or perform any other operation, is always some kind of expert. And an expert would *not* expect to make a profit out

(And in the *Theages* it is quite possible that we ought to read προσποιοῦμαι.) He objects to the use of προσαγορεύειν in the sense of " to name," which is justified by parallels at *Sophist.* 251a, *Polit.* 291e, *Phileb.* 12c, 54a, and the phrase ἅρματα κυβερνᾶν, a mere piece of " Gorgianism " with a close parallel in *Laws*, 641a 2. The only really suspicious *word* in his list is ἰδιολογεῖσθαι, apparently used nowhere else before Philo Judaeus. But as the noun ἰδιολογία occurs in Epicurus, three centuries before Philo, the suspicion does not amount to much. Ritter (*Untersuchungen*, 94) finds the mannerisms in agreement with Plato's earlier style, though inconceivable in a dialogue later than the *Theaetetus*, on which the *Theages* is dependent.

[1] See also H. Brünnecke, *de Alcibiade II, qui fertur Platonis* (Göttingen, 1912), 113. H. Dittmar (*Aeschines von Sphettos*, 64) thinks of Heraclides of Pontus and his friends, which comes to much the same thing.

[2] This is not in Plato's manner. Apart from the purposely anonymous chief speakers in the *Sophistes-Politicus* and *Laws*, he only introduces unnamed ἑταῖροι as persons to whom Socrates reports the conversation (e.g. in the *Protagoras*), never as interlocutors in the dialogue proper. It is also not his practice to name a dialogue after a character who is not an interlocutor, though Aeschines seems to have done this in his *Miltiades*.

of worthless material or by using worthless instruments, as we may readily convince ourselves by taking simple examples. This disposes of the suggestion that *cleverness* is part of the definition of the φιλοκερδής. We try a second formula : the greedy are those who are insatiably eager for *petty* profits. (The emphasis now falls on the paltriness of the gain.) Still, they cannot be supposed to *know* how petty the profit is. Also, *ex hyp.* they are *eager* for the gain. Gain is the " opposite " of detriment, detriment is always an evil and *therefore* men are made worse by it, *therefore* it is always an evil (227a, a singular argument in a circle). Gain, then, being the " opposite " of something which is *always* an evil, must always be a good. A man who loves gain is one who loves " good," as we all do. With the first definition it would seem that no one could be greedy, with the second that everyone must be greedy. If we try a third suggestion, that the greedy man is one who is not " above " making gain from sources to which the respectable (οἱ χρηστοί, 227d) will not stoop, it may still be replied that if it is true (a) that to make a gain is to be benefited (ὠφελεῖσθαι), and (b) that all men desire good, it must follow that the " respectable " are as much " fond of *all* gain " as others. And it would not help us to say that they do not desire to gain by that which will do them harm, or to make a " wicked " gain. For to be harmed = to suffer loss of some kind, and it is meaningless to talk of losing by a gain ; and if gain is *always* good, how can there be any " wicked " gain ?

Here the friend complains that Socrates is " gulling " him. But that, says S., would be a shocking act and would violate the precept of that good and wise man Hipparchus, the eldest of the Pisistratids. He introduced Homer's poetry to Athens, regulated its recitation, patronized Anacreon and Simonides, all out of zeal for improving his fellow-citizens. For the country-folk he set up Hermae by the roads engraved with maxims intended to surpass the wisdom of the famous Delphian inscriptions. One of these maxims was ΜΗ ΦΙΛΟΝ ΕΞΑΠΑΤΑ, " never gull a friend." *After* the murder of this great and good man, his brother Hippias ruled like a tyrant, but so long as he lived, Athens enjoyed a golden age. The true story of his death is that Harmodius murdered him from jealousy because Aristogiton preferred the wisdom of Hipparchus to his own.[1]

To return : we cannot give up any of our theses, but perhaps we might *qualify* one of them, the thesis that gain is always good. Perhaps some gain may be bad. But at least, gain is always gain, as a man, good or bad, is always a man. In a definition we should

[1] The story makes a deliberate point of contradicting the facts in every possible detail. It is thus certainly not meant to be taken seriously, but should be regarded as a not quite successful attempt to recapture the " irony " of Plato's Socrates. Stallbaum's denunciation of the *homuncio* who could make such a string of blunders is wasted. So is the labour of those who have gone to the passage for light on the " Homeric problem." The dialogue gets its name from this intercalated piece of awkward pleasantry.

indicate the common character of all gain, as we do that of all
" meats," wholesome or not, when we call them " solid nutriment "
(ξηρὰ τροφή). We might try, as a last attempt, the definition that
gain is " anything acquired at no outlay, or an outlay less than
what accrues from it." But we reflect that one might acquire
an illness, not only at no expense, but by being feasted at another's
expense, and yet this would not be a gain. If we add the qualification that the thing acquired must be a good, we shall be thrown back
on a difficulty which has already given us trouble. And the words
" with no outlay, etc." also have their difficulties.[1] To make their
meaning clear, we need to introduce the notions of *value* (ἀξία 231d)
and a *standard* of value. The profitable = the valuable, and the
valuable = that of which the possession, or ownership, is valuable.
But this seems to mean just the " beneficial " or " good." We
have ended by equating " gain " with " good " a second time and
are thus baffled by the plain fact that there appear to be " wicked "
gains which good men do not desire, and by the notorious common
employment of φιλοκερδής as a term of reproach.

The thoughts of the trifle are, all through, as Platonic as it;
language, and, apart from the one awkward " circle " in the reasoning, the main argument seems to me worthy of Plato in his more
youthful vein. The interest shown in economic facts is thoroughly
intelligent. The real evidence of non-Platonic authorship is, to
my mind, the anonymity of the interlocutor and the inferiority and
irrelevant length of what is meant to be the humorous interlude
about Hipparchus. The dialogue should be assigned to an Academic
of the earliest period with an excellent style and an intelligent
interest in economics.[2]

Clitophon. The work is no more than a brief fragment, but
raises interesting questions. Clitophon, a minor character in the
Republic,[3] is conversing with Socrates, who has been told that he is
a great admirer of Thrasymachus, but inclined to be critical of
Socrates himself. Clitophon explains his real position. He holds
that as long as S. confines himself to preaching the need for " learning justice " his discourse is most awakening. He is convincing,

---

[1] The point is that you might, *e.g.*, exchange gold for twice or four times
its weight in silver and yet lose by the transaction, though you acquire a
greater weight of metal (since the ratio of the value of gold to that of silver
is 12 : 1).

[2] It stands " stylometric " tests well. C. Ritter (*Untersuchungen*, 91)
thinks—or thought—its genuineness an open question. I agree with him
that the writer has " learned more than his style " from Plato, and am content
to believe that his work may actually have been read by Plato.

[3] He is mentioned there at 327b in a way which suggests that he has
come to the party in company with Thrasymachus. At 340a–b he says a
few words urging that Thrasymachus shall be allowed " fair play." Presumably he is the Clitophon mentioned by Aristotle, Ἀθηναίων Πολιτεία, 34,
as one of the more moderate supporters of the establishment of the 400 in 411
B.C., whose object was to return to the institutions of Clisthenes. Aristotle
classes him with Theramenes, Archinus and Anytus.

again, when he is exposing the error of the belief that injustice is ever " voluntary," [1] and the folly of trying to use what you have not yet learned how to use, or insisting that if a man does not know how to " use " his ψυχή, he would be better dead, or under the control of another who has this knowledge, which is the " art of the statesman." [2] (That is, Cl. accepts the whole of the theoretical Socratic ethics.) But when one has been converted to the necessity of " learning justice " and is anxious to set about the task, Socrates fails one. We may illustrate the nature of the failure thus. A medical man can do two things with his knowledge. He can make another man a medical specialist by imparting it ; over and above this, he can *cure* a patient. Socrates should not merely tell us that by " learning justice " we shall become specialists in the subject ; he should also explain what justice produces, as medicine produces health in the patient (409*b*). We want to know what " health of soul " is. Some say that the *product* of justice is the *expedient* (συμφέρον), some that it is the *right* (δίκαιον), some that it is the *profitable* (λυσιτελοῦν), or the *beneficial* (ὠφελιμόν). None of these answers—they are taken from *Rep.* 336*c–d* where Thrasymachus says he will not be fobbed off with any of them as a definition —are very enlightening. An associate of S. has said that justice produces *friendship* (φιλία) in *cities*. But he went on to say that some φιλίαι, those with boys or animals, are not good. True φιλία is ὁμόνοια, the concord of two minds, and ὁμόνοια is a *science* (ἐπιστήμη). The argument went no further, because no one could explain what it is about which all just men are " of one mind." Clitophon referred the question to Socrates, who told him that justice makes us able to " do good to our friends and harm to our enemies." Yet, on being pressed, S. admitted that a " just " man will do no harm to any one. [3] It looks, then, as though one of two things must be true. Either Socrates has the same limitations as a man who can speak eloquently in praise of a science in which he is himself only a layman, or, more probably, Socrates did not choose to explain himself fully. Clitophon is sure he needs a physician of the soul, but, unless S. can do more for him than he has so far done, he will be left to fall into the hands of Thrasymachus or another for practical treatment (410*a–e*).

It is not quite clear to what conclusion the writer is leading up, but it should be plain that the apparent commendation of Thrasymachus at the expense of Socrates is ironical. Clitophon's point is that unless Socrates can do more for him than simply preach on the

[1] 407*d–e*, where the allusion is to the treatment of this topic in the *Protagoras*.

[2] 407*e* ff. The allusions seem to be to the " protreptic " discourse of Socrates in the *Euthydemus* ; 408*b* 3 seems to refer to the simile of the mutineers in the *Republic* itself (488*a* ff.).

[3] The allusion is to *Rep.* 332*a–d*, but there it is Polemarchus who offers the definition and Socrates who criticizes it on the very ground mentioned by Clitophon.

necessity of " tending " the soul, he is in the position of a sick man in danger of falling into the hands of a confident " quack." I suspect that if the writer had gone on with his argument, Socrates would have been made to explain why the physician of the soul cannot simply give his " patient " a set of rules for moral regimen, why, in fact, morality is not a professional specialism. Such an argument would furnish a sound Academic commentary on the discourse between Socrates and Polemarchus in *Rep.* I. We might understand the piece better and, perhaps, discover something about its origin, if we could be sure how to interpret the reference to the *ἑταῖρος* of Socrates who maintained that "justice" produces *ὁμόνοια* in cities and that *ὁμόνοια* is a science.[1] Since the passage cannot be explained out of the *Republic* itself, we clearly have here an allusion to some actual controversy[2] ; the very irrelevance of the thesis to its immediate context shows that the point is one to which the writer attaches importance. That this writer is not Plato seems to be proved by his manifest dependence on *Republic, Euthydemus, Protagoras.* There would, so far as I can see, be no linguistic difficulty in admitting Plato's authorship. Hence I should ascribe the piece to some fourth-century Academic.[3]

Minos. Like the *Hipparchus*, this dialogue gets its name from the introduction of an historical narrative ; the respondent is anonymous. The question discussed is the nature of *law,* and the point is to be made that it is not of the *essentia* of law to be a *command.* A law is the *discovery* (ἐξεύρεσις) of a truth,—the view common to all champions of " eternal and immutable " morality. The piece opens, in an un-Platonic way, by a direct question from Socrates, " What is law ? " (The abruptness seems to be copied from the opening of the *Meno,* but there the abrupt question is put into the mouth of Meno and is dramatically appropriate.) The answer given is that " the law " is a collective name for τὰ νομιζόμενα, the aggregate of " usages." But this is like saying that sight (ὄψις) is the aggregate of visibles (ὁρώμενα). The statement, that is, tells us nothing about the *formal* character of the " legal " as such. A new definition is

---

[1] That justice produces φιλία and ὁμόνοια is said at *Rep.* 351d by Socrates himself.

[2] The question in what " goodness " makes men of one mind is, as we saw, raised in *Alc. I.,* but the allusion cannot well be to that dialogue as Adam thought, since there is nothing there about the φιλίαι of " boys and animals." H. Dittmar suggests Aristippus as the ἑταῖρος of S. intended. It seems improbable, however, that he wrote any Σωκρατικοὶ λόγοι. I fancy the guess is based on the fact that the ἑταῖρος is said to be κομψός and the mistaken identification of the κομψοί of the *Philebus* with Cyrenaics. φιλία was a standing topic with writers from the Academy ; Speusippus, Xenocrates, Aristotle all treated of it.

[3] See C. Ritter, *Untersuchungen,* 93, who finds the language closely akin to that of the latest Platonic dialogues. Perhaps there may be an allusion to the view that ὁμόνοια is an ἐπιστήμη in Aristotle's remark that agreement about astronomy is not ὁμόνοια since the sphere of " concord" is τὰ πρακτά (of which there is no ἐπιστήμη, *E.N.* 1167a 25). *E.E.* 1236b 2 ff., which has some remarks about φιλίαι with θηρία, may allude to the same discussion.

offered : a law is δόγμα πόλεως, a pronouncement of the community.
(*I.e.* it is the *authority* of the " sovereign " which gives to " use "
the formal character of law—the view of Hobbes and Austin.)
S. treats this statement as equivalent to saying that a law is an
opinion (δόξα) of the community, and, in spite of the contemptuous
comments of Stallbaum, the equation is a sound one. On the
proposed definition, a law *is* an embodied " judgement " of society,
or its representative, the " sovereign." But we also hold that
οἱ νόμιμοι, " respecters of law," and they only, are δίκαιοι and that
δικαιοσύνη, regard for right, is good and preserves society ; its
contrary, ἀνομία, disregard for law, is bad, and destroys society.
Now a given enactment may be a " *bad* law." But how can a
bad δόγμα πόλεως really be law, if law is what really exalts a nation ?
It is suggested that we should define law as a *sound* judgement
(χρηστὴ δόξα) of society. But here *sound* is a mere synonym
for *true*, and truths are not manufactured but *discovered*. It seems,
then, that formally a law is ἐξεύρεσις τοῦ ὄντος, a *discovery* about
(moral) *reality*. This is the main point of the *Minos*, and it is a
perfectly just one.[1]

What are we to say about the notorious divergences between
the laws of different communities or different generations ? One
thing is clear ; no society ever fancies that right can really be
wrong. A law not based on reality (τὸ ὄν) is an *error* about τὸ
νόμιμον. (It may be accepted as law, but it *ought* not to be so
accepted.) And we see from the examples of medicine, agriculture
and other arts that the laws of an art are the regulations of the
ἐπιστήμων, the man who has expert knowledge about some region
of τὸ ὄν. So the true " laws " of civic life are the directions given
by " kings " and good men (the experts in *moral* knowledge), and
therefore will not vary ; a mistaken direction has no right to be
called " law."

Now, who knows how to " distribute " (διανεῖμαι) seeds to different soils properly ? The farmer who knows his business. The
physician's " distributions " of food and exercise are the right
distributions for the body, the shepherd's distributions the right
ones for the flock. Whose distributions are the right ones for
men's *souls* ? Those of the *king* who knows his business.[2] In
ancient days, there were such " divinely " wise experts in kingship,
of whom Minos of Crete was one. The current story is that he

[1] Cf. Sir F. Pollock, *Spinoza*,[2] 304, " Law is not law merely because the
State enforces it ; the State enforces it because it is law," and the definition
in the *Institutes*, iurisprudentia est divinarum et humanarum rerum notitia,
iusti atque iniusti scientia.

[2] There is here a conflation of the language of the *Politicus* about the
king as tender of the human herd with that of *Laws*, 713c–714a, where νόμος,
" law," is playfully derived from νέμειν in the sense *to divide, distribute,
assign*, and law is said to be the " assignment " (διανομή) made by νοῦς.
The allusion to this passage explains the awkward double use of νομεύς in
the *Minos* as covering at once the meanings *herdsman* and *dispenser*.

was a savage tyrant, though his brother Rhadamanthys is proverbial for righteousness. This is a mere calumny of Attic poets on a successful antagonist of Athens. Homer and Hesiod speak very differently. Homer says that Minos used to "converse" with Zeus every ninth year.[1] Zeus was a superlative sophist and Minos his pupil. Rhadamanthys was not taught by Minos the whole art of royalty, but only how to do the "understrapper's" share of the work.[2] He and Talus—the iron man of the tale—policed Crete under Minos. Now what does the wise king "distribute" to souls as the wise trainer "distributes" food and exercise to bodies? If we find ourselves unable to say, we must confess that this inability to say what is good or bad for our souls is disgraceful. (Thus we end with the familiar point that a man's first duty is to get knowledge of good, to "tend" his soul.)

The thought of the *Minos* is Platonic; not so Platonic is the eulogy of Minos, of whose institution the *Laws* speaks with some severity.[3] Since the use of the *Laws* is unmistakable, the date of composition must be after Plato's death. This disposes of the unhappy suggestion of Boeckh that the *Hipparchus* and *Minos*, with two of the νοθευόμενοι (*de Iusto, de Virtute*), are the work of the cobbler Simon, who was believed in later antiquity to have circulated "notes" (ὑπομνήματα) of conversations held in his shop by Socrates (D.L. ii, 128). The language is really open to no exceptions.[4] Stallbaum's theory that the work is an Alexandrian forgery is excluded by the known fact that Aristophanes of Byzantium placed it in one of his "trilogies." The right inference is not Stallbaum's, that Aristophanes brought the work into the Platonic canon, but that he found it there. The language points to a date after the death of Plato, but still in the fourth century. Aristophanes and Thrasylus both evidently regarded the *Minos* as a kind of "introduction" to the *Laws*. The discrepancy between its estimate of Minos and Cretan institutions and that of *Laws, I.* shows that the piece can hardly have been intended so.

I subjoin here some brief notes on the contents of those among

[1] An allusion to *Laws*, 624a–b, where Homer's obscure phrase ἐννέωρος ὀαριστής is explained in the same way.

[2] The distinction between the king and his "underling," as Boeckh and Stallbaum saw, comes from the *Politicus*. The explanation given of the bad repute of Minos is strictly true, in spite of Stallbaum's ridicule. The venom of the *Attic* versions of the legends about him and his family (Pasiphae, Phaedra, the Minotaur) is accounted for by the hostile relations between Attica and the prehistoric rulers of Cnossus. To the Athenian ear the name Minos suggested "chains and slavery."

[3] At *Laws*, 630d, the Cretan complains τὸν νομοθέτην ἡμῶν ἀποβάλλομεν εἰς τοὺς πόρρω νομοθέτας.

[4] See C. Ritter, *Untersuchungen*, 92–93, though he holds that the *style* is more like that of the *Gorgias* than of any other dialogue. Stallbaum took offence at the use of ἁρμόττειν = *convenire*, to be fitting, at 314e, as only found elsewhere in *Ep.* viii. 356d. But the author of *Ep.* viii. *was* Plato, and our writer is imitating him.

the *Epistles* of which I have given no account in the body of this book.

I. By an unknown and turgid writer to an unknown recipient, who seems to be, virtually at least, an autocrat. The writer has long held the highest ἀρχαί in " your city," and has had to shoulder the odium of false steps taken against his advice. He has now been dismissed with contumely, and so washes his hands of the " city " and returns an insultingly small sum of money sent him for his present expenses. The situation answers to none in the life of Plato, nor, so far as one can see, in that of Dion, to whom Ficinus wished to transfer the authorship. Yet the style seems fourth-century, and its total unlikeness to that of all the other *Epistles* shows that we can hardly be dealing with a deliberate forgery meant to pass as Plato's. If the "city" is Syracuse, the writer might be a Syracusan who has been sent into actual or virtual banishment and therefore poses as no longer a citizen. But why does he write in Attic ? Or is our text a transcription into Attic ? (I have sometimes thought of the historian Philistus— who had been sent into virtual exile at Adria by Dionysius I but returned at his death and was the chief opponent of Dion—as a possible author.[1])

V. *Plato to Perdiccas of Macedonia.* A letter recommending Euphraeus of Oreus as a political adviser. Constitutions, like animals, have their distinctive " notes " ; Euphraeus is skilled in the knowledge of these, and would not be likely to recommend measures " out of tune " with monarchy. An unfriendly critic might discount the recommendation by urging that its author has not even caught the " note " of the democracy in which he lives. But the truth is that " Plato was born too late in the day " for his country to listen to advice which he would have rejoiced to give. Objections to the letter will be found in the works of C. Ritter and R. Hackforth,[2] but seem to me trivial. I cannot think Plato, who wrote the *Politicus* and played the part he did at Syracuse, would have thought it unreasonable to give advice to a Macedonian king, and the influence of Euphraeus with Perdiccas is attested as a fact. (Athenaeus 506*e*.) The attacks on the very intelligible language about the " notes " of different constitutions seem to rest on the arbitrary assumption that the writer must be recalling and mis-understanding the words of *Rep.* 493*a–b* about the cries of the demo-cratic *belua*. Ritter can urge nothing against the language, which he regards as very much like that of *Ep.* iv. ; he gives away his whole case, to my mind, by suggesting that v. is a genuine letter

[1] The same suggestion is thrown out by L. A. Post, *Thirteen Epistles of Plato*, 130, but rejected on the ground that the writer appears not to be a citizen of Syracuse. As explained above, I think this inconclusive. But why should Philistus write in Attic ?

[2] C. Ritter, *Neue Untersuchungen*, 327–398. R. Hackforth, *Authorship of the Platonic Epistles*, 73–75.

of Speusippus. (*I.e.* his real reason for denying it to Plato is that he cannot rid his mind of the notion that Plato must have been " above " corresponding with a Macedonian king. I think Plato understood the political situation better than this.) The letter, if genuine, falls some time in the reign of Perdiccas (365–360 B.C.).

VI. *Plato to Hermias, Erastus and Coriscus.* The two young Academics (Coriscus is Aristotle's friend whose name figures so often in his " logical examples ") are introduced to Hermias, who had made himself " tyrant " of Atarneus and was soon to be the patron of Aristotle, as well as the first martyr in the Hellenic " forward movement " against Persia. He needs confidants of high character ; the two young men have character and intelligence, but need an ἀμυντικὴ δύναμις, a " protector," whom they can find in him. The writer hopes that his letter will lay the foundation for an intimate friendship. We are not likely to hear any more of the " spuriousness " of vi. since the vigorous defence of it by Wilamowitz in his *Platon* and the throwing of a flood of light on the philosophical and political importance of the " Asiatic branch " of the Academy at Assos by Jaeger.[1] The letter is valuable as showing that the foundation of the " colony " at Assos was undertaken in Plato's lifetime and on his initiative. The letter must belong to the last years of his life.

IX. *Plato to Archytas.* Archytas has complained of the heavy burdens and anxieties of public life. He should remember that our country and our family have both as much claim on our thought and our time as our personal concerns.[2] A promise is made to care for a young man named Echecrates, from regard to Archytas no less than on his own and his father's account. No one has alleged anything suspicious in the language of ix. The difficulty which has been made about the youth of Echecrates arises from the assumption that he is the man of that name who appears in the *Phaedo.* Archer-Hind rightly called attention in his edition of the dialogue to the mention of an Echecrates of Tarentum, the city of Archytas, in Iamblichus's list of Pythagoreans. The date of the letter cannot be fixed. Plato and Archytas were already friends in 367 B.C. (*Ep.* vii. 338*a*) and we do not know how much earlier.

X. *Plato to Aristodorus.* A mere note commending the loyalty of the recipient to Dion and expressing the conviction that " loyalty, fidelity, honesty " (τὸ βέβαιον καὶ τὸ πιστὸν καὶ ὑγιές) are the true " philosophy." There are no materials for judgement either way, but, as Ritter says, the tone " seems genuine." And why should one forge such a note ?

XI. *Plato to Leodamas.* A meeting would be desirable, but

---

[1] Jaeger, *Aristoteles*, 112–124, 303–305.

[2] Cicero quotes the sentiment with approval, *de Finibus*, II., xiv. 45 : ut ad Archytam scripsit Plato, non sibi se soli natum meminerit, sed patriae, sed suis, ut perexigua pars ipsi relinquatur.

L. cannot contrive a visit to Athens and Plato is not equal to a journey which would probably bear no fruit. He might have sent Socrates, *i.e.* the Academic of that name who figures in the *Politicus* —but he is ill. One hint may be given to L. in connection with the colony he is projecting. A sound public life requires an authority which can exercise vigilant supervision of daily life. Such an authority can only be created if there is an adequate supply of persons fit to undertake the charge. It is useless to dream of setting up such a body if its members would first have to be educated for the position. The date of the letter, if genuine, is probably about 360 B.C.[1] That Leodamas, a mathematician and member of the Academy,[2] as well as a statesman, should have consulted Plato about the founding of a " city " and received an answer is in keeping with all we know of the interests and position of the Academy in Plato's advanced age. C. Ritter, who finds linguistic affinities between xi., ii. and xiii., has only rather pointless objections to urge. He thinks that the precise character of the " illness " of Socrates would not be given in a genuine letter. But surely we all, even if we are philosophers, do give such information to friends at a distance, and there is real point in making it plain that the illness is not "diplomatic." Ritter also thinks the reason given for Plato's unwillingness to face the journey himself "unworthy." (It seems to be a polite way of saying that he is too old.) Finally, it is " not Platonic " to say that when a situation is desperate, one can only " pray " for better things. But why not ? Plato says the very thing at *Ep.* vii. 331d. And the way in which the younger Socrates is mentioned is far too natural for the Hellenistic forger.[3]

XII. *Plato to Archytas.* A note acknowledging the receipt of certain " papers " (ὑπομνήματα) and expressing admiration of their author as fully worthy of his legendary ancestors. The writer sends certain unrevised " papers " of his own in return. Our chief MSS. append a note that the authenticity of this letter was disputed,— when or why is not known. C. Ritter inclines to attribute it to the author of ii., vi. and xiii. (that is, as I hold, to Plato). The strongest argument on the other side is its apparent connection with the pretended letter from Archytas to Plato prefixed to *Ocellus* (or *Occelus*) *the Lucanian on the Eternity of the Cosmos.*[4] If this were genuine, xii. would be Plato's reply to Archytas, and the " papers " sent to Plato would have to be identified with " Ocellus." There is no doubt that " Ocellus " is a fabrication of the first or second century B.C. or that the " letter of Archytas " is part of the fabrica-

---

[1] Post, *op. cit.*, 37.

[2] Proclus in *Euclid. I.* (Friedlein), 66, 212.

[3] A forger, even if he knew of the younger Socrates, would have been afraid to make his document look suspicious to the purchaser by a reference which would seem like a bad chronological blunder about the great Socrates.

[4] The fiction is that " Ocellus " is an ancient Pythagorean of the sixth century, whose work has just been unearthed after long concealment.

tion. Hence Zeller suggested the now widely accepted view that *Ep.* xii. is also the work of the same hand. This plausible view has, to my thinking, one fault. It assumes that the fabricator had the wit and sense to avoid introducing into Plato's "reply" a single word which would definitely identify the "papers" spoken of with "Ocellus." Of course the introduction of such language is just the way in which the ordinary fabricator "gives himself away," but the cleverness of avoiding the blunder seems to me a little too clever for the sort of persons who "faked" Pythagorean remains. I think it possible, then, that *Ep.* xii. *may* be a genuine note from Plato to Archytas about matters otherwise unknown, and that its existence *may* have suggested to the fabricator of "Ocellus" the basis of his romance.[1] But appearances are certainly strongly against xii. I take no account of the few additional "letters" which figure in the *Life* of Plato in Diogenes. They were never included in the "canon," or in any known Platonic MS. It was a mistake in principle on the part of C. F. Hermann to prejudice the case for the collection of the "thirteen epistles" by printing these items in his edition of Plato.[2]

B. The Ὅροι.

This is a collection of definitions of terms of natural and moral science. The total number of terms defined is 184, but a good number of them receive two or more alternative definitions. In the "canon" the collection was definitely marked off from the genuine work of Plato by exclusion from the "tetralogies." Since our collection was thus known to Dercylides and Thrasylus, it must be older than the Christian era. I do not know that there is any further evidence to show when or where it was made. The genuineness of the contents as old Academic work is fairly guaranteed by two considerations. Many of the definitions are simply extracted from the dialogues ; others are quoted and criticized by Aristotle, whose *Topics*, in particular, are rich in allusions of this kind. I think it will be found that there are no signs of Stoic influence, and this suggests that the collection, or a larger one of which it is what remains, goes back to a time before the *rapprochement* between Academicism and Stoicism under Antiochus of Ascalon in the second quarter of the first century B.C. There seems also to be no serious trace of Aristotelian influence. No use is made of the great Aristotelian *passe-partout* ἐνέργεια ; the genus of εὐδαιμονία is actually given (412*d*) as δύναμις; the Aristotelian distinction

---

[1] Since Zeller, the fabrication of "Ocellus" and the correspondence connected with it has usually been assigned to the first century B.C. The latest editor, R. Harder, argues strongly for an earlier date in the *second* century (Harder, *Ocellus Lucanus*, 149 ff.).

[2] On the *Epistles* generally see also the *Introduction* to J. Souilhé's edition of them in the *Collection des Universités de France*. But the conclusions reached there seem to me vitiated by a violent animus against admitting authenticity.

between σοφία and ἐπιστήμη, the speculative, and φρόνησις, the practical exercise of intelligence, has not affected the terminology. On the other side, ὄρεξις, Aristotle's technical word for " conation," unknown elsewhere in the Platonic *corpus*, occurs twice, in the definitions of *wish* (413c) and of *philosophy* (414b). The statement that νόησις is ἀρχὴ ἐπιστήμης (414a) and the definition of δεινότης (413c) also sound Aristotelian. But these are trifles when set against the absence of the distinction between ἐπιστήμη and φρόνησις. On the whole I believe we should be reasonably safe in saying that the collection fairly represents Academic terminology as it was in the time of Xenocrates and Aristotle. Since we know that Speusippus was keenly interested in terminology, and that a collection of ὄροι was included among his works (D.L. iv. 5), we may infer that he is likely to be the ultimate source of much of our document. The *Divisions* of Xenocrates (D.L. iv. 13) are also likely to have contributed. As Aristotle quotes and criticizes Academic definitions not found in the collection, it is clear that we possess only an extract from more copious materials.

C. νοθευόμενοι.

de Justo. A conversation between Socrates and an unnamed friend on the nature of τὸ δίκαιον. Justice, the art of the judge (δικαστής), like counting, measuring, weighing, is an art of *distinguishing*. It distinguishes the rightful from the wrongful. A given act, *e.g.* the utterance of a false statement, may be sometimes right, sometimes wrong: right when it is done "in the appropriate situation" (ἐν δέοντι), wrong in all other cases. It is *knowledge* which enables a man to recognize the appropriate occasion. Wrongdoing, then, is due to ignorance, and so is involuntary.

de Virtute. This conversation also is held by Socrates with a friend who is anonymous in most of the MSS. In the Vatican MS. called by Burnet O he has a name, Hippotrophus. The piece is thus presumably that mentioned by Diogenes Laertius under the alternative names *Midon* and *Hippotrophus*. It has the same type as the last. The question is whether "goodness" can be taught. In both pieces Socrates is made, as in the *Minos*, to originate the problem. The example of the various "arts" is used to show that if you would acquire special knowledge, you must put yourself under a specialist's tuition. But "goodness" apparently cannot be acquired thus, since Themistocles, Aristides, Thucydides, Pericles were all unable to impart it to their sons. Again "goodness" does not seem to come "by nature." If it did, we might have specialists in human nature, as we have fanciers of dogs and horses, and they would be able to tell us which young persons have the qualities that will repay careful training. "Goodness," then, like prophecy, seems to depend on an incalculable "divine" inspiration.

Boeckh, as we have said, regarded these trifles as the genuine work of an acquaintance of Socrates, the cobbler Simon.[1] They cannot be that for several reasons. For (1) they are slavishly close imitations, often reproducing whole sentences of Plato's text. Thus the argument about the parallel between " justice " and the arts of number and measure in the *de Iusto* has been directly copied, as Stallbaum said, from *Euthyphr.* 7b ff. The *de Virtute* is largely made up of similar "liftings" from the *Meno* and *Protagoras*. (2) The discourses ascribed to the cobbler Simon must have been shorter even than our two νοθευόμενοι, for there were thirty-three of them in a single roll (D.L. ii. 122). (3) The work ascribed to Simon was almost certainly a forgery. (The learned Stoic Panaetius said that the only certainly genuine dialogues by " Socratic men " were those of Plato, Xenophon, Antisthenes, Aeschines ; those ascribed to Euclides and Phaedo were doubtful, all others spurious. D.L. ii. 64.) In fact, it is hard to doubt that we are dealing with late exercises in imitation of Plato's style, " atticizing " copies of a classic. The purity of the language is partly explained by this, partly by the presence of *verbatim* extracts.

Demodocus. This hardly even pretends to be a dialogue. It is a direct harangue of Socrates to an audience which includes Demodocus (? the father of Theages). The style is halting to the verge of inarticulateness. The drift, obscured by verbiage, is that Socrates has been asked to advise the audience on some decision they are about to take. The request implies that there is a " science of giving advice." Either the present audience possess this science or they do not. If they all possess it, there is nothing to discuss ; if none of them possess it, discussion is waste of time. If one or two possess it, why do not they advise the others ? Where is the use of listening to rival counsellors, or of taking a vote when their counsel has been heard ? How can persons who do not know for themselves which is the advisable course vote to any purpose on the advices of rival counsellors ? Socrates will certainly not advise such a set of fools.

At this point the shambling speech ends. What follows seems to be a detached set of anecdotes, having nothing in common with what has gone before, except that Socrates is apparently the narrator, and that each anecdote embodies a rather puerile dilemma.

(a) I once heard a man blame his friend for accepting the story of the plaintiff in a suit without troubling to hear the other side. This, he said, was unfair and a violation of the dicast's oath. The friend retorted that if you cannot tell whether one man is speaking the truth, you will be still more at a loss if there are two speakers with different stories. If they should both tell the same story, why need you listen to it twice ?

(b) A man is reproached by a friend to whom he has refused

---

[1] For a statement of Boeckh's case see his essay *In Platonis qui vulgo fertur Minoem* (Halle, 1806). It is fairly met and disproved by Stallbaum in the introduction to his own commentary on the *Minos*.

a loan. A bystander comments, " Your rebuff is your own fault. For a *fault* means a failure to effect one's purpose, and you have failed to effect yours. Also, if your request was an improper one, it is a fault to have made it ; if it was proper, it is a fault not to have made it successfully. Also, you have not gone to work the right way, or you would not have been refused ; *ergo*, you have made a fault.'' A second bystander urged that any man may fairly complain if one whom he has helped refuses to help him in turn. But the first speaker said, " The man either is able to do what you ask, or he is not. If he is not, you should not make so unreasonable a request ; if he is, how is it you did not succeed with him ? '' " Well, a man at least expects better treatment for the future if he remonstrates.'' " Not if the remonstrance is as groundless as it is in this case.''

(c) A man is blamed for giving ready credence to the random utterances of irresponsible persons. Why ? Because he believes the tale of " anyone and everyone '' without investigation. But would it not be an equal fault to believe the tales of your most particular intimates without examination ? If a speaker is an intimate of A and a stranger to B, will A be right in believing his tale and B equally right in disbelieving the same story ? If the same tale is told you by an intimate and a stranger, must it not be equally credible on the lips of both ?

The shambling and helpless style of these anecdotes shows that they come from the same hand as the foolish harangue to Demodocus. The writer must have been a person of low intelligence, with no power of expression and a taste for futile "eristic.'' I doubt whether his scraps were meant to form a connected whole.

Sisyphus. Socrates is in conversation with a Pharsalian of the singular name of Sisyphus,[1] whom he expected to have seen the day before among the audience at an *epidexis* or show-speech. Sisyphus explains that he was kept away by " our rulers,'' who commanded his presence at an important consultation.[2] But what is consultation (τὸ βουλεύεσθαι) ? A process of inquiry (τὸ ζητεῖν). Inquiring is trying to get fuller knowledge of something of which we have some preliminary notion, but not full knowledge. It is the presence in us of ignorance which makes this process difficult. But men do not " consult '' about what lies beyond the range of their knowledge ; hence the business of yesterday should have been called an *inquiry* into the interests of Pharsalus. Why did not the inquirers take the course of " learning '' the truth from some

---

[1] Presumably the Sisyphus of Pharsalus mentioned also by Theopompus, Fr. 19 (*ap.* Athenaeus, 252*f*). Sisyphus was perhaps a " nickname.'' Xenophon (*Hellenica*, iii. 1, 8) says that the Spartan commander Dercylidas was called so for his "artfulness.'' Athenaeus (500*b*), quoting from Ephorus, gives the *sobriquet* in his case as σκύφος, an obvious corruption (CK for CIC).

[2] Then is Socrates supposed to be in Thessaly, or were the " government offices '' of Pharsalus at Athens ?

one who already knew it, rather than the inferior course of trying to puzzle it out for themselves ?   And can there really be a difference between better and worse advice ?   Advice always has reference to the future, the future is what " has not happened " and therefore has no determinate character (οὐδὲ φύσιν ἔχει οὐδεμίαν). One guess about it cannot well be better or worse than any other.

The writer is perhaps the same man as the author of the *Demodocus* ; he has the same foible for childish eristic, the same interest in the alleged puzzle about " deliberation " and the same helplessness of style, though the *Sisyphus* is not quite so helpless as the *Demodocus*.   He has read the *Meno* [1] and he has one real point, though he does not know how to manage it.   He is playing with the conception of the future as something which is, as yet, nothing at all,[2] and therefore not a subject for rational consideration. Possibly he is thinking of the Cyrenaic doctrine that the future, being unreal, is " nothing to us," [3] and trying to " expose " it ?

Eryxias.   This is a much more serious production than any of the four just examined.   The writer has provided a definite audience, scene and date.   Socrates is talking in the portico of Zeus Eleutherius [4] with Critias (the " oligarch "), Eryxias and Erasistratus, nephew of Phaeax (the contemporary and rival of Alcibiades).   The date is supposed to be between the Peace of Nicias and the determination taken in 416 by Athens to attack Syracuse, as we see from the opening remarks made by Erasistratus on the necessity of taking a firm line with that " wasp's nest." The subject of the discussion, which is made to arise quite naturally, is the nature and worth of πλοῦτος, " capital," as we should say. Erasistratus holds that " the richest man is he who owns what is worth most."   If so, may not a poor man in lusty health be said to be richer than an opulent invalid with whom he would never dream of changing places ?   And there may be things of higher worth than health.   It is evident, also, that the thing of highest worth is happiness (εὐδαιμονία).   It should follow that the richest of men are the " wise and good," because they do not impair their happiness by making false steps in life : " the man who knows what is good is the only real capitalist,"—a clear allusion to the Stoic paradox, *solus sapiens dives*.   Eryxias objects that a man might be as wise as Nestor and yet in want of the bare necessaries of life.   Still, says S., such a man's wisdom might have a high value in exchange in any district where it was esteemed.   A man

---

[1] As we see not only from his reference to the old eristic quibble about τὸ ζητεῖν, but from his allusion to " inquiring " into the ratio of " diagonal " to " side," to which he adds the later problem of the " duplication of the cube."

[2] The view adopted by Dr. C. D. Broad, *Scientific Thought*, 66 ff.

[3] Cf. the saying ascribed to Aristippus, μόνον ἡμέτερον εἶναι τὸ παρόν, μήτε δὲ τὸ φθάνον μήτε τὸ προσδοκώμενον· τὸ μὲν γὰρ ἀπολωλέναι, τὸ δὲ ἄδηλον εἶναι εἰ πάρεσται, R.P. 267.

[4] For which see Pausanias, i. 3, 2.   It is also the scene of the *Theages*.

who understood the direction of life might make capital of his knowledge, if he chose. Eryxias treats this as a verbal quibble, and this leads to a dispute between him and Critias in which S. acts as seconder to Eryxias. Leaving on one side the verbal paradox that the wise man is the true capitalist, we may more profitably ask what ways of acquiring wealth are honourable, and whether wealth itself is or is not good. Eryxias thinks it is, Critias that it is not, since *for some persons*, those whose wealth leads them to perpetrate follies or crimes, wealth is so clearly not good ; but what is not good for *everyone* is not properly called a good. That argument, says S., is a mere borrowing from Prodicus, who had publicly defended the thesis that everything is good for the man who knows how to *use* it, bad for the man who does not, but had been silenced and put to shame by a mere lad. The lad's counter-argument was that only a fool expects to get as answers to prayer things he might learn from a teacher, or find out for himself. Prodicus, like other men, asks in his prayers that " his lot may be good " : on his own theory this amounts to praying that he may himself *become* good, and also, according to his own theories, good-ness is something a man can learn from a teacher. Critias is borrowing the argument of Prodicus, and if he is not hooted down, that is only because reasoning which would be seen to be bad in a " sophist " imposes on hearers who respect Critias as a gentleman and man of the world.

Here S. directs attention to the original and still more funda-mental question what wealth *is*. You may say, " abundance of χρήματα, means." But what are means ? It is argued, with a little needless display of general information, that means are " possessions which are of *use* to us." Hence a cartload of Car-thaginian currency would not be " means " at Athens, where it will not exchange for anything. Coin is popularly confused with wealth simply because it exchanges freely for clothes and all other com-modities. Now a professional man can exchange his professional services for commodities, and thus ἐπιστῆμαι, knowledge of pro-fessions, seems to be one form of capital. Again an article is only capital to one who knows how to use it, and the καλοὶ κἀγαθοί are the persons who know how to make the right use of everything. Thus there is a sense in which to make a man wiser is to make him richer. Critias still protests that possessions are not wealth, but the argument is continued. In any trade, a man's capital clearly includes not only his materials but his implements, and sometimes also appliances for making those implements. If a man were once fully equipped with all that his body requires, money and such things would be useless to him. Again, since to learn you must be able to hear, the money a man pays his doctor for taking care of his hearing is actually useful as a means to " goodness." This money may have been made in a " base " calling, and thus a " base " thing *may* be useful for good. We are almost tempted to say that, since a man can only become wise, healthy, good, if he has previously been ignorant, unwell, bad, ignorance, disease, vice are conditions *sine quibus non* of their opposites, and therefore useful, and ought, by consequence, to be called wealth. But apart from this paradox, we may ask ourselves one question, " When is a man happier and better, when he has the most or when he has the least numerous and expensive wants ? " Since this amounts to asking whether a man is happier in disease or in health, the question answers itself. The rich, who have many and expensive wants, are not the truly happy.

I think it clear that the purpose of the dialogue, which is very interesting for its economic theses, is to canvass the Stoic doctrine that wisdom, virtue, wealth are identical, and that the sage is the only " capitalist." This is the thesis which Eryxias treats as idle playing with words and Socrates " side-tracks," in order to discuss the more than verbal question whether riches are good or bad. It is part of the anti-Stoic polemic that S. supports Eryxias against Critias who denies that " property " is wealth. The author means to protest against " pulpit declamation " which amounts to nothing but words and to replace it by the dispassionate Academic view that wealth and wisdom are different things, the one at the bottom, the other at the top of the scale of good. The Greek of the dialogue is not the Attic of Plato, yet it is hardly the vulgar κοινή. I should conjecture that the work belongs to the beginnings of the Academic polemic against Stoicism, in the early decades of the third century. The writer seems to have drawn some of his material from the *Callias* of Aeschines,[1] in which the wealth of the famous " millionaire " family was a prominent topic and Prodicus received some notice. Suidas ascribes an *Eryxias* to Aeschines himself, but there seems to be no other evidence for the existence of such a work. Presumably our *Eryxias* is meant, and Suidas has made a mistake about its authorship.

Axiochus. In style this dialogue is far inferior to the *Eryxias*. The language is a vulgar κοινή, full of non-Attic words and phrases. The *mise-en-scène* shows complete ignorance of the personages of Plato's dialogues. The principal figure, apart from Socrates, is Axiochus of Scambonidae, the uncle of Alcibiades. The supposed date is fixed by a reference to the trial of the generals after Arginusae (368*d*) as not earlier than 405, and Axiochus represents himself as having supported the protest of Socrates against the unconstitutionality of the proceedings. The writer has forgotten that Axiochus was, next to Alcibiades, the chief victim of the scandals of 415 and shared the capital sentence.[2] In the opening

---

[1] See H. Dittmar, *Aeschines von Sphettos*, 198–199, who, however, perhaps mistakes a probability for a demonstration.

[2] Andocides, i. 16, Agariste, wife of Alcmeonides and widow of Damon, gave information against Alcibiades, Axiochus and Adimantus, καὶ ἔφυγον οὗτοι πάντες ἐπὶ ταύτῃ τῇ μηνύσει. Alcibiades afterwards had his hour of

scene (364*a*) Damon is mentioned as the music-master of Axiochus'
son Clinias (the Clinias of the *Euthydemus*), and Socrates sees the
two " running towards him," though Damon, a contemporary of
Anaxagoras, would have been almost a centenarian if he had been
living at the supposed date. The scheme of the dialogue is simple.
Axiochus has been seized by a severe " fit " and apprehends death ;
Socrates is called in to " console " him. He does this by the
arguments that (1) death is utter unconsciousness and after it
there are no more pains to fear ; (2) life in the body is one unbroken
scene of anxiety and suffering, so that it is a positive good to have
done with it. This second point, intended to rule out the possible
rejoinder to (1) that even if death brings no posthumous disagree-
ables with it, it is still dreadful because it puts an end to the *joie
de vivre*, is argued at length in a speech professedly taken from
the eminently wise Prodicus. (3) A further argument, also ascribed
to Prodicus, is the dilemma, " death matters neither to the living
nor to the dead ; while we live, *death* is not there, and when we
have died, *we* are not there." Axiochus rejects these " consolations " scornfully. They are the " superficial twaddle " which is
coming into vogue just now with empty-headed lads. It all sounds
fine, but when one is face-to-face with death it proves idle bravado
(369*d*). In the remainder of the dialogue Socrates drops the pretence of holding the views of Prodicus and discovers himself as
a convinced believer in the blessed immortality of the soul. This,
he says, is proved (1) by the achievements of man in his ascent
from barbarism to civilization, (2) and particularly by his great
intellectual triumph, his creation of astronomy, the science which
reveals to us the *magnalia Dei*. Man could not have done all
this, " were there not indeed the breath of God in his soul." This
message goes home to the heart of Axiochus, who feels himself
now delivered from his terrors. Socrates then completes his good
work by relating a myth, in the Orphic style, of the blessedness
of souls in the next life, professing to have learned it from a Persian
magus. The myth leaves Axiochus actually " in love " with death.

I feel personally convinced that Immisch is right in the view
taken of the purpose of the dialogue in his edition of it.[1] As he
points out, the third of the pretended " consolations " produced
by Socrates is the familiar Epicurean dilemma, " death is nothing
to us, for while we are, death is not, and when death is, we are
not." [2] This is the argument of which Axiochus speaks with
marked contempt as superficial " twaddle " momentarily fashion-

triumph and restoration, but he had been banished again before 405 and
all his connections were then in the worst odour. The alleged " support "
given to Socrates is unknown to the historians, and the reference to προεδροι
in the *ecclesia* (368*e*) seems to show ignorance of the fifth-century method and
procedure.

[1] O. Immisch, *Philologische Studien zu Plato. Erster Heft. Axiochus*,
Leipzig, 1896.
[2] Epicurus, *Ep.* iii. 125 (Bailey), Lucretius iii. 830.

able with mere boys. Immisch seems also to have shown that there are numerous distinctively Epicurean turns of speech throughout the so-called discourse of Prodicus on the misery of existence. Hence I cannot reject his conclusion that the dialogue is a piece of anti-Epicurean polemic, intended to contrast the Platonic with the Epicurean answer to the perennial question *What may I hope for?* and to insinuate that the "wisdom" of Epicurus is not even original. It is a mere revival of the ideas of a second-rate sophist, and a "doctrine of despair" into the bargain. It is natural, though not absolutely necessary, to draw Immisch's further conclusion that, in the writer's day, Epicureanism was just beginning to be in vogue among *fin-de-siècle* youths. In that case we must date the composition as early as somewhere *c.* 305–300 B.C., since Epicurus established himself at Athens in 307/6. Other scholars, such as Wilamowitz and H. Dittmar, reject this date as too early, but, though I do not want to be over-confident, I suspect they may be ascribing to "lateness" faults of style and vocabulary which may only mean that the writer is neither an Athenian [1] nor a person with a literary sense. I see no need to suppose a date later than the time of Epicurus, whose Greek is much of the same stamp. There was an earlier *Axiochus* by Aeschines of Sphettus of which all that is known is that, as we learn from Athenaeus, it painted an unfavourable picture of the debauched life of Alcibiades, and presumably of his uncle also. It can hardly have supplied our author with material. [2]

It is hardly necessary to say anything of the little trifle, not contained in our Plato MSS., called the *Alcyon* and attributed, in MSS., variously to Plato or to Lucian. (It is commonly included in printed texts of Lucian ; the only recent editor of Plato to print it is C. F. Hermann.) This piece of silly prettiness is certainly neither Plato's nor Lucian's ; since it was already known to Favorinus of Arles, [3] it must be the work of some Atticist earlier than Lucian. It describes Socrates and Chaerephon as walking by the Bay of Phalerum, where they hear the cry of the (mythical) halcyon. Socrates relates the legend that the bird is a transformed woman, argues that, since God's power is incomprehensibly great, we must not be too ready to reject such "miracles," and commends the story for its moral of wifely devotion.

Diogenes Laertius (iii. 62) gives the following list of νοθευόμενοι : *Midon* or *Hippotrophus, Eryxias* or *Erasistratus, Alcyon*, [a corrupt

---

[1] The attempt to argue from 365*e*, 368*d* that the writer must be an Athenian because he makes his characters talk of *their* national heroes as they naturally would, does not deeply impress me.

[2] On the *Axiochus* of Aeschines see H. Dittmar, *Aeschines von Sphettos*, 159–163.

[3] Favorinus ascribed it to a certain Leon (D.L. iii. 62). Athenaeus (516*c*) calls the author " Leon the Academic," on the authority of Nicias of Nicaea. If this means the fourth-century mathematician Leon, the ascription is most improbable.

word], *Sisyphus, Axiochus, Phaeaces, Demodocus, Chelidon, Hebdome, Epimenides.* The only "work" we possess not included in this list is the *de Iusto*. This is absent, unless it is covered by the corrupt entry ἀκεφάλοις or ἀκέφαλοι or ἀκέφαλος ἤ (Schanz, ἤ), before the *Sisyphus*. As there was a dialogue *Cephalus* ascribed to Speusippus (D.L. iv. 4), the reference of Diogenes may be to that, as the Basle editors of the *Vita Platonis* suggest. Athenaeus (506*d*), apparently following Hegesander of Delphi, the author of a foolish diatribe against Plato, refers to an otherwise unknown *Cimon*, alleged to contain invectives against Themistocles, Myronides, Alcibiades and Cimon himself. Some of the statements made in this attack on Plato are so absurd that one may wonder whether the *Cimon* ever existed, except in the imagination of a careless scribbler.

There still survives in Syriac a translation of a "Socratic" dialogue, *Herostrophos* [1] dealing with the soul. The text was published by Lagarde in his *Analecta Syriaca* (1858); there is a German version with a discussion of *provenance* by V. Ryssel in *Rheinisches Museum*, N.F. xlviii. 175–196, on which the following remarks are based. The dialogue is shown by its vocabulary and other peculiarities to be a genuine version of a Greek original; the translator, according to Ryssel, was the priest and physician Sergius of Rāsain, a student of Aristotle who died at Constantinople soon after 536 A.D. The name of the interlocutor Herostrophos appears to be a miswriting of Aristippus. (He is represented as a stranger attracted to Socrates by his reputation for wisdom, exactly as Aeschines of Sphettus (D.L. ii. 65) related that Aristippus was drawn to Athens κατὰ κλέος Σωκράτους. The two names, as written in Syriac, only differ by a single letter.) The problem to which he desires an answer is that of the fate of the soul at death. Does it perish with the body, enter a new body, or die for a time and revive again with the same body? (The last alternative seems to be suggested by the Christian dogma of the "resurrection of the flesh," but might allude only to the Pythagorean and Stoic conception of "cyclical recurrence"?) I do not myself understand the confused reply of Socrates. He seems to be combining insistence on the thought that the soul is imperishable and immutable with the notion that it has fire as its chief component, and the suggestion of an analogy between death and sunset. As the sun rises again to-morrow, so the soul reappears again with a new body after the death of the present body. It does not appear that the lost Greek original was ever taken by anyone for a work of Plato, and I find it hard to believe that it is not influenced by Stoicism. This might account for the apparent materialism and also for the suggestion of the reappearance of the same body, if this is not actually a borrowing from Christianity.

[1] My attention was first drawn to the point by Mr. W. L. Lorimer of St. Andrews University.

The *Anthology* contains a number of epigrams ascribed to Plato (though, in one or two cases, to other authors also). The fact of the ascription does not prove authenticity. On the other side, the manner and diction of Greek epigram is so stereotyped that it would probably be impossible to prove any of these compositions spurious on linguistic grounds. The collection will be found most conveniently in Hiller-Crusius, *Anthologia Lyrica*,[3] *Pt. I.* The items which, if genuine, would throw some light on Plato's personality are 1, the well-known couplet on Agathon, translated by Shelley ; 8, the lines on Alexis and Phaedrus ; 14, 15, two famous couplets on a beautiful boy, *perhaps* called Aster ; 7, a fine epigram commemorative of Dion. 1 and 8, at any rate, if genuine, would prove Plato to have had the "erotic" temperament. To my own mind, the occurrence of the names Agathon and Phaedrus is proof of spuriousness. The author clearly has in his mind the parts taken by Agathon the poet and Phaedrus of Myrrhinus in Plato's great ἐρωτικὸς λόγος the *Symposium*, and has forgotten that both were grown men when Plato was under twelve. I see no reason why most of the other epigrams should not be Plato's, except that there is no particular reason why they must be. Even the lines on Dion, though worthy of Plato, can hardly be said to contain anything which might not be said by any other good epigrammatist. And it is, perhaps, hardly likely that Plato, writing after he was seventy about his devotion to a friend who had lived to be over fifty, would use the word ἔρως to describe the attachment. I fear we must be content to say that though some of the verses may be Plato's, none need be so.

A more interesting personal document is Plato's Will (D.L. iii. 41–43). The probability is that this and the Wills of Aristotle and Theophrastus are genuine. The Academy would have legal reasons for safeguarding the document, just as a society to-day preserves its charter of incorporation or its title-deeds. The Will runs thus : " Plato leaves possessions and devises them as hereunder. The property at Iphistiadae bounded on the N. by the road from the shrine at Cephisia, on the S. by the shrine of Heracles at Iphistiadae, on the E. by the land of Archestratus of Phrearria, on the W. by the land of Philippus of Chollidae, shall be neither sold nor alienated, but secured in every way to the boy Adimantus.[1] The property at Iresidae purchased from Callimachus and bounded on the N. by the land of Eurymedon of Myrrhinus, on the S. by the land of Demostratus of Xypate, on the E. by the land of the said Eurymedon, on the W. by the Cephisus.[2] . . . *Item*, three *minae* of silver. *Item*, a silver goblet, weight 165 dr. *Item*, a cup, weight 45 dr. *Item*, a gold finger-ring and earring, com-

---

[1] Presumably a descendant (? grandson) of Plato's eldest brother.

[2] There is no statement about the way in which this property is devised. Either the text is defective or we must understand that this property also is part of the settlement on Adimantus.

bined weight 4½ dr. Euclides the stone-cutter owes me three *minae*. I give Artemis her freedom. I leave the following household slaves, Tychon, Bictas, Apollonides, Dionysius. Also the household furniture specified in the annexed schedule of which Demetrius has the duplicate. I leave no unpaid debts. I appoint as executors Leosthenes, Speusippus, Demetrius, Hegias, Eurymedon, Callimachus, Theopompus."

By comparison with the similar wills of Aristotle and Theophrastus we can see that Plato was by no means in affluent circum·stances.

See further on the works dealt work above :

SHOREY, P.—*What Plato Said* (pp. 415–444, " Doubtful and Spurious Dialogues ").

SOUILHÉ, J.—*Platon, Dialogues Suspects* (Paris, 1930. The author tends to accept the *Clitophon*, and *Alcibiades* I) : *Platon, Dialogues Apocryphes*. (Paris, 1930.)

FRIEDLÄNDER, P.—*Die Platonischen Schriften* (Berlin and Leipzig, 1930), pp. 117–127 (on *Hipparchus*), 147–155 (on *Theages*), 233–245 (on *Alcibiades* I). All these are accepted.

INDEXES

I. INDEX OF PROPER NAMES

(This index makes no pretensions to be exhaustive, but it is trusted that it will be found sufficient)

II. INDEX OF SUBJECTS

(The list is unavoidably far from exhaustive)

Analysis (logical). See Division (logical)

Analysis (mathematical), 511 ff.

Arithmetic, 290 ff., 323–324, 342, 430, 485, 507–513

Art (fine), 279–280

Art (the statesman's), 97–98, 530–531, 539

Association (of " Ideas "), 136, 186–187

Astronomy (Platonic), 447, 452, 485, 498–500, 518

Beauty, 34, 113, 229–231, 280, 308

Being and Becoming, 95, 202 ff., 226 ff., 326 ff., 337, 383 ff., 414–415, 427 ff., 440 ff.

Being and Not-Being, 85–86, 96, 388–392

Categories (Platonic), 386 ff.

Causality, 34, 202 ff., 415, 441, 453, 491

Classes (in *Republic*), 275–276

Comic, the, analysis of, 425–426

Conceptualism, 357

Constitutionalism, 375, 393, 401-404, 470–474

Copula, the, 392

Courage, 57 ff., 248–249, 257 ff., 280–282, 466–467

Creation, 391, 442–444

Definition, 47, 132, 149, 151, 248

Democracy, 126 ff., 140 ff., 157, 296, 401 ff., 471 ff.

Depletion and Repletion, 120, 217, 297, 418 ff., 453, 458

Dialectic, 82, 98, 224, 230, 291 ff., 313, 387, 412, 430, 497

Division (logical), 153, 313, 375–395 *passim*, 398–400, 412

Drama, criticism of, 279–280

Dyad, the Platonic, 512–513

Earth, motion of, 448 ff., 485

Economics 273-275, 276, 478, 534 ff., 548 ff.

Education, 237 ff., 241 ff., 278 ff., 480, 482–486

Eristic, 86 n., 89 ff., 380

Eros, Platonic conception of, 224–231, 305–309

Evil, involuntariness of, 26–27, 37–38, 112, 259, 459, 476 ; source of, 455, 476, 491–492

Family, the, in *Republic*, 277–278 ; in *Laws*, 480–482

Forms, in minor Socratic dialogues, 30 n. (*Hippias I*), 70–71 (*Lysis*), 81 (*Cratylus*) ; in *Gorgias*, 112 n., 121 n. ; in *Meno*, 132 ; in *Euthyphro*, 149 ; in *Phaedo*, 181 n., 190 n., 202–203, 204–206 ; in *Symposium*, 230 ff. ; in *Protagoras*, 257 ; in *Republic*, 286–289 ; in *Phaedrus*, 308 ; why absent from *Theaetetus*, 348 ; in *Parmenides*, 349–359 ; in *Sophistes*, 384–386, 388–389 ; in *Philebus*, 417–418 ; in *Timaeus*, 442, 456

Forms, Aristotelian criticism of, 508 ff., 518

Forms and numbers, 503 ff.

Forms and sensibilia, 188, 190, 202, 353–359, 411, 442, 508, 514

Friendship, 64–74, 537

Geometry, 137–138, 186–188, 289–291, 324, 361, 485, 501, 504, 513–514

God, Platonic doctrine of, 442, 489–494. See also *s.v.* Good, Form of

Good, Form of, 231–232, 285–289, 441–442

Good, Goods, nature of, 26–28, 227, 257 ff., 410 ff., 431 ff., 475 ff.

Goods, hierarchy of, 27–28, 73, 93, 99, 114–115, 144–145, 180 ff., 227 ff., 295 ff., 304, 431 ff., 475 ff., 522 ff.

Goodness. See Virtue

Guardians (in *Republic*), 275–276, 280, 282–284, 295

" Gymnastic," 111, 460, 482, 486

MERIDIAN BOOKS

MERIDIAN BOOKS
17 Union Square West, New York 3, New York